M000191772

THE THEORY OF THE FIRM: MICROECONOMICS WITH ENDOGENOUS ENTREPRENEURS, FIRMS, MARKETS, AND ORGANIZATIONS

The Theory of the Firm presents a path-breaking general framework for understanding the economics of the firm. The book addresses why firms exist, how firms are established, and what contributions firms make to the economy. The book presents a new theoretical analysis of the foundations of microeconomics that makes institutions endogenous. Entrepreneurs play a central economic role by establishing firms. In turn, firms create and operate markets and organizations. The book provides innovative models of economic equilibrium that endogenously determine the structure and function of economic institutions. The book proposes an "intermediation hypothesis" – the establishment of firms depends on the effects of transaction costs and on the extent of the market.

Daniel F. Spulber is the Elinor Hobbs Distinguished Professor of International Business and Professor of Management Strategy at Northwestern University's Kellogg School of Management and the founder of Kellogg's International Business and Markets Program. He is the founding editor of the *Journal of Economics and Management Strategy.* His current research is in the areas of entrepreneurship, international economics, economics of organizations, industrial organization, management strategy, and law. Spulber is the author of 11 books, including *Networks in Telecommunications: Economics and Law* (with Christopher Yoo, 2009), *Global Competitive Strategy* (2007), *Market Microstructure: Intermediaries and the Theory of the Firm* (1999), and *Deregulatory Takings and the Regulatory Contract: The Competitive Transformation of Network Industries in the United States* (with J. Gregory Sidak, 1997), all from Cambridge University Press, and *Management Strategy* (2004), *The Market Makers* (1998), and *Regulation and Markets* (1989), from other publishers.

The Theory of the Firm

Microeconomics with Endogenous Entrepreneurs, Firms, Markets, and Organizations

Daniel F. Spulber

Northwestern University

CAMBRIDGE
UNIVERSITY PRESS

CAMBRIDGE UNIVERSITY PRESS
Cambridge, New York, Melbourne, Madrid, Cape Town, Singapore, São Paulo, Delhi

Cambridge University Press
32 Avenue of the Americas, New York, NY 10013-2473, USA

www.cambridge.org
Information on this title: www.cambridge.org/9780521736602

First published 2009

Printed in the United States of America

A catalog record for this publication is available from the British Library

Library of Congress Cataloging in Publication data
Spulber, Daniel F.
The theory of the firm : microeconomics with endogenous entrepreneurs,
firms, markets, and organizations / Daniel F. Spulber.
p.   cm.
Includes bibliographical references and index.
ISBN 978-0-521-51738-6 (hbk.) – ISBN 978-0-521-73660-2 (pbk.)
1. Industrial organization (Economic theory)   I. Title.
HD2326.S723   2009
338.501 – dc22   2008039228

ISBN   978-0-521-51738-6 hardback
ISBN   978-0-521-73660-2 paperback

Contents

Preface and Acknowledgments

This book presents a general theory of the firm. *The Theory of the Firm* seeks to explain (1) why firms exist, (2) how firms are established, and (3) what firms contribute to the economy. The book addresses the foundations of microeconomics by making institutions endogenous. In the models presented in the book, the following are endogenous: entrepreneurs, firms, markets, and organizations.

The general theory of the firm begins with the individual consumer. The characteristics of consumers are the theory's exogenous data. Consumers can do practically anything without firms. Consumers can produce goods and services by operating technology. Consumers can transact directly with each other through bilateral exchange. Finally, consumers can form organizations such as clubs, buyers' cooperatives, workers' cooperatives, and basic partnerships.

The firm is an economic institution that differs fundamentally from a consumer organization. This book introduces a new definition of the firm that is highly useful in developing the theory: The firm is a transaction institution whose objectives are separate from those of its owners. Consumer organizations such as clubs and basic partnerships are not firms. The objectives of consumer organizations cannot be separated from those of their owners.

Why do firms exist? *The Theory of the Firm* shows that firms exist only when they improve the efficiency of economic transactions. The efficiency of firms is compared to the alternative of direct exchange between consumers. Direct exchange between consumers involves search, bargaining, barter, and contracts. Direct exchange between consumers also can involve forming consumer organizations. To be economically viable, firms must improve on the efficiency of what consumers can achieve without firms.

How are firms established? Individual consumers can choose to become entrepreneurs and establish firms. *The Theory of the Firm* thus makes the entrepreneur endogenous in microeconomics. Because entrepreneurs establish firms, the firm also is endogenous in microeconomics. Entrepreneurs and firms arise based on the underlying characteristics of consumers who possess the judgment, knowledge, skills, and technology that are needed to set up a firm. Individuals provide the effort, investment, and planning that are needed to start up a business. If firms will enhance economic efficiency, entrepreneurs can earn a return from establishing a firm.

What do firms contribute to the economy? Firms are institutions that coordinate transactions by acting as intermediaries. Among the many instruments that firms use to coordinate transactions are two major ones. First, firms intermediate exchange by creating and operating markets. This makes markets endogenous in the theory of the firm. Firms create markets by marketing and selling goods and services, by setting up facilities such as stores and Web sites, and by arranging exchanges for commodities and financial assets. Firms adjust prices to balance their purchases and sales and thereby clear markets. Second, firms create and manage organizations that employ personnel and financial capital; intermediate transactions; internally allocate capital, labor, and resources, and carry out production. This makes organizations endogenous in the theory of the firm.

The theory of the firm constitutes a unified field with its own set of questions. The analysis departs from the neoclassical general equilibrium framework that takes both firms and markets as given exogenously and that does not consider either entrepreneurs or organizations. The theory of the firm incorporates advances in the study of firms from industrial organization, contract theory, game theory, law and economics, institutional economics, the economics of organizations, and finance.

The general theory of the firm is not based on a specific "silver bullet" theory of why firms exist. The general theory of the firm includes the full range of transaction costs, including the absence of a double coincidence of wants, communication costs, search costs, bargaining costs, moral hazard, adverse selection, contracting costs, and free riding.

Microeconomics seeks to address the purpose and functions of firms, markets, and organizations. Understanding why firms exist, how firms are established, and what firms contribute to the economy is essential to this task. The framework develops some critical empirical implications that require further investigation. In addition, the general theory of the firm helps to understand management decision making. The field of management strategy seeks to develop policies for managers, which require a framework that can evaluate the effectiveness of alternative strategies.

A general theory of the firm also is useful for teaching economics. Economics courses, including principles of economics, intermediate microeconomics, and graduate microeconomics, rarely mention entrepreneurship. In the neoclassical economics course, firms and markets are given exogenously. Firms lack an explicit organizational structure and are fully described by their production technology. Markets are operated by an invisible hand. Students are often perplexed, because firms are said to be price-takers and yet, at the same time, firms often are said to adjust prices in response to surpluses or shortages, an obvious contradiction to price-taking behavior. The theory of the firm contributes to teaching economics by introducing a more complete picture of the economy. The contributions of entrepreneurs often provide appealing narratives. Discussion of eBay's Internet auctions or the now publicly traded New York Stock Exchange yields insights into the market-making activities of firms.

The book is organized as follows. Part I of the book provides the foundation for the endogeneity of the firm. Chapter 1 provides the exogenous preconditions for the theory of the firm by defining the consumer. The characteristics, endowments, and transaction costs encountered by the consumer form the basis for the endogenous decisions of consumers to become entrepreneurs and establish firms. The chapter defines direct exchange between consumers and also explains why consumer organizations are not firms. Chapter 2 explores the formal definition of the firm, examines the separation criterion, and introduces the intermediation hypothesis. Chapter 3 introduces the separation theorems, which explain the separation of consumer decisions from those of the firm. The chapter extends the neoclassical and Fisher separation theorems to a model with oligopoly competition between price-setting firms.

Part II of the book introduces the entrepreneur as the central figure in microeconomics. Chapter 4 presents a formal definition of the entrepreneur and reviews the literature and historical context of entrepreneurship. The discussion highlights the critical importance of the entrepreneur in the economy and emphasizes the role of the entrepreneur in establishing firms. The chapter identifies three types of competition faced by the entrepreneur: competition among entrepreneurs, competition between the entrepreneur and direct exchange between consumers, and competition between the entrepreneur and established firms. Chapter 5 presents a set of models in which entrepreneurs establish firms in economic equilibrium. Entrepreneurs compete to establish firms, with various factors determining the number of entrepreneurs, including such factors as set-up costs, rates of time preference, risk aversion, and wealth.

Part III of the book considers the role of the firm in obtaining human capital and finance capital. Chapter 6 contrasts management of the firm with worker cooperatives and examines the implications of human capital for size and structure of organizations. Chapter 7 considers how financing the firm's capital investment affects the organization of the firm and compares sole proprietorships, partnerships, and corporations.

Part IV of the book develops the economic role of the firm as an intermediary. In Chapter 8, the firm alleviates the absence of a double coincidence of wants and provides a substitute for money. The absence of a double coincidence of wants is examined in the context of transportation and travel costs, allocation over time, and uncertainty. In Chapter 9, the firm addresses the free rider problem when joint production involves economies of scale, public goods, or common property resources.

Part V of the book considers the economic contribution of the firm as a market maker. In Chapter 10, the firm acts as a market maker and a matchmaker in markets with homogeneous products and in markets with differentiated products. The market-making activities of the firm contrast with costly search when consumers engage in direct exchange. Chapter 11 examines the firm's economic role as a market maker in comparison to bilateral contracts between buyers and sellers. The discussion highlights the role of the firm in mitigating transaction costs associated with underinvestment and renegotiation, moral hazard, and adverse selection. Chapter 12 concludes the book.

Acknowledgments

I am particularly grateful to the Ewing Marion Kauffman Foundation for a grant that made it possible for me to carry out and complete this research study. I thank Carl Schramm, Bob Litan, and Bob Strom of the Ewing Marion Kauffman Foundation for their interest in this work, their helpful comments, and their encouragement of entrepreneurship research.

I am grateful to Dean Dipak Jain and Dean Kathleen Hagerty for their support for my research. I am pleased to acknowledge the research support of the Kellogg School of Management. I also acknowledge the support of a grant from the Searle Fund for earlier research on historical aspects of the firm that helped to lay the foundation for this work.

I thank my students Alexei Alexandrov, Ramon Casadesus-Masanell, and Joaquin Poblete for helpful discussions. I have presented parts of the book over a number of years to my graduate economics class. I thank my graduate students for their helpful reactions and penetrating questions. I thank the Searle Center on Law, Regulation and Economic Growth for the opportunity to present the book at a Research Roundtable conference, and I thank participants at the Searle Center conference for their valuable input. I thank Henry Butler, the director of the Searle Center, for his encouragement and support of the project. For their helpful and constructive comments, I particularly wish to thank Michael Baye, George Deltas, Shane Greenstein, David Haddock, Gillian Hadfield, Peter G. Klein, Jin Li, Henry Manne, Scott Masten, Troy Paredes, Jens Prüfer, Steve Ramirez, Larry Ribstein, John Rust, Scott Stern, and Joshua Wright. Also, I thank Aaron Spulber for his cover illustration, "The Firm" oil on canvas © 2008.

I drew upon the following publications in preparing this book:

Daniel F. Spulber, "The Intermediation Theory of the Firm: Integrating Economic and Management Approaches to Strategy," *Managerial and Decision Economics*, 24, 2003, pp. 253–266.

Daniel F. Spulber, "Market Microstructure and Incentives to Invest," *Journal of Political Economy*, 110, April, 2002, pp. 352–381.

Daniel F. Spulber, "Transaction Innovation and the Role of the Firm," in *The Economics of the Internet and E-Commerce*, edited by Michael R. Baye, Advances in Applied Micro-Economics, v. 11, JAI Press/Elsevier Science, 2002, pp. 159–190.

David Lucking-Reiley and Daniel F. Spulber, "Business-to-Business Electronic Commerce," *Journal of Economic Perspectives*, 15, Winter, 2001, pp. 55–68.

Daniel F. Spulber, "Market Making by Price Setting Firms," *Review of Economic Studies*, 63, 1996, pp. 559–580.

Joaquin Poblete and Daniel F. Spulber, *Entrepreneurs, Partnerships, and Corporations: Incentives, Risk, and the Organization of the Firm*, Northwestern University, 2008.

Daniel F. Spulber, "Discovering the Role of the Firm: The Separation Criterion and Corporate Law," *Berkeley Business Law Journal*, 6.2, Spring, 2009.

Introduction

The purpose of this book is to present a general theory of the firm. The theory provides a microeconomic framework in which entrepreneurs, firms, markets, and organizations are endogenous. The models help to explain why firms exist, how firms are established, and what firms contribute to the economy. Because firms create and operate markets, *The Theory of the Firm* helps to explain how markets arise and how they work, and provides a basic analysis of the formation and design of organizations.

The structure of the theory of the firm is as follows. Consumers and their preferences, endowments, and intellectual property, are exogenous to the model. Consumers choose to become entrepreneurs by working to establish firms, which makes entrepreneurs endogenous. Through the actions of entrepreneurs, firms are established endogenously. Firms act as market makers by creating and operating markets, so that markets also are endogenous. Firms also create and manage organizations that transact internally and in the marketplace, making organizations endogenous. Economic equilibria are the result of consumer-entrepreneurs who establish firms and, in turn, of firms that create and manage markets and organizations. Firms, markets, and transactions are the results of economic equilibria. This framework is summarized in Figure I.1.

Economics is a social science. Economic relationships between individuals in society are its essential elements. Accordingly, the theory of the firm rests upon the characteristics and actions of individual consumers and their relationships. Acting together they form families, communities, social institutions, and governments. Consumers carry out market transactions through direct exchange. Consumers generate a wide variety of organizations that are alternatives to firms.

The critical first step in the theory of the firm is to begin with the individual consumer – and without firms or markets. Consumers have preferences over consumption bundles. They have initial endowments of factors of production and of goods and services. Consumers also have technological knowledge regarding production processes, product designs, transaction mechanisms, and organizational

1

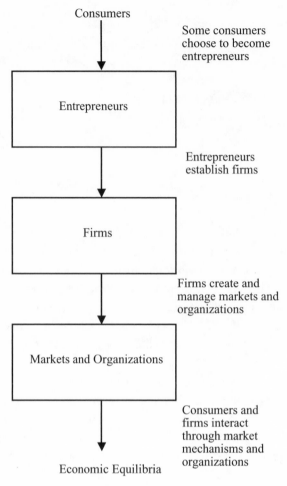

Figure I.1. Microeconomics with endogenous entrepreneurs, firms, markets and organizations.

management. They make purchasing decisions and labor supply decisions. Consumers are inventors, artists, managers, investors, and property owners. Consumers can act as producers and operate manufacturing technology, either individually or collectively. They are capable of technological and scientific invention, and they can commercialize their inventions.

Consumers also are able to set up and manage organizations. They can obtain benefits by transacting with one another through barter and bilateral contracts. They can form clubs, interest groups, and other associations. Consumers can devise more complex economic institutions, such as workers' cooperatives, consumers' cooperatives, and basic partnerships. Consumers can choose to form all kinds of social institutions to facilitate their economic interaction, and they can carry out economic transactions without the need for firms.

Although consumers realize gains from trade through direct exchange and cooperative agreements, they also encounter transaction costs. Such transaction costs include the time and effort required to search for trading partners. Consumers must communicate with one another, calculate the benefits from trade, negotiate the terms of exchange, design contracts, and observe the performance of contract terms by their partners. Consumers' net gains from trade will depend on how efficient direct transaction methods are in achieving gains from trade and how costly those transaction methods are.

Consumers, acting as entrepreneurs, choose to establish firms when doing so improves economic efficiency. An entrepreneur spends time, effort, and resources to establish a firm in order to receive the returns to ownership once the firm is established. The value generated by the firm must be greater than the costs of establishing the firm.

Transaction costs help to explain why consumers need firms and markets. A firm is a particular type of social institution that can improve the efficiency of transactions. Firms enhance net gains from trade by offering transaction methods not available to individual consumers or even to groups of consumers. The firm achieves transaction efficiencies by creating markets and organizations. To be economically viable, a firm must increase net gains from trade in comparison with direct exchange between consumers. Although consumers may develop and own such transaction technologies, they must establish a firm to implement them. The firm is an instrument for carrying out transactions.

A critical source of the firm's transaction efficiencies is that its objectives differ from those of its owners. The objectives of the firm are distinct from those of its customers, suppliers, managers, or employees. After establishing the firm, the entrepreneur becomes an owner. Therefore, the objectives of the firm are also separate from those of the entrepreneur who established it.[1] The separation of the entrepreneur and the firm allows for a development of a theory of the entrepreneur.

Separation helps a firm to improve the efficiency of transactions in comparison to direct exchange between consumers. By extending the neoclassical separation theorem, separation implies that the firm maximizes profits. Separation allows the firm to be an independent economic actor and decision maker. The firm is an additional player in the economic game. By adding a new player, an entrepreneur gives the economy additional degrees of freedom and new economic instruments. As an additional economic player, the firm performs economic functions not available to consumers. The firm can handle multilateral transactions simultaneously and thus improve efficiency relative to bilateral transactions between consumers.

---

1 Richard Cyert and James March (1963, p. 10) once observed with regard to the neoclassical paradigm, "If we take seriously the concept of a firm as something distinct from an individual entrepreneur, there is no consensus on a theory of the firm." Cyert and March (1963), in their behavioral approach to the firm, criticized the basic profit maximization framework of neoclassical economics, which in their view was based on the notion that the entrepreneur and the firm were one and the same. By separating the entrepreneur and the firm, the analysis presented here provides a theory of the firm that is consistent with optimization by rational economic agents.

The firm is much more than a nexus of contracts. It is an autonomous player that acts as the counterparty in contracts with customers, suppliers, investors, and employees. The firm enters into many contracts simultaneously as a central player. By acting as a contracting hub, the firm can achieve more than would a complete set of contracts directly linking its trading partners. The firm is a market maker, with instruments such as posted prices and auctions that can aggregate and balance supply and demand. The firm is a matchmaker that can coordinate and connect buyers and sellers. The firm is a centralized clearinghouse that can aggregate transactions and process information.

Because the firm's objectives are separate from those of its owners, it offers incentive mechanisms without the budget-balancing requirement of a buyers' cooperative, a workers' cooperative, or a business partnership. Budget-balancing requirements limit the efficiency of incentive mechanisms. The firm's ability to earn a profit enhances its ability to design incentive contracts for consumers, suppliers, and employees. The firm manages an organization with internal transactions that motivate managers and employees.

Because its objectives are separate from those of its owners, the firm offers other advantages. The firm has longevity, with a lifetime that stretches beyond its particular economic relationships and exceeds the lifetimes of its trading partners. The firm also can transcend geographic limits on its trading partners by operating in a convenient central location or by operating simultaneously in multiple locations. The firm has a brand identity and business reputation beyond those of its individual owners, managers, and employees.

The firm, in the form of a corporation or complex partnership, allows its investors to have both limited liability and liquidity. Investors in corporations are residual claimants. The analysis shows that corporations can provide incentives for managers that cannot be achieved within a basic partnership. Investors can withdraw their capital by selling their shares without disrupting the corporation's business and without selling the company to realize the value of its assets.

The theory of the firm as presented here provides an important insight about economic institutions. In a variety of economic settings, the theory of the firm yields the following result. The establishment of complex economic institutions depends on the extent of the market. The greater the extent of the market, the more economic institutions such as firms, markets, and organizations are established. This recalls Adam Smith's observation that the realization of economies of scale depends on the extent of the market. The greater the extent of the market, the greater the contribution of firms in improving transaction efficiencies. This suggests why the establishment of firms, markets, and organizations is associated with economic growth, economic development, and international trade.

A key variable repeatedly emerges in a variety of different contexts – the number of consumers. When there are few consumers, direct exchange may be the most efficient economic process. Consumer transactions and consumer organizations are most efficient. When there are many consumers, firms intermediating exchange

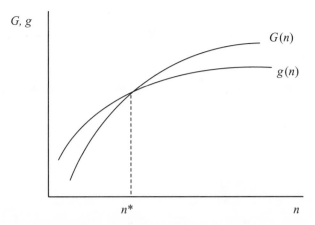

Figure I.2. Entrepreneurs establish firms when the number of consumers is sufficiently greater than n^*. The establishment of complex economic institutions depends on the extent of the market.

becomes the most efficient way to organize the economy. Establishing firms and creating markets and organizations provide economic efficiency relative to direct exchange. The greater the size of the economy, in terms of the number of consumers, the greater are the efficiencies that can be realized by establishing firms.

When there are many consumers, direct exchange may not perform as effectively as intermediated exchange due to transaction costs associated with search, communication, and bargaining, and due to such problems as free riding. As the number of consumers increases, the economy realizes benefits from setting up firms, which are due to economies of scale in transaction technologies. The economy also realizes returns to centralization of exchange through the use of market mechanisms and organizations.

In many models, there is a critical size at which the economic equilibrium switches from direct exchange between consumers to intermediated exchange through firms. It is useful to illustrate the effects of the extent of the market on economic institutions. Let $g(n)$ represent the consumers' total net gains from trade with direct exchange when there are n consumers in the economy. Let $G(n)$ represent the total net gains from trade when there is intermediated exchange through firms. As the number of consumers increases, net gains from trade with direct exchange may increase more slowly than net gains from trade with intermediated exchange through firms. The effects of the extent of the market are illustrated in Figure I.2. Entrepreneurs become active when the size of the economy is greater than n^*. When there are costs to establishing firms, there must be a sufficient increase in net gains from trade relative to direct exchange.

The importance of the size of the economy for the formation of firms has not been recognized elsewhere. The main point is that direct exchange between consumers through decentralized institutions may be preferable with a small number of people. Intermediated exchange through firms becomes preferable when there is a large number of people. One forerunner of the idea that transaction costs depend on the number of people is Ronald Coase's (1960) discussion of externalities in the classic article "The Problem of Social Cost." Coase observes that with a smoke nuisance "a large number of people are involved and . . . therefore the costs of handling the problem through the market or the firm may be high." Coase declines to suggest whether markets or administrative decisions within firms are better at handling many transactions.

The Theory of the Firm explores the great variety of economic conditions under which the establishment of firms may or may not be worthwhile. The theory provides a unified framework for studying firms and markets that attempts to integrate much of the previous work on the firm. Within a general framework, different reasons for firms to undertake an activity will be valid depending on economic conditions. Some explanations may have greater resonance than others in empirical applications. All of these explanations are highly valuable for organizing our thoughts about firms. The theory of the firm should not advocate any particular explanation for the boundaries of the firm. Rather, it provides a set of methods that can be used to compare and evaluate the various explanations for firms' activities.

The Theory of the Firm introduces a general analysis of the entrepreneur. The analysis builds on the classic work of Richard Cantillon, Jean-Baptiste Say, Frank Knight, and Joseph Schumpeter. Knight (1971) emphasizes the essential role of the firm as a means of handling incentives. Entrepreneurs exercise judgment in the face of uncertainty and earn profit as a residual return that depends on the uncertain outcome.

The role of the firm in creating and operating markets is central. The firm is an intermediary that reduces the costs of market transactions; see Daniel Spulber (1996a, 1996b, 1999). The firm is instrumental in solving problems due to the absence of a double coincidence of wants. It allows consumers to engage in risk sharing. The firm coordinates exchange over time and provides services that substitute for money in an economy without fiat money or without a store of value. The firm acts as a matchmaker to alleviate the costs of search. The firm sets up markets to improve coordination between buyers and sellers. The firm creates markets for contracts that improve efficiency in comparison to bilateral contracting.

In the theory of the firm, firms also coordinate transactions within organizations. Governance within the firm provides an alternative to market contracts. Ronald Coase (1937, 1988, 1994) explains the firm as an oasis of planning and organizational administration that is an alternative to transactions in the market. Firms choose whether to buy an input and thereby incur a transaction cost or to make the input in-house, thereby benefiting from management and control of activities within the organization. Coase's insights, particularly the introduction of transaction costs into economics, are reflected throughout the discussion.

Firms manage investments in risky projects. A potential advantage of firms over direct exchange is that firms are mechanisms for separating ownership and control. The discussion includes the classic work on the theory of the firm due to Michael Jensen and William Meckling (1976). They characterize the public corporation as a "nexus for a complex set of voluntary contracts among customers, workers, managers, and the suppliers of materials, capital, and risk bearing." In their view the firm is a mechanism for allocating control when there is economic risk. "Corporations, like all organizations, vest control rights in the constituency bearing the residual risk" (Jensen 2000, p. 1).

The discussion examines the financial structure of the firm and compares the sole proprietorship, the partnership, and the corporation. Research on the corporation in economics and finance tends to emphasize moral hazard and adverse selection problems that result from delegating authority to the CEO. In the traditional framework, the corporation's investors are principals and must design incentives for the manager, who acts as their agent. The financial literature examines the inefficiencies that result from the separation of ownership and control using the benchmark of first-best efficiency. In contrast, it is suggested here that the shortcomings of the corporation should be measured against the yardstick of the best organizational alternative. The organizational alternative that combines ownership and control is the partnership. The discussion gives conditions under which either the partnership or the corporation is more efficient, based on Poblete and Spulber (2008b).

An important task of the firm is the employment and management of labor. Firms manage production operations whether they are used to manufacture goods and services or to generate transactions. The role of the firm is examined in comparison to that of the labor-managed organization. The firm chooses employment at the margin to maximize profit. In contrast, the labor-managed firm chooses employment to maximize the average benefit of its members. The firm provides efficiencies as a consequence of profit maximization.

The general theory of the firm differs from neoclassical economics in a number of critical areas.[2] In the general theory of the firm, the entrepreneur is the central player because the entrepreneur establishes the firm. In neoclassical economics, there are no entrepreneurs because firms already are established.

In the general theory of the firm, the firm is responsible for intermediating transactions. In contrast, neoclassical economics limits the function of the firm to that of being a producer that operates a technology. Arrow and Hahn (1971, p. 17),

---

2 The classical economists include Adam Smith, David Ricardo, and John Stuart Mill. See Sowell (2006) for a highly illuminating overview and discussion of classical economics. By neoclassical economics, I refer to economics since the marginalist revolution, including the work of Léon Walras, William Stanley Jevons, and Carl Menger. I also use the term neoclassical economics as shorthand for the general equilibrium model that was developed by Kenneth Arrow, Gerard Debreu, Robert Hahn, and many others. The neoclassical theory of value refers to the concept that the value of goods and services is determined by a market equilibrium in a general equilibrium setting based on consumer preferences, initial consumer endowments, and producer technologies.

for example, observe that households and firms "are distinguished by the property that firms do, and households do not, take production decisions." Firms take prices as given and make no organizational, management, purchasing, or marketing decisions. Firms do little more than choose the input-output mix that maximizes profits.

The general theory of the firm is founded on transaction costs. In contrast, neoclassical economics is without frictions because markets are established and operate without transaction costs. In the neoclassical general equilibrium framework, a fictitious Walrasian auctioneer clears markets by exogenously selecting prices. Neoclassical economics presents a theory of value that does not consider the institutions of exchange. The market equilibrium with endogenous firms provides a more general theory of value because it reflects transaction costs.

In neoclassical economics, the firm is a veil that covers the decisions of consumers as well as those of suppliers, customers, and owners of firms. Once the veil of firms is removed, all the action in the neoclassical tradition is on the consumer side. Consumers own firms and unanimously agree on the profit-maximizing input choice, so the production decision coincides with the consumer-owners' decision. Consumers are the suppliers of firms, providing the firm with all of its primary factors of production, because consumer endowments include labor and all other resources. Consumers purchase all of the outputs of firms that are not used as inputs for other firms. The transformation of inputs into outputs through production is absorbed into the economy's excess demand function. The production activity could just as well be owned and operated by consumers, who then supply outputs to firms or to other consumers.

The general theory of the firm draws from neoclassical economics and institutional economics. Neoclassical economics offers an analysis of the benefits of transactions through its study of the theory of value. Institutional economics offers an analysis of the costs of transactions through its study of the mechanisms of exchange. By considering both the benefits and costs of transactions, the general theory of the firm combines the strengths of these two important traditions.

The general theory of the firm presented here contains a number of new models and results. The discussion presents equilibrium models in which entrepreneurs choose to establish firms. The discussion examines equilibrium models that contrast the decisions of consumer organizations with those of firms. The analysis compares how consumer organizations and firms choose the size of the organization, obtain capital investment, provide incentives, and allocate resources. The discussion considers how firms create and operate markets. The general theory of the firm helps to explain the vital economic role played by the firm in the contemporary economy. Microeconomics with endogenous entrepreneurs, firms, markets, and organizations provides insights into the nature and function of economic institutions.

PART I

THE THEORY OF THE FIRM

1

The Consumer

The main tasks of the economic theory of the firm are to determine why firms exist, how firms are established, and what functions firms perform. Firms are economic institutions whose objectives, decisions, and activities are the result of fundamental economic forces. To explain the economic role of firms, economic analysis must derive firms endogenously from initial conditions.

Take firms away from microeconomics and what is left? – consumers! This immediately suggests that the theory of the firm should begin with an economy in which there are only consumers. Starting with consumers as the givens of the model has a key implication. Consumers will establish firms if and only if doing so improves economic efficiency. The theory of the firm necessarily derives the existence of firms from fundamental assumptions about the characteristics of consumers who have exogenously given preferences and endowments. Therefore, consumers are the basic building blocks of the theory of the firm.

The purpose of this chapter is to examine the characteristics of consumers and economic interaction between consumers. Consumers are defined by their preferences and endowments. Consumers own ideas, business methods, technologies, and other intellectual property. Consumers can engage in research and development (R&D) to find new technology. Consumers own production technologies and they can act as producers by operating the production technology themselves. Consumers obtain benefits from exchange with one another and incur transaction costs.

This chapter introduces the *intermediation hypothesis*. Firms play an economic role when intermediated exchange is more efficient than direct exchange. *Intermediated exchange* refers to transactions between consumers that go through firms. *Direct exchange* refers to transactions between consumers that do not involve firms. Consumers have the ability to engage in transactions with each other, in the form of either spot transactions or contracts. Consumers can form various organizations to coordinate their transactions, including clubs, cooperatives, associations, nonprofits, and partnerships. There are economic benefits to establishing firms when they improve efficiency in comparison to direct exchange.

11

The distinction between the firm and direct exchange depends on the *separation criterion.* The critical difference between firms and direct exchange is the separation of the firm's objectives from those of its consumer-owners. A transaction institution is defined to be a *firm* if its objectives can be separated from those of its owners. The next chapter examines how the objectives of firms differ from those of their owners. Consumer organizations have objectives that cannot be separated from those of their owners, so they are not firms. Direct exchange between consumers is the benchmark for evaluating the economic contribution of the firm. This chapter examines direct exchange between consumers as the alternative to intermediation by firms.

1.1 The Intermediation Hypothesis and the Scope of the Firm

Consumers in the economy are connected by all kinds of personal interactions – "no man is an island, entire of itself."[1] Consumers are linked economically through their roles as buyers, sellers, workers, entrepreneurs, managers, investors, and owners. Their economic relations are embedded within complex ties of family, friendship, society, and nation. Yet, despite these many connections, there remain economic forces that divide individuals – these forces are transaction costs. Firms play an economic role by mitigating transaction costs and improving the efficiency of transactions. This section presents the intermediation hypothesis.

1.1.1 Transaction Costs and the Intermediation Hypothesis

A *transaction* is the creation of value by voluntary cooperation between two or more economic actors. The value created by a transaction equals the benefits to the parties that are generated by their cooperation minus the costs to the parties of arranging the cooperation. Economic actors structure transactions to maximize their net gains from trade, that is, transaction benefits net of transaction costs.

Consumers encounter transaction costs when they engage in direct exchange. Consumers encounter transaction costs in pure exchange of goods. Consumers also encounter transaction costs in forming and operating organizations such as clubs, consumer cooperatives, worker cooperatives, nonprofits, and basic partnerships. Organizational transaction costs sometimes are referred to as governance costs. Consumers incur transaction costs of communication, information processing, search, matching, bargaining, moral hazard, adverse selection, free riding, and contracting.

The key question is "Why do consumers need firms?" To be profitable, firms must provide better transactions in comparison with direct exchange between consumers. To improve the efficiency of transactions, the firm creates both markets

---

1 John Donne, Meditation XVII, 1975 [1572–1631].

Table 1.1. *The firm improves the efficiency of transactions by creating and managing markets and organizations*

Consumer transaction costs	The firm's transaction mechanisms	
	Market transactions	Organizational transactions
Communication and information processing	Communication networks and platforms	Organizational hierarchies and information technology
Search and matching	Centralized marketplace Match-making Intermediation	Internal coordination Assignments to tasks Internal allocation
Bargaining	Posted prices, auctions	Relational contracts
Moral hazard	Monitoring and incentives	Monitoring and incentives
Adverse selection	Incentive contracts and quality certification	Incentives and quality management
Free riding	Incentive contracts	Incentives and coordination
Contracting	Market for contracts	Vertical integration

and organizations. A *market* is a mechanism that brings buyers and sellers together. A market can be a store, a Web site, a matchmaker, or an auction. The firm's *market transactions* are those that the firm conducts with individuals and firms outside of its organization. The firm creates markets by designing the institutions of exchange.

An *organization* can involve hierarchies, bureaucracies, groups, teams, and networks. The firm's *organizational transactions* are those that it conducts with its managers, employees, and business units. The firm creates organizations by hiring managers and delegating authority to them, by establishing internal rules and mechanisms for communication, by defining tasks for employees, and by assigning employees to those tasks. The firm provides incentives for performance to its managers and employees and monitors their performance.

The *scope* of the firm's activities is the *combination* of its market-making and organizational activities. The firm expands its scope by increasing its market transactions and its organizational transactions. The scope of the firm is determined by its ability to improve the efficiency of economic transactions relative to direct exchange and consumer organizations. The firm plays an economic role if it provides greater efficiency than direct exchange between consumers. Firms intermediate exchange through markets and through organizations. Table 1.1 provides an overview of how the firm addresses transaction costs that consumers face in direct exchange. The general theory of the firm suggests a set of empirical implications that are referred to as the "intermediation hypothesis."

Intermediation Hypothesis. Higher consumer transactions costs of direct exchange, in comparison to firms' transaction costs, lead to firms intermediating exchange between consumers.

The intermediation hypothesis compares the costs of direct exchange between consumers to the costs of intermediated exchange through firms. The hypothesis makes predictions about what types of institutions of exchange will be observed.

The intermediation hypothesis involves comparison of alternative institutions of exchange. The comparison applies whether costs are rising or falling. The development of electronic commerce, including improvements in telecommunications, information systems, and the Internet, lowers transactions costs for a wide variety of transactions. This implies that the costs of direct exchange and the costs of intermediated exchange are both likely to fall. If improvements due to electronic commerce lower transaction costs of intermediated exchange more than those for direct exchange, the intermediation hypothesis predicts more intermediation by firms. The advent of electronic commerce thus may explain the entry of a wide variety of highly specialized firms that intermediate transactions. Even though the costs of direct exchange decrease, the costs of intermediated exchange decrease even more, leading to a restructuring of institutions of exchange.

1.1.2 The Firm versus Direct Exchange

Transaction costs can be either explicit or implicit. Transaction costs such as those associated with communication, information processing, and search involve resource expenditures. The presence of explicit transaction costs can result in additional implicit transaction costs in the form of inefficient transactions. Transaction costs associated with matching, bargaining, moral hazard, adverse selection, free riding, and contracting can be implicit and appear only in the form of efficiency distortions. To highlight the role of the firm, it is useful to consider the basic framework with implicit transaction costs.

Suppose that there are n consumers. Denote each consumer's allocation by q_i, which may be a vector. The allocation takes values in the set Y_i. Let q be the vector of consumer allocations, which takes values in the set $Y = Y_1 \times \cdots \times Y_n$. Each consumer has an additively separable utility function of the allocation vector, q, and a scalar numeraire good, x:

(1) $$U_i(q, x_i) = U_i(q) - x_i.$$

The vector of allocations, q, can represent externalities and public goods. In the case of private goods, the effect on utility of the vector of allocations, q, is restricted to consumer i's allocation, q_i. Let u_i be consumer i's opportunity costs of trade. For ease of presentation, the opportunity costs of trade are assumed to be independent of allocations. The discussion can be extended to include more general opportunity costs.

Let $C(q)$ represent the costs of production and other joint costs. Then the gains from trade can be represented by

(2) $$\Gamma(q) = \sum_{i=1}^{n} U_i(q) - C(q) - \sum_{i=1}^{n} u_i.$$

Denote a socially optimal allocation by q^*, where

$$q^* \in \arg\max_q \Gamma(q).$$

Consider direct exchange between consumers. Let q_{-i} denote the vector of allocations excluding consumer i's allocation. Define the payment function $p_i(q_i, q_{-i})$ for consumers $i = 1, \ldots, n$. The gains from trade for an individual consumer equal

(3) $$V_i(q_i, q_{-i}, p_i) = U_i(q_i, q_{-i}) - p_i(q_i, q_{-i}) - u_i.$$

Consumers participate in direct exchange only if they obtain gains from trade. Consumer i's individual rationality condition is

$$U_i(q_i, q_{-i}) - p_i(q_i, q_{-i}) \geq u_i.$$

In direct exchange, the payments are subject to a budget-balancing condition,

(4) $$\sum_{i=1}^{n} p_i(q_i, q_{-i}) = C(q).$$

Combining the individual consumer gains from trade definition with the budget-balancing condition gives total gains from trade

(5) $$\sum_{i=1}^{n} V_i(q_i, q_{-i}) = \Gamma(q).$$

Consider direct exchange between consumers in the absence of either explicit or implicit transaction costs. Consumers can coordinate their choices of allocations and payments. The allocations, q, are observable and consumers can form contractual agreements. Consumers can play a cooperative game in which they choose among allocations that maximize their net gains from grade. For example, allocations and payments can be determined by outcomes in the Core of a cooperative game. It follows from equation (5) that consumers will maximize net gains from trade.

Proposition 1. Without transaction costs, direct exchange between consumers maximizes gains from trade.

Suppose now that there are explicit or implicit transaction costs of direct exchange. Transaction costs such as search, moral hazard, adverse selection, free riding, or contracting costs can prevent consumers from attaining the efficient outcome. These costs prevent consumers from coordinating their activities to choose cooperatively among allocations that maximize gains from trade. One possibility is that direct exchange entails explicit transaction costs. Sufficiently large transaction costs result in autarky, with consumers choosing their outside option u_i.

Suppose that there are implicit transaction costs. These can limit exchange to bilateral transactions or they can limit the types of payment functions that consumers can choose. Another implicit form of transaction costs requires that consumers can only choose allocations in a noncooperative fashion. Thus, a Nash noncooperative equilibrium, q^0, is defined by

$$q_i^0 \in \arg\max_{q_i} V_i\left(q_i, q_{-i}^0\right), \quad i = 1, \ldots, n.$$

Designate the equilibrium gains from trade with direct exchange by

(6) $$g = \Gamma(q^0).$$

Suppose that the payment functions are given exogenously. For many payment functions, the noncooperative equilibrium does not correspond to the efficient outcome. Due to the budget balancing condition, there are settings in which there do not exist payment functions such that the noncooperative outcome is efficient. This implies the following result.

> **Proposition 2.** With transaction costs, direct exchange between consumers may not maximize gains from trade.

For example, in the classic prisoners' dilemma game, the outcome fails to be efficient. The prisoners' dilemma has exogenous payments that result from legal penalties. The payoffs are represented in the table below. The unique outcome of the game occurs when the prisoners do not cooperate with each other, they both confess and receive the payoffs $(0, 0)$. Transaction costs appear in the form of infinite costs of communication. The prisoners cannot communicate with each other to make an agreement on their strategies. If the two prisoners could form an agreement on their strategies they would cooperate with each other and receive the payments $(2, 2)$.

	Cooperate	Do not cooperate
Cooperate	2,2	−1,3
Do not cooperate	3,−1	0,0

Suppose that the players in the prisoners' dilemma game can make binding agreements with action-contingent side payments. There exist side payments that transform the payoffs in the game; see for example Gutman (1978, 1987). As a result of these transfers, the players achieve the efficient outcome, which is cooperate-cooperate, as a noncooperative equilibrium. However, Jackson and Wilkie (2005) show that when players choose side payments noncooperatively, there is no equilibrium that results in the efficient outcome. Thus, even with endogenous action-contingent side payments, the outcome is inefficient. Again, when transaction costs result in noncooperative behavior, the outcome is inefficient.

The firm is able to intermediate exchange. The firm offers consumers different payment schedules $P_i = P_i(q_i, q_{-i})$. The firm's objective is to maximize profit, although this objective is derived endogenously in later chapters. The firm's profit equals

$$\text{(7)} \qquad \Pi(q) = \sum_{i=1}^{n} P_i(q) - C(q).$$

Define the allocation achieved by a profit-maximizing firm by

$$q^F \in \arg\max_q \Pi(q).$$

Let gains from trade with a profit-maximizing firm be denoted by

$$\text{(8)} \qquad G = \Gamma(q^F).$$

Suppose that the firm chooses allocations and payments that are subject only to the consumers' individual rationality constraints,

$$U_i(q_i, q_{-i}) - P_i \geq u_i.$$

Suppose that the firm exercises monopoly power by choosing allocations and payments such that consumers' individual rationality constraints are strictly binding. For example, the firm can engage in first-degree price discrimination, setting payments that extract all of the consumers' gains from trade. Then, substituting from the individual rationality constraints into the profit function (7), it follows that the firm's profit function exactly equals total gains from trade,

$$\text{(9)} \qquad \Pi(q) = \Gamma(q).$$

This implies that the profit-maximizing firm chooses the efficient allocation. This result is standard for firms with private goods that can engage in first-degree price discrimination; see for example Spulber (1979). For a similar result with externalities in a full information setting, see Segal (1999).

> **Proposition 3.** When the firm can choose both allocations and payments subject only to consumers' individual rationality constraints, the profit–maximizing allocation is efficient, $q^F = q^*$.

This result implies that when consumers cannot form cooperative agreements, firms play an economic role by providing coordination.

More generally, suppose that the firm has incomplete information about the characteristics of consumers. The firm chooses allocations and payment schedules to maximize profits subject to consumer individual rationality constraints and incentive compatibility constraints,

$$\max_P \sum_{i=1}^{n} P_i(q) - C(q),$$

subject to

$$U_i(q_i, q_{-i}) - P_i(q_i, q_{-i}) \geq u_i,$$
$$q_i \in \arg\max_{q_i} U_i(q_i, q_{-i}) - P(q_i, q_{-i}), \quad i = 1, \ldots, n.$$

In a multiple-agent model with externalities and asymmetric information, Spulber (1988b) shows that the full-information optimum can be achieved by incentive contracts if and only if the individual rationality conditions for agents are nonbinding. In a regulation model with asymmetric information about both supply and demand, Spulber (1988a) shows that the full-information optimum can be achieved with sufficient gains from trade. In both of these analyses, the principal must give agents information rents to induce truthful revelation of information. When gains from trade at the full-information optimum are sufficient to cover information rents, the optimum is attained. Conversely, when gains from trade at the full-information optimum do not cover information rents, the optimum is not attained. The profit-maximizing firm will depart from the social optimum because of the trade-off between increasing profits and inducing revelation of information.

The comparison of the firm with direct exchange between consumers has two main implications. First, the firm can serve as a means of exchange. Suppose that the transaction costs of direct exchange are sufficiently large so that they result in autarky. Then the firm plays a role when $G \geq 0$ by providing gains from trade. This role is the basis of the neoclassical separation theorem, which essentially identifies the firm as a vehicle for achieving gains from trade.

Second, the firm provides intermediated exchange that competes with direct exchange. Generally, with transaction costs, both direct exchange between consumers and intermediated exchange with firms depart from the optimum. The value created by the firm is G, which equals gains from trade adjusted for the firm's transaction costs. If direct exchange is feasible, $g \geq 0$, the firm's added value relative to direct exchange is $G - g$. Then, the firm improves economic efficiency if and only if it increases gains from trade,

$$G \geq g.$$

This fundamental inequality describes the economic role of the firm. What distinguishes direct exchange from intermediated exchange is the intervention of an additional player with a distinct objective. If the firm adds value relative to direct exchange, there are benefits to consumers from establishing an institution with a distinct objective.

1.1.3 Example 1: Explicit Transaction Costs

Suppose that transaction costs are explicit. The basics of the model can be illustrated for a simple economy with two consumers and two goods, q_1 and q_2. Suppose that the first consumer derives a per-unit benefit v from consuming the first good and has a unitary marginal utility of the second good, so that the consumer's utility function is

$$U^1(q_{11}, q_{12}) = vq_{11} + q_{12}.$$

The second consumer derives a per-unit benefit c from consuming the first good and has a unitary marginal utility of the second good,

$$U^2(q_{21}, q_{22}) = cq_{21} + q_{22}.$$

The first consumer has an endowment $(0, \omega)$ and the second consumer has an endowment $(1, 0)$. The two consumers can obtain gains from trade by exchanging some or all of their endowments.

Suppose that the first good is not divisible and is available in discrete units, such as hats or chairs. The second good is a perfectly divisible commodity, such as wheat or wood. The second good can be used as commodity money providing a store of value, a medium of exchange, and a unit of account. In the pure-exchange economy with two consumers, the first consumer can be seen as a buyer and the second consumer as a seller.

Suppose that the two consumers live on different islands. If the buyer and seller engage in trade, they jointly encounter transaction costs that consume t units of the second good.[2] Transaction costs are distinct from the buyer's enjoyment of the good and from the seller's cost of providing the good. Suppose that the initial endowment of the divisible good is sufficient to cover transaction costs and to compensate the second consumer for transferring the first good, $\omega > t + c$.

Consider first the state of autarky. The buyer's initial benefit is $U^1(0, \omega) = \omega$. The seller has an endowment that consists of one unit of the discrete good and no endowment of the monetary good, so that the seller's initial benefit is $U^2(1, 0) = c$.

Next, compare the state of autarky with direct exchange between the two consumers. For simplicity, assign all of the transaction costs to the seller. If the buyer obtains a unit of the discrete good and pays a price $p < \omega$ of the monetary good, the consumer's benefit is $U^1(1, \omega - p) = v + \omega - p$. If the seller trades the unit of the discrete good to the first consumer in return for p units of the monetary good and incurs the joint transaction costs, the second consumer's benefit is $U^2(0, p - t) = p - t$.

The first consumer will wish to trade only if there are gains from trade,

$$U^1(1, \omega - p) - U^1(0, \omega) = v - p \geq 0.$$

The second consumer also will wish to trade only if there are gains from trade,

$$U^2(0, p - t) - U^2(1, 0) = p - c - t \geq 0.$$

For both consumers to obtain positive gains from trade requires that there are positive net gains from trade, $v - c - t > 0$. Both consumers have positive gains

---

2 Alternatively, transaction costs might be consumer-specific, where $t_1 + t_2 = t$.

from trade for p in $(c + t, v)$. The buyer makes any payment p that does not exceed the minimum of the buyer's benefit and the initial endowment of the monetary good, $p \leq \min\{v, \omega\}$. The seller accepts any payment that covers the opportunity cost of selling the good plus transaction costs, $p \geq c + t$.

Direct exchange between the buyer and seller yields transaction benefits net of transaction costs,

$$g = U^1(1, \omega - p) - U^1(0, \omega) + U^2(0, p) - U^2(1, 0) = v - c - t.$$

Direct exchange takes place only if there are net gains from trade, $g \geq 0$. This requires that gains from trade cover transaction costs, $v - c - t \geq 0$. If the net gains from trade are negative, the buyer and seller choose not to trade; that is, autarky results. Transaction costs are hidden under autarky because no trade occurs. Thus, implicit transaction costs are the forgone returns to trade, $v - c$.

The value created by a transaction equals the net gains from trade g between the buyer and the seller. The economy's transactions create value that equals the benefits of transactions net of the costs of organizing those transactions. Many of the economy's institutions of exchange are determined endogenously by the activities of consumers and firms maximizing the net benefits of transactions. The value created by the economy depends on the realization of gains from trade and the types of institutions of exchange that develop.

Firms establish institutions of exchange that supplement direct transactions between individual consumers. A firm offers the seller and the buyer an alternative set of transaction opportunities and mechanisms of exchange. To represent this, suppose that when transacting with the firm, the buyer obtains value V from the transaction and the seller incurs cost C in providing the good. This means that firms can improve the goods and services received by consumers through product and transaction innovations, potentially raising V. Also, firms can improve productivity and efficiency through process and transaction innovations, potentially lowering C.

The firm creates a transaction in many different ways. The firm can purchase a good from the seller and resell it to the buyer. The firm can match buyers and sellers and broker transactions. The firm can bring buyers and sellers together by transforming the good in some way through manufacturing, transportation, and so on. The transaction technology T refers to the firm's mechanisms of exchange that are distinct from those available for direct exchange between consumers. For example, consumers can engage in bilateral negotiation to complete an exchange. However, a firm can employ multilateral pricing mechanisms such as auctions. The types of transaction mechanisms specific to firms are discussed more fully in subsequent chapters.

Consider a firm that performs the basic functions of a dealer. The firm obtains the good from the seller and in return makes a payment to the seller. The firm supplies the good to the buyer and collects a payment from the buyer. The firm's intermediation activities consume resources. Let T represent the total of per-transaction costs for the seller, the buyer, and the firm. Transaction costs require using T units of the divisible good. Assume that there is a sufficient endowment of the divisible good to cover the transaction costs and compensate the seller, $\omega > C + T$.

For ease of presentation, suppose that the firm bears all of the transaction costs in its dealings with the buyer and the seller. This is equivalent to assuming that the firm compensates the seller and the buyer for the costs that they incur. The first consumer pays P to the firm and obtains gains from trade relative to autarky equal to

$$U^1(1, \omega - P) - U^1(0, \omega) = V - P \geq 0.$$

The second consumer receives W from the firm and obtains gains from trade relative to autarky equal to

$$U^2(0, W) - U^2(1, 0) = W - C \geq 0.$$

The firm's profit equals the bid-ask spread net of transaction costs,

$$\Pi = P - W - T.$$

The firm's creation and coordination of transactions through intermediated exchange yields gains from trade net of transaction costs equal to

$$G = U^1(1, \omega - P) - U^1(0, \omega) + U^2(0, W) - U^2(1, 0) + \Pi = V - C - T.$$

In comparison to autarky, the buyer and seller will trade through the firm only if the gains from trade are greater than total transaction costs, $G \geq 0$. The firm improves economic efficiency relative to direct exchange if and only if it increases net gains from trade, $G \geq g$, or equivalently,[3] $V - C - T \geq v - c - t$.

Suppose that there are n consumers and that consumers are restricted to bilateral transactions due to limits on their time and the costs of effort devoted to transactions. Suppose also that a firm can implement a transaction technology that permits multiple transactions. The firm's transaction technology has a fixed cost, T. Then, if the firm's transactions and the consumers' direct transactions are otherwise identical, the firm improves on direct exchange through economies of scale in transactions. Thus, $G \geq g$ when the firm offers lower total transaction costs in comparison to n bilateral transactions, $T \geq nt$. When the economy is sufficiently large, intermediated exchange through firms replaces direct exchange.

Figure 1.1 summarizes the comparison between the firm and direct exchange. The transaction triangle shows the alternatives. The line connecting the seller and the buyer represents direct exchange. The lines connecting the seller and the buyer to the firm represent the intermediated transactions. After a firm is established, the buyer and the seller choose between direct exchange with gains from trade g and intermediated exchange with gains from trade G. The firm plays an economic role if and only if intermediation of transactions yields greater benefits than does direct exchange.

3 If direct exchange is not feasible, the firm's added value equals its value created, G. Thus, if direct exchange is not feasible, the firm improves the efficiency of exchange relative to autarky if and only if $G \geq 0$.

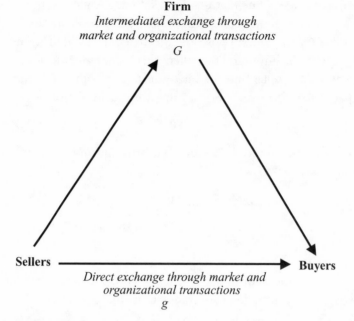

Firm

Intermediated exchange through
market and organizational transactions

G

Sellers ⟶ **Buyers**

Direct exchange through market and
organizational transactions

g

Figure 1.1. Comparison of intermediated exchange by firms with direct exchange between consumers. Intermediated exchange through the firm is efficient if and only if $G \geq g$ for $g \geq 0$, and $G \geq 0$ otherwise.

1.1.4 Example 2: Search versus Market-Making Firms

To illustrate the firm's role in intermediating exchange, consider an example with imperfect matching in a search market. Transaction costs are implicit because they take the form of imperfect matches of buyers and sellers. Suppose that there are two buyers with willingness to pay v_L and v_H, where $v_L < v_H$. Also, suppose that there are two sellers with costs c_L and c_H, where $c_L < c_H$.

Denote the expected value of the buyers' willingness-to-pay levels by

$$v = (1/2)v_L + (1/2)v_H.$$

Also, denote the expected value of the sellers' costs by

$$c = (1/2)c_L + (1/2)c_H.$$

A high-willingness-to-pay buyer can trade with both types of seller, $v_H > c_H$. A low-cost seller can trade with both types of buyer, $v_L > c_L$. Assume that $v_L < c_H$, so that a high-cost seller cannot trade with a low-willingness-to-pay buyer. This assumption means that the supply curve crosses the demand curve.

Before entering the market, buyers and sellers do not know the type of their trading partners. Assume that after a buyer and a seller decide to trade, they learn each other's type. At that point, trade occurs if and only if they have gains from trade. A buyer and a seller split the gains from trade evenly.

Given $v_L < c_H$, the search market is inefficient. It is easy to demonstrate that otherwise, if $v_L \geq c_H$, all matches are feasible, so that direct exchange is efficient. Moreover, if $v_L \geq c_H$, there do not exist any prices at which a monopoly firm is viable.[4] Thus, consumers would have no need for a firm to intermediate exchange.

With random matching, the expected gains from trade for the high-willingness-to-pay buyer equal $(v_H - c)/2$. The expected gains from trade for the low-cost seller equal $(v - c_L)/2$. However, because $v_L < c_H$, a low-willingness-to-pay buyer has expected gains from trade in the direct exchange market equal to $(v_L - c_L)/4$, because he has only one other potential trading partner. A high-cost seller has expected gains from trade equal to $(v_H - c_H)/4$.

Consider a firm with fixed transaction costs, T. The profit-maximizing firm chooses the highest ask price, p, and the lowest bid price, w, that will attract the high-willingness-to-pay buyer and the low-cost seller,

$$p^M = v_H - (v_H - c)/2 \quad \text{and} \quad w^M = c_L + (v - c_L)/2.$$

The firm's profit equals

$$\Pi = p^M - w^M - T = (c_H - v_L)/2 - T.$$

The low-willingness-to-pay buyer and high-cost seller are inactive because they do not gain from direct exchange with each other.

Direct exchange between consumers, that is, exchange without the presence of firms, yields expected gains from trade equal to

$$g = (1/2)(v_H - c_L) + (1/2)[(v_H - c_H) + (v_L - c_L)].$$

The expected gains from trade with a firm equal

$$G = (v_H - p^M) + (w^M - c_L) + p^M - w^M - T$$
$$= v_H - c_L - T.$$

The firm improves economic efficiency relative to direct exchange if and only if it increases net gains from trade. This is equivalent in this case to the requirement that the firm is profitable,

$$G - g = \Pi = (c_H - v_L)/2 - T \geq 0.$$

The firm obtains profit equal to the increase in the gains from trade. The firm improves efficiency if and only if the gap between the high-cost seller and the low-willingness-to-pay buyer is greater than or equal to the firm's fixed transaction costs. A larger gap, all other things equal, reduces the gains to consumers from direct exchange. A larger gap correspondingly increases the profits to the firm from intermediating exchange. This illustrates the intermediation hypothesis.

---

4 If $v_L \geq c_H$, all combinations of buyers and sellers can trade in the direct exchange market. Then, because they are uninformed about the type of their trading partners, the expected gains from trade of a type-i buyer and a type-j seller from the direct exchange market are respectively $(v_i - c)/2$, $i = L, H$, and $(v - c_j)/2$, $j = L, H$.

1.1.5 Example 3: Clubs versus Firms

Consider a club whose members share the fixed costs of producing an excludable public good. Let the fixed costs of the good equal c. The number of members of the club equals n. Members of the club derive benefits $u(n)$ from consuming the public good. The club is subject to problems of congestion, so that the member benefits $u(n)$ are decreasing and concave in the size of the club. Suppose that individuals may obtain a substitute good without joining the club, with net benefits v.

The identification of the club's objectives with its members' consumption benefits is what distinguishes a club from a firm. The members of the club determine the size of the club. Their objective is to maximize their individual consumption benefits,

$$u(n) - c/n.$$

The optimal size of the club, n^0, therefore solves

$$-u'(n^0) = c/(n^0)^2.$$

The club is viable if it offers benefits over competing alternatives, $u(n^0) - c/n^0 \geq v$.

Consider a profit-maximizing firm that offers the excludable public good. The firm charges the highest price subject to the constraint from the outside alternative. Thus, the firm's price equals

$$p = u(n) - v.$$

The firm's profit is then

$$\Pi(n) = pn - c = n(u(n) - v) - c.$$

The firm chooses the number of customers to maximize its profit, trading off congestion effects that reduce consumer benefits with the revenue advantages of serving more customers. The firm's profit-maximizing number of customers, n^F, solves

$$-u'(n^F) = (u(n^F) - v)/n^F.$$

The firm maximizes total benefits and thus is more efficient than the club, which maximizes average benefits.[5] The profit-maximizing firm serves more customers than the club, $n^F > n^0$.[6]

The members of the club would not prefer to organize the club as a firm. This is because club membership maximizes the members' individual benefits. Suppose

---

5 The fixed costs of producing the public good do not enter into the firm's choice of the number of customers. If there were variable costs associated with the quantity of a public good, these would affect the firm's choices.

6 From the firm's first-order condition, it follows that $-u'(n^F) = (u(n^F) - v)/n^F > c/(n^F)^2$. Comparing to the first-order condition for the club, and noting that $u''(n) < 0$, implies that $n^F > n^0$.

that members could purchase the good from the firm and obtain a share of the firm's profits. Then a member of the club would obtain greater benefits than a customer/owner of the firm:

$$u(n^0) - c/n^0 \geq u(n^F) - c/n^F = u(n^F) - p^F + \Pi(n^F)/n^F.$$

Suppose, however, that the original members of the club are considered as owners of the club, and that there is a market for club memberships. A membership market for labor-managed firms induces profit maximization; see Dow (2003, p. 149).

Consider how a membership market affects the club's objectives. Let n^0 be the number of original members and let n be the expanded size of the club. All members of the club would obtain benefits net of shared fixed costs, $u(n) - c/n$. A new member is charged a membership fee equal to the difference between net benefits and the value of the outside opportunity, $u(n) - c/n - v$. Insiders choose the number of total members to maximize their individual benefits plus their share of earnings from selling new memberships,

$$U(n) = u(n) - c/n + (u(n) - c/n - v)(n - n^0)/n^0.$$

Simplifying this expression yields

$$U(n) = (1/n^0)\Pi(n) + v.$$

Maximizing each member's benefits over the size of the club yields the profit-maximizing size, n^F. Therefore, when insiders sell shares in the club to new members, they will choose the profit-maximizing membership.

This provides a separation theorem. The objectives of a club can be separated from those of its members when the club's inside members sell memberships to new members. The inside members are the owners of the firm. When inside members choose to sell shares to outside members, the objectives of the club become separate from their consumption objectives and the club becomes a firm.

When consumers form a club, the gains from trade in direct exchange equal

$$g = n^0 u(n^0) - c - n^0 v.$$

Establishing a firm that intermediates exchange yields gains from trade equal to

$$G = n^0 U(n^F) - n^0 v = n^F u(n^F) - c - n^F v.$$

Profit maximization implies that gains from trade increase when a firm intermediates exchange,

$$G - g = \Pi(n^F) - \Pi(n^0) > 0.$$

Because the firm's objectives are separate from the consumption objectives of its owners, establishing a firm increases gains from trade.

1.2 Consumer Characteristics

The general theory of the firm begins with consumers. There is a set of consumers in the economy, $N = \{1, 2, \ldots, n\}$. Denote by i an individual consumer. In the theory of the firm, the preferences and endowments of consumers generally are taken as givens.[7] The preferences and endowments of consumers are the foundations of the theory of the firm.

The discussion follows standard usage in designating all individuals as "consumers." In addition to being buyers of goods and services, consumers also play important economic roles as workers, managers, suppliers of resources, owners of assets, and entrepreneurs. The number of consumers n will turn out to have significant effects on transaction benefits and costs. This is perhaps the critical determinant of whether or not firms will be established in the economy.

1.2.1 Consumer Endowments

In describing consumer endowments, the theory of the firm incorporates the neoclassical theory of the consumer, but with some notable extensions and additions. Consumer endowments of commodities can be represented as a vector ω^i in the consumption set X^i in the product space R^L, where i is an element of N and where L is the number of products. The number of goods in the economy can be taken as given or the number of goods can be determined endogenously through product innovation.

Consumer endowments can be final consumption goods. Consumer endowments also can be factors of production such as land and natural resources or commodities that are used as both productive inputs and consumption goods. Consumers can have an initial endowment of time that can be used for leisure, labor, and other time-consuming tasks. The consumer can also have an endowment of fiat money or a numeraire good, if these exist. These possibilities conform to the standard neoclassical model.

Consumers in the theory of the firm own production technologies. In the neoclassical framework, consumers own production technologies through their ownership of firms. In the present framework, consumers can operate production technologies without the need for firms. Consumer i owns a production technology Y^i in the product space R^L, where i is an element of the set of consumers N. A

---

7 Some models consider consumers in a transferable utility setting. Other models apply the neoclassical theory of the consumer, in which each consumer i has ordinal preferences over consumption bundles in their consumption set within a product space. The preferences of the consumer are generalized in standard ways. In particular, consumers can value time spent on leisure. Consumers can evaluate consumption bundles that have goods that are consumed at different points in time. They can apply subjective rates of discount to future consumption. Some models examined in later chapters also consider consumers with von Neumann-Morgenstern utility functions exhibiting risk aversion. As in agency models, consumers can experience disutility of effort.

consumer can operate a production technology either individually or in concert with other consumers. In the neoclassical setting, firms are defined as production technologies and only firms can be producers. Here, firms are institutions rather than production technologies.

Consumers in a general theory of the firm possess practically any knowledge that people have in practice. The theoretical analysis should not artificially limit consumer knowledge while *a priori* assigning that knowledge to firms. Consumers possess information, ideas, and other types of intellectual property. Consumers have scientific and engineering information and many other forms of knowledge as part of their endowments. Consumers can have private information about their own preferences and endowments that is not observable by others. Consumers, in some cases, can have information about the preferences and endowments of other consumers.

The technologies and intellectual property owned by consumers can be established exogenously. Alternatively, the production technologies owned by consumers can be determined endogenously through process innovation. Consumers can transfer technologies to other consumers or to firms, including the sale of intellectual property.

In addition to production technologies, consumers can own transaction technologies. Such a transaction method t^i, where i is a member of the set of consumers, can be used to represent a vast array of possible ways of interaction between consumers. They can include search, communication, negotiation, payment methods, and contract formation. These types of transaction methods are referred to as direct exchange or decentralized exchange to indicate that they operate without firms. These types of transaction technologies do not operate through intermediaries such as firms.

A consumer i also can own a transaction method T^i that represents centralized exchange through firms, where i is an element of the set of consumers N. These types of transaction technologies include centralized market mechanisms such as posted prices, auctions, and matchmaking services.

Consumer-entrepreneurs may establish firms and provide the firms with their transaction technology. The transaction technology T^i can be viewed as the intellectual property of the consumer. The transaction technology also can be interpreted as the result of invention of a new business method. Spulber (2002c) introduces the concept of a "transaction innovation."

1.2.2 Consumer Activities

Consumers play many economic roles. They can engage in a wide variety of activities, some of which are consistent with the neoclassical model and some of which clearly are not. As in the traditional neoclassical setting, consumers purchase final consumption goods and supply primary goods to other consumers and to firms. Consumers provide labor services, acting as consumer-workers.

Consumers can operate production technology, acting as consumer-producers. As already noted, this departs from the neoclassical setting in which only firms can be producers. Consumers are skilled craftsmen, manufacturers, and farmers. Consumers are merchants and intermediaries between other consumers. They provide services as physicians, attorneys, and accountants. Consumers create works of art as musicians, composers, dancers, authors, painters, and sculptors.

Also, consumers are inventors, devising new products or new production processes. They generate new information by imagination, observation, calculation, and reasoning. They can create scientific research and are owners of intellectual property. Consumer-inventors can employ inventions in production or they can sell the intellectual property to other consumers.

Consumers also participate in financial markets by borrowing, saving, and investing in firms. Once firms are established, consumers then transact with firms as customers buying the firms' output. Consumers also supply the firm with capital, resources, production technology, and transaction methods. Consumers are the managers and employees of the firm.

Perhaps most critically for the theory of the firm, consumers establish firms by acting as entrepreneurs. Having established a firm, a consumer-entrepreneur becomes an owner of the firm. This will be spelled out more fully in Chapters 4 and 5.

1.3 Consumer Cooperation and Transaction Benefits

Establishing firms can improve the efficiency of transactions relative to exchange between consumers without firms. To understand transactions, it is necessary to know the purpose of transactions. Because transactions are voluntary, they must yield benefits for each of the parties. Consumers transact with other consumers to obtain those benefits. Identifying potential gains from trade allows a classification of transactions. Such a classification suggests what types of costs are required to accomplish the transaction. Such a classification also shows the purpose of firms, because their objective is to increase transaction benefits net of transaction costs.

The Pareto ranking of economic allocations, which is at the heart of neoclassical economics, welfare economics, and international trade, tells us much about transaction benefits. Neoclassical analysis considers economic equilibria that are attained without transaction costs. Direct exchange between two consumers results in an allocation of goods on the contract curve. If there are no costs of establishing and operating a price system with a Walrasian auctioneer, then the two theorems of welfare economics hold. Any market equilibrium will be an allocation on the contract curve, and any allocation on the contract curve can be supported by a price system with a suitable redistribution of initial endowments. More generally, any market equilibrium is a Pareto optimal allocation and any Pareto optimal allocation can be supported by a market equilibrium given a suitable redistribution of initial endowments.

Representing transaction benefits using neoclassical efficiency conditions does not suggest that the economy reaches a Pareto optimum. Pareto improvement is a necessary but not a sufficient condition for a transaction. The choice of transactions for individuals and in the aggregate will depend on transaction costs and the institutions of exchange.

Although neoclassical economics has tended to neglect the institutions of exchange, it provides a solid foundation for understanding the benefits of exchange. The literature on transaction costs, in rejecting the frictionless equilibrium of neoclassical economics, tends to bypass many of the major contributions of classical and neoclassical economics. But these are the rules of economics – the returns to specialization and division of labor that have been studied at least since Adam Smith. A comprehensive understanding of the institutions of exchange necessarily incorporates the benefits of exchange.

Transaction benefits explain the incentives of individuals to participate in transactions. They illustrate the types of trading partners and the types of exchanges that would be preferred in a frictionless world. The complexity of transaction benefits helps to suggest the diverse types of transactions that would be needed to achieve some of these benefits. Some transaction benefits are more subtle and involve some types of cooperation that do not necessarily correspond to the neoclassical efficiency conditions. Of course, the types of trades that will occur in the economy cannot be determined without introducing transaction costs, which are the subject of the next section.

In what follows, many of the potential gains from trade result from pure exchange and from cooperation in production. The discussion is presented in terms of the benefits that consumers receive when they engage in direct exchange with each other. This includes exchange between consumers who own endowments of goods and services or consumers who own and operate production technology. This helps to distinguish gains from trade from institutions of exchange.

1.3.1 Marginal Rates of Substitution

Consider a pure exchange economy in which each consumer has an initial endowment of goods. The slope of a consumer's indifference curve is the marginal rate of substitution. For a given allocation of endowments of goods, marginal rates of substitution differ across consumers. By trading endowments, two consumers can reduce the differences between their marginal rates of substitution. Each consumer will receive an allocation of goods that they prefer to their initial endowment.

Consider a standard pure exchange economy with two consumers and two goods. Each consumer i has an initial endowment of the two goods, $\omega^i = (\omega_1^i, \omega_2^i)$, $i = 1, 2$. The consumers have preferences represented by continuously differentiable and concave utility functions $U^i(q_1^i, q_2^i)$, $i = 1, 2$. If the two consumers cannot meet to trade for some reason, then they are restricted to consumption of their initial endowments.

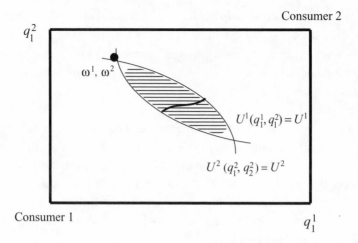

Figure 1.2. Potential gains from trade and the contract curve.

Gains from trade refer to the improvement of consumer benefits relative to what they obtain by consuming their initial endowments. Figure 1.2 depicts the classic Edgeworth-Bowley box. The set of allocations that make both consumers at least as well off and one consumer better off than they are at their initial endowments is represented by the lens-shaped shaded area in Figure 1.2. The contract curve is the set of Pareto-efficient allocations. Along the contract curve, the two consumers' marginal rates of substitution are equalized. The Core is the portion of the contract curve within the lens, which is shown as a bold line. The Core is the set of allocations that are Pareto efficient and Pareto superior to the initial endowment point.

These gains from trade cannot be attained unless the two consumers are able to carry out a transaction. Those transactions outside the lens are Pareto inferior to the allocation of initial endowments, because both consumers are worse off. Those transactions within the lens are Pareto superior to the allocation of initial endowments, while those allocations on the contract curve are Pareto superior to all other allocations. Each consumer is made better off without making the other consumer worse off.

In the neoclassical model of the pure exchange economy, consumers engage in direct exchange without transaction costs. Consumer exchange is mediated through markets that are established exogenously and the Walrasian auctioneer exogenously adjusts prices. Consumers maximize preferences subject to budget constraints where consumer wealth is the market value of initial endowments, evaluated at market-clearing prices. Consumers take prices as given exogenously. At the market equilibrium, each consumer's market basket is chosen independent of the choices of other consumers, although the preferences of all consumers affect aggregate demand and thus determine equilibrium prices along with the supply of initial endowments. In the neoclassical framework, therefore, prices separate consumer decisions in comparison with bilateral exchange through barter. When there is a complete set of markets, that is, a market is established corresponding to each good, the economy attains a Pareto optimum.

If transactions are costly, gains from trade must be greater than or equal to transaction costs for trade to occur. Economic agents will choose those transactions that produce the greatest net gains from trade, that is, with the greatest transaction benefits net of transaction costs. The resulting transactions need not be those with the greatest gains from trade, because other transactions may be more convenient or efficient. With many goods and many consumers, reducing differences in marginal rates of substitution across the economy is likely to require many bilateral trades.

1.3.2 Marginal Rates of Technical Substitution

The neoclassical production technology when there are multiple inputs has isoquants that represent combinations of inputs necessary to produce a given output level. The slope of the isoquant is the marginal rate of technical substitution. Suppose that producers are consumers who own and operate production technologies. For a given allocation of input endowments, marginal rates of technical substitution differ across producers. By trading endowments of inputs, two producers can reduce the differences between their marginal rates of technical substitution. Each producer will receive an allocation of inputs that lets them increase output relative to the output they could produce with their initial endowment of inputs.

With many inputs and many producers, reducing differences in marginal rates of technical substitution is likely to require many bilateral trades. Chapter 2 further examines the economy with production.

1.3.3 Relative Factor Productivities

In the classic Ricardian gains from trade, two countries have different relative factor productivities. For a given allocation of input endowments, and fixed coefficients technology, each of the two countries can change their output mix by altering the underlying allocation of inputs. By trading outputs, the two countries each can increase available outputs relative to their initial output mix. The two countries can be viewed as individual consumers who have endowments of inputs and each own and operate different production technologies. Such gains from trade apply to many other situations. For example, they extend to two producers who each potentially produce the same set of goods. Gains from trade are achieved by each producer specializing in different subsets of goods. With many producers and many goods, taking full advantage of potential gains from trade likely will require many bilateral trades.

1.3.4 Marginal Rates of Transformation

Suppose that a producer is a consumer who owns and operates a multiproduct technology. A producer with a given multiproduct technology and a given endowment of inputs will have a production possibilities frontier that represents the combinations of products that can be produced. The marginal rate of transformation is the slope of the production possibilities frontier. Two producers with production possibilities frontiers can have different marginal rates of product transformation. By trading outputs, two producers can obtain classic gains from trade. The gains from trade result from moving along the production possibilities frontiers such that the producers reduce the differences between their marginal rates of transformation. The potential gains from trade reflect differences in underlying endowments of productive resources or differences in technologies. For example, the classic Heckscher-Ohlin theorem in international trade states that each country exports the good that makes relatively more use of the input that it has in greater abundance. Technology differences also lead to specialization. With many goods and many producers, more complex patterns of trade are likely to be necessary to take full advantage of gains from trade.

1.3.5 Producer Marginal Rates of Transformation and Consumer Marginal Rates of Substitution

In the present framework, consumers can own and operate multiproduct production technologies. Consumers also have endowments of final goods. When producer marginal rates of transformation differ from consumer marginal rates of substitution, there are opportunities to change the mix of products produced and to exchange those products with other consumer-producers and with other consumers. Gains from trade are realized when producer marginal rates of transformation move closer to consumer marginal rates of substitution. These type of transactions require coordination of both consumption and production decisions. As before, when there are many producers and many goods, taking full advantage of these types of potential gains from trade likely will require many bilateral trades.

1.3.6 Economies of Scale and Scope

Suppose that consumers have access to a common production technology that exhibits economies of scale. Then consumers will benefit from cooperation to jointly produce the good. This will require coordination across multiple consumers to take advantage of joint production economies. There will be a need to coordinate production and consumption decisions. Gains from trade are realized as a result of lower total costs of production when output production is combined. Additional gains from trade are obtained from increased consumption that can be achieved from lower costs. In addition, lower production costs due to economies of scale permit consumers to produce a greater variety of goods.[8] A related type of gains

---

8 This type of gains from trade is observed in models of international trade, such as Krugman (1979).

from trade results from economies of scope that would result from joint production of different products. Gains from trade are realized from lower total costs when products are produced together. Further gains from trade from economies of scope are realized from increased consumption and greater product variety. Coordination of multiple consumers to take advantage of economies of scale and scope will require multilateral trades or a coordinated set of exchanges.

1.3.7 Risk Aversion

Consumers who are risk averse can obtain gains from trade by sharing risk through insurance and other types of risk-sharing contracts. Consumers who face different types of risk can benefit from pooling their risks. Consumers with different marginal rates of substitution across states of the world can benefit by reallocating resources across states through risk-sharing agreements. Gains from trade are realized by narrowing the differences between their marginal rates of substitution across states of the world. More consumers with diverse risks widen the pool and increase gains from trade. Taking advantage of risk pooling requires multiple trades.

1.3.8 Rates of Time Preference

Consumers can obtain gains from trade by exchanging goods over time. Consumers may have different marginal rates of substitution across time periods. These differences may be due to different rates of time preference or to the allocation of endowments. Consumers realize benefits by transferring goods over time and narrowing differences in their marginal rates of substitution. Consumers also realize gains from trade through borrowing and lending. Realizing the benefits from differences in rates of time preference could require multiple trades because consumers will benefit from debts and loans of varying size and duration.

1.3.9 Delegation

A consumer acting as a principal can benefit from delegating authority to another consumer acting as an agent. There are gains from trade for the principal and agent if the agent has some particular skill or expertise that the principal does not have. Total productivity is increased by delegating a productive task to an agent. There are also gains from trade if the principal has a different opportunity cost of time than the agent. The agent can act as the principal's representative in dealing with third parties.

1.3.10 Cooperative Production

Consumer-workers may have complementary skills that allow them to produce efficiently in a team, producing more together than they could produce separately.

Consumer-workers who initially have similar skills may obtain gains from trade from a division of labor and from the expertise that comes from specialization. This is one aspect of Adam Smith's key insight that specialization and division of labor depend on the extent of the market and was exemplified by Smith's classic example of the pin factory. To obtain these benefits of joint production requires consumer-workers to participate in transactions that support joint production. Some types of benefits from specialization and division of labor can be realized simply by trading the output produced by individuals and realizing gains from trade. Other types of benefits of specialization require working together directly to manufacture goods and services.

1.3.11 Public Goods

Public goods have the property that consumption is not competitive, so that multiple consumers can benefit from consuming the same good. For example, multiple consumers can benefit from sharing information. Multiple consumers can enjoy illumination from the same street light. There are also local public goods for which access can be excluded. Public goods provide potential gains from trade because consumers can share the costs of jointly producing a public good instead of each consumer bearing the full costs of separately producing the same public good. For example, it is efficient to produce a movie that is seen by many people, rather than producing a different movie for each person. Obtaining the benefits of a public good requires coordinating the production and joint consumption of the public good so that consumers can share the cost savings. The cost savings from joint production of public goods generate additional gains from trade because they permit increases in the quantity, quality, and variety of the public goods that are provided.

1.3.12 Externalities

When there are externalities there are potential gains from trade. This is the situation described by Coase (1960), who considered bargaining over the extent of externalities. Suppose that there are two consumers, and one creates pollution that harms the other. The pollution provides benefits to the polluting consumer because it is a byproduct of consumption. For example, suppose that the pollution consists of the noise from a loud radio. Suppose that there are no legal restrictions on pollution. Then there are potential gains from trade that can be achieved if the consumer creating the pollution reduces the pollution in return for compensation from the consumer being harmed by the pollution. Alternatively, suppose that there are legal restrictions on pollution if another is harmed. Then there are potential gains from trade that can be achieved if the consumer creating the pollution is able to continue some pollution by paying compensation to the consumer being harmed by the pollution.

1.4 Consumer Coordination and Transaction Costs

Consumer coordination to achieve transaction benefits entails transaction costs. Neoclassical economics generally assumes frictionless transactions. Markets establish prices and allocate goods and services without consuming resources. When transactions are costly, however, the economy can only move toward outcomes that satisfy the traditional neoclassical efficiency conditions. Consumers can achieve some but not all potential transaction benefits. The neoclassical efficiency conditions must be modified to take transaction costs into account.

Consumers expend time, effort, and resources in arranging transactions. The great diversity of institutions of exchange reflects the potential benefits and the relative costs of alternative transactions. Transaction costs are economic forces that deter or prevent exchange. The many type of exchanges are designed to overcome such frictions and obtain gains from trade. The many types of gains from trade require different types of coordination between consumers. Thus, the structure of transactions depends on the underlying transaction benefits and transaction costs. This section examines some of the major categories of transaction costs.

1.4.1 Communication and Information Processing

Consumers must communicate with one another to arrange trades or to form consumer organizations. Even the most basic bilateral trade requires communication and information processing. Forming consumer organizations requires more complex communication and information processing. Consumers must make and receive offers and evaluate economic alternatives. Consumers can experience cognitive limits in processing market information and attempting to make rational decisions based on that information. Simon (1976, pp. 81–84) cautions that there are limits to rationality: incomplete knowledge, imperfect anticipation of future events, and difficulty in identifying all possible alternatives.[9] Williamson (1985, p. 45) observes that "[b]ounded rationality is the cognitive assumption on which transaction cost economics relies."

For consumers to achieve transaction benefits often requires either simultaneous multilateral transactions or at least a series of bilateral transactions. In the context of mitigating externalities, Coase (1960) emphasized that the more parties are involved, the greater will be the costs of bargaining. This fundamental insight can be applied to the theory of the firm. The more consumers are involved, the greater will be the costs of arranging bilateral transactions.

With multiple goods and multiple consumers, achieving gains from trade requires multilateral trades or a complex series of trades. Moving toward equality

---

9 Rubinstein (1998) examines diverse attempts at economic modeling of bounded rationality. He considers models that address procedural decision making, defining knowledge, limited memory, choosing what to know, and limits on strategic decision making in games.

of marginal rates of substitution entails a reallocation of initial endowments. Also, consumers prefer greater variety, due to convex preferences. If consumers have sufficiently different endowments, multiple trades realize higher gains from trade.

For many types of transaction benefits, the more consumers that are involved the better. For example, the benefits of risk sharing are enhanced when the number of consumers that pool risks is greater. Multiple consumers are needed to realize the benefits that result from economies of scale. Realizing the benefits of joint production of public goods requires many consumers.

Multiple consumer-workers must be involved for the benefits of joint production to be attained. Consumer-workers can offer complementary skills or realize the benefits of specialization and division of labor. Multiple consumer-workers are needed to achieve the benefits of delegation of authority. Achieving the benefits of joint production is likely to require a complex set of transactions to coordinate the consumer-workers who will cooperate in production.

Further transactions are then needed for the group of consumer-workers engaged in productive activities to trade with other consumers or other groups of consumer-workers who will provide financing, materials and productive inputs. Also, the group of consumer-workers engaged in joint production may need to sell or trade its output with other consumers or other groups of consumer-workers to achieve gains from trade.

The transaction costs of carrying out and coordinating multiple transactions are likely to increase substantially the transaction costs identified for bilateral exchange. The costs of searching for multiple trading partners are likely to increase more than proportionately. Compare the cost of arranging a meeting between two people with the costs of arranging a meeting with more than two people. Scheduling conflicts are likely to multiply.

Consider the potential number of interactions between n people. There are $\frac{1}{2}n(n-1)$ potential contacts, so that the number of potential contacts increases with the square of the number of people. Often this point illustrates the benefits of belonging to a network, because having more members means more potential contacts. However, when contacts are costly, the need to make more potential contacts implies that costs tend to increase with the square of the number of people involved. Thus, communication can become more difficult with a larger group of consumers.

The costs of assembling and managing a team for joint production can be substantial. Finding the members of the team involves the costs of search and negotiation required for group transactions. The costs of putting a group together are likely to increase more than proportionally with the size of the group.

1.4.2 Search and Matching

When there are few consumers, transaction costs tend to be small and consumers can achieve efficient allocations through barter and bargaining. They can transact within families and social groups. They can form cooperatives to coordinate efforts and share the fruits of productive activities. In contrast, when there are many consumers, the transaction costs of coordination will tend to be large. With many consumers, transaction costs are likely to increase disproportionately, sometimes outweighing the benefits of greater opportunities for trade.

Search costs involve time, effort, and resources. There are costs to finding the right type of trading partner when there are diverse buyers and diverse sellers. Consumers must cope with the effects of asymmetric information that make the characteristics of potential trading partners costly to observe. As a means of dealing with search costs, consumers can incur the costs of forming various types of social and business networks. In addition, consumers may bear the costs of establishing travel and communications networks. The transaction costs of finding trading partners involve both the direct costs of search and the indirect costs of imperfect matches. Product differentiation increases the costs of finding a suitable trading partner. For example, search costs are greater in real estate markets because houses are differentiated products.

The problem of "the absence of a double coincidence of wants" refers to the situation in which such costs are prohibitive and lead to autarky. A consumer with apples who is seeking oranges must find a trading partner with oranges who is seeking apples. Additionally, the consumer must find such a trading partner at the desired time and place. Generally, the benefits from exchange must exceed transaction costs to avoid the problem of the absence of a double coincidence of wants.

1.4.3 Bargaining

Bargaining is necessary for bilateral exchange between consumers. Consumers also need to bargain with each other to establish and manage an organization. Bargaining requires time and effort. Similarly to the labor-leisure choice, individuals will value the time spent on transactions in comparison to their opportunity costs of time. Consumers determine the benefits from goods and services taking into account the convenience of the transactions needed to acquire them. Because bargaining takes time, there is a transaction cost from the delay in consumption. The present value of benefits derived from goods and services will reflect a consumer's rate of time preference and the time needed to complete the transaction. The cost of bargaining also depends on consumers' disutility of effort spent on negotiation. Some consumers may enjoy the social interaction in market exchange more than others. Consumers may differ in the effectiveness or productivity of effort devoted to transactions. Some consumers are more skilled at search or bargaining.

Bargaining costs have efficiency implications. Consumers will forego some transactions if bargaining costs exceed gains from trade. For more complex negotiations, bargaining costs can result in incomplete contracts that imperfectly share risks. Costly bargaining can lead to mistakes in transactions. The costs of bargaining may prevent the formation of some types of consumer organizations or limit the size of such organizations.

1.4.4 Moral Hazard

Consumers engaged in bilateral exchange encounter transaction costs due to moral hazard. Consider a consumer who contracts with another consumer to produce a good. Suppose that the effort of the producer is unobservable. The transaction may be inefficient relative to the outcome under full information. For example, in the moral hazard model of agency, the principal pays the agent to carry out a designated task and the agent decides how much effort to devote to the task. The principal hires an agent because she does not have the time or capability to do the work herself. The principal's problem is to design an incentive schedule that motivates the agent to choose a desired level of effort.

The principal must rely on performance-based rewards such as bonuses and commissions to induce the agent to work. The contract could potentially induce the agent to devote an efficient level of effort by allowing the agent to keep all the returns to his effort. Yet such a performance-based rewards system has the significant drawback that it shifts risk to the agent. Suppose that the principal is risk-neutral but the agent is risk-averse. The principal needs to compensate the agent for the cost of risk-bearing to induce him to enter the relationship. Accordingly, to reduce the risk borne by the agent, thus reducing the cost of compensating the agent for that risk, optimal contracts consist generally of a fixed payment plus some performance-based rewards. Sharing output between the principal and the agent necessarily results in some shirking because the agent's rewards do not capture the full effects of his effort.

1.4.5 Adverse Selection

Asymmetric information creates various types of adverse selection problems. These problems affect the efficiency of bilateral exchange between consumers. Akerlof's (1970) model of the "market for lemons" showed that bad cars can drive out good cars. In product markets with unobservable quality, buyers will make their participation decisions on the basis of expected quality.

Asymmetric information can affect the extent of trade. When a buyer and a seller have bilateral asymmetric information, they may decide not to trade even though the buyer's willingness to pay exceeds the seller's cost; see Myerson and Satterthwaite (1983). Asymmetric information affects bilateral exchange between an investor and producer. Diamond (1984) considers a model in which investors make loans to producers who observe the outcome of an uncertain investment project. Producers have an incentive to understate the outcome of the investment project. The optimal contract between an investor and a producer takes the form of debt. The debt contract provides incentives for the producer to report the outcome of the investment project.

Principal-agent transactions are subject to adverse selection problems. The principal designs the menu of contracts so that at a separating equilibrium she will know with certainty the agent's preferences by observing the agent's choice from the menu. Thus, contracts are self-selecting and the agent will end up revealing his type. Each contract in the menu consists of a payment and an effort level and it is tailored to one of the agents' types. In the case of two types of agents, the contract written for the low-cost agent provides a large payment in exchange for large effort. The contract written for the high-cost agent has lower payment but also requires lower effort. If both contracts gave the same payment, both types of agent would choose the same contract, the one that required less effort. The high-cost agent ends up getting the income that he could get elsewhere in the market, his reservation utility. The low-cost agent obtains informational rents to induce revelation of private information.

1.4.6 Free Riding

The costs of group decision making are likely to be substantially greater than the costs of bilateral negotiation. Achieving a consensus becomes more difficult when many people are involved. As the number of parties to the negotiation increases, different devices such as committees and voting may be required, with all the attendant inefficiencies of collective decision making.

Even after the team is assembled, coordination requires group negotiation costs. In addition, the group will face the costs of selecting and rewarding leaders and the possibility of malfeasance by the leaders. Forming a hierarchy to deal with group coordination entails problems that result from moral hazard, adverse selection, and collusion on the part of subordinates.

An association of consumers is likely to engage in noncooperative behavior that results in free riding. Associations of consumers include buyers' cooperatives, workers' cooperatives, and partnerships. Consumers may offer contributions to the group that fail to maximize joint benefits. They may shirk as a best response to anticipated equilibrium behavior by other group members. Consumers may also misrepresent their preferences as a best response to anticipated equilibrium disclosure of other group members.

An important source of transaction costs for group decision making is due to the budget balancing constraint. An allocation mechanism for a group of consumers must satisfy a balanced budget. In many cases, such break-even mechanisms fail to achieve efficient allocations.

1.4.7 Contracting

Buyers and sellers face a contracting process with several stages, each of which brings its own transaction costs. Transaction costs can introduce inefficiencies at each stage of the process. Moreover, transaction costs in one stage of the contracting process can affect decisions and efficiency at another stage in the contracting process. It is useful to consider three general stages of contracting. First, potential

contracting partners must engage in costly search to find each other. Second, potential contracting partners must negotiate and formalize the terms of the contract,
which entails communication costs, the time costs of bargaining, and the costs of
writing the contract. A buyer and seller who face bargaining costs may negotiate
an incomplete contract that yields lower expected gains from trade than would the
complete contingent contract that might be chosen in the absence of transaction
costs. Third, after the contract has been formed, the contracting partners must
make decisions about performance of the agreed-upon terms, monitoring of performance, settlement of payments, verification of states of the world, and possible
contract renegotiation. In the event of a breach of contract, there are legal and
transaction costs of contract enforcement.

There has been considerable discussion in economics of the problem of contract
hold-up. Although contract law enforces efficient contracts, it is not always possible
to write complete contingent contracts. One of the parties may seek to renegotiate
the agreements after the other party has made an investment in the relationships.
When such investments are specific to the relationship, renegotiating contract terms
takes advantage of relationship-specific investment. In making investments that are
relationship-specific, the parties will anticipate the possibility that the agreement
will be renegotiated. This can lead to inefficient investment.

The standard underinvestment result arises from the inability of the parties to
make a binding commitment; see for example Grout (1984). The buyer and seller
division of the ex post returns to trade lowers the marginal returns to investment
below the ex ante returns to investment. Also, the value of the outside option for the
buyer and seller enters into their investment decisions, as shown by Hart and Moore
(1990). The return to investment is lowered because it is a weighted average of the
outside option and the ex ante return, and the marginal effect of investment on
the outside option is lower than that of the ex ante return. Moreover, the externality
effects operating through the outside option functions influence the equilibrium
investment levels of the buyer and seller.

1.5 Consumer Organizations and the Separation Criterion

Consumers form all sorts of transactions, contracts, and organizations that should
not be classified as firms. These institutions may perform some functions that
are similar to those carried out by firms, including intermediation of transactions.
These organizations may be precursors to firms and may evolve into firms. However,
many types of consumer organizations make decisions that are often not separable
from the interests of consumers who establish, own, manage, or are members of
the organization.

An institution satisfies the *separation criterion* if the objectives of the institution
can be distinguished from those of its owners. This section applies the separation
criterion to demonstrate that consumer transactions and organizations are not

firms. Chapter 2 further develops the theory of the firm based on the separation criterion.

1.5.1 Autarky

Under autarky, the consumer's production and consumption decisions are intertwined. The consumer produces a mix of outputs and combines inputs to maximize his net benefits subject to his production possibilities. Therefore, autarkic production by the consumer is not a firm, based on the separation criterion.

Autarky, as applied in the present discussion, refers to consumers who choose not to exchange goods with others or to participate in consumer organizations. Consumers remain on separate islands and fend for themselves, as did Robinson Crusoe.[10] Consumers can choose to avoid exchange by consuming their initial endowments. Because consumers own and operate production technology, they can be producers as well. In addition, consumers can develop their own production technology. Autarky can refer to production and consumption by families and extended households. Autarky provides a natural benchmark for evaluating gains from trade between consumers, as well as gains from trade once firms are introduced into the economy. Market exchange is voluntary because consumers have the option of autarky.

Although autarky is a useful theoretical construct, it has rarely been observed on a large scale. The most primitive of village communities engage in sharing of goods through gift exchange, feasts, cooperative production, and trade. Throughout recorded history, individuals have traded goods at the local, regional, and even international level, as the discussion of merchants in the next chapter demonstrates.

1.5.2 Exchange Transactions and Contracts

Consumers together can form bilateral or multilateral transactions. Groups of consumers engaged in multilateral exchange, or in multilateral contracts, do not constitute firms. There is no independent economic institution with objectives that are distinct from those of the parties to the transactions. The transactions are simply a group of economic exchanges between consumers.

The parties to a transaction or contract often have conflicting interests. A buyer is maximizing his consumption interest and a seller is maximizing his earnings. Transaction costs aside, the buyer wishes to obtain the maximum net benefit $v - p$ and the seller wishes to obtain the maximum earnings $p - c$. Speaking informally, the buyer and the seller jointly own the transaction. The objective of the transaction is the combination of the objectives of the buyer and the seller and cannot be separated from them.

---

10 Robinson Crusoe is the character in the classic novel of the same name by Daniel Defoe, who finds himself "some hundreds of leagues out of the ordinary course of the trade of mankind."

Contracts between consumers, that is, transactions with a promise to provide a good in the future, also do not constitute firms. Jensen and Meckling (1976) refer to the firm as a "nexus of contracts." Although firms are centers of many contracts, not every nexus of contracts is a firm. Consumers form bilateral or multilateral contracts without intermediation by firms. Principals can form contracts with agents. Collections of contracts, no matter how complex they are, do not constitute independent economic actors. They represent the offers and acceptances of the parties to the contracts. In a bilateral contract, the parties to the contract divide the gains created by the exchange. Each of the parties seeks to maximize their share of the value created by the exchange. The contract reflects the objectives of the parties. Some contracting costs can be alleviated by intermediaries that separate the interests of the contracting parties, as the discussion in Chapter 11 emphasizes.

1.5.3 Business Enterprises

Consumers establish business enterprises in any sector of the economy, including manufacturing, agriculture, and commerce. Consumers become entrepreneurs by establishing firms, as will be discussed in later chapters. In the contemporary economy, business enterprises are likely to be organized as firms with objectives separate from those of their owners. A consumer chooses to establish an enterprise as a firm to obtain the benefits from separating the firm's decisions from his consumption decisions. The advantages of separation are discussed further in the next chapter.

A consumer enterprise that is managed as a combination of consumption interests and commercial activities should not be viewed as a firm. The enterprise may be a family farm, a service provider, a small manufacturing business, or a merchant enterprise. The consumer may adjust his labor effort, his investment, and the output of the enterprise on the basis of consumption needs as well as commercial returns. The enterprise is not a firm when the consumer connects business decisions with consumption decisions.

A family business is not a firm when it does not meet the separation criterion. Historically, most family enterprises were not firms as defined here. The business activities of their owners were closely connected to their consumption activities. Agricultural, artisanal, and merchant enterprises traditionally were intertwined with the personal activities of the merchant. Even highly developed merchant banking enterprises, such as that of the Medicis, were closely tied with the personal finances, consumption, artistic endeavors, political activities, and religious contributions of the merchant's family.[11] The business was part of the family, which supplied labor, management, and capital to the enterprise. The objectives of the family businesses were closely tied to the consumption objectives of the family that operated the business.

11 See Parks (2006).

Consider, for example, the Antinori family, which has been making wine for over six centuries and over twenty-six generations. According to the *Wall Street Journal*, "The Antinoris have flourished in part because of their willingness to flout conventional wisdom over how a family company should be run. Instead of creating clear lines that separate the family's interests from the company's, the Antinoris blur the two beyond recognition." The interconnections between the enterprise and the family reflect practices from the Middle Ages: "The Marquis, his wife and their youngest daughter still live on the top two floors of the 15th-century Palazzo Antinori, a few steps from the Florence cathedral, where the family has resided for the past five centuries. The business is still run on the palazzo's bottom two floors, and the three daughters are top executives." The palace is filled with artwork of Renaissance masters including Tintoretto. Employees address the head of the company "by his nobleman's title, *marchese*." According to the Marquis, the company's board, with four family members and two outsiders, only meets "for formalities." The real board meeting "happens every Sunday, when we sit down to lunch," which "often takes place in one of the family's nearby vineyards, either in the hills of Chianti, or along the Tuscan coast." Rather than maximizing quarterly profits, the family is concerned with maintaining succession by family members; "the Antinoris plan far into the future, laying the foundations for a company their grandchildren can run." The family's enterprise reflects a combination of its consumption objectives and business objectives.[12]

1.5.4 Intermediaries

Firms are not required for intermediation. Consumers can act as intermediaries in coordinating transactions. However, consumers who act as intermediaries are distinct from firms because their intermediation activities also reflect their consumption interests.

The consumer's attitude toward risk and rate of time preference will affect his consumption interests and thus affect the intermediation transactions. Individual consumers are limited in their ability to intermediate transactions since they cannot be in multiple locations at once. The consumer may not have the time and ability to engage in multiple transactions simultaneously. The consumer's ability to intermediate transactions may be reduced by transaction costs associated with communication and information processing. The following chapter examines how firms can improve the efficiency of intermediation.

An intermediary, as residual claimant, allows the separation of the transaction from the buyer's and the seller's objectives. The intermediary breaks the budget-balancing condition of bilateral exchange. By offering a bid price w to the seller and an ask price p to the buyer, the intermediary separates the buyer and the seller.

---

12 Gabriel Kahn, 2008, "A Vintage Strategy Faces Modernity," *Wall Street Journal*, http://online.wsj.com/article_print/SB120734217745590759.html 4/10/2008.

The intermediary's objective is to maximize his returns, $p - w$. There are now two transactions, between the buyer and the intermediary and between the seller and the intermediary. Although these transactions are the combination of the objectives of the three parties involved, there is an additional degree of freedom in comparison to the bilateral exchange between the buyer and the seller. The consumer acting as intermediary may combine consumption objectives with the maximization of the returns to intermediation.

1.5.5 Clubs

Clubs and other social organizations are associations of consumers with common interests. The members of a club can be united by similar affinities deriving from common professional, social, ethnic, national, or religious backgrounds. The members of the group may have a common purpose such as education, recreation, charity, or social interaction. Consumers obtain benefits from interaction with others. Consumers can form a club to share the costs of producing public goods or to share the fixed costs of private goods such as recreational facilities.[13] Clubs and other social organizations reduce transaction costs relative to multilateral contracts by coordinating interaction between their members.

Clubs and other social organizations are not firms. Their objectives are collections of those of their members. The members of the club often are its owners. The objective of the club is generally to maximize the consumption benefits of its members. Clubs tend to be limited in terms of organizational structure and the use of incentive mechanisms. A club only becomes a firm when its objectives can be separated from those of its members.[14] When consumer clubs develop independent economic and legal identities and make decisions that become separate from their members, they begin to take on the characteristics of firms.

Albert Dicey (1905) was concerned with the paradox that the freedom to make contractual commitments and the right of association could potentially limit individual freedom both of the members of an organization and of others in society who are not in the organization. He pointed out that "whenever men act in concert for a common purpose, they tend to create a body which, from no fiction of law, but from the very nature of things, differs from the individuals of whom it is constituted" (1905, p. 153). In addition to the *esprit de corps* of its members, the organization benefits from the power of coordinated action. To obtain these benefits, members of clubs voluntarily choose to relinquish some autonomy. Although clubs and organizations may attain an independent identity,

---

13 See Buchanan (1965) and Cornes and Sandler (1996).

14 This differs from Prescott and Townsend (2006), who suggest that clubs are firms. They argue that contracts between economic agents are club goods. They note that McKenzie (1959, 1981) identified firms with entrepreneurial inputs supplied to the market in a general equilibrium setting. As the present discussion emphasizes, however, something more than shared contractual associations is needed to establish a firm.

their objectives are still dependent on the consumption objectives of their members. Clubs and social organizations do not meet the separation criterion.

1.5.6 Merchants' Associations and Exchanges

An important forerunner of the contemporary firm is the merchants' association. Merchants formed professional guilds to limit market entry, to establish commercial rules, and to share information. Merchants' associations served to coordinate prices and product quality and to facilitate interaction with governments. Merchants' associations formed central marketplaces to enhance the convenience of retail trade with consumers. Merchants' associations formed trading posts and trade fairs to engage in wholesale trade.

Merchants' associations lowered the costs of international trade by forming cooperative networks. International merchant networks offered access to trusted trading partners in foreign countries. In the contemporary economy, firms form industry associations that engage in political lobbying, generic marketing to share the costs of advertising, establishment of technological and product standards, and gathering and exchange of market information.

Organized exchanges for financial assets and commodity contracts are an important form of a merchants' association. Intermediaries such as market makers and brokers form exchanges to engage in wholesale trading of financial securities and commodities. Most of the major organized exchanges, such as the New York Stock Exchange, began as associations. Such associations provide their members with market power by restricting entry. A seat on an exchange often has a high market value. Associations that form organized exchanges demonstrate that individuals acting together can create and operate markets. This means that market making is not the exclusive function of firms.

Exchanges are clubs that provide their members with the benefits of interaction. Traders who are members of the exchange can find each other conveniently without search costs. The more members there are in the exchange, the greater the opportunities for trade, which provides liquidity in financial markets and immediacy in commodity markets. As with clubs, exchanges provide members with shared resources such as facilities for trading, mechanisms for price adjustment, information gathering, and dissemination, communication services, joint marketing, and management of the exchange. Traditional exchanges relied on floor trading and thus experienced congestion. As with clubs, exchanges faced a trade-off between the transaction benefits and congestion costs of increased membership.

A major development in the governance of financial and commodity exchanges is the replacement of member associations by a corporate form of ownership. Advances in information technology replace the congestion costs of floor trading with the nearly unlimited capacity of electronic trading; see Steil (2002). Exchanges that incorporate are able to raise capital to improve their ability to engage in mergers and acquisitions; see Brito Ramos (2006). Hart and Moore (1996) compare the

governance of exchanges by member cooperatives with outside ownership; see also
Pirrong (1999).[15] They suggest that outside ownership may be useful when diversity
of membership raises the costs of voting. Hart and Moore argue that an exchange,
whether it is organized as a cooperative or owned by an outside investor, serves to
consolidate residual rights of control over its "agglomeration" economies.[16]

Steil (2002, p. 65) states that "separation of ownership and membership is
fundamental to the concept of demutualization." Stoll (2002) observes that the
reorganization of exchanges may not be the replacement of mutual associations
by profit-maximizing firms but rather the replacement of members. He points out
that ownership of some exchanges is changing from traditional intermediaries such
as brokers and dealers to large firms such as major market makers and brokerages.
The large market makers and broker-dealers operate the exchange to benefit from
its services as with joint-venture firms.[17]

1.5.7 Buyers' Cooperatives

A buyers' cooperative is an association of consumers formed to consolidate and
coordinate purchases. Its purpose may be to achieve economies of scale and scope in
transaction costs. Alternatively, by combining purchases, the consumer cooperative
may seek market power in its dealings with suppliers.

Buyers' cooperatives are not firms because their objectives cannot be separated
from those of their owners. The buyers' cooperative performs various tasks that
can also be performed by firms, including retailers, wholesalers, and the purchasing
function of manufacturers. The buyers' cooperative provides an alternative arrangement for handling transactions that does not require the establishment of firms.
Firms provide alternatives to the organizational structure and types of incentives
that exist within a buyer's cooperative.

Buyers' cooperatives are rarely observed in the economy, although they are more
prevalent in some industries than others.[18] There are buyers' cooperatives composed
of associations of firms that engage in wholesale transactions, but these are simply other forms of transactions between firms rather than consumer cooperatives.

---

15 Hart and Moore (1996) model the cooperative using a median-voter model. Members vote based
    on benefits that they receive from using the services of the exchange to carry out trades. Outside
    ownership substitutes profit maximization for voting.

16 Hart and Moore's (1996) classification of the cooperative as a firm is based on their definition of
    a firm as a means of consolidating residual rights of control over nonhuman assets; see Grossman
    and Hart (1986), Hart and Moore (1990), and Hart (1995). Thus, they view the exchange as a
    firm whether it is governed by a member cooperative or by an outside owner. In contrast, the
    theory of the firm presented here does not necessarily identify cooperatives as firms because the
    cooperative's objectives are based on members' consumption objectives.

17 Although the objectives of the exchange reflect the interests of its parent companies, these
    organizations can be viewed as firms because their objectives are distinct from the consumption
    objectives of the investors who own the parent companies.

18 See Heflebower (1908) and Hansmann (1988).

Cooperative housing, such as the condominium association, is another type of consumer cooperative, although the number of members in such cooperatives tends to be relatively small. Cooperative housing constitutes a small share of total housing. There are consumer-owned public utilities such as rural electric cooperatives, although federally subsidized loans played a role in their development, creating a cost advantage over privately owned firms (Hansmann, 1988). Barzel and Sass (1990) find that in establishing housing cooperatives, profit-maximizing developers structure the constitution of the cooperative to reduce expected costs of decision making.

1.5.8 Workers' Cooperatives

Workers' cooperatives are associations of consumers for the purpose of production of goods and services. Workers can form cooperatives to obtain the benefits of joint production, including scale economies. They can also seek to obtain efficiencies in transacting with input suppliers and final customers. Smaller worker cooperatives that are owned and operated by their members are not necessarily firms, primarily because they tend to have objectives that correspond to the consumption objectives of their members. Also, worker cooperatives are limited in their choice of organizational structures and incentives.

Larger producer cooperatives tend to take on many features of firms. However, there are some difficulties in classification. For example, there are several thousand large-scale agricultural cooperatives in the United States that compete with investor-owned firms.[19] These cooperatives are intermediaries that act in the interests of their producer-owners but tend to have a distinct economic identity. The U.S. Department of Agriculture set forth three principles that define the agricultural cooperative: it must be owned by its users, it must be controlled by its users, and the benefits must accrue to users on the basis of their use.[20] According to the U.S. Department of Agriculture, equity investment by nonmembers "disrupts" the connection between owners and users. Also, although the cooperative should be profitable, the three "cooperative principles provide an additional framework through which options for business strategies, organizational structures, and operations must be analyzed." The report concludes that "Those who suggest that a cooperative can be run just like any other business either do not understand or do not respect the significance of these differences."[21] This suggests that it might be useful from the point of view of economic theory to treat even large-scale producer cooperatives as distinct from firms.

The worker cooperative connects the labor-supply decisions of workers with the employment decisions of the organization. This implicitly requires that workers

---

19 Rural Business-Cooperative Service (2002, p. 20).
20 Rural Business-Cooperative Service (2002, p. 1).
21 Rural Business-Cooperative Service (2002, p. 2).

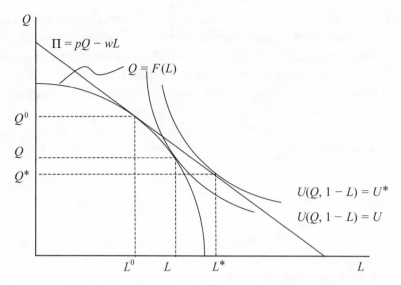

Figure 1.3. The neoclassical separation theorem for the labor-managed firm.

prefer to manage the organization that employs them. However, when there are gains from trade in product markets and labor markets, workers may prefer to separate their labor supply decisions from the organization's employment decisions. Suppose that technology can differ across organizations or suppose that worker preferences are heterogeneous. This creates gains from trade in product and labor markets. Different technologies or heterogeneous preferences imply that the neoclassical separation theorem applies to the labor-managed firm.

Consider a consumer who owns a firm. The consumer is endowed with one unit of time that can be used for labor, L, or for leisure, $1 - L$. The consumer's preferences over consumption Q and leisure are represented by the utility function $u(Q, 1 - L)$. The consumer-owner chooses labor to maximize net benefits. Given the production function $Q = F(L)$, the consumer's net benefits equal

$$U(L) = u(F(L), 1 - L).$$

The consumer-owner maximizes his net benefits by choosing the labor supply that equates his marginal rate of substitution to the marginal product of labor,

$$\frac{u_2(F(L^0), 1 - L^0)}{u_1(F(L), 1 - L^0)} = F'(L^0).$$

Consider the neoclassical separation theorem in the context of the labor-leisure choice. Suppose that the consumer can provide labor services to the market at wage w. The firm can hire labor services at the wage w and sell output at price p. For almost any wage-price ratio, w/p, the consumer-owner prefers to separate the firm's production and employment decisions from his consumption and labor-supply decisions. This is illustrated in Figure 1.3. The consumer-owner is better off at the consumption-labor combination Q^* and L^*. Both the firm and the consumer take advantage of arbitrage opportunities in the product and labor markets.

The consumer-owner receives the firm's profit as income and prefers that the firm maximize profit. The consumer-owner supplies his labor services in the labor market and purchases the consumption good on the product market. The separation theorem for the labor-managed firm thus is equivalent to the standard neoclassical separation theorem. Consumer-owners will unanimously prefer separation. This implies that when market alternatives are available, the owners of labor-managed firms will prefer that the firm maximize profits.

Chapter 6 shows that members of basic workers' cooperatives prefer their situation to working for a profit-maximizing firm where they receive a wage and a share of the firm's profits. The worker cooperative maximizes the benefit per member. The profit-maximizing firm sets employment such that the marginal revenue product of labor equals the outside wage. The profit-maximizing firm chooses the efficient employment level. This is greater than the workers' cooperative employment level, which maximizes the average benefits of workers.

The objectives of the basic workers' cooperative are altered substantially when there is a market for membership shares. This is an argument that is similar to the club considered earlier. Suppose that the members of the worker's cooperative are its owners and they can sell additional memberships. The result is a separation of the objectives of the members of the workers' cooperative from those of the organization. By the separation criterion, this implies that the workers' cooperative with tradeable membership shares becomes a firm. Then, as shown in Chapter 6, the workers' cooperative that sells membership shares chooses the number of members that maximizes profit; see Dow (2003, p. 149). This yields a separation theorem. The worker-owners of a firm with tradeable membership shares unanimously prefer that the firm maximize profits.

1.5.9 Nonprofit Organizations

Nonprofit organizations operate in many sectors of the economy, including social advocacy, political lobbying, environmental conservation, education, the arts and culture, health care, religion, social services, and charity.[22] Nonprofit organizations generally are a form of consumer cooperative. Nonprofit organizations earn profits, but these are often referred to as a "financial surplus." Nonprofit organizations are not firms because their objectives generally cannot be separated from those of their owners. Some types of nonprofits may achieve separation of objectives by specifying and following donors' intent (Schramm 2006c).

Nonprofit organizations are a form of consumer cooperative when they provide consumption benefits to their members. Often nonprofit organizations provide public goods to their members such as arts, entertainment and culture. Nonprofit

22 See for example Clotfelter (1992) and Bilodeau and Steinberg (2006).

organizations engaged in philanthropy provide public goods to their donors, who derive benefits from altruism. Nonprofit organizations engaged in advocacy provide public goods to their members, who derive benefits from influencing public policy makers and social institutions.

Nonprofit organizations differ from firms in terms of ownership. The owners of firms have property rights that are complete, exclusive, and transferable. Nonprofit organizations tend not to have formal ownership. Nonprofits generally have governing boards that oversee the managers of the organizations. Some nonprofit organizations have formal memberships whereas others do not. An essential feature of nonprofit organizations is that their profits cannot be distributed to their owners; see Hansmann (1980). Hansmann (1996) argues that nonprofits do not have owners.

The managers and boards of trustees of nonprofits have limited property rights. They can exercise control rights, but they cannot receive earnings nor can they sell control rights or rights to earnings. Nonprofit organizations cannot distribute their earnings to their members. Nonprofit organizations delegate authority to managers, with boards of trustees providing oversight. Ben-Ner and Gui (2003) argue that the absence of formal ownership gives managers and boards of nonprofit organizations greater autonomy that those of for-profit firms. Some nonprofit organizations have features of workers' cooperatives that operate for the benefit of their managers and employees.

Nonprofit organizations that operate for the benefit of their members maximize the provision of services. Nonprofit organizations that operate for the benefit of their managers and employees maximize their compensation and perks. This accords with Tullock (1966), who finds that due to asymmetric information and limited monitoring, managers of nonprofit organizations engage in some combination of service maximization and budget maximization. Weisbrod (1988, 1998) finds that nonprofit organizations are owned by their members in a manner similar to the way government agencies are "owned" by citizens.

Kuan (2001) argues that nonprofit organizations arise when consumers "integrate into production" to produce a public good for their own consumption, such as the classical performing arts, but also in health care, R&D, and education. Consider a simplified version of her model that illustrates the basic issues. Suppose that there are two consumers with willingness to pay v_L and v_H, where $v_L < v_H$. They wish to consume a nonrival public good such as a symphony orchestra that is produced with cost c. The willingness to pay of the high-value consumer is less than the cost of the public good, $v_H < c$. The combined values of the two consumers are sufficient to pay for the good:

$$v_H + v_C > c.$$

Suppose that the consumers' willingness-to-pay levels are not observable, so that a firm cannot price discriminate. Each consumer knows their own willingness to pay, so that each consumer correctly infers the other consumer's willingness to pay.

There are two possibilities depending on whether $c > 2v_L$ or $c \leq 2v_L$. Suppose first that $c > 2v_L$. Then a firm cannot operate because the lowest uniform price it can charge would be $c/2$, which would exclude the low-willingness-to-pay consumer, and so would not yield revenue to cover costs. Charging the maximum price to the high-willingness-to-pay consumer also would not yield sufficient revenues to cover costs.

The high-value consumer can form a nonprofit organization that takes advantage of price discrimination. Ticket prices are set at the benefit of the low-willingness-to-pay consumer, $p = v_L$. The high-willingness-to-pay consumer provides charity equal to the shortfall in revenues, $c - 2v_L$. The high-willingness-to-pay consumer obtains positive benefits equal to the value created by the nonprofit organization,

$$v_H - p - (c - 2v_L) = v_H + v_L - c.$$

The nonprofit organization generates an efficient outcome. There is no need for a firm in this case.

Suppose that $c \leq 2v_L$. A consumer cooperative could produce the public good in this case as well by charging break-even prices equal to $c/2$. Imagine an alternative scenario that is the reverse of the previous case. The founding consumer again charges ticket prices equal to the benefit of the low-willingness-to-pay consumer, $p = v_L$. However, rather than making a charitable contribution, the founding consumer receives perks equal to $2v_L - c$. This might take the form of a charity ball or an opening night gala event. As before, the founding consumer receives all of the surplus, $v_H + v_L - c$.

A firm could provide the good at a uniform price that covered costs and attracted both consumers when $c \leq 2v_L$. Competition between firms or competition between the firm and the nonprofit organization would result in a break-even price of $c/2$.

This example assumes that the consumers know each other's types, whereas the firm cannot identify the consumers' types. Chapter 9 compares the provision of public goods under asymmetric information and compares the firm to a consumer cooperative. When choosing the amount of a public good to produce, the consumer cooperative encounters transaction costs in the form of the free rider problem. The consumer cooperative performs better than a monopoly firm with a small number of members. With a large number of members, the monopoly firm performs better than the cooperative.

1.5.10 Basic Partnerships

A *basic partnership* is an association of consumers that owns and controls an organization. The basic partnership shares its surplus among its members. The members of the partnership provide management and are the owners of the partnership. Such a basic partnership is a collection of the consumers that are its members and reflects little more than the relationships between them. The objective of the partnership is to maximize the benefits of its owners. Therefore, the basic partnership as defined here is not a firm.

There are more complex forms of partnerships that separate the objectives of the organization from those of its owners. These more complex partnerships are firms as defined here. Many of the key issues in the theory of the firm arise in the context of partnerships. A partnership becomes a firm when it begins to take on an independent identity and the ability to make autonomous decisions that are independent of its owners. Members of more complex partnerships act as entrepreneurs, managers, producers, or investors. Larger partnerships are more likely to be complex organizations with the features of firms, although smaller partnerships can be firms as well.

Some concepts from partnership law and business law shed light on the economics of partnerships. Partnership law has evolved in a manner reflecting the development of the modern firm. The legal controversies in debates over the statutory regulation of partnership help to clarify some related issues in the theory of the firm. The main point of contention in partnership law is whether the partnership should be treated as the aggregate of its members or whether it forms a separate entity, that is, a legal person capable of independent action.

The partnership as defined in law traditionally differs from the corporation, which is a legal entity distinct from its owners. Increasingly, however, the partnership has taken on many of the features of the corporation. This is closely related to our discussion of whether an enterprise is a collection of consumers or whether the enterprise is a firm that is an independent economic actor.

The common law traditionally viewed a partnership as an *aggregate* of the relationships between its members.[23] The law of partnerships dates back to the Roman Empire. Partnerships were regulated by statutes in the European commercial cities of the Middle Ages (Mechem, 1896, p. xxxvii).[24] British statutes incorporated and superseded some aspects of the common law of partnerships.[25] In the United States, until the end of the nineteenth century, the legal view of the partnership was firmly grounded in the common law.

In a classic treatise, Justice Nathaniel Lindley (1888, p. 110) wrote that "Partners are called collectively a firm."[26] Lindley emphasized that "The firm is not recognized by lawyers as distinct from the members composing it."[27] The members of a partnership are the joint owners of the partnership's property and are fully responsible for the partnership's liabilities. The members of the partnership also make common usage of the partnership's property in operating the joint business.[28] Lindley (1888) argues that a member of a partnership is both a principal and an

---

23 See Rosin (1989, p. 396) and also Mechem (1896).
24 Interestingly, Bromberg and Ribstein (1988) trace the origins of the partnership back to share-cropping in Babylonian times, cited in DeMott (1991, p. 491).
25 This begins with the English Partnership Act of 1890; see DeMott (1991, p. 491).
26 Lindley also is quoted in Mechem (1896, p. 5).
27 See English Partnership Act, 1890, 53 & 54 Vict, ch. 39, § 1 (1), Lindley (1888), Mechem (1890), Lewis (1915), and Rosin (1989).
28 See Rosin (1989, p. 397); see also Lewis (1915) and Drake (1917).

agent. As a principal, the partner is bound by his own actions and those of his partners, and as an agent he binds his partners by his actions.[29] Gary S. Rosin (1989, p. 397) observes that the "early common law view of partnership as a purely aggregate concept was fatally defective" because it emphasized the individual rights of each partner while neglecting the collective rights of all of the partners.

Of great relevance to the theory of the firm is that business people held the view that the partnership was a separate entity. Justice Lindley (1888, p. 110) noted that "merchants and lawyers have different notions respecting the nature of a firm":

> Commercial men and accountants are apt to look upon a firm in the light in which lawyers look upon a corporation, *i.e.*, as a body distinct from the members composing it, and having rights and obligations distinct from those of its members.

To end the "hopeless confusion in law and practice,"[30] the Uniform Partnership Act (UPA) of 1914 attempted to take a middle position, treating a partnership as a collective for some purposes and as a separate entity for other purposes.[31]

The entity versus aggregate debate has been resolved for all practical purposes. The dual approach continued through the twentieth century with many states continuing to use the UPA. The Revised Uniform Partnership Act of 1997 (RUPA) began to be adopted by many states. The RUPA continues to define a partnership as "an association of two or more persons to carry on as co-owners of a business for profit."[32] However, in contrast to the UPA, the RUPA clearly states that "A partnership is an entity."[33] Thus, partnership law has moved toward the corporate law view of the firm as an entity that is distinct from its owners.[34]

Hillman (2005) observes that "there seems to be little practical distinction between corporations and partnerships when either form of firm is populated by a large number of shareholders or partners, as the case may be." Hillman (2005)

---

29 Justice Lindley (1888, p. 112) states that "the name under which a firm carries on business is in point of law a conventional name applicable only to the persons who, on each particular occasion when the name is used, are members of the firm." Lindley's use of the word "firm" reflects the traditional usage that designates a partnership. This derives from the Latin "firmare" or signature that confirmed an agreement by designating the name of the business. The use of the word "firm" to indicate a partnership continues only in a limited sense for certain types of partnerships, such as in law or accounting. Generally, the meaning of the word "firm" has evolved to designate an entity separate from its members, thus mirroring commercial usage. The standard meaning of "firm" thus conforms to its usage in the present book.

30 Lewis (1915, p. 162) quoted in Rosin (1989, p. 399).

31 Rosin (1989) approvingly calls this a functional approach and argues for rejecting the "legal-person fiction" as well as the concept of the aggregate.

32 RUPA § 101.

33 RUPA § 201.

34 See Hillman (2005) for further discussion.

further observes that even small partnerships may depart from the egalitarian model, with hierarchical relationships between dominant and subordinate partners and little or no bargaining over operations and the form of the organization. There are over 2.5 million partnerships in the United States, with an average of six members.[35] Partnerships with hundreds of owners, or even thousands of owners, exist in the professional services industry, including accounting, consulting, medicine, and law. However, large partnerships are rare in other economic sectors.[36] Such large partnerships are characterized by centralized management and an organizational hierarchy in which the status and authority of individual partners vary considerably, so that in practice many large partnerships take on the characteristics of corporations.

Just as with entrepreneurs, partnerships face financial decisions associated with "getting in" and "getting out." Establishing the partnership requires raising capital and contributions from the partners. Over time, partners may wish to restructure the partnership by adding new partners or through the departure of partners. The partnership may require additional funds for growth. The choice of the partnership as an organizational form is affected by the imperfect separation of the consumption-savings decisions of individual partners from the investment decisions of the partnership.

Consumer-entrepreneurs form a partnership by entering into a set of multilateral contracts with one another. Members of the partnership jointly establish and own the enterprise. The partners act as investors, providing the enterprise with financial capital and other productive assets such as land, equipment, and intellectual property. Members of the partnership are joint owners of the enterprise and share in the profits and losses of the business.[37] The partners are managers of the business, contributing effort to run the business and supervise operations and employees. The partners contribute their productive efforts to the enterprise achieving economies of scale through specialization of function and division of labor. The partners obtain cost economies from complementary inputs.

As with individual entrepreneurs, the partnership can self-finance or raise capital from investors. Partners choose to self-finance if they believe that they have better information about the potential of the business than outside investors. Also, the partners invest in a business because holding an equity share has incentive

---

35 Partnerships include both general partnerships and limited partnerships. Statistics are based on tax data for 2004; see http://www.irs.gov/taxstats/index.html. See also Eisenberg (2000, p. 24) on the average size of partnerships.

36 According to the U.S. Census Bureau, "Fourteen percent of all U.S. firms operated in professional, scientific, and technical services and accounted for 4.5 percent of the total gross receipts." *Survey of Business Owners 2002*, http://www.census.gov/csd/sbo/companysummaryoffindings. htm.

37 According to *Black's Law Dictionary*, "Under the Uniform Partnership Act, a partnership is presumed to exist if the persons agree to share proportionally the business's profits or losses."

properties that motivate effort. When partners have unique knowledge and skills, they may wish to be owners of the business to capture the returns from their efforts.

Partners encounter various transaction costs in the process of establishing and operating the partnership. They must spend time and effort in the search for potential partners. This problem is more difficult than matching pairs of buyers and sellers because the partnership may involve multiple parties. The costs of search and communication are substantially greater because multilateral matching is required. Forming compatible groups is significantly more complicated than pairwise assignments.[38]

Once they have found each other, the partners need to negotiate a partnership contract. The partnership depends on the identities, preferences, financial endowments, and abilities of each of its partners. Macneil (1978, pp. 44–8) identifies a host of questions that a lawyer would need to have answered *by each of the individual partners* before drafting a partnership agreement. In addition to determining the nature of the business, the lawyer preparing the partnership agreement must determine for each of the individual partners ownership of assets of the proposed business, skills, experience, expectations about the business, financial resources, family circumstances, and tax problems. In addition, the partnership agreement must specify for each of the individual partners how much money or property the partner will contribute, what share of property or money of the business the partner will own, whether the partner will receive interest, a profit share, or a salary, whether the partner will have an expense account, what will be the partner's management authority and responsibilities, what are prohibited acts for the partner, and what will be the provisions for death, disability, bankruptcy, expulsion, or withdrawal of the partner.[39]

The partnership agreement necessarily entails transaction costs needed to make the agreement conform to the individual characteristics of its partners. Just as a complete contract is costly because it is contingent on multiple states of the world, a partnership contract is costly because it is dependent on details about the multiple parties to the agreement.

The partnership contract also must specify the nature of the business and the common objectives of the partners. The transaction costs of negotiations needed to form the partnership are likely to increase as the number of partners becomes greater. Because the partnership is a multilateral contract, it requires a cooperative

---

38 Farrell and Scotchmer (1988) consider a cooperative game of partnership formation. They restrict attention to equal sharing among coalition members and full information about player characteristics. Individuals have different abilities. They show that there is a (generically) unique partition of players into coalitions such that no new coalition could form and make all its members strictly better off. Finding the unique partition of the Core would be likely in practice to present computational difficulties.

39 See Macneil (1978, pp. 44–8).

agreement, with multiple parties involved in the negotiation. As the number of parties increases, so does the complexity of communications, with a greater number of potential bilateral or multilateral discussions and more extensive group meetings. As the number of potential partners increases, negotiating the interconnected contractual provisions also becomes more difficult because the partnership contract becomes more detailed. It is extremely costly to design a contract that is both a complete contingent contract and a multiparty partnership agreement; see Blair and Stout (1999) and Blair (2003).

With a small number of partners, direct negotiations concerning the contract remain feasible. With a large number of partners, there is a need for collective decision-making techniques such as voting, division of labor through committees, and hierarchical authority. With a small number of partners, there may be trust between the parties that allows for simpler contracts. With a large number of partners, there are likely to be diverse levels of trust between individuals that will increase the need for contractual solutions.

After the formation of the partnership agreement, the members must operate the business. They must collectively make decisions needed to manage the business. These decisions concern products, pricing, sales, marketing, purchasing, finance, employment, and innovation. These decisions are likely to involve difficulties of collective decision making that are similar to those encountered in negotiating the partnership agreement. In addition to collective decision making, the partners must make individual decisions about their contributions to the business.

All partners are agents of the group of members. The typical agency problems of moral hazard and adverse selection may occur. Partners may shirk by devoting less than efficient effort to running the business. If the profit of the business depends on the effort of the partners, they may choose to free ride on each other. With small numbers of partners, there can be ways for partners to coordinate their efforts and reduce free riding. When the number of partners is large, coordination becomes more difficult and it might be useful to describe the behavior of the partners as a noncooperative game.

All of the partners are also principals. They each need to monitor the performance of the business and that of their fellow partners. Again, the partners are likely to free ride on each other. The result will be that monitoring efforts are below the jointly optimal levels. Inefficiencies due to free riding in effort and in monitoring will increase when the number of partners is greater.

Partnerships combine ownership and control. The partnership encounters incentive problems because the decisions of its owners are not separate from the decisions of the firm. The partners own the firm and thus prefer to obtain more profit. However, the partners also supply productive effort and monitoring. With profit sharing, a member of the partnership chooses effort or monitoring to maximize his individual net benefit rather than the profit of the partnership.

The absence of separation between ownership and control is reflected in the partnership's profit-sharing rule. This results in a balanced budget, which affects the design of incentives for performance in many situations with asymmetric information; see Groves (1973). Because partners share the profit among themselves, any incentive mechanism for partners to perform is subject to a balanced-budget constraint. As a result, partners will free ride by selecting less effort than the jointly optimal effort levels.

This corresponds to the well-known problem of moral hazard in teams.[40] Hölmstrom (1982) shows that the introduction of a residual claimant who manages the team resolves the budget-balancing problem. By applying an incentive rule in the form of a forcing function, the manager can induce optimal effort in the absence of uncertainty. The forcing function rewards the members of the team if and only if the total output exceeds the target level. This overcomes incentives to shirk. The manager as residual claimant collects a profit if any individual member of the team shirks. This would only occur out of equilibrium. Accordingly, the team's budget balances in equilibrium.

The forcing function approach can be problematic because it gives the principal an incentive to prevent the team from completing the task in order to avoid paying the bonus. Innes (1990) makes a similar observation for principal-agent models. Innes (1990) requires that the agent contract exhibit monotonicity for the principal to avoid such conflicts of interest.[41]

Introducing a residual claimant may alleviate the problem of moral hazard in teams, but it does not solve the problem of designing a partnership. As soon as a residual claimant is introduced, the organization ceases to be a basic partnership. A centrally managed organization that acts as a residual claimant achieves some separation between the organization and workers. The organization begins to resemble a corporation more closely than it does a partnership.

Other theoretical solutions to the problem of incentives in teams attempt to solve the partnership problem by departing from the organizational form of the basic partnership in one way or another, particularly in terms of the equal sharing rule. For example, Miller (1997) and Huddart and Liang (2005) show that a partnership could improve joint surplus by designating one member as a specialist monitor.[42] Rasmusen (1987) examines risk-averse partners and induces efficiency by unequal distribution, with either one member being punished for an inefficient outcome or all but one member being punished. Such "scapegoat" or "massacre" contracts do not correspond to the definition of a partnership. Marino and Zábojník (2004) split the partnership into two competing teams who engage in a tournament.

---

40 Partnerships exhibit free riding due to moral hazard in teams and limited liability; see particularly Holmstrom (1982) and Legros and Mathews (1993). Partnerships have equal sharing of profits; see Farrell and Scotchmer (1988), Kandel and Lazear (1992), Levin and Tadelis (2005), and Morrison and Wilhelm (2005).

41 See Poblete and Spulber (2008a) for a principal-agent model that builds on Innes (1990).

42 Legros and Matthews (1993) examine approximate efficiency in partnerships in terms of total output (rather than the benefits of individual members). They show that free riding causes inefficiency in partnerships to the extent that members' liability is limited.

Such an organization may describe how profit sharing and team production work in some types of firms, but it cannot be interpreted as a basic partnership.

Partnerships combine ownership and control not only in terms of operation but in terms of dissolution. After the partnership contract is formed and the business is established, one or more partners may wish to withdraw from the agreement. For some types of partnerships, this means that the partnership must be dissolved because it is only the aggregate of its members. Because there is no separation of ownership and control, the departure of a member can end the partnership even if the enterprise would have value if it continued to function.

The dissolution of a partnership due to the withdrawal of one or more members limits the liquidity of partners' investments. Partners can recover some share of the value of dissolving the partnership rather than a share of the value of the ongoing business. Limits on liquidity will reduce incentives to invest in partnerships. This drawback of unified ownership and control creates a disadvantage for the partnership form of organization in comparison to the corporation.

The dissolution of a partnership when members depart also creates moral hazard problems. A member has an incentive to quit the partnership if the expected return from continuing is less than what the member expected to receive from exiting. This means that the partnership could be dissolved inefficiently. It is efficient to continue operating the business if the value of continuing exceeds the total value that members of the partnership could obtain by dissolving the partnership.

Because any individual member of the partnership can force dissolution by withdrawing, any member of the partnership can force a renegotiation of the partnership agreement. Ideally, renegotiation would lead to an efficient outcome because the remaining partners could continue the business and buy out the partner that wished to withdraw. Renegotiation raises a number of problems, however. The renegotiation of the partnership agreement means that initial contractual commitments are not binding. The partnership agreement is enforced by partnership law and by trust between partners motivated by social norms, personal ethics, and business reputation.

Limits on the ability of potential partners to make initial commitments through the partnership agreement can reduce the potential value of partnership. Renegotiation entails transaction costs just as the initial partnership agreement is costly to negotiate. With asymmetric information, the renegotiation may fail to be efficient. For example, each of the partners may have private information about the value of their outside opportunity. Also, the remaining partners may encounter financial capital constraints in obtaining the funds to compensate the member who wishes to withdraw.

The member who is withdrawing also may possess unique abilities and knowledge without which the partnership cannot continue. Even if the remaining partners can continue to operate the enterprise, the goods, services, or reputation of the business may be altered fundamentally. Thus, the partnership form of organization can be inefficient if transaction costs prevent continuation of a viable business. If the partnership contract does not fully protect the expectation interests of its investors, then some efficient partnerships will not form.

Traditional joint venture partnerships have their origins in the *societas* addressed by the law of ancient Greece and ancient Rome. Partners contributed capital or labor and were liable for the debts of the partnership, so that the partners often were family members. During the twelfth century, the *compagnia* began to replace the *societas*. Partners were still liable for debt, but the *compagnia* offered partners the ability to raise additional capital and allowed the extension of partnerships beyond families. The *compagnia's* financing could be obtained through the retained earnings of partners, additional investment by partners, and time deposits from outside investors.[43]

Blair (2003b) points out that in 1800 there were only 335 chartered business corporations in the United States, of which most were chartered after 1790.[44] However, by 1890, the U.S. led the world, with almost 50,000 chartered business corporations.[45] Unincorporated joint stock companies, which evolved out of partnership law, died out, while businesses increasingly switched to the corporate form.[46] Ribstein (2006) finds that liquidation does not explain the switch to corporations because partners can prevent liquidation through the partnership agreement and the partners can contract for buyout rights.[47] Ribstein (2006) argues that partnerships already had developed continuity and other entity features by the early nineteenth century. The ability to lock in capital thus need not help to distinguish between organizational forms.[48]

Partnerships exhibit transaction costs associated with team production. Partners benefit from sharing investment costs and from combining complementary skills to operate the business. Partners encounter transaction costs in forming the

43 The history and description of the *societas* and *compagnia* rely on Baskin and Miranti (1997, p. 38).

44 See also Davis (1965).

45 Blair (2003b) citing Votaw (1965) and Wright (2002).

46 See Blair (2003b). Note that in the modern context, "stock" refers to the capital invested in the company rather than its earlier interpretation as goods for trade. Note further that the U.S. "unincorporated joint-stock company" is similar to what Adam Smith termed private copartneries, whereas the U.S. corporation is similar to Adam Smith's joint-stock company, because members can transfer their shares to others but cannot withdraw their membership or capital.

47 Ribstein (2004) notes that partnerships, in contrast to corporations, let members transfer economic interests in the firm but not necessarily control rights. Ribstein (2004) also states that any member of the partnership has the power to dissolve a partnership or to seek to be bought out by the partnership.

48 Blair (2003a) argues that unincorporated joint stock companies could be easily broken up by the partners or their heirs seeking to remove their capital from the firm. Corporations became the dominant legal form because courts recognized them as "separate legal entities with potentially unlimited life," whose assets would be protected from owners who could then sell their shares to others based on the market value of the company.

partnership, in coordinating investment and management efforts, and in dissolving the partnership. Firms can reduce these transaction costs through different managerial, financial, and ownership arrangements.[49]

1.5.11 Public Enterprises

Governments, whether representative or not, are the creations of individual consumers, yet governments are not firms. In centrally directed or planned economies, governments attempted to supplant markets and firms entirely, replacing them with government directives. These attempts have failed largely because of the complexity of private transactions. Friedrich A. Hayek (1988) criticized the view that governments could solve such complex economic problems as the "fatal conceit" of socialism. Authoritarian governments applied controls to the economy in the belief that "man is able to shape the world around him according to his wishes."

Governments are participants in economic transactions, often as major purchasers of goods and services. Governments regulate private transactions through a vast array of entry restrictions, price and quality controls, product safety standards, workplace health and safety standards, environmental regulations, and financial regulations. Governments also influence the economic activities of consumers and firms through taxes and subsidies.

Public enterprises are not firms because their objectives are those of the state. Government ownership substantially alters the objectives of public enterprises, substituting such goals as increased employment, growth, subsidization, or lower prices for profit maximization. In many countries governments own and operate public enterprises, often in the utility sector (telecommunications, energy, and water), but also including transportation and postal systems and assorted industries. The past extent of government control of firms is suggested by 8,000 acts of privatization around the world between 1985 and 1999 worth over $1 trillion, not counting the privatization by voucher of assets by former socialist countries.[50] However, many state enterprises remain and the public sector is a major part of most economies around the world.

Government bureaucracies, present under the earliest civilizations, also are forerunners to the modern firm. Sovereigns established organizations to collect taxes, to manage lands and agriculture production, to maintain irrigation, to construct public works, and to provide for defense. States and specialized state enterprises engaged in transactions needed to conduct trade with other governments. They also engaged merchants to serve as intermediaries in the transactions with other states and their representatives. For example, Moore and Lewis (1999, p. 71) observe that "Babylonian trade remained a mixed enterprise, with the crown and private merchants each contributing 50% of the capital."

49 The corporate organization of the firm is compared to the partnership in Chapter 7.
50 Brune et al. (2004).

Government bureaucracies developed large-scale hierarchies that influenced the organization of major corporations. Joseph Schumpeter observes that beginning in the fourteenth century and continuing for several centuries thereafter, numerous works in economics on the "economic problems of the nascent modern state" conceive of the national economy as "a sort of sublimated business unit . . . something which needs to be managed like a big firm" (1966, pp. 163–4). The culmination of this idea is Saint-Simon's (1975) utopian socialist view of the government as an administrative industrial manager of the economy and the industrial planning ministries that became a common feature of centrally planned economies.

The organizational structure of the contemporary corporation also has its origins in military hierarchies. Beginning with the earliest civilizations, the army general solves the problem of designing and managing an organization that will carry out chosen strategies. Armies require a hierarchy, a chain of command, rules of conduct, and incentives.

Military organizations were also among the first large private enterprises. According to Max Weber, "the procurement of armies and their administration by private capitalists has been the rule in mercenary armies, especially those of the Occident up to the turn of the Eighteenth Century" (1968, pp. 981–2). Weber (1968, p. 982) writes that in the eighteenth century, the "regiment" was "an economic management unit created by the entrepreneurial position of the colonel. Semiofficial sea-war ventures (such as the Genoese *maone*) and army procurement belong to private capitalism's first giant enterprises with a largely bureaucratic character." Weber compares the nationalization of the military to that of the railroads, which were also private enterprises under control of the state. Weber (1968, p. 980) observes that "The bureaucratically led army of the Pharaohs, the army of the later period of the Roman Republic and of the Principate, and, above all, the army of the modern military state are characterized by the fact that their equipment and provisions are supplied from the magazines of the lord." The bureaucratic army structure he notes is necessary for centralized provisioning, military discipline, and technical training.

The organizational structure of the modern corporation derives from prior public agencies, government, hierarchies, and military organizations. Generally, the public sector performs many functions that also are performed by firms, including the provision of public and private goods and the allocation of resources. However, public enterprises are not firms because their objectives cannot be separated from those of the governments that own and control them.

1.6 Conclusions

The general theory of the firm begins with consumers. Based on assumptions about the preferences, endowments, and activities of consumers, the theory identifies conditions under which the economy gives rise to firms. The analysis derives firms endogenously, rather than exogenously specifying firms as in the neoclassical setting. Consumer transactions, contracts, and organizations perform economic functions that are substitutes for the services that firms provide. Establishing a firm requires more than forming an association between consumers. The firm is an independent economic actor and decision maker. The firm's objectives are distinct from those of its consumer owners.

When consumers form partnerships or cooperatives, they maximize average benefits per member. In contrast, the profit-maximizing firm makes decisions at the margin. For example, a worker cooperative will hire the number of workers that maximizes average benefits. The profit-maximizing firm hires based on the marginal revenue product of employees in comparison to the wage. In contrast to direct exchange, the firm resolves the budget-balancing problem by acting as a residual claimant. This allows for allocation mechanisms that are not available in direct exchange between consumers.

The role of firms in the economy depends on their advantages in comparison to direct exchange and consumer organizations. Consumers choose between direct exchange and intermediated exchange. With greater transaction costs between consumers, as compared to the firm's market and organizational transaction costs, firms replace direct exchange and consumer organizations. The "intermediation hypothesis" posits that increases in transaction costs experienced by buyers and sellers, relative to the firm's transaction costs, explain greater intermediation of those transactions by firms.

2

The Firm

The *firm* is defined to be a transaction institution whose objectives differ from those of its owners. This separation is the key difference between the firm and direct exchange between consumers. Consumer organizations that generally fail to satisfy the separation criterion include groups of contracting individuals, clubs, workers' cooperatives, buyers' cooperatives, nonprofits, and basic partnerships. This chapter examines how separation provides the firm with capabilities that improve the efficiency of transactions in comparison to direct exchange.

The *scope of the firm* is the combination of the firm's market-making and organizational activities. The "intermediation hypothesis," as set forth in the previous chapter, states that increases in consumer transaction costs relative to those of the firm lead to growth in the scope of the firm. This chapter examines in greater detail how firms address transaction costs through both markets and organizations. The major role that firms play in the contemporary economy suggests that firms possess substantial transaction cost advantages over direct exchange.[1]

The discussion then reviews the "internalization hypothesis," otherwise known as the "make-or-buy" choice, which suggests that firms address some types of transaction costs by vertical integration. This determines how the firm divides its scope between its market-making activities and organizational activities, and is complementary to the "intermediation hypothesis."

The separation criterion has important implications. Under some conditions, firms maximize profits rather than owners' consumption benefits. With separation, ownership of firms represents financial assets that facilitate divestiture, acquisition, and mergers. The ability to trade ownership of firms as financial assets provides liquidity to investors and allows market valuation of the firm, thus helping firms to raise capital. Separation is the basis of the market for corporate control, which

---

1 See Spulber (1998, 1999) on the role of firms in establishing and operating markets and in the design of market microstructure. Spulber (2007) points out that firms provide markets with mechanisms of spontaneous order in addition to prices, including marketing, sales, media, and other types of mass communication.

provides incentives for managers. Separation helps firms to choose efficient employment levels and to provide incentives for its employees.

Separation allows the firm to achieve greater economic efficiency than direct exchange between consumers. Owners prefer that the firm choose prices to maximize profits; see Chapter 3. The separation of objectives is essential to the establishment of firms because it helps to provide incentives to entrepreneurs. The *foundational shift* occurs when the firm is established and the entrepreneur becomes an owner of the firm, as discussed in Chapter 4. The incentives for entrepreneurs provide returns for the endogenous establishment of firms in equilibrium; see Chapter 5. The separation of objectives enhances the firm's ability to hire an efficient number of workers in comparison to consumer organizations; see Chapter 6. The separation of objectives underpins the separation of the owner's decisions from the firm's management decisions, referred to as the separation of ownership and control, which enhances the firm's ability to raise capital relative to consumer cooperatives; see Chapter 7.

Intermediated exchange through firms improves upon direct exchange as a result of the separation of objectives. Separation allows the firm to serve as a profit-maximizing intermediary in economic transactions. The firm addresses the problem of the absence of a double coincidence of wants; see Chapter 8. The separation of objectives allows the firm to act as a residual claimant, thus mitigating the free riding that occurs in consumer organizations; see Chapter 9. The firm creates markets that separate demand decisions from supply decisions, thus coordinating buying and selling throughout the economy; see Chapter 10. Finally, the separation of objectives allows the firm to become a contracting hub, resolving problems of adverse selection, moral hazard, and hold-up that can occur with direct exchange between consumers; see Chapter 11.

2.1 The Separation Criterion

The *separation criterion* holds when the objectives of an institution are separate from the objectives of its owners. The separation criterion provides a bright line distinction between firms and consumer organizations. By definition, the firm's business objectives differ from the consumption objectives of its owners. As the preceding chapter showed, consumer organizations are not firms because they do not satisfy the separation criterion. Separation provides the institution with "superpowers" that are unavailable both to individual consumers and to consumer organizations. The purpose of this section is to show how separation provides the firm with enhanced transaction capabilities.

2.1.1 Conditions for Separation

Before turning to the implications of separation, it is useful to consider the conditions under which separation occurs. Fisher (1906, 1907, 1930) addressed the separation of the firm's investment decisions from the owners' consumption and saving objectives. The firm's optimal investment decisions are independent of the preferences of its owners and independent of how the investment is financed. The firm's owners are only affected by the firm's decisions through their wealth. They carry out their consumption and saving decisions through product markets and financial markets. Fisher's separation theorem is in the neoclassical tradition and requires price-taking behavior by both consumer-owners and firms. The Fisher separation theorem assumes that there are no transaction costs and that there exists a complete set of competitive markets.

Price-taking behavior is not a necessary condition for separation of objectives. In Chapter 3, separation of objectives is shown to hold when firms engage in monopolistic competition and choose prices. Because of product differentiation, the effect of the firm's profit on owner's income is substantial while the expenditure effect of the firm's price is negligible.Chapter 3 also generalizes the Fisher separation theorem to price-setting firms and shows that with product differentiation, the owners' consumption-saving decisions can be separated from the firm's investment decisions.

Separation of objectives is closely connected to gains from trade. When individual consumers cannot achieve gains from trade due to transaction costs, they will engage in autarkic production, essentially managing production for their consumption benefit. When there are few or no transaction costs and markets exist, consumers achieve gains from trade by decoupling production and consumption decisions. The neoclassical separation theorem is based on two sources of gains from trade. The consumer obtains part of the gains from trade by adjusting consumption and buying and selling goods at given prices. The firm obtains part of the gains from trade by adjusting production and by buying and selling goods at given prices, generating profit that adds to the income of its consumer-owners.

Market opportunities to buy and sell goods imply that groups of consumers do not need to rely on operating production to achieve their consumption objectives. Firms can choose the best mix of products based on their technology and consumer demands, and consumers can choose the best mix of goods to buy based on their preferences and endowments. Market opportunities to share risk imply that consumers do not need to operate production to allocate resources under uncertainty. Market opportunities for contracts imply that consumers do not need to operate production to transfer resources over time.

Consumer organizations internalize transactions and maximize the consumption benefits of their members. Gains from trade with others outside the group of members generate returns from separation. The ability to sell memberships, for example, generates gains from trade. Consumers do not need to operate a club or cooperative to obtain benefits from economies of scale or from local public goods.

Property rights are fundamental to the firm because they allow gains from trade. Property rights allow individuals to trade goods and services and to realize the returns on investments. Consumers need not rely on autarkic production or internalization of exchange within consumer organizations. When a club's members cannot sell memberships, the club maximizes average consumption benefits for its members. When the club's "insiders" can sell memberships, the club changes its objectives. The insiders view the club as an asset and their consumption objectives become separate from the club's objectives. As a result, the inside members unanimously prefer that the club maximize profits. With a market for membership shares, the club becomes a firm.

Well-defined property rights are essential to the establishment of firms. Property rights provide owners with rights to the firm's returns and rights to control the firm. The firm's owners cannot manage the firm without exercising control rights. The firm's owners will not devote effort to operating and monitoring the firm unless they obtain returns to their efforts. Entrepreneurs will not devote resources to establishing firms unless they will become owners, and receive returns and rights of control. The firm has a greater ability to secure capital when it can provide investors with collateral based on the firm as an asset.

Efficient markets require property rights to be complete, exclusive, and transferable. Consumer organizations may fail to satisfy any or all of these requirements. Consumer organizations such as clubs, cooperatives, nonprofits, and associations are owned in common by their members, so that shares are not owned exclusively. In basic partnerships, common ownership poses problems of free riding and moral hazard. Collective ownership in basic partnerships restricts the ability of members to transfer ownership shares. Transferable ownership shares allow members to realize gains from trade through separation of objectives, giving them incentives to establish a firm.

Henry Hansmann and Reinier Kraakman (2000a, p. 390) ask "what, if any, essential role does organizational law play in modern society?" They further ask "do the various legal entities provided by organizational law permit the creation of relationships that could not practicably be formed by contract alone?" Hansmann and Kraakman (2000a, 2000b) argue that the main role of organizational law is *asset partitioning*. Not only are investors' assets protected from claims of the corporation by limited liability, but the converse is also the case. The assets of the corporation and the personal assets of its owners and managers are protected from claims by investors. Effectively, organizational law establishes a system of property rights for the corporation, rather than just rules for contracts. Hansmann and Kraakman (2000a, p. 393) emphasize that "the separation between the firm's bonding assets and the personal assets of the firm's owners and managers – is the core defining characteristic of a legal entity, and establishing this separation is the principal role that organizational law plays in the organization of enterprise."[2]

---

2 Hansmann et al. (2006) examine the development of asset separation shielding the firm in ancient Rome, medieval Italy, early modern England, and the contemporary United States.

2.1.2 Separation Implies That the Firm's Objective
Is Profit Maximization

Separation implies that the firm's objective is profit maximization. With separation, the firm's owners are affected by the firm's decisions only through the impact of the firm's profit on their income. The firm's owners make consumption decisions by choosing the most preferred consumption bundle given their income. As a result, the firm's owners unanimously prefer that the firm maximize profits.

Profit maximization by the firm yields decisions that differ from those of consumer organizations. Firms and consumer organizations generally choose different prices, outputs, product quality, investment levels, employment levels, and technologies. The differences in the choices made by firms and by consumer organizations determine the economic impact of firms.

The differences in the decisions of a firm from those of consumer organizations result in greater economic efficiency under some conditions. Generally, consumer organizations are concerned with maximizing average benefits, which often results in inefficient outcomes. Firms consider the marginal benefits of their decisions, which often results in greater economic efficiency. Economic profits provide incentives for firms to carry out their activities, including price setting. Increased competition between firms limits their market power and can enhance economic efficiency. Firms play an economic role when the combination of profit maximization and competition leads to outcomes that are more efficient than those for consumer organizations.

As a consequence of the separation of objectives, the firm is an additional player in the economy. Essentially, a firm adds degrees of freedom to a set of economic transactions. If there are n consumers, adding a firm means that there are $n + 1$ economic actors, and potentially n additional economic relationships between the consumers and the firm itself. This fundamentally changes the set of feasible transactions. The firm is an independent decision maker as a result of separation from its owners, employees, and trading partners. Because firms maximize profits, they are players with strategic objectives different from those of consumers.

The separation criterion implies that the firm is a transferable asset. Suppose that property rights to firms are well defined, so that owners of firms potentially can transfer these rights. The separation between the owners' consumption objectives and the objectives of the firm implies that owners do not need to own the firm to achieve their consumption objectives. The firm's owners can realize the value of the firm by transferring ownership to others, thus realizing the value of the firm by selling it. Separation implies that the owners of the firm are only affected by the firm through the income that the firm generates. As a result, the firm is a transferable financial asset.

Firms allow a system of complete, exclusive, and transferable property rights. Ownership of firms is complete and exclusive. Firms are divisible assets whose shares can be transferred. The transferability of shares of firms has a number of important benefits. The owners of the firm can sell their ownership to other consumers or to firms, providing liquidity to inventors and to entrepreneurs. Transfers of ownership determine the market value of the firm. Firms engage in many transactions with investors, customers, suppliers and others. The returns to this set of transactions can be capitalized in the form of ownership shares of the corporation. The firm provides a mechanism for converting the value of future transactions into a tradable asset.

2.1.3 Separation of Objectives Allows the Separation of Ownership and Control

With separation of objectives, the firm's owners can delegate decision making to managers, thus separating ownership and control. Consumer organizations such as cooperatives and basic partnerships do not separate ownership and control. More complex organizations, such as closely held firms, corporations, and some types of partnerships, allow the separation of ownership and control.[3] The advantages of separating ownership and control include delegation of authority to specialized managers. In corporations, owners of the firm can delegate monitoring of the firm's managers to a board of trustees.

The separation of ownership and control allows individuals to buy and sell shares of firms. Prices in securities markets reflect investor information about the anticipated performance of the firm. The owner of the firm obtains the residual returns from the firm's earnings and exercises residual control over the firm's operations. Individuals can build portfolios of securities, allowing them to obtain the benefits of diversification of investments. The separation of ownership and control thus enhances the ability of the firm to raise financial capital in comparison with consumer organizations. Financing investment is one of the most important functions of the firm.

Another major benefit from the separation of ownership and control is the development of a market for corporate control. The importance of the market for corporate control originally was identified by Manne (1965, 1966). Corporate managers operate under the supervision of the firm's shareholders, its board of directors, and its investors. The firm's managers must act in shareholders' interests or they will be replaced by either the firm's current or its future shareholders.

The separation of ownership and control allows market valuation of the firm, providing information to managers, investors, and the firm's owners. Markets for corporate ownership make it easier to combine firms through mergers and

---

3 Ribstein (2007) examines more complex partnership forms, which he refers to as "uncorporations." He considers variations on the partnership form such as master limited partnerships, real estate investment trusts, private equity firms, hedge funds, and venture capital funds. More complex partnerships with general governance structures are firms because they allow the separation of objectives.

acquisitions. This allows the firms' owners to obtain gains from consolidating different firms. Markets for corporate ownership make it easier to reorganize firms by divestiture, allowing the firm's owners to benefit from assigning the firm's assets and capabilities to different tasks.

Blair (2003a, 2004) points out that corporate law performs an important function by giving the firm entity status through the separation of ownership and control. Corporate law provides incentives for the firm to accumulate enterprise-specific physical capital, organizational capital, and human capital (Blair 1995, 2003a, 2004). The entity perspective emphasizes that the firm has value as an ongoing concern. The separation of ownership and control provided by corporate law allows investors to withdraw capital without necessarily blocking the continued operation of the firm. Also, managers can withdraw from the firm without necessarily changing its continued operation. Investors and managers need not have their decisions dependent on how their withdrawal affects the survival of the entity, as in the case of the basic partnership.

The question of separation of ownership and control has generated some controversy. Although corporations are the main form of organization in developed economies, they have traditionally been the object of criticism. Adam Smith (1998, p. 850) observed that directors of joint-stock companies

> being the managers rather of other people's money than of their own, it cannot well be expected, that they should watch over it with the same anxious vigilance with which the partners in a private copartnery frequently watch over their own. . . . Negligence and profusion, therefore, must always prevail, more or less, in the management of the affairs of such a company.

The inefficiencies of the corporate form are a frequent theme in the economics, finance, and law literatures. A large literature on corporate governance offers myriad suggestions for private reforms and public regulation.[4]

Berle and Means (1932), writing in the shadow of the Great Depression, expressed great concern that the separation of ownership and control would replace efficient markets with inefficient corporations. In their classic study, Berle and Means (1932) examined the wide dispersion of share ownership of major corporations. They lamented what they perceived to be a divergence, and even opposition, of interests between owners and managers and also noted the general absence of dominant shareholders. Berle and Means argued that such diffuse ownership reduced the incentives for shareholders to monitor management in comparison to those in a closely held company. For Berle and Means, this situation represented a corporate revolution that outdid the effects of the industrial revolution. Because of the separation of ownership and control, the management of corporations exercised significant autonomy and consequently might not maximize profit. Means indeed attributed the Great Depression to the corporate revolution, which in his view led

---

4 See, for example, Blair (1995) and MacAvoy and Millstein (2003).

to inflexible "administered prices." Administrative action by managers replaced market forces in determining prices, "thus inhibiting any general fall in the price level and converting a general fall in demand into a recession and unemployment."[5] Corporate scandals have led to public policy debates regarding the efficiency of the corporate form. Regulation by the Securities and Exchange Commission and laws such as the Sarbanes-Oxley Act reflect these continued concerns.

The Berle and Means view is inconsistent with the success of the corporate form of organization of the firm. As Jensen and Meckling (1976, p. 357) observe, "Whatever its shortcomings, the corporation has thus far survived the market test." Contrary to Berle and Means, Demsetz and Lehn (1985) find no correlation between accounting profits and concentration of ownership; see also Demsetz (1983). Corporations remain the dominant form of organization for firms. They continue to be established and to attract most investment. The corporate sector is a major engine of economic growth. The industrial organization of developed economies clearly shows that corporations have passed the market test. Share ownership has grown increasingly diffuse across the population. The fact that corporations are the main form of business organization strongly suggests that they provide greater economic benefits than other institutional arrangements.

Corporations offer a number of features that improve transaction efficiencies. The corporate form of organization reduces transaction costs by providing a standard legal form. Additional features of the corporation include delegation of monitoring to a board, delegation of authority to management, limited liability of shareholders, transferable control rights, limits on dissolution through the board, and protecting creditors by limiting shareholders to residual returns.[6]

Ruback and Jensen (1983) point out that the market for corporate control involves not only competition between potential owners of the firm, but also competition between potential managers for the opportunity to manage corporate resources. They show empirically that corporate takeovers generate gains from trade, both for target shareholders and for acquiring firm shareholders, and that these gains come from efficiency rather than market power.

Alchian and Demsetz (1972) observe that the organizational structure of firms (sole proprietorship, partnership, and corporation) provides ways to monitor team production. Jensen and Meckling (1976), based on the principal-agent model, emphasize the effects of incentives on the performance of managers. As the agent of the corporation's shareholders, the manager is subject to moral hazard. If the manager has a substantial ownership share, he or she will be overly cautious and will avoid risky projects that might increase the firm's expected value. If the manager has a small ownership share, he or she may shirk in terms of insufficient effort or in terms of excessive perks. The manager's actions may depart from the interests of

---

5 See Means in the introduction to Berle and Means (1967). See also Means (1934, 1935, 1939, and 1940).
6 See Ribstein (2004).

shareholders in various ways. The manager may not devote sufficient effort to his tasks, may not accurately share information with owners, may have a time horizon that is too short, may avoid risk, and may overinvest in the firm's activities rather than distributing returns to shareholders; see Butler (1989).

Some important benefits of separation of ownership and control are those associated with agency. Delegation to managers provides benefits from specialization and the division of labor. The managers of the firm are specialists in strategy, administration, and functional areas such as accounting, marketing, finance, operations, information technology, and R&D. The managers of the firm provide knowledge and expertise, so that the firm is not limited by the capabilities of its owners. The managers of the firm devote their time and effort to management, so that the firm is not limited by the opportunity costs of its owners' time and effort.

Delegation of authority to a manager replaces multiple contracts among owners with two types of contracts. The firm's owners contract with the firm through ownership shares, and in turn, the firm contracts with the manager. The firm provides transaction cost advantages when ownership shares, combined with a contract between the firm and the manager, are less costly than multiple contracts among members of a consumer organization. The manager unifies the control of the firm in comparison with multiple conflicting managers of a consumer cooperative or a basic partnership. The contract between the firm and the manager is a relational contract that specifies the manager's duties in general terms without the need for continual renegotiation that might occur within a basic partnership.

Separation of ownership and control provides incentives for management that differ from those in consumer organizations such as basic partnerships. The firm provides the manager with incentives for performance. This relationship is subject to problems of moral hazard because the manager's effort may not be observable. The relationship is subject to problems of adverse selection because the manager may have information that is hidden from the firm's owners, such as the manager's ability. Consumer organizations experience moral hazard in the form of free riding and adverse selection due to asymmetric information. The relative effects of these costs determine whether there are advantages to the separation of ownership and control. The firm performs better if the transaction costs associated with agency are less than the transaction costs associated with free riding. The unity of control offered by delegation to a manager can offer benefits by replacing costly group decision making.

2.1.4 Returns to Entrepreneurs

The separation of objectives has profound implications for the establishment of firms. The resulting separation of ownership and control helps to specify the returns to entrepreneurs. After the firm is established, the entrepreneur becomes an owner of the firm. The entrepreneur realizes a return to entrepreneurship by obtaining the firm's profits once the firm is established. If there is a market for firms, the entrepreneur realizes a return by selling the firm. The return to entrepreneurship is the owner's share of the value of the firm once it is established.

As an illustration, consider an entrepreneur who identifies an opportunity to bring an invention to market by purchasing the invention from an inventor and then selling it to several producers. One way to obtain the returns from this idea would be for the entrepreneur to carry out all of the necessary transactions with the inventor and the producers. The entrepreneur would invest time and effort in completing the necessary transactions. The entrepreneur would realize returns through contracts with the inventor and producers. Alternatively, the entrepreneur could establish a firm to carry out the necessary transactions. After establishing the firm, the entrepreneur would receive a share of the profits of the firm or the entrepreneur could sell the firm to investors. The value of the firm would reflect the expected return to the entrepreneur's idea. Forming a firm gives the entrepreneur the benefit of liquidity by allowing the entrepreneur to realize the value of his idea through operating the firm or through selling ownership of the firm. The potential entrepreneur chooses between contracts and establishing a firm based on the relative efficiency of the transactions.

2.1.5 The Firm Provides Multilateral Transactions and Networks of Relationships

The separation of objectives between the firm and its consumer-owners supports the firm's role as an intermediary in economic transactions. Through multilaterial transactions, the firm overcomes time constraints faced by individuals. By creating market mechanisms and organizational structures, firms are able to manage many transactions simultaneously.

Consumers cannot be in two places at once. This limits their ability to engage in multiple transactions. Consumers have a limited amount of time to allocate between labor, leisure, and transaction activities. It is reasonable to suppose that consumers can only engage in one transaction at a time, and because transactions take time, a consumer is limited in the number of transactions per unit of time. Firms overcome such time limitations through organizations with multiple members, so that firms can engage in multiple transactions simultaneously.[7] The firm faces practically no limits on the number of transactions per unit of time. The application of information technology further extends the ability of the firm to enter into many transactions.

By transacting with many buyers and sellers, the firm creates a network that gives its customers access to many suppliers and its suppliers access to many customers. The firm as intermediary is thus at the center of a hub-and-spoke network.[8] Jensen

---

7 For example, the Federal Reserve Bank's FedWire in 2003 handled 123 million transactions with an aggregate value of $447 trillion (Lyon, 2004).

8 Such hub-and-spoke economies are well known in marketing (Alderson, 1954; see also Townsend, 1978).

and Meckling's (1976) view of the firm as a nexus of contracts reflects the efficiency of centralized contracting. Buyers and sellers transact with the firm in contrast to making every possible connection between individual buyers and sellers. Efficiency is improved because the number of connections is significantly lower. Efficiency is further enhanced if the firm adds additional matchmaking activities that reduce search costs for members of the network.

The firm has advantages over individual consumers by serving as a contracting hub. Many different types of transactions can be connected. The firm contracts with customers, suppliers, partners, investors, and employees. This simplifies the content of each transaction. For example, a customer buying a gallon of milk at a supermarket need not consider all of the underlying transactions that were necessary to establish, finance, staff, and provision the store. The customer further benefits from one-stop shopping, filling a shopping basket with one transaction at the store, without the need to shop at many specialized stores for each item in the basket.

Firms can also perform clearinghouse activities that consolidate transactions. In a clearinghouse, members make multiple trades and settle with the clearinghouse only the net payments. Clearing reduces the number of necessary settlements to at most one transaction per member. Banks benefit from processing payments between their own accounts, known as "on us" transactions, rather than payments between banks, which double the number of transactions, referred to as "transit transactions."[9]

The firm's market transactions and organizational transactions are voluntary. Firms apply market mechanisms and organizational incentives rather than command and control. The firm's customers, suppliers, and employees make decisions on the basis of their preferences, endowments, and information. The voluntary response of individuals to incentives such as prices, wages, and contracts generates "spontaneous order" in the sense of Friedrich Hayek (1977, v. 2, p. 109). Market transactions are the result of voluntary agreements between buyers and sellers who receive gains from trade. Organizational transactions also are the result of voluntary agreements between the firm and its employees, who each receive gains from trade. Alchian and Demsetz (1972, p. 777) emphasize the voluntary nature of employment. They point out that "managing, directing, or assigning workers to various tasks" is just a form of continual contract renegotiation within organizations.

2.1.6 The Firm Has Longevity

The separation of the firm's objectives from those of its owners provides the firm with an important feature. Although the firm's owners have finite lifetimes, the firm can overcome this limitation. By living longer than individual consumers, firms create many kinds of transactions that consumers cannot. By operating in multiple periods, firms transfer value over time. Firms develop transactions that

9 Shaffer (1997).

connect consumers who wish to transact in different time periods. Firms transfer value and goods over time through contracts with consumers and suppliers in multiple periods. Shares of the firm are tradable assets that provide a store of value to investors.

Because firms can live longer than consumers, they can invest in developing long-term reputations. In practice, the firm's name is a brand that stands for the firm's reputation for product quality, expertise, trustworthiness, or possibly lack thereof. Such reputation effects can reduce potential problems of moral hazard or adverse selection. The long-term returns to reputation provide incentives for behavior by firms that allow transactions not necessarily available to consumers.

The longevity of firms permits investments in activities such as research and development that take a long time to bear fruit. Because firms can live longer than their employees, firms can receive returns to efforts that have a long-term payoff. Firms can reward employees for efforts whose returns may exceed the employees' tenure or even their lifetime.

Firms also can outlive their owners. This valuable aspect of longevity is reflected in the corporate form, which allows owners to withdraw their capital by selling their ownership shares to others without interfering in the life of the company, as discussed in the previous chapter. Entrepreneurs earn returns from establishing a firm that outlives them. Such a transaction might be difficult to achieve through direct exchange between shorter-lived consumers.

2.1.7 The Firm Offers Identity and Anonymity

Consumers generally have well-defined identities. Firms offer both identity and anonymity to markets. The firm has its own name and identity that are known to its customers, suppliers, partners, and investors. The firm's identity provides returns to building a brand name and reputation, as already noted. In turn, the firm may keep track of the identity of its trading partners as a means of gathering market information.

However, by being at the hub of transactions, the firm often confers some amount of anonymity on its transaction partners. Although the firm and its trading partners know each others' identities, the firm allows its trading partners to retain their anonymity with each other. Customers need not know each others' identities or those of the firm's suppliers or investors. Transactions become somewhat removed from their social context in comparison with direct exchange.

Two consumers participating in direct exchange often are aware of each other's individual characteristics; they may know each other socially or they may have traded together before. Such social connections may have advantages; the two consumers may have built up trust, for example. However, such social connections may have disadvantages as well. The transaction may involve time-consuming conversations and social rituals that increase the costs of bargaining. The terms of trade may reflect social obligations between the parties that may prove advantageous for some. In contrast, firms standardize transactions in terms of prices and the characteristics of goods and services. They confer anonymity on their customers and other trading partners. A customer can purchase a product at a store with a minimum of interaction beyond the transaction. This allows firms to develop markets for goods and services in which transactions are more convenient for customers and suppliers.

Firms also offer some anonymity in employment. There may be advantages in working with family members or members of a social group, as in the case of merchant associations. However, there are high transaction costs involved in establishing and maintaining a team or partnership. Negotiations can be affected by family or social relationships. By standardizing employment relationships, firms allow potential employees to develop standard skills that can be offered to different firms. Firms standardize wages and job descriptions for potential employees. Firms organize labor markets by making employment relationships more convenient for employees.

2.1.8 The Firm Realizes Economies from Specialization and Division of Labor

The many different types of firms are specialists in particular types of transactions. The great variety of economic transactions helps to explains the many types of firms in the economy. A buyer forms a contract with a seller to obtain a future service. A factory owner engages workers and coordinates their productive efforts to manufacture a good. A contractor engages skilled labor to complete a project. A principal hires an agent, often to represent the principal in a further transaction with a third party. An investor provides financing for a productive activity. Practically any economic activity from exchange to manufacturing can be fully described in terms of transactions.

The specialization and division of labor in society that Adam Smith emphasized is enhanced by adding firms to the population of consumers. Entrepreneurs can establish a firm to undertake a highly specific task. Firms can specialize in particular types of transactions in a manner that may not be feasible for consumers. A consumer may purchase a wide variety of goods. A consumer may have diverse interests, combining labor and leisure pursuits. Consumer-owners can invest in a specialized firm, while holding a diverse portfolio of other investments.

The specialist firm improves transactions by developing expertise in completing a particular type of exchange. Firms employ and train personnel with the necessary skills and develop knowledge within the organization needed to conduct a particular type of business. Firms develop business routines to carry out repetitive tasks, such as production assembly lines or checkout stands at retail stores. Chandler (1990b) identifies organizational capabilities in management strategy and in functional areas such as innovation, marketing, and purchasing. As a result of specialization, firms can get better at communicating, learning, and making decisions.

The specialist firm takes advantage of economies of scale and scope in transaction technology. Firms have fixed costs of transactions; that is, the costs do not depend on the volume of transactions, such as information-processing equipment.[10] Firms can also take advantage of many sources of economies of scale including automation, standardization of the terms of transactions, and specialization and division of labor in the processing of transactions. Firms can obtain economies of scope by using such methods to handle a variety of different transactions. For example, a retailer handles many different products with a common transaction technology. The specialist also benefits from network economies as a center of transaction activity. Specialists also take advantage of market information obtained by handling many similar transactions.

2.2 Firms Create and Manage Markets

Firms create and manage markets, so markets are endogenous institutions. The allocation mechanisms offered by firms are the "microstructure" of markets (Spulber 1998, 1999). Firms intermediate exchange through their markets and organizations. Firms provide economic value by enhancing the net benefits of transactions, by coordinating transactions, and by developing innovative types of transactions.

2.2.1 Communication and Information Processing

Consumers face communication costs in direct exchange and in forming consumer organizations. Communication takes time and effort and is subject to mistakes. Interaction between individuals may be constrained by social networks. Consumers also face costs of information processing due to human limits on cognition. Groups of consumers face coordination costs in forming social organizations due to costs of communication and information processing.

Firms use both markets and organizations to coordinate the activities of many individuals. Through centralized market mechanisms and organizational processes, firms improve communication and information processing in comparison to what can be achieved by consumers with direct exchange. Some firms specialize in communications services, such as telecommunications companies, cable television companies, Internet service providers, and Internet backbone providers. Retailers, wholesalers, financial firms, and specialized intermediaries provide communication services.

---

10 Banks have economies of scale in handling accounts and processing transactions. See empirical studies by Sealey and Lindley (1977), Gilligan et al. (1984), and Ferrier and Lovell (1990). Advertising agencies have economies of scale and scope deriving from transactions in placing media advertisements for their clients; see Silk and Berndt (1994). Retail stores use computers, cash registers, bar coding, and point-of-sale terminals.

Distinguishing individuals on each side of the market raises two fundamental issues. First, how do buyers and sellers engage in communication to find each other for the purpose of economic transactions? Buyers and sellers can communicate directly or they can communicate indirectly through firms that act as matchmakers. Second, how do buyers and sellers carry out the computation that is needed to operate the allocation mechanism? Buyers and sellers can handle their own computation through bilateral or multilateral transactions or they can rely on firms that act as matchmakers and market makers. The role of the firm depends on a comparison of the performance of markets in which buyers and sellers engage in direct exchange with that of markets in which firms intermediate between buyers and sellers.

Firms centralize markets by intermediating transactions. Without firms acting as intermediaries, markets tend to be decentralized, with individual buyers and sellers handling all communication and computation tasks. Allocations in decentralized markets are characterized by constraints on communication and computation. Costly communication is likely to lead to random search and inefficient matching of buyers and sellers. Costly computation is likely to involve asymmetric information and inefficient allocation mechanisms. Individuals thus encounter network constraints that limit the efficiency of decentralized exchange.

Firms create centralized markets by providing communication and computation services to buyers and sellers. Firms establish and operate information systems that supply buyers and sellers with some of the means to communicate and process information. Firms engage in communication with buyers and sellers to gather information about their characteristics and to provide information about terms of exchange, such as prices and product features. Firms also engage in computation, through their match-making and market-making activities.

Firms address transaction costs by applying information systems to economic transactions. *Information systems* contain two essential components. *Communication* in an information system refers to the exchange of information between individuals and *computation* in an information system refers to the processing of data that is being exchanged. Information systems generally comprise physical networks involving telecommunications and connected computers.[11] Information systems must interact with economic and social networks and human intelligence. Generally, the functions of communication and computation are complementary.

11 An industry definition of *information system* is "1. A system, whether automated or manual, that comprises people, machines, and/or methods organized to collect, process, transmit, and disseminate data that represent user information. 2. Any telecommunications and/or computer related equipment or interconnected system or subsystems of equipment that is used in the acquisition, storage, manipulation, management, movement, control, display, switching, interchange, transmission, or reception of voice and/or data, and includes software, firmware, and hardware.... 3. The entire infrastructure, organization, personnel, and components for the collection, processing, storage, transmission, display, dissemination, and disposition of information." See Committee T1A1 (2000).

Table 2.1. *Classification of allocation mechanisms based on the costs of communication and computation*

	Costless computation	Costly computation
Costless communication	Decentralized exchange is feasible Core allocations Walrasian equilibria	Buyers and sellers engage in bilateral exchange on complete networks Firms provide computation services: Matchmaking and market making
Costly communication	Buyers and sellers engage in cooperative equilibria on incomplete networks Buyers and sellers hold auctions on incomplete networks Firms provide communication services: Gathering and distributing information	Buyers and sellers engage in bilateral exchange on incomplete networks Buyers and sellers engage in bilateral exchange on random networks Firms provide separate or bundled communication (gathering and distributing information) and computation services (matchmaking and market making)

Internet users require both the communications capability of the Internet to link to Web sites and the computational ability of search engines to locate Web sites. Internet auction sites, such as eBay, offer both communication between buyers and sellers and computation in the form of automated auctions. Traditional telecommunications systems transmit voice and data and provide guidance through telephone directories.

Markets require the services of information systems to function. Markets consist of transactions between buyers, sellers, and firms. Individuals must communicate to find each other, negotiate the terms of transactions, and monitor performance. Individuals must perform computations to choose between trading partners and to evaluate alternative terms of exchange. Costly communication and computation translate into transaction costs. When communication is costly, buyers and sellers deal with incomplete networks. There is a role for firms in providing communication in the form of matchmaking services. When computation is costly, buyers and sellers engage in bilateral transactions rather than more complex multilateral transactions such as those represented by the core. There is a role for firms in providing computation in the form of market-making services. A market classification based on the properties of information systems is shown in Table 2.1.

Firms employ information systems in creating and managing markets. Firms such as eBay apply information systems to manage online auctions. Firms such as Amazon employ information systems for online retailing. Bricks-and-mortar retailers and wholesalers employ information systems to manage their market places.

The theory of the firm distinguishes between the firm and its production technology, in contrast to the neoclassical firm. In electronic commerce, for example, firms are distinct from their information technology. Firms are also distinct from their core competencies and capabilities, which can include operational routines, organizational capital, and management strategies. Moreover, firms are distinct from the products and services that they offer to their customers, which can include technologies for implementing electronic commerce. A retailer's costs of establishing a market include the costs of the retail stores themselves. Firms that create financial markets incur costs of operating exchange trading systems.

Market-making costs for practically any type of firm include the costs of price adjustment. These are sometimes referred to as menu costs, because restaurants with paper menus must print new menus when prices change. Zbaracki et al. (2004) find that in addition to the physical costs associated with communicating price changes, there are substantial managerial and customer costs involved in adjusting prices. Zbaracki et al. (2002) point out that firms invest in pricing capital such as electronic shelf-labeling systems.

Market-making costs in electronic commerce include the costs of computer software, hardware, and management needed to operate Web sites. Firms offer customers electronic commerce services through the use of information system platforms. A *platform* is a collection of related technological standards. The term "platform" is sometimes used in the economics literature to designate firms that act as intermediaries in electronic commerce. The term is a shorthand reference indicating that these firms use information systems that obey common technical standards.

Platforms play an important role in information systems, both in communications and in computing. In computers, a platform is a "reconfigurable base of compatible components on which users build applications" and is identified with "engineering specifications for compatible hardware and software" (Bresnahan and Greenstein 1997; see also Bresnahan and Greenstein 1999 and Greenstein 1998). For example, IBM devised standards for the personal computer that were adopted by manufacturers of software, internal components, such as memory and microprocessors, and peripheral devices, such as printers and monitors. In turn, Microsoft's standards for personal computer operating systems are used by designers of software applications that are compatible with operating systems.

In communications networks, platforms permit compatible transmission of communications and interconnection of equipment; see Spulber and Yoo (2005). Platforms in telecommunications include hardware and software standards for computer-based switching and transmission systems. Platforms in communications include computer software standards such as the Transmission Control Protocol/ Internet Protocol (TCP/IP) used for Internet communication between computers. A network is said to be *modular* or to exhibit an *open architecture* if most suppliers of complementary services can gain access to the network.

Collections of technical standards exist in many industries where independent producers supply substitute products that are interchangeable and complementary products that must work together. Thus, cameras and film share technological standards that allow the products to be used together, and there are multiple providers of cameras and of film that follow the technical standards. These standards exist in many high-tech industries such as audio systems, video systems, and mobile phones. Platforms exist in many other types of industries in which compatible components are needed, including automobiles, aircraft, and industrial machinery.

Platforms exist in electronic commerce, in the form of technical standards for the electronic exchange of data between companies. Innovations in communications and computation as applied to business documents avoid the need to translate computer files into paper documents, thereby increasing the speed and accuracy of transactions. There is a wide-ranging set of standards for electronic data interchange (EDI) on private networks that pre-dates the Internet. Extensible Markup Language (XML) provides standards for documents and data transmission over the Internet developed by the World Wide Web Consortium. The advantage of document standardization is ease of communication and computation between businesses, including retailers, wholesalers, manufacturers, and parts suppliers.

Electronic commerce is the automation of economic transactions through the use of information systems. Electronic commerce lowers transaction costs by enhancing communications and computation in exchange between consumers, between consumers and firms, and between firms. Electronic commerce substitutes capital for labor services in the production of transactions, and potentially displaces costly labor services applied to routine commercial tasks, such as communicating with customers and suppliers regarding prices, product availability, ordering, billing, and shipping. Moreover, electronic commerce enhances the productivity of labor services in commercial activities such as sales, distribution, and procurement. Firms improve efficiency by linking external transaction systems with their internal computer systems, thus increasing the frequency, rapidity, and accuracy of communication and allowing links to production and inventory management systems within each organization.[12]

Electronic commerce further enhances communication of transaction information by allowing buyers and sellers to transact with the firm at remote locations and at different times. Thus, the buyers and sellers in an auction on eBay need not be present at the same location and can participate in the auction at different times. This reduces transaction costs by avoiding the costs of travel and the costs

12 See Lucking-Reilly and Spulber (2001).

of holding meetings, whether those costs would be borne by the firm or by its customers and suppliers. Thus, technological change in information processing and communication results in innovations in transaction methods and changes in the organization of firms.

2.2.2 Search and Matching

Through centralization of transactions, firms can improve the efficiency of transactions between consumers. Markets, whether stores, Web sites, auction houses, or exchanges, provide central locations where buyers and sellers can meet and transact. The firm's intermediation and market-making functions are examined in detail in Chapters 8 to 11.

Firms reduce search costs by matching buyers and sellers. There are many types of specialized intermediaries and matchmakers that bring buyers and sellers together. Matchmakers operate in markets with homogenous products, introducing buyers and sellers. Matchmaking and brokerage services are of particular importance in markets with differentiated products. Matchmakers take into account buyer and seller characteristics and the features of the products or services to be exchanged. Some types of matchmakers offer mechanisms for exchange, particularly in the case of online auctions and marketplaces, which provide mechanisms for price adjustment and market clearing.

Brokers are common in financial asset markets, including markets for securities, commodity futures, derivatives, insurance, and loans. Brokers bring buyers and sellers together in return for commissions or fees without taking ownership or directly providing the goods and services being exchanged. Firms gather and disseminate buyer and seller information to improve matches and reduce the costs of search. Pure information providers include directories such as the Yellow Pages; print and broadcast media that carry advertisements, Internet-based portals with seller or buyer listings, Web portals, and Internet search engines (Yahoo, Microsoft Live Search, Google); publishers of classified advertisements; and media (book publishers, newspapers, journals, and terrestrial and satellite broadcasters).

The many types of matchmaking services include the following: residential and commercial real estate brokers; employment and recruiting agencies; staffing and temporary agencies; representative agents (literary, talent, sports); and travel agents and freight transportation brokers. Other types of specialized intermediaries include dating and marriage matchmakers; interest group matchmakers (meetup.com); business brokers (for buyers and sellers of businesses); technology and intellectual property brokers; commodity and metals brokers; ship brokers; art brokers; and consignment and resale stores. Firms intermediate between businesses through various brokerage activities and business-to-business marketplaces. The Chinese web site Alibaba.com brings buyers and sellers together across country borders for over 200 countries in practically every industry, illustrating its motto "Global trade starts here."

Firms reduce search costs by aggregating buyer demands and seller supplies. Such aggregation avoids inefficiencies that result from mismatches between individual buyer demands and individual seller supplies. Firms can break up large orders, combine small orders, and match total demand and supply. Large-scale firms also improve market efficiency by bringing together many buyers and sellers, thus reducing reliance on small-scale dealers. By posting prices, market makers provide efficiencies in comparison with a market in which consumers must search across dealers for the best price.

Buyers participate in markets based on their expectations of seller participation and sellers participate in markets based on their expectations of buyer participation. To reduce search costs in financial markets, many types of firms perform market-making functions that bring liquidity to the market. Firms stand ready with funds needed to buy assets if there are not sufficient buyers and they stand ready with financial assets if there are not sufficient sellers. Buyers and sellers can enter the centralized market with confidence that they are unlikely to be rationed due to the absence of a trading partner.

Market makers are dealers that offer to buy and sell financial assets at posted prices. They assure buyers and sellers of liquidity if there are not sufficient counter parties available. Firms that provide liquidity in financial markets include block traders, who are dealers that handle large trades; value traders, who speculate based on superior information about price movements and asset values; and arbitrageurs, who identify differences in the supply and demand for liquidity across markets.[13] In addition, organized exchanges for securities and derivatives provide specialists who act as market makers by quoting bid and ask prices and acting as dealers. Buyers and sellers of financial assets benefit from the liquidity supplied by market makers. Investors can hold assets without being concerned about selling the asset in the future. Other financial firms such as banks and mutual fund companies act as market makers by standing ready to make loans or take deposits or to buy and sell financial assets.

Firms in product markets act as market makers by providing immediacy to their suppliers and customers.[14] Retailers and wholesalers stand ready to buy from their suppliers and they keep inventories on hand to serve their customers. By aggregating demands and suppliers, specialized firms pool demand-side and supply-side risk.[15] With market making by firms, consumers need not hold inventories, because they can rely on firms to have products on hand when needed. Suppliers can bring products to market when it is convenient to provide them, because they can rely on firms to purchase the products. Demsetz (1968a) notes that in securities markets "the ask-bid spread is the markup that is paid for predictable immediacy of exchange

---

13 See Harris (2003) for a practical guide to these financial firms. These definitions are adapted from the institutional discussion in Harris.

14 See Clower and Leijonhufvud (1975).

15 See Lim (1981) and Spulber (1985).

in organized markets; in other markets it is the inventory markup of retailer and wholesaler."

Matching problems arise even without search costs. Consumers face the absence of a double coincidence of wants when they cannot achieve an efficient allocation through bilateral trades. Firms alleviate this problem by serving as intermediaries, thus replacing money as a medium of exchange. Firms also create money by providing various payment systems, including checks and credit cards. The absence of the double coincidence of wants can also arise when a buyer and a seller cannot transact with each other at the same time.[16] The firm addresses such timing issues through market making, standing ready to buy and sell. The absence of a double coincidence of wants can occur when trading partners are in different locations. Firms can solve this problem by intermediating between consumers in different locations. By operating in multiple locations, the firm also reduces the costs of communication and search for consumers who deal with the local branch of the firm. Consumers encounter the absence of a double coincidence of wants when they cannot trade in different states of the world. By creating financial assets, firms allow consumers to carry out exchange under uncertainty and transfer resources across uncertain states. These issues are addressed further in Chapter 8.

2.2.3 Bargaining

Consumers incur bargaining costs in direct exchange and in establishing consumer organizations. Coase (1937) points out that "[t]he costs of negotiating and concluding a separate contract for each exchange transaction which takes place on a market must also be taken into account." Coase observes that in certain markets, techniques are devised for minimizing but not eliminating these costs, such as exchanges for fresh produce.

Firms have an arsenal of mechanisms for improving the efficiency of transactions relative to bargaining between consumers. These transaction mechanisms might not be feasible for consumers. Firms offer standardized contracts and other routine business processes that reduce bargaining costs. Firms standardize business processes and achieve economies of scale in transactions. By centralizing exchange, firms can post prices, operate auctions, and standardize exchange.

The firm's posted prices or its auction mechanisms create a critical separation between buyer demands and seller supplies. With posted prices, the firm trades with buyers who have a willingness to pay above the firm's ask price and the firm trades with sellers who have a cost below the firm's bid price. With double auctions, the firm identifies high-willingness-to-pay buyers and low-cost sellers and separates demands and supplies through the equilibrium prices chosen by the auction.

Firms consolidate the demands of many customers or the supplies of many sellers. The firm then can post prices on the basis of aggregate information about

---

16 See also Clower and Leijonhufvud (1975).

the demand of its customers or the supply offered by its sellers. Alternatively, the firm can gather more detailed information about demand and supply through auction mechanisms or through repeated observation of purchases and sales.

There are advantages to posted prices in comparison with bilateral negotiation. Posted prices are convenient for buyers or sellers relative to the time and effort required in negotiating exchange. Transacting at posted prices also removes the uncertainty that may be present in bilateral exchange if consumers have imperfect information about trading partners and thus do not know the outcome of bargaining. Transacting at posted prices improves the value of transactions relative to random matching of buyers and sellers. By adjusting prices to maximize profits, firms balance supply and demand, thus establishing market-clearing prices.

Firms design markets and allocation mechanisms to overcome the effects of imperfect information. The firm adjusts prices so that its purchases and sales clear the market. Thus, the firm performs the market-clearing function that neoclassical economics ascribes to the Walrasian auctioneer. Market clearing further reduces inefficiencies that might accompany search and bilateral exchange.

Net gains from trade in an economy with firms are increasing in the number of consumers if the firm obtains economies of scale in transactions. Such scale economies can be due to fixed costs of communication and information processing. There may also be benefits from dealing with many consumers if the firm aggregates information. The firm also benefits from dealing with many consumers if it can pool risks. Finally, the firm increases efficiency by dealing with many consumers if doing so improves the effectiveness of market making. When there are many buyers and sellers market makers benefit from increased liquidity.

Firms are intermediaries that coordinate buyers and sellers; see Spulber (1998, 1999). Buyers and sellers transact with a firm rather than engaging in direct exchange if the firm increases the benefits minus the costs of the transaction. In practice, firms incur many of the costs of buying and selling, including searching for trading partners, establishing prices, communicating price and product information, negotiating and writing contracts, arranging payments, recording exchange data, and monitoring contractual performance. Firms can reduce the costs of transactions by internalizing some parts of the exchange. Wholesalers and retailers are specialized firms that focus on distribution and sales.

Firms aggregate transactions to create benefits from coordination and scale, thus acting as market makers. In other cases, firms disaggregate transactions to create benefits from matching buyers and sellers more precisely, thus acting as intermediaries. In still other cases, firms create new types of transactions bringing buyers and sellers together in innovative ways. Chandler (1977) identifies large corporations and their managers as the "visible hand" responsible for a large share of economic decision making.

Consider market making by a firm that is a monopoly intermediary. Let $D(p)$ be the demand function of the firm's customers and let $S(w)$ be the supply function of the firm's suppliers. The firm's ask price is p and the firm's bid price is w. The

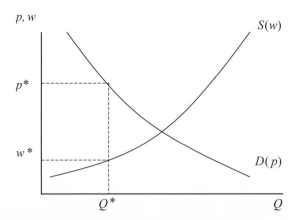

Figure 2.1. The market-making firm.

profit-maximizing firm chooses an ask price p^* and a bid price w^* that clear the market. The firm's profit-maximizing prices depart from the Walrasian "law of one price." The firm's ask price and bid price are respectively above and below the Walrasian price, $w^* < p^W < p^*$. The firm's output is below the Walrasian input, $Q^* < Q^W$. The firm's profit-maximizing bid and ask prices are shown in Figure 2.1.

2.2.4 Moral Hazard

The firm addresses the problem of moral hazard through market contracts and within its organization through incentives for managers, employees, and business units. The firm can reward agents based on their performance and a measure of aggregate performance. Holmstrom (1982) shows that with common uncertainty, by the theory of sufficient statistics, the optimal incentive scheme need only use aggregate information about the performance of peers. Nalebuff and Stiglitz (1983) point out that when all of the outputs are independent, the optimal compensation scheme can be based on each seller's individual output, so there is no advantage to joint compensation schemes. When the outputs of individuals are linked through common uncertainty, joint compensation schemes dominate rewards based strictly on individual performance.

A firm can contract simultaneously with many principals and many agents. The firm can organize the market differently from bilateral exchange. The firm can act as a central intermediary between the group of principals and the group of agents. This yields two potential advantages for the firm. The firm can aggregate information about agent performance. This can reveal information when there is statistical interdependence between the random shocks to agent outputs. This allows the firm to connect contracts and improve their performance. The firm can reward agents based on their relative performance. This can induce agents to compete with each other. Agents may devote more effort to production in a competitive situation than in a bilateral contract. The firm's coordination of multiple contracts subject to moral hazard is discussed in Chapter 11.

2.2.5 Adverse Selection

Markets and organizations provide solutions to the problem of adverse selection. Through market mechanisms, firms address asymmetric information that impedes bilateral exchange. The firm's reputation, quality certification, and economies of scale in gathering information help to mitigate some types of adverse selection problems.

When parties to economic relationships have asymmetric information, inefficient transactions can be the result. Buyers and sellers that have asymmetric information about their preferences and costs, respectively, may engage in inefficient levels of trade. In the relationship between a principal and agent, asymmetric information can result in departures from efficiency. Parties with private information command information rents that are necessary to induce them to reveal their private information. Providing information rents tends to distort economic interactions.

Firms can address asymmetric information in bilateral exchange by acting as intermediaries. In Myerson and Satterthwaite (1983), an intermediary designs a trading mechanism for a buyer and a seller who are exchanging a single object. By the revelation principle, a direct mechanism can represent the outcomes of bargaining under asymmetric information.[17] The direct mechanism determines the payment and likelihood of trade given the announcements by the buyer and the seller of their respective private information. The direct mechanism represents the outcome of such bargaining procedures as first-and-final offers by either the buyer or the seller or alternating offers. It also encompasses double auctions, where the good is exchanged at some average of the buyer's bid and the seller's bid, as long as the buyer's bid exceeds that of the seller.

The intermediary modifies the bargaining process by designing a profit-mazimizing mechanism that taxes the exchange. The intermediary's direct mechanism creates a spread between the payment to be made by the buyer and the payment to be received by the seller. As with direct bargaining, intermediated exchange also can fail to take place under asymmetric information, even when the buyer and seller would realize gains from trade. Because the buyer and seller have an incentive to conceal their private information, they must be compensated by information rents to induce them to reveal their information. If the gains from trade are not sufficiently large to cover these rents, even intermediated trade will break down.

Firms can reduce some effects of adverse selection through market mechanisms. Asymmetric information can create losses for an intermediary if some agents are better informed about the value of the assets that are being exchanged. The firm

---

17 See Dasgupta et al. (1979) and Myerson (1979).

compensates for expected losses by extracting rents from less informed agents. Adverse selection has a specific effect on the bid-ask spread in financial markets; see Copeland and Galai (1983) and Glosten and Milgrom (1985). The market maker must deal with informed and uninformed traders. The informed traders may have better information than the intermediary about the value of the asset. Thus, the informed traders may know that the value of the asset is above the ask price or below the bid price. In this case, trading with informed traders results in losses for the intermediary. Uninformed traders are said to trade for liquidity and purchase at the ask price or sell at the bid price, depending upon their estimates of the asset value of liquidity requirements. The firm can set bid and ask prices to recover losses from trades with informed agents through trades with uninformed agents. This allows the firm to provide liquidity services to the uninformed traders.

Firms can reduce the effects of adverse selection by offering monitoring efficiencies as well.[18] Diamond (1984) considers a firm that invests in a group of individual producers. The firm extends a debt contract to each of the producers, each of whom invests in a risky project. The firm is able to observe the outcome of the project perfectly by purchasing a monitoring technology. Individual investors provide financing to the firm through debt contracts. Diamond compares the outcome to a situation in which investors contract directly with producers. The investors are not able to observe the outcome of the risky projects. When there are few producers, direct contracting performs better than the firm. When there are many producers, the firm performs better than direct contracting because the firm benefits from risk pooling. The benefits of risk pooling are sufficient to cover the cost of the firm's monitoring technology.

2.2.6 Contracting

Consumers engaged in bilateral exchange may encounter contracting costs. These costs include the costs of negotiating and writing contingent contracts, monitoring performance, and enforcing the terms of contracts.

The reluctance of parties to invest in relationships subject to renegotiation is known as the "hold-up" problem. Economic analyses of the hold-up problem emphasize internalization through vertical integration. As is discussed in the next section, a buyer and a seller vertically integrate to avoid contracting problems and to improve incentives for investing. Even with contracting costs, however, the hold-up problem need not lead to vertical integration.

Firms can address the hold-up problem with market transactions that intermediate between buyers and sellers. By creating and managing markets, firms reduce

---

18 Melumad et al. (1997) show the advantages of delegated contracting when contract contingencies are costly. The analyses of Diamond (1984), Ramakrisnan and Thakor (1984), Williamson (1986), Krasa and Villamil (1992), and others establish that delegated monitoring is superior because of diversification by intermediaries.

the potential for renegotiation. Centralized markets reduce contracting costs in comparison with decentralized exchange, which requires search and bargaining. Buyers and sellers are not tied to a bilateral relationship. The efficiency of markets improves returns to investment in comparison to direct exchange. The standardization of transactions and allocation based on price mechanisms allows buyers and sellers to make investments that are not subject to hold-up. The market for contracts is discussed further in Chapter 11.

2.2.7 Free Riding

Free riding arises in a variety of contexts. Partnerships that engage in joint production encounter free riding when the efforts of partners are unobservable. There are incentives for free riding because the benefits are divided among the members. Each member receives only a share of the marginal contribution of their effort to the output of the partnership. The firm addresses this type of free riding by consolidating management in the hands of a single CEO. The corporation's shareholders delegate management to the CEO, which can lead to moral hazard problems, because the CEO's effort is unobservable and the CEO's ownership share is constrained by limited liability. Smaller partnerships perform better than corporations, because agency costs of delegating management to the CEO exceed the costs of free riding in the partnership. The corporation performs better than larger partnerships, because agency costs of delegating management to the CEO are less than the costs of free riding in the partnership. The effects of incentives and moral hazard on the financial organization of the firm are discussed further in Chapter 7.

Consumer cooperatives encounter free rider problems in allocating joint costs. Free rider problems affect the provision of public goods and the joint use of common property resources. The firm addresses free riding in cost allocation for both private goods and public goods through the use of pricing mechanisms that may not be available to consumer cooperatives. The firm reduces consumption externalities when there are common property resources through unifying the control of the resource. These issues are addressed further in Chapter 9.

2.3 Firms Create and Manage Organizations

Firms incur organizational transaction costs. The firm must decide how to divide its activities between markets and organizations. For any given scope of activities, such a division determines the firm's extent of vertical integration.[19] The

---

19 This is often referred to as the "boundaries of the firm" but might more accurately be termed the "boundaries of the organization." Because the firm encompasses both market activities and organizational activities, its scope extends beyond the organization.

extent of vertical integration refers to the activities carried out by the firm's organization. The "internalization hypothesis" states that firms will substitute organizational transactions for market transactions when doing so lowers transaction costs.

Economic analysis of firms has focused much attention on explaining vertical integration. The comparison of market transactions and organizational transactions is an important theme in the literature on institutional economics; see Commons (1931), Coase (1937, 1988, 1994), Williamson (1975, 1985), Spulber (1999), and Furubotn and Richter (2000). Commons (1931) distinguishes between bargaining transactions, which take place in the market, and managerial transactions, which take place within the organization.[20] The empirical literature on the firm has extensively tested the effects of transactions costs on vertical integration. The "internalization hypothesis" posits that increases in market transaction costs, relative to the firm's organization costs, explain greater internalization of those transactions through vertical integration.[21]

Coase (1937) states that "a firm will tend to expand until the costs of organizing an extra transaction within the firm become equal to the costs of carrying out the same transaction by means of an exchange on the open market or the costs of organizing in another firm." Coase emphasizes that firms engage in economic planning within the organization. As Coase points out: "Marshall introduces organization as a fourth factor of production; J. B. Clark gives the co-ordinating function to the entrepreneur; Knight introduces managers who co-ordinate. As D. H. Robertson points out, we find 'islands of conscious power'." Focusing on the firm's internal activities (rather than on its external activities), Coase asserts that "the distinguishing mark of the firm is the supersession of the price mechanism" and assigns organizational activities to the entrepreneur-coordinator. In the general theory of the firm presented here, the firm's external market-making activities also reflect conscious power and coordination.

---

20 According to John R. Commons (1931): "Transactions, as derived from a study of economic theories and of the decisions of courts, may be reduced to three economic activities, distinguishable as bargaining transactions, managerial transactions and rationing transactions." Finally, Commons refers to rationing transactions as those originating from courts, legislatures, or regulatory bodies. For Commons, "The bargaining transaction derives from the familiar formula of a market, which, at the time of negotiation, before goods are exchanged, consists of the best two buyers and the best two sellers on that market." In the case of managerial transactions "by which wealth itself is produced," there are hierarchical relationships: "The master, or manager, or foreman, or other executive, gives orders – the servant or workman or other subordinate must obey."

21 Harold Demsetz (1991) suggests that because making and buying each entail both management and transaction costs, the question is "whether the sum of management and transaction cost incurred through in-house production is more or less than the sum of management and transaction cost incurred through purchase across markets, since either option entails expenditures on both cost categories."

2.3.1 Communication and Information Processing

Firms establish organizations as a means of implementing market transactions and as a way of managing organizational transactions. Firms can improve the efficiency of transactions by substituting transactions within an organization for arms-length transactions, as Coase (1937) emphasizes. Firms can be complex organizations with many members and many trading partners. They allocate resources within their organizations, including labor services, capital financing, parts and components, and intellectual property. Firms coordinate the activities of their employees through many types of management procedures and organizational relationships.

Within the organization, firms have extensive communication systems, including the hierarchical chain of command, internal networks of relationships, and information technology networks. The firm's organization addresses the problem of bounded rationality. The collective efforts of members of the organization overcome some of the limits on the cognition of individuals. Individuals working together in an organization can presumably collect and analyze greater amounts of information than individuals working separately. These affect the ability of individuals to make complex decisions. Of course, there are well-known limits on the abilities of organizations as well, such as organizational conflict and bureaucratic inertia.

Herbert Simon (1955, 1972, 1976) examines the implications of limited cognition for organizations. The organization must deal with limits on an individual's ability to perform tasks and make decisions (Simon 1976, p. 39). The bounded rationality of managers and subordinates results in the need to delegate authority and share information within the organization.[22] The decisions of managers and employees may involve satisficing, rather than optimizing, which must be addressed by the design of incentives for individual performance. Because of limits on the knowledge, computation, and decision-making capacity of individuals, the organization breaks large tasks into smaller ones, achieving organizational goals by assigning subgoals to units of the organization.[23] March and Simon (1958) conclude that organizations engage in adaptive behavior to deal with complexity in decision making. Cyert and March (1963) present a behavioral theory of the firm that is based on a systems view of strategy making. They describe decision making by firms as a process of goal setting, feedback, adaptation, and search.[24] By combining the forces of many decision makers and taking advantage of specialization and division of labor, organizations can potentially improve information processing

---

22 However, Simon (1976, pp. 81–4) cautions that there are limits to rationality that affect the functioning of the organization: incomplete knowledge, imperfect anticipation of future events, and difficulty in identifying all possible alternatives.

23 March and Simon (1958, p.168).

24 Williamson (1975, p. 40) observes that organizations may facilitate "adaptive, sequential decision making, thereby to economize on bounded rationality."

and the accuracy of decision making. Knight (1965) finds that assignment of individuals to managerial positions may reflect greater capacity for decision making and information processing. Stinchcombe (1990, p. 29) suggests that the "social structure of organizations can be explained by the structure of the information problem they are confronted with." Arrow (1974, p. 68) argues that because information is costly, it is more efficient to transmit the information centrally, that is, through the upper levels of the hierarchy. The bounded rationality of economic actors and costly interaction within the organization in turn create bureaucratic inertia and impose limits on the performance of organizations in handling uncertainty.

Limits on the rationality of individuals constrain their ability to form productive teams. Organizations develop mechanisms to reduce the resulting inefficiencies yielding transaction benefits that might not be achieved through market transactions between team members. The costs of communication channels are highlighted by Marschak and Radner's (1972) classic model of communication in teams in which each member of a team imperfectly observes the current state of the world at some cost, with the decisions of the team depending on what (costly) channels of communication are established. In their framework (1972, p. 313), an organizer is faced with the problem of designing an organizational network that yields the highest expected payoff "net of the costs of observation, communication and computation" incurred by members of the team. They further point out that the activities of the organizer also are likely to entail similar costs of decision making, as well as costs of resolving conflicts and allocating tasks.

Firms offer management and unity of purpose. This contrasts with basic partnerships and cooperatives, which are subject to group decision making. Operating an organization as a collective agreement can be difficult and inefficient when transaction costs are present. Consumers face all of the complexities and inefficiencies of collective decision making. They face the costs of communication and negotiating with each other. Even if consumer-owners were to agree unanimously, they also face the costs of continually monitoring the complex activities of the enterprise to ensure conformity with their plans. They may need to make frequent adjustments in their strategies and instructions. These types of transaction costs suggest the need for managers. Rubinstein (1998) examines the organizational implications of bounded rationality in terms of the complexity of group decision making. Groups have difficulties in making optimal decisions because of the cost of establishing channels of communication between members of the organization, the time costs of sequential communication, and the costs of aggregating preferences in group decision making. As is well known from the social choice literature, group decision making can fail to rank alternatives in transitive manner. Firms provide a hierarchical structure in which managers assign tasks, design incentives, and monitor the performance of subordinates. Firms may offer efficiencies in comparison to consumer organizations due to differences in governance.

2.3.2 Search and Matching

Organizations offer an alternative to search in the marketplace. Within its organization, the firm reduces search costs by designing activities that match managers and employees with diverse capabilities. The firm's organizational units combine economic activities that benefit from repeated interaction without the need to search for trading partners. As organizational designer, the firm provides centralized mechanisms for planning, management, resource allocation, and task assignment. Firms benefit from economies of scale in information technology.

The firm searches in the labor market for managers and employees with various skills and capabilities. The firm benefits from scale economies in search, hiring, and personnel management. The firm matches its managers and employees to specific tasks without the need for individuals to search for each other in the market place. Relationships between jobs within the organization can remain stable even as personnel enter and depart the firm.

Organizations reduce search costs through internal allocation mechanisms for financial capital and other resources. Firms reduce search costs by holding inventories and engaging in multiple activities. Vertically integrated firms combine multiple tasks to address demand-side and supply-side risks. Vertically integrated firms avoid some costs of searching for new suppliers when they change product specifications or update their production technology.

Coase (1937, p. 390) emphasizes vertical integration as a means of avoiding the "disadvantages" of using the price mechanism. The costs of market transactions that Coase identifies include the use of short-term contracts in comparison with longer-term contractual relations within the firm. The firm has a wide range of mechanisms within its organization that differ fundamentally from what can be done in the marketplace, either between the firm and its trading partners or between consumers engaged in direct exchange. These mechanisms can lower the costs of organizational transactions relative to market transactions.

Coase finds that firms carry out various production tasks to reduce the costs of searching for prices, negotiating individual transactions, and specifying contingencies in long term contracts. Thus, "by forming an organization and allowing some authority (an 'entrepreneur') to direct the resources, certain marketing costs are saved" (Coase, 1937, p. 392). Coase adds that "[t]he main reason why it is profitable to establish a firm would seem to be that there is a cost of using the price mechanism." Coase observes that "[t]he most obvious cost of 'organizing' production through the price mechanism is that of discovering what the relevant prices are."

For Coase, the firm's make-or-buy decision is based on comparing the costs of market transactions with the costs of organizational transactions. If market transactions are more costly that organizational transactions, the production activity should be located within the firm. If market transactions are less costly than organizational transactions, the productive activity should be located outside the firm, with the firm relying on suppliers for the good or service. Transaction costs are the determinants of the firm's collection of activities. The make-or-buy choice shows that the critical activity is not production of goods, because any production activity could be outside or inside any particular firm. The critical activity is the transaction.

2.3.3 Bargaining

By establishing organizations, firms centralize transactions within the firms. This has the potential to reduce bargaining costs though internal allocation and pricing systems and managerial decision making. Through hierarchies, relational contracts, and managerial assignment of tasks, organizations can reduce the need for negotiation in comparison with market alternatives.

The ability of organizations to reduce transaction costs is offset by internal rent seeking, political conflicts, and the inertia that afflicts bureaucratic systems. Workers engage in "influence" activities, seeking promotions, perks, and job assignments.[25] Internal politics gives organizations a distinct disadvantage in comparison with market contracts.[26] Workers compete to change the firm's objectives and strategy. Such activities can be useful when they motivate employees to improve their performance or to reveal information. However, such activities can be costly when they displace productive effort with political effort. The firm may expend considerable costs in mitigating the influence activities of employees. The firm's choice between market contracts and forming an organization must weigh the benefits and costs of organizational politics.

Within the organization, the firm establishes systems for communication and information processing. The firm establishes a hierarchy and defines responsibilities and authority for managers and employees. The firm provides a set of rules and conventions. In coordinating transactions within the firm, firms use planning, commands, and incentive mechanisms. The firm creates internal allocation mechanisms, transfer prices, and incentives for performance. Organizational transactions include exchange of goods and services, distribution of financial capital and allocation of labor services.

Organizational transactions are costly. There are costs of coordinating managers and employees. There are costs of managing operations and distribution, human resource administration and personnel employment, accounting and financial reporting, investment, R&D, and use of communications and information

---

25 See Milgrom and Roberts (1988).

26 Milgrom and Roberts (1990, p. 58) suggest that "efficient organization is not simply a matter of minimizing transaction costs" and compare the costs of bargaining over short-term market contracts with the influence costs that result from centralized control of organizations. Influence costs refer to political rent-seeking within the firm; see also Milgrom and Roberts (1988, 1992). Scharfstein and Stein (2000) find that rent-seeking by division managers results in greater overall compensation from the CEO in the form of capital budget allocations that reduce the efficiency of internal capital markets.

technology. Organizational costs also arise from transactions that cross organizational boundaries. Organizational costs thus include the costs of supporting the firm's market transactions.

The firm's organizational costs should be compared with those of consumer organizations. Such organizations include buyers' cooperatives, workers' cooperatives, and basic partnerships. Firms may have advantages if they reduce bargaining costs relative to consumer organizations. However, Aoki (1986) argues that firms engage in extensive bargaining within their organizations.

The firm's organizational activities support its market-making functions. Firms establish purchasing departments to locate suppliers, to learn about prices and product features, and to communicate their purchasing requirements. The firm's employees keep track of transactions with suppliers, including preparing bills and receipts and monitoring supplier performance. Within the organization, managers allocate equipment and facilities, control inventories, and assess input requirements. Firms establish finance departments that carry out transactions to obtain capital in additional to financial management. Firms communicate with lenders and investors regarding the firm's performance and the firm's need for funds. Within the organization, firms undertake the transactions necessary to account for costs and revenues, to allocate funds to various projects, and to budget over time.

Firms establish personnel departments to handle labor market transactions in addition to labor management tasks. Due to imperfect information, firms must find potential employees and communicate wages and job descriptions. Within the organization, firms evaluate job performance and provide employees with various performance incentives. The personnel departments of firms handle payment of wages as well as the complex transactions associated with human resources. Personnel departments manage such things as work schedules, benefits, health insurance, retirement funds, and tax payments.

2.3.4 Moral Hazard

Firms address moral hazard problems through organizational transactions. Within organizations, firm gather information about the performance of managers and employees. They also obtain signals about the efforts of managers and employees through investment in monitoring. Firms employ various types of incentive contracts to induce revelation of private information that may enhance productive performance and improve the assignment of managers and employees to tasks.

Principal-agent relationships encounter transaction costs due to unobservable effort leading to moral hazard. Vertical integration between firms in an agency relationship may be more efficient if organizational transactions are more effective than market transactions. The firm's organization has advantages over market transactions if it does better at addressing moral hazard problems. Organizational transactions offer benefits if the principal can design tasks within the organization to reduce the effects of unobservable effort, if the principal can improve monitoring of agent performance within the organization, or if the principal can improve incentives for performance by agents.

Riordan (1990a) considers the make-or-buy decision as the choice between hiring a manager and contracting with an upstream firm. He finds that vertical integration can yield better information about upstream variable costs even if it reduces managerial incentives for cost reduction. Riordan and Sappington (1987) consider the effects of information on the choice between contracting and vertical integration. They consider a two-stage process corresponding to development and production of a good in which only the party performing each task observes the cost of that task. When the costs of production and the costs of improving product quality are positively correlated, the principal prefers to undertake production and rely on the agent for development. When the costs of development and the costs of production have a small negative correlation, the principal prefers to contract with the agent for both tasks. The principal wishes to observe the second-stage costs due to a monitoring effect. The principal also is aware of a "linkage" effect. The agent's incentive to overstate the second-stage costs is worsened or improved depending on whether these costs are positively or negatively correlated.

Lafontaine and Slade (2007) point out that empirical studies of forward integration into retailing tend to be based on incentives and moral hazard arguments. In franchising, Lafontaine (1992) finds that the importance of effort by the downstream firm results in less vertical integration while the need for franchisee experience results in more vertical integration. In soft drinks, Muris et al. (1992) consider the incentives for effort by the upstream firm, the soft drink manufacturer, in its relationship with bottlers downstream. Geographic expansion of customers leads to greater vertical integration between manufacturers and bottlers as a means of serving final customers such as grocery chains. Nickerson and Silverman (2003) emphasize agency costs in trucking. They find that vertical integration takes the form of ownership of the vehicle by the trucking company due to difficulties in contracting over maintenance effort.

The costs of monitoring agent efforts may drive internalization. Holmstrom and Milgrom (1991) present a model in which pay for performance, asset ownership, and task design are complementary instruments. Organizational transactions have an advantage over market transactions if they improve the firm's ability to monitor performance. Gertner et al. (1994) distinguish between internal and external capital markets on this basis. In their framework, the firm is better able to allocate capital internally when it can observe the progress of projects at intermediate stages. Internal capital allocation leads to greater monitoring and allows managers to reallocate funds from projects that are not performing well to more successful projects. A problem with such intervention at the intermediate stage of a project is a reduction in entrepreneurial behavior by managers. Markets provide better capital allocation than organizations when entrepreneurial effort and creativity are required.

Based on empirical studies of sales forces by Anderson (1985) and Anderson and Schmittlein (1984), Holmstrom and Milgrom (1991) consider an application of their model that groups the agent's responsibilities into four tasks: direct selling, investing in future sales to customers, nonselling activities, and selling the products of other manufacturers. They show that the returns to the principal of increasing the rewards to performance in any activity are enhanced by the increase in the rewards to performance of any other activity. For example, increasing commission rates and sharing of transferable returns are complementary. Anderson (1985) considers sales efforts in electronics and finds that monitoring costs result in firms hiring sales personnel rather than contracting with outside sales agents.

2.3.5 Adverse Selection

Unobservable information reduces the efficiency of market transactions. Firms can mitigate adverse selection problems within the organization if principals are better able to design incentives for agents to reveal information, if principals can gather information more effectively, or if principals can better motivate performance. A key element of the firm's contribution is to break the budget-balancing constraint. Thus, for any set of consumers, all bilateral and multilateral transactions balance. With asymmetric information about actions or player types, bilateral and multilateral transactions are subject to moral hazard, adverse selection, free riding, and other inefficiencies.

The firm acts as residual claimant in transactions with employees and with trading partners. This allows the firm to create transactions that enhance consumer benefits. With bilateral exchange, for example, two consumers share the net gains from trade. With intermediated exchange through a firm, the net gains from trade are shared between the two consumers and the firm. This opens up an infinite variety of ways to divide the surplus between the consumers, with the firm acting as the residual claimant.

The same applies with many consumers. By acting as a residual claimant, the firm can improve the performance of economic transaction in comparison to a group of consumers sharing the total returns from cooperation. Acting as the residual claimant, the firm can design transactions that improve incentives for consumers to supply effort thus alleviating the moral hazard problem. The firm can improve incentives for consumers to report information truthfully and reduce adverse selection problems.

The budget for the group of n consumers plus the firm still must balance in the absence of free disposal. However, the budget for the group of consumers can run a deficit because the firm earns a profit. To break the budget-balancing constraint for a group of consumers, the firm must be a separate and independent entity. The firm cannot simply be an aggregate of consumers.

Separation of objectives gives the firm the ability to improve economic efficiency. The firm's addition of degrees of freedom can significantly reduce transaction costs. Consumers may form a buyers' cooperative, a workers' cooperative, or an investors' partnership. Also, consumers may engage in bilateral and multilateral transactions or form bilateral and multilateral contracts. All of these situations are subject to collective budget-balancing restrictions.

The theory of mechanism design shows that strategic interaction between economic actors can be represented as an incentive mechanism. Consumers face the problem of finding allocation mechanisms that are incentive-compatible when actions are imperfectly observable or when information is distributed asymmetrically. Such an allocation mechanism must be individually rational to guarantee that consumers will choose to participate in the collective action. Consumers must be made at least as well off as they would be outside the cooperative, partnership, or contract.

Well-known results from the theory of mechanism design find that the balanced budget requirement is highly restrictive. Green and Laffont (1977, 1979) show that a mechanism that can be implemented using dominant strategies and that satisfies the budget-balancing condition will fail to maximize total benefits of the economic agents involved.[27] Suppose that implementation with Bayesian Nash strategies is allowed. Also, suppose that individual rationality must be satisfied to guarantee participation. Then, under some conditions, the mechanism again may fail to maximize expected benefits if budget balancing is required. With asymmetric information and voluntary participation, there is generally no mechanism that is ex post efficient.[28]

The departures from efficiency that are associated with budget balancing highlight the problems faced by consumers acting without firms. In bilateral and multilateral transactions, problems of moral hazard and adverse selection can occur. In consumer groups, such as the buyers' cooperative, workers' cooperative, or investors' partnership, free riding can occur. The firm, as a residual claimant, can employ a wider class of mechanisms by relaxing the budget-balancing constraint for the group of consumers. With the establishment of the firm as an independent entity, the budget surplus from the mechanism is the firm's profit. In fact, the Vickrey-Clarke-Groves mechanism maximizes the budget surplus as compared to other efficient mechanisms.[29] Thus, the firm can offer consumers a mechanism that maximizes its profit over all efficient mechanisms.[30] The firm can improve

---

27 A mechanism that maximizes total benefits is one due to Groves (1973); see Vickrey (1961), Clarke (1971), and Groves and Loeb (1975).

28 See Arrow (1979), d'Aspremont and Gérard-Varet (1979) and Mas-Colell et al. (1995).

29 See Krishna and Perry (1998) and Krishna (2002).

30 As long as the firm's decisions are separate from the decisions of consumers, redistribution of the firm's profit to its consumer-owners need not eliminate the beneficial budget-breaking effect of profits. With separation of consumer and firm decisions, redistribution of firm profits allows a general equilibrium representation of the economy with firms, as will be discussed in later chapters.

efficiency relative to the budget-balancing mechanisms available to consumers without the firm.

Organizations offer advantages over decentralized exchange by combining principal-agent relationships in various ways. In hierarchies, principals delegate some types of contractual design and monitoring to subordinates, creating principal-supervisor-agent relationships with supervisors acting as "middle principals."[31] In McAfee and McMillan (1995), only the agent has private information, with the supervisor designing the contract. The supervisor extracts information rents in return for reporting the agent's information to the principal. As a result, adding layers to the organization causes information rents to increase exponentially with the length of the hierarchy. Moreover, due to the costs of incentives, the principal's marginal cost of producing output also increases with the length of the hierarchy, thus reducing the organization's chosen output.

Melumad et al. (1995) point out that delegated contracting can be a means of distributing information processing among members of the organization. The advantages of overcoming bounded rationality come at the cost of loss of control. They consider a model of a principal and two agents and compare a centralized arrangement, in which the principal contracts directly with both agents, with a decentralized arrangement, in which the principal contracts with only one agent who in turn contracts with the other agent. They derive a delegation mechanism that eliminates the incentive problems inherent in delegated contracting. The result relies on the principal being able to monitor the contribution of the intermediary to the joint product and to design the sequence of contracts. Melumad et al. (1995) show that if the principal cannot monitor the intermediate agent's contribution, the intermediary takes advantage of his monopoly power, creating a problem that resembles that of "double marginalization" is a successive monopoly. The intermediary will bias the assignment of production task by shifting production away from the final agent.

Melumad et al. (1997) show the advantages of delegated contracting when contract contingencies are costly. In models for which the Revelation Principle applies, centralization of decision making dominates delegation arrangements. However, when the cost of incorporating contract contingencies is prohibitive, the number of contingencies will not be sufficient for the Revelation Principle to hold. In such a setting, it is advantageous to the principal to forego some control over agent decisions as a means of obtaining greater flexibility. They consider centralized contracting in which the principal offers a contract to both agents who report information to the principal. They show that with centralized contracting, the principal is better off when the agents act sequentially rather than simultaneously. They compare centralized contracting with decentralized contracting, as represented by a three-tier hierarchy in which one of the agents acts as an intermediary within the organization. Under delegated contracting, the principal offers a contract to the intermediary. The intermediary commits to the contract with the principal before designing a

---

31   See for example Geanakoplos and Milgrom (1991) and Qian (1994).

contract for the agent. The intermediary reports to the principal before the agent. However, the intermediary chooses productive effort only after the agent. In this setting with limited communication, delegated contracting dominates centralized contracting.

Firms may derive competitive benefits from forming organizations. The firm's organization and centralization of contracting may be necessary to respond to competition from other firms. Gal-Or (1997) discusses the literature on decentralization versus consolidation of contracting rights when there is competition in the product market. Gal-Or (1992) shows that product market competition increases the incentives of principals to vertically integrate because otherwise their agents have better market information. Gal-Or (1993) further shows that competition affects the allocation of tasks within the organization, leading to organizational differences across firms. Some firms may prefer to consolidate tasks within their organization while others prefer to departmentalize. These decisions depend on the intensity of competition, information asymmetries, and equilibrium behavior by competitors. Competition affects how firms choose between creating markets and forming organizations.

2.3.6 Free Riding

Consumer organizations such as workers' cooperatives, buyers' cooperatives, and basic partnerships divide the benefits among their members. The division of benefits affects incentives of members. When effort is not observable, the members of a partnership have an incentive to free ride on the efforts of others. The division of benefits divides the marginal return to effort, thus discouraging effort at the margin. When members of the partnership choose efforts noncooperatively, effort levels are below efficient levels. This is referred to as moral hazard in teams (Holmstrom 1982).

Alchian and Demsetz (1972) explain the purpose of the firm based on the difficulties of monitoring team production. They describe the firm as a form of contract, with the owner as the centralized contracting actor for the team. They suggest (1972, p. 790) that self-monitoring partnerships will arise when team production requires artistic or professional skills and when there are few partners. Firms require a residual claimant as the central monitor. Firms emerge when the cost of managing the team's inputs is less than the cost of metering marginal outputs. The firm's owners are themselves monitored because they are residual claimants to the firm's profit, which is in turn subject to the discipline of the market.

Holmstrom (1982) emphasizes the firm's role as a designer of incentives rather than as a monitor.[32] As a residual claimant, the firm can employ incentive mechanisms that are not subject to budget-balancing constraints that are faced by

---

32 Holmstrom (1982, p. 328) states that "The primary role of the principal is to administer incentive schemes that police agents in a credible way rather than to monitor agents as in Alchian and Demsetz' story."

partnerships. Although mechanisms such as penalties and rewards work well under certainty, this need not hold under uncertainty. When outcomes are subject to shocks, the efficacy of such schemes is constrained by limits on the liability of either the principal or of the agents in the team. The firm's ability to use such incentive mechanisms is limited by its ability to make credible commitments, as Innes (1990) points out for the standard principal-agent framework.

The firm offers mechanisms for reducing free riding in the formation and dissolution of relationships. The firm's organization establishes internal responsibilities and relationships between positions that are separate from the particular people that occupy those positions. Thus, an organization can continue to function with the replacement of particular individuals employed by the organization. The organization can operate with established relationships that do not need to be reestablished when personnel change. The coordination of organizational transactions by firms helps to explain why firms design, build, and administer organizations.

2.3.7 Contracting

Contracting costs are a critical determinant of the firm's extent of vertical integration. The traditional explanations for vertical integration can be reexamined from a transaction costs perspective. One explanation for vertical integration is that firms seek to avoid the inefficiencies of double marginalization due to market power at both stages. However, avoiding double marginalization can be achieved through contracts without the need for vertical integration. The firm can implement marginal cost pricing through lump-sum transfers. Firms will integrate vertically when doing so is less costly than such contracts. Another source of vertical integration is due to economies of combining stages of production. The transaction cost approach emphasizes that separate firms could combine stages of production contractually without vertical integration. For example, auto manufacturers house input suppliers within their plants.

Another traditional explanation for vertical integration is to reduce either demand-side or supply-side risk. The transaction cost approach suggests that this problem could also be solved through market contracts, since contracts are ways for parties to share risk. In practice, risk may reduce vertical integration. In franchising, Lafontaine and Bhattacharrya (1995) find that the risks associated with sales dispersion reduce vertical integration. This may occur because independent units are better at reacting to market conditions. Woodruff (2002) suggests that frequent fashion changes reduce vertical integration in the Mexican footwear industry.

The literature on vertical integration has focused attention on contracting costs that result in "hold-up." Lafontaine and Slade (2007) find that studies of backward integration into production tend to be based on contracting cost arguments.[33]

---

33 See also Klein (2005) on empirical analysis of the make-or-buy decision and the survey by Joskow (2005).

When investments are specific to the contractual exchange and contracts are not fully enforceable, parties to the contract may have an incentive to choose investments below efficient levels. Various types of assets can be specific to contractual relationships, including physical capital and human capital. Building on Coase and Commons, Williamson (1975, 1985) views the firm's hierarchy as a means of mitigating enforcement problems in market contracts. Williamson (1985, p. 32) observes that firms "organize transactions so as to economize on bounded rationality while simultaneously safeguarding them against the hazards of opportunism." He concentrates on imperfections in market contracts that lead to opportunism, which he defines as "self-interest seeking with guile," resulting in contract renegotiation.[34] Numerous studies examine the choice between vertical integration and market contracts.

Masten et al. (1991) test the effects of asset specificity on the vertical integration decision in naval shipbuilding. Before construction is complete, the ship is an immobile asset. Production is performed in stages, so that hold-up can take the form of strategic delay rather than price negotiation. They find that physical capital, human capital, and the need for timely performance increase the costs of market transactions more than the costs of organizational transactions. Uncertainty and complexity also raise market transactions costs more than organizational costs. They conclude that firms have an incentive to internalize transactions in naval shipbuilding.

Offering a property-rights view of the firm, Grossman and Hart (1986), Hart and Moore (1990), and Hart (1995) explain vertical integration based on the consolidation of asset ownership. Firms own assets to mitigate the effects of incomplete contracting and asset specificity. They argue that ownership of productive assets improves incentives for investment in complementary transaction-specific capital, such a human capital. For Hart (1995, p. 29), "ownership is a source of power when contracts are incomplete." In contrast, Holmstrom and Roberts (1998) point out that property rights to assets are not sufficient to explain the boundaries of the firm, because market contracts can be created that replace many of the functions of vertical integration. They find that contracts in the market place can allocate decision rights just as does ownership. The firm thus chooses between market contracts and internal transaction for many reasons other than asset ownership.

Monteverde and Teece (1982) examine evidence of a limited form of vertical integration in which assemblers of automobiles own specialized equipment used by suppliers. Miwa and Ramseyer (2000), however, find evidence for an absence of relationship-specific physical or human capital in the Japanese automobile industry. Casadesus-Masanell and Spulber (2000) examine the classic case of vertical integration between General Motors and Fisher Body and find evidence

---

34 See Klein et al. (1978), Grout (1984), Grossman and Hart (1986), Hart and Holmstrom (1986), Hart and Moore (1988), and Hart (1995).

that contract hold-up was not a driver of vertical integration; see also Coase (2000, 2006).[35]

2.4 The Development of the Firm

The firm is a relatively modern phenomenon. The genesis of the contemporary firm accompanies the emergence of the industrial economy. The establishment of an enterprise that has objectives different from those of its owners begins to take shape in the nineteenth century. The development of the firm reflects increases in agricultural productivity beginning in the seventeenth century that expanded the output of farms in England and Holland. It also reflects the industrial revolution, which led to the creation of large manufacturing enterprises starting in the late eighteenth century. These developments coincided with the expansion of merchant trading companies. The role of firms in creating and coordinating both market and management transactions expanded considerably across the economy in many countries.

The establishment of firms is a critical component of economic growth. As economies develop, entrepreneurs establish a great variety of firms. The traditional merchant, family farm, and artisan producer are features of developing economies. Consumer organizations such as workers' cooperatives and buyers' cooperatives are rare in developed economies. Highly specialized firms and large-scale multibusiness firms characterize practically every sector of developed economies.[36]

2.4.1 Precursors to the Firm

Merchants are the primary forerunner of the contemporary firm. Merchants played an important role in many of the great empires, including the Greek and Roman empires, traveling the trade routes of the Silk Road from North China to Asia Minor and the Mediterranean beginning before the Christian era. Merchants engaged in extensive retail and wholesale trade, laying the groundwork for the development of market economies. Merchant guilds and associations also have features that are

---

35 These articles reexamine and correct the historical record of the Fisher Body acquisition as discussed in Klein et al. (1978).

36 The North American Industry Classification System (NAICS) includes (1) agriculture, (2) mining, utilities and construction, (3) manufacturing, (4) wholesale trade, retail trade, transportation, and warehousing, (5) information, finance and insurance, real estate, and rental and leasing, professional, scientific, and technical services, management of companies and enterprises, administrative and support and waste management and remediation services, (6) educational services, health care and social assistance, (7) arts, entertainment, and recreation, accommodation and food services, and (8) other services (except public administration). http://www.census.gov/epcd/naics/naicscod.txt.

related to the later design of firms. Other precursors of the contemporary firm include families themselves (Ben-Porath, 1980), feudal estates, religious organizations (Ekelund and Burton, 1996), armies, and government bureaucracies.

Merchant enterprises in Europe begin to separate from the activities of their owners as they developed and expanded from the sixteenth to the eighteenth centuries. The industrial revolution gave rise to large-scale manufacturing and distribution and the establishment of large-scale enterprises. Alfred D. Chandler (1977, p. 16) observes that "In the 1790s American businessmen still relied entirely on commercial practices and procedures invented and perfected centuries earlier by British, Dutch and Italian merchants."

Farmers, artisans, and merchants from the earliest times to the eighteenth century are precursors to the contemporary firm. What distinguishes these economic actors from firms is that their enterprises tended to be integrated with the personal economic affairs of the entrepreneur. There was no separation between the owner's commercial activities and their personal consumption activities. Most merchants operated as family businesses, so that the merchant family was closely tied to the firm: "the business being in the family and the family being in the business."[37] The finances of the merchant family and their business were intertwined and family members managed the business and generally served as its representatives.

From the earliest times, merchants and merchant houses established enterprises to finance and manage ventures necessary to conduct trade.[38] Merchants engaged in a wide range of local, regional, and international trade from nearly the beginning of civilization. The activities of merchants became increasingly sophisticated, reaching a high level during the commercial revolution in Europe in the first half of the Middle Ages.[39] Merchants' capabilities continued to develop from the fourteenth century to the end of the eighteenth century.

Business enterprises were engaged in creating and coordinating transactions, in addition to manufacturing and agriculture. Merchants traded a wide variety of goods and engaged in retail and wholesale trade, banking, insurance, and other transactions. They kept detailed records of transactions and contracts, provided local and long-distance transportation, arranged the financing of stocks of goods for trading, and negotiated with governments to facilitate exchange. Merchants

---

37 Reynolds (1952, p. 352).

38 The linguistic connection between merchants, markets, and commerce is long established. The words "merchant" and "market" have the same Latin origins. Merchant comes from the word *mercari*, which means to trade, and market comes from *mercatus*, which is the past participle of *mercari*. The word *mercari* itself derives from the Latin word *merx*, meaning wares, merchandise, or goods for trade. The word "commerce" also derives from *commercium*, which is bringing together goods for trade (Webster's New World Dictionary of the American Language, 2nd College Edition).

39 Gies and Gies (1972) refer to the development of merchants and finance in Europe between 1000 and 1500 as "the commercial revolution." The term also appears in Polanyi (2001, p. 29).

formed large-scale associations and other types of organizations and established foreign outposts and colonies.

The central importance of transactions in economic development is highlighted by Adam Smith's 1776 *Wealth of Nations*. Economic development, for Smith, depends primarily on the division of labor, which generates "the greatest improvement in the productive powers of labour" (p. 13). The division of labor, which yields the benefits of specialization, is achieved through the propensity in human nature "to truck, barter and exchange one thing for another" (p. 13). Because "the division of labour is limited by the extent of the market," industry is improved by transactions that increase the size of markets, so that the industry can specialize ("subdivide and improve itself," p. 20). Trading in local, regional, national, and international markets is thus critical to development. Smith highlights the effects of the costs of trade and demonstrates how having access to water transportation, as opposed to costly land routes, drives improvements in agriculture and manufacturing.

Adam Smith emphasizes that "the power of exchanging" explains the success of early civilizations in Egypt, India, and China. When the division of labor has been thoroughly established, "Every man thus lives by exchanging, or becomes in some measure a merchant, and the society itself grows to be what is properly a commercial society" (p. 25). Smith argues that merchants, artificers (craftsmen), and manufacturers increase the productivity of agricultural labor "by leaving it at liberty to confine itself to its proper employment" (p. 767). In the corn trade, for example, Smith distinguishes between the inland dealer, the merchant importer, the merchant exporter, and the merchant carrier (import for reexport). Smith also mentions retailers when he criticizes medieval European laws that protected shopkeepers and prevented manufacturers from operating their own retail shops, requiring them to sell at wholesale to dealers and shops.

Karl Moore and David Lewis (1999), in their stimulating work *Birth of the Multinational*, examine the forerunners of the international business firm in four ancient empires that together span two millennia: the Assyrian, the Phoenician (succeeded by the Carthaginian), the Greek, and the Roman empires. Mesopotamian merchants in the Assyrian empire, initially in the employ of a ruler or a religious temple, eventually assumed the roles of private traders, creditors, speculators, and agents for the government and creditors.[40] Among the goods they traded were textiles, fish, barley, wheat, copper, tin, lumber, spices, wines, and cattle. Merchant communities in large Sumerian port cities formed private guild associations that regulated commerce and exercised commercial, legal, and administrative duties.[41] The Phoenician and Carthaginian merchants created a "vast and well-organized network of trade and investment which spanned three continents."[42]

---

40 Moore and Lewis (1999, p. 56).
41 Moore and Lewis (1999, p. 58).
42 Moore and Lewis (1999, p. 69).

Merchants engaged in retail and wholesale trade, banking, and other transactions in ancient Greece and during the Roman Empire. The presence of some 167 corporations or guilds representing associations of Roman retail and wholesale merchants as well as craftsmen of various kinds gives some indication of the diversity of Roman trade. These include, for example, *aromatarii*, merchants of perfumes, spices, and groceries; *magnarii*, wholesale merchants; *mercatores frumentarii*, wheat merchants; and *negotiates vinarii*, wine merchants.[43] There were "innumerable numbers of entrepreneurs and contractors trading beneath the Roman eagle from Iberia to India, large family firms, partnerships and semipublic corporations."[44] Enterprises in Greece and Rome share many features with contemporary firms.[45]

Periodic markets and commercial fairs operated in the urban areas within the Roman empire.[46] In the last centuries of the Roman period, there is evidence of markets and commercial fairs in the ports of Merovingian Gaul and Visigothic Spain.[47] Fairs provided merchants with a means of wholesale exchange.[48]

Significant development of commercial, manufacturing and banking enterprises occurred in medieval Europe, particularly in Italy from the eleventh to the fourteenth century, followed by the growth of trade centers in northern France, Flanders, and the lower Rhineland.[49] Businesses kept records of transactions, employed legal counsels, and by 1200, in Genoa, Florence, and elsewhere, kept detailed business accounts.[50]

Merchants conducted wholesale transactions with suppliers and resold goods to retailers. Merchants also conducted wholesale goods trade in commercial fairs such as those in Champagne in the twelfth and thirteenth centuries. The commercial fairs were important meeting places for large numbers of merchants. They provided convenient ways of exchanging goods as well as economic information. By the thirteenth century the commercial purpose was well established; "all fairs were markets, but not all markets were fairs."[51] Fairs eventually were supplanted by

---

43 A complete list appears in Waltzing (1979, v. IV).

44 Moore and Lewis (1999, p. 225).

45 The classic history by Carcopino (1968) notes the many retailers and wholesalers who purveyed their wares in Roman trade. Temin (2001, 2002) argues for the existence of a market economy and financial intermediaries in the early Roman empire.

46 De Ligt (1993).

47 Verlinden (1965).

48 After the seventh century, as Islam spread over Arabia, Persia, Egypt, North Africa, and Southern Europe, so did extensive commercial development. Muslim merchants traveled the silk road to cities such as Isfahan, Rayy, Bukhara, and Samarkand and visited China: "Muslim ships and caravans brought rubies and emeralds from Persia and Arabia, pearls from the Persian Gulf, silk and porcelain, camphor, musk, and spices from China, fur, skins, and amber from Russia, sandalwood, ebony and coconuts from India, linen from Egypt, carpets from Persia and Armenia, gold and slaves from Africa" (Gies and Gies, 1972, p. 4).

49 Pounds (1994, p. 364).

50 Reynolds (1952, p. 353).

51 Hunt and Murray (1999, p. 26).

year-round commercial centers such as those that were established in Italy at least by the 1100s.[52] Merchants established permanent branches in Paris, London, and Bruges that supplanted the Champagne fairs and other commercial fairs.[53]

Merchants created and coordinated transactions through their extensive activities in trading goods, buying goods in one location and reselling them in another. In the Middle Ages, merchants created markets between countryside and town, between towns, between regions, and between foreign countries. Merchants established commercial links between buyers and sellers for a wide variety of traded goods including textiles, furs, dyes, spices, wine, grains, prepared foods, wood, metals, weapons, and jewels.

Merchants engaged in significant commercial communication and handled substantial amounts of information. They examined supply and demand conditions in areas where they transacted. Merchants monitored prices, kept track of changing customer preferences, evaluated competitors, and considered potential partners. They obtained information about new types of goods and novel production techniques. Merchants knew about taxes and duties assessed by nobles and municipalities and gathered intelligence about politics, wars, piracy, festivals, and general economic conditions. They were aware of monetary exchange rates, transportation costs, and financing costs. Merchants established extensive information networks to obtain the most up-to-date intelligence.[54]

The transactions created and coordinated by merchants extended far beyond traded goods. Merchants contracted for many types of transportation services. They engaged in banking and monetary exchange in foreign markets rather than relying on simple barter. They obtained or provided financing for goods and the costs of transportation. They arranged to insure their merchandise or to share business risks. They contracted with intermediaries to share their goods abroad or with local brokers and business partners in foreign markets.[55] Some merchants diversified into banking and manufacturing, particularly beginning in the fourteenth century: "the onetime merchant began to figure as a businessman and prime mover of industrial change."[56]

Associations of merchants presage the firm in many ways. Merchants formed trading associations to share risk and to lower the transaction costs of doing business. Individual merchants established societies that increased the scale of their businesses; thus the Galliani Society of Siena brought together thirty-two merchants, and the Rapondi of Lucca had branches in Paris, Bruges, and Avignon.[57] In addition, as in the Roman period, merchant guilds regulated local competition,

---

52 Reynolds (1952, p. 363).
53 See de Roover (1965) and Favier (1998).
54 See Favier (1998) for a detailed description of merchants' information gathering.
55 Favier (1998, pp. 70–76).
56 Favier (1998, p. 190).
57 Favier (1998, p. 61).

set standards for admission of members, set quality standards for goods, helped merchants exchange information, and participated in municipal government.[58] English merchants formed cartels in the fourteenth and fifteenth centuries to export wool (the Merchants of the Staple) and to export broadcloths (the Merchant Adventurers).[59] On a broader scale, in Italy, Germany, and France, there were associations of towns to promote international trade. The Hanseatic League was a commercial organization of merchants' associations in German and Baltic towns led by the city of Lübeck.[60] Merchants in the Hanseatic league could transact with other merchants located anywhere within Europe.[61]

Merchants formed trading networks to further extend their reach and lower the costs of transacting in distant locations. As merchants increasingly relied on agents to deliver goods and transact with distant counterparts, they obtained the benefits of dealing through specialized intermediaries. Merchants retained agents both to travel with goods and to provide resident representation. However, relying on agents created other types of transaction costs. Merchant networks were ways of ensuring that merchants could trust their representatives to act in accordance with the merchant's interests and to report information accurately.

Some merchant associations were based on ethnic or religious groups with settlements in trade routes. Avner Greif (1989, 1993) studied the Maghribi Traders' Coalition in the eleventh century, whose settlements served as end points and transshipment points of trade on the Mediterranean. The Maghribi traders felt that transacting through agents was crucial despite the risks that relying on agents posed for the business.[62] Greif (1993, p. 526) observes that "Expectations, implicit contractual relations, and a specific information-transmission mechanism constituted the constraints that affected an individual trader's choice of action. In particular, these constraints supported the operation of a reputation mechanism that enabled the Maghribis to overcome the commitment problem. In turn, the reputation mechanism reinforced the expectations on which the coalition was based, motivated traders to adhere to the implicit contracts, and led to entry and exit barriers which ensured the sustainability of the coalition." The Maghribi traders had a "Merchants' Law" that specified a set of rules governing behavior that served as a "default contract" between merchants and their agents.[63]

Merchant houses became less tied to families as merchants hired greater numbers of salaried employees and made greater use of commission agents and as

---

58 See for example Dahl (1998, pp. 47–55) and Hunt and Murray (1999, pp. 35–7).
59 Day (1987, p. 168).
60 Day (1987, p. 168).
61 Favier (1998, p. 26).
62 Greif (1993, p. 528) illustrates the importance of agency relationships with two examples: "one trader wrote to his business associate who served as his overseas agent that 'all profit occurring to me comes from your pocket' [. . .] while another mentioned that in trade 'people cannot operate without people.'"
63 Greif (1993, p. 543).

merchant families formed associations.[64] Family-controlled firms currently account for over a third of companies in the Fortune 500, including Ford, Wal-Mart, and Anheuser-Busch, and 60% of the publicly held companies in the United States are family-controlled (Garcia, 2004). Family firms account for 40% of U.S. GDP, and around 65% of Germany's GDP.[65] Family firms represent over 80% of all business enterprises in North America and a large share of firms internationally.[66]

There were large trading companies that carried out international commerce, such as those that operated in Tuscany in the thirteenth to the fifteenth century, although most medieval merchants still operated through small family firms or through partnerships.[67] The large international companies of merchants were sometimes referred to as merchant banks, but they actively participated in a wider range of activities. For example, Benedetto Zaccaria of Genoa in the late thirteenth and early fourteenth centuries owned a large-scale firm with interests in shipping, trading, and mining.[68] "Super companies" such as the Bardi, Peruzzi, and Acciaiuoli of Florence were partnerships with ownership shares proportional to initial investment, and with subsidiaries that operated as branches of the parent company.[69]

The industrial revolution saw the rise of large-scale manufacturing, but also the development of large-scale merchant firms engaged in international trade. Between the sixteenth and the eighteenth century, European "chartered trading companies" such as the English and Dutch East India Companies and the Hudson's Bay Company participated in international trade.[70] From the sixteenth to the nineteenth century, Indian trading firms based in the Indian diaspora traded with Iran, Afghanistan, Central Asia, and Russia.[71] In the twentieth century, Japanese general trading companies handled a large share of Japan's imports and exports. These companies include Itochu, Kanematsu, Marubeni, Mitsubishi, Mitsui, Nichimen, Nissho Iwai, Sumitomo, and Tomen. Major U.S. companies engage in significant market making in international trade, such as the international wholesaler Ingram Micro in computer products or the trading company Cargill in agricultural products.

The contemporary firm is in many respects the descendant of merchant houses of the Middle Ages. The general merchant of the 1790s was "an exporter,

64 See Ball (1977, pp. 24–5). Ball observes further that "In Genoa, the process of evolution towards a more impersonal form of company organization had gone even further. In the fifteenth century companies were often founded for more specialized purposes, such as the transport of salt, alum or mercury, though still investing some of their capital in subsidiary activities. In such firms the domination of a single individual or family had disappeared both in the title of the company and in practice." These companies presaged the joint-stock companies of the seventeenth century in Northern Europe (Ball, 1977, pp. 24–5).
65 "The Family Connection," *The Economist*, October 5, 1996.
66 Astrachan and Shanker (2003).
67 Day (1987, p. 171).
68 See the discussion in Gies and Gies (1972, pp. 98–113) and Hunt and Murray (1999, pp. 99–100).
69 Hunt and Murray (1999, pp. 102–9).
70 There is a substantial literature in this area; see for example Jones (2000).
71 See Markovits (2000) and Levi (2002).

wholesaler, importer, retailer, shipowner, banker, and insurer."[72] Firms in Europe and in the United States in the late 1800s still employed many business methods dating back to the fifteenth century.[73] They employed double-entry bookkeeping, used the partnership for business, sold goods on their own account and on consignment for commission rates, maintained Adventure and Merchandise accounts, employed ship captains and supercargoes as consignees, used formal exchanges for market transactions, employed sophisticated credit instruments, and made use of commercial law.[74]

Merchants then begin to specialize in one or two types of goods, "concentrating more and more on a single function: retailing, wholesaling, importing, or exporting" over the fifty years after the 1790s.[75] Significantly, in the 1840s, the traditional mercantile firm begins to be replaced by more modern types of firms. According to Chandler (1977, p. 209), "In the 1850s and 1860s the modern commodity dealer who purchased directly from the farmer and sold directly to the processor took over the marketing and distribution of agricultural products. In the same years, the full-line, full-service wholesaler began to market most standardized consumer goods. Then, in the 1870s and 1880s the modern mass retailer — the department store, the mail order house, and the chain store — started to make inroads on the wholesaler's markets." These mass marketing enterprises employed extensive administrative coordination, reduced the number of total transactions, increased the speed and regularity of the flow of goods, and took advantage of the railroads, the telegraph, the steamship, and improved postal services (Chandler, 1977).

Although the contemporary corporation has roots in the large-scale manufacturing and trade that begins with the industrial revolution, it takes a more recognizable shape in the mid-nineteenth century. At that time, as Chandler (1990a, 1990b) points out, companies seeking to benefit from technological change invested not only in production facilities, but also in distribution and in management. Manufacturing firms had significant costs of selling, purchasing, hiring, financing, and other market functions, as well as internal costs of management, accounting, and information technology. At the same time, companies were established that engaged in large-scale retail and wholesale distribution.

2.4.2 The Firm in the Contemporary Economy

Firms in the contemporary economy carry out diverse productive tasks including agriculture, mining, construction, and manufacturing. Firms engage in wholesale and retail trade, transportation, and warehousing. Firms provide a broad set of transaction services including information, finance, insurance, and real estate

---

72 Chandler (1977, p. 15).

73 Ball (1977, p. 23) notes that by the late fifteenth century, "the greater Italian cities had evolved business methods to a point which neither saw nor needed much further change until the emergence of the modern industrial economy."

74 Chandler (1977, p. 16).

75 Chandler (1977, p. 15).

brokerage. They also supply professional, scientific, technical, and management services. Firms provide education, health care, entertainment, recreation, and accom-
modations.

Firms are dominant features of developed market economies. The name brands
of companies are instantly recognizable, whether Ford, Coca-Cola, Nabisco, American Airlines, MasterCard, IBM, General Electric, or countless others. Firms provide practically all goods and services in the economy, from the corner restau-
rant, garage, bakery, or hairdresser to supermarkets, wholesalers, manufacturers,
and utility companies. Many government activities rely on outsourcing to private
firms, including freeway construction, military procurement, and information technology.

In the United States alone, there are more than 20 million firms. Of those,
there are 5 million firms with paid employees, having a total employment of more
than 100 million people and a combined sales revenue of about $18 trillion.[76] In
the United Kingdom, there are more than 1.35 million firms with one or more
employees.[77] Japan counts approximately 6.28 million establishments.[78] There are
millions more firms in other developed economies and a growing number of firms
in the developing countries.[79]

Firms are present in all countries, and many firms operate in multiple countries.
There are over 64,000 multinational firms that operate across national boundaries.[80]
Generally, multinational firms are identified with the country in which their head-
quarters is located, so that the food products company Nestlé is Swiss and the
aircraft manufacturer Embraer is a Brazilian company. The total sales of foreign
affiliates of multinational firms exceeds $17 trillion. The total assets of foreign
affiliates of multinational firms is greater than $26 trillion. The foreign affiliates
of multinational firms employ over 53 million people. Multinational firms handle
most cross border investment in the form of foreign direct investment (FDI), with
world FDI inward stock exceeding $7 trillion.[81] Multinational firms handle most of
the transactions associated with international trade in goods and services, as well
as handling most international financial transactions.

Firms vary considerably in size, from the smallest sole proprietorships to the
major corporations. The largest companies in the world, based on sales volume,
include Wal-Mart Stores, ExxonMobil, General Motors, Royal Dutch/Shell, British

---

76 The 1997 U.S. Census lists 5,295,152 firms with paid employees, having a combined sales revenue
    of $17.9 trillion, and counts 20,821,935 firms overall, with sales receipts of over $18.5 trillion.
    http://www.census.gov/epcd/mwb97/us/us.html.
77 Census 2001, National Statistics, United Kingdom.
78 2001 Census, Japan Statistics Bureau, www.stat.go.jp.
79 See Bartelsman and Doms (2000) and Scarpetta et al. (2002) on cross-country studies of firms
    in the developed economics and Tybout (2000) on firms in developing economies.
80 United Nations Conference on Trade and Development (2003). For additional discussion see
    Gabel and Bruner (2003).
81 Data on FDI and sales and assets or foreign affiliates are for the year 2002. United Nations
    Conference on Trade and Development (2003).

Petroleum (BP) Ford Motor Company, DaimlerChrysler, Toyota Motor, General Electric, and Allianz. Wal-Mart, for example, had annual sales of $244 billion, a market value of $232 billion, and annual profits of $8 billion.[82] Wal-Mart employed almost 1.3 million people worldwide, was served by 30,000 suppliers, and operated about 4,300 stores, 1000 super centers, and 500 Sam's Clubs wholesale outlets.

Firms operate widely diverse technologies. Some firms employ the most traditional skills, such as restaurants, shoe repair, or beauty parlors. Other firms employ the most advanced research and development (R&D) in biotech, microprocessors, aerospace, or satellite systems. Microeconomic studies of manufacturing reveal great differences in firm behavior in terms of the distribution of output, choice of what types of goods to produce, selection of technology, employment, investment and productivity, even within the same industry (Scarpeta et al. 2002; Bartelsman and Doms 2000).

Firms have a great variety of lifespans. Some firms have a short lifespan due to changing economic conditions or faulty business decisions. Many new firms are established each year and many firms go out of business each year. Some new firms represent attempts to profit from a new production technology or a new type of good or service. Some firms are engaged in R&D and are established without having yet developed a specific product or service. One of the interesting features of firms is that they can represent a venture formed for a specific purpose. The firm can be established by entrepreneurs to complete a particular project and then closed when the project is complete. Firms can change their purpose by choosing to exit a market and to enter another.

Some firms have long lives that far exceed human lifespans. The Italian family business Camuffo was founded in 1438 and remains in the shipbuilding business. Their boats have been called "the Stradivarius of the sea" and were supplied to "Mohammed the Second, the Venetian Republic, Napoleon, the Asburg Imperial and the Royal Italian navies."[83]

The family business Kongo Gumi in Japan was founded in 578 and remained in the construction business for 40 generations. "Prince Shotoku brought Kongo family members to Japan from Korea more than 1,400 years ago to build the Buddhist Shitennoji Temple, which still stands. Over the centuries, Kongo Gumi has participated in the construction of many famous buildings, including the 16th-century Osaka castle."[84] Based in Osaka, the family continued to engage in general contracting and the construction of religious temples. A business downturn in Japan and problems with real estate debt resulted in the company being acquired and absorbed into Takamatsu, a large Japanese construction company.[85]

---

82 *Business Week* July 2003 Global 1000, Update July 2004. http://www.finfacts.ie/Private/curency/busweek.htm.

83 O'Hara and Mandel (2004).

84 See O'Hara and Mandel (2004).

85 J. O. Hutcheson, "The End of a 1,400-Year-Old Business," *Business Week*, April 16, 2007, www.businessweek.com.

Competition and technological change affect the entry and exit of companies. In the industries shown in the first part of Table 2.2, the number of establishments has fallen considerably, giving an indication of the attrition of individual firms. In the industries shown in the second part of Table 2.2, such as computer and data processing services, there has been substantial entry and growth. A pattern of growth, shakeout, and leveling off has been observed in many industries, including compressors, electrocardiographs, gyroscopes, jet-propelled engines, lasers, outboard motors, nylon, paints, ball point pens, photocopy machines, radar, heat pumps, nuclear reactors, transistors, and zippers.[86] Shakeouts in wholesaling occurred in over a dozen industries, including flowers, woodworking machinery, locksmithing, specialty tools and fasteners, sporting goods, wholesale grocers, air conditioning and refrigeration, electronic components, wine and spirits, waste equipment, and periodicals.[87]

The entry and exit of firms and technological change substantially alter the market structure and performance of industries. Changes in management practices and technological change also modify the activities and organization of firms. Most significantly, firms differ considerably in their extent of vertical integration. The firm's degree of vertical integration reflects its relative reliance on market transactions and on organizational transactions.

Some firms are highly focused on some specific tasks with minimal vertical integration. Other firms are highly vertically integrated, providing many of their own inputs and simultaneously engaging in manufacturing, wholesaling, and retail distribution of their own products. The major oil companies are classic examples of such vertical integration. Companies such as British Petroleum and Exxon Mobil explore for crude oil, extract the oil, transport the oil in their own supertankers, process the crude oil in their own refineries, transport and wholesale petroleum products, and operate service stations for retail distribution. The vertical integration of such companies may represent the complex engineering aspects of the petroleum industry and the high transaction costs of international operations.

The high level of vertical integration exhibited by such firms provides an illustration of the case where the transaction costs of market transactions exceed the transaction costs of organizational transactions, so that many activities are moved within the firm. Many large-scale vertically integrated manufacturing companies developed in the early part of the twentieth century. According to Chandler (1977, p. 34) there was extensive vertical integration in American business between 1900 and 1917.

This development suggests that business executives in many industries anticipated greater returns from internalizing transactions through vertical integration. Henry Ford's slogan was "from mine to finished car, one organization." By 1920, General Motors "had extended its scope so that not only all the engines used in

---

86 See Gort and Klepper (1982) and Klepper and Graddy (1990).
87 See Fein (1998).

Table 2.2. *Selected shrinking and expanding industries*

	Number of establishments	
	1970	1996
Selected shrinking industries		
Fur goods	980	133
Barber shops	24,577	4,499
Asbestos products	133	30
Drive-in theaters	1,567	408
Leather and leather products	3,430	1,938
General merchandise stores	25,032	14,797
Glass containers	128	78
Brooms and brushes	449	278
Trailer parks and campsites	6,419	3,984
Bowling centers	9,215	5,735
Concrete block and brick	1,332	901
Manufactured ice	800	578
Variety stores	14,439	10,848
Radio and television repair	7,953	6,212
Labor organizations	20,376	19,536
Selected expanding industries		
Videotape rental	0	20,816
Computer and data processing services	6,517 (1975)	88,911
Carpet and upholstery cleaning	816	8,879
Prepackaged software	1,522 (1975)	9,084
Vocational schools	1,188	6,816
Movie production and services	2,922	14,680
Semiconductors and related devices	291	1,052
Amusement parks	362	1,174
Chocolate and cocoa products	51 (1975)	165
Car washes	4,624	13,334
Political organizations	928	2,579
Office and computing equipment	923	2,112
Eating and drinking places	233,048	466,386
Colleges and universities	1,855	3,663
Florists	13,865	26,728
Tour operators	2,464 (1988)	4,725
Dental offices	63,817	113,054
Internal combustion engines	162	277
Passenger car rental	2,556	4,231
Pharmaceuticals	1,041	1,637
Aircraft	163	255
Plastic bottles	280 (1988)	437
Aircraft engines and parts	247	355
Physical fitness facilities	7,723 (1990)	10,720
Hotels and motels	34,674	45,252
Travel agencies	22,609 (1988)	28,735
Space vehicle equipment	39 (1975)	45
Beauty shops	70,967	81,872

Source: Cox and Alm (1999) based on data from United States Bureau of the Census County Business Patterns, various years. Establishments are classified based on their major activity.

its cars, but a large proportion of such units as gears, axles, crankshafts, radiators, electrical equipment, roller bearings, warning signals, spark plugs, bodies, plate glass, and body hardware, were produced either by a General Motors unit or by a subsidiary" (Edmonds, 1923).

Chandler attributes increasing vertical integration to the returns obtained from internalizing the market processes connecting mass production to distribution and to the efficiencies of the "visible hand of administrative coordination." Chandler (1962, p. 37) also notes the desire of companies to assure a more certain supply of parts, raw materials and other supplies. Some of the vertical integration may have been due to the high costs of transportation and communication, which favored internal provision of critical inputs to the manufacturing process. Extensive vertical integration was observed in the automobile industry as companies sought economies of internal coordination.[88] Managers could choose a variety of mechanisms to allocate resources within the firm. Chandler further observes that the modern multiunit business arose "when administrative coordination permitted greater productivity, lower cost, and higher profits than coordination by market mechanisms."[89]

Some economists of the period who observe such increasing vertical integration consider reasons that firms might have for replacing market transactions with organizational transactions. Knight (1971, p. 259), for example, concludes that "The problem of meeting uncertainty thus passes inevitably into the general problem of management, of economic control." The firm is organized as a means of mitigating the effects of uncertainty regarding production and final demand. Another economist, Frank (1925, pp. 179, 187, 191), goes further, arguing that "coordinated operation calls for the ownership or control by some organization of all other stages" and suggests that "the price system, in so far as it affects the conduct of industry at least, is being rendered obsolete" due to vertical integration.

The emphasis on vertical integration in business practices and economic analysis at the start of the twentieth century may have been due in part to a distrust of markets. There was an early fascination with planned economies that existed long before the collapse of the Soviet Union would demonstrate the drastic inefficiencies of such systems. Planned economies attempted to supplant the market by vertical integration of the entire economy through trade ministries that allocated inputs and directed production.[90] From 1928 on "the Soviet manufacturing

88 See Casadesus-Masanell and Spulber (2000).
89 Chandler (1977, p. 6); see also Williamson (1970).
90 Central planning in the Soviet economy reflected the Marxist view that just as factories organized production, the government could replace the market: "Anarchy in social production is replaced by systematic definite organization" (Engels, 1989). Such a view carried over into industrial organization in planned economies. Enterprises strove for all-embracing vertical integration and staggering size, known as gigantism. Reflective of this approach, the former Soviet Union "constructed the most enormous hydro-electric dam, the roomiest hotel, the tallest TV tower, the largest transport plane, the heaviest battle tank, and the mightiest particle accelerator. A

industry operated within the framework set by detailed central directives enforced and supervised by the party and by a hierarchical, complex planning and managerial administration."[91] The distinction between the division of labor in markets and within firms that appears in Karl Marx (1992) dates back to the classical economists such as Adam Smith.

Chandler (1977, p. 109) finds that the "managers of large American railroads during the 1850s and 1860s invented nearly all of the basic techniques of modern accounting," including financial, capital, and cost accounting. After 1900, with the growth of mass production, comes the development of modern factory cost accounting.[92] The management innovations at Du Pont beginning in 1903 combined financial, capital, and cost accounting and thereby "helped lay the base for modern asset accounting."[93] The firms' managers began to allocate capital between competing activities within the firm based on the rate of return.[94] Advanced management techniques developed at large diversified firms such as General Electric, Du Pont, and General Motors were widely adopted during the 1920s, particularly the multidivisional organization structure, and accounting, budgeting, and forecasting methods.[95]

Alfred P. Sloan's 1919 study of the organization of General Motors was adopted as a plan of reorganization for the company the following year. The plan, which was to become influential for the organization of large-scale companies, sought to bring some central coordination to the very decentralized General Motors company. Sloan's book about General Motors, completed in 1954, emphasizes the importance of determining the rates of return to individual divisions as a guide to the corporation's strategic investment decisions (1963, p. 50). Sloan sets out general principles that recognize the tradeoffs between central control of the company by the chief executive officer and independence of the company's divisions. The decentralizations carried out by General Motors and by Du Pont in the 1920s are important to the history of management because they represent attempts to address management incentives and performance through changes in organizational design.

popular joke from the 1980s went that the Soviet computer industry produced 'the world's biggest microchip.'" Such gigantism persisted until the collapse of the Soviet Union: "The world's largest building, according to the Guinness Book of Records, is workshop no. 55 here at Sevmash, an off-limits shipyard in Russia's far north that built some of the biggest submarines, including the ill-fated Kursk. Everything about this sprawling city-within-a-city, with 25,000 workers and dozens of huge workshops and floating docks, seems vastly outsized." Fred Weir, "Kursk Recovery May Salvage Russian Shipyard, too," *Christian Science Monitor*, August 3, 2001.

91 See Nicolas Spulber (2003, p. 224).

92 Chandler (1977, p. 278).

93 Chandler (1977, p. 447).

94 Johnson and Kaplan (1986, p. 86).

95 Chandler (1977, p. 464). Drucker's (1946, p. 49) study of General Motors states that "decentralization . . . is not considered as confined to top management but a principle for the organization of all managerial relationships."

The later twentieth century and the early part of the twenty-first century saw significant reduction of vertical integration in many industries in industrialized market economies. Automobile companies, for example, divested their parts manufacturing units. Diverse industries such as computer manufacturing had separate firms manufacturing individual components with other firms specializing in assembly and distribution. The period also witnessed increased reliance on outsourcing both domestically and through international trade. In business practice, there was less emphasis on the notion that firms exist solely to replace markets with organizations, and greater emphasis on lowering market transaction costs.

These developments coincided with reductions in the costs of both market transactions and organizational transactions. Technological developments dramatically improved information processing, communications, and transportation. Lower transaction costs may have reduced the impetus for vertical integration and helped establish new forms of economic exchange. The functions and tasks of management changed but by no means reduced the need for firms. Rather, these economic developments highlighted the dual nature of firms in managing both market transactions and organizational transactions.

The vertical integration of the early twentieth century has given way to vertical disintegration through outsourcing and specialized intermediaries. Some manufacturers are primarily engaged in transactions and maintain minimal manufacturing operations. For example, Dell Computer is classified as a manufacturer of computer equipment but is primarily a direct marketer of computers, relying on other companies for distribution, assembly, software, hardware components, and design. Original equipment manufacturers (OEMs) often outsource manufacturing to companies that organize supply chains and handle contract manufacturing. In electronics, many OEMs who supply electronics products rely on supply-chain managers, such as Flextronics, which in turn subcontract with many different smaller manufacturers. Fashion companies outsource production to specialized supply-chain managers such as Li & Fung.

The reduction of vertical integration was accompanied by a greater focus on the efficiency of market transactions. The role of firms in creating and coordinating transactions is particularly apparent in the retail, wholesale and financial sectors. Firms in these sectors account for approximately a quarter of gross domestic product in the United States (Spulber, 1996b). Retailers are intermediaries between final consumers and wholesalers and manufacturers. Two-thirds of wholesale transactions are sales made by wholesale merchants (including also distributors, jobbers, drop shippers, import/export merchants, grain elevators, and farm product assemblers) and agents (including also brokers, commission merchants, import/export agents and brokers, auction companies, and manufacturers' agents). The remaining one-third of wholesale transactions are sales conducted through manufacturers' sales branches and offices to wholesalers, retailers, and other manufacturers (United States Census Bureau, 2000). Financial firms, including banks, securities brokerages, mutual funds, and insurance companies, also primarily create transactions.

Others engaged in intermediation activities include attorneys, sales agents, real estate brokers, and other specialized agents.

All types of companies, including manufacturing firms, spend substantial resources on transactions through their marketing and sales, input purchasing, financing, and other market functions. Large-scale commodity firms such as Exxon-Mobil or BP in petroleum or Cargill in grains and agricultural products play a major role in organizing international markets. Transaction activities are an essential part of the establishment and operation of firms.

2.5 The Social, Legal, and Political Context of the Firm

Firms are transaction institutions designed and established by entrepreneurs. The firm functions within the context of social, legal, and political constraints. The concept of a firm is related to social conventions such as language, norms, rules, or customs. The firm is defined by legal concepts such as those governing business transactions and organizations.

2.5.1 The Social Context of the Firm

The economic role of the firm is heavily influenced by its social context. Transactions take place within networks of already-established social relationships. Parties to transactions often share social customs, business practices, a common language, and common knowledge of goods and services. If the social context promotes trust, the transaction costs of bilateral and multilateral exchange are often reduced, thereby making exchange between consumers more efficient. For example, a high-trust society can reduce free riding in a consumer cooperative. A high-trust society might increase revelation of information, thus reducing adverse selection problems in markets. This can reduce the need for firms.

However, a social context that promotes trust and lowers transaction costs also enhances the efficiency of the firm's market transactions. The social context also can enhance relationships within organizations, which also improves the efficiency of the firm's organizational transactions. Whether the social context increases or decreases the need for firms depends on the relative effects of the social context on transactions between consumers and transactions mediated by firms.

According to John R. Commons (1931) "Transactions are the means, under operation of law and custom, of acquiring and alienating legal control of commodities, or legal control of the labor and management that will produce and deliver or exchange the commodities and services, forward to the ultimate consumers." He distinguishes institutional economics from classical economics and hedonic economics as follows: "transactions are, not the 'exchange of commodities,' but the alienation and acquisition, between individuals, of the rights of property and liberty created by society, which must therefore be negotiated between the parties concerned before labor can produce, or consumers can consume, or commodities be physically exchanged."

The notion that transactions take place within the framework of social relationships is fundamental in sociology and anthropology.[96] Karl Polanyi (2001) argued that "man's economy, as a rule, is submerged in his social relationships," through reciprocity, redistribution, and the household. Economic transactions are said to be "embedded" within social relations. There are many social institutions including conventions, customs, kinship, and traditional relationships. Firms are a very special type of enterprise within the vast set of possible associations and organizations within a society. The theory of the firm makes no claim to broader implications, but rather views transactions and the firm as residing within the social context.

Ian R. Macneil (1980, p. 1) argues that "Contract without the common needs and tastes created by society is inconceivable; contract between totally isolated, utility-maximizing individuals is not contract, but war; contract without language is impossible; and contract without social structure and stability is – quite literally – rationally unthinkable. The fundamental root, the base, of contract is society." Macneil (1980, p. 10) defines a "discrete contract" as "one in which no relation exists between the parties apart from the simple exchange of goods. Its paradigm is the transaction of neoclassical microeconomics." However, Macneil argues that such a contract is rarely observed because "every contract is necessarily partially a relational contract, that is, one involving relations other than a discrete exchange." For Macneil (1974), a relational contract has many characteristics, including significant duration, close personal relations as in employment, social reputation and norms, anticipation of future cooperative behavior, and a view that the relationship will evolve over time rather than being fully specified at the outset.

The family is a particular social institution that is worth emphasizing. Apart from their explicit business activities in merchant houses, small-scale manufacturing, or farms, families are precursors of firms in a more fundamental way. The family or household in general is an important means of organizing exchange. Ben-Porath (1980, p. 1) points out that the "family plays a major role in the allocation and distribution of resources."[97] Family members engage in transactions involving implicit contracts. Ben-Porath notes that between the two extremes of the family transaction and the market transaction are a range of transaction modes and institutions including transactions between friends, business partners, and employers and employees.

2.5.2 The Legal Context of the Firm

Market transactions and organizational transactions exist within a framework of laws and regulations. Many of these rules raise the value of transactions, increasing

---

96 In anthropology see the classic work on the gift by Mauss (1954), Malinowski (1966 [1922]) on trade in the Trobriand islands, and Sahlins (1974) on stone-age economics.

97 See also Ben-Porath (1982).

transaction benefits and lowering transaction costs, although some types of rules complicate and deter transactions. Government statutes, regulations established by administrative agencies, and the Uniform Commercial Code also affect transaction costs. The financial organization of the firm depends on financial regulations and laws governing partnerships, corporations, and other forms of organization.

The firm operates in the context of the common law of property, which is a foundation of market exchange. It is difficult to conceive of a market forming in the absence of ownership. A producer owns outputs and transfers ownership to consumers. Such transactions would have little meaning without legal protection for ownership by the seller and its subsequent transfer to the buyer. Legal protection of private ownership rights reduces the costs of protecting property and transferring property rights. Property rights allow entrepreneurs to establish and own firms. They are essential to financing firms because the firm sells ownership shares. Property rights are necessary to the market for corporate control because owners can transfer shares of the firm on financial markets.

Property rights assure investors that they will obtain residual returns, thus preserving incentives for individuals to commit effort and capital resources. Property rights protect ownership of land, natural resources, capital equipment, and intellectual property. Property rights allow the market to function well when those rights are complete, exclusive, and transferable. Completeness means that all resources and other assets are fully accounted for. Property rights are exclusive if there are no assets that are owned in common by competing interests. Rights are transferable when the legal system recognizes and permits the transfer of ownership between parties. Property rights never fully satisfy these three ideal criteria. Some environmental resources are not fully accounted for by the system of property rights. Few assets are subject to fully exclusive use without such restrictions as zoning laws. There are legal restrictions that limit transferability of assets such as land.

Contract law helps to reduce the costs of private enforcement and allows parties to enter into efficient agreements in the absence of reputation or prior transactions. The credibility of contractual promises made by individuals is enhanced by the presence of legal enforcement mechanisms. There are some market mechanisms that can arise to enforce contracts, such as the posting of a bond, the development of long-term relationships, or the establishment of reputations for contract performance or breach.

Contract law helps to reduce the costs of contracting by providing standard terms and spelling out general purpose contingencies, such as remedies for breach of contract. Because it is costly to identify all possible contingencies and to write contracts that depend on many contingencies, contracts are of necessity incomplete; that is, they do not spell out all possible contingencies and the associated performance that is expected. Contracts often address only those events whose occurrence is readily verifiable.

Contract terms are agreed upon as a result of a voluntary bargaining process, so that each party must receive positive net gains from trade. In legal terms, each party to a contract must receive *consideration*; that is, each party must expect to be made better off by the exchange. A party making a promise to perform a given service must expect to receive compensation. Moreover, the contracting process cannot involve deceit, coercion, or duress, and requires the informed consent of both of the parties. This ensures that the contract is a voluntary agreement and that both parties are aware of the terms of the exchange. These conditions are generally sufficient to ensure that each of the parties enters into the contract anticipating gains from trade. The contractual agreement is expected by each of the parties to lead to a net improvement of their economic position before they entered into the contract.

Because there are economic costs to creating contracts, a contractual agreement may be enforced whether it is an express or implied agreement. An *express agreement* is a formal contract that is either written or oral. An *implied agreement* can be the result of an informal agreement and actions taken by the parties. In many cases parties may find it worthwhile to incur the costs of writing down the contract terms or spelling them out orally. In other instances, it may be more convenient or less costly to enter into informal agreements. The parties to a contract may signify their commitment to the contractual agreement by incurring costs, by making expenditures, or by taking certain irreversible actions in return for the other party's promises and in anticipation of the other party's performance.

Most transactions do not involve simultaneous performance, as with a simple exchange. It takes time to produce capital equipment, to build production facilities, or to develop inventions. Contracts are needed to handle the problems that may arise with the passage of time. Generally, there is a delay between the time the contract is entered into and the time that performance is completed. During this time there are often foreseen and unforeseen changes in the circumstances of the parties. The contract is designed to adjust the terms of the transaction to handle some contingencies. The parties to a contract incur costs or obligations in anticipation of the other party's performance.

When circumstances change, parties to contracts can decide to renegotiate the terms of their agreements. By providing legally enforceable rights, contract law helps to address problems of contract risk or hold-up in which a party to a contract takes advantage of the reliance of other parties to the contract.[98] In the absence of such rights, the parties to a transaction would seek to reduce their risk by reducing the level of transaction-specific investment in a particular contractual arrangement. This would reduce efficiency by causing departures from the investment levels that maximize the joint benefits of the parties to the agreement. Moreover, people would seek out agreements of shorter duration, again reducing economic efficiency. Other market mechanisms for building trust and reducing contract risk include business

---

98 Posner (1986, p. 81) observes that "the fundamental function of contract law (and recognized such at least since Hobbes' day [see Thomas Hobbes, *Leviathan* 70–71 (1991)] is to deter people from behaving opportunistically toward their contracting parties, in order to encourage the optimal timing of economic activity and make costly self-protective measures unnecessary."

reputations and long-term relationships. Social pressure to conform to norms also reduces contract risk.

Jensen and Meckling (1976), Fama and Jensen (1983a) and Easterbrook and Fischel (1989, 1991) offer a contractarian view of the corporation as a "nexus of contracts." Easterbrook and Fischel (1989, 1991) recommend that courts be guided by an implicit but efficient contract in which the firm's owners seek jointly to maximize their wealth. Fischel (1982) argues that courts should be guided by the role of the manager as a fiduciary; that is, the manager is guided by the duties of loyalty and care. He observes that "optimal fiduciary duties should approach the bargain that investors and managers would reach if transaction costs were zero" (1982, p. 1265).[99] Casadesus-Masanell and Spulber (2005) examine the implications of trust for the economic model of the principal-agent relationship.

Butler (1989) points out that although corporations receive a charter from the state, the corporation is founded on private contracts. He points out that owners and managers will negotiate the optimal mix of market and legal restraints on agency costs. The market for corporate control will provide further incentives for owners and managers to form efficient contracts. Shareholders are unanimous about the corporation's objective function so that corporate law should provide a framework for shareholder value maximization.

The firm also operates within the tort system of common law. A consumer buying a good is concerned about its quality or safety. Reduction of risks associated with purchasing products raises the consumer's willingness to pay. A consumer who is concerned about product risks may choose to invest in additional information or safeguards, leading to a reduction in demand. Tort rules provide incentives to producers to mitigate potential damages. Tort law provides mechanisms that handle general problems associated with product quality and work place health and safety. When administered efficiently, tort rules can reduce transaction costs, because they avoid the need for specifying certain contract contingencies related to negligence and compensation for damages.

2.5.3 The Political Context of the Firm

The economic role of the firm is profoundly affected by its political context. Government policies significantly affect the benefits and costs of transactions. Many public policies mitigate transaction costs whereas other public policies increase

99 Kornhauser (1989, p. 1449) finds that contracts and trust offer two metaphors that "lead us awry or abandon us altogether through ambiguity." Kornhauser argues that the contracts view is problematic because in practice there are transaction costs and information asymmetries in contracting. He adds that trust falls short because of the multitude of corporate principals including directors, shareholders, and bondholders, who have conflicting interests. Kornhauser argues for mandatory rules that restrict the types of bargains parties can strike when the corporation is formed, thus allocating rights over the life of the corporation. This approach would complement trust as a means of reducing contracting costs.

them. Thus, firms create and coordinate transactions in the context established by public policy. However, discussion of public policy is beyond the scope of our discussion.

Government activities that are likely to reduce transaction costs include the establishment of a judicial system, the management of a dependable monetary system, the development of transportation infrastructure, the maintenance of public safety, and standards such as weights and measures. Conversely, many types of public regulations such as price controls, product quality, licensing requirements, and mandated access to facilities of regulated industries are likely to increase transaction costs; see Spulber (1989b). Governments also raise transaction costs by creating entry barriers to the establishment of new business and by imposing tariff and nontariff barriers to international trade. Taxes and other public policies have significant impacts on business productivity, particularly in developing countries.[100]

Transaction costs are likely to be much higher in international trade than in the domestic economy. In the international economy, there are substantial distances between some countries that require greater transportation costs. In addition, international trade crosses country borders and is subject to a wide variety of tariff and nontariff barriers. Along with trade barriers created by individual countries, there are complex international trade regulations overseen by associations of countries through customs unions and bilateral and multilateral trade agreements. This includes general trade agreements achieved through the World Trade Organization.

International transaction costs, referred to as the costs of trade, are substantial. Buyers and sellers in different countries are separated by diverse time zones, currencies, languages, social customs, business practices, legal jurisdictions, and political systems. Buyers and sellers are likely to have less information about each other than if they were in the same economy. Therefore, the transaction costs of search, negotiation, contract formation, and contract monitoring are likely to increase accordingly in the international context.

Empirical analysis demonstrates the substantial level of transaction costs in the international context. Anderson and van Wincoop (2004) estimate that average trade costs correspond to a proportional markup equal to 170% of the initial price. This includes transportation costs, trade barriers, and retail and wholesale margins. In addition to direct measurements of trade costs, a substantial amount of research has attempted to infer trade costs from trade volumes and prices. Empirical gravity models show substantial effects of distances and country borders on bilateral trade volumes, while accounting for the effects of country sizes and prices on trade; see Anderson and van Wincoop (2003). Empirical analysis consistently shows that the law of one price fails to hold across international borders; see Goldberg and Knetter (1997). Also, baskets of goods do not have the same average prices across borders, so

100 Lewis (2004).

that currencies do not satisfy purchasing power parity, with very slow adjustment of average prices towards parity; see Rogoff (1996). Trade costs help to explain a wide variety of puzzles in international macroeconomics, including the home-country bias of trade; see Obstfeld and Rogoff (2000).

The presence of international transaction costs solves another major puzzle – why are there international firms? The international trade literature has long wondered about the reasons for the existence of multinational firms, that is, firms that own and operate in multiple countries. A Coasian explanation is that such firms reduce transaction costs by internalizing trade, transferring inputs, outputs, payments, and technology between international units of the firm, because the costs of doing so are lower than those of international market transactions.

International firms also create and coordinate international transactions, bringing together buyers and sellers across national borders. International firms achieve international gains from trade and reduce the costs of trade. This analysis helps explain the existence of international companies that do not necessarily operate facilities in multiple countries and do not necessarily create value through internalization of transactions. Many international firms, such as financial firms and wholesalers, enhance the benefits and reduce the costs of international transactions by helping to establish international markets.

2.6 Conclusions

The firm is a transaction institution whose objectives differ from those of its owners. The general theory of the firm provides a unified framework for studying firms, markets, and organizations. The firm's activities efficiently combine market mechanisms and organizational mechanisms. The scope of the firm is the full range of its market transactions and organizational transactions. The economic equilibrium involves the endogenous choice of consumers to become entrepreneurs. This leads to the endogenous establishment of firms. By creating and managing markets and organizations, firms help to determine the equilibrium prices and allocation of resources in the economy.

Coordination of transactions is central to the theory of the firm. Entrepreneurs establish firms and transact through firms when doing so enhances the benefits of transactions net of the costs of transactions. Firms create value by making possible transaction efficiencies that consumers could not realize through direct exchange and consumer organizations. The transactions that are observed in equilibrium will involve some combination of direct exchange between consumers and intermediated exchange through firms.

The "intermediation hypothesis" examines the economy's reliance on firms as intermediaries. The "intermediation hypothesis" suggests that as a result of transaction costs, the extent of the market explains the establishment of firms to replace consumer organizations and direct exchange. The general theory of the firm yields useful insights that can be tested empirically using contemporary and historical data. The diversity of firms in the contemporary economy provides substantial information for studying the activities of firms. The following chapters examine the economic role of the firm in a variety of environments.

3

The Separation of Consumer Objectives
and Firm Objectives

The separation criterion is fundamental to the theory of the firm. A firm is defined as a transaction institution whose objectives differ from those of its consumer-owners. To understand the firm's economic contribution, it is necessary to derive the firm's objectives endogenously from the choices made by the firm's owners. The neoclassical separation theorem shows that the firm's objective is profit maximization. Although the neoclassical separation theorem provides essential guidance, it is based on several critical assumptions: transaction costs are absent, the firm is defined as a producer of goods, firms take prices as given, and the Walrasian auctioneer chooses market-clearing prices. This chapter extends the separation theorem to accommodate a more general model of the firm. The theory of the firm emphasizes that the firm is more than a producer of goods. The firm chooses prices and creates markets. The discussion in this chapter shows that when firms choose prices, the firm's owners continue to want the firm to maximize profits.

The firm's profit-maximization objective is distinct from the consumption objectives of its owners. Profit maximization by firms is a critical feature of neoclassical analysis of general equilibrium, industrial organization models of imperfect competition, and models of market microstructure. In the theory of the firm, profit maximization drives the firm to select allocations that are more efficient than direct exchange, under some conditions. Profit maximization gives the firm enhanced capabilities in comparison to consumer organizations such as cooperatives, non-profits, and basic partnerships. The analysis also extends the Fisher Separation Theorem to show the separation of consumer saving objectives and firm investment objectives with price-setting firms.

The neoclassical separation theorem makes three important assertions: (1) *firms maximize profits*, (2) *firms generate gains from trade compared to autarky*, and (3) *firm decisions are separate from consumer decisions*. First, with price-setting firms, the chapter shows that the consumer-owner wants the firm to maximize profit because the consumer-owner receives the firm's profits as income. Competition between many firms selling differentiated products plays an important role in extending the separation theorem. The consumer-owner spends the profit earned

125

from the firm on many goods and thus does not benefit much from cutting prices on the products produced by the firm that he owns. The returns to profit maximization thus outweigh changes in the prices and production decisions of the firm that would benefit the owner as a consumer. The analysis justifies profit maximization by firms in industrial organization models of imperfect competition and in market microstructure models with market-making firms.

Second, firms generate gains from trade because consumer-owners do better operating price-setting firms in the market than by operating the technology in direct exchange or under autarky. The consumer-owner obtains gains from trade by buying goods in the marketplace and by using the firm to sell goods in the marketplace, rather than managing the firm entirely for his own consumption purposes. The size of the economy is critical to generalizing the separation theorem. With many consumers, the consumer-owner's purchase is a small share of the firm's sales and the profit effect of price greatly exceeds the effect of the price on the consumer's own expenditure. When there are many consumers, the extent of the market is greater, which provides benefits from economies of scale. The greater the extent of the market, the greater will be the number of goods produced, which provides benefits from product variety. Consumers experience gains from trade in comparison with autarky due to economies of scale and product variety.

Third, firm decisions are separate from consumer decisions because firms choose prices and coordinate transactions. The intermediation hypothesis goes further. Firms as transaction institutions separate demand and supply decisions in the economy. In the neoclassical tradition, markets separate consumption from production decisions. Markets and the Walrasian auctioneer stand between demand and supply, coordinating the two sides of the market with equilibrium prices. Separation of decisions by the equilibrium price vector yields the neoclassical separation theorem, proving incentives to firms and consumers. In contrast, firms stand between demand and supply in the general theory of the firm. Firms make price-setting decisions and allocation decisions that coordinate demand and supply. The theory of the firm does not presume the existence of markets, but rather studies how firms create and operate markets and other institutions of exchange. The theory of the firm examines how firms clear markets through price adjustment, quantity rationing, and matchmaking.

The implications of removing the neoclassical assumptions are not well understood. In discussing the neoclassical separation theorem, Mas-Colell et al. (1995, p. 153) observe that "If prices may depend on the production of the firm, the objective of the owners may depend on their tastes as consumers." This suggests that when firms choose prices, instead of a Walrasian auctioneer setting prices, the separation theorem does not hold. This poses a problem with potentially serious consequences for economic theory because it suggests that the profit-maximization hypothesis is no longer valid when firms set prices. This would call into question models of imperfect competition or models of market microstructure.

The separation theorem has important implications for the role of the entrepreneur. To understand why firms exist, it is important to understand the entrepreneur's motivation. After the firm is established, the entrepreneur becomes an owner. The separation of the objectives of the firm from those of its owners means that the entrepreneur does not establish the firm to realize consumption benefits. The separation theorem comes into force *after* the firm is established. The separation theorem therefore implies that *before* the firm is established, the entrepreneur's objective is to obtain the value of the firm, that is, the present value of the firm's profit stream. The entrepreneur establishes the firm to obtain the monetary reward from ownership of the firm rather than future consumption benefits. By this process of backward induction, one may conclude that the entrepreneur maximizes the net benefits obtained from establishing the firm. The entrepreneur's profit is the discounted value of the firm when it is established net of the costs of establishing the firm, as will be discussed in Chapter 4.

This chapter examines conditions under which there is a separation between consumer and firm objectives when firms choose prices. The discussion maintains the assumption of price-taking behavior by consumers because firms can commit to prices and consumers make purchasing decisions after prices are posted. With price competition between firms that offer differentiated products, the consumer-owner wants the firm to choose its price without taking into account the impact of price changes on the consumer's expenditures. When the number of consumers is sufficiently large, the effect of the firm's price on the profit the consumer obtains outweighs any consumption benefits that might result from a departure from profit maximization. The discussion extends this result to a two-period setting with consumer saving decisions and firm investment decisions. The Fisher separation theorem applies when there is price competition between firms that offer differentiated products. The consumer-owner obtains gains from trade by buying goods in the market place and by using the firm to sell goods in the market place, rather than managing the firm entirely for his own consumption purposes.

3.1 The Neoclassical Separation Theorem

In the neoclassical framework the idea that firms maximize profit is based upon the objectives of consumers who own a firm. Consumers choose to purchase their most-preferred consumption bundles within the limits of their budget, taking market prices as fixed and not dependent on the firm's input-output choices. The consumer-owner obtains a share of the firm's profit which adds to the consumer's income. Any consumer wishes to obtain the greatest possible income so that if multiple consumers share ownership of a firm, they will unanimously prefer that the firm choose its production activities to maximize its profit. This type of reasoning is known as a *separation theorem*; the objective of the firm is separate from the objectives of its consumer-owners.

In neoclassical economics, the firm is a producer *by assumption*. As Arrow and Hahn (1971) put it, households and firms "are distinguished by the property that firms do, and households do not, make production decisions." The neoclassical firm is fully described by its production possibilities set, so the neoclassical firm is synonymous with a producer of goods and services. Because transactions are costless, markets are already established, and prices are determined exogenously, the firm's role is reduced to choosing a profit-maximizing input-output vector while taking prices, products, and technology as givens.

Separation of consumption and production decisions in the neoclassical framework requires the assumption of price-taking behavior both by consumers and by firms. The assignment of demand decisions to consumers and supply decisions to firms makes possible the separation between demand and supply. Confining the firm to choosing activities within a production possibilities set requires an exogenous and costless market mechanism, the Walrasian auctioneer, to establish prices for all commodities. The market-clearing price vector rations demand for inputs and outputs and stimulates the supply of inputs and outputs. By assumption, prices cannot depend on production decisions because otherwise, consumers with different endowments or different preferences would disagree on what should be the firm's production decision. Unanimity of consumers regarding the firm's production decision establishes the profit-maximization objective of the firm.

The separation theorem demonstrates that there are *gains from trade* available in established markets for outputs. The firm need not sell to its consumer-owners, and in turn consumer-owners need not rely directly on the firm that they own to satisfy their consumption requirements. Instead, firms sell outputs and purchase inputs in the market and consumer-owners in turn purchase outputs and sell inputs in the market. The profit-maximizing production decisions of the firm and the preference-maximizing consumption decisions of the consumer-owners both realize gains from trade with others. At prevailing market prices, firms earn greater profit and consumer-owners fare better than if they were to rely exclusively on the firm's production for the goods that they consume.

In addition to the assumption of price-taking behavior and the assumption that the firm is a producer, the neoclassical separation theorem depends on an absence of transaction costs. Sufficiently high transaction costs lead to autarky. The firm and its consumer-owners would not obtain gains from trade, leading owners to manage the firm for their own consumption purposes.

Even if transaction costs did not lead to autarky, they would be inconsistent with the neoclassical separation theorem. The separation result assumes that there exist complete markets, which implicitly presumes that markets are costlessly established and operated. Consumers and firms observe and respond to the same market-clearing prices, which must satisfy the law of one price. This rules out price dispersion, which might arise when consumer search was costly. Also, there cannot be different buying and selling prices, because the separation theorem depends on a single price for each good. If there were a bid-ask spread, as is commonly observed in many markets, the firm would face different prices depending on whether it was

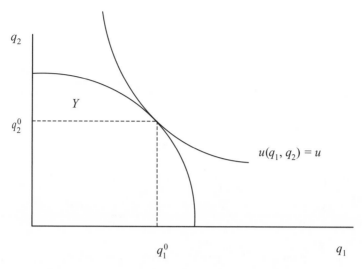

Figure 3.1. The Robinson Crusoe economy with preference-maximizing outputs (q_1^0, q_2^0).

buying or selling a particular good. As a consequence, consumer-owners would disagree on the desired production decisions of the firm. Again, absence of unanimity removes the conditions used to establish the firm's objective of profit maximization.

Suppose that each consumer owns a production technology. This corresponds to a Robinson Crusoe economy in which a single consumer owns and operates a production technology. Assume that there are only two goods and let the consumer's preferences be represented by the utility function $u(q_1, q_2)$. The production possibilities set Y and the consumer's indifference curve are shown in Figure 3.1. The output levels (q_1^0, q_2^0) maximize the consumer's preferences subject to the production possibilities set. It is evident that consumers with different preferences would choose a different pair of outputs along the production possibilities frontier, defined as the curved boundary of the production possibilities set, Y.

The standard statement of the separation theorem is as follows. A firm with production possibilities set Y is owned by consumers $i = 1, 2, \ldots, n$. Let the input-output vector y be the firm's production decision, which must be within the production possibilities set Y. Each consumer has a share $\theta_i \geq 0$ of the firm's profit, where $\sum_1^n \theta_i = 1$. Each consumer has a utility function $u_i(q_i)$ of the vector of consumption goods q_i and an initial endowment of the vector of goods ω_i. The consumer takes the price vector as given exogenously and chooses $q_i \geq 0$ to maximize utility subject to the consumer's budget constraint,

$$\max_q u_i(q) \text{ subject to } p \cdot q \leq p \cdot \omega_i + \theta_i p \cdot y.$$

From the consumer's maximization problem, it follows that consumers prefer the greatest possible profit for the firm, because a share of that profit adds to the consumer's income.[1]

---

1 See Mas-Colell et al. (1995, pp. 152–3) for additional discussion.

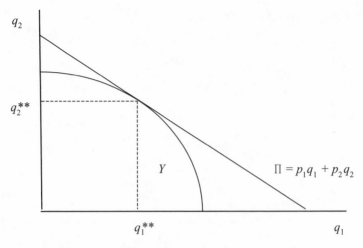

Figure 3.2. The profit-maximizing output mix.

In the general equilibrium framework, it is assumed that the firm's production decision y does not affect prices. We will return to this critical assumption. Firms take prices as given exogenously and do not recognize any effect that their supply would have on equilibrium prices. Therefore, consumer-owners unanimously prefer that the firm should choose an input-output vector y to maximize profit subject to the production possibilities constraint:

$$\max_y \ p \cdot y \ \text{subject to} \ y \text{ in } Y.$$

If p were to depend on the production decision y, then changes in y would affect the market value of the consumer's endowment, which would lead to disagreements about the preferred production decision among consumer-owners with different endowments. Also, if p were to depend on y, then changes in y would affect the cost of the consumer-owner's purchase, which again would lead to disagreements about the preferred production decisions of the firm based on different preferences. Accordingly, if p does not depend on y, consumers agree unanimously on the profit-maximization objective of the firm.

Suppose that market prices for the two goods are p_1 and p_2. For a price-taking producer the profit-maximizing outputs q_1^{**}, q_2^{**} are shown in Figure 3.2. All consumers would agree that a firm with the production possibilities set Y should maximize profit.

A consumer who receives profit Π as income will choose to purchase a mix of outputs q_1^*, q_2^* that differs from the output mix q_1^0, q_2^0 that is chosen strictly to satisfy the needs of the consumer-owner; see Figure 3.3. These differ in turn from the profit-maximizing output mix, q_1^{**}, q_2^{**}. The consumer-owner is better off choosing outputs on the budget line than at the preference-maximizing consumption bundle. There are two reasons for this. First, the consumer-owner's budget line is generated by the income from the firm. Thus, the firm's profit-maximizing production decision provides the consumer-owner with the greatest possible income, which is equal to the market value of the firm's outputs; that is, $\Pi = p_1 q_1^{**} + p_2 q_2^{**}$.

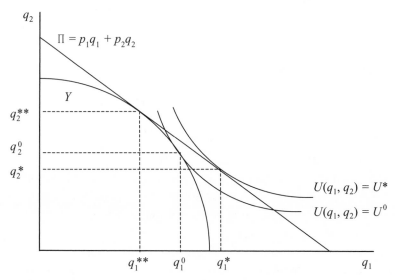

Figure 3.3. Production and consumption decisions with product markets (q_1^0, q_2^0).

Second, given the firm's profit, the consumer's budget line reflects all possible market opportunities to purchase outputs. This means that the consumer benefits from *gains from trade* with other consumers and firms by making purchases in the market place. This is shown by the consumer choosing the best consumption bundle along the budget line $p_1 q_1 + p_2 q_2$.

The standard neoclassical welfare conditions hold because the consumer's marginal rate of substitution equals the marginal rate of transformation along the production possibilities frontier, because both are equal to the price ratio. All potential gains from trade are realized if the rest of the economy satisfies similar efficiency conditions.

Financial markets allow the decoupling of the financial contracts of the firm and those of its owners. Both the firm and its consumer-owners rely on financial markets to transfer income over time and across states of the world. The Fisher Separation Theorem generalizes to the case of uncertainty when markets are complete – see Hirshleifer (1965) and Drèze and Modigliani (1972) – and in some settings when markets are incomplete – see Diamond (1967), DeAngelo (1981), Krouse (1985), Makowski and Pepall (1985), MacMinn (1987), and Kamara (1993).

The Fisher Separation Theorem does not specify the firm's financial decisions or its organizational structure. Modigliani and Miller (1958) and Miller and Modigliani (1961) showed that the firm's financial structure, in terms of its debt-equity ratio or its dividend policy, did not affect the firm's value. If decisions regarding financial structure are neutral in terms of value, it is not possible to determine why firms in practice make different financial structure decisions. Neoclassical analysis also does not consider the effects of the firm's financial decisions and organizational structure on managerial decision making. In this setting, corporate governance has no effect, and there is no need for a market for corporate control. Incentives for performance are not needed. The firm is a black box, and there is no need to specify its organizational structure. Chapter 7 will consider the interaction between the firm's financial decisions and its organizational form.

3.2 The Separation Theorem with Price-Setting Firms

This section introduces a separation theorem with price-setting firms. Consumers purchase a continuum of differentiated products. The production technology for each product exhibits economies of scale. Because there are many products, a price change for any product has a very small impact on the consumer. Accordingly, consumer-owners prefer that the firm choose the profit-maximizing price. Also, with differentiated products and economies of scale, consumer-owners prefer to operate a profit-maximizing firm that participates in the market in comparison to operating the firm for their own consumption needs. Consumers' preference for product variety provides gains from trade. Economies of scale in production also create gains from trade because consumers want to consolidate production.

3.2.1 Profit Maximization

Consider an economy with a continuum of single-product firms. The measure of the number of firms is m. The number of firms is taken as given for now but will be made endogenous in Chapter 5. A firm i earns a profit that depends on the price of good i and the prices of other goods, $\Pi_i(p_i, p_{(i)})$.

Consumers have identical utility functions, $u(x)$, where x is a vector of consumption goods. The utility function is increasing and concave. Suppose that there is a continuum of goods, x_j, where the index j takes values on the interval $[0, m]$. Let p_j be the price of good j and denote the consumer's income by I. Each consumer chooses to purchase all m differentiated goods. The consumer takes the price vector as given exogenously when making consumption decisions. Consumer-owners take the profit of the firm that they own as a given part of their income when making their consumption decision.

The consumer's problem is to maximize utility subject to the budget constraint

(1)
$$\max_x u(x) \text{ subject to } \int_0^m p_j x_j \, dj \leq I.$$

The consumer's desired consumption bundle then depends on income and the vector of prices, $x = x(p, I)$. Let λ be the Lagrange multiplier for the consumer's budget constraint. The consumer's first-order conditions are

(2)
$$u_j(x) = \lambda p_j, \quad \text{for all } j \text{ in } [0, m],$$

(3)
$$\int_0^m p_j x_j \, dj = I.$$

Suppose that a consumer owns a share of a firm that produces one of the goods, say good i. The consumer's profit share is θ_i. The consumer-owner's income equals the share of the profit obtained from the firm, $I = \theta_i \Pi_i(p_i, p_{(i)})$. The consumer-owner chooses the firm's price to maximize benefits from being an owner,

$$\max_{p_i} u(x^*(p, \theta_i \Pi_i(p_i, p_{(i)}))).$$

The first-order condition for the consumer-owner's problem is

(4)
$$\int_0^m u_j(x^*) \left(\frac{\partial x_j}{\partial p_i} + \frac{\partial x_j}{\partial I} \frac{\partial \theta_i \Pi_i(p_i, p_{(i)})}{\partial p_i} \right) dj = 0.$$

Applying equation (2), the first-order condition for the consumer-owner's problem can be written as

(5)
$$\lambda \int_0^m p_j \left(\frac{\partial x_j}{\partial p_i} + \frac{\partial x_j}{\partial I} \frac{\partial \theta_i \Pi_i(p_i, p_{(i)})}{\partial p_i} \right) dj = 0.$$

Differentiating the consumer's budget constraint with respect to I implies that

(6)
$$\int_0^m p_j \frac{\partial x_j}{\partial I} dj = 1.$$

Differentiate the consumer's budget constraint with respect to p_i. For any good j other than i, the derivative of the consumer's expenditure is $p_j \frac{\partial x_j}{\partial p_i}$. For good i, the derivative of the consumer's expenditure is $p_i \frac{\partial x_i}{\partial p_i} + x_i$. This means that the function that is being integrated in equation (6) has a discontinuity at i. Since x_i is bounded, and there is a continuum of goods, the integral is well defined. The discontinuity does not affect the convergence of the integral.[2] Differentiating the consumer's budget constraint with respect to p_i implies that

(7)
$$\int_0^m p_j \frac{\partial x_j}{\partial p_i} dj = 0.$$

Now, substitute from equations (6) and (7) into equation (5). Then the consumer-owner's first-order condition reduces to

(8)
$$\frac{\partial \Pi_i(p_i, p_{(i)})}{\partial p_i} = 0.$$

Therefore, the consumer-owner chooses the price to maximize the firm's profit. This establishes that consumer-owners want the firm to maximize profit, even when the firm chooses prices. The reason is that with a continuum of goods, the effect of the price of the good on the consumer-owner's expenditure is negligible. The solution does not depend on the owner's consumption preferences or on the owner's share

---

2 This follows from the standard definition of the Riemann integral. The function being integrated is continuous almost everywhere. There is a discontinuity at i. The improper integral converges when it is continuous and bounded in the open interval; see Courant and John (1989, pp. 302–3).

of profits. Consumer-owners will unanimously prefer profit maximization. When there are many differentiated products and price-setting firms, consumer decisions can be separated from firm decisions.

3.2.2 Gains from Trade

In addition to profit maximization, a separation theorem must show that consumer-owners obtain gains from trade by operating a firm. To compare the equilibrium when there are firms to autarky in a consistent manner, suppose that the number of consumers, n, and the number of goods, m, are integers. The number of consumers is assumed to be large for consistency with the preceding discussion of price setting by firms. Each consumer has an endowment of one unit of labor, so that total labor in the economy equals n. Labor is the numeraire good. To produce q_j units of good j requires $\alpha + \beta q_j$ units of labor, where $\alpha > 0$ represents fixed costs and $\beta > 0$ is marginal cost. For ease of discussion, suppose that the consumer utility function is symmetric. Assume that $\alpha < 1$, so that consumers under autarky can produce at least one good.

To examine gains from trade it is necessary to consider the returns to autarkic production. Suppose that consumers own the production technology for producing any good. Although each final product is unique, the production technology for every good is identical and exhibits increasing-returns-to-scale technology. Let benefits $u(x)$ be symmetric across goods. Under autarky, the consumer chooses the number of goods, m, and production of each good, x_j, to maximize net benefits $u(x_1, \ldots, x_m)$ subject to the labor constraint, $m(\alpha + \beta x) \leq 1$. Let m^0 denote product variety under autarky and let x^0 denote the level of production of each good under autarky. The consumer devotes his entire labor endowment to production, so that the amount of each good produced under autarky equals

$$(9) \qquad\qquad x^0 = (1/m^0 - \alpha)/\beta.$$

In the Robinson Crusoe economy, the consumer suffers from limited product variety due to an absence of opportunities to trade. The consumer also suffers from high unit production costs because the consumer only produces for his own consumption and does not obtain the benefits of economies of scale.

Now, suppose that consumers establish m firms that produce for the market. Each firm produces a differentiated good. Consumers sell their labor to firms and receive a unit wage in labor units. Each consumer obtains an equal share of the profits of each firm, $\Pi_j(p_j, p_{-j})/n$. This allows consolidation of production if there are more consumers than firms. Each consumer's income is the sum of profits and the wage,

$$I = 1 + (1/n) \sum_{j=1}^{m} \Pi_j.$$

Profits will be equal across firms in equilibrium, so that total demand for good i can be written as

$$q_j(p_j, p_{-j}) = nx_j(p_j, p_{-j}, 1 + (m/n)\Pi).$$

Profit is suppressed in the consumer demand functions to simplify notation.

From the preceding discussion, consumer-owners unanimously prefer that the firm choose the profit-maximizing price when there are many goods. Each firm produces a differentiated good and sells that good to all consumers. Firms engage in Bertrand–Nash price competition. The profit from producing q_j units of good j equals

(10) $$\Pi_j(p_j, p_{-j}) = (p_j - \beta)q_j(p_j, p_{-j}) - \alpha.$$

The profit-maximizing price for each firm is a best response to the equilibrium prices of other firms.

Firm j's first-order condition is

(11) $$(p_j - \beta)\frac{\partial q_j(p_j, p_{-j})}{\partial p_j} - q(p_j, p_{-j}) = 0.$$

By symmetry, a consumer devotes the same amount of income to each good. Prices are equal across firms, and each firm produces the same output, $q(p^*)$. Let p^* be the equilibrium price vector. The benefit of each consumer is given by $u(x, \ldots, x)$, where

(12) $$x^* = x(p^*, 1 + (m/n)\Pi(p^*)) = q(p^*)/n.$$

From the consumers' budget constraints, it follows that the economy's labor constraint is satisfied. The labor constraint equates the total demand for labor to the number of consumers, n:

$$m(\alpha + \beta q^*) = n.$$

This determines the equilibrium output of each firm,

(13) $$q^* = (1/\beta)(n/m - \alpha).$$

The separation theorem holds if consumers obtain gains from trade from the establishment of firms. When there are firms, the consumer purchases m goods and the number of units of each good equals $x^* = q^*/n = (1/\beta)(1/m - \alpha/n)$.

Firms provide gains from trade when there is greater product variety than under autarky, $m \geq m^0$.[3] Compare consumption of each good when there are firms with

---

3 If the market equilibrium with firms were to provide less product variety than under autarky, $m < m^0$, then consumption of each good would be greater in the equilibrium with firms than under autarky:

$$x^* = (1/\beta)(1/m - \alpha/n) > (1/m^0 - \alpha)/\beta = x^0.$$

Less variety and economies of scale increase consumption of each good with firms relative to autarky. The equilibrium with firms yields gains from trade if the benefits of increased consumption outweigh the benefits of variety. Consumption in the equilibrium with firms is increasing in the number of consumers n.

rescaled consumption of each good under autarky. Consumption of each good with firms is greater than rescaled consumption,

$$x^* > (m^0/m)x^0,$$

if and only if the number of consumers is greater than or equal to the ratio of the number of goods with firms to the number of goods under autarky, $n > m/m^0$. This condition always holds when the number of consumers is greater than or equal to the number of firms, $n \geq m$. If the number of consumers is less than the number of firms, then the inequality holds when there is a sufficient number of consumers. For example, if the equilibrium with firms doubles the number of goods, then the condition $x^* > (m^0/m)x^0$ holds whenever there are two or more consumers. Increasing utility then implies that

$$u(x^*, \ldots, x^*) \geq u(m^0 x^0/m, \ldots, m^0 x^0/m).$$

Concave utility and symmetry imply that the consumer derives greater utility from consuming $(m^0/m)x$ units of each good when there are m goods than x units of each good when there are m^0 goods. The consumer has greater utility from consuming a given number of units divided among more goods. Thus, the consumer is better off with firms than under autarky if $n > m/m^0$. Consumers obtain gains from trade because they benefit from increased product variety and from sharing fixed costs.

With a sufficiently large number of consumers, the sufficient condition holds for there to be gains from trade, $n > m/m^0$. Also, with a sufficiently large number of consumers, consumer-owners prefer that the firm choose prices to maximize profit. This gives the following separation theorem.

> **Separation Theorem.** With many consumers, many differentiated products, and oligopoly competition between price-setting firms, consumer-owners unanimously prefer that the firm choose prices to maximize profits. Consumer-owners obtain gains from trade from owning firms in comparison to operating production for consumption under direct exchange.

3.3 The Fisher Separation Theorem

The traditional Fisher Separation Theorem depends on price-taking behavior by firms and consumers and the presence of neoclassical markets for consumer goods, investment goods, and financial capital. The Fisher Separation Theorem provides a foundation for the study of the firm's investment decisions. The firm is owned by consumers who have preferences over current and future consumption bundles. The Fisher Separation Theorem shows that the firm's investment decisions are independent of the consumption decisions of its owners. Consumer-owners receive a share of the present value of the firm's profits. Accordingly, consumer-owners unanimously agree that the firm should maximize the present value of profits.

The Fisher Separation Theorem further shows that the firm's investment decisions are independent of how the firm finances its investment. The level of investment maximizes the present value of profits, so that the efficient investment level equates the marginal return to investment to the marginal cost of investment. Investment might be financed from an initial endowment of funds or through borrowing, or in some other manner, such as issuance of securities. This will not affect the investment decision in Fisher's framework.

The Fisher Separation Theorem is planted firmly in the neoclassical tradition. It explains why firms make investment decisions and why consumers do not. It provides a foundation for the study of investor decisions in financial markets. However, the Fisher model maintains the neoclassical assumptions that markets are established and operate without costs. This section reexamines the Fisher separation analysis when there are transaction costs.

Consider a consumer who lives for two periods and consumes the same good in each period. Let c and C represent the amounts of consumption good consumed in the two periods. The consumer's preferences are represented by the separable utility function

$$(14) \qquad U(c, C) = u(c) + \frac{1}{1+\rho}u(C),$$

where ρ is the consumer's rate of time preference. The function $u(c)$ is differentiable, increasing, and concave. The consumer has an initial endowment of the consumption good equal to ω that is available in the first period and an endowment Ω that is available in the second period. There is a market for the consumption good in each period. The consumer can purchase or sell the good in either period. Let p be the price of the good in the first period and let P be the price of the good in the second period. The consumer takes the prices of the goods as given exogenously. The consumer has access to a capital market and can borrow money or save money at interest rate r, also taken as given exogenously. Suppose that the consumption good is not storable. The consumer's budget constraint expressed in present value terms is

$$(15) \qquad pc + \frac{PC}{1+r} = p\omega + \frac{P\Omega}{1+r}.$$

The consumer borrows $p(c - \omega)$ if $\omega < c$ or saves $p(\omega - c)$ if $\omega > c$. The consumer maximizes utility subject to the budget constraint, so that first and second period consumption solve

$$(16) \qquad u'(c^*) = \frac{1}{1+\rho}u'(C^*)(1+r)\frac{p}{P},$$

where $C^* = (1+r)(p/P)(\omega - c^*) + \Omega$.

Suppose that the consumer owns a firm. The firm is described by its production function as in the neoclassical model. The input to the production function is the consumption good in the first period and the output of the production function is the consumption good in the second period. The input to production is K and the output of the production process is Q. The investment level K results in a capital stock of equal amount that only provides services for a single period before being used up. Production involves a one-period lag so that output only is available in the second period. The production function is $Q = f(K)$, which is differentiable, increasing, and concave, and $f(0) = 0$.

Consider the financing and investment decisions of the firm. If the firm has no initial endowment, it can fully finance investment by borrowing money at interest rate r. The firm purchases K units of the consumption good at price p to invest in production. The firm's investment decision will be the same regardless of whether or not it has an initial endowment of the consumption good. The firm sells its output in the second period at market price P. The firm's profit in present-value terms is

$$(17) \qquad \Pi = \frac{Pf(K)}{1+r} - pK.$$

The firm's optimal investment decision equates the marginal revenue product of investment to the per-unit cost of investment,

$$(18) \qquad Pf'(K^{**}) = p(1+r).$$

The per-unit cost of investment is the purchase price of the consumption good times the cost of borrowing. The profit-maximizing investment is shown in Figure 3.4.

Consider a Robinson Crusoe economy in which the consumer owns the firm. Suppose further that there is no capital market, so that there is no possibility of borrowing or lending money. Suppose further that there is no possibility of buying or selling the consumption good. Then the consumer will manage the firm to maximize the consumer's benefit subject to the production function. The consumer solves

$$\max_{c,C} u(c) + \frac{1}{1+\rho} u(C)$$

subject to $C = f(\omega - c) + \Omega$ and $c \le \omega$. The optimal consumption c^0 solves

$$(19) \qquad \frac{u'(c^0)}{u'(C^0)/(1+\rho)} = f'(\omega - c^0),$$

where $C^0 = f(\omega - c^0) + \Omega$, if there is an interior solution $c^0 < \omega$. The solution for the Robinson Crusoe economy is represented in Figure 3.5 with investment on the x axis and second-period consumption on the y axis, letting second-period endowment Ω equal zero.

Consider now the situation in which a consumer owns the firm but both the consumer and the firm have access to product and capital markets. The firm's investment decision is independent of the preferences of its consumer-owner. The consumer-owner wishes to obtain the greatest present value of profit, so the firm

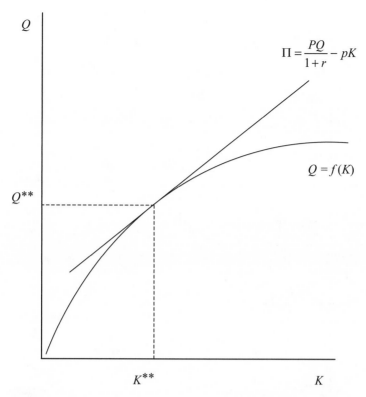

Figure 3.4. Profit-maximizing investment by a price-taking firm.

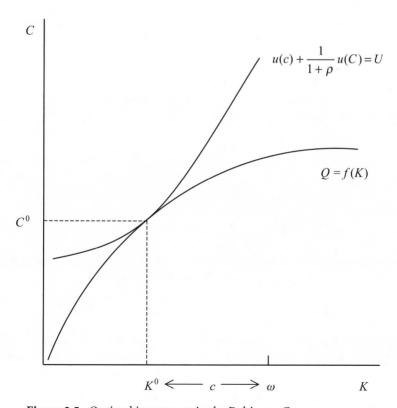

Figure 3.5. Optimal investment in the Robinson Crusoe economy.

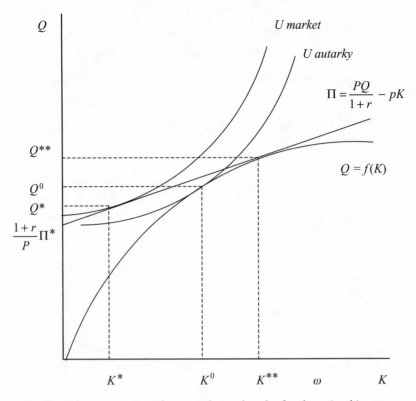

Figure 3.6. The Fisher Separation Theorem shows that the firm's optimal investment decision is independent of the preferences of a consumer-owner.

chooses the profit-maximizing investment. Then, taking the firm's profit as given, the consumer maximizes utility subject to the consumer's endowment plus the firm's profit. The consumer problem is

$$\max_{c,C} u(c) + \frac{1}{1+\rho} U(c)$$

subject to

$$(20) \qquad pc + \frac{1}{1+r} PC = p\omega + \Pi + \frac{P\Omega}{1+r}.$$

The first-order condition for the consumer's problem is the same as in equation (16), with second-period consumption equal to

$$(21) \qquad C^* = (1+r)(p/P)(\omega - c^*) + \Omega + (1+r)(1/P)\Pi.$$

The Fisher Separation Theorem demonstrates that the consumer is better off letting the firm choose the profit-maximizing investment instead of the utility-maximizing investment. This is depicted in Figure 3.6. The consumer has a consumption profile in the Robinson Crusoe economy different from that in the market economy. With initial endowment ω, the consumer invests K^0 and consumes $c^0 = \omega - K^0$ and $C^0 = f(\omega - K^0)$ in the Robinson Crusoe economy. The consumer in the market economy consumes $c^* = \omega - K^*$ and $C^* = (1 + r)(p/P)K^* + (1 + r)(1/P)\Pi^*$. The consumer in the case depicted in Figure 3.6 has a greater amount of consumption in the first period in the market economy as compared to the Robinson Crusoe economy, because the consumer uses less of the initial endowment, $K^* < K^0$. In the case shown, the consumer consumes less in the second period in the market economy as compared to the Robinson Crusoe economy, but is still better off. The benefits of additional consumption in the first period outweigh the benefits of less consumption in the second period. The additional consumption in the first period occurs because the firm purchases more of the investment good in the market than the consumer supplies to the market: $K^* < K^0 < K^{**}$. The firm invests more in the market economy than in the Robinson Crusoe economy in the case shown in Figure 3.6. The consumer supplies less of the endowment of the investment good in the market economy than in the Robinson Crusoe economy in the case shown in Figure 3.6. This illustrates how the market for goods and the market for capital investment allow the decoupling of the firm's investment decision and the consumer's saving and consumption decisions.

The Fisher Separation Theorem depends critically on the existence of three types of markets: for the investment good, for the consumption good, and for financial capital. This dependence is obscured in the standard presentation by the triple nature of the good, which can be used for investment, consumption, and financial transactions. The Fisher Separation Theorem depends also on the absence of transaction costs. Not only are markets established exogenously, but also neither the consumer nor the firm faces a bid-ask spread in their market transactions. Again, the consumer is made better off when consumer decisions and firm decisions are separated because of the presence of outside opportunities. Both the consumer and the firm realize gains from trade through their market transactions with other unobserved consumers and firms. These gains from trade are achieved without transaction costs.

The Fisher Separation Theorem explains why consumption and firm investment decisions can be separated, but does not identify an economic role for the firm. The framework is neoclassical, with the firm being fully described by its production technology. Both the consumer-owner and the firm are price takers. The firm chooses an investment and output plan taking prices as given and the consumer solves a consumption-saving problem. The decisions of the consumer and the firm are separable because both the consumer and the firm realize gains from trade with other trading partners. The consumer wants the firm to maximize its profit because the consumer is only interested in the firm as a source of income. The consumer makes consumption and saving transactions and the firm makes sales and investment transactions in established markets.

3.4 The Fisher Separation Theorem with Price-Setting Firms

This section extends the Fisher Separation Theorem to allow for price setting by firms. Consumer-owners choose to separate their saving decisions from the investment decisions of the firms that they own. The analysis applies the differentiated products approach developed in the previous section to include a capital market.

3.4.1 Profit Maximization

Consider a two-period model of the economy. There is a single good in the first period that can be consumed or invested. The good is not storable; it can either be used immediately for consumption or employed as a capital good to manufacture a second-period consumption goods.

Every firm's manufacturing process results in a unique consumption good. The second-period consumption goods differ from the first-period consumption good. To illustrate this idea, consider manufacturing processes that can produce a great variety of goods even though they have the same basic input. The assumption that there is a single capital good is made for convenience of exposition, although this assumption is not overly restrictive.

In practice, a single consumption good that also serves as a capital good can be employed to make a variety of products in the second period. For example, a person's endowment of time can be consumed in the form of leisure in the first period. The person's time can be invested in the form of human capital. The consumer's human capital then provides services in production that can be employed to manufacture an unlimited variety of goods.

As another example, suppose that the consumer has an endowment of milk. The good can be consumed in the first period. Alternatively, the good can be invested through time-consuming fermentation processes to produce many types of cheese, yoghurt, and other dairy products.

There are m second-period consumption goods j, where j is a continuous index that takes values in the interval $[0, m]$. Let q_j be the output of a second-period consumption good j and let K_j be the capital investment in the production of the second-period consumption good j. All second-period consumption goods have the same production function,

$$(22) \qquad\qquad\qquad q = \gamma K,$$

where γ is a productivity parameter.

Consumers live for two periods and make consumption and saving decisions. All consumers have the same preferences and the same endowment, which is equal to one unit of the first-period consumption good. Consumers discount second-period benefits with the subjective discount rate ρ. Consumers consume c units of the first-period consumption good and therefore save $z = 1 - c$ units. Consumers consume m goods in the second period, which can be represented for notational convenience by a composite good, C. The second-period composite good corresponds to a CES utility function with elasticity of substitution $s > 1$,

$$
(23) \qquad C = \left(\int_0^m x_j^{(s-1)/s} dj \right)^{s/(s-1)}.
$$

The consumer's two-period utility function is given by

$$
(24) \qquad U(c, C) = u(c) + \frac{1}{1+\rho} u(C).
$$

The consumer's utility function within each period is twice differentiable and strictly concave.

Consumers receive a market-determined rate of return on savings equal to r. Let z_i denote consumer i's savings. There is a continuum of consumers $[0, n]$, m of which own firms. If consumer i does not own a firm, then consumer i's second-period income is simply the return on savings, $I_i = (1 + r)z_i$. If consumer i owns a firm, then consumer i's second-period income equals profit plus the return on savings, $I_i = \Pi + (1 + r)z_i$.

The consumer's problem is to maximize utility subject to the first- and second-period budget constraints. Consider the problem of a consumer-owner. The problem solved by a consumer who does not own a firm is the same with profit equal to zero. The consumer-owner solves the constrained maximization problem

$$
\max_{c,x} U(c, C)
$$

subject to equation (23) and

$$
(25) \qquad c + z = 1,
$$

$$
(26) \qquad \int_0^m p_j x_j dj = \Pi + (1 + r)z.
$$

The consumer's problem can be decomposed into two problems and solved by backward induction. The consumer solves a first-period consumption-saving problem that determines income in the second period. Then the consumer solves a second-period consumption problem in which he allocates second-period income across the differentiated products.

The second-period problem is to maximize the value of the composite good given the consumer's second-period income I,

$$
\max_x u \left(\left(\int_0^m x_j^{(s-1)/s} dj \right)^{s/(s-1)} \right),
$$

subject to

$$
(27) \qquad \int_0^m p_j x_j dj = I.
$$

The solution to the consumer's second-period problem is

$$(28) \qquad x_i = \frac{I/p_i^s}{\int_0^m (1/p_j)^{s-1} dj}.$$

The value of the second-period composite consumption good then can be written as a product of a price index, P, and second-period income, I,

$$(29) \qquad\qquad C = IP,$$

where the price index equals

$$(30) \qquad P = \left[\int_0^m (1/p_j)^{s-1} dj \right]^{1/(s-1)}.$$

The consumer-owner's problem can be written as a function of first-period saving by substituting for the first-period budget constraint and the second-period composite good:

$$\max_z u(1-z) + \frac{1}{1+\rho} u([\Pi + (1+r)z]P).$$

The consumer-owner's choice of savings equates the marginal rate of substitution to $(1+r)$ times the price index:

$$(31) \qquad \frac{u'(1-z^*)}{u'([\Pi + (1+r)z^*]P)/(1+\rho)} = (1+r)P.$$

Consider next the consumer-owner's pricing problem. Given profit as a function of the price of good j, the consumer owner chooses the price of good j to maximize utility:

$$\max_{p_j} u(1-z^*) + \frac{1}{1+\rho} u([\Pi(p_j) + (1+r)z^*]P).$$

Consideration of the saving problem shows that the consumer-owner prefers that the firm maximize profit.

By the envelope theorem and equation (31), the marginal effect of profit on the consumer's benefit is zero at the consumer's optimal savings level. The effect of the firm's price change on the aggregate price index P is negligible. Therefore, the solution to the consumer-owner's pricing problem is simply profit maximization,

$$(32) \qquad [1/(1+\rho)]u'([\Pi(p_j) + (1+r)z^*]P)\Pi'(p_j) = 0,$$

which implies that $\Pi'(p_j) = 0$. Therefore, the firm's owners prefer that the firm choose prices that maximize profits.

Consider the equilibrium with profit-maximizing firms. Because the production function is $q = \gamma K$, the firm's profit is

$$(33) \qquad\qquad \Pi = pq - (1+r)q/\gamma.$$

With many differentiated products, the elasticity of demand equals the parameter of the CES utility function, for every good j, $\eta_j = s$. Substituting for the elasticity of demand into the firm's first-order condition for profit maximization shows that prices are equal in equilibrium:

$$(34) \qquad p^* = [s/(s-1)][(1+r)/\gamma].$$

Because prices are equal across goods, the price index equals

$$(35) \qquad P = \frac{s-1}{s}\frac{\gamma}{1+r}m^{1/(s-1)}.$$

The quantities of goods produced also are equal, so that $q_j = q$ for all j. With m firms and n consumers, the investment-savings constraint is $mq/\gamma = nz^*$, so that the output of each good equals

$$(36) \qquad q = nz^*\gamma/m.$$

Substituting for the price and output into the firm's profit function gives

$$(37) \qquad \Pi = [1/(s-1)](1+r)nz^*/m.$$

Each firm earns positive profits at the competitive equilibrium.

3.4.2 Gains from Trade

It remains to determine conditions under which the consumer-owner obtains gains from trade by operating the firm independently. Suppose that under autarky, the consumer can only produce a single good. Then gains from trade will depend on the benefits of product variety.

Under autarky, the consumer chooses consumption in the first period to maximize net benefits:

$$\max_{c,C} u(c) + \frac{1}{1+\rho}u(C) \text{ subject to } c + C/\gamma = 1.$$

The consumer's first-order condition equates the marginal rate of substitution to the productivity parameter:

$$(38) \qquad \frac{u'(c^0)}{u'(\gamma(1-c^0))/(1+\rho)} = \gamma.$$

In the market equilibrium with a firm, consumption of the composite good in the second period equals $C = IP$. Consumption of the composite good can be written as a function of first-period savings, z:

$$C = P[\Pi + (1+r)z].$$

Solving for first-period savings, z, as a function of the composite good implies that

$$z = [1/(1+r)](C/P - \Pi).$$

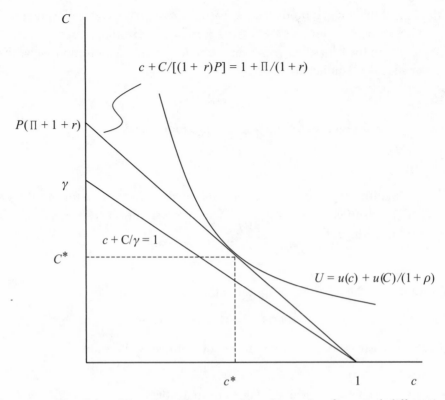

Figure 3.7. The Fisher Separation Theorem with price-setting firms and differentiated products.

Substitute for z in the consumer's first-period budget constraint, $c + z = 1$, to obtain a budget constraint with first-period consumption and the second-period composite good. The consumer's problem can then be recast as a choice of consumption in the two periods. The consumer chooses c and C to solve the following problem:

$$(39) \quad \max_{c,C} u(c) + \frac{1}{1+\rho} u(C) \text{ subject to } c + \frac{C}{(1+r)P} = 1 + \frac{\Pi}{1+r}.$$

The equilibrium with firms can be compared to autarky using Figure 3.7. The figure shows the consumer-owner's choice of first-period consumption and the second-period composite good when there are firms. The budget constraints are the only difference between autarky and ownership of the firm. The y-axis intercept of the budget constraint under autarky is simply the productivity parameter, γ. The y-axis intercept of the budget constraint when the consumer owns the firm equals $P(\Pi + 1 + r)$. The consumer obtains gains from trade from owning the firm if the y-axis intercept increases: $P(\Pi + 1 + r) > \gamma$.

Substituting for the price index, the y-axis intercept with ownership of the firm equals

$$P(\Pi + 1 + r) = \frac{s-1}{s}\frac{\gamma}{1+r}m^{1/(s-1)}(\Pi + 1 + r).$$

Because firms are profitable in equilibrium,

$$P(\Pi + 1 + r) > \frac{s-1}{s}\gamma m^{1/(s-1)}.$$

The right-hand side is greater than or equal to the parameter γ when the number of goods, m, is sufficiently large. Because each consumer owns a firm, the number of goods is bounded by the number of consumers, so there must be a sufficient number of consumers. A sufficient condition for the consumer to obtain gains from trade by operating a firm is for the number of goods to satisfy

$$m \geq [s/(s-1)]^{s-1}.$$

For example, if $s = 2$, there must be at least two goods for the consumer to obtain gains from trade. If $s = 3/2$, two goods are sufficient for the consumer to obtain gains from trade. With many goods, the condition is easily satisfied.

The Fisher Separation Theorem holds when investment is used to produce a variety of goods. When there are many consumption goods in the second period, consumer-owners will want the firm that they own to maximize profit. With a sufficient number of goods, consumer-owners will be better off with the firms participating in the market than they are producing under autarky. This extends the Fisher Separation Theorem to an economy in which firms set prices.

> **Fisher Separation Theorem with Price-Setting Firms.** With investment in the production of many differentiated goods, the investment objectives of firms are separate from the consumption and saving objectives of consumer-owners.

3.5 Conclusions

Firms maximize profit, generally acting independent of the consumption objectives of their consumer-owners, whether the firms are publicly traded or privately held. The separation of consumer objectives from firm objectives does not occur because firms are engaged in production, but rather because consumer-owners benefit from profit maximization. The separation theorem is valuable for our later discussion of the entrepreneur because the entrepreneur's reward from establishing the firm reflects the value of the firm.

The discussion in the chapter extended the separation theorems to a more general economic setting and showed that the firm's owners want the firm to maximize profit. The separation theorem applies to economic situations that are of interest to the theory of the firm. The firm's objectives are distinct from those of its owners when firms play an enhanced role in the economy by adjusting prices and intermediating transactions between buyers and sellers. The firm's objectives also are distinct from those of its owners when price-setting firms make investment decisions. The separation of the firm's objectives from those of its owners is fundamental to the economic role of the firm.

The analysis in the chapter can be extended in two ways. First, the separation theorem should apply for many types of gains from trade. The analysis shows that firms generate gains from trade due to product variety and economies of scale. Firms will have objectives separate from those of their owners when gains from trade result from other sources, including differences in consumer marginal rates of substitution, differences in marginal rates of technical substitution of inputs, and differences between consumer marginal rates of substitution and marginal rates of transformation. Separation of objectives also results from sharing the costs of producing public goods, allocating common property resources, and mitigating positive and negative externalities. The separation theorem should apply in comparison to direct exchange in general. The discussion in the chapter examined gains from trade relative to autarky. The firm potentially provides gains from trade relative to direct exchange and consumer organizations. These types of gains from trade are examined further in the following chapters.

PART II

THE ENTREPRENEUR IN EQUILIBRIUM

4

The Entrepreneur

Pierre Omidyar set up a Web site to help his fiancée Pamela collect and trade Pez candy dispensers, which were colorful toys molded in the form of cartoon characters. He launched an auction Web site as a sole proprietorship and it soon sparked the interest of many different types of collectors and hobbyists. The company incorporated as demand flourished and it expanded its scope. Omidyar renamed the company eBay, and a year later Omidyar relinquished his position as CEO when the company went public. The company diversified its market-making activities as it grew to become "the world's online marketplace."[1] Pierre Omidyar's founding of eBay illustrates the role of entrepreneurs in establishing firms.

Entrepreneurs play a central role in the economy because they are the prime movers – the makers of firms. A consumer becomes an entrepreneur by deciding to establish a firm, so entrepreneurs are endogenous to the economy. The question – Why do firms exist? – is closely connected to another question – Why do consumers choose to become entrepreneurs? Answering this question provides fundamental insights into the theory of the firm. By examining the decisions of the entrepreneur, this chapter provides an analysis of the economic role of the entrepreneur.

The general theory of the firm places the entrepreneur at the center of microeconomic analysis. The entrepreneur engages in transactions that are needed to establish firms. In turn, firms create and operate markets and organizations. Firms manage transactions through markets and organizations, which ultimately results in equilibrium prices and allocation of resources. Thus, the actions of the entrepreneur are essential forces that drive the economy toward equilibrium. The entrepreneur's activities lead to the establishment of most economic institutions.

This chapter presents a dynamic theory of the entrepreneur. The theory has two critical events: the decision of the individual to become an entrepreneur and the establishment of the firm. Initially, an individual consumer chooses whether or

---

1 Academy of Achievement, http://www.achievement.org/autodoc/page/omi0bio-1.

not to become an entrepreneur based on market opportunities and individual preferences, endowments, and other characteristics. The consumer is an entrepreneur
during the period in which he devotes effort and resources to establishing a firm.
If the entrepreneur succeeds in establishing a firm, he then becomes an owner of
the firm. The entrepreneur receives the residual returns and the residual rights of
control to the firm once it is established. The value of the ownership rights provides
the basis for the returns to the entrepreneur.

To describe the change in the individual's role from entrepreneur to owner,
I introduce the concept of the *foundational shift*. Before the foundational shift
occurs, the objectives of the startup enterprise cannot be separated from those of
the entrepreneur. The startup enterprise is not a fully formed firm for this reason.
After the foundational shift occurs, the firm is established and the entrepreneur
becomes an owner of the firm. Because a firm's objectives are separate from those
of its owners, the entrepreneur's objectives become distinct from those of the firm
once it is established. The foundational shift is important because it helps to explain
the entrepreneur's activities. Before the foundational shift takes place, the financial, labor, and technology decisions of the startup enterprise are interconnected
with the consumption, human capital, and innovation decisions of the individual
entrepreneur.

The dynamic theory of the entrepreneur considers the individual consumer's
decision whether or not to become an entrepreneur. The individual chooses to
become an entrepreneur only if he expects that establishing a firm improves economic efficiency relative to competing alternatives. The entrepreneur faces three
types of competition. In type I competition, entrepreneurs compete with each
other to establish firms. The many personal attributes of entrepreneurs that are
critical include preferences, income, wealth, judgment, knowledge, ability, ideas,
and opportunity costs. In type II competition, entrepreneurs compete with consumer organizations. Entrepreneurs will be successful only if the newly established
firms create efficiencies of intermediated exchange that consumers cannot achieve
through direct exchange. In type III competition, entrepreneurs compete with
established firms, because the entrepreneurial startup must provide incremental
economic benefits that cannot be achieved by expanding or restructuring incumbent firms. To add value, the entrepreneur must launch a firm that can offer
scarce capacity, more effective organizations, better market transactions, more efficient technologies, or differentiated goods and services. Successful entry generally
requires innovations in transactions, business methods, technologies, and products. The entrepreneur competes in the market by proxy because the entrepreneur
becomes an owner after the firm is established.

The chapter concludes with an overview of the classical literature on the
entrepreneur. The study of the entrepreneur has undergone cycles of revival and
neglect throughout the history of economic thought. At the dawn of the field of economics, Richard Cantillon (1755) introduced the entrepreneur in 1732 in his path-
breaking treatise. Jean-Baptiste Say (1841, 1852) provided the first comprehensive

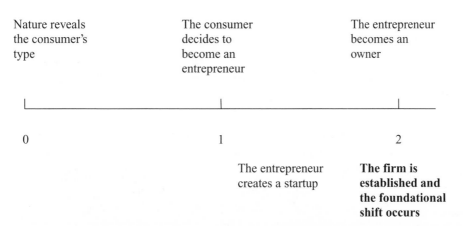

Figure 4.1. A dynamic theory of the entrepreneur.

discussion of the entrepreneur in economic analysis, emphasizing the effects of the entrepreneur's reputation, judgment, and risk-bearing on profit. Frank Knight's (1971) discussion of risk, uncertainty, and profit addresses the supply of and demand for entrepreneurship. Joseph Schumpeter (1997, p. 75) identifies entrepreneurship as "the fundamental phenomenon of economic development."

4.1 A Dynamic Theory of the Entrepreneur

An *entrepreneur* is a consumer who establishes a firm. The definition of the firm given previously provides content to this straightforward definition of the entrepreneur. Recall that the firm is a transaction institution whose objectives are distinct from those of its owners. The entrepreneur creates the startup enterprise as a means of establishing a firm. During the period of entrepreneurship, the startup generally does not fit the definition of a firm because its objectives cannot be separated from those of the entrepreneur.

Entrepreneurship is a dynamic process with two phases. First, the individual consumer decides whether or not to become an entrepreneur. Second, the entrepreneur makes a set of economic decisions needed to establish a firm. The entrepreneur does not become an owner until the firm has been established successfully. This decision framework represents a dynamic theory of the entrepreneur. The timeline for the dynamics of the entrepreneur is illustrated in Figure 4.1.

4.1.1 The Entrepreneur in the Contemporary Economy

The entrepreneur is at the heart of the theory of the firm because his actions and motivation help to explain why firms exist. The entrepreneur's decisions, costs, and profits are fundamental to the development of the theory of the firm. Although many individuals contribute to the value of a firm, including investors, inventors, employees, managers, suppliers, and partners, these contributors are rewarded directly for their contributions through return to capital, royalties for technology, wages, salaries, factor payments, and shared returns. These payments are deducted from the firm's earnings. The entrepreneur's reward is based on the economic value of the firm.

Entrepreneurs are major contributors to economic growth, development, and prosperity; see Audretsch et al. (2006), Schramm (2006b), and Baumol et al. (2007). Entrepreneurs are responsible for a large share of technological innovation in products and production processes, driving economic transformation and international trade.[2] Entrepreneurs establish new forms of organizations and employ new types of business methods. Understanding the fundamental contributions of entrepreneurs is essential for formulating economic policies that do not restrict productive entrepreneurs.

Classical economics identifies the firm with the entrepreneur; that is, the firm and the entrepreneur are one and the same. This approach has some merit because the entrepreneur's objectives are closely tied to those of the startup enterprise. However, the entrepreneur and the firm are distinct economic actors. Once the foundational shift takes place, the firm has its own objectives that are separate from those of its owners. This provides an important dividing line between the classical literature and the theory of the firm.

The traditional view of the entrepreneur and the firm as a single entity results from accurate observation of commerce up to the mid-nineteenth century. Individuals established enterprises as means for them to carry out their own business activities. Merchants, manufacturers, and farmers tended to own and manage the enterprises that they established and were closely identified with those enterprises. Founders who wished to extend the life of the business often relied on family involvement. The importance of the family in the establishment and operation of businesses is illustrated by David Landes (2006), who studies great dynasties in a variety of sectors, including banking and automobiles.

The entrepreneur establishes a firm to accomplish an economic objective. Although all firms involve market mechanisms and organizational structures, each firm's activities involve different combinations of these activities. Some examples are helpful for illustrating the main concepts. Jeff Bezos left a successful Wall Street career to establish an online bookstore based in Seattle that became the virtual marketplace Amazon.com. The firm in turn created a vast set of online markets for a wide range of products. These products were grouped into such broad categories as (1) books, music, and movies, (2) toys and video games, (3) consumer electronics, (4) computer and office, (5) tools and automotive, (6) food and household, (7) home and garden, (8) clothing and jewelry, (9) health and beauty, (10) kids and baby, and (11) sports and fitness. Within these broad categories,

---

2 Spulber (2007) examines entrepreneurial strategies for the international business. Khanna (2008) discusses entrepreneurs in India, China, and other emerging economies.

there are over forty product categories containing many thousands of products from many manufacturers. These represented thousands of markets where Amazon brought together buyers and sellers. Amazon served tens of millions of buyers and over one million sellers. Amazon also offered startup sellers an alternative to "heavy lifting" by providing Web hosting and transaction intermediation.

Entrepreneurs Bob Noyce and Gordon Moore established Intel, which has a complex organization. About forty years after its founding, the firm's organization had more than 90,000 employees. The firm was structured around five groups: three groups were based on the company's technology platforms for mobility, the digital enterprise, and the digital home, another group was concerned with digital applications in healthcare, and another group dealt with worldwide distribution. The firm had a worldwide network of R&D laboratories; the firm's researchers focused on advanced computing, communications, and wireless technologies. The firm operated manufacturing plants for producing microprocessors, component assembly, and quality testing and conducted research on manufacturing processes.

Practically all firms are established by entrepreneurs, whether in retail, wholesale, finance, manufacturing, agriculture, mining, utilities, construction, transportation, information, services, health care, or arts and entertainment. Some firms are set up by other firms or result from spin-offs, but even here individual entrepreneurs usually initiate the formation of the new firm. Some firms are the result of government privatization, although entrepreneurs often establish the new firm by acquisition of public assets.

Because there are millions of firms, there is no shortage of information on individual entrepreneurs, especially on the most successful ones. William Crapo ("Billy") Durant of Durant-Dort Carriage Company, Flint, Michigan, after taking control of the Buick Motor Company, established General Motors in 1908. Sam Walton set up shop in Arkansas, and built the retail giant, Wal-Mart, one of the largest companies in the world. Michael Dell, founder of Dell Computer, began by ordering parts and assembling computers in his college dormitory room. The idea for what became the leading global freight company, FedEx, started with founder Frederick W. Smith's undergraduate economics term paper on a night-time delivery service. Richard Branson set up a mail-order company to sell recordings. With the earnings from producing a hit record he built an empire of 200 companies that includes an airline, mobile communications, financial services, Internet, rail, and hotels. Liu Chuanzhi and 10 colleagues at the Chinese Academy of Sciences started a computer company in a small bungalow near the Academy that became Lenovo computers and acquired IBM's personal computer division.

Debra J. Fields ran her own bakery in Palo Alto, California and grew the company into the retail chain Mrs. Fields Cookies. Her description of what it means to be an entrepreneur illustrates the possibilities:

> Entrepreneurship sees no boundaries, no limits and no discrimination. Entrepreneurship requires vision, passion, perseverance and boundless energy.

> It allows dreamers, inventors, scientists, artists and engineers . . . any and
> all . . . that share a common belief that they can make a world of difference
> and refuse to accept can't as a possibility. Entrepreneurship has no age or time
> limits . . . it thrives on hope and inspiration. Those who choose to participate
> can only make the world a better place.[3]

Firms are not part of the economy's initial endowment. Rather, they arise from the efforts and imagination of the entrepreneur.

Beyond the stories of extremely successful entrepreneurs, there are millions of startups per year. The U.S. Small Business Administration estimates that there were over 612,000 new firms with employees in the year 2000 (United States Small Business Administration, 2001). Reynolds (1997, 2000) estimates that about 4% of the U.S. labor force participates in the entrepreneurial process (with the labor force exceeding 110 million people). Reynolds et al. (2004) estimate that in the year 2000 there were over 11.8 million "nascent entrepreneurs" and about 6.5 million startup efforts in progress. Reynolds (1997, p. 460) finds that over 80% of those trying to establish a firm are self-employed in an existing business or are part-time or full-time employees.

Reynolds (2000) reviews the National Panel Study of U.S. Business Startups, which provides an extensive and detailed statistical overview of new businesses and the personal characteristics of entrepreneurs. The personal information that is studied includes all of the usual demographic data such as age, sex, ethnic background, education, and household income. In addition, interviews and questionnaires are used to obtain information about the entrepreneur's motivation, expectations, knowledge, career experiences, competitive strategy, decision-making style, and risk preferences.

4.1.2 The Economic Contribution of the Entrepreneur

The entrepreneur has played practically no part in neoclassical economics.[4] There are two main reasons for the absence of the entrepreneur in microeconomics. First, firms already are given exogenously, so that no entrepreneur is needed to establish them. Second, institutions of exchange such as markets also are given exogenously in standard models. In neoclassical general equilibrium and partial equilibrium models, markets attain equilibrium by means of the invisible auctioneer, so that

---

3 http://www.societyofentrepreneurs.com/members/bio.asp?ID=113.

4 William Baumol (2006) points out that the entrepreneur is mentioned virtually never in the modern theory of the firm. The entrepreneur also tends to be absent from economics courses. Dan Johansson (2004) studies Ph.D. programs and textbooks in economics and finds that required Ph.D. courses in microeconomics, macroeconomics, and industrial organization and the related textbooks completely exclude the concept of the entrepreneur. Although the study was performed in Sweden, the textbooks are the ones used in practically any Ph.D. program. Johansson concludes that "there is a need for economics Ph.D. training based on theories that incorporate entrepreneurship and institutions." The present discussion attempts to redress this oversight.

firms are not needed to create or manage markets. Neoclassical economics is silent on entrepreneurs because they serve no purpose, because firms are confined to production.

The general perception that it is difficult, if not impossible, to represent entrepreneurs in economic models appears to be supported by neoclassical theory. As Baumol (1993, p. 12) observes, "Virtually all theoretical firms are entrepreneur-less – the prince of Denmark has been expunged from the discussion of *Hamlet*." Baumol finds this absence "not difficult to explain" because the "theoretical firm must choose among alternative values for a small number of rather well-defined variables: price output, perhaps advertising outlay." Thus, the management of the firm maximizes profit but "There is no room for enterprise or initiative."[5] Baumol (1993) suggests that there may be some hope in studying the relative pay-offs to alternative entrepreneurial activities and the entrepreneurial role in allocating resources.[6]

Schumpeter first raised the issue of economic modeling of the entrepreneur. The entrepreneur has no place in a deterministic economic equilibrium model without uncertainty because there is no consideration of the entrepreneur's risk-taking activities. For Schumpeter, if equilibrium is described as a timeless, deterministic outcome, then the entrepreneur cannot play a part. In Schumpeter's view, the entrepreneur only disrupts such an equilibrium. He suggests that the entrepreneur, by bringing an innovation to the economy, ends the existing equilibrium. This is what Schumpter termed the process of "creative destruction." After the entrepreneur's disruption has occurred, there being no other sources of uncertainty, the economy may once again regain its equilibrium.

The issues raised by Schumpeter do not pose insurmountable problems for economic theorists. Economic models that incorporate incomplete information, uncertainty, and dynamic adjustment are commonplace. Players that react to or anticipate random shocks are standard in decision theory and game theory. An entrepreneur, upon observing the occurrence of a scientific invention, which is by its very nature unexpected, discerns the economic value of introducing such an invention into the market place. The model can be viewed as being out of equilibrium, in the sense of Schumpeter, as long as the invention is known but not introduced. The model can be characterized as being in equilibrium once the entrepreneur introduces the invention and collects a reward for the innovation. The economy moves to a new equilibrium that includes the new production processes or products that result from the innovation.

Kirzner (1973, p. 81) states that entrepreneurship in Schumpeter is "disruption of the circular flow, the creation of disequilibrium out of equilibrium." Kirzner

5 Baumol (1993, pp. 12–13); see also Baumol (1968).
6 There is some controversy over whether the actions of an entrepreneur can be described adequately in an equilibrium economic model. Many question whether economic theory can do justice to the creativity, leadership, energy, and courage that many real-life entrepreneurs exhibit. However, the personal attributes and social contributions of entrepreneurs and other outstanding individuals can be addressed empirically.

argues that "it is entrepreneurial alertness to unnoticed opportunities which creates the tendency toward the even circular flow of equilibrium." These positions of Schumpeter and Kirzner are consistent in a dynamic setting in which entrepreneurial innovations disrupt existing market outcomes and help to realize new market outcomes. However, the function of entrepreneurs is far more complex and far-reaching than innovation.

In the general theory of the firm, the entrepreneur plays a pivotal role in economic equilibrium. The entrepreneur's decision as to whether or not to establish a firm is itself part of the economic equilibrium. The entrepreneur chooses to establish a firm only if doing so creates sufficient economic value. The entrepreneur finds it worthwhile to incur the costs of establishing a firm only if the value of the firm exceeds those costs.

When firms make markets, entrepreneurs are needed to provide the market-making mechanism. The entrepreneur changes the equilibrium market outcome by establishing a new firm. Once established, the new firm creates markets and chooses prices. The new firm competes with direct exchange between consumers, with other newly established firms, and with existing firms. The result is a change in the market structure due to the entry of the new firm and possibly the exit of competitors. The newly established firm has a fundamental effect on economic equilibrium. Because firms intermediate transactions, they foster the resulting market equilibrium. Therefore, by establishing firms, entrepreneurs create mechanisms that generate market equilibria. The entrepreneur establishes firms because he notices opportunities to create a new market equilibrium.

The entrepreneur's activities are necessary for the economy to perform efficiently. Although entrepreneurs implement innovations that disrupt existing prices and products, the entrepreneur contributes to the economic equilibrium. The entrepreneur's actions are themselves part of the economic equilibrium. Further, by establishing firms, entrepreneurs help the economy to reach a new equilibrium. After being founded by entrepreneurs, firms create markets and organizations that generate equilibrium transactions.

The economic contribution of the entrepreneur can be deduced from the observation that practically all existing firms were established by entrepreneurs, whether in retail, wholesale, finance, manufacturing, agriculture, mining, utilities, construction, transportation, information, services, health care, or arts and entertainment. Firms occasionally establish other firms through joint ventures, divestitures, and initial investment, contributing to the value of the parent firm. Managers and employees who help the firm establish new enterprises are known as intrapreneurs. Governments also establish firms by privatizing public enterprises, in some cases by selling assets to entrepreneurs.[7]

---

7 Some privatizations of government enterprises involve selling shares to investors, which occurs somewhat more frequently in countries undergoing a transition from socialist to market economies.

Casson (1982, 2003) describes the entrepreneur as a coordinator and middleman. Casson (1982, p. 84) identifies various *obstacles to trade* including no contact between buyer and seller, no knowledge of reciprocal wants, no agreement over price, need to exchange goods and pay taxes, no confidence in product descriptions, and no confidence that restitution will be made for default. Casson (1982, p. 84) argues that the firm provides *market-making* activities to address each of these: contact making via search or advertising, specification and communication of the trade to each party, negotiation, transport and administration, monitoring of quality, and enforcement. Casson (1982, p. 97) points out that

> For information flows as complex as those required for the operation of a market, social convention is usually unable to provide the degree of structure required. Greater sophistication is called for and this necessitates the use of purpose-built organizations. Among these purpose-built organizations are market-making firms.

Casson (1982, Chapter 9) concludes that the entrepreneur "specializes in providing market-making services." He builds the firm as a "market-making organization" to reduce the transaction costs of intermediation.

Highlighting the critical role of entrepreneurs in intermediation, Casson (2003, p. 15) observes that the "rationale of the market-making firm is that it produces trade at minimum cost." He notes further that "Compared with the material-transforming firm, the market-making firm is of much greater significance" for economic analysis (2003, p. 15); see also Casson (1997).

The definition of the entrepreneur as someone who establishes a firm serves to narrow the wide range of conflicting definitions of the entrepreneur in the law, economics, and management literatures. These definitions are often very broad and fail to distinguish entrepreneurship from practically any other economic activity. For example, Shane (2003, p. 4) defines entrepreneurship as "an activity that involves exploitation of opportunities."[8] Yet practically any economic actor, including a consumer or a firm, seeks to exploit economic opportunities. The entrepreneur is someone who exploits economic opportunities by establishing a firm.

Some researchers define the entrepreneur as someone who is self-employed. This does not provide a useful definition of the entrepreneur. As Lazear (2004, 2005) correctly points out, self-employment is quite different from someone who "responds affirmatively to the question, 'I am among those who initially established the business.'" The self-employment choice has value in studying labor market data. However, the self-employment category includes independent contractors and workers for hire, but misses some types of individuals who establish firms.

---

8 Shane emphasizes that entrepreneurship involves interaction between the individual characteristics of entrepreneurs and the set of market opportunities and stresses the effects on opportunities of changes in technology, regulation and public policy, and social and demographic conditions.

It is important to distinguish the entrepreneur from the innovator. Entrepreneurs are innovators in the sense that they commercialize inventions by establishing a firm. Not all innovators are entrepreneurs because some innovators may choose to commercialize inventions by licensing the inventions to existing firms. The entrepreneur chooses to innovate specifically by establishing a firm that embodies the invention. Entrepreneurs need not be inventors because they may commercialize the inventions of others. Although entrepreneurs are innovators, their commercialization activities may replicate certain aspects of incumbent firms or firms that have exited the market. Entrepreneurs can engage in such replicative entry if there is additional need for productive capacity in the market. Innovative entry generates rents even when capacity is scarce, because firms with lower costs or better products earn additional profits. When capacity growth outruns demand growth, innovative entry becomes necessary, as firms can require a competitive advantage to survive a shakeout.

There are many other uses of the term "entrepreneur" that should be distinguished from the usage of the term in the theory of the firm. David Pozen (2008) observes that "we are all entrepreneurs now" and notes the increasingly frequent use of the term to designate all kinds of activities, including "social entrepreneurs," "public policy entrepreneurs," "norm entrepreneurs," and "moral entrepreneurs." These terms emphasize the creativity of individuals and the creation of innovations in society and public policy. Individuals such as "social entrepreneurs" help to establish social institutions. For our purposes, we restrict the use of the term entrepreneur to individuals who establish firms.

4.1.3 The Entrepreneur's Decision

Entrepreneurs are endogenous to the economy because consumers decide whether or not to become entrepreneurs based on their individual characteristics and the potential rewards from establishing a firm. Entrepreneurs can establish a firm, either acting alone or in concert with other entrepreneurs.

In the theory of the firm, the exogenous data of the model are the characteristics of consumers. Consumers have preferences over consumption bundles. They own endowments of goods and services. They own production technologies and can carry out manufacturing using those technologies. Consumers also possess ideas, capabilities, skills, blueprints, transaction methods, and other types of intellectual property. Consumers can invent new technologies and can exchange them. Consumers also have the capacity to perform various activities, acting as inventors, investors, managers, and workers.

Consumers choose to become entrepreneurs based on two primary considerations: personal characteristics and market conditions. Individual characteristics of the consumer that affect the decision to start a firm include the consumer's preferences and endowments. Preferences are important because the entrepreneur may derive greater satisfaction from the creative process of establishing a firm in contrast to management positions or various types of employment.

Consumers act rationally and purposefully in making the decision to establish firms. The consumer weighs the net benefits of entrepreneurship against alternative activities. The consumer takes into account the expected costs of entrepreneurship and the expected benefits of establishing a firm. The consumer weighs alternative activities such as employment by an existing firm, self-employment as an independent contractor, education, and leisure.

The entrepreneur establishes the firm as an instrument to achieve a desired economic objective. As with any type of instrument, the firm augments the abilities and capacity of the entrepreneur who creates it. The consumer becomes an entrepreneur because establishing a firm allows the consumer to accomplish something that otherwise could not be done as effectively. The entrepreneur seeks to commercialize an invention by establishing a firm.

Von Mises (1998, p. 255), in his classic analysis of human action, states that in economic theory, "Entrepreneur means acting man in regard to the changes occurring in the data of the market."[9] For von Mises (1998, p. 259), "The market process is entirely a resultant of human action." He (1998, p. 312) observes that "The market is a social body; it is the foremost social body. The market phenomena are social phenomena."

Individual members of the society establish firms to facilitate, formalize, and enhance economic relationships. The social and economic origins of the firm should be reflected in the structure of the economic theory of the firm. Rather than being given exogenously, firms arise endogenously because consumers choose to become entrepreneurs. Consumer characteristics are the givens and firms are the result of consumer decisions. The existence of firms, their purpose, and their organizational structure depend on the decisions of the entrepreneur.

The consumer's endowments have a major effect on the entrepreneurship decision. The entrepreneur's wealth affects his ability to self-finance the new venture and to attract capital investment. The individual's endowment includes personal capabilities, interests, creativity, education, training, and business judgment. The consumer's endowment also includes intellectual property, such as patents, copyrights, industrial processes, brands, and trademarks. In addition, the consumer's access to information about market opportunities is critical to making business decisions.

---

9 Von Mises (1998, p. 255) distinguishes the usage of the term entrepreneur as establishing firms from the more commonplace usage by economists and others as "those who are especially eager to profit from adjusting production to the expected changes in conditions, those who have more initiative, more venturesomeness, and a quicker eye than the crowd, the pushing and promoting pioneers of economic improvement." Von Mises (1998, p. 255) suggests that the notion of the entrepreneur as a highly eager person is actually the narrower one and should perhaps be called "promoter." Owners and managers can have entrepreneurial qualities.

The consumer's decision to become an entrepreneur has been studied as a self-employment decision. Kihlstrom and Laffont (1979, 1982) assume that establishing firms is risky in comparison to working for others at a fixed wage. In a general equilibrium setting, they show that consumers who choose to become entrepreneurs are those who are the least risk-averse. Lucas (1978) shows how the size distribution of business firms may be based on an underlying distribution of managerial talent across individuals. Jovanovic (1994) considers the allocation of individuals to jobs when managerial and labor skills are correlated and Jovanovic (1982) considers the evolution of an industry when firms gradually learn about their efficiency, which has implications for entrepreneurs who gradually discover their capabilities.

Following Manne's (1965) suggestion that the size distribution of firms reflects the allocation of resources to managers based on their differences in abilities, Lucas considers how individuals move from the position of an employee to that of a manager. Increases in national income increase the average size of firms, which depends on the ratio of managers to employees. Holtz-Eakin et al. (1994a, 1994b) show that the entrepreneur's endowment matters; see also Evans and Jovanovic (1989), and Blanchflower and Oswald (1998). Evans and Leighton (1989) find that wealth increases the likelihood of a switch to self-employment. Holmes and Schmitz (1990, 1995, 1996) consider the role of the entrepreneur in business turnovers.

The self-employment decision of entrepreneurs provides useful insights into the entrepreneur's decision process. However, establishing a firm is much more than a labor market choice. The consumer entrepreneurship decision addresses opportunities in the market for firms. The founding entrepreneur realizes the returns from his judgment and innovation in addition to his work in setting up the firm. Large-scale enterprises such as General Motors, Amazon.com, or Intel provide employment for many, not just self-employment for their founder. The rewards from entrepreneurship reflect the firm's contribution to economic efficiency.

Market opportunities for new firms are crucial to the consumer's decision to become an entrepreneur. Industrial structure, taxes, and technological change affect the entrepreneur's decision; see Blau (1987) for a general equilibrium model of self-employment. The interaction between the entrepreneur's characteristics and the menu of market opportunities recalls a traditional framework in the field of management strategy. The manager of the firm examines the firm's opportunities and competitive threats. The manager then considers the firm's strengths and weaknesses. The manager formulates a competitive strategy by making the best match between the firm's characteristics and the choice of opportunities.[10] The

---

10 The notion that both external analysis and internal analysis are vital for strategy making draws upon Kenneth R. Andrews (1971, p. 48), who wrote that "Economic strategy will be seen as the best match between qualification and opportunity that positions a firm in its product/market environment." Andrews stated that "Determination of a suitable strategy for a company begins in identifying the opportunities and risks in its environment" (p. 48). Andrews observed that "opportunism without competence is a path to fairyland" (p. 70). Bourgeois (1985), citing

entrepreneur makes a similar choice by making the best match between his own personal characteristics and market opportunities. The entrepreneur establishes a firm that involves the best combination of his personal talents and endowments and the choice of available opportunities.

The consumer who chooses to become an entrepreneur acts in pursuit of entrepreneurial profit. The reward of the entrepreneur is his share of the economic value of the firm. In turn, the firm's economic value depends on its provision of transaction efficiencies that the economy cannot attain otherwise. Accordingly, consumers choose to establish firms if and only if doing so increases transaction benefits net of transaction costs in comparison with the best institutional alternative.

4.2 The Entrepreneur's Decisions and the Foundational Shift

The consumer is an entrepreneur only during the time period that he endeavors to establish a firm. Before the firm is established, the entrepreneur creates and operates a startup enterprise. Upon the establishment of the firm, the entrepreneur becomes an owner. As Schumpeter (1997) points out, being an entrepreneur is "not a lasting condition." After the firm is established and the entrepreneur becomes an owner, the individual can continue his association and keep working to develop the firm. Alternatively, the consumer can divest his ownership share. After the foundational shift takes place, the firm operates as a separate enterprise with distinct objectives.

4.2.1 The Entrepreneur's Decisions

The key to understanding the entrepreneur's decisions is that the entrepreneur's objectives tend to be interconnected with those of the startup. As a result, the entrepreneurial startup enterprise does not satisfy the separation criterion. Therefore, the startup differs from an established firm.

An important implication of the absence of separation of objectives is that the startup enterprise may not maximize profit. The constraints faced by the entrepreneur place limits on the actions of the startup. The entrepreneur may not have sufficient funds for the startup to undertake the profit-maximizing level of investment. The entrepreneur's financial constraints can cause the firm to be established more quickly or more slowly than the pace that would maximize profit. The incomplete separation of the entrepreneur's objectives from those of the startup implies that the entrepreneur's personal preferences impact the startup's business decisions.

The close ties between the entrepreneur's consumption objectives and the objectives of the startup enterprise do not allow the separation of ownership and

Andrews, describes "strategic fit" as follows: "The central tenet in strategic management is that a match between environmental conditions and organizational capabilities and resources is critical to performance, and that a strategist's job is to find and create this match."

control. The entrepreneur's choice of management strategy – rate of growth, what markets to serve, what suppliers to contract with – reflects the limitations and constraints imposed by the entrepreneur's personal consumption decisions.

The entrepreneur must devise a business plan to guide the new enterprise and to attract investment. Typically, the business plan includes the entrepreneur's vision of the business and a description of the objectives of the new enterprise. The business plan also features a strategic analysis of the markets that will be served by the firm and the competitors that will be encountered. The entrepreneur formulates a competitive strategy and examines potential sources of competitive advantages for the new business.

The planning process also includes an examination of what production technology will be used, what types of products and services the business expects to provide, and how the firm will market, sell, and distribute its offerings. The business plan features a preliminary organizational structure for the new enterprise. The business plan includes projected costs and revenues and a financial analysis of the capital resources needed to establish the firm. The entrepreneur usually bears the costs of preparing the business plan.

The entrepreneur determines when to create the startup, how long the period of entrepreneurship will be, and when the firm will be established. These decisions depend on the nature of competition the entrepreneur faces and on changing market opportunities. They are affected by the entrepreneur's personal resources, including financial capital, human capital, and intellectual property. The interconnection between the entrepreneur's objectives and those of the startup enterprise has important implications in three main areas: investment, employment, and innovation.

Investment

The entrepreneur's investment decisions are combined with his consumption-savings decisions. These objectives are closely connected because the entrepreneur contributes his own money to financing the startup, along with family and friends. The entrepreneur's consumption objectives are closely tied to his objectives in managing the startup. The entrepreneur often provides financing so that his personal budget constraint is interconnected with the startup's costs and revenues. When the entrepreneur provides financing, his consumption and savings decisions can be connected to the amount of investment in the startup. This implies that the Fisher Separation Theorem may not apply.

The interconnection between the entrepreneur's personal budget and the startup's financing is due to transaction costs in the relationship between the entrepreneur and sources of financial capital. This may result from asymmetric information, which creates incentives for the entrepreneur to contribute to the financing of the startup. This illusrates the "pecking-order" theory in finance; see Myers and Majluf (1984). The entrepreneur's contribution to financing the startup implies that his wealth affects the startup's financing decisions. The entrepreneur, rather than the startup, often is a party to contracts with venture capitalists and others involved in the startup enterprise.

The decision about the date at which to launch the firm also depends on the entrepreneur's own consumption objectives. The entrepreneur's realization of income from the project depends on the timing of the establishment of the firm. Again, asymmetric information plays a fundamental role because of difficulties that outside investors face in determining the value of the prospective firm.

Before the foundational shift occurs, transaction costs often are the most important type of costs incurred by the entrepreneur. The entrepreneur learns about the industry and makes contacts with potential customers and suppliers. There are substantial transaction costs associated with search, communication, negotiation, and forming relationships with prospective customers and suppliers. The entrepreneur incurs transaction costs in assembling the productive inputs and technology needed to establish the firm.

Employment

The entrepreneur's effort decisions are combined with his labor market decisions. These objectives are closely tied because the entrepreneur contributes to the management and labor of the startup. As with financing, the entrepreneur's hiring decisions can be based on personal relationships, with family and friends compensated through informal arrangements. Asymmetric information prevents the entrepreneur from making full use of the labor market to hire workers and managers, thus requiring the entrepreneur to do much of the initial work or to obtain additional labor inputs through contracts with venture capitalists. Asymmetric information also may affect the entrepreneur's ability to realize returns from his ideas through an employer, which can lead to the decision to quit a job and create a startup.

The entrepreneur takes time to establish a firm. For example, Kaplan et al. (2005) study 49 venture-capital-financed companies and find that the average time elapsed from early business plan to public company is almost six years. The relative importance of human capital, especially the entrepreneur's expertise, declines over time, whereas there is an increase in the importance of intellectual property and physical assets.

Due to the entrepreneur's participation in financing the startup and providing management and labor to it, the entrepreneur's labor-leisure decisions are not separable from the employment decisions of the startup. The entrepreneur's labor-leisure tradeoffs are affected by income effects that depend on his investment in the startup and anticipation of earnings from establishing the firm. This may explain why many researchers emphasize the entrepreneur's personal enjoyment, creativity, drive, preferences, attitude toward risk, and rate of time preference. The entrepreneur's preferences and other characteristics drive effort decisions so that the consumption objectives of the entrepreneur are not separable from the employment decisions of the startup.

The entrepreneur often devotes significant effort to raising financial capital from banks and investors. Financial transaction costs are thus part of the entrepreneur's costs. In addition, the entrepreneur's costs include the effort and resources devoted to information gathering and learning. To establish the firm, the entrepreneur is likely to require information about the needs and characteristics of potential consumers, the availability and features of alternative products, the technology required to manufacture the product, and the business methods involved in supplying the product. The entrepreneur must gather other types of market knowledge, including the prices of comparable products and the prices of productive inputs needed to provide the good. The entrepreneur may need to purchase the technology used to provide the good.

The entrepreneur takes into account the opportunity cost of his time, given his skills and other abilities. The entrepreneur will spend time researching and developing the idea of the business. The entrepreneur may need to devote time and effort to developing the skills needed to understand and apply the technology. The entrepreneur will invest time in the process of setting up the business and forming the organization. The entrepreneur's ability to contribute time and effort to the startup may depend on whether he is employed elsewhere.

The entrepreneur's personal satisfaction can offset some of the costs incurred to establish the firm. The entrepreneur may derive consumption benefits from establishing the firm. The process of establishing a firm can be creative, entertaining, informative, and enjoyable. Then, the per-period costs of establishing the firm reflect the entrepreneur's costs net of the benefits of being an entrepreneur. The costs of establishing a firm reflect the consumer-entrepreneur's idiosyncratic productivity and costs of effort. The costs also include the entrepreneur's use of resources, labor and capital.

Innovation

The entrepreneur's innovation decision is combined with a technology market decision. Asymmetric information about the entrepreneur's ideas prevents full use of the market. This helps to explain why the entrepreneur chooses to embody the technology in the new firm rather than to license the technology to other individuals or to other firms. This applies to new products, new processes, new business methods, and new forms of organization. The innovation decisions of the entrepreneur are closely tied to the entrepreneur's personal knowledge, information, and creativity.

The entrepreneur's intellectual property is an essential aspect of the entrepreneur's innovation decision. The entrepreneur's intellectual property may be in the form of patents, trademarks, copyrights, and business plans. The entrepreneur may own trade secrets, industrial designs, and other intangible assets. The entrepreneur attempts to commercialize his intellectual property by establishing a firm. The entrepreneur contributes his creativity and intellectual property to the startup. As with the entrepreneur's contribution of finance capital and labor to the startup, the entrepreneur's personal intellectual property is connected to the inventions used by the startup enterprise.

4.2.2 After the Foundational Shift

What makes the foundational shift so important is that once the entrepreneur becomes an owner, the firm's objectives are separate from those of the entrepreneur. After becoming an owner, the entrepreneur can choose whether or not to continue to exercise control and obtain returns from the firm without necessarily affecting the survival of the firm. The firm is an offspring with an independent identity and its own objectives.

The transaction costs that are required to establish a firm provide a solution to a longstanding puzzle. It is often asserted that entrepreneurs face a dilemma because entrepreneurial profit will be eroded by competitive entry. However, the cost of establishing a firm limits entry and reduces the erosion of profit. Moreover, costly transactions mean that competitors will encounter difficulties in discerning and in imitating entrepreneurial innovations. Economic frictions reduce the prospect of perfect competitive challenges. Economic frictions further provide opportunities for entrepreneurs to establishing market-making firms that earn rents from mitigating transaction costs.

The entrepreneur's costs of establishing the firm should be distinguished from the firm's costs, which it incurs after it begins to operate. The entrepreneur incurs costs during the period when he is establishing the firm. The entrepreneur necessarily bears risk in practice because of the delay between the time when he begins to establish the firm and the time when the firm begins to operate. This time lag introduces uncertainty about the firm's profit. The dynamic nature of the entrepreneur's activity implies that starting a firm is a type of investment.

The entrepreneur may have supplied some essential inputs to the firm, such as reputation, talents, creativity, and other unique services, but the entrepreneur could continue to supply these to the firm on a contractual basis once the firm is established. After the foundational shift occurs, there is a separation of the owner's consumption decisions from the firm's decisions.

The entrepreneur can maintain a connection to the firm after the foundational shift by remaining as an owner and also by performing such functions as manager, consultant, supplier, or customer. The entrepreneur can still be creative and innovative as an owner and manager, or he can delegate these duties to managers and employees. After the foundational shift, the entrepreneur can choose to end all economic ties to the firm by divesting the ownership share. Even after divesting his ownership share, the consumer can maintain other economic relationships with the firm.

The foundational shift, from entrepreneur to owner, is what makes the firm such a valuable economic actor. The firm pursues activities that maximize its profit. The foundational shift allows the firm to provide limited liability for its owners.

The firm is an additional economic actor that augments the number of actors in the economy. The firm is a social institution with capabilities that differ from those of the entrepreneur. The firm becomes a financial asset at the date when it is established. As an owner, the consumer obtains rights of *residual control* over the firm's activities. The consumer-owner also obtains *residual returns* equal to the firm's revenues net of expenditures including debt payments and residual claims of other owners.

4.2.3 The Returns to Entrepreneurship

Is the entrepreneur's interest in the firm after it is established purely financial? The Fisher Separation Theorem implies that the entrepreneur has a financial interest in establishing a firm. The consumer-entrepreneur seeks the rewards of ownership rather than, for example, the goods and services produced by the firm.

After the foundational shift, the consumer takes on the economic role of an owner. The consumer-entrepreneur no longer acts in the economic capacity of an entrepreneur, having completed the task of establishing the firm. The owner of the firm can divest his share of the firm or direct the firm's activities using rights of residual control. The firm acts under the authority delegated to it by its owners. Because the firm satisfies the separation criterion by definition, the firm's objective is designated by its owners. The entrepreneur's objective changes from establishing a firm to the objectives of an owner of the firm.

The owner who also manages the firm supplies his human capital to the firm. The market for human capital provides potential gains from trade to the owner and the firm. The owner may derive benefits from selling his human capital in the market (or consuming leisure). The firm can maximize profits by hiring a manager in the market for human capital. The owner finds the best opportunity for his human capital and the firm finds the best manager for the particular needs of the firm. In this way, the separation of ownership and control realizes gains from trade.

Fama and Jensen (1983b) explain the survival of organizations that have separation of decision and risk-bearing functions. For Fama and Jensen, the benefits of separation result from specialization of management in decision making and risk bearing. They also emphasize the mechanisms that help separation to be more effective, particularly the corporation's board of directors' role in monitoring major decisions and in designing rewards for managers.

After it is established, the firm is a new economic actor. The firm plays various economic roles as a seller of outputs, a buyer of resources, a borrower of finance capital, an employer of workers, and a party to contracts. The firm is an intermediary that matches buyers and sellers and makes markets. The firm's managers choose goals, strategies to achieve the goals, and means to implement strategies. Although it acts under delegated authority, the newly established firm is an additional decision maker in the economy.

The entrepreneur does not earn money directly. The entrepreneur often does not earn anything while he is establishing the firm because he receives payments by becoming an owner of the firm. The entrepreneur is rewarded based on the quality of his product. As in professions such as science and art, the entrepreneur earns money indirectly by creating something new. This indirect payment may explain why entrepreneurs say that they do not do it for the money. Of course, entrepreneurs also may enjoy the creative process involved in designing the firm and seeing it take shape.

The motivation of the entrepreneur is to obtain the value of the firm. The value of the firm is the present discounted value of the firm's profit stream. The value of the firm depends on the entrepreneur's market knowledge, organizational design, and intellectual property. The value of the firm can depend on the entrepreneur's production technology, Y^i, and the entrepreneur's transaction technology for firms, T^i. The consumer-owner receives part of the value of the firm based on his ownership share of the firm. The consumer also makes consumption decisions that are independent of the firm's profit maximization decisions. The separation of consumer and firm decisions is explored in greater depth in subsequent chapters.

The entrepreneur's profit is equal to the value of the firm, discounted to account for the time it takes to establish the firm, less the costs incurred in establishing the firm. The entrepreneur's profit is the value of the firm, discounted to the present, minus the present value of the costs of establishing the firm. The entrepreneur's profit is the consumer's incentive to become an entrepreneur. The value of the firm is affected by market demand and supply conditions and by transaction benefits and transaction costs. Competition with other firms is a major determinant of the firm's value. The entrepreneur usually begins to receive a return after the foundational shift takes place.

The entrepreneur obtains the value of the firm by becoming an owner of the firm at the time the firm is established. As an owner, the entrepreneur receives the firm's profit by remaining an owner of the firm over time and thereby receiving the residual returns from the firm's operation. Alternatively, the entrepreneur can realize the value of the firm by selling the firm to others after it is established. The entrepreneur also can form contracts with potential buyers that allow the firm to be sold before it is established.

The entrepreneur's profit is a standard net-present-value (NPV) statement. The establishment of a firm differs from a standard investment project because the payoff of the project is the value of the firm, which is an initial value. However, the standard results from NPV analysis still apply. The entrepreneur should establish the firm only if it yields a positive return. Given a choice among alternative firms that could be established, the entrepreneur should choose the type of firm that yields the greatest return.

Basic theories of investment yield some insights into the entrepreneur's decision. The entrepreneur may experience adjustment costs in establishing the firm. The faster the firm is established, the greater the costs of establishing the firm.

The entrepreneur may face a tradeoff between the high cost of rapidly establishing a firm and the cost of delay in obtaining the value of the firm.

The basic statement of the entrepreneur's profit can be generalized easily to incorporate uncertainty about the future value of the firm. With uncertainty and learning, the entrepreneur should apply more sophisticated techniques. The entrepreneur may wish to delay establishing the firm as a means of learning more about the market. The entrepreneur can decide on the start date by using stochastic dynamic programming to find an optimal rule for when to stop the process of developing the firm.[11] Also, the entrepreneur can apply real options analysis to the problem of choosing a start date under uncertainty.[12]

The date at which the firm becomes established can be uncertain as well. If the start date depends randomly on the stream of expenditures made to establish the firm, the entrepreneur's problem resembles a standard research and development (R&D) problem.[13] The entrepreneur can choose the optimal level of investment at each date that reflects the tradeoff between the cost of investment and the forgone return due to the expected delay in establishing the firm. As in any standard investment problem, the entrepreneur can choose the amount to invest in the firm. More generally, the entrepreneur chooses the characteristics of the firm that he plans to establish, which in turn affect the value of the firm and also determine the costs of establishing the firm.

The entrepreneur's problem is much more complicated than choosing an optimal level of investment. The entrepreneur's profit is a reduced form that derives from a complex situation. The entrepreneur must evaluate market opportunities and competing alternatives. The entrepreneur must make decisions that determine the market activities, internal operations, and organizational design of the firm. The entrepreneur must secure initial financing for the firm from personal funds, partners, banks, venture capitalists, and other investors.

4.2.4 Establishing the Firm

To give some indication of the number of entrepreneurs that start sole proprietorships, consider the United States Small Business Administration (2001) estimate that there were over 612,000 new firms with employees in the year 2000. Reynolds et al. (2004) estimate that in the year 2000 there were over 11.8 million "nascent entrepreneurs" and about 6.5 million start-up efforts in progress. There are over 17.5 million sole proprietorships in the United States, with revenues approaching $1 trillion.[14] These firms exist in practically every sector of the economy.

---

11 For example, stochastic dynamic programming yields a stopping rule for a research and development project; see Spulber (1980).
12 See Dixit and Pindyck (1994).
13 This can be modeled as in the patent race literature; see Reinganum (1981, 1982) and see Reinganum (1989) for a survey.
14 See BizStats.com, http://www.bizstats.com/numbersp.htm.

The entrepreneur seeks finance for two purposes that can be summarized as "getting in" and "getting out." Getting in represents the first stage of the entrepreneur's decision-making – *establishing* the firm. Getting out represents the second stage of the entrepreneur's decision-making – *restructuring* both the established firm's capital structure and the owner's portfolio. The purpose of financing in each stage affects financial decisions. In each stage, finance helps to accomplish the separation of the entrepreneur's decisions from the decision of the firm. Also, in each stage, finance affects the incentives of the entrepreneur/owner and those of the firm.

The entrepreneur innovates by establishing a firm. The entrepreneur needs funds to pay for initial costs of labor, capital equipment, resources, and technology. The entrepreneur also encounters substantial transaction costs and costs of marketing, learning, and innovation. The entrepreneur may self-finance all or part of the new venture. The entrepreneur may turn to investors including partners, banks, equity markets, and venture capitalists.

The financial needs of the entrepreneur are substantially different from those of an established firm. First and perhaps foremost, the entrepreneur seeks finance as a means of separating personal consumption-savings decisions from the activity of establishing the firm. Second, the entrepreneur seeks capital to create a new business, rather than to extend or transform an existing business. Established firms that seek financing for new business activities are likely to have a financial track record as well as other sources of revenue. In contrast, the entrepreneur often seeks capital for untested and innovative products, production techniques, or business methods. Accordingly, the entrepreneur and the investors in the new venture often encounter greater uncertainty in comparison with that faced by existing firms.

The different needs and financial choices of entrepreneurs result in specialized financial institutions. Entrepreneurs may choose to borrow from venture capitalists rather than banks or equity markets. This difference is more than a matter of degree. Venture capitalists offer different types of financial contracts, engage in closer monitoring of performance, provide business advice, and make connections to potential customers and suppliers. Contracts with venture capitalists are a means of providing information to the capital markets for the initial public offering (IPO). For an in-depth examination of the role of venture capital in funding entrepreneurs, see Lerner and Gompers (2001) and Gompers and Lerner (1999).

The highly speculative nature of new ventures and information asymmetries can lead to credit rationing and costly financing. Barzel (1987) argues that due to costly monitoring and the possibility of moral hazard, the entrepreneur supplies the production factor "performing the least routine role." For this reason, the entrepreneur is a residual claimant and often supplies his own capital (Barzel, 1987, p. 115).

In choosing to self-finance, the entrepreneur benefits from independence in business decisions. The entrepreneur can make full use of his skills, knowledge, ingenuity, creativity, vision, and most of all, judgment. There are many decisions to be made in the process of establishing a firm. These decisions include the firm's mission, goals, strategy, products, personnel, technology, and organizational structure. The self-financing entrepreneur avoids transaction costs of raising capital and negotiating with investors after obtaining capital. The entrepreneur need not be an agent of the firm's investors, avoiding performance contracts targeting the entrepreneur's moral hazard. The entrepreneur avoids having his interests aligned with those of investors.

The entrepreneur who self-finances obtains the full marginal returns of the firm and has an incentive to supply effort optimally and to make optimal decisions in establishing the firm. Knight (1971, p. 252) originally identified the moral hazard problem in entrepreneurial finance: "not less important is the incentive to substitute more effective and intimate forms of association for insurance, so as to eliminate or reduce the moral hazard." Knight (1971, p. 252) recognized the risk to investors and suggested "the application of the insurance principle of consolidation to groups of ventures too broad in scope to be 'swung' by a single enterpriser."

There are many costs to self-financing that motivate the entrepreneur to seek investors. The most important problem, of course, arises when the entrepreneur's assets are not sufficient to cover the necessary capital investment. Even if the entrepreneur has sufficient funds, avoiding risk requires portfolio diversification so that the entrepreneur does not invest too great a share of assets in the new venture. Through the use of debt, the entrepreneur benefits from leverage by self-financing only a share of the enterprise. By obtaining financing, the entrepreneur can engage in multiple ventures. The entrepreneur benefits from the expertise of investors, particularly when investors are venture capitalists.

Entrepreneurs raise capital from outside investors because, as Penrose (1959, p. 38) points out, doing so indicates a "very rare sort of entrepreneurial ability." This ability allows new firms to enter markets and compete with incumbents even though larger established firms may have lower costs of raising capital. Obtaining financing to establish the firm begins the process of separating the entrepreneur from the firm. The entrepreneur's innovation skills may apply specifically to the process of creating the firm. This implies that the establishment of the firm should not depend exclusively on the entrepreneur's assets.

Following Knight (1971), various studies identify agency problems in the relationship between entrepreneurs and investors. These agency costs entail moral hazard and adverse selection. Extensions of the basic agency model of finance provide insights into the effects of financial contracts on the incentives of the entrepreneur.[15] Agency costs arise when the entrepreneurs' revenue is unobservable; see Diamond (1984) and Bolton and Scharfstein (1990, 1996). Agency costs exist when effort in the form of investment is unobservable; see for example

---

15 See Sahlman (1990) and Kaplan and Strömberg (2003, 2004) on the agency approach to entrepreneurship.

Innes (1990), Zender (1991), Hart and Moore (1998), and Biais and Casamatta (1999).[16]

The entrepreneur and investors may have conflicting interests while the firm is being established. Both the entrepreneur and the venture capitalists supply productive effort that affects the prospective success of the firm. This results in a situation with double moral hazard; see Schmidt (2003) and Repullo and Suarez (2004). The entrepreneur and the venture capitalists write contracts to address these double moral hazard problems. Convertible securities are bonds or stocks that can be exchanged for common stock at a specified price and such securities are used often in venture capital financing. Schmidt (2003) shows that convertible securities can be used to improve investment efficiency when there is double moral hazard. Cornelli and Yosha (2003) demonstrate that a combination of convertible debt and stage financing works better than a mixture of stock and debt in addressing problems of asymmetric information between the entrepreneur and the venture capitalists. Aghion and Bolton (1992) and Hellmann (1998) examine the allocation of control rights between an entrepreneur and venture capitalists as a means of affecting the threat points in renegotiation.

In addition to agency conflicts between venture capitalists and entrepreneurs, start-up companies experience conflicts between investors themselves. Bartlett (2006) finds that preferred stock has advantages in reducing conflicts between venture-capital investors. A new venture can have multiple investors for the same reason that the entrepreneur does not self-finance. Venture capitalists may have limited funds to invest, they may seek to diversify their portfolios, or they may reduce their agency risk by partnering with other investors. As the new venture expands, more capital is needed, which requires more investors.

Venture capitalists provide human capital inputs in addition to financial capital. Smith (1999) identifies such inputs as serving as a sounding board for the entrepreneur, obtaining alternative sources of financing, recruiting managers, intermediating with other investors, and formulating business strategy. Accordingly, for Smith (1999), the entrepreneur and venture capitalists form a team that is "more like a partnership than a principal-agent relationship." Multiple venture capital investors thus create opportunities for free riding in monitoring and managing the start-up firm. Additionally, venture capitalists may have limited time and expertise required to monitor the start-up firm, so that additional venture capitalists are brought in to share the burden.[17]

Because investors participate differently in multistage financing, Bartlett (2006) points out that the prices they pay for the firm's securities and the amounts of preferred stock they hold will vary across investors, thus creating the potential for conflict. He argues that the contrast that typically is drawn between public and private corporations is inaccurate. Publicly held corporations often are said to

---

16 Both revenue and investment are unobservable in Povel and Raith (2004).
17 See Bartlett (2006).

have (vertical) agency problems in which the interests of managers conflict with dispersed shareholders. Privately held (closely held) corporations have (horizontal) agency problems in the form of conflict between shareholders. The entrepreneurial startup can exhibit both types of agency conflicts.

4.2.5 Restructuring: The Firm's Financial Structure and the Owner's Portfolio

After the firm is established, financial restructuring often is necessary. The entrepreneur becomes an owner and seeks to restructure his portfolio and to separate ownership from control of the firm. The firm may seek to raise capital for initial growth and to change the firm's organizational structure.

The firm issues debt and equity that help to decouple the entrepreneur-owner's consumption-saving decisions from the firm's investment decisions. The advantages of separation observed after the firm is established are related to the advantages of external financing during the start-up phase. The newly established firm's capital requirements for growth are likely to exceed the combination of the entrepreneur's assets and the firm's ability to generate revenue for investment. The entrepreneur may not wish to invest all of his assets in the firm. The entrepreneur is likely to diversify his investment portfolio after the firm is established by seeking additional investors.[18]

The entrepreneur's responsibilities can change considerably as an owner. The entrepreneur's skills in innovation and establishing the firm may not apply once the firm is established. The firm employs a chief executive officer (CEO) and other managers to replace the entrepreneur's strategy-making and supervisory functions. The entrepreneur's time constraints may require divesting his ownership share if his outside opportunities provide a greater return than does monitoring the firm's managers. Financial arrangements to divest the entrepreneur-owner's share of the firm allow the entrepreneur to obtain the market value of the firm.

The IPO is a financial mechanism that helps the entrepreneur to divest some or all of his ownership share. The entrepreneur and venture capitalists give up some of the private benefits of control.[19] Going public provides additional funds for capital investment. The firm changes its capital structure replacing debt with equity. The ownership shares of the entrepreneur owner and venture capitalists are replaced with publicly traded equity. The firm's owners learn about the market value of the firm.

The agency costs observed during the establishment phase are replaced by the firm's agency cost. Ang et al. (2000) measure agency costs empirically and find that in small corporations, agency costs are significantly higher when an outsider

---

18 See, for example, Benninga et al. (2005), Bodnaruk et al. (2007), and Pastor (2006).
19 See Dyck and Zingales (2004).

manages the firm, are inversely related to the manager's ownership share, and increase with the number of nonmanager shareholders.

At the restructuring phase, the entrepreneur and the venture capitalists may disagree about the timing of the sale of the firm. The entrepreneur may prefer to liquidate the firm more or less rapidly than would the venture capitalists. The entrepreneur may prefer to continue as owner to realize the benefits of firm-specific investments particularly in human capital. The entrepreneur may have better information about the prospects of the firm and the value of its assets than either the venture capitalists or a perspective buyer. Berglöf (1994) points out that the contract between the entrepreneur and the venture capitalists allocates decision rights pertaining to the sale of the firm. The entrepreneur and the venture capitalists both want the right to bargain with a prospective buyer, particularly if the terms of sale favor one side or the other. Berglöf (1994) shows that standard debt and equity have complementary effects in mitigating conflicts between the entrepreneur and the venture capitalists regarding the sale of the firm. Gompers (1995) finds that staged capital investments are used when there are agency costs.

The entrepreneur and the venture capitalists also may disagree on whether to invest more in the development of a firm or to abandon the project when difficulties arise. Bergemann and Hege (1998) examine this conflict in a dynamic agency model. Over time, the entrepreneur and the venture capitalists learn and revise their estimates of the likelihood that the firm will succeed. The entrepreneur controls the allocation of investment using some of the funds to improve the likelihood of success and possibly diverting the rest for personal gain. Long-term contracts resembling options mitigate some of these types of moral hazard problems.

Restructuring the firm's financing through an IPO changes the agency relationships that existed during the establishment phase. Conflicts between the interests of the entrepreneur and venture capitalists and between venture capitalists themselves are avoided when these contracts are replaced with the incentive structure of a publicly traded corporation.

4.3 Type I Competition: Competition among Entrepreneurs

Entrepreneurs compete with each other by determining whether or not to establish firms. Entrepreneurs consider the relative costs of establishing a firm and the relative value that the firm will add to the market. In determining the value of the firm, entrepreneurs must weigh potential entry by other firms. The entrepreneurial process helps to determine what will work best in the market place. Entrepreneurs effectively conduct economic experiments that test the relative effectiveness of the production and transaction technologies. Entrepreneurs who compete to establish firms perform the valuable function of comparing and selecting the best technologies. Entrepreneurs also compete for inputs such as resources, labor, and capital.

Entrepreneurs also compete to obtain inventions, product designs, and other intellectual property.

Entrepreneurs take into account their personal characteristics and those of competing entrepreneurs. Entrepreneurs must examine their preferences and endowments in comparison with other potential entrepreneurs. For example, entrepreneurs consider their relative risk tolerance, patience, judgment, and costs of effort. Entrepreneurs evaluate their relative knowledge of market opportunities and technological endowments. Entrepreneurs consider their relative wealth in determining their ability to finance the firm through personal funds and through investors. Entrepreneurs examine their relative capabilities in innovation, negotiation, management, planning, strategy making.

Suppose, for example, that two consumers have full information about each other's transaction technologies, T^1 and T^2. Both transaction technologies produce the same benefits excluding transaction costs, that is, a benefit V for the buyer and an opportunity cost C for the seller. Suppose that one transaction technology is more efficient than the other, $T^1 < T^2$. Suppose that there are no capacity constraints and the services of the firm are not differentiated, so that one firm can serve the market. Then only consumer 1 chooses to become an entrepreneur and establish a firm.

In this situation, the firm is a monopoly intermediary and earns monopoly rents. If direct exchange is feasible, $g \geq 0$, the firm earns monopoly profit equal to

$$\Pi = G - g.$$

The entrepreneur establishes a firm to provide intermediated exchange only if the discounted value of the firm is greater than or equal to the cost of establishing the firm, where δ is a discount factor,

$$\delta(G - g) \geq k.$$

If direct exchange is not feasible, the firm earns monopoly profit equal to $\Pi = G$. The entrepreneur will establish a firm to provide intermediated exchange only if the discounted value of the firm is greater than or equal to the cost of establishing the firm, $\delta G \geq k$.

More generally, suppose that there are capacity constraints per firm of one unit and suppose that the market can support only m firms. Suppose further that there are $n > m$ potential entrepreneurs, with transaction technologies, $T^1 < T^2 < \cdots < T^n$. Assume that entrepreneurs have the same costs of establishing a firm, and normalize those costs to zero. Then, as a result of competition between entrepreneurs, only the m most efficient entrepreneurs will choose to establish firms to enter the market. Competition between entrepreneurs will result in the selection of the most efficient transaction technologies.

Suppose in contrast that two entrepreneurs have the same transaction technologies T but differ in terms of their costs of establishing a firm, $k^1 < k^2$. Without capacity constraints and with homogeneous products, only consumer 1 chooses to become an entrepreneur and establish a firm. Suppose that firms have capacity constraints and that there are n potential entrepreneurs with different entry costs, $k^1 < k^2 < \cdots < k^n$. Then there will be entry of entrepreneurs until the profit of each firm is greater than the cost of the marginal entrepreneur and less than the cost of the next-highest entrepreneur. Competition between entrepreneurs results in the selection of entrepreneurs who are most efficient at establishing firms. Chapter 5 presents a series of models in which entrepreneurs compete to enter the market.

4.4 Type II Competition: Competition between Entrepreneurs and Consumer Organizations

Entrepreneurs who establish a firm compete with consumer organizations. The firm can be profitable only if intermediated exchange is more efficient than direct exchange between consumers. Entrepreneurs decide whether or not to establish a firm based on their knowledge of the potential economic contribution of the firm. The actions of the firm in intermediating exchange allow for the endogenous establishment of firms. Entrepreneurs evaluate the efficiency of their endowments of firm transaction technologies in comparison to the efficiency of direct exchange.

There are many forms of type II competition between entrepreneurs and direct exchange. Firms create markets by setting up and managing allocation mechanisms, including posted prices and auction markets. Firms provide services as intermediaries and design market microstructure; see the analysis presented in Spulber (1996a, 1996b, 1998, 1999, 2002b, 2002c, 2003a). Firms centralize exchange by creating networks and matching buyers and sellers; see Spulber (2006). Firms establish and operate information systems that supply buyers and sellers with some of the means to communicate and process information. Firms engage in communication with buyers and sellers to gather information about their characteristics and to provide information about terms of exchange, such as prices and product features. Firms also provide computation to improve the efficiency of matchmaking and market-making activities, helping buyers and sellers search for each other, adjusting prices, and providing immediacy. In these ways, firms provide alternatives to direct exchange between consumers by intermediating transactions.

Firms also establish organizations that provide alternatives to direct exchange. The firm's organization manages its internal transactions and its market transactions. Transactions within the firm provide an alternative to market transactions between consumers. For example, consumers can combine their inputs, technology, and capabilities by supplying labor services to a firm rather than through market contracts with each other. The firm as a contracting hub reduces transaction costs through standardization and scale and avoids the complexities of multilateral contracting between many individuals.

The firm's organization also provides an alternative to consumer organizations. It is the autonomy of the firm that distinguishes it from consumer organizations such as consumer cooperatives, worker cooperatives, and basic partnerships. The firm provides transaction efficiencies through relational contracts, delegation of authority, incentives for performance, monitoring, communication, and information gathering; see the discussion of contracts and of agency in Spulber (1999).

Compare intermediated exchange through the firm and with direct exchange in the basic example. Because the firm operates for a single period, the value of the firm corresponds to its single-period profit Π. If direct exchange is feasible, the firm improves efficiency only if total gains from trade rise relative to direct exchange: $V - P + W - C \geq v - c - t$. Thus, if $g \geq 0$, the firm's profit Π cannot exceed the added net gains from trade:

$$\Pi \leq G - g.$$

If direct exchange is not feasible, the firm improves efficiency only if it offers gains from trade: $V - P + W - C \geq 0$. Without direct exchange, the firm's profit is limited by the gains from trade it provides:

$$\Pi \leq G.$$

These inequalities specify the potential returns to the firm's transaction activities. The extent of competition between firms determines the firm's profit.

The profit of the firm is a key element of the entrepreneur's decision. Suppose that an entrepreneur incurs a cost of establishing a firm equal to k. After the entrepreneur establishes the firm, the firm begins to operate. The consumer-entrepreneur becomes an owner and receives the value of the firm, Π. The entrepreneur establishes a firm only if the discounted value of the firm is greater than or equal to the cost of establishing the firm, where δ is the discount factor,

$$\delta\Pi \geq k.$$

The entrepreneur competes with direct exchange only through the newly established firm.

The entrepreneur chooses the most effective organizational structure of the firm. In establishing the firm, the entrepreneur chooses between intermediated market transactions or internal management transactions. If a firm is preferable to direct exchange, the entrepreneur's incentive to establish a firm depends on the value added by the firm. The value of the firm is less than or equal to the value added by the firm's market transactions and management transactions. The scope of the firm is the combination of its market-making and organizational activities, as previously noted, see Table 1.1. The entrepreneur thus plays a fundamental economic role in determining the initial scope of the firm.

The entrepreneur does not engage in head-to-head competition with direct exchange because it is the firm, once it is in operation, that must contend with direct exchange between consumers. The entrepreneur's contribution is to anticipate the need for the firm as an intermediary and as an organization. The entrepreneur has an incentive to establish the firm only if the firm will add value relative to direct exchange.

4.5 Type III Competition: Competition between Entrepreneurs and Established Firms

The entrepreneur chooses to establish a firm if it will address market conditions more effectively than existing firms. The entrepreneurial entrant introduces capacity in response to growth in market demand or provides products that respond to changes in customer preferences. The entrant competes with established firms that can expand, diversify, or change their products. The entrepreneur also establishes a new firm if it offers improvements in market transactions, organizational transactions, production technology, or products. The entrepreneurial entrant competes with existing firms that can innovate by introducing their own new transaction methods, production processes, or new products. Finally, the entrepreneur establishes a firm that offers new organizational structures. The entrepreneurial entrant competes with established firms that can restructure their organization to increase its efficiency.

Entrepreneurs compete with established firms in terms of incentives for managerial performance. All other things equal, a new firm must offer greater efficiency if incentives for performance and opportunities to monitor performance are greater than within an established firm. Otherwise, an established firm could offer the same products by expanding or diversifying. Established firms also can offer organizational innovations by restructuring to increase their efficiency. The entrepreneur must offer innovations more effectively than existing firms.

The entrepreneur's establishment decision thus results in a more efficient organization of the industry. The entrepreneur's entry decision plays an important economic role by displacing less efficient incumbents and stimulating innovation by existing firms. In the absence of demand growth and capacity constraints on existing firms, displacing incumbents requires innovation. But innovation in itself is not enough. The entrepreneur must offer innovations that create greater value than incumbents. This explains the great emphasis on innovation in economic discussions of the entrepreneur, particularly by Schumpeter.

4.5.1 Entry

Entrepreneurs compete with existing firms through their newly established firms. The entrepreneur establishes a firm only if it adds value in competition with existing firms. Being newly established, the entrepreneur's firm necessarily is an entrant, and the entrepreneur devises the firm's strategy towards incumbents. The entrepreneur's competitive role ceases once market entry takes place.

Competition between entrepreneurs and established firms can be modeled using the plethora of industrial organization models of entry; see for example Spence (1977), Dixit (1980), and Spulber (1981a). It is straightforward to interpret these models in terms of entrepreneurship, because all entrepreneurs must make a market entry decision. The entrant's strategies are also those of the entrepreneur.

The strategies of incumbent firms in entry models also shed light on entrepreneurial decisions, because the entrepreneur considers the impact of future entry on the firm. The entrepreneur also takes into account the firm's future position as an incumbent in evaluating the value of the firm being established.

The entrepreneur's costs of establishing a firm should be considered as an important component of the entry costs that are examined in economic models of industrial organization. One of the key strategic aspects of entry is the need to make irreversible investments in transaction costs such as planning the new venture, marketing, conducting market research, and obtaining financing. Firms also must make irreversible investments in R&D to develop new products and production technologies.

The empirical industrial organization literature on entry sheds light on the entrepreneur. Geroski (1995) provides a useful overview of data and results in this area and finds that entry appears relatively easy but survival is not. Ease of entry calls into question many empirical studies that suggest the presence of high barriers to entry. The importance of entry as a means of introducing innovations helps to reconcile these opposing observations. Geroski suggests that entry may be imperfect as a means of short-term price competition. However, entry is a valuable mechanism for introducing product and process inventions, with the best products and processes selected through competition between firms once they are established and operating within the industry. Empirical analysis of entry thus supports the view of the entrepreneur as innovator.

Entrepreneurs can apply creative entry strategies and innovations to surmount potential advantages of incumbent firms. Growing market demand or changes in consumer tastes generate opportunities for entry. Technological change allows entrants to arrange novel transactions, introduce new products, or lower production costs. Bayus and Agarwal (2007), in a study of the computer industry, find that technology strategies employed after entry are critical for firm survival.

If the incumbent and entrant offer differentiated products, price competition tends to be reduced. Both the incumbent and entrant will have the opportunity to earn profits in postentry competition. Because a price lower than a competitor's causes only some customers to switch their purchases, the incumbent and the entrant will not have an incentive to engage in an all-out price war. Because the incumbent and the entrant earn positive profits in competition after entry, it is more likely that the entrant can earn a sufficient margin above operating expenses to recover the sunk costs of entry. Other factors that lessen price wars are customer switching costs, customer brand loyalty, different convenience features, and imperfect information. If these factors are present, the entrant can expect a reduction in the severity of postentry competition, allowing the recovery of sunk costs. Therefore, with product differentiation and other factors, sunk costs are less likely to be a barrier to entry.

If the entrepreneur establishes a firm that will offer a differentiated product, the firm's value is greater and the entrepreneur has a better chance of recovering costs incurred in establishing the firm. An entrant could offer products that deliver sufficiently greater value to the customer than do the products of established companies. In return, the entrant will earn margins that allow the recovery of sunk costs incurred in entering the market.

Generally, with technological change, the need to sink cost is not an insurmountable barrier to the entry of new competitors. If an entrant employs new technologies to reduce its operating costs, it can enjoy a cost advantage over an incumbent operating outdated technology. Even if the incumbent and entrant compete on price, an entrant with an operating cost advantage over the incumbent will earn positive margins that allow for the recovery of sunk costs.

Moreover, sunk costs need not be an entry barrier because the entrant's sunk cost is a matter of strategic choice. The entrepreneur makes various decisions about how much to spend on planning, marketing, R&D, and so on. The choice of products, production processes, and transaction methods impacts the new firm's costs. The entrant can serve different sets of customers than the incumbent, thus changing the entrant's need for distribution facilities and marketing expenditures.

The entrepreneur can adopt different production or distribution technologies than incumbent firms, often drastically changing the mix of investment and operating costs. For example, entrants into telecommunications employ wireless systems with lower sunk cost in facilities in comparison to incumbents that operate traditional wireline systems.

Even with similar products and technology, an entrepreneur can reduce the risk associated with making investment commitments in a variety of ways. The entrepreneur can lessen the risk of postentry competition by forming *contracts with customers* before irreversible investments are made. The entrant can compete with the incumbent for customers before deciding to enter the market and then only incur entry costs if the customer contracts will generate sufficient revenues. The company can find out if their product will be successful before making substantial investments in facilities. For example, aircraft manufacturers such as Boeing and Airbus sign up prospective customers on a contingent basis before starting a production run on an aircraft.

The success of the contracting strategy also depends on the level of transaction costs. Efficiencies in contracting can mitigate the impact of entry costs and entrepreneurs can use contracts as an entry strategy when there are substantial costs for establishing the firm. If the transaction costs of contracting with customers are relatively low in comparison with the sunk costs of entry, then testing the waters through contracts is worthwhile. The entrepreneur can use contracts to establish prices and customer orders before the established firm operates in the market, thus reducing the risk of irreversible investments and avoiding price wars after entry.

4.5.2 Transaction Costs

The entrepreneur enters the market if it offers more efficient transactions than incumbents. A firm that performs transactions with greater efficiency than its competitors has a *transaction advantage*; see Spulber (2002c, 2003b). Also, the entrepreneur can enter the market with transactions that create new combinations of buyers and sellers, as Schumpeter (1997, p. 229) emphasized. Transaction advantages are likely to erode quickly limiting their potential effects as entry barriers. Entrepreneurs devise strategies to address the incumbent's transaction advantage. They can create their own innovative transaction methods or they can identify new combinations of buyers and sellers.

To surpass incumbent advantages, the entrepreneur must establish a firm that lowers transaction costs relative to those for incumbents or that offers transactions that create greater value for suppliers and customers. At the most basic level, there may be economies of scale and scope in the transaction technology itself. Retail stores have fixed costs of transactions, that is, costs that do not depend on the volume of transactions, such as information-processing equipment such as computers, cash registers, bar coding, and point-of-sale terminals. These cost economies need not translate into barriers to entry. As with production cost advantages, the entrant can offer transaction innovations. For example, an entrant could apply new types of enterprise software, point-of-sale equipment, or communications devices as means of lowering transaction costs.

Transaction technologies such as back-office information technology or point-of-sale systems can involve substantial sunk costs. Entrants may perceive an entry barrier if incumbent firms may have made substantial irreversible investments in such transaction technology. However, sunk costs in transaction technology can be overcome by continued innovations. Moreover, entrants can pursue different distribution channels that lower transaction costs.

A critical transaction advantage for a firm stems from identifying innovations and bringing them to market faster than competitors. However, incumbent firms that achieve success from such a strategy often build their business by producing products based on a particular generation of technology. The successful incumbent has an incentive to stick with a particular generation of technology to provide service to its installed base of customers. The incumbent may choose to incrementally improve its products because continually changing their basic technology would involve substantial investment and costs of adjustment. As a result, entrants can gain a transaction advantage by embracing later generations of technology.

An entrepreneur may believe that the incumbent firm has a transaction advantage resulting from supplier and customer relationships that are difficult to duplicate. Moreover, the established firm may have experience in coordinating its supplier and customer transactions. For entrants to overcome such advantages, it is necessary to offer different types of transactions that improve upon existing types of exchange. For example, Amazon.com was able to enter the retail book business by selling through the Internet even though established bookstores had longstanding relationships both with customers and with publishers.

If the entrepreneur establishes a firm with innovative transactions, the sunk costs of establishing the firm need not be a barrier to entry. Through innovative intermediation between buyers and sellers, the entrant can earn operating profits after entry. By reducing transaction costs, the entrant will earn returns that allow the entrepreneur to recover sunk costs. Accordingly, entrants can make investments in information technology, communications systems, customer support, supplier connections, and back office processes. The entrant recovers its investment costs as a result of transaction advantages over incumbent firms.

4.5.3 Competition and Innovation

Entrepreneurs compete with established firms to be innovators. In particular, suppose that an inventor makes a discovery of a new production process, product design, or transaction method. How shall the discovery be introduced into the market? Entrepreneurs and established firms are alternative mechanisms for introducing the invention to the market. Both entrepreneurs and established firms can serve as intermediaries between the inventor and users of the invention.

The entrepreneur can start a new firm to commercialize the invention. Alternatively, an established firm can employ the invention to improve or replace its existing processes, products, or transaction methods. The key question is why new firms are needed for innovation.

In many cases, a new firm is needed because no existing firm is available. The invention opens up a completely new line of business that does not correspond to the activities of any established enterprise. Often, the new line of business, although related to the activities of existing firms, is sufficiently distinct so that established firms lack the knowledge and resources to employ the invention. Also, it may be that the diversification required to employ the invention would distract the company's managers and employees from their existing activities, thus overcoming any potential economies of scope.

A new firm may be needed for innovation if existing firms do not correctly judge the economic value of the invention. As is often the case in practice, the managers of existing firms may underestimate the competitive threat posed by the invention. This management problem commonly is referred to as "management myopia."[20] The managers of existing firms follow such a narrow definition of their market that they fail to identify technological changes that create products that are substitutes in demand. Thus, managers of fax machines do not see the value of e-mail because they believe that they are in the fax machine business rather than in the communication business. Similarly, managers may not understand the impact of technologies that create substitute production processes or improved transactions. For example, Levitt (1960) notes that neighborhood grocery store chains believed that supermarkets did not pose a competitive threat.

The entrepreneur's incentive to adopt an invention may differ from that of the established firm. Arrow (1962) identified a displacement effect faced by a

---

20 The term comes from Theodore Levitt (1960), who wrote about "marketing myopia," in which managers do not understand the implications of inventions for their business.

monopolist. The firm earning a profit operating a business evaluates an invention on the basis of its incremental contribution to profit, in contrast to a competitive industry that has a zero profit benchmark. This same analysis would apply to an entrepreneur who evaluates an invention de novo in contrast to a profitable incumbent.

The vast literature on R&D yields insights into entrepreneurial innovation. Entrepreneurs can compete with established firms through R&D. An entrepreneur that obtains an invention before an incumbent could establish a firm that displaces the existing firm. This can be analyzed using models of racing to invent in which the winner obtains an exclusive monopoly patent and enters the market; see Reinganum (1989) for a survey. Gans and Stern (2000) look at a race where there is only one winner but licensing and imitation are feasible; see also Salant (1984) and Katz and Shapiro (1987).

In the literature on research tournaments, a sponsor designs the prize for the best innovation and contestants devote effort to producing inventions; see for example Taylor (1995) and Che and Gale (2003). The tournaments approach studies the design of incentives for inventive effort. The contestants in a tournament could be existing firms and entrepreneurs. Entrepreneurs could establish a firm by providing the best invention and supplying the sponsor of the tournament with the desired product.

These examples consider competitions with a single winner. However, even if inventions are scientifically unique, difficult to copy, or protected by patent, there are alternative inventions that are substitutes in demand. As Edmund Kitch (2000, p. 1730) cogently observes, "patents that confer monopoly market power are rare." Kitch discusses "elementary and persistent errors in the economic analysis of intellectual property," noting particularly the incorrect assertion that exclusivity in intellectual property confers an economic monopoly. In the same way, copyrighted works compete with each other; see Goldstein (1992) and Yoo (2004). The Justice Department recognizes the possibility of competition. The Antitrust Guidelines for Licensing of Intellectual Property state that "The Agencies will not presume that a patent, copyright, or trade secret necessarily confers market power upon its owner."[21]

In short, the market for inventions can be competitive. Inventions with different scientific and engineering details and patent protections can offer comparable cost savings. These inventions yield process innovations that are substitutes in demand within such categories as machine tools, industrial robots, enterprise software, factory designs, lasers, or chemical processes. Different inventions can be used to develop new products with competing features. These inventions yield product innovations that are substitutes in demand within such categories as appliances, electronic gadgets, automobiles, cameras, fabrics, or medications.

---

21 See U.S. Department of Justice and Federal Trade Commission, Antitrust Guidelines for the Licensing of Intellectual Property §§ 2.0, 2.2 (1995), *reprinted in* 4 Trade Reg. Rep. (CCH) ¶ 13,132, at 20,734–5. This is quoted in Yoo (2004).

The presence of competing inventors provides entrepreneurs with a means of competing with existing firms. By obtaining inventions in the market for ideas, entrepreneurs introduce innovations that compete with the existing products or the innovations of established firms. Shane (2001) finds that an invention is more likely to be commercialized by an entrepreneur than by an established firm the greater is the innovation's importance, impact, and patent scope. Hellman and Puri (2000) show that venture capital financing favors innovators over imitators and tends to speed the time to market for new high-tech ventures.

Anton and Yao (1995) look at entrepreneurs who are employees of firms, discover significant inventions, and then leave to start new firms. The employee has three options: keep silent and leave to start a new firm, reveal the invention to the employer in hopes of a reward, or negotiate a reward with the employer before revealing the invention. Dealing with the employer can also result in a new firm in the form of a "spin-off." Here general inventions result in spin-offs whereas specific inventions lead to "start-ups." Thomas Hellmann (2005) uses a multitask incentives model and shows how the choice of organizational structure of new ventures (start-ups, spin-offs, or internal ventures) depends on corporate policies toward employee inventors and the allocation of intellectual property rights.

4.5.4 Incentives

Economists and management researchers contrast the incentives of entrepreneurs with those of managers. The profit of the entrepreneur is the discounted value of the firm when established minus the costs of establishing the firm. In contrast, the manager receives contractual incentives that are based on the measured performance of the firm. The entrepreneur acts to maximize his return, whereas the manager often responds to incentives designed by the owners of the firm. Barzel (1987) argues that the entrepreneur takes the role of the residual claimant because his actions are more costly to monitor than those of other factors of production.

Gromb and Scharfstein (2005) consider a partial equilibrium model in which an investor owns two potential projects that depend on managerial ability. The projects must be completed one after the other. The manager must devote effort to improve the chances the first project will be successful. The outcome of the projects provides information about the manager's ability. They interpret the first project as that of an established firm, and they interpret outsourcing of the second project as an entrepreneurial firm. The distinction between existing and new firms has to do with different labor-market incentives for managers, with higher-ability managers preferring to become entrepreneurs.

The incentives of entrepreneurs and managers differ because their tasks differ. The entrepreneur is concerned with defining the new firm, which is by definition a market entrant. The manager who works for an established firm takes into account the potential continuation of existing business. The entrepreneur is building an organization and works independently. In contrast, the manager of an established firm is part of an existing hierarchy, often with bureaucratic inertia, risk aversion, and inefficiencies that are observed in many large business organizations; see Carl Schramm (2006a).

4.6 The Classical Theory of the Entrepreneur

The classical theory of the entrepreneur offers many important insights in a literature that spans over two and a half centuries. The classical literature provides the background, context, and conceptual tools that are required for developing the theory of the entrepreneur. The main contributors to the classical theory include Richard Cantillon, Jean-Baptiste Say, Frank Knight, and Joseph Schumpeter.

The classical theory suffers from a serious shortcoming: the absence of a clear distinction between the entrepreneur and the firm. The classical theory views the activities of the entrepreneur in combination with those of the firm that the entrepreneur establishes. The entrepreneur's role in establishing the firm is not separated from the entrepreneur's transformation into an owner and manager. The profit of the entrepreneur is not distinguished from the profit of the new enterprise.

The conceptual combination of the entrepreneur and the enterprise can be explained as according with classical economists' observations of the economy in earlier times. The small farm, retail shop, merchant, or artisanal producer often is closely identified with its founder, who usually continues as operator and manager. However, with the widespread development of the modern firm in the mid-1800s, observation requires economists to distinguish between the entrepreneur and the enterprise.

4.6.1 The Entrepreneur's Activities

The entrepreneur establishes the firm as a means of carrying on an economic activity. Cantillon, likely the first celebrated economist to use the term entrepreneur, makes clear their economic function as early as 1732: "all of the exchange and circulation of the State is conducted by the intermediation of these entrepreneurs."[22] It bears emphasis that Cantillon understands the role of the firm in conducting nearly all of the transactions of the economy. He highlights the actions of the firm in carrying

---

22 The quotations from Richard Cantillon are all my translation from the French version. Cantillon's *Essai sur la nature du commerce en général* likely was written in 1732, although it is not clear whether the essay originally was written in English or in French. The first available version is in French and is dated 1755, although it claims on the cover to be a translation from an English text: "Traduit de l'anglois." The English version that is commonly available is a translation done in 1931 by Henry Higgs that was published by Macmillan & Co. and reissued for the Royal Economic Society in 1959. I prefer my translation of these quotations to that of Higgs for various reasons. For example, Higgs renders the French term "entrepreneur" as "undertaker," and the French term "entremise" as "medium."

out the circulation of goods and services. Moreover, Cantillon already observes that the role of the entrepreneur is to be a central economic intermediary. Cantillon's early essay was to influence later economists whether directly or indirectly, including notably Adam Smith, Jean-Baptiste Say, W. Stanley Jevons, Alfred Marshall, Frank Knight, and Joseph Schumpeter.

Cantillon, as in the present discussion, views the entrepreneur as someone who establishes an enterprise. For example, he speaks of some farmers who "establish themselves as entrepreneurs" to transport produce for farmers to the market of the nearest town. Also, "people in the town establish themselves as merchants or entrepreneurs, to buy agricultural produce from those who bring it, or to order it to be brought on their account." Further, noting that shopkeepers are entrepreneurs, Cantillon observes that if there are too few hat makers in a town or street, "it would be a profitable enterprise, which would encourage some new hatters to open shops."

Writing in 1841, Jean-Baptiste Say provides the most important discussion of the entrepreneur after that of Cantillon. Say is careful to distinguish the income of the entrepreneur from that of the capitalist. This is because the income of the entrepreneur is a return to the entrepreneur's effort, knowledge, and risk-taking. The capitalist provides funds to the entrepreneur that are used to establish the firm. The entrepreneur pays the capitalist a return on that investment.[23]

The entrepreneur establishing a firm is precisely what Joseph Schumpeter (1997, p. 75) identifies as "the fundamental phenomenon of economic development. The carrying out of new combinations we call 'enterprise'; the individuals whose function it is to carry them out we call 'entrepreneurs.'" Schumpeter (1997, p. 66) further observes that "new combinations are, as a rule, embodied, as it were, in new firms which generally do not arise out of the old ones but start producing beside them."

Moreover, Schumpeter (1997, pp. 45–6) suggests a distinction between the entrepreneur and the manager or owner of the firm: "If we choose to call the manager or owner of a business 'entrepreneur,' then he would be an *entrepreneur faisant ni bénéfice ni perte*, without special function and without income of a special kind."[24] Here, as in Cantillon, the entrepreneur is defined both by the specific functions he performs and by the presence of uncertainty.

---

23 See Koolman (1971) for an excellent overview of Say's discussion of the entrepreneur, including the importance of judgment and the differences between the entrepreneur and the investor.

24 Emphasis in original. Schumpeter believes that the manager and the owner of the firm do not make any profit or loss because in his highly stylized equilibrium system there is no uncertainty and all profits equal zero. It should be emphasized that Schumpeter's equilibrium model does not represent an accurate description of the economy and most likely was not intended to do so. In practice, owners experience uncertainty in income because firms have uncertain profits. Managers experience uncertainty particularly when they have ownership shares of the firm and when their pay is based on the performance of the firm. Theoretical models of the economy, whether in a general equilibrium setting or in industrial organization setting, routinely incorporate uncertainty.

The entrepreneur can establish an enterprise in any industry, whether it be in retail, wholesale, finance, farming, transportation, construction, or manufacturing. Cantillon lists as entrepreneurs all of the following: farmers, transporters of agricultural goods, merchants, wholesalers, bakers, butchers, manufacturers, drapers, hatters, shopkeepers, and retailers. Cantillon further identifies among others those in charge of mines, theaters, buildings, merchants by sea and land, tavernkeepers, restauranteurs, pastry chefs, journeymen and skilled craftsmen, seamstresses, chimney sweeps, shoemakers, tailors, carpenters, and wigmakers. Cantillon also includes artists, scientists, doctors, and attorneys due to the uncertainty of their earnings.

Say points out that all the three categories of producers of useful products, the farmer, the manufacturer, and the merchant, should be given the common designation of entrepreneur.[25] Say (1841, p. 79) specifies that "it is the industrial entrepreneur who, at his own expense, for his profit, and at his risk, attempts to create some product."[26]

The consumer who establishes a firm is an entrepreneur regardless of the size of the resulting firm. The new firm may be small, with few employees, little initial investment, and a narrowly defined mission. Say (1841, p. 76) gives the example of a humble itinerant knife-grinder, whose capital is on his back and whose skill is at his finger tips. Also, for Say (1841, p. 76), a mason with his trowel or an apprentice tailor with his own thimble and needles are entrepreneurs, who also contribute a small part of the capital investment. Conversely, the new firm may be

---

25 Say (1841, p. 79) points out that there is no term in English for "entrepreneur." He observes that this makes it difficult for English economists to distinguish the services rendered by the capacity and talent of the entrepreneur who employs capital, from that of the capitalist who supplies capital. Say also points out that Italian offers multiple alternatives: "imprenditore, impresario, intraprenditore, and intraprensore."

26 The quotations from Jean-Baptiste Say are my translation. Say has two major works. I am not aware of an English translation of Say (1852), *Cours Complet d'Économie Politique: Pratique.* The other major work, Say (1841), refers to the sixth edition of the *Traité d'Économie Politique,* which was first published in 1803. There is only one English translation of this work. Say was not well served by his translator, Charles Robert Prinsep, who states in a footnote to his 1832 translation, p. 18, "The term *entrepreneur* is difficult to render in English; the corresponding word, *undertaker,* being already appropriated to a limited sense. It signifies the master-manufacturer in manufacture, the farmer in agriculture, and the merchant in commerce; and generally in all three branches, the person who takes upon himself the immediate responsibility, risk, and conduct of a concern of industry, whether upon his own or a borrowed capital. For want of a better word, it will be rendered into English by the term *adventurer*" (emphasis in original). Say's contribution to the study of the entrepreneur may have been obscured by his translator's word choice. Moreover, the translator inserts various footnotes that argue with various assertions of Say. The neglect of Say by economists is not new. A discussion of his work by Teilhac (1927, p. 1) points out that "About J.-B. Say, people speak a lot. They speak a lot about him without having read him, and to not say anything good about him."

large, with many employees, substantial initial investment, and a broadly defined mission. Say (1841, p. 82) attributes England's "immense riches" to the "remarkable talent of its entrepreneurs." Say (1841, p. 82) illustrates this observation with a discussion of England's industrial revolution and that country's large-scale industrial manufacture of cotton and wool garments "for the whole world."

The entrepreneur can use traditional methods or new technology to establish the firm. The firm may depend on traditional technology, being no more than a bakery on the corner. Contrary to many accounts, the definition of an entrepreneur does not depend on some arbitrary standards of scientific or technological innovation. Recall Cantillon's list of basic farming, artisanal, and merchant activities. Say (1852, I, p. 94) speaks of the watchmaker as an entrepreneur who "informs himself of the knowledge necessary for the exercise of his art; he has brought together all the means of execution that this art requires, and he has made or caused to be made the useful products that we call clocks or watches."

Alternatively, the new firm may represent the cutting edge of technology, with its establishment starting a new type of industry as well. Say (1852, I, Chapter 29) discusses at length the revolution in the cotton industry based on machines for spinning cotton. He observes that the English barber Arkwright around the year 1769 asked himself why one could not spin hundreds of threads of cotton simultaneously on large spinning wheels.[27] Arkwright not only improved the spinning machine, he built a water-powered cotton-spinning mill in 1771. Arkwright's innovation was the first factory and it signaled the start of the industrial revolution.

4.6.2 The Sources of the Entrepreneur's Profit

Previously, I stated that the profit of the entrepreneur was the discounted value of the firm once established, net of the cost of establishing the firm. In the present framework, the entrepreneur earns a positive profit if the firm adds value relative to direct exchange, the firms established by competing entrepreneurs, or existing firms. Also, the entrepreneur must succeed in capturing some of that added value through efficient decisions.

It is likely that the entrepreneur's profit will be subject to *uncertainty* due to randomness in demand, costs, technology, and competition. However, in the present framework, uncertainty is not a prerequisite for the entrepreneur to earn a profit. In contrast, in the classical theory of the entrepreneur, uncertainty is an essential part of the definition of the entrepreneur.

Cantillon designates two economic classes (other than the Prince and landowners): those who receive fixed wages and those who do not. Those without fixed wages are entrepreneurs: "whether they establish themselves with capital to

---

27 Say's mention of Arkwright and his discussion of cotton spinning brings to mind Schumpeter's (1997) discussion of the introduction of the power loom.

manage their enterprise, or if they are entrepreneurs through their own labor without any capital, and they may be considered as living under uncertainty." Cantillon lists a multitude of sources of uncertainty. For example, the farmer faces price variation due to uncertainties in weather, demand, population, and supply. Entrepreneurs who are wholesalers, shopkeepers, manufacturers, and merchants of every kind face uncertanties in demand and competition: "all of this causes so much uncertainty among all these entrepreneurs, that everyday one sees some of them go bankrupt."

The connection between profit and risk certainly is established early in economic thought. Adam Smith (1998, p. 130) states that "In all the different employments of stock, the ordinary rate of profit varies more or less with the certainty or uncertainty of the returns." However, Smith suggests that the profit of entrepreneurs does not fully compensate them for risk in the most uncertain industries. Referring to entrepreneurs as adventurers, Smith writes

> The presumptuous hope of success seems to . . . entice so many adventurers into those hazardous trades, that their competition reduces their profit below what is sufficient to compensate the risk. To compensate it completely, the common returns ought, over and above the ordinary profits of stock, not only to make up for all occasional losses, but to afford a surplus profit to the adventurers of the same nature with the profit of insurers. But if the common returns were sufficient for all this, bankruptcies would not be more frequent in these than in other trades.

Say (1841, pp. 368–71) attributes only a part of the entrepreneur's profit to the presence of risk. The entrepreneur's profit is a return to his "industrial abilities, that is to say his judgment, to his natural or acquired talents, to his occupation, to his spirit of order and conduct." Say identifies three explanations for the entrepreneur's profit. First, the entrepreneur must raise the necessary capital, which requires the entrepreneur to have a good *reputation*. Second, the entrepreneur must possess the necessary combination of personal attributes: "He needs judgment, reliability, knowledge of men and things." Third, risk affects the entrepreneur's profit because it "limits in another way the amount of this type of services that are offered and makes them a bit more expensive." For Say, all three sources of profit are due to the scarcity of entrepreneurial efforts that are supplied relative to the amount demanded.

Say (1852, I, p. 97) emphasizes that it is the entrepreneur who "judges needs and most of all the means to satisfy them, and who compares the ends with these means; also, his main quality is judgment." Say (1852, II, p. 67), differing with Smith, distinguishes the profit of the entrepreneur from that of capital. The entrepreneur's intelligence, talent, and efforts bring additional value to capital investment.

The idea that the entrepreneur earns profit based on uncertainty is taken up by Knight (1971) as the foundation of his theory of profit. Knight (1971, pp. 41–7) quotes F. B. Hawley (1901, p. 610) in this regard:

> This surplus of consumer's cost over entrepreneur's cost, universally regarded as profit . . . is the inducement for the assumption by the entrepreneur . . . of all the risks, whatever their nature, necessitated by the process of production.[28]

To this, Knight (1971, p. 41) adds "Enterprise is the only really productive factor, strictly speaking, land, labor and capital being relegated to the position of 'means' of production."

Entrepreneurship is the central element of Knight's framework. Knight modifies Hawley by making his now well-known distinction between risk and uncertainty. For Knight (1971, p. 268), uncertainty is "the fact of ignorance and necessity of acting upon opinion rather than knowledge." Knight (1971, p. 285) states that "true profit, therefore, depends on an absolute uncertainty in the estimation of the value of judgment." The entrepreneur receives profit in return for his private knowledge of the quality of his own judgment. The size of entrepreneurial profits varies inversely with their "optimism." The entrepreneur's profit is a return to the quality of his judgment. Knight's analysis of risk, uncertainty, and profit is entirely within the context of the entrepreneur.

Smith (1998, p. 10) observed that many economic improvements were made by the "ingenuity . . . of those who are called philosophers or men of speculation, whose trade is not to do anything, but to observe everything; and who, upon that account, are often capable of combining together the powers of the most distant and dissimilar objects." Smith's gains from the specialization of function and division of labor also apply here: "In the progress of society, philosophy or speculation becomes, like every other employment, the principal or sole trade and occupation of a particular class of citizens." Entrepreneurship is, for Smith, another type of specialization and division of labor. Entrepreneurs are specialists in making business judgments.

Casson's (1982, p. 23) definition builds on these earlier approaches: "an entrepreneur is someone who specializes in taking judgmental decisions about the coordination of scare resources."[29] Casson characterizes judgment in terms of contemporary decision theory, referring as well to the entrepreneur's skills in delegation and organizational management. Following Say (1852) and John Bates Clark (1894), Casson emphasizes the entrepreneur's coordination of scarce resources, particularly the productive factors of land, labor, and capital.

---

28 See also Hawley (1893, 1907, 1901).
29 See Casson (1982, 2003) and the references therein.

4.6.3 The Entrepreneur as Intermediary

The entrepreneur perhaps may best be described as an intermediary. The entrepreneur engages in many economic transactions that are needed to establish the firm. The entrepreneur is an intermediary between the providers of inputs to the firm and the prospective owners of the firm.

It is important to distinguish the entrepreneur's role as intermediary from that of the firm. In Spulber (1999), I presented a portrait of the firm as an intermediary between the firm's customers and its suppliers. This theme is emphasized in a number of later chapters in the present work. Thus, when Cantillon states that "all of the exchange and circulation of the State is conducted by the intermediation of these entrepreneurs," I believe he is combining the intermediation activities of entrepreneurs in setting up firms with those of the firms that they establish.

Say (1841, p. 349) identifies many ways in which entrepreneurs act as intermediaries. Say (1841, p. 349) argues that the entrepreneur becomes an intermediary by acquiring productive services that will ultimately satisfy consumer demand: "Industrial entrepreneurs are only, so to speak, intermediaries who require those productive services needed for producing a good in proportion to the demand for that good." According to Say, the entrepreneur brings together the productive services of land, labor, and capital so as to satisfy consumer demand.

Say (1852, I, p. 94) notes that the "entrepreneur profits from the most elevated and the most humble abilities of humanity. He receives directions from the scientist and transmits them to the worker." Say (1852, I, p. 97) points out that the "industrial entrepreneur is the main agent of production. The other operations certainly are indispensable for creating products, but it is the entrepreneur who puts them to work, who givens them a useful impulse, who obtains value from them." Say (1841, pp. 579–82) states that "the entrepreneur applies acquired knowledge, the services of capital and those of natural agents to produce goods that people value."

Schumpeter (1997) implicitly views entrepreneurs as intermediaries because they establish firms to carry out "new combinations." The entrepreneur brings a power loom to a textile industry that had previously relied on manual labor. The entrepreneur earns a return to introducing the innovation by acting as an intermediary. The entrepreneur obtains the invention from the inventor and capital equipment from the producers of the equipment. Then the entrepreneur supplies the invention and the equipment to the manufacturer that will use them.

> Now to whom does it fall? Obviously to the individuals who introduced the looms into the circular flow, not to the mere inventors, but also not to the mere producers or users of them. Those who produce them to order will only receive their cost price, those who employ them according to instructions will buy them so dearly at first that they will hardly receive any profit. The profit will fall to those individuals whose achievement it is to introduce the looms, whether they produce and use them or whether they only produce or only use

them. . . . The introduction is achieved by founding new businesses, whether for production or for employment or for both.

Schumpeter adds that the entrepreneur is an intermediary in the market for productive inputs including financial capital,

> What have the individuals under considerations contributed to this? Only the will and the action: not concrete goods, for they bought these – either from others or from themselves; not the purchasing power with which they bought, for they borrowed this – from others or, if we also take account of acquisition in earlier periods, from themselves. And what have they done? They have not accumulated any kind of goods, they have created no original means of production, but have employed existing means of production differently, more appropriately, more advantageously.

Schumpeter's characterization of entrepreneurs as intermediaries shows how entrepreneurs focus their efforts on establishing firms. The entrepreneur obtains the invention from others, or equivalently self-produces the invention in an earlier period. The entrepreneur obtains financing from others, which is equivalent to self-financing at market rates. The entrepreneur need not be a manufacturer, either of the capital equipment or of the final product. It is equivalent whether the entrepreneur procures the equipment from others or establishes a firm that produces the equipment.

Entrepreneurial profit in Schumpeter is a return to innovative transactions that create new combinations. The arrangements made for production, purchasing, finance, and innovation are incidental to carrying out the innovative combinations. The entrepreneur's return derives from being able to "produce a unit of product with less expense and thus to create a discrepancy between their existing price and their new costs" (1997, p. 133). The entrepreneur's new combinations realize arbitrage profit. The entrepreneur acts as an intermediary to make the new combinations that are needed to establish a firm.

Hellmann (2007) explicitly models the entrepreneur as an intermediary in the market for inputs needed to establish a firm. He show how the entrepreneur convinces two suppliers of complementary resources to commit to the new venture. The entrepreneur's sequential bargaining strategy depends on the potential partners' costs of evaluating the quality of the entrepreneur's project.

4.6.4 Entrepreneurial Innovation and Creative Destruction

Say (1852) distinguishes the entrepreneur from the scientist, who studies nature, and from the worker, who takes directions from the scientist and the entrepreneur. Say (1852, I, p. 94) emphasizes that the entrepreneur innovates by applying scientific inventions: "This art of application, which constitutes such an essential component of production, is the occupation of a class of men that we call *industrial entrepreneurs.*"[30] The entrepreneur's role as an innovator is evident in Say's (1852, I, pp. 97–8) discussion,

> Personally, he can do without science, by making a judicious application of that of others; he can avoid manual labor by employing the services of others; but he would not know how to do without judgment; because he could incur high costs in making something without any value.

For Say (1841, pp. 579–82) the entrepreneur makes new combinations: "the entrepreneur applies acquired knowledge, the services of capital and those of natural agents to produce goods that people value."

Positing economic equilibrium as a static state without change or uncertainty, Schumpeter's entrepreneur disrupts matters through "gales of creative destruction." He (1964, p. 114) emphasizes that many types of innovation create opportunities for entrepreneurs who then move the economic system away from an equilibrium position in the upturn of the cycle and toward another equilibrium position in the downturn of the cycle.

Schumpeter (1964, p. 59) famously distinguishes invention from innovation. Not only the introduction of new commodities, but also "Technological change in the production of commodities already in use, the opening up of new markets or of new sources of supply, Taylorization of work, improved handling of material, the setting up of new business organizations such as department stores – in short, any 'doing things differently' in the realm of economic life – all these are instances of what we shall refer to by the term innovation."

Schumpeter's entrepreneur establishes a new business as a means of providing "innovations in business organization and all innovations in commercial combinations." The entrepreneur identifies new suppliers through "the choice of a new and cheaper source of supply for a means of production." The entrepreneur provides new products that allow "replacing one production or consumption good by another" that is cheaper or that satisfies needs more adequately. Finally, the entrepreneur earns profit from the "search for new markets in which an article has not yet been made familiar and in which it is not produced."

Schumpeter's theory of economic development encompasses nonentrepreneurial suppliers who simply copy the products and technology of the entrepreneur. The followers generally earn just enough returns to cover the costs of the factors of production. This does not mean that markets have only one successful entrepreneur. In a dynamic economy, a succession of firms introduce entrepreneurial innovations, so that over time many different firms can be entrepreneurs in the same market.

The entry of new firms can cause incumbent firms to go out of business. A *shakeout* happens when there are too many firms chasing too few consumers.

---

30 Emphasis in original.

Shakeouts often are part of a *boom-and-bust cycle* that begins with innovation and considerable entry of entrepreneurs into an industry, rapidly followed by intense competition that results in exit of firms and consolidation of capacity. Many commentators attribute these boom-and-bust cycles to irrational exuberance of entrepreneurs, who are said to overestimate the rewards to entry, thereby wasting capital investment and disturbing the economy.[31]

Far from being irrational or wasteful, however, boom-and-bust cycles serve an important economic function – selecting the best technologies. Schumpeter (1964, p. 116) finds that "most people will link up recessions with errors of judgment, excesses, and misconduct" but argues against that view, emphasizing that "it is understandable that mistakes of all sorts should be more frequent than usual (i.e. when untried things are being put into practice and adaptation to a state of things becomes necessary the contours of which have not yet appeared)."

Traditionally, significant boom-and-bust cycles have been associated with major innovations such as the development of the steam locomotive, the power loom, petroleum for lighting, the sewing machine, and electric current (Schumpeter, 1964). Innovations are observed to precede boom-and-bust cycles in many industries, such as automobiles (Bresnahan and Raff, 1991) and pharmaceutical wholesaling (Fein, 1998). According to Fisher (1933, p. 348), events start with "*new opportunities to invest at a big prospective profit* as compared with ordinary profits and interest, such as through new inventions, new industries, development of new resources, opening of new lands or new markets."[32]

After significant innovations, entry and expansion tend to create industry capacity that substantially outruns market demand. Joseph A. Schumpeter (1997, p. 229) observed the "appearance of entrepreneurs in clusters." The resulting shakeout denotes much more than the effects of random fluctuations in demand or the occasional exit of badly managed firms. Industry capacity expands above the level that is needed to serve the market as a result of the investment and entry. A period of vigorous competition then follows, eventually leading to capacity reduction and the exit of firms.

Many industries experience shakeouts, including supermarkets, motor vehicle manufacturers, pharmaceutical wholesalers, computer manufacturers, television producers, airlines, media companies, Internet companies, on-line publishers,

---

31 For example, Charles P. Kindleberger (1996, p. 13) states that "Overestimation of profits comes from euphoria, affects firms engaged in the productive and distributive processes, and requires no explanation." Fisher (1933, p. 349) emphasizes the "public psychology of going into debt for gain" as a cause of a boom-and-bust cycle, including "the lure of big prospective dividends or gains in *income* in the remote future," the hope of "a *capital* gain in the immediate future," "the vogue of reckless promotions, taking advantage of the habituation of the public to great expectations," and "downright fraud" (emphasis in original).

32 Emphasis in original. Fisher is discussing debt problems leading to the Great Depression, as quoted in Schumpeter's discussion of business cycles (1964, pp. 122–3).

beer brewers, law firms, and clothing designers.[33] Fein (1998) finds shakeouts in wholesaling in over a dozen industries, including flowers, woodworking machinery, locksmiths, specialty tools and fasteners, sporting goods, wholesale grocers, air conditioning and refrigeration, electronic components, wine and spirits, waste equipment, and periodicals.

4.7 Conclusions

Upon the establishment of the firm, a foundational shift takes place as the entrepreneur becomes an owner. The foundational shift represents more than a change in the entrepreneur's role; it is the time when the firm and the entrepreneur can be separated and the firm can continue to function. Historically, the entrepreneur was closely identified with his enterprise. Merchants, farmers, and artisans mingled their business activities with their personal affairs. The modern firm represents a distinct economic actor, with autonomous decisions that maximize profit. It is the separation between the firm and its owners that provides the entrepreneur with a means of accomplishing economic objectives.

The entrepreneur is a consumer who takes action to establish a firm. The entrepreneur's economic role is combine personal capabilities, including judgment and knowledge, with recognition of market opportunities. The entrepreneur's profit is the value of the firm net of the costs of establishing the firm. Firms generate gains from trade and also incur transaction costs in both their market transactions and their management transactions. Consumer-entrepreneurs establish firms if doing so generates added value to the economy.

The newly established firm adds value if it increases economic efficiency relative to three types of competitive alternatives: Potential competition from entrepreneurs who contemplate establishing firms, direct exchange between consumers, and established firms' prospective offerings. Entrepreneurs establish firms to add capacity to the economy in response to growth and change in economic demand. Entrepreneurs further realize the economic value of innovations in transactions, products, and technologies by embodying innovations in new firms.

---

33 Shakeouts are observed in many industries including supermarkets (Craswell and Fratrick, 1985–6), motor vehicle manufacturers (Bresnahan and Raff, 1991), and pharmaceutical wholesalers (Fein, 1998). Books on shakeouts examine the computer industry (McClellan, 1984), airlines (Peterson and Glab, 1994; Morrison and Winston, 1995), and media companies (Maney, 1995). Many types of shakeouts have been noted in press reports, including, for example, Internet companies (Tedeshi, 2000), online publishing (Schiesel, 1997), beer brewing (Moriwaki, 1996; Horvath et al., 2001), law firms (Deutsch, 1995), and clothing designers (King, 1998).

5

Competition among Entrepreneurs

Entrepreneurs are the genesis of firms. Through the actions of entrepreneurs, firms obtain their initial missions, goals, business definitions, employees, financing, technology, and organizational structure. The economic theory of the firm must therefore recognize that entrepreneurial decisions endogenously create firms. The purpose of this chapter is to examine the endogenous establishment of firms by entrepreneurs.

The chapter presents a gallery of general equilibrium models with endogenous entrepreneurs. Consumers choose whether to become entrepreneurs and establish firms or whether to become workers. The analysis features competition among entrepreneurs, that is, Type I competition. The analysis demonstrates that important features of entrepreneurship can be analyzed in equilibrium models. In all of the models presented in this chapter, the separation theorem applies, so that firms maximize profit. The analysis further demonstrates that firms can be made endogenous in economic models.

In the first model, entrepreneurs establish firms that offer differentiated products and engage in oligopolistic price competition. The equilibrium number of entrepreneurs depends on differences in the setup costs of establishing a firm. In the second model, consumers solve a two-period consumption-saving problem and entrepreneurs invest in the cost of establishing firms and invest in productive capital. The equilibrium number of entrepreneurs depends on differences in investment costs required to establish a firm. In the third model, entrepreneurs bear the risks that result from uncertain start-up costs. The equilibrium number of entrepreneurs depends on differences in their risks of establishing the firm, with all entrepreneurs having the same risk preferences. In the fourth model, entrepreneurs bear the risks that result from uncertain start-up costs, with all projects having the same level of risk. The equilibrium number of entrepreneurs depends on differences in their degree of risk aversion. In the fifth model, entrepreneurs encounter delays in establishing firms. The equilibrium number of entrepreneurs depends on differences in rates of time preference. Finally, in the sixth model, entrepreneurs obtain financing to establish firms, and endowments affect the incentives of entrepreneurs to devote effort to the firms. The equilibrium number of entrepreneurs depends on differences in endowments.

The analysis builds on the general equilibrium model of Kihlstrom and Laffont (1979, 1982). Kihlstrom and Laffont (1979) present an important general equilibrium model in which consumers act as entrepreneurs and establish firms. All consumers can employ the production technology without cost. This assumption is consistent with the assumption in the present analysis that consumers are endowed with production technology. Consumers choose between establishing firms and working at a fixed wage. All consumers are risk-averse and production is subject to uncertainty. A consumer who becomes an entrepreneur operates the production technology and chooses the number of workers to hire. The consumer-entrepreneur thus is a residual claimant and bears risk because of the uncertainty in the production process. The consumer-entrepreneur chooses the number of workers to maximize the expected utility of income, which equals the profit of the firm. The wage is determined by a Walrasian auctioneer, as in the standard general equilibrium model. All consumers have an indivisible unit of labor that can be used either to be an entrepreneur or to be a worker.

Kihlstrom and Laffont's (1979) analysis demonstrates that endogenous formation of firms by entrepreneurs is consistent with an economic equilibrium model. They show that the equilibrium number of firms and the equilibrium prices depend on consumer risk aversion. Consumers who are more risk-averse become workers, whereas those who are less risk-averse become entrepreneurs. Entrepreneurs operate larger firms the lower is their degree of risk aversion. The equilibrium is second-best efficient, taking into account institutional constraints that rule out risk trading between consumers.[1] A key difference between Kihlstrom and Laffont's model and the present analysis is that in their model there is a Walrasian auctioneer and firms are price-takers. The models presented in this chapter examine entrepreneurship in which oligopoly firms offer differentiated products and engage in oligopolistic price competition. In their analysis, risk-averse consumer-owners do not maximize expected profit because production plans are adjusted to reduce risk. In contrast, the models presented in this chapter obey the separation criterion, with firms maximizing profits.

5.1 Set-Up Costs

Consider an economy in which any consumer may become an entrepreneur and start a firm. The model examines the establishment of firms by entrepreneurs in a

---

1 Kihlstrom and Laffont (1982) extend their analysis by adding a stock market. They show that all consumers are indifferent between being or not being entrepreneurs. With opportunities to share risks through a capital market, the economy with entrepreneurs performs more efficiently. This result depends on there being not only uncertainty in setting up a firm but also fixed costs that can be shared across multiple owners.

general equilibrium setting. The creativity of entrepreneurs is represented by assuming that every firm produces a unique product. Once established, firms engage in monopolistic price competition. The entrepreneur encounters transaction costs when establishing a firm. These costs represent the efforts required to conduct market research, commercialize inventions, design the organization, gather factors of production, and negotiate with potential customers, suppliers, employees, investors, and partners.

The equilibrium analysis of competing entrepreneurs makes the entrepreneurship decision endogenous. The model examines the effects of the size of the economy and the effects of demand and cost parameters on the equilibrium number of entrepreneurs. In addition, the model shows the effects of the choice by consumer-owners to maximize profit. The model applies the separation theorem with differentiated products that was developed in Chapter 3. Once established, firms engage in price competition with differentiated products. The oligopoly model presented here draws on Dixit and Stiglitz (1977) and Lancaster (1980).

A key feature of the model is that each potential entrepreneur has a different cost of establishing a firm. The differences in set-up costs represent the ability, judgment, and knowledge of the consumer-entrepreneur. The consumer-entrepreneur's cost of establishing a firm in labor units equals $1 + k$. The consumer-entrepreneur supplies the first unit of labor and employs other consumers for the incremental labor units. The incremental set-up costs k are distributed uniformly with unit density on the interval $[0, n]$. The measure of the number of consumers equals n.

Each consumer owns a production technology for producing a good. Although each final product is unique, the production technology for every good is identical and exhibits increasing-returns-to-scale technology. To produce q_j units of good j requires $\alpha + \beta q_j$ units of labor, where $\alpha > 0$ represents fixed costs and $\beta > 0$ is marginal cost. The consumer can operate the technology for his own benefit, or establish a firm and sell the product to other consumers, thereby earning profit from sales.

Each consumer has an endowment of one unit of labor. A consumer must choose between becoming a worker and becoming an entrepreneur. The consumer-worker receives a wage in return for supplying a unit of labor, and the wage is normalized to equal 1. The consumer-worker either works for an entrepreneur to establish a firm or works for a firm once it is established. The consumer-entrepreneur becomes an owner of the firm once it is established and receives the profit of the firm, Π, net of the incremental labor cost of establishing the firm, k.

A consumer chooses to become an entrepreneur only if the profit net of the incremental labor cost of establishing the firm exceeds what the consumer would earn elsewhere as a worker,

$$\Pi - k \geq 1.$$

The worker's labor earnings are the entrepreneur's opportunity cost. At the competitive equilibrium with differentiated products, it will be shown that all firms earn the same profit. This means that consumers with low costs of establishing firms will become entrepreneurs whereas those with high costs will become workers. In equilibrium, consumers with incremental labor costs k in the interval $[0, m]$ will choose to become entrepreneurs, whereas consumers with incremental labor costs k in the interval $(m, n]$ will choose to become workers. Because each firm produces a unique product, the number of goods that will be produced in equilibrium will equal m. The number of entrepreneurs will be determined by consumer decisions at the market equilibrium.

Every consumer has a utility function with the CES form,

$$(1) \qquad u(x) = \left(\int_0^m x_j^{(s-1)/s} dj \right)^{s/(s-1)}.$$

The demand parameter is greater than one, $s > 1$, which is necessary and sufficient for products to be substitutes. Let I be the consumer's income. The consumer's problem is to maximize utility subject to the budget constraint

$$(2) \qquad \max_x u(x) \quad \text{subject to} \quad \int_0^m p_j x_j dj \leq I.$$

The solution to the consumer's problem yields the level of consumption of each good i,

$$(3) \qquad x_i = \frac{I/p_i^s}{\int_0^m (1/p_j)^{s-1} dj}.$$

Recall that the own-price elasticity of demand is $\eta_i = s$ for any consumer i because the derivative of the price index with respect to any price is zero when there is a continuum of goods.

Substitute the consumption levels from equation (3) into the consumer's utility function in equation (1) to obtain the consumer's benefit as a function of price and income,

$$(4) \qquad u(p, I) = I \left[\int_0^m (1/p_j)^{(s-1)} dj \right]^{1/(s-1)}.$$

The income of a consumer-worker is $I = 1$. The income of an entrepreneur equals the profit from the firm minus the cost of establishing the firm, $I = \Pi - k$.

Consider the market equilibrium in which m consumers choose to become entrepreneurs and establish firms. Each consumer-entrepreneur will then become an owner of a single-product firm. Each firm produces a differentiated good and sells that good to all consumers. The profit from producing q_j units of good j equals

$$(5) \qquad \Pi_j(p_j) = p_j q_j - \alpha - \beta q_j.$$

The separation theorem obtained in Chapter 3 demonstrates that each consumer-owner maximizes profit when there are many differentiated products.

Profit maximization by consumer-owners implies that the mark-up above marginal cost equals price divided by demand elasticity,

(6) $$p_j - \beta = p_j/\eta_j.$$

Substituting the elasticity of demand into the firm's first-order condition for profit maximization shows that prices are equal in equilibrium,

(7) $$p^* = s\beta/(s-1).$$

Because prices are equal across goods, the amounts of the goods that are produced also are equal, $q_j = q$ for all j. The profit of a firm at the competitive equilibrium equals

(8) $$\Pi = p^*q - \alpha - \beta q = [s\beta/(s-1)]q - \alpha - \beta q.$$

The equilibrium number of entrepreneurs is determined by the critical incremental labor cost at which profit minus the incremental labor cost of setting up a firm equals what the entrepreneur could earn as a worker, $\Pi - k = 1$. Letting $k = m$ be the critical cost, the marginal entrepreneur is determined as follows:

(9) $$[s\beta/(s-1)]q - \alpha - \beta q - m = 1.$$

The number of firms m is equal to the incremental labor cost of the marginal entrepreneur.

Consider now the economy's labor resource constraint. The total amount of labor in production equals the number of goods times the labor cost of each good, $m(\alpha + \beta q)$. In addition, the number of workers employed in setting up firms equals $\int_0^m k\,dk = m^2/2$. Recall that entrepreneurs provide the first unit of labor in establishing a firm, which equals m units of labor. The economy's labor constraint equates the total demand for labor to the number of consumers, n:

(10) $$m(\alpha + \beta q) + m^2/2 + m = n.$$

Equations (9) and (10) determine the equilibrium number of entrepreneurs and the amount of each good that is produced. One way to think about the equilibrium is to consider equation (9) as the output-entrepreneur pairs consistent with the determination of the number of entrepreneurs. This marginal-entrepreneur relationship between output and the number of entrepreneurs is an upward-sloping line,

$$q^E(m) = (1 + \alpha + m)(s - 1)/\beta.$$

Also, consider equation (10) as the output-entrepreneur pairs consistent with the labor constraint. This labor-constraint relationship between output and the number of entrepreneurs is a downward-sloping line,

$$q^L(m) = (n/m - 1 - m/2 - \alpha)/\beta.$$

Using these curves, the equilibrium is represented in Figure 5.1.

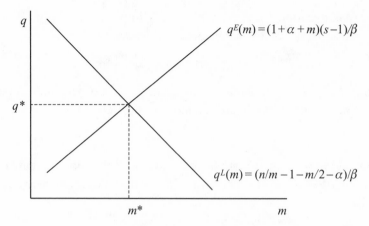

Figure 5.1. The equilibrium number of entrepreneurs and output of each product.

Solving equations (9) and (10) gives the number of entrepreneurs and the amount of each good that is produced,

$$(11) \qquad m^* = -\frac{s(1+\alpha)}{2s-1} + \left[\frac{s^2(1+\alpha)^2}{(2s-1)^2} + \frac{2n}{2s-1} \right]^{1/2},$$

$$(12) \qquad q^* = \frac{(s-1)^2(1+\alpha)}{\beta(2s-1)} + \frac{s-1}{\beta} \left[\frac{s^2(1+\alpha)^2}{(2s-1)^2} + \frac{2n}{2s-1} \right]^{1/2}.$$

The equilibrium number of entrepreneurs and the equilibrium output depend on the number of consumers in the economy, n.

An increase in the number of consumers, n, results in greater output of each good and more entrepreneurs. The presence of more entrepreneurs implies that there is an increase in the total of firms' fixed costs. Moreover, having more entrepreneurs increases the total cost of establishing firms as well as the marginal cost of establishing a firm. The presence of more consumers provides the additional demand for final goods and the additional labor resources to support these higher costs. Even though entrepreneurship becomes more costly at the margin, a larger economy results in more entrepreneurial activity overall. Consumers in the larger economy benefit both from greater product variety and from greater economies of scale in production.

Comparative statics analysis yields additional results. An increase in the marginal production costs, β, lowers the output of each good but does not affect the number of entrepreneurs in equilibrium. An increase in the fixed cost of production, α, raises the amount of each good that is produced but lowers the number of entrepreneurs that choose to establish firms. An increase in the substitution parameter, s, increases the amount of each good that is produced and lowers the number of entrepreneurs that choose to establish firms.

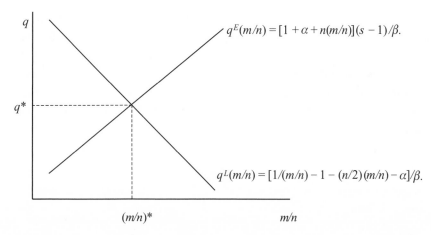

Figure 5.2. The equilibrium number of entrepreneurs and output of each product.

Consider the equilibrium number of entrepreneurs as a proportion of the population, m^*/n. The equilibrium output curves in Figure 5.1 can be written based on the number of entrepreneurs per capita:

$$(13) \qquad q^E(m/n) = [1 + \alpha + n(m/n)](s - 1)/\beta,$$

$$(14) \qquad q^L(m/n) = [1/(m/n) - 1 - (n/2)(m/n) - \alpha]/\beta.$$

The axes are output q and entrepreneurs per capita m/n. See Figure 5.2. A greater number of consumers shifts the first curve upward and shifts the second curve downward. More consumers thus lead to less entrepreneurial activity per capita, so that m^*/n is decreasing in n. This result is due to increases in the costs of establishing a firm as the number of entrepreneurs increases. The result also is due to increased scale of firms as the number of consumers increases. Entrepreneurs become less efficient at the margin, whereas firms become more efficient.

We now compare firms to direct exchange. We determine conditions under which consumers prefer the outcome with endogenous entrepreneurs and firms to direct exchange. Suppose that consumers can form cooperative organizations to take advantage of economies of scale in production and to obtain the benefits of product variety. All of the members of a cooperative contribute their labor to jointly produce goods. Each cooperative shares its benefits equally among its members by allocating an equal share of the output of each good to each of the members. Each cooperative is assumed to operate efficiently by maximizing the benefit of each member.

To represent market transaction costs, assume that cooperatives only transact internally, so that trade between cooperatives is not possible. Assume that consumers encounter transaction costs in assembling the members of the cooperative. Consumers also face coordination costs once the cooperative is established. To represent costs of establishing and operating a cooperative, let the population of consumers be evenly divided into cooperatives of size L. The size of the cooperative, L, is a measure of the number of consumers in a cooperative. The greater the transaction costs of cooperatives, the smaller will be the size of cooperatives.

A cooperative produces m goods at a scale of q units for each good. A consumer in a cooperative of size L obtains consumption $x = q/L$ of each good. This means that each member of a cooperative of size L obtains benefits equal to

$$(15) \qquad\qquad u(x) = m^{s/(s-1)}q/L.$$

Each member of a cooperative contributes a unit of labor. The labor constraint of the cooperative is thus

$$(16) \qquad\qquad L = m(\alpha + \beta q).$$

Solve the resource constraint for the scale of production of each good, q, and substitute into the consumer's benefit function. This yields an expression that depends on the number of goods produced by the cooperative and on the size of the cooperative,

$$(17) \qquad\qquad u(m, L) = m^{s/(s-1)}\left(\frac{1}{\beta m} - \frac{\alpha}{\beta L}\right).$$

The cooperative chooses the variety of goods to maximize the benefits of each of its members. Choosing the number of goods to maximize the benefit function in equation (17) yields the optimal variety for a cooperative of size L,

$$(18) \qquad\qquad m = L/(\alpha s).$$

Substitute the optimal number of goods into the benefit function of a member of the cooperative. The consumer's benefit will depend on the size of the cooperative,

$$(19) \qquad\qquad u(L) = \left(\frac{L}{\alpha s}\right)^{1/(s-1)}\left(\frac{s-1}{s\beta}\right).$$

The consumer's benefit is increasing in the size of the cooperative. Note that as the size of the cooperative gets small, the consumer's benefit approaches that under autarky. As the size of the cooperative approaches the size of the population, the consumer's benefit approaches the social optimum.

Consider now competition between entrepreneurs and direct exchange. In the equilibrium with entrepreneurs, all workers obtain the same benefits and all inframarginal entrepreneurs obtain additional benefits from profit net of the costs of establishing a firm. The benefit of a worker in the equilibrium with entrepreneurs equals

$$(20) \qquad\qquad u^* = (m^*)^{1/(s-1)}\left(\frac{s-1}{s\beta}\right).$$

All entrepreneurs except the marginal entrepreneur obtain benefits greater than u^*. If the presence of entrepreneurs makes workers better off than they would be in cooperatives, then all entrepreneurs are also better off than they would be in an equilibrium with cooperatives. Thus, when workers are made better off at the equilibrium with entrepreneurs, all consumers are better off than they would be with cooperatives.

The condition for the activities of entrepreneurs to make workers better off is obtained by comparing equations (19) and (20),

$$L \leq \alpha s m^*.$$

Otherwise, workers will be as well off or better off with cooperatives than with firms established by entrepreneurs. Every consumer is made better off by entrepreneurs establishing firms if cooperatives are sufficiently small. The condition is also necessary for the market equilibrium with entrepreneurs to compete with the equilibrium with cooperatives. If firms paid workers more, the market equilibrium would result in lower product variety, so that workers would be worse off.

The comparison of cooperatives and firms yields a separation theorem. Because the cooperative is limited in size, the market with firms offers advantages of greater scale in production and greater product variety. When the cooperative encounters transaction costs in the market, the firm offers advantages due to gains from trade. The market mechanism operates through price-setting by firms. Gains from trade result because each firm sells to many consumers and each consumer buys from many firms to obtain the benefits of scale and variety. The firm differs from the consumer cooperative because its objectives differ from those of its owners. Consumers obtain gains from trade by establishing profit-maximizing firms rather than operating cooperatives.

Consumers unanimously prefer separation when the condition $L \leq \alpha s m^*$ holds. The equilibrium with entrepreneurs (weakly) Pareto dominates the equilibrium with cooperatives. Recall that the number of entrepreneurs is increasing in the size of the population; that is, $m^*(n)$ is an increasing function. This implies that the greater the population, n, the more competitive is the market equilibrium with entrepreneurs in comparison with direct exchange between consumers. This yields a critical population size, n^{**}, which is shown in Figure 5.3. When the population exceeds the critical size n^{**}, consumers unanimously prefer the equilibrium with firms to the equilibrium with cooperatives of size L. The greater the transaction costs of direct exchange, that is, the smaller the size of a cooperative, the lower is the critical size of the population at which consumers unanimously prefer the market equilibrium with firms.

5.2 Investment

Consider a dynamic equilibrium model with endogenous entrepreneurship. The economy exists for two periods and all consumers live for two periods. Any

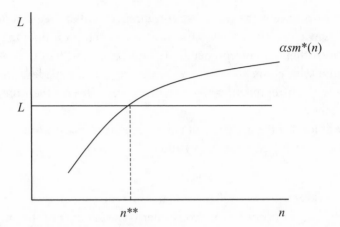

Figure 5.3. The market equilibrium with endogenous firms is preferred to direct exchange when the population exceeds the critical size n^{**}.

consumer can choose to become an entrepreneur and to establish a firm. Firms are established in the first period by young consumers.

An entrepreneur incurs costs of setting up the firm in the first period. To pay for the costs of establishing a firm, the entrepreneur must obtain investment capital in the first period. The firm carries out production in the second period. As a consequence, the firm is a store of value for consumers, in terms of both investment in set-up costs and investment in productive capital.

There is a single good in the first period that can be consumed or invested. The good is not storable; it must either be immediately consumed or invested. As an investment, the first-period consumption good can be used to establish the firm or employed as a capital good to manufacture a second-period consumption good.

Every consumer has the potential to become an entrepreneur. Each consumer has a different cost of establishing a firm due to differences in the transaction costs of innovation. In contrast to the preceding model, the costs in this section are investment costs rather than labor costs. There is a continuum of consumers, each of whom has a different cost k of setting up a firm, which is uniformly distributed on the interval $[0, n]$.

Each firm established by an entrepreneur offers a unique consumption good in the second period. There are m second-period consumption goods j, where j is a continuous index that takes values in the interval $[0, m]$. The number of entrepreneurs, or equivalently, the number of second-period consumption goods is determined endogenously.

All second-period consumption goods have the same production function,

$$(21) \qquad\qquad\qquad q_j = \gamma K_j,$$

where γ is a productivity parameter, q_j is the output of a second-period consumption good j, and K_j is the capital investment in the production of the second-period consumption good j.

All consumers have same endowment, which is equal to one unit of the first-period consumption good. Consumers consume c units of the first-period consumption good and therefore save $z = 1 - c$ units. Consumers consume m goods in the second period, which can be represented for notational convenience by a composite good, C. The second-period composite good corresponds to a CES utility function,

$$(22) \qquad C(x) = \left(\int_0^m x_j^{(s-1)/s} dj \right)^{s/(s-1)}.$$

Consumers have the same preferences, which are represented by the two-period utility function with the subjective discount rate ρ:

$$(23) \qquad U(c, C) = u(c) + \frac{1}{1+\rho} u(C).$$

The consumer's utility function within each period is concave and given by $u(c) = c^{1/2}$. Let the consumer's elasticity of substitution across second-period consumption goods be $s = 3/2$. Given the parametric values, the consumer's two-period utility function is

$$(24) \qquad U(c, C) = c^{1/2} + \frac{1}{1+\rho} \left(\int_0^m x_j^{1/3} dj \right)^{3/2}.$$

The return on savings is normalized to 1 without loss of generality because only relative prices matter in equilibrium. Let z_i denote consumer i's savings. A consumer's savings can be positive or negative because consumers are allowed to borrow from each other.

The consumer's problem is solved by backward induction, as shown in Chapter 3. The second-period problem is to maximize the value of the composite good given the consumer's second-period income I,

$$(25) \qquad \max_x u \left(\left(\int_0^m x_j^{(s-1)/s} dj \right)^{s/(s-1)} \right),$$

subject to the budget constraint $\int_0^m p_j x_j dj = I$. The consumer solves a first-period consumption-saving problem that determines income in the second period.

Given $s = 3/2$, the solution to the consumer's problem is

$$(26) \qquad x_i = \frac{I / p_i^{3/2}}{\int_0^m (1/p_j)^{1/2} dj}.$$

The composite good as a function of second-period income thus equals

$$(27) \qquad C(I) = I \left[\int_0^m (1/p_j)^{1/2} dj \right]^2.$$

Let $P = [\int_0^m (1/p_j)^{1/2} dj]^2$ denote the price index in equation (27), so that $C(I) = IP$.

If a consumer with cost parameter k establishes a firm, then that consumer's second-period income equals profit minus the cost of establishing the firm plus the return on savings,

$$(28) \qquad\qquad I_k = \Pi - k + z_k.$$

If a consumer with cost parameter k does not establish a firm, then that consumer's second-period income is simply the return on savings, $I = z$.

The entrepreneur's saving problem is

$$\max_z (1 - z)^{1/2} + \frac{1}{1 + \rho}\{[\Pi - k + z]\, P\}^{1/2}.$$

The first-order condition for the entrepreneur's savings problem can be solved for savings z. The type-k entrepreneur's savings are

$$(29) \qquad\qquad z_k = \frac{P - (\Pi - k)(1 + \rho)^2}{P + (1 + \rho)^2}.$$

Clearly $z_k < 1$, so that first-period consumption is positive.

The saving problem of a consumer who is not an entrepreneur is the same, with profit and set-up costs set equal to zero:

$$\max_z (1 - z)^{1/2} + (zP)^{1/2}/(1 + \rho).$$

A consumer who does not become an entrepreneur has savings

$$(30) \qquad\qquad z = \frac{P}{P + (1 + \rho)^2}.$$

Clearly z is an interior solution such that $0 < z < 1$, so the consumer saves some of his income. The entrepreneur saves less than a consumer who is not an entrepreneur because he anticipates income as an owner of a firm. The entrepreneur may borrow to finance first-period consumption and borrows the cost of establishing the firm.

An entrepreneur chooses to establish a firm if and only if the firm's profit is greater than or equal to its capital cost, $\Pi \geq k$. Therefore, the marginal entrepreneur, $k = m$, is given by

$$(31) \qquad\qquad \Pi = m.$$

This determines the number of entrepreneurs and also the number of products that will be offered in the second period.

By arguments given in Chapter 3, the Fisher Separation Theorem applies in the two-period economy with product variety. Entrepreneurs establish a firm to receive the firm's profit net of the costs of establishing the firm. The entrepreneur becomes an owner and separates his consumption-saving decision from the firm's profit-maximizing decision. The firm thus chooses its price to maximize profit as a best response to the equilibrium prices of other firms. Because the production function is $q = \gamma K$, the firm's profit is

$$(32) \qquad \Pi = pq - q/\gamma.$$

With many differentiated products, the elasticity of demand equals the parameter of the CES utility function for every good j, $\eta_j = s = 3/2$. Substitute the elasticity of demand into the firm's first-order condition for profit maximization,

$$(33) \qquad p - 1/\gamma = p/s.$$

In equilibrium, each firm chooses the price

$$(34) \qquad p^* = 3/\gamma.$$

Because prices are equal across goods, the amounts of the goods that are produced also are equal, $q_j = q$ for all j. Each firm earns the same profit at the competitive equilibrium,

$$(35) \qquad \Pi = (2/\gamma)q.$$

Because $\Pi = m$, the number of entrepreneurs and the output of each good are related as follows, using profit from equation (35):

$$(36) \qquad m = (2/\gamma)q.$$

The economy's total investment has two components. First, the total cost of establishing firms equals $\int_0^m k\,dk = m^2/2$. Second, the total cost of productive capital equals

$$(37) \qquad mK = mq/\gamma.$$

From equations (36) and (37), total productive capital is

$$(38) \qquad mK = m^2/2.$$

Therefore, the economy's total investment equals $m^2/2 + m^2/2 = m^2$.

The economy's total savings equals the savings of entrepreneurs and those of other consumers,

$$(39) \qquad Z = \int_0^m z_k\,dk + (n - m)z.$$

The equilibrium price $p^* = 3/\gamma$, so that the price index is $P = m^2\gamma/3$. Using equations (29) and (30), total savings equal

$$(40) \qquad Z = \frac{n\gamma/(1 + \rho)^2 - 3/2}{\gamma/(1 + \rho)^2 + 3/m^2}.$$

Equating total investment, m^2, and total savings, Z, gives the number of entrepreneurs in equilibrium,

$$(41) \qquad m^* = [n - 9(1 + \rho)^2/(2\gamma)]^{1/2}.$$

A sufficient condition for entrepreneurs to establish firms is that the number of consumers is sufficiently large, $n > n^*$, where

(42) $$n^* = 9(1 + \rho)^2/(2\gamma).$$

The equilibrium number of entrepreneurs, m^*, is increasing in the number of consumers. The number of entrepreneurs is also increasing in the productivity parameter, γ. Because starting a firm is a form of saving, the number of entrepreneurs is decreasing in the subjective discount rate, ρ. The equilibrium number of entrepreneurs per capita, m^*/n, is increasing in the number of consumers, n, when n is sufficiently close to n^*. As the population of consumers increases beyond a critical level, entrepreneurs per capita are then decreasing in population size.

Entrepreneurs borrow the cost of establishing the firm. In addition, lower-cost entrepreneurs may borrow to finance additional first-period consumption beyond their initial endowment. A sufficient condition for entrepreneurs not to consume more than their initial endowment is to guarantee that the least-cost entrepreneur does not borrow to finance consumption, $z_0 \geq 0$. This holds if the total number of consumers is sufficiently large:

$$n \geq \frac{9(1 + \rho)^2}{2\gamma} \left[1 + \frac{2(1 + \rho)^2}{\gamma}\right] = N^*.$$

The necessary and sufficient condition for entrepreneurs not to consume more than their initial endowment in the first period requires more consumers than are needed to guarantee that firms are established, $N^* > n^*$. In the range of the population $[n^*, N^*]$, entrepreneurs establish firms and some entrepreneurs borrow to finance consumption. They use the firm's profit to repay borrowing for consumption as well as borrowing to finance the cost of establishing the firm.

Compare the equilibrium with entrepreneurs with direct exchange between consumers. To provide a benchmark, suppose that consumers can form cooperatives to combine their technologies so as to produce a variety of goods. Assume that the size of cooperatives is limited due to the transaction costs of establishing and operating cooperatives. Assume that the population is evenly divided into cooperatives of the same size and let L represent the measure of the number of consumers in a cooperative. Suppose further that cooperatives can produce L goods so that the benefit of a cooperative is that it provides product variety that is not available with autarky.

The total savings of the members of a cooperative, $L(1 - c)$, are invested evenly among the $m = L$ goods that the cooperative produces. Thus, the output of each good from the cooperative equals $q = \gamma(1 - c)$. Each individual's second-period consumption of any good equals $x = q/L = \gamma(1 - c)/L$. Substituting into equation (24) gives the utility of each consumer in a cooperative,

(43) $$U^0(c, C) = c^{1/2} + m\gamma^{1/2}(1 - c)^{1/2}/(1 + \rho).$$

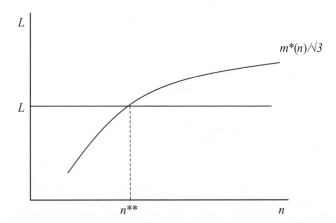

Figure 5.4. With savings and investment, the market equilibrium with endogenous firms is preferred to direct exchange when the population exceeds the critical size n^{**}.

The consumption that maximizes each individual's utility equals

$$c^{-1/2} = m\gamma^{1/2}(1-c)^{-1/2}/(1+\rho).$$

Substituting into the consumer's utility function yields the consumer's benefit as a function of the size of the cooperative,

(44) $$U^0(L) = [(1+\rho)^2 + \gamma L^2]^{1/2}/(1+\rho).$$

At the market equilibrium with entrepreneurs, the price index is $P = m^2\gamma/3$, so that the savings of a consumer who is not an entrepreneur equal

$$z = \frac{m^2\gamma/3}{m^2\gamma/3 + (1+\rho)^2}.$$

Substituting into the consumer's utility function, $U = (1-z)^{1/2} + (zP)^{1/2}/(1+\rho)$, gives the equilibrium utility of a consumer who is not an entrepreneur,

(45) $$U^*(m) = [(1+\rho)^2 + \gamma m^2/3]^{1/2}/(1+\rho).$$

At the market equilibrium, the number of goods is $m^*(n) = [n - 9(1+\rho)^2/(2\gamma)]^{1/2}$.

Consumers are made better off by firms when the market equilibrium provides greater product variety than the cooperative. The additional product variety must be sufficient to offset the costs of establishing firms and the efficiency distortions from oligopoly pricing. Compare the benefits of a consumer with firms with the benefits of a consumer in a cooperative. Then, $U^*(m^*) \geq U^\circ(L)$ when

$$m^*(n) \geq L\sqrt{3}.$$

This condition is illustrated in Figure 5.4. From equation (41), this requires

$$n \geq n^{**} = 9(1+\rho)^2/(2\gamma) + 3L^2.$$

When the number of consumers is greater than the critical number n^* there will be sufficient incentives for nonentrepreneur consumers to participate in the economy. Because entrepreneurs are better off than consumers who do not establish firms, all consumers are better off when the condition holds. The critical number of consumers n^{**} guarantees that the economy with firms generates greater benefits for consumers than the economy with direct exchange through cooperatives. When the condition is satisfied, the benefits of product variety and scale economies outweigh the costs of establishing firms and the distortions from oligopoly pricing.

The condition $n \geq n^{**}$ provides a separation theorem. Consumers obtain gains from trade by operative profit-maximizing firms rather than cooperatives when the condition holds. The critical number for firms to create gains from trade is greater than the critical number of consumers required for an entrepreneur economy to be viable, $n^* = 9(1 + \rho)^2/(2\gamma)$. Thus, $n \geq n^{**}$ implies $n \geq n^*$ for all values of L. When the economy with firms generates greater benefits than the economy with direct exchange, entrepreneurs have incentives to set up firms.

5.3 Time Preferences

A consumer's rate of time preference is likely to affect his choice between becoming an entrepreneur and seeking employment. If employment offers immediate wages whereas entrepreneurship offers delayed earnings, only more patient consumers are likely to become entrepreneurs. This section presents an overlapping-generations model in which consumers have different rates of time preference. Those consumers who are more patient are more willing to delay consumption and choose to become entrepreneurs.

Consumers live for two periods and have an endowment of one unit of labor in each period. Consumers have an initial endowment of a numeraire good h in the first period. The numeraire good cannot be stored. The measure of consumers in each generation equals one. Consumers discount utility of future consumption with a factor δ. Consumers have different discount factors that are uniformly distributed on the unit interval.

Consumer preferences are represented by the two-period utility function

$$U(x, X) = u(x) + \delta u(X),$$

where x and X are the consumption vectors for the two periods. There are m goods produced in each period. The utility function in each period is a CES function with substitution parameter $s > 1$,

$$u(x) = \left(\int_0^m x_j^{(s-1)/s} dj \right)^{s/(s-1)}.$$

The consumer maximizes $U(x, X)$ subject to his budget constraints for the two periods. Consumption in each period is given by $x_j(p, I)$, where I is the consumer's income in that period.

The solution to the consumer's problem yields the level of consumption of each good i,

$$x_i = \frac{I/p_i^s}{\int_0^m (1/p_j)^{s-1} dj}.$$

Each consumer chooses whether to be a worker or an entrepreneur. A worker provides a unit of labor in each period in return for a wage of 1 in each period. An entrepreneur provides a unit of labor to establish a firm when young and a unit of labor to operate the firm when old. The firm only operates during the second period of the entrepreneur's life. The worker's income is $I_1 = h + 1$ when young and $I_2 = 1$ when old. The entrepreneur's income is $I_1 = h$ when young and $I_2 = \Pi$ when old.

Substituting for the optimal consumption levels, the consumer's net benefit equals

$$U = (I_1 + \delta I_2) \left[\int_0^m (1/p_j)^{s-1} dj \right]^{1/(s-1)}.$$

Establishing a firm provides a means of consuming more when the consumer is old, whereas working provides a means of consuming more when the consumer is young. The consumer is indifferent when the present value of income is the same when he is a worker and when he is an entrepreneur. The consumer's initial endowment is the same in each case and so plays no role. The marginal consumer's discount factor is such that the present discounted value of labor income equals the discounted profit from the firm,

$$1 + \delta^* = \delta^* \Pi.$$

Let δ^* be the discount factor of the marginal entrepreneur. Consumers with discount factors greater than or equal to δ^* choose to become entrepreneurs. Accordingly, the number of entrepreneurs in each generation equals $m = 1 - \delta^*$. This equals the number of firms at any date, because each firm operates for only one period.

Each firm produces a unique product, with firm j producing q_j units of good j. There is a continuum of differentiated products with measure m, which also indicates the number of entrepreneurs. Good j has a price p_j, where j is an index that takes values in the interval $[0, m]$. At the steady-state equilibrium, prices remain stationary. Firm j employs $\alpha + \beta q_j$ units of labor. Each firm's profit-maximizing price is $p^* = s\beta/(s - 1)$ at the monopolistically competitive equilibrium. The firm's profits from producing q_j units of output are given by

$$\Pi(q) = \beta q/(s - 1) - \alpha.$$

The marginal entrepreneur is indifferent between being an entrepreneur and being employed by a firm. Substitute for the firm's profit into the marginal entrepreneur's indifference condition and let $\delta^* = 1 - m$,

$$(2 - m) = (1 - m)[q\beta/(s - 1) - \alpha].$$

The marginal entrepreneur's indifference condition provides a relationship between output and the number of entrepreneurs. Solving for output as a function of the number of entrepreneurs gives

$$q^E(m) = [(s - 1)/\beta][1 + \alpha + 1/(1 - m)].$$

The output level is increasing in the number of entrepreneurs in each generation, m.

Consider the labor market equilibrium in each period. There are m entrepreneurs in each generation. The total number of workers at each date equals the total population minus the number of young and old entrepreneurs, $2 - 2m$. The demand for labor at each date equals the number of firms times the amount of labor per firm, $m(\alpha + \beta q)$. The labor constraint thus is

$$m(\alpha + \beta q) = 2 - 2m.$$

The relationship between the output of the firm and the number of entrepreneurs is thus

$$q^L(m) = (1/\beta)(2/m - 2 - \alpha).$$

The output level that solves the labor constraint is decreasing in the number of entrepreneurs in each generation, m.

Combining these two conditions gives the equilibrium output per firm and number of entrepreneurs,

$$q^* = q^E(m^*) = q^L(m^*).$$

The equilibrium is shown in Figure 5.5. The substitution parameter s shifts the entrepreneur curve upwards, leading to greater output per firm and more entrepreneurs at the equilibrium. An increase in the marginal cost β does not affect the equilibrium number of entrepreneurs but reduces the equilibrium scale of the firm. A reduction in fixed costs α reduces the equilibrium number of entrepreneurs.

5.4 Risky Projects

Say, Knight, Schumpeter, and other contributors to the classical literature on entrepreneurship emphasize the role of entrepreneurs as risk takers. Entrepreneurs face uncertainty because establishing firms typically involves new products, new

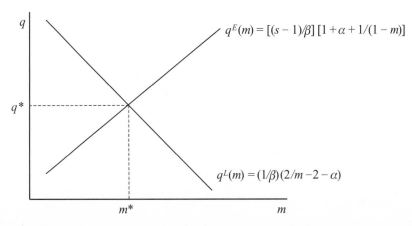

Figure 5.5. The market equilibrium output and the number of entrepreneurs when consumers have different rates of time preference.

technologies, new transactions, and new combinations of buyers and sellers. Kihlstrom and Laffont (1979) present a general equilibrium model in which establishing a firm entails risky production. Consumers are risk-averse, so only those consumers who are less risk-averse choose to become entrepreneurs.

The model in this section modifies and extends the analysis of Kihlstrom and Laffont. In their model, firms are price-takers and offer a homogenous product, and the Walrasian auctioneer clears the market. In our setting, firms set prices and compete with differentiated products. In contrast to Kihlstrom and Laffont, we assume that all consumers have the same preferences, so that all consumers are equally risk-averse. Consumers differ in terms of the risks they face in establishing a firm. Consumers with less risky projects become entrepreneurs, whereas those who would face greater risk as entrepreneurs choose to become wage earners.

There is a continuum of consumer types distributed uniformly with unit density on the interval $[0, n]$. A consumer of type θ on the interval $[0, n]$ has a labor cost $1 + k$ of establishing a firm, where k is a random variable. Set-up costs k are independently distributed across consumer-entrepreneurs. Uncertain set-up costs can represent the risky process of innovation carried out by the consumer-entrepreneur.

Consumer θ selects costs from the uniform probability distribution defined on the interval $[h - \theta/n, h + \theta/n]$. The probability distribution has a mean of $h \geq 1$ and a variance of $(\theta/n)^3$. Thus, a greater value of θ increases the spread of the distribution without changing its mean. Higher θ–type consumers face greater risk if they choose to become entrepreneurs.

Consumers have identical preferences. Consumer utility exhibits constant absolute risk aversion (CARA), so that a consumer's wealth does not affect their degree of risk aversion. Consumers utility has the form $u(C) = -e^{-aC}$, where C is consumption and a is the degree of absolute risk aversion, $a = -u''(C)/u'(C)$.

Each consumer buys m goods, where the number of goods is to be determined endogenously. The consumption level C refers to a composite good that has a CES form,

$$C = \left(\int_0^m x_j^{\frac{s-1}{s}} dj \right)^{\frac{s}{s-1}}.$$

The consumer takes prices as given and maximizes utility subject to a budget constraint. The consumer's problem is

$$\max_x - \exp\{-\alpha C\}$$

subject to the budget constraint $\int_0^m p_j x_j dj \leq I$. The consumer does not face uncertainty in choosing the consumption bundle, because income and prices are known at the time when the consumption choice is made.

By earlier arguments, the consumer's purchase of good i is

$$x_i = \frac{I/p_i^s}{\int_0^m (1/p_j)^{s-1} dj}.$$

The elasticity of demand is $s > 1$ and the composite consumption good is

$$C = I \left[\int_0^m (1/p_j)^{s-1} dj \right]^{1/(s-1)}.$$

Let $P = \left[\int_0^m (1/p_j)^{s-1} dj \right]^{1/(s-1)}$ represent a price index. If all prices equal p, the price index equals $P = m^{1/(s-1)} p$.

Every consumer has an initial endowment of one unit of labor. A consumer must decide between being a worker and being an entrepreneur. If the consumer chooses to be a worker, the consumer supplies a unit of labor to the market and receives a wage, which is normalized to one without loss of generality. The worker's income thus equals $I = 1$. If the consumer chooses to be an entrepreneur, the consumer pays a labor cost of $1 + k$. The consumer-entrepreneur must supply the first unit of labor himself and must obtain the incremental labor cost k from the labor market. The consumer-entrepreneur receives the firm's profit, Π, after the firm is established, so that the consumer-entrepreneur's income is $I = \Pi - k$. The potential consumer-entrepreneur faces risk from the cost of establishing the firm. Accordingly, the consumer chooses to become an entrepreneur if and only if the expected utility of being an entrepreneur is greater than or equal to the utility obtained as a worker,

$$E_\theta u(P(\Pi - k)) \geq u(P),$$

because $C = PI$ from the value of the composite good.

As a result of CARA, the uncertainty due to the costs of establishing a firm is multiplicatively separable,

$$(46) \qquad\qquad E_\theta u(P(\Pi - k)) = -u(P\Pi) E_\theta u(-Pk).$$

This means that the risk stemming from the set-up cost does not affect the consumer's profit maximization decision. Because profit is not uncertain, the consumer's attitude toward risk does not affect the consumer-owner's utility of income from profit. This would still hold if profit also were subject to additive uncertainty. With many differentiated products, consumer-owners do not take into account the effect of the firm's price on the aggregate price index. The separation theorem thus applies, and the consumer-owner prefers that the firm choose its price to maximize profit.

Each consumer-entrepreneur establishes a firm that offers a unique product. The labor cost of production for any good j equals $\alpha + \beta q_j$, where α is the firm's fixed cost, β is the firm's marginal cost, and q_j is the firm's output. The firm's profit has the form

$$\Pi = (p - \beta)q_j - \alpha.$$

Because the separation theorem applies, the firm chooses the profit-maximizing price according to the standard oligopoly model,

$$p - \beta = p/s.$$

So the equilibrium price for any good j is

$$p^* = s\beta/(s - 1).$$

Given the equilibrium price, the firm's profit function can be written as a function of output,

(47) $$\Pi(q) = \beta q/(s - 1) - \alpha.$$

Using the values of prices in equilibrium, the price index equals

(48) $$P = m^{1/(s-1)}(s - 1)/(s\beta).$$

The economy's aggregate labor constraint equates the total labor supply n to the total demand for labor. The total labor employed in production equals $m(\alpha + \beta q)$. The total labor employed in establishing firms equals the total labor supplied by entrepreneurs, m, plus the total incremental cost of establishing firms. By the law of large numbers, the realization of the total incremental cost of establishing firms equals the total of the common expected values of the incremental labor costs $\int_0^m k_j \, dj = mh$. Therefore, the economy's labor constraint is

(49) $$m(\alpha + \beta q) + m + mh = n.$$

The labor constraint can be solved to obtain the output of each good, q, as a function of the number of entrepreneurs, m:

(50) $$q^L(m) = (n/m - \alpha - 1 - h)/\beta.$$

The output level that satisfies the labor constraint is decreasing in the number of entrepreneurs due to the tradeoff between scale and variety.

The number of entrepreneurs remains to be determined. The consumer chooses between becoming a worker or an entrepreneur, and takes into account prospective prices and income from owning a firm. Given equation (46), the marginal entrepreneur of type $\theta = m$ is indifferent between being an entrepreneur and being a worker:

(51) $$- u(P\Pi) E_m u(-Pk) = u(P).$$

Using CARA and rearranging terms gives

(52) $$u(P(\Pi - 1)) = 1/(E_m u(-Pk)).$$

Recall that in the certainty case in Section 5.1, the marginal entrepreneur had an incremental set-up cost equal to the profit of the firm net of the entrepreneur's opportunity cost, which was equal to foregone wages, $\Pi - 1 = k$. There is an analogous condition in the case of uncertainty. At the marginal entrepreneur's cost type k, the utility of a consumer with income of $\Pi - 1$ equals the reciprocal of the expected utility of consumption with income foregone equal to cost k.

Using the form of the consumer's utility function and the probability distribution of costs for a consumer of type $\theta = m$, it follows that

(53) $$E_\theta u(-Pk) = - \int_{h-\theta/n}^{h+\theta/n} e^{aPk} dk/(2\theta/n).$$

Therefore, a type m consumer has expected utility of costs

(54) $$E_m u(-Pk) = - \frac{e^{aP(h+m/n)} - e^{aP(h-m/n)}}{aP2m/n}.$$

Therefore, equation (52) can be written as

(55) $$- e^{-aP(\Pi-1)} = - \frac{aP2m/n}{e^{aP(h+m/n)} - e^{aP(h-m/n)}}.$$

Substitute into equation (55) from the profit function, $\Pi(q) = \beta q/(s - 1) - \alpha$, and the price index, $P = m^{1/(s-1)}(s - 1)/(s\beta)$. Then equation (55) can be solved implicitly for output as a function of the number of entrepreneurs, $q = q^E(m)$. It can be shown that this function is increasing in m.

The analysis yields two relationships between output and the number of entrepreneurs. The labor constraint yields output as a decreasing function of the number of entrepreneurs, $q^L(m)$. The marginal entrepreneur condition yields output as an increasing function of the number of entrepreneurs. These conditions determine the equilibrium output and the equilibrium number of entrepreneurs,

$$q^* = q^L(m^*) = q^E(m^*).$$

The equilibrium is represented in Figure 5.6.

Some properties of the equilibrium emerge from consideration of Figure 5.6. An increase in the mean of set-up costs, h, reduces the equilibrium number of

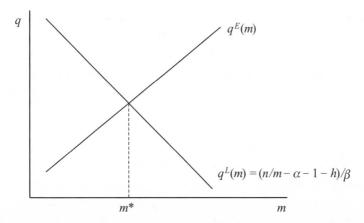

Figure 5.6. The equilibrium number of entrepreneurs when set-up costs are uncertain.

entrepreneurs because it shifts up the entrepreneur curve and shifts down the labor curve. An increase in the fixed costs of production, α, shifts up the entrepreneur curve and shifts down the labor constraint curve, thus lowering the equilibrium number of entrepreneurs. An increase in the marginal costs of production, β, shifts down both curves and lowers the equilibrium output of each good, although the effect on the number of entrepreneurs cannot be determined. An increase in the substitution parameter s shifts up the entrepreneur curve but not the labor constraint curve, thus reducing the equilibrium number of entrepreneurs and increasing equilibrium output. This is because an increase in the substitution parameter increases the firm's profit for each level of output.

With risky projects, entrepreneurs who establish firms have set-up costs with the lowest risks. Entrepreneurs are rewarded for taking risks but not for being less risk-averse than other consumers in the economy. Establishing firms is risky, but entrepreneurs receive rewards for their knowledge of how to avoid risk. Entrepreneurs with less risky projects obtain greater expected utility, whereas the most risky projects are not undertaken.

5.5 Risk Aversion

Following Kihlstrom and Laffont (1979), this section assumes that all consumers have the same technology but differ in terms of their attitudes toward risk. The discussion modifies their analysis by allowing product differentiation and price competition between firms. The analysis obtains their result that only those consumers who are less risk-averse choose to become entrepreneurs, whereas those who are more risk-averse choose to become wage earners. It is shown that with price competition, owners of the firm prefer that the firm maximize profits. Kihlstrom and Laffont (1982) point out that shareholder unanimity can occur in an entrepreneur model with a stock market when consumer utility exhibits CARA.

There is a continuum of consumer types a distributed uniformly with unit density on the interval $[0, n]$. Consumers differ in terms of their degree of risk aversion. Consumer utility exhibits constant absolute risk aversion, so that a consumer's wealth does not affect their degree of risk aversion. Consumers' utility has the form $u(C) = -e^{-aC}$, where C is consumption and a is the degree of absolute risk aversion, $a = -u''(C)/u'(C)$.

Entrepreneurs face a labor cost $1 + k$ of establishing a firm, where the incremental set-up cost k is a random variable. The entrepreneur supplies the first unit of labor. Incremental set-up costs k are independently random variables that are uniformly distributed on the unit interval. Uncertain set-up costs can represent the risky process of innovation carried out by the consumer-entrepreneur.

Each consumer buys m goods, where the number of goods is to be determined endogenously. The consumption level C refers to a composite good that has a CES form,

$$C = \left(\int_0^m x_j^{\frac{s-1}{s}} dj \right)^{\frac{s}{s-1}}.$$

The consumer takes prices as given and maximizes utility subject to a budget constraint. Given the composite good C, the consumer's problem is

$$\max_x - \exp\{-aC\} \quad \text{subject to} \quad \int_0^m p_j x_j dj \leq I.$$

The consumer does not face uncertainty in choosing the consumption bundle, because income and prices are known at the time that the consumption choice is made.

By earlier arguments, the consumer's purchase of good i is

$$x_i = \frac{I/p_i^s}{\int_0^m (1/p_j)^{s-1} dj}.$$

The elasticity of demand is $s > 1$ and the composite consumption good is

$$(56) \qquad C = I \left[\int_0^m (1/p_j)^{s-1} dj \right]^{1/(s-1)}.$$

Let $P = \left[\int_0^m (1/p_j)^{s-1} dj \right]^{1/(s-1)}$ represent a price index. If all prices equal p, the price index equals $P = m^{1/(s-1)} p$.

Every consumer has an initial endowment of one unit of labor. A consumer must decide between being a worker and being an entrepreneur. If the consumer chooses to be a worker, the consumer supplies a unit of labor to the market and receives a wage, which is normalized to 1 without loss of generality. The worker's income thus equals $I = 1$. If the consumer chooses to be an entrepreneur, the consumer pays a labor cost $1 + k$. The consumer-entrepreneur must supply the first unit of labor himself and must obtain the increment labor cost k from the labor market. The consumer-entrepreneur receives the firm's profit, Π, after the firm is established, so that the consumer-entrepreneur's income is $I = \Pi - k$. The potential consumer-entrepreneur faces risk from the cost of establishing the firm. Accordingly, the consumer chooses to become an entrepreneur if and only if the expected utility of being an entrepreneur is greater than or equal to the utility obtained as a worker,

$$E u(P(\Pi - k)) \geq u(P),$$

because $C = PI$ from the value of the composite good. Therefore, the marginal entrepreneur, m, has a coefficient of risk aversion, a, such that the participation constraint is binding:

$$(57) \qquad E u(P(\Pi - k)) = u(P).$$

Consumers with a lower level of risk aversion, $a \leq m$, choose to become entrepreneurs.

As a result of CARA, the uncertainty due to the costs of establishing a firm is multiplicatively separable. The left-hand side of equation (57) can be written as

$$(58) \qquad E u(P(\Pi - k)) = -u(P\Pi) E u(-Pk).$$

This means that the risk stemming from the set-up cost does not affect the consumer's profit maximization decision. Because profit is not uncertain, the consumer's attitude toward risk does not affect the consumer-owner's utility of income from profit. This would still hold if profit also were subject to additive uncertainty. The separation theorem again applies, and the consumer-owner prefers that the firm choose its price to maximize profit.

Each consumer-entrepreneur establishes a firm that offers a unique product. The labor cost of production for any good j equals $\alpha + \beta q_j$, where α is the firm's fixed cost, β is the firm's marginal cost, and q_j is the firm's output. The firm's profit has the form

$$\Pi = (p - \beta)q_j - \alpha.$$

Because the separation theorem applies, the firm chooses the profit-maximizing price, because according to the standard oligopoly model,

$$p - \beta = p/s.$$

So the equilibrium price for any good j is

$$p^* = s\beta/(s - 1).$$

The price index as a function of the number of entrepreneurs is thus

$$P(m) = m^{1/(s-1)}(s - 1)/(s\beta).$$

Given the equilibrium price, the firm's profit also can be written as a function of output,

(59) $$\Pi = \beta q/(s-1) - \alpha.$$

The economy's aggregate labor constraint equates the total labor supply n to the total demand for labor. The total labor employed in production equals $m(\alpha + \beta q)$. The total labor employed in establishing firms equals the total labor supplied by entrepreneurs, m, plus the total incremental cost of establishing firms. By the law of large numbers, the realization of the total incremental cost of establishing firms equals the total of the common expected values of the incremental labor costs $mEk = m/2$. Therefore, the economy's labor constraint is

(60) $$m(\alpha + \beta q) + m + m/2 = n.$$

The labor constraint can be solved to obtain the output of each good, q, as a function of the number of entrepreneurs, m:

(61) $$q^{L}(m) = (n/m - \alpha - 3/2)/\beta.$$

The output that solves the labor constraint is decreasing in the number of entrepreneurs, m.

The consumer chooses between becoming a worker or an entrepreneur and takes into account prospective prices and income from owning a firm. It can be shown that entrepreneurs are those consumers with the lowest levels of risk aversion. Combining equations (57) and (58), and given CARA, the marginal entrepreneur of type m is indifferent between being an entrepreneur and being a worker:

(62) $$u(P(\Pi - 1)) = 1/(E_{m}u(-Pk)).$$

Recall that in the certainty case in Section 5.1, the marginal entrepreneur had an incremental set-up cost equal to the profit of the firm net of the entrepreneur's opportunity cost, which was equal to foregone wages, $\Pi - 1 = k$. There is an analogous condition in the case of uncertainty. At the marginal entrepreneur's cost type k, the utility of a consumer with income of $\Pi - 1$ equals the reciprocal of the expected utility of consumption with income foregone equal to cost k.

By CARA, it follows that

(63) $$e^{-mP(\Pi-1)} = \frac{mP}{e^{mP} - 1}.$$

Given the price index $P(m)$ and profit as a function of output, $\Pi(q)$, the marginal entrepreneur's condition in equation (63) implicitly defines output as a function of the number of entrepreneurs, $q = q^{E}(m)$. It can be shown that $q^{E}(m)$ is increasing in the number of entrepreneurs.[2] Combining with the labor market constraint gives

---

2 Substitute into equation (63) for the price index $P(m)$ and profit as a function of output, $\Pi(q)$, and implicitly differentiate with respect to m. The derivative is characterized at $q = q^{E}(m)$ for $mP(m)$ greater than, equal to, or less than one.

the equilibrium output per firm and the number of entrepreneurs,

$$q^* = q^L(m^*) = q^E(m^*).$$

An increase in the number of consumers shifts up the labor curve without shifting the other curve, and as a consequence, increases the equilibrium output per firm and the equilibrium number of entrepreneurs.

5.6 Endowments and Incentives for Effort

Consider an economy with consumers that have different initial endowments h. The consumer endowments are uniformly distributed on the interval $[h_0, h_1]$. The consumer's endowment can be invested in establishing a firm. The resource cost of establishing a firm is K. Let $K > h_1$ so that any consumer with endowment h who establishes a firm must borrow $K - h$ from other consumers. Each consumer chooses between being an investor and being an entrepreneur. A consumer who establishes a firm expends effort z to generate a firm with value F, where

$$F(z) = z^\gamma/\gamma.$$

The parameter γ is positive and less than one.

The entrepreneur finances the firm by selling shares, $(1 - s)$, to investors. The entrepreneur's cost of effort equals z. The entrepreneur's effort is not observable. He chooses effort to maximize net benefits,

(64) $$V = sF(z) - z.$$

The entrepreneur's effort level is a function of his share of the firm's value,

(65) $$sF'(z^*) = 1.$$

The entrepreneur's net benefits are increasing in his share of the firm. By the envelope theorem,

(66) $$V'(s) = F(z^*(s)).$$

Given the form of the production function, F, the entrepreneur's effort level equals

$$z^*(s) = s^{1/(1-\gamma)}.$$

An entrepreneur with endowment h must obtain $K - h$ from investors to establish a firm. Consider a very basic representation of a capital market equilibrium. Assume that the equilibrium return per unit of investment is equal across firms. Let R represent the endogenous return per unit of investment. The assumption requires that for each firm, the share s retained by the entrepreneur is such that the

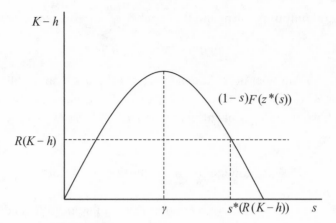

Figure 5.7. The entrepreneur's share of the firm, $s^*(x)$, is a decreasing function of the payment to investors.

payment to investors is given by the common per unit return on investment times the amount financed by the entrepreneur,

$$(67) \qquad (1 - s)F(z^*(s)) = R(K - h).$$

Assume further that the endogenous return per unit of investment equates the demand for investment to the supply of investment. The capital market equilibrium corresponds to a Walrasian equilibrium. A more general model of the capital market would include market-making firms.

In equilibrium, the share retained by the entrepreneur is a function of the amount owed to investors, $s^* = s^*(R(K - h))$. From equation (67) and the form of the production function, $s^* = s^*(R(K - h))$ solves

$$(68) \qquad (1 - s^*)s^{*\gamma/(1-\gamma)}/\gamma = R(K - h).$$

Implicit differentiation gives

$$(69) \qquad s^{*\prime}(F(K - h)) = \frac{\gamma(1 - \gamma)}{(\gamma - s^*)s^{*(2\gamma-1)/(1-\gamma)}}.$$

This means that the function $s^*(x)$ that solves equation (68) is decreasing (or increasing) in x as s^* is greater than (or less than) γ. The investors' return on investment condition is represented in Figure 5.7. There are two possible solutions for investor's share, because the left-hand side of equation (68) is increasing for $s^* < \gamma$ and decreasing for $s^* > \gamma$. The entrepreneur's share in equilibrium, s^*, must be the larger value since the entrepreneur's net benefit is increasing in his share of the firm. This means that the entrepreneur's share of the firm, $s^*(x)$, is decreasing in the total payment to investors. Therefore, the entrepreneur's share, $s^*(R(K - h))$, is increasing in the entrepreneur's endowment level, h.

The entrepreneur's effort level is increasing in the entrepreneur's endowment, because effort is increasing in the share s and the share s is increasing in the endowment h,

$$\frac{d}{dh}z^*(s^*(R(K-h))) = -Rz^{*\prime}(s^*(R(K-h)))s^{*\prime}(R(K-h)) > 0.$$

In addition, the entrepreneur's net benefits are increasing in the entrepreneur's endowment,

$$\frac{d}{dh}V(s^*(R(K-h))) = -RF(z^*(s))s^{*\prime}(R(K-h)) > 0.$$

Substituting for $s^{*\prime}(x)$, obtained by differentiating equation (67),

$$\frac{d}{dh}V^*(s^*(R(K-h))) = \frac{RF(z^*(s))}{F(z^*(s^*)) - (1-s^*)F'(z^*(s^*))z^{*\prime}(s^*)}.$$

Because $dV(s^*(R(K-h)))/dh$ is positive, it follows that

$$\frac{d}{dh}V(s^*(R(K-h))) > R.$$

The entrepreneur's net benefits are increasing in his endowment at a rate greater than the per-unit return R.

This determines the marginal entrepreneur. The consumer becomes an entrepreneur only if the benefits of establishing a firm are greater than or equal to the benefits of investing the initial endowment:

$$V(s^*(R(K-h))) \geq Rh.$$

The marginal entrepreneur has an endowment $h = h^*(R)$ that solves

(70) $$V(s^*(R(K-h^*))) = Rh^*.$$

This is shown in Figure 5.8. The equilibrium number of entrepreneurs equals

(71) $$m^* = h_1 - h^*,$$

because all consumers with endowments that are greater than the marginal endowment, h^*, strictly prefer to be entrepreneurs. From Figure 5.8, an increase in the per-unit return on investment, R, shifts up the return to investment Rh and shifts down the entrepreneur's benefit $V(s^*(R(K-h)))$, thus increasing the marginal endowment, h^*, and reducing the number of entrepreneurs.

Consider the equilibrium demand and supply of investment. The entrepreneur's total demand for investment equals

(72) $$D(R) = (h_1 - h^*(R))K - \int_{h^*(R)}^{h_1} h\, dn.$$

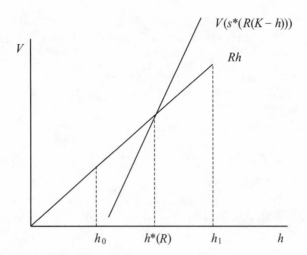

Figure 5.8. The marginal entrepreneur, h^*, as a function of the return on investment when effort is unobservable.

The total available endowment of consumers who are not entrepreneurs equals

(73)
$$S(R) = \int_{h_0}^{h^*(R)} h\,dh = \left[(h^*(R))^2 - h_0^2\right]/2.$$

The equilibrium return on investment equates the demand for investment, R^*, to the supply of investment. The marginal entrepreneur's endowment must be such that

$$h^*(R^*) = h_1 - \left(h_1^2 - h_0^2\right)/(2K).$$

The number of entrepreneurs equals

(74)
$$m^*(R^*) = h_1 - h^*(R^*) = \frac{h_1^2 - h_0^2}{2K}.$$

The number of entrepreneurs, m^*, is decreasing in the cost of establishing the firm K. The equilibrium return on capital, R^*, is increasing in the cost of establishing the firm, because $h^*(R)$ is increasing in R, so that

$$\frac{dR^*}{dK} = \frac{h_1^2 - h_2^2}{2K^2 h^{*\prime}(R^*)} > 0.$$

5.7 Conclusions

Entrepreneurs play a fundamental role in economic equilibrium by establishing firms. This important activity of entrepreneurs readily lends itself to economic modeling. In the models presented in this chapter, entrepreneurs differ in terms of their preferences, endowments, or their costs of establishing a firm. The most efficient entrepreneurs choose to establish firms. The equilibrium number of successful entrepreneurs is determined by various economic conditions.

In a static general equilibrium setting, labor resource constraints and the relative returns to being an entrepreneur and being a worker determine the equilibrium number of active entrepreneurs. In a dynamic general equilibrium setting, the rate of time preference, the productivity of investment, and the size of the population affect the equilibrium number of active entrepreneurs. In a general equilibrium setting with risk, consumers' level of risk aversion and the labor resource constraint affect the equilibrium number of active entrepreneurs.

Entrepreneurs compete with each other to establish firms. Only the most efficient entrepreneurs will choose to establish firms. A larger economy, in terms of the number of consumers, tends to increase entrepreneurship. However, the number of entrepreneurs per capita is likely to decline when the costs of establishing a firm increase at the margin. Entrepreneurs establish firms to obtain the value of the firm as an owner. The firm's value derives from activities that extend beyond the neoclassical view of the firm as a producer. The firm creates value by adjusting prices and by mitigating transaction costs through market making. The returns to these activities provide incentives for entrepreneurs to establish firms.

PART III

HUMAN CAPITAL, FINANCIAL CAPITAL, AND THE ORGANIZATION OF THE FIRM

6

Human Capital and the Organization
of the Firm

Why are firms needed to manage the services of human capital? After all, it is individual workers who provide their abilities, knowledge, information, ideas, designs, productive effort, monitoring, supervision, and decision making. Consumers do not require a firm to coordinate their efforts because they can organize themselves into productive teams. Yet most production and distribution take place within organizations established by firms. To determine why this is so, this chapter examines the economic role of the firm in the management of human capital.

Instead of establishing firms, consumer-workers can combine their human capital to produce output through worker cooperatives. These basic labor partnerships feature equal sharing of surplus and democratic control over production and hiring decisions. The worker cooperative maximizes net benefit per member, as do clubs and other types of partnerships. The worker cooperative is an organization that consists of its members. The worker cooperative provides an alternative to the formation of firms.

The basic worker cooperative is a type of partnership that shares profits equally among its members and maximizes returns per member. Such equal sharing may not be the optimal contract among members. In practice, the partnership may perform more complex functions such as sharing joint costs and building reputations. However, the basic worker cooperative as described here has been widely studied. The basic partnership serves as a useful benchmark for understanding the economic role of the firm. This chapter examines the consequences of modifying the partnership with more sophisticated institutional features. The main modification of the partnership is a market for memberships. The partnership with and without modification is compared to the profit-maximizing firm.

The worker cooperative's hiring decisions generally are inefficient because the cooperative does not maximize profit. The worker cooperative's organizational structure is necessarily restricted due to the requirements of equal sharing of surplus and democratic control. These features of the worker cooperative restrain its ability to form an organizational hierarchy and to assign different rewards to its members. Increasing the complexity of the worker cooperative to solve these problems does not replace firms, because the changes required essentially convert the worker cooperative to a firm.

Modifying the worker cooperative to separate ownership and control begins the process of forming a firm. Implementing such institutional features as a membership market effectively separates ownership and control. A complex organization is the hallmark of the firm. In comparison to the worker cooperative, the firm has the advantage of designing hierarchical structures of authority. The firm can design incentive mechanisms that provide rewards that are based on individual and group performance. When the partnership differentiates among its members by developing a hierarchical organization and individual incentives, it takes on the characteristics of a firm.

Although the firm's performance is enhanced by the quality of its employees' human capital, the firm is distinct from its employees. The firm employs the services of its managers and workers, but the firm has an identity that differs from those of its employees. The firm has its own market reputation that is not the same as the reputations of its employees in labor markets. The firm's decisions are different from those of individual employees. The firm's economic contribution depends on its being an independent economic actor.

This chapter emphasizes the role of the firm in forming organizations. The discussion compares the input and output choices of the basic worker cooperative with those of the firm. Then the analysis looks at how the worker cooperative and the firm select the number of employees based on the quality of their human capital. The chapter considers how incentives in teams affect the size of the worker cooperative and that of the firm. The chapter examines how the worker cooperative and the firm coordinate worker participation decisions. In each of these settings, the firm plays a critical role in determining the number of workers in a team.

The chapter then examines how the firm chooses between market contracts with workers and employment contracts. The discussion compares the benefits and costs of market transactions with management transactions within the organization. Both market transactions and management transactions are voluntary and involve instruments of spontaneous order. Organizations can offer advantages when the firm can coordinate multiple contracts in ways that are not feasible in markets.

6.1 The Worker Cooperative versus the Firm

Human capital is central to economic activity. Consumers invest in their human capital through education and training. Applying their human capital, consumers engage in scientific research, develop new products and industrial processes, and create works of art. Consumers provide medical, legal, accounting, and consulting services. Workers provide the labor services necessary to manufacture products and to conduct economic transactions.

Because individual consumers perform practically every conceivable productive task, why are firms needed? To understand why firms are useful institutions, it is necessary to identify their economic contributions relative to those of associations of workers. Consumers can form associations to combine the services of their endowments of human capital and to coordinate their productive efforts. Such associations need not be firms, but they presumably can achieve anything that could be done by a firm.

Worker cooperatives provide mechanisms for joint production without establishing firms.[1] A basic worker cooperative is not a firm because the organization is not an entity that is separate from its workers. A basic worker cooperative is a set of contracts and transactions between its workers. More complex worker cooperatives become firms by introducing some separation between the firm and its employees. By separating ownership from labor participation, the organization begins to take on the characteristics of a firm. Also, as the decisions of the organization are separated from those of its employees, the organization performs the functions of a firm.

In practice some workers' cooperatives have some types of separation between the organization and its employees. Partnerships, particularly those with many employees, exhibit the features of corporations when they have a legal status as separate entities, hierarchical organizational forms, and separation of ownership and control. For purposes of discussion, the basic worker cooperative is an organization with equal sharing that chooses to maximize the returns per partner. In contrast, a firm is an organization that has some separation of ownership and control and therefore chooses to maximize profit.

A clue to the contribution of firms is the scarcity of worker cooperatives, also known as labor-managed firms.[2] In the United States, the plywood cooperatives of Washington and Oregon have been studied widely.[3] In many economies, taxicab companies, trucking, and other transportation companies' services often are organized as worker cooperatives.[4] What tends to distinguish worker cooperatives is worker ownership and democratic control, "one worker, one vote."[5] The labor-managed firm also may give workers control in proportion to the amount of labor supplied.[6]

It is important to distinguish between a basic worker cooperative and more complex organizations that are clearly firms. For example, Spain's Mondragon group is a massive conglomerate with over 150 member cooperatives engaged

---

1 Such organizations also are called labor-managed firms. Ward (1958) refers to economies with such systems as "market syndicalism."

2 The U.S. Federation of Worker Cooperatives estimates that there are only 3,500 people employed by some form of worker cooperative, www.usworker.coop/aboutworkercoops.

3 See Berman (1967), Bellas (1972), and Dow (2003).

4 See Hansmann (1996, p. 68).

5 See www.usworker.coop/aboutworkercoops.

6 See Dow (2003), who refers to an economic system with labor-managed firms as "laborism."

in manufacturing, international business, and corporate takeovers.[7] Italy's Lega Cooperatives have thousands of member co-ops and benefit from subsidies, tax advantages, government procurement, and other public support.[8] Professional partnerships in the United States in such areas as law, accounting, consulting, and medicine have hierarchical organizations and other features that resemble corporations, as noted previously. Many firms in the United States are majority-owned by their employees through employee stock ownership plans (ESOPs). Dow (2003, p. 81) points out that such organizations should not be classified as labor-managed firms because votes are proportional to invested capital and not to labor.

A firm can be owned and controlled by its employees. What distinguishes a worker cooperative from a firm is the degree to which the enterprise can be separated from its employees. The most basic worker cooperative is not distinguishable from its employees. It is a basic partnership, often with equal sharing of profits, that consequently maximizes the benefits of its members. The consumption and labor supply decisions of the firm's owners are connected closely with the production and hiring decisions of the worker cooperative. The discussion in this section shows that when workers own a firm, they prefer to separate their decisions from those of the firm. Thus, even when the enterprise is owned by workers, it chooses to maximize profits.

The "symmetry principle" is a useful approach to understanding the contribution of the firm; see Drèze (1976, 1989) and Dow (2003, p. 118). The basic idea is that when finance capital and human capital can be viewed as symmetric, there need not be differences in the behavior of a "labor-managed" firm and that of a "capital-managed" firm. Of course, finance capital can be sold but human capital cannot.[9] However, labor services are provided in markets in return for wages, salaries, and other compensation. Many things are transferable in a labor-managed firm. Workers can invest capital in the firm. The labor-managed firm can sell memberships; see Dow (2003). The labor-managed firm can distinguish between insiders, who are original owners, and outsiders, who are prospective owners. These features imply that a labor-managed firm with complex institutional features can do many of the same things as a corporation. This suggests that the relative scarcity of labor-managed firms is due to the transaction costs associated with these institutional features.

Consider the basic worker cooperative as described by Ward (1958). Suppose that all workers are identical. Each worker is supplied with one unit of labor and can

---

7   See Cheney (1999) and Dow (2003).

8   See the discussion in Holmstrom (1989) and Dow (2003).

9   Dow (2003, p. 17) states that labor-managed firms are rare because "capital is alienable, while labor is not." Dow (2003, p. 107) concludes that "no one can own a firm because a firm is a set of human agents." The problem with this conclusion is the incorrect definition of a firm. The legal ownership of firms is well established. It might be more accurate to conclude that because people own firms, it follows that a firm must be something other than a set of human agents.

earn a market wage w that serves as an opportunity cost of joining the partnership. The production technology is described by a production function

$$(1) \qquad\qquad\qquad Q = F(L),$$

where L is units of labor and Q is the output produced. The production function is increasing in labor and exhibits diminishing marginal returns: $F'(L) > 0$, $F''(L) < 0$. Every consumer-worker has access to the production technology. There is a fixed cost of production, K. Consumer-workers form partnerships to take advantage of economies of scale. The worker cooperative sells its output at price p.

The worker cooperative chooses employment to maximize each member's share of profits,

$$(2) \qquad\qquad\qquad u^P(L) = \frac{pF(L) - K}{L}.$$

The size of the worker cooperative, L^P, equates the average revenue product of labor to the marginal revenue product of labor:

$$(3) \qquad\qquad\qquad \frac{pF(L^P) - K}{L} = pF'(L^P).$$

The partnership attracts employees if and only if it offers each worker a share that is greater than or equal to the wage: $u^P(L^P) \geq w$.

Compare the partnership to the profit-maximizing firm.[10] The firm's profit is

$$(4) \qquad\qquad\qquad \pi(L) = pF(L) - wL - K.$$

The standard neoclassical profit maximization condition results:

$$(5) \qquad\qquad\qquad pF'(L^F) = w.$$

The participation constraint for the worker partnership, $u^P(L^P) \geq w$, and equations (3) and (5) imply that worker partnerships have a higher marginal revenue product of labor than do firms:

$$pF'(L^F) \leq pF'(L^P).$$

Due to the diminishing marginal product of labor, the worker cooperative hires fewer workers than does the firm:

$$L^P \leq L^F.$$

The worker cooperative produces a lower output than the firm: $Q^P \leq Q^F$.

Compare the benefits of a member of the worker cooperative with a worker in a firm when the worker has an ownership share. The member of a firm with an ownership share receives a wage, w, and a share of profits, $\pi(L^F)/L^F$. The maximization of each member's share of profits implies that

$$u^P(L^P) \geq u^P(L^F) = \pi(L^F)/L^F + w.$$

10 See Ward (1958), Domar (1966), and Vanek (1970) on the labor-managed enterprise.

A member of the basic worker cooperative is better off than a worker in a firm who has an ownership share. The members of a worker cooperative prefer the cooperative to a firm.

Consider the implications of a market for membership shares. The membership market for the worker cooperative provides incentives for profit maximization; see Dow (2003, p. 149). Suppose that the members of the worker cooperative are "insiders." The "insiders" sell membership shares to "outsiders." After the new members join the worker cooperative, every member receives an equal share of the firm's profit, $u^P(L)$. Outsiders are willing to join as long as their benefits are greater than or equal to the wage, $u^P(L) \geq w$, so that each new member pays $u^P(L) - w$. Insiders receive the share at the new level of membership, $u^P(L)$, plus an insider's share of the total membership fees paid by new members:

$$\text{Insider's share} = u^P(L) + (L - L^P)(u^P(L) - w)/L^P.$$

Maximizing the insider's share with respect to the size of the expanded partnership, L, gives

$$u^{P\prime}(L) + (L - L^P)u^{P\prime}(L)/L^P + (u^P(L) - w)/L^P = 0.$$

The first-order condition simplifies to

(6) $$L u^{P\prime}(L) + u^P(L) - w = 0.$$

The first-order condition reduces to the profit maximization condition for the firm, $pF'(L^F) = w$. This implies that the partnership that sells membership shares chooses the same number of workers as the profit-maximizing firm, L^F.

The worker cooperative with tradeable membership shares satisfies the separation criterion. The ability to sell membership shares separates the members' objectives from those of the worker cooperative. Thus, the worker cooperative with tradeable membership shares is equivalent to a firm. Selling membership shares yields a separation theorem. The owners of the worker cooperative, who are the "insiders," unanimously prefer that the worker cooperative choose employment to maximize profit.

The difference between the basic worker cooperative and the firm also depends on the market equilibrium prices for goods and labor services. The result that the equilibrium share per member is greater than the market wage depends on the assumption that the labor partnership and the firm have market power in the product market. Suppose instead that there is competition with free entry in the product market. Entry occurs until the market price p adjusts so that the average product of labor equals the wage, $u^P(L^P) = w$, which from equations (2) and (3) implies that the labor partnership chooses the number of members such that the marginal revenue product of labor equals the wage, $pF'(L^P) = w$. Accordingly, the labor partnership and the firm choose the same number of workers in a competitive market. Note also that free entry of firms drives profits to zero, so that the firm also equates the average revenue product of labor to the marginal revenue product of labor. With competitive entry, the labor partnership and the firm behave identically.

6.2 Hiring Workers with Diverse Abilities

The hiring decisions of a worker cooperative must adjust to reflect differences in the abilities of workers. Levin and Tadelis (2005) adapt Ward (1958) to consider the effects of worker abilities on the organization of the firm. Following their model, suppose that the pool of potential workers has abilities a that are uniformly distributed on the unit interval. Let w be the outside market wage, which represents a common opportunity cost for workers. Assume that $w < 1$. Establishing an organization, whether it is a basic worker cooperative or a firm, requires a fixed cost of capital, K.

An organization is a basic partnership if it shares profits equally among its members. A firm pays the same wage w to all of its employees. Assume also that the firm distributes shares to its employees like an ESOP. The firm is fully owned by its employees but maximizes profit due to a separation of ownership and control. Later in the following discussion, these definitions will be modified. Any organization that differs from the basic worker partnership will be classified as a firm.

Assume that only one organization can exist in equilibrium. Assume further that the organization is a monopoly in the product market. It can be shown that the basic partnership and the firm will hire only higher-quality workers. If an organization hires a worker of a particular quality level, a', then that organization would hire all workers with a higher quality level.

The quality of output of an organization equals the *average quality* of the workers in the organization. Let a be the *marginal quality* of a worker in the organization, where $1 - a$ is the number of workers in the organization as well as the total output of the organization. Then, the quality of the organization's output, that is, the average quality of its workforce, equals

(7) $$q(a) = [1/(1 - a)] \int_a^1 \tilde{a} d\tilde{a} = (1 + a)/2.$$

Assume that customers of the organization have a willingness to pay equal to the quality of the organization's output. Also, because the organization is a monopoly, it sets a price equal to customers' willingness to pay. The organization is assumed to be able to sell all of its output at that price.

The organization's customers cannot perfectly observe its quality. Suppose that quality is revealed to customers with probability μ. Otherwise, customers form expectations about quality that are based on a point expectation of the organization's marginal quality, a^e. Expectations are fulfilled in equilibrium. In the case of a basic partnership, the equilibrium is denoted by a^P, whereas in the case of a firm, the equilibrium is denoted by a^F. The expected quality offered by an organization with marginal worker quality a equals

(8) $\mu(1 + a)/2 + (1 - \mu)(1 + a^e)/2 = [1 + \mu a + (1 - \mu)a^e]/2.$

Expectations are fulfilled in equilibrium, so that $a^e = a$.

In equilibrium, consumers pay a price equal to average quality, so that equilibrium profits equal

(9) $$\Pi(a) = \int_a^1 (\tilde{a} - w)d\tilde{a} - K.$$

Profits are concave, with a maximum at $a = w$. Thus, first-best marginal quality is $a = w$ and first-best profits are

(10) $$\Pi(w) = (1 - w)^2/2 - K.$$

Assume that first-best profits are positive, so that $(1 - w)^2/2 > K$.

The basic partnership shares its profits equally among its members. The share per member in a partnership with marginal quality a and market expectations a^e equals

(11) $u(a, a^e) = [1 + \mu a + (1 - \mu)a^e]/2 - K/(1 - a).$

Maximizing each partner's share with respect to marginal quality implies that hiring continues until the marginal revenue effect equals the marginal cost-sharing effect:

(12) $u_1(a, a^e) = \mu/2 - K/(1 - a)^2 = 0.$

Customer expectations do not affect the partnership's choice of marginal quality. The partnership's marginal quality thus equals

(13) $a^P = 1 - (2K/\mu)^{1/2}.$

The customers' expectations are fulfilled in equilibrium: $a^e = a^P$. Each member of the partnership receives a share of benefits equal to $u(a^P) = u(a^P, a^P)$. The number of workers, $1 - a$, is increasing in fixed costs, K, due to the need to capture economies of scale. The number of workers is decreasing in the market monitoring level, μ, due to the need to maintain product quality. The partnership will choose the size that maximizes each partner's share as long as each partner receives more than the outside wage, $u(a^P) \geq w$.

The equilibrium benefit per member of the partnership equals

(14) $u(a^P) = (1 + a^P)/2 - K/(1 - a^P).$

The partnership is profitable if and only if

$\pi^P = (1 - a^P)(u(a^P) - w) \geq 0.$

Substituting for a^P, and simplifying, implies that the partnership is profitable if and only if

$$\frac{2\mu(1-w)^2}{(1+\mu)^2} \geq K.$$

The profit of a firm with marginal worker quality a and market expectations a^e equals

(15) $$\pi(a, a^e) = (1-a)\{[1+\mu a+(1-\mu)a^e]/2 - w\} - K.$$

Maximizing profit with respect to marginal quality implies that

(16) $$\pi_1(a, a^e) = -[1+\mu a+(1-\mu)a^e]/2 + \mu(1-a)/2 + w = 0.$$

Expectations are fulfilled in equilibrium, $a^e = a^F$, so that marginal quality equals

(17) $$a^F = (2w + \mu - 1)/(1+\mu).$$

The profit of the firm equals $\Pi(a^F) = \pi(a^F, a^F)$:

(18) $$\Pi(a^F) = (1-a^F)[(1+a^F)/2 - w] - K$$
$$= \frac{2\mu(1-w)^2}{(1+\mu)^2} - K.$$

The firm is profitable if and only if $\Pi(a^F) \geq 0$, or equivalently

$$\frac{2\mu(1-w)^2}{(1+\mu)^2} \geq K.$$

This means that the firm is profitable if and only if the basic partnership is profitable.

To compare the marginal worker quality in the partnership with that in the firm, consider the two optimization problems. Given $u(a, a^e) \geq w$, the marginal benefit for each partner is

$$u_1(a, a^e) \geq \mu/2 + w/(1-a) - [1+\mu a + (1-\mu)a^e]/2 = \pi_1(a, a^e)/(1-a).$$

Because $a < 1$, it follows that

$$u_1(a, a^e) \geq \pi_1(a, a^e).$$

The partnership will choose a marginal worker quality that is greater than that chosen by the firm, for the same level of market expectations. The partnership's choice of marginal quality does not depend on market expectations. At a^P, $u_1(a^P, a^P) = 0$ and $\pi_1(a^P, a^P) \leq 0$. Because $\pi_1(a, a)$ is decreasing in a, and $\pi_1(a^F, a^F) = 0$, it follows that $a^P \geq a^F$. The partnership hires fewer workers than the firm, as was the case with identical workers in the previous section.

Consider which type of organization consumer-workers prefer to establish. There is a tradeoff between employment and quality as a result of market expectations. The partnership hires fewer workers than the firm and benefits from customers' willingness to pay for higher quality. The partnership, by hiring fewer workers, bears greater fixed costs per employee.

Since $u(a^P, a^e)$ is the highest benefit per worker for any a^e, it follows that

$$u(a^P, a^P) \geq u(a^F, a^P) = \frac{\pi(a^F, a^P)}{1 - a^F} + w.$$

Profit $\pi(a, a^e)$ is increasing in the market expectation of marginal quality. Because quality is greater under a basic partnership, it follows that

$$\pi(a^F, a^P) \geq \pi(a^F, a^F) = \Pi(a^F).$$

This implies that a member of a basic partnership is better off than a worker in a firm who has an ownership share:

$$u(a^P) \geq \Pi(a^F)/(1 - a^F) + w.$$

Consumer-workers always will choose to establish basic partnerships rather than firms.

The benefit of a member of a partnership is therefore greater than that of a worker in a firm because partnerships maximize benefits per member and because the partnership offers its customers a commitment to greater average quality. This has an important implication. Consumers always choose to form a basic partnership in equilibrium. This conclusion depends on the limits placed on the structure of the two types of organization. If the organizational structure of the basic partnership or that of the firm is modified, the market equilibrium outcome will change. In particular, note that a partnership is inefficient because it results in greater unemployment than does a firm. As we will see, modifying the organizational structures will improve efficiency in equilibrium.

Consider the effect of customer monitoring on the outcome. With perfect monitoring, the marginal worker quality of a firm exactly equals the outside wage. From equation (17), setting $\mu = 1$, it follows that $a^F = w$ and the firm earns the first-best profit. If $\mu = 1$, the partnership sets $a^P = 1 - (2K)^{1/2}$. The partnership's share per member is

$$u^P = 1 - (2K)^{1/2} > w,$$

by the assumption that $(1 - w)^2/2 > K$. Thus, the partnership must choose a^P such that $a^P > w$. So the firm earns profits strictly greater than does the partnership. If customer monitoring is not perfect, $\mu < 1$, and customer monitoring μ is chosen such that a^P is optimal, $a^P = w$, then

$$\mu^P = 2K/(1 - w)^2.$$

This is strictly less than one by the assumption that first-best profit is positive. Given $\mu < 1$, the firm chooses quality strictly less than w, so the firm earns profits strictly less than the partnership.

This implies that there is a critical value of the monitoring parameter, μ^* in $(\mu^P, 1)$, such that the partnership is more profitable for $\mu < \mu^*$ and the firm is more profitable for $\mu > \mu^*$; that is,

$$\Pi(a^F) \gtreqless \Pi(a^P) \text{ as } \mu \gtreqless \mu^*.$$

This follows from the concavity of Π (a) and a comparison of $\Pi(a^F(\mu))$ and $\Pi(a^P(\mu))$.

In equilibrium, consumers form a basic partnership. The basic partnership operates by hiring the best workers and thus excluding more workers than does the firm. When the partnership is at least as profitable as the firm, this is an efficient outcome. However, when the firm is more profitable than the partnership, the market equilibrium is inefficient. The problem is that the additional workers who would be hired by a firm are excluded from the partnership. There are two equivalent ways to modify the organizational forms to remedy this problem.

One way to address inefficient hiring is to modify the basic partnership to allow a membership market. The members of the partnership with high quality, $a \geq a^P$, would be "insiders," whereas the workers with lower quality a such that $a^F \leq a < a^P$ would be "outsiders" who purchased membership in the partnership. The insiders would receive the revenue from membership sales. After the new members join, every member receives an equal share of the firm's profit, $u^P(a, a^e)$, as defined in equation (11). Outsiders are willing to join as long as $u^P(a, a^e) \geq w$, so that each new member pays $u^P(a, a^e) - w$. Insiders receive the share at the new level of membership, $u^P(a, a^e)$, plus an insider's share of the total membership fees paid by new members:

$$\text{Insider's share} = u^P(a, a^e) + \frac{(a^P - a)(u^P(a, a^e) - w)}{1 - a^P}.$$

Maximizing the insider's share with respect to the size of the partnership gives

(19) $$u_1^P(a, a^e) + \frac{(a^P - a)u_1^P(a, a^e) - u^P(a, a^e) + w}{1 - a^P} = 0.$$

The first-order condition simplifies to

(20) $$(1 - a)u_1^P(a, a^e) - u^P(a, a^e) + w = 0.$$

Consumer expectations are fulfilled in equilibrium, so that $a = a^e$. So we have

$$(1 - a)\mu/2 - (1 + a)/2 + w = 0.$$

The first-order condition reduces to the profit maximization condition for the firm; see equation (16). This implies that the partnership with membership fees chooses the same number of workers as the profit-maximizing firm, $a = a^F$.

Suppose instead that there is no membership market for partnerships. Instead, let the profit-maximizing firm divide its workforce, offering profit shares and wages to the high-quality workers while only paying wages to the low-quality workers. The high-quality workforce is defined as those workers with quality greater than or equal to a^P. Then high-quality workers are "insiders" who each receive $\Pi(a^F)/(1 - a^P) + w$. If the firm makes more profit in equilibrium than a firm with the size of a partnership, it follows that

$$\Pi(a^F)/(1 - a^P) + w > \Pi(a^P)/(1 - a^P) + w = u^P(a^P).$$

This implies that a firm with selective profit shares is preferred by high-quality workers in comparison to a basic partnership. Other workers do not object because they would not be employed by the basic partnership, so they are indifferent between the two market outcomes. This means that a partnership with a membership market and a firm with selective profit shares are equivalent ways of establishing a firm.

When a firm has the more complex organizational form, the equilibrium depends on the consumer monitoring parameter. If market monitoring is low, $\mu \leq \mu^*$, a firm with the size of a basic partnership makes a greater profit than the profit-maximizing firm. Thus, the equilibrium form of organization will be the basic partnership with marginal quality a^P. If market monitoring is high, $\mu > \mu^*$, a profit-maximizing firm makes a greater profit than a firm that has the size of a basic partnership. Thus, the equilibrium form of organization is a profit-maximizing firm.

When markets are not good at determining product quality, the market equilibrium organizational form is a basic partnership. Such a partnership consists of workers with a high level of human capital. The profit-maximizing firm emerges in equilibrium when there are efficiencies from separating ownership from labor. When markets can better observe product quality, there are efficiencies that derive from increasing employment and segmenting the workforce. Thus, the market equilibrium organizational form is a firm.

6.3 Hiring with Moral Hazard in Teams

The traditional discussion of incentives in teams has emphasized the dual role of the firm as a monitor and as a designer of incentives; see Alchian and Demsetz (1972) and Holmstrom (1982). The problem of incentives in teams has important implications for the efficient size of the team. A worker cooperative is a self-organized team in which workers determine how many members to have in their team. In contrast, a firm selects the number of employees who will be in its productive team.

The firm plays an economic role when it provides the best method of selecting the size of the team, in comparison to the worker cooperative.

Selecting the size of the team adds an essential dimension to the problem of incentives in teams. This aspect of teams is important because a greater number of team members worsens moral hazard problems and increases free riding. At the same time, adding more team members can increase or decrease the team's total effort, depending on the severity of the moral hazard problem. More team members also offer benefits because a larger team can take advantage of economies of scale. Larger teams benefit from scale economies either by sharing fixed costs or through specialization and division of labor.

The firm thus has an advantage over the partnership for reasons other than monitoring or incentive design. The firm's owners are residual claimants and the firm chooses the number of employees to maximize profit. The firm's choice of number of employees generally differs from the number of members that is chosen by a worker cooperative that maximizes benefits per member. Thus, the firm's advantage stems from its residual claimant status, which affects the size of the team. When incentives and monitoring are similar in the partnership and in the firm, the size of the team affects the organization's productivity and performance.

Each consumer-worker derives utility from consuming a good y and disutility from providing effort z. Each consumer has a utility function of the form

$$(21) \qquad u(y, z) = y - c(z).$$

The effort cost function, $c(z)$, is increasing and convex. Total work effort is the sum of the efforts of individual workers,

$$(22) \qquad Z = \sum_{i=1}^{n} z_i.$$

Both the worker cooperative and the firm benefit from diverse efforts because marginal costs of individual efforts are increasing. Let w be the outside wage, which is the workers' opportunity cost of joining either the worker cooperative or the firm.

Establishing any type of organization requires a fixed cost K, denominated in units of the consumer good. There exists a common production technology that is available to all consumers. Let Y be the final good produced by the organization. The technology is represented by the production function

$$(23) \qquad Y = F(Z).$$

The worker cooperative is a basic partnership with equal sharing of returns. In the partnership with n members, each worker receives the net benefit

$$(24) \qquad u^P(n) = (1/n) F \left(\sum_{j=1}^{n} z_j \right) - c(z_i) - K/n.$$

A worker participates in the cooperative if net benefits exceed opportunity costs:

$$u^P(n) \geq w.$$

The members of the cooperative play a noncooperative game in effort levels. Let z_i^P be the Nash equilibrium effort levels, $i = 1, \ldots, n$. Each worker's effort level is a best response to the other workers' effort levels. The equilibrium effort level for each worker equals z_i^P, which solves

(25) $$(1/n)F'\left(\sum_{j=1}^{n} z_j^P\right) = c'(z_i^P).$$

In equilibrium, each worker chooses the same effort level, $z^P = z^P(n)$. It can be shown that due to free riding, the effort of each worker is decreasing in the size of the partnership.

The worker cooperative chooses the number of members to maximize net benefits per member, $u^P(n)$. The worker cooperative sets marginal benefits per member equal to zero:

(26) $$u^{P\prime}(n) = 0.$$

Applying the envelope theorem and the first-order condition for equilibrium effort levels (25) gives the condition

(27) $$F'(nz^P(n))[(n-1)z^{P\prime}(n) + z^P(n)] = (F(nz^P(n)) - K)/n.$$

The partnership chooses the number of members to equate the marginal productivity of an additional worker to the average productivity per worker.

Condition (27) determines the optimal size of the partnership with moral hazard in teams. Denote the size of the partnership by n^P. Substituting for the size of the partnership gives the equilibrium effort levels, $z^P = z^P(n^P)$. The partnership provides its members with benefits equal to $u^P(n^P)$. The condition for the optimal size of the partnership can be rewritten using the definition of average benefits per partner to obtain

(28) $$F'(nz^P(n))[(n-1)z^{P\prime}(n) + z^P(n)] = u^P(n) + c(z^P(n)).$$

Because the partnership maximizes benefits per member, the size of the partnership differs from that of a profit-maximizing organization. For purposes of comparison, suppose that the profit-maximizing organization gives each member an equal share of returns just as the partnership does, so that effort per member is the same for any given size, $z^P = z^P(n)$.

If we require the organization to use contracts that are monotonic for the principal, the best incentives are to give each team member a share of returns. As Innes (1990) points out for principal-agent contracts, the monotonic contract constraint can be motivated either by the need to rule out sabotage by the principal or by the ability of the agent to revise his performance report upward costlessly.[11]

The monotonic contract constraint has similar implications for the problem of a principal with multiple agents working as a team. Without the monotonic contract requirement, the principal could design a "forcing function" to induce optimal efforts by all members of the team. However, the "forcing function" approach is ruled out whether the principal offers group penalties or bonuses. Such contracts introduce a discontinuity in the payoffs of the principal and those of the team. The principal does not have an incentive to honor his commitment. In the case of group bonuses, for example, the principal would have an incentive to sabotage the team to avoid paying the bonuses. The monotonic contract requirement restricts the set of contracts offered by the principal. The monotonic contract requirement means that the profit-maximizing organization does not have an advantage over the partnership in terms of designing incentives.

The profit-maximizing organization gives each worker an equal share of output net of fixed costs, so that in equilibrium, each worker chooses the same effort level as in the partnership of size n, $z^P = z^P(n)$. The firm's profit equals output net of the total costs of effort, the total opportunity costs, and fixed costs. The firm chooses the number of workers to maximize profit:

$$(29) \qquad \Pi = F(nz^P(n)) - nc(z^P(n)) - nw - K.$$

Assume that the firm's profit is concave in the number of workers. Applying the first-order condition for equilibrium effort levels (25), the first-order condition for the firm's profit-maximization problem can be written as

$$(30) \qquad F'(nz^P(n))[(n-1)z^{P\prime}(n) + z^P(n)] = w + c(z^P(n)).$$

Let n^F denote the employment chosen by the profit-maximizing firm. The comparison between the profit-maximizing firm and the partnership depends on whether the benefits per member of the partnership, $u^P(n^P)$, are greater than or equal to the worker's opportunity cost, w.

If the labor market is competitive, the benefit per member of the partnership, $u^P(n^P)$, equals the worker's opportunity cost, w. This implies that equations (28) and (30) are identical, so that the partnership and the profit-maximizing firm choose the same number of workers.

If the benefits per member of the partnership, $u^P(n^P)$, are greater than the worker's opportunity cost, w, equation (28) implies that

$$F'(nz^P(n^P))[(n-1)z^{P\prime}(n^P) + z^P(n^P)] > w + c(z^P(n^P)).$$

By concavity, it follows that the profit-maximizing firm hires more workers than the partnership, $n^F > n^P$. This accords with the basic model in which the worker

---

11 Innes (1990) shows that the optimal principal-agent contract with uncertainty and limited liability takes form of a standard debt contract.

cooperative chooses labor to maximize average product and thus chooses a smaller number of workers than the firm.

Due to free riding, effort per worker, $z^P(n)$, is a decreasing function of the number of workers. This implies that effort per worker is greater in the partnership than in the firm, $z^P \geq z^F$. Total effort, $Z(n)$, can be either increasing, decreasing, or constant in the number of workers. This implies that total effort in the partnership can be less than, equal to, or greater than total effort in the firm. Thus, the partnership's output can be less than, equal to, or greater than the firm's output. Recall that in the basic worker cooperative model without moral hazard in teams, the partnership's lower employment results in a lower output than the profit-maximizing firm.

Consider the difference between the worker cooperative and the firm for an example. Let the consumer's effort cost function have the form

$$c(z) = z^\beta / \beta,$$

where $\beta > 1$. Let the production function have the form

$$F(z) = z^\gamma / \gamma,$$

where the production technology parameter is such that $\gamma < 1$. Given the form of the effort cost function and the production function, effort-per-worker in either the worker cooperative or the partnership equals

$$z = (n)^{(\gamma-2)/(\beta-\gamma)}.$$

Each worker's effort is an interior solution, $0 < z < 1$. Also, total effort is such that $0 < Z < 1$, because $Z = (n)^{(\beta-2)/(\beta-\gamma)}$. The total-effort function $Z(n)$ is increasing in n for $\beta > 2$, decreasing in n for $\beta < 2$, and constant for $\beta = 2$.

The firm earns a greater profit than does the worker cooperative by profit maximization. This implies that there are efficiency gains from increasing the size of the worker cooperative through a membership market. The difference between the worker cooperative and the firm with free riding depends on the worker participation constraint being nonbinding, as was the case with the full-information model without free riding.

Consider the introduction of a membership market. Members of the worker cooperative sell memberships to new members. After joining the partnership, a new member obtains benefits, $u^P(n)$. New members will pay up to the difference between the benefits of being in the partnership and their opportunity costs, w. Letting n^P be the number of insiders, the benefit per inside member equals

(31) $$U(n) = u^P(n) + (u^P(n) - w)(n - n^P)/n^P.$$

Maximizing the insider's return yields the first-order condition

(32) $$u^{P\prime}(n)n + u^P(n) - w = 0.$$

Note that

$$(33) \qquad u^{P\prime}(n) = (1/n)F'(nz^P(n))[(n-1)z^{P\prime}(n) + z^P(n)]$$
$$- (1/n)(u^P(n) + c(z^P(n))).$$

Substituting into equation (32) gives

$$(34) \qquad F'(nz^P(n))[(n-1)z^{P\prime}(n) + z^P(n)] - c(z^P(n))) - w = 0.$$

This is again the condition for profit maximization. The partnership with moral hazard in teams thus chooses the profit-maximizing number of members. The introduction of a membership market results in the partnership acting as a profit-maximizing firm.

6.4 Market Contracts versus Organizational Contracts

The organizational structure of the firm primarily reflects the requirements of human interaction. The organization must allow interpersonal communication within the firm and between the firm's employees and customers, suppliers, and others outside the firm. Firms generally have hierarchies with authority relationships in which managers provide instruction and incentives to subordinates and monitor their performance. The firm's hierarchy serves the needs of communication between managers and subordinates. The firm's organization specifies job titles, responsibilities, and authority relationships between employees. The positions within the firm's organization usually are defined independent of the person who occupies that position, although responsibilities often are adjusted based on individual capabilities.

6.4.1 Market Transactions versus Organizational Transactions

Firms can coordinate workers in two ways: through markets and through organizations. Firms can coordinate workers through market transactions with individuals acting as independent contractors. Firms also can coordinate workers by hiring them as employees and managing their interactions. Firms choose the best mix of market transactions and management transactions, depending on the relative costs. Typically, firms employ a combination of independent contractors and employees that varies depending on the task at hand. For example, a firm may have independent sales agents for some products and sales personnel for other products.

Firms play an important economic role by coordinating workers. The relative abundance of firms and the relative scarcity of worker cooperatives suggest that firms are more efficient. The discussion thus far in this chapter shows that under some market conditions, firms are more efficient than basic worker cooperatives in choosing the size of productive teams. Firms also provide greater efficiency than worker cooperatives because firms can operate more complex organizations with hierarchical structures and rewards that vary across workers. The boundaries of the firm's organization reflect a choice between market contracts and employment contracts.

Organizations primarily serve to facilitate coordination between workers. The discussion identifies some similarities and differences between market transactions and management transactions. One advantage of organizations is that the firm can form multilateral contracts with its workforce, whereas market contracts often require bilateral contracts between the firm and independent contractors.

Just as they do in markets, firms employ instruments of spontaneous order within their organizations. In the employment process itself, large-scale firms hire many workers by marketing employment positions and by offering standardized wages and benefits. Retail giant Wal-Mart has a work force of over 1.2 million employees, which it maintains through continual hiring at a rate of 600,000 employees per year.[12] This example illustrates the role of the firm in assembling and coordinating teams.

Once the large-scale firm has hired workers, it employs many additional instruments of spontaneous order. Once it is established, the hierarchy itself is an instrument of spontaneous order, allowing information gathering and dissemination up and down the organization. The firm's central office communicates with its managers and workers through the hierarchy's channels. The firm's managers coordinate the activities of the work force through internal price signals such as transfer prices, bonuses, and raises. Managers employ various nonprice signals including announcements of company objectives, meetings, design of production procedures, and administrative rules. Such workplace features as building architecture, uniforms, and corporate culture norms provide additional nonprice instruments. Because employment is a voluntary agreement, these function as mechanisms of spontaneous order rather than as command-and-control.

Markets and organizations are different instruments for firms. The choice between these instruments determines the boundaries of the firm's organization – not necessarily the scope of the firm itself. The firm's scope extends to its contractual relations with customers, suppliers, and partners. Because firms engage in a mix of market transactions and management transactions, there cannot be a systematic advantage that always favors one or the other approach. Otherwise, a market advantage would eliminate organizations or an organizational advantage would result in nearly unlimited growth of organizations.

One difference beween markets and organizations is in the effects of legal rules. Masten (1988, p. 196) finds that law does recognize differences between market transactions and organizational transactions. He suggests that legal distinctions support the view that internal transactions have advantages in terms of authority,

---

12 See "Is Wal-Mart Good for America: Wal-Mart at a Glance," http://www.pbs.org/wgbh/pages/ frontline/shows/walmart/secrets/stats.html.

flexibility, and information. He adds, however, that laws promoting obedience and disclosure may discourage employee initiative and incentives to gather information. Legal rules that apply to a firm's relationships with customers, suppliers, and partners generally differ from rules governing the employment relationship. These rule differences can introduce variation in the transaction costs of market and organizational interactions.

Organizations allow standardization of information and communication that may not be feasible in market transactions with diverse customers and suppliers. This can give organizations advantages in terms of record-keeping, accounting, monitoring, and performance evaluation. These cost advantages of standardization are subject to diminishing returns as organizations require large bureaucracies to manage personnel and operations. Bureaucracies function through rules and standardization that generate economies of scale. The same standardization can limit the bureaucracy's ability to respond to uncertainty and to tailor services to individual needs.

A critical question is whether contracts create benefits and costs that differentiate between markets and organizations. If the firm has the ability to create market contracts or to structure employment contracts that achieve similar outcomes, contracts cannot explain the formation of organizations. Levin (2003) argues that organizations offer advantages from informal incentives when aspects of performance such as teamwork, leadership, or initiative are difficult to measure. This difficulty can raise the costs of writing and enforcing market contracts and so may favor typical organizational incentives such as promotion and compensation that are tied to subjective performance evaluations. Levin (2003) characterizes principal-agent contracts when there is repeated interaction. Both market contracts and organizational relationships involve repeated interactions so that either type of agreement can be self enforcing. If repeated interactions are achieved at lower cost in markets or in organizations this can generate greater contract efficiencies.

Firms are organized to handle market transactions and management transactions in the most efficient manner. An important reason that a firm establishes an organization is simply to handle its market transactions. The firm employs personnel to carry out market making, intermediation, and entrepreneurial activities. The firm's personnel consolidate market demand and supply, calculate and adjust prices, keep track of information about purchases and sales, gather information about buyers and sellers, and match individual buyers and sellers. The firm's merchant activities involve contacts with consumers and other firms in the market. Many of the firm's organizational activities support its market actions. These activities include management of sales personnel and purchasing staff. Organization activities also include back-office processes that handle the record keeping, computation, and communications needed to carry out transactions.

Firms also establish organizations where there are advantages from internalizing transactions, thus replacing some market transactions, as Coase emphasized.

The firm has many transaction techniques within the organization that are not feasible in arms-length transactions. The firm can employ management techniques to coordinate and control the activities of employees. For example, the firm establishes relational contracts within organizations that broadly specify the duties of managers and employees with less detail than might be necessary in a contract with external buyers and sellers.[13] Organizations realize benefits from centralization of some forms of communication and control (Arrow, 1974, p. 68).

Typically, the firm's organization is engaged in some combination of market transactions and management transactions. The costs of market transactions and management transactions help to explain the structure of the organization. Organizations tend to be hierarchies because of the need to delegate authority. Transaction costs associated with finance, ownership, and management affect the company's relationship with its shareholders and creditors. Transaction costs in the market for corporate control influence the structure of the corporation and the relationship between the company's board of directors and its management.

There are numerous benefits from coordination within organizations. The structure of the organization takes advantage of the returns to specialization of function and division of labor. Such returns are not confined to manufacturing operations, but are also present in market transactions and management transactions. Organizations involve *horizontal* specialization. The company's divisions reflect its diverse lines of business. Functional units such as marketing, sales, or purchasing are based on differences in activities and skills. Members of the organization provide complementary or substitute inputs to common activities, so that joint optimization is required to achieve efficiency. Organizations also involve *vertical* specialization with differences between the tasks of managers and employees. Herbert Simon (1945, p. 9) observes that vertical specialization allows coordination across tasks, specialization of managers in making decisions, and accountability to superiors in the hierarchy.

Chester Barnard (1938, p. 81) defines formal organizations as "a system of consciously coordinated activities or forces of two or more persons." Barnard observes that "the individual is always the basic strategic factor in organization" and that therefore "the subject of incentives is fundamental in formal organizations" (p. 139). Barnard stresses the role of managerial leadership and concludes that "the most general strategic factor in human cooperation is executive capacity" (p. 282). He emphasizes the cooperative aspects of organizations, the distinction between the objectives of the organization and those of individuals in the organization, and the elaboration of the role of communication in organizations (see also Simon, 1955, 1972, 1976).

---

13 Arrow (1974, p. 33) suggests that "organizations are a means of achieving the benefits of collective action in situations in which the price system fails." However, this definition is too restrictive because it presumes that external transactions are limited to the neoclassical price system. It is more useful to view both markets and organizations as offering a wide variety of alternative forms of transactions.

Incentives are a critical aspect of the choice between employees and independent contractors. Within the firm, it is possible to apply all kinds of subjective performance evaluations and implicit rewards.[14] The firm will establish an organization when managers are best at monitoring and supervising employees. The firm will turn to independent contractors and suppliers when these market contracts are better for addressing problems of moral hazard and adverse selection. Management transactions are designed to mitigate problems that result from unobservable effort (moral hazard) and from unobservable information (adverse selection).

What will motivate subordinates in the organization to carry out the objectives of management? Further, what will motivate subordinates in the organization to report information truthfully to management? Principal-agent models provide a framework that is useful in examining the delegation of authority and the design of incentives. The agency model applies to both market transactions and management transactions.

The employees of the firm that deal with suppliers, distributors and customers are agents of the firm. In law, *agents represent principals in dealing with third parties.* Agents are intermediaries and business representatives. The firm delegates authority to its sales personnel, purchasing staff, and other employees who engage in transactions on behalf of the firm. The principal-agent model can be adapted to study the firm's relationships with consumers and firms outside of the organization. The theory of the firm shows that the firm is organized to handle market transactions.

Agency models also apply to delegation of authority to employees who handle tasks within the organization. In the case of internal relationships, the focus is on the design of incentive contracts between managers acting as principals and subordinates in the organization who act as their agents. This aspect of the organization of firms has been studied intensively. Agency models are useful in understanding incentives for action and communication within hierarchies. Moreover, agency models are useful in guiding the design of incentive schemes to motivate subordinates. Agency models have been used to make important advances in the fields of accounting, finance, and marketing.

The standard agency model in which agents exert effort specifies a production function relationship between the agent's effort and uncertain outcomes. The productive input is unobservable to the firm's manager and therefore is not subject to direct control. The firm's management decisions regarding delegation of authority and the design of incentives must take into account the personal characteristics of the agent, including degree of risk aversion, disutility of effort, and reservation utility. In hidden knowledge models, the description of the firm includes the allocation of information between the principal and the agent. Each may have information that is unavailable to the other. Management transactions are affected by the strategic interactions between managers and employees within the organization.

---

14 See Prendergast (1999) for a comprehensive survey of incentives in firms.

Interactions between members of organizations are as complex and intricate as are human relationships in general. This complexity likely will be reflected in the explicit and implicit aspects of employment contracts. The firm's choice between market contracts and employment contracts thus will depend on many different aspects of organizational interaction. Organizations typically involve hierarchies with upper level managers, middle level managers, and employees. Personnel at higher levels supervise, motivate, and reward personnel at lower levels. Market contracts do not feature such hierarchies. The firm may hire another firm that in turn supervises its own employees, but this is an indirect sort of hierarchy intermediated by another firm. The firm will favor employment contracts if there are advantages from an organizational hierarchy in comparison to market contracts with intermediated supervision of workers.

Organizations typically involve delegation of authority from the firm's owners to the CEO, and from the firm to other managers and employees. Managers exercise delegated authority in supervising employees. The firm's personnel apply delegated authority by acting as agents who make binding commitments with third parties, including the firm's customers and suppliers. The costs and benefits of delegation affect the relative performance of employment contracts in comparison with market contracts. The firm may prefer to employ sales personnel when delegated authority poses substantial risks for the firm. The firm may be able to reduce these risks through supervision of an in-house sales force in comparison with an independent sales force.

Each worker in a firm performs multiple tasks; see Holmstrom and Milgrom (1991). With multitasking, increased supervision and subjective performance evaluation may be needed to avoid biased efforts that focus on specific activities. With explicit incentives, workers may neglect some tasks such as product quality or workplace safety that are important to the firm. There are tradeoffs between employment contracts and market contracts; each offer advantages in addressing the multitasking problem.

Workers make investments in their human capital through education and training. Worker decisions about human capital investment are based on plans for their careers. Such human capital decisions are long-term and transcend current employment opportunities. Firms have an interest in workers' human capital because the qualifications and abilities of workers affect the quality of the labor services that they provide to the firm. The firm compares the human capital of workers who are available through the employment relationship with what is available through market contracts. The firm will form an organization when doing so improves its ability to obtain better workers. The firm may be able to improve incentives for workers to invest in firm-specific human capital through compensation, career development, incentives, and training programs. Conversely, the firm will turn to market contracts when access to highly qualified workers requires arms-length relationships. For example, large corporations typically rely on both an in-house legal staff and contracts with law firms.

The essence of the organization is that it involves multiple contracts with employees. Holmstrom (1999) observes that handling multiple contracts together has advantages. Multiple performance measures can be used to provide incentives to groups of workers. When workers produce output as a team, the use of multiple performance measures allows more precise targeting of rewards, so that individual workers have greater incentives to perform. Organizations offer benefits over market contracts if they provide the firm with additional performance measures for worker teams. This requires that the firm design and administer multilateral contracts targeted to teams of workers.

Laffont and Martimort (1997) describe the firm as a "multicontract organization," in which there are multiple principals. In their framework, the firm's stakeholders act as principals. These stakeholders include owners, lenders, customers, and suppliers. The firm's managers are the agents of these principals. They also consider multiple principals in multidivisional firms and in multilayer hierarchies. This would suggest an advantage for organizations when the firm is able to mediate conflicts between principals better when these conflicts occur in house. Conversely, the firm should reduce the number of internal principals when conflicts of interest between principals are better handled through market relationships. The firm can reduce the number of in-house principals by removing layers of its hierarchy, divesting divisions, and outsourcing production, distribution, and other tasks.

6.4.2 The Firm's Choice between Market Contracts and Organizational Contracts

Firms create an organization when doing so improves its ability to coordinate contracts in comparison with separate market contracts. The firm chooses between market contracts and organizational contracts. To understand this choice, suppose that the firm's market contracts are a set of bilateral relationships. The firm cannot make commitments across its market contracts. In contrast, suppose that the firm can structure its organizational contracts as a multilateral relationship with its employees. Levin (2002) points out that firms have contractual relationships with "their workforce as a whole" rather than with individual employees. This may discourage selective pay cuts or layoffs that would affect worker perceptions and performance.[15]

Firms will prefer organizational contracts over market contracts if multilateral contracts perform better than sets of bilateral contracts. The firm effectively promises to its workers that they will be part of a productive team. The firm promises to its managers that they will be members of a management team. The firm promises its managers that it will hire workers and the firm promises workers that it will hire managers. Such promises are implicit but essential components

---

15 See Doeringer and Piore (1971) and Bewley (1999) on the differences between market contracts and firms' relations with their workforces.

of the employment relationship. The firm's implicit contractual commitment thus involves the creation of the organization itself. The advantages of multilateral contracts then affect the firm's choices between market contracts and organizational relationships. This section examines a simplified version of Levin's (2002) model to gain some insights into the choice between market contracts and employment contracts.

Let $N = \{1, \ldots, n\}$ be the set of potential workers. Suppose that workers are agents who supply effort at each date t, z_t^i, where $z^i \in [0, 1]$, $i \in N$. The firm produces output using the total inputs of its workers,

$$Q = F(Z),$$

where $Z = \sum_{i=1}^{n} z^i$. The production function is increasing and concave, $F' > 0$, $F'' < 0$. Worker inputs thus are assumed to be substitutes. Levin (2002) points out that when worker efforts are substitutes, multilateral contracts can be better than bilateral contracts. The two types of contracts are equally effective when worker efforts are complements.[16]

Suppose that the firm and workers have a common discount factor δ. Workers have an opportunity cost in the form of an outside wage, w. Worker i has a cost of effort at date t, $c^i(z_t^i)$. The firm offers each worker i a fixed wage, W^i, and a discretionary bonus, B^i. A worker i obtains $W_t^i + B_t^i - c(z_t^i)$ if he is employed at date t and otherwise receives an outside wage, w. The firm's profit at date t equals

$$\Pi_t(M) = F\left(\sum_{i \in M} z_t^i\right) - \sum_{i \in M}(W_t^i + B_t^i),$$

where M is the subset of workers that are employed by the firm.

The firm and its workers play a repeated game. The firm cannot commit to reward performance in the static model, so in such a setting workers would choose the minimum effort and the firm would not operate. Repeated interaction between the firm and the workers results in relational contracts that are self-enforcing. There is a range of contracts in which firms honor their contractual commitments and workers exert effort.

Consider first self-enforcing bilateral contracts. To simplify notation, assume that the firm's optimal contract involves employing all of the workers. We rule out the possibility that the firm can identify a subset of employees, I, with which to recontract, while terminating the others. To rule this out as unprofitable requires that for any I, the incremental profit from terminating workers not in I exceed the cost of paying bonuses to workers not in I,

$$\frac{\delta}{1 - \delta}[\Pi(N) - \Pi(I)] \geq \sum_{j \notin I} B^i.$$

---

16 Levin (2002) obtains this result for the case of two workers.

A worker i will choose not to shirk or quit if and only if

$$\frac{\delta}{1-\delta}(W^i + B^i - c^i(z^i) - w) \geq \max\{0, c^i(z^i) - B^i\}.$$

Substitute from the worker's inequality constraints $W^i + B^i$ in the firm's profit functions. Then the firm's inequality constraint can be written as

$$\frac{\delta}{1-\delta}\left[\left(F\left(\sum_{i \in N} z^i\right) - \sum_{i \in N} c^i(z^i)\right) - \left(F\left(\sum_{i \in I} z^i\right)\right.\right.$$
$$\left.\left. - \sum_{i \in I} c^i(z^i) + \sum_{i \notin I} w\right)\right] \geq \sum_{i \notin I} c^i(z^i).$$

This condition states that the *incremental surplus* generated by each group of employees must be greater than their current costs of effort. The incremental surplus condition is a necessary condition for bilateral contracts to be self-enforcing. It is also a sufficient condition. To see this, let $W^i = w$ and $B^i = c(z^i)$ for each employed worker. Then the incremental surplus condition yields the firm's profit inequality. Also, $W^i = w$ and $B^i = c(z^i)$ for each employed worker easily implies that the workers' inequality conditions hold. Each worker's participation constraint holds. To summarize, there exists a set of bilateral contracts that supports performance level $z = (z^1, \ldots, z^n)$ if and only if the incremental surplus condition holds for any subset I of employed workers.

Consider multilateral contracting. The effort-supply decisions of individual workers are governed by a common condition. The firm will make bonus payments in each period if and only if

$$\frac{\delta}{1-\delta}\Pi(N) \geq \sum_{i \in N} B^i.$$

Summing the workers' constraints and the firm's constraint implies the following. There exists a self-enforcing multilateral contract with performance $z = z^1, \ldots, z^n$ if and only if

$$\frac{\delta}{1-\delta}\left(F\left(\sum_{i \in N} z^i\right) - \sum_{i \in N} c^i(z^i) - \sum_{i \in N} w\right) \geq \sum_{i \in N} c^i(z^i).$$

This self-enforcing multilateral contracts condition states that surplus generated by each group of employees, N, must be greater than their total costs of effort.

Let us compare the two conditions for the special case of n identical workers. For self-enforcing bilateral contracts, the incremental surplus condition states that the incremental surplus generated by each group of employees must be greater than their current cost of effort,

$$\frac{\delta}{1-\delta}[F(nz) - F(mz) - (n-m)c(z) - (n-m)w] \geq (n-m)c(z),$$

$[\delta/(1-\delta)](F(nz)/n - c(z) - w)$

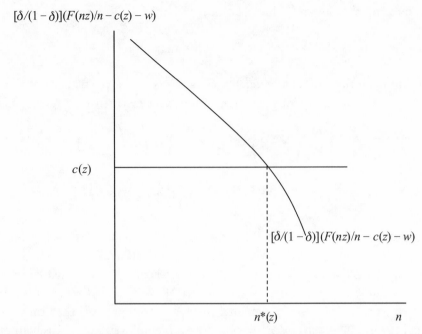

Figure 6.1. The feasibility of multilateral contracting can be limited by the size of the team.

where $m < n$. For self-enforcing multilateral contracts, the necessary and sufficient condition reduces to the requirement that the average surplus generated by each employee exceed each employee's current cost of effort:

$$\frac{\delta}{1-\delta}[F(nz)/n - c(z) - w] \geq c(z).$$

The self-enforcing multilateral contracts condition with identical workers is illustrated in Figure 6.1 for z constant. For any given effort level z, multilateral contracts are feasible if and only if the number of workers is below the critical cutoff $n^*(z)$ at which discounted average surplus per employee equals the cost of effort. The condition suggests that the feasibility of multilateral contracting can be limited, depending on the size of the organization. With unobservable effort and free riding, product per worker can decrease, placing stricter limits on the feasibility of multilateral contracting.

6.5 Hiring by the Firm versus a Cooperative with Open Membership

The firm chooses the size of its labor force to maximize profits. This provides coordination to employees in comparison to partnerships. To examine the costs of coordination in partnerships, consider a worker cooperative that has open membership. Each worker decides whether or not to join the partnership. Workers form expectations about the benefits of joining the cooperative based on what the equilibrium choices of other workers will be. Workers decide whether or not to join the cooperative as a best response to the equilibrium decisions of other potential members, so that the number of members of the worker cooperative is the result of a Nash noncooperative equilibrium.

Workers seeking to form a cooperative necessarily encounter coordination costs. They must search to find each other and negotiate contractual agreements to form the basic partnership. A critical problem is determining who should be a member of the cooperative. The models of the worker cooperative in the preceding sections assumed that coordination costs were zero. Workers form the partnership costlessly. The workers decide on the size of the partnership by agreeing to maximize net benefits per member. When workers are identical, this means simply choosing the number of members. When workers have diverse abilities and those abilities are observable, the best workers form the partnership and determine the size of partnership by choosing the marginal worker quality that maximizes net benefits per member.

Workers have opportunity costs of supplying effort to the cooperative. The opportunity costs of workers are represented by an index i that is uniformly distributed on the unit interval. The decision of a worker i to join the cooperative is represented by z_i, where $z_i = 1$ if the worker joins the cooperative and $z_i = 0$ if the worker does not join the cooperative. It can be shown that if a worker i' joins the cooperative, all workers with lower costs, $i \leq i'$, also will join the cooperative. Accordingly, the number of workers who join the cooperative can be represented by a measure n that takes values in the unit interval.

Let $F(n)$ be the cooperative's production function, where F is increasing with diminishing marginal returns. Let K be the fixed cost of establishing the cooperative. The total effort costs of the members of the cooperative equal $\int_0^n i \, di = n^2/2$. The total net benefits of the cooperative equal $F(n) - K - n^2/2$. The efficient size of the cooperative solves

$$F'(n^0) = n^0.$$

Assume that the efficient-sized cooperative has average benefits capable of supporting the marginal worker's opportunity costs:

$$(F(n^0) - K)/n^0 - n^0 \geq 0.$$

This implies that at the efficient size, the average product of the cooperative is greater than or equal to the marginal product:

$$(F(n^0) - K)/n^0 \geq n^0 = F'(n^0).$$

Let $\bar{n}$ be the employment level that maximizes average net product. Then the efficient size of the cooperative is greater than or equal to employment at the maximum average net product, $n^0 \geq \bar{n}$; see Figure 6.2.

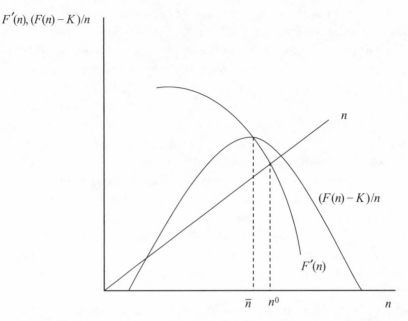

Figure 6.2. The efficient size of the cooperative, n^0, is greater than or equal to the number of workers that maximizes the cooperative's average net product.

Consider now the equilibrium size of the partnership. Every worker i chooses z_i as a best response to the equilibrium choices of other workers $z^*_{(i)}$. Worker i chooses to join a cooperative of size n if

$$(F(n) - K)/n \geq i.$$

With a continuum of workers, an individual worker's decision does not affect net product per member. There are three possible Nash equilibria denoted by I, II, and III in Figure 6.3. In equilibrium I, no workers join the cooperative. A worker will choose not to join the cooperative as a best response to other workers not joining. Equilibrium II is a small cooperative in which a small output is shared among few workers, whereas equilibrium III is a large cooperative in which a large output is shared among many workers. The possibility of multiple Nash equilibria complicates the coordination problem.

With a small number of potential members, workers presumably can communicate with each other at low cost and choose an outcome that maximizes their net benefits. With costless communication, workers can choose the size of the partnership that maximizes benefits per member, $(F(n) - K)/n - n/2$. The first-order condition is

$$F'(n^*) - (F(n^*) - K)/n^* = n^*/2.$$

This is a feasible solution because marginal product is greater than average product, so that average product exceeds the cost of the marginal worker n^*.

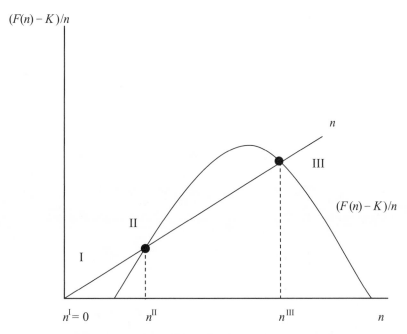

$(F(n)-K)/n$

n

III

$(F(n)-K)/n$

II

I

$n^{\mathrm{I}}=0$ n^{II} n^{III} n

Figure 6.3. Nash equilibria for the worker cooperative.

Suppose that there are few workers, so that coordination costs are low. Suppose, however, that transaction costs prevent workers from forming a central authority to choose the optimal membership. Instead, workers must decide individually whether or not to join the cooperative. This means that the membership size can be determined by a Nash equilibrium, although the multiplicity of equilibria creates difficulties. With a small number of workers, they may communicate with each other to choose between Nash equilibria. One possibility is that workers choose the Pareto-dominant Nash equilibrium. Here, the highest-membership Nash equilibrium at n^{III} Pareto dominates the other two equilibria. However, this is not a necessary consequence of the Nash equilibrium. Workers may not choose the Pareto-dominant outcome unless they expect others to do so.

If there are many workers, communication costs can be substantial. It is then difficult to rule out any Nash equilibrium. The outcome cannot be predicted because it is not evident which equilibrium outcome will be observed or whether there will be other outcomes, because workers may make out-of-equilibrium decisions. This adds another problem that may help to explain the rarity of worker cooperatives. The costs of coordination may affect the willingness of potential members to form a partnership. The problem is similar to that observed in many other types of coordination games, such as markets with network effects or financial markets with the possibility of bank runs.[17]

17 On markets with network effects, see Katz and Shapiro (1985, 1994) and Economides (1996). On markets with the possibility of bank runs, see Diamond and Dybvig (1983). For a discussion of consumer coordination in markets with network effects, see Spulber (2008a).

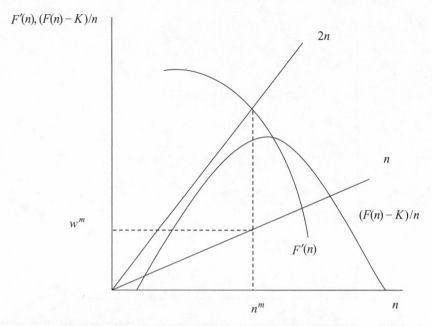

Figure 6.4. The size of the firm chosen by a monopsony firm.

Costly coordination in forming partnerships creates an economic role for a firm. The firm helps to resolve coordination problems by announcing a wage w and job openings. Workers make decisions based on the wage and the availability of job openings without having to make strategic choices. Workers decide to join only if the wage exceeds their effort costs, $w \geq i$. The firm faces a supply curve equal to w. The firm is a monopsonist in the labor market in the present model, so the firm chooses the wage $w = n$ to maximize profit,

$$\Pi(n) = F(n) - K - n^2.$$

The monopsony firm chooses the wage such that the size of the firm solves

$$F'(n^m) = 2n^m.$$

See Figure 6.4. Because of the firm's market power, the size of the firm is always less than the efficient-sized cooperative, $F'(n^0) = n^0$. The size of the firm may be greater than, equal to, or less than the size that maximizes average product, $\bar{n}$.

Suppose that in addition to paying wages, the firm distributes profit shares to its employees, so that they receive the average net product of the firm. Compare the benefits per employee of the firm with the benefits received by a member of the worker cooperative in the Nash equilibria II and III. If $n^{III} = n^0$, that Nash equilibrium yields the highest average net benefits, so that the firm provides its employees with lower benefits and cannot block that equilibrium. This outcome is unlikely because $n^{III} \geq n^0$. If n^{III} takes any value strictly greater than n^0, there is a range between n' and n^{III} where n' is the lower value of n at which average net product equals n; see Figure 6.5. If the firm chooses employment n^m in the interval

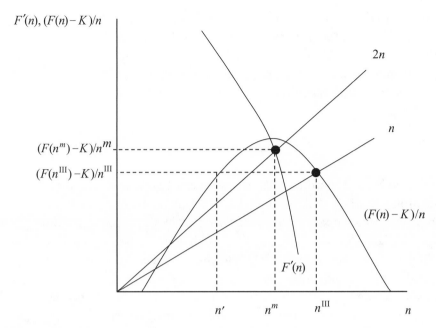

Figure 6.5. The monopsony firm's employment level yields a greater net benefit than the equilibrium employment levels for the workers' cooperative with open admission.

between n' and n^{III}, the firm generates a greater average net product for each of its worker-owners, as is shown in Figure 6.5. The worker-owners prefer separation because the profit-maximizing firm excludes workers, in comparison to the worker cooperative. If the firm restricts employment too much, so that n^m is less than n', the worker cooperative performs better.

The size of the range from n' to n^{III} depends on the size of fixed costs. The greater are fixed costs, the smaller is the range in which the firm performs better, because the worker cooperative spreads the fixed costs over more members, whereas the firm restricts employment. With zero fixed costs, average product is everywhere decreasing, so that the firm always performs better than the worker cooperative with open membership. The advantage of the firm goes away if K is sufficiently large so that the size of the worker cooperative is close to the size at which average net product is maximized.

The firm improves the outcome relative to the Nash equilibria (and most out-of-equilibrium outcomes) by providing coordination to workers. If the number of workers is small, their coordination costs are likely to be low, so that the workers can form an efficient-sized partnership. If the number of workers is large, their coordination costs are likely to be high. Then a firm provides centralized coordination through price signals in the form of posted wages, advertised job openings, and profit maximization to decide the size of the firm. Accordingly, the firm is more likely to form than the worker cooperative when workers face coordination costs.

When fixed costs are not too high, there is a range of employment levels such that if the firm's employment level is in the range, the firm performs better than the worker cooperative with open membership. The firm provides average net benefits greater than those at the three Nash equilibria. The low-opportunity-cost workers prefer to join the firm rather than the worker cooperative.

6.6 Conclusions

Firms assemble and coordinate teams of workers. To assemble worker teams, firms make hiring decisions that maximize profits. This can increase the productivity of worker teams in comparison to worker cooperatives that hire to maximize benefits per worker. This holds whether worker abilities are homogeneous or diverse. Modifying the worker cooperative by allowing a market for memberships to operate results in profit maximization. However, such membership markets begin the process of separating ownership and control. The organization then takes on the characteristics of a firm with profit-maximizing hiring decisions.

Firms coordinate teams of workers through market transactions and through management transactions within the organization. The boundaries of the organization depends on the firm's choice between market contracts and employment contracts. Firms create organizations to take advantage of systems of monitoring and subjective evaluation that may not be feasible in market transactions. The organization provides a way for firms to form multilateral contracts with its workforce. Such multilateral contracts can improve incentives for worker performance by improving the firm's ability to make commitments. Firms use organizational contracts rather than market contracts if multilateral contracts perform better than a set of bilateral contracts.

7

Financial Capital and the Organization of the Firm

One of the most important economic functions of the firm is to raise financial capital. By definition, the firm is a transaction institution whose objectives are separate from those of its owners. The separation of objectives plays a critical role in raising financial capital. The firm chooses its investment policies separately from its owners' consumption and savings decisions, as the Fisher Separation Theorem shows; see Chapter 3. Because the firm's owners need not rely on the firm as a means of saving, they benefit from gains from trade in financial markets. The firm's owners are affected by the firm's decisions only through its profits so that they prefer that the firm maximize profits. The firm generates gains from trade by obtaining capital investment from investors, which generates additional profits for the firm's owners.

The purpose of this chapter is to examine how firms can enhance transaction efficiencies in financing investment. The firm provides two types of transaction efficiencies in capital investment. First, the firm provides efficiencies in its *market transactions* with investors. Separation of ownership and control provides liquidity to investors, who are able to buy and sell ownership shares of the firm depending on their consumption and savings objectives. Ownership shares offer both residual returns and residual control, which allows the development of a market for corporate control.

Second, the firm provides efficiencies in its *management transactions* within the firm. Separation of ownership and control allows the firm to benefit from delegating authority to professional managers. In practice, such separation corresponds to the corporation and more complex forms of partnership. The corporation separates ownership from control by delegating management authority to a chief executive officer (CEO). The firm designs incentives that attempt to align the incentives of managers with those of the firm. The market for corporate control also serves the purpose of providing incentives to managers to act in the interests of the firm's investors.

Consumer organizations also have the ability to transact with investors and to employ finance capital in investment projects. To highlight the economic role of the firm, this chapter considers the basic partnership as a benchmark. The basic partnership shares benefits equally among its members and maximizes benefits per member. The members of the basic partnership are also its owners, so that the objectives of the partnership are not separate from those of its owners. The basic partnership combines ownership and control, with partners providing both ownership and management effort. The basic partnership suffers from free riding, with its members subject to the problem of moral hazard in teams. This chapter considers basic partnerships that raise finance capital both from investors and from their members.

The chapter considers the incentive effects of investment in the firm and the basic partnership. The discussion examines incentives for team production in the firm and in the basic partnership. The discussion presents a market equilibrium model that compares the incentives and performance of the corporations with sole proprietorships and partnerships. We examine equilibrium contracts in the aggregate rather than studying a single debt contract in isolation. The financial structure of the firm is determined endogenously in equilibrium as are the opportunity costs of borrowers and investors and the rate of return to capital. The number of partners in the partnership and the number of investors in the corporation also are determined endogenously. The chapter examines the implications for finance of the separation of ownership and control. It shows that the corporation serves to separate ownership and control to avoid free rider effects due to the combination of ownership and control that occurs in the partnership.

7.1 The Basic Model

The analysis in this section examines the self-financing sole proprietorship and the corporation. Because we do not consider the effects of taxes, it is not necessary to address legal distinctions between financial structures.[1] The corporation is compared to the partnership in later sections. Zingales (2000) points out that the theory of the firm should have important implications for the foundations of finance. The discussion in this chapter illustrates the interaction between financing decisions and organizational form in equilibrium.

Firms in the United States have three basic financial structures: corporations, partnerships, and sole proprietorships. In terms of total numbers of firms, corporations make up over 19%, partnerships are about 9%, and sole proprietorships represent over 72%.[2] However, in terms of annual revenue, corporations

---

1 In practice, there are different types of corporations. An S corporation has a limited number of shareholders who are taxed as sole proprietors or as partners, whereas a C corporation is taxed as a separate entity that can retain or distribute profits and earnings. A limited liability company (LLC) offers limited liability and taxation as a partnership.

2 Sole proprietorships exist in practically every sector of the economy. To give some indication of entrepreneurial startups of sole proprietorships, consider the United States Small Business Administration (2001) estimate that there were over 612,000 new firms with employees in the

earn almost 85% of total revenues, whereas partnerships earn about 11%, and sole proprietorships earn about 4% of total revenues. Corporations account for the bulk of employees, partnerships tend to be small, with an average of six members, and sole proprietorships have even fewer employees. Although there are partnerships with hundreds or even thousands of owners in the professional services industry, including accounting, consulting, and law, such large partnerships are rare in other economic sectors.[3]

The investment costs of corporations are substantial, with corporations accounting for nearly $1 trillion in annual capital expenditures. Using annual depreciation as a proxy for capital investment, corporations account for 84%, partnerships for 11%, and sole proprietorships for 5% of total investment.[4] Large partnerships are characterized by centralized management and an organizational hierarchy in which the status and authority of individual partners varies considerably, so that in practice many large partnerships take on the characteristics of corporations. Hillman (2005) observes that "there seems to be little practical distinction between corporations and partnerships when either form of firm is populated by a large number of shareholders or partners, as the case may be."

Consider an economy in which any consumer can act as an entrepreneur and establish a firm. The economy is composed of countably many consumers, each of whom is endowed with one unit of time and with h units of a consumption good, y. When acting as a borrower or as an investor, the consumer's endowment of the good h can be interpreted as the consumer's financial liability. Thus, each consumer has limited liability.

The consumer provides managerial effort if the individual is an entrepreneur who creates a sole proprietorship, a member of a partnership, or the CEO of a corporation. The individual consumer may provide z units of managerial effort in terms of time, $0 \le z \le 1$. The consumer derives utility from consuming the good

year 2000. Reynolds et al. (2004) estimate that in the year 2000 there were over 11.8 million "nascent entrepreneurs" and about 6.5 million start-up efforts in progress.

3 According to the U.S. Census Bureau, "Fourteen percent of all U.S. firms operated in professional, scientific, and technical services and accounted for 4.5 percent of the total gross receipts." *Survey of Business Owners 2002*, http://www.census.gov/csd/sbo/companysummaryoffindings. htm.

4 The U.S. economy has approximately 5.56 million corporations representing over $22.8 trillion in annual receipts and depreciation of $707 billion. Corporations includes both S corporations and C corporations. There are over 2.55 million partnerships in the United States, with over 15.56 million partners, $3 trillion in receipts, and $90 billion in depreciation. Partnerships include both general partnerships and limited partnerships. There are over 20.59 million nonfarm sole proprietorships in the United States, with receipts approaching $1.14 trillion, and depreciation of $44 billion. The number of firms is based on the number of tax returns. Statistics are based on tax data for 2004; see http://www.irs.gov/taxstats/index.html. Based on census data, reported depreciation for nonfinancial corporations was $692 billion, for partnerships $84 billion, and for sole proprietorships $42 billion; see U.S. Census Bureau, *Statistical Abstract of the United States: 2007*, Washington, DC.

y and disutility from providing effort z. Each consumer has a utility function of the form

(1) $$u(y, z) = y - c(z).$$

If the consumer does not own or manage a firm, the consumer's benefit equals $u(h, 0) = h$.

The managerial effort of an individual, z, is unobservable. An individual's choice of effort depends on incentives for performance. Performance is based on the outcome of production which is observable. The net benefits to an individual depend on the organization's financing arrangements and incentive contracts. The individual's choice of effort depends on the amount of financial capital that the organization obtains. The individual's choice of managerial effort also depends on the way that the organization compensates its members.

The consumer's effort cost function has the form

(2) $$c(z) = \alpha z + z^{\beta}/\beta.$$

The form of the effort cost function guaranties that the marginal cost of effort is bounded away from zero, $\alpha > 0$. Assume that the effort cost function is increasing and convex, so that $\beta > 1$. The convexity of the effort cost function implies that there are returns to cooperation. Let Z be the total effort of n individuals,

(3) $$Z = \sum_{i=1}^{n} z_i.$$

There are benefits of diverse efforts because marginal costs of individual efforts are increasing:

$$c(Z) > \sum_{i=1}^{n} c(z_i).$$

Establishing a firm requires an investment cost K, denominated in units of the consumer good. The investment cost represents capital costs such as plant and equipment, technology procurement, and other initial fixed expenditures. This cost also includes the transaction costs the entrepreneur encounters in establishing the firm, including the costs of designing the firm, complying with regulations, securing financial capital, and negotiating with input suppliers.

There is an important relationship between the cost of establishing a firm and the endowment of consumers. If the cost of setting up a firm is less than or equal to the consumer's endowment, $K \leq h$, the entrepreneur can engage in production without obtaining financial capital. This outcome is the self-financing sole proprietorship. If the cost of setting up a firm exceeds the consumer's endowment, $K > h$, then the entrepreneur must obtain financial capital to engage in production. This can be achieved by forming a corporation or a partnership.

There exists a common production technology that is available to all consumers. Let Y be the final good produced by the firm and let the parameter $\tilde{x}$ be a random variable representing production uncertainty. The technology is represented by the production function

$$(4) \qquad Y = \tilde{x}F(Z) = \tilde{x}(Z^{\gamma}/\gamma).$$

The production function exhibits expected decreasing marginal returns, so that the technology parameter satisfies $\gamma < 1$.

The shock $\tilde{x}$ equals 1 with probability $(1 - p)$ and equals $x < 1$ with probability p. The expectation of the shock equals

$$(5) \qquad E(\tilde{x}) = 1 - p + px.$$

Assume that the low realization of the shock is bounded above, $x < \gamma h$. It will be shown that the entrepreneur's optimal effort z is always less than one. The entrepreneur incurs costs of effort and will not invest when his endowment h is greater than or equal to expected output.

In the self-financing sole proprietorship, the owner finances and manages the firm. Establishing such a sole proprietorship is feasible only if the cost of establishing the firm is less than or equal to the consumer's endowment, $K \leq h$. The entrepreneur's net expected benefit as the owner and manager of the firm is given by

$$(6) \qquad u^{S}(z) = E(\tilde{x})F(z) - c(z) - K + h.$$

The entrepreneur-manager chooses effort to maximize his net expected benefit. The first-order condition for the entrepreneur's problem is to equate the expected marginal product of managerial effort to the marginal cost of effort. This level of effort is optimal for the organizational form because the entrepreneur is sole owner and obtains all of the returns of the firm.

Total managerial effort of the sole proprietor, z^{S}, maximizes $u^{S}(z)$:

$$(7) \qquad E(\tilde{x})F'(z^{S}) = c'(z^{S}).$$

The manager's effort is shown in Figure 7.1. The entrepreneur achieves the first-best level of effort given this form of organization but is unable to exploit benefits from diversification or specialization. The net benefit of the entrepreneur who decides to set up a sole proprietorship is given by

$$(8) \qquad u^{S} = E(\tilde{x})F(z^{S}) - c(z^{S}) - K + h.$$

Because sole proprietorships do not suffer from agency, they generate more surplus than corporations. An individual entrepreneur will form a corporation only to finance the firm's capital expenditures that exceed the entrepreneur's endowment.

Define a *market equilibrium* as an allocation of consumers to organizations such that the allocation is not blocked by any coalition of consumers. An allocation is blocked if a group of individuals can form their own organization and at least one individual gets higher net benefits, and all other individuals are at least as well off. An

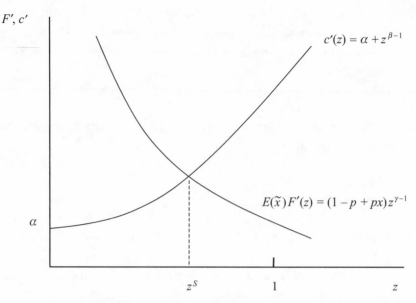

Figure 7.1. The managerial effort of the self-financing sole proprietor.

allocation refers to the benefits received by owners of sole proprietorships, members of partnerships, investors in corporations and partnerships, and consumers who are employed as the managers of corporations.

7.2 The Corporation in Equilibrium

The corporation separates the objectives of the firm's owners from those of its managers. The corporation decouples the firm's financial investment from the endowments of its manager. In contrast to the self-financing sole proprietorship, the corporation can obtain additional capital investment. This allows for a separation between ownership and control. The corporation's owners can delegate control to the firm's CEO. The benefits of additional capital investment are offset by the transaction costs of delegating authority to a CEO.

7.2.1 The Corporation and Managerial Incentives

The theory of finance has applied agency theory extensively to address financial and managerial decision making. Following Jensen and Meckling (1976) and others, extensive empirical and theoretical research applies agency to study the structure of financial contracts and the market for corporate control.[5] The firm's financial structure and the terms of the firm's contracts with investors significantly affect

---

5 See for example Myers and Majluf (1984), Shleifer and Vishny (1997), Vives (2000), and the references therein.

incentives for managerial performance. This helps to explain why firms choose different financial structures and address the functions of the market for corporate control.

Although the agency approach to finance has proved to be highly fruitful, the theory of the firm views separation as a source of value rather than as a problem. The corporation may fall short of efficiency as compared to a neoclassical outcome with full information and without transaction costs. However, evaluating the efficiency of financial decisions requires a comparison of alternative institutions. The natural alternatives to the corporation are the sole proprietorship and the partnership. Each type of organization offers different financial choices and incentives. In this general setting, financial decisions achieve the best mix of incentives and separation of ownership and control. The benefits and costs of separation help to explain the firm's financial decisions and organizational structure.

Managerial decisions and financial choices can differ depending upon whether the decision makers are corporate managers or members of a partnership, as the discussion in the present chapter demonstrates. Generally, the firm's organizational structure will vary with risk, incentives, liability, and the need for capital investment. In turn, the firm's organizational structure will affect the firm's financial contracts, including debt and equity.

The agency literature on the corporation examines the transaction costs associated with separation of ownership and control. The seminal study by Jensen and Meckling (1976) points out that the separation of ownership and control creates agency costs.[6] They emphasize that managers necessarily fail to maximize the value of the firm. If managers have too great an ownership share, they inefficiently avoid risk. If managers have too small an ownership share, they may shirk in their duties. They suggest (1976, p. 309) that problems attributed by observers to the separation of ownership and control in "the modern diffuse ownership corporation are intimately associated with the general problems of agency."

The legal separation of the firm's assets from those of its owners and managers is related to the independence of the firm from its owners and managers. Asset separation, although not sufficient, is necessary for the separation of firm decisions from those of owners and managers. The corporation also provides organizational structures that are essential for separating decision making and for improving incentives.

The corporation provides financial mechanisms for separating the owner's consumption-savings decisions from the firm's investment decisions. The shares of the corporation are transferable, allowing the firm's investors to benefit from liquidity in acquiring and divesting their shares. The divestiture of shares by an

---

6 There is a vast literature on agency costs in the corporation. See, for example, Fama (1980), Fama and Jensen (1983a, 1983b), Hart (1983), Holmstrom and Weiss (1985), Agrawal and Mandelker (1987), Scharfstein (1988a, 1988b), Ricart i Costa (1988), and Schmidt (1997). For the agency perspective on the firm in law, see Easterbrook and Fischel (1991) and the references therein.

investor does not affect the value of the firm as a going concern. Shareholders can adjust the sizes of their portfolios of investments based on their personal savings decisions. The firm, in turn, can issue debt and securities to fund capital investment through capital markets.

The market for the firm's shares is part of the market for corporate control, allowing investors to trade residual returns and residual control based on information about the corporation's performance. Manne (1965) provides the seminal introduction to the market for corporate control. In addition to financial mechanisms, the corporation provides organizational mechanisms for separating the decisions of its owners from those of the firm. Owners delegate decision making to the firm's CEO. Also, owners delegate monitoring of management to the firm's board of directors. The corporate board hires and fires the CEO, oversees the CEO's compensation, approves the CEO's general strategy, reviews the CEO's performance, and examines the firm's financial information.

Delegating authority to the corporation's CEO provides the firm with unity of control. The CEO manages a hierarchy of subordinate managers and employees. The CEO is a single decision maker who guides the firm's organizational activities and its actions in the marketplace. Through delegation of authority by owners to the CEO, the firm becomes an independent economic actor.

Delegation of authority by owners to the CEO also achieves the benefits of agency. Principals hire agents for a number of economic purposes. A principal cannot be everywhere at once. The agent represents the interest of the principal when the principal cannot be present. In general, the agent is an *intermediary* who represents the principal in economic transactions; see Spulber (1999). The agent negotiates for the principal, buys and sells for the principal, has the authority to bind the principal in contractual relations, and reports information to the principal. The agent is a fiduciary, acting for the principal with duties of loyalty and care.[7] When the principal's opportunity cost of time is greater than that of the agent, there are potential advantages to hiring an agent. The firm's CEO provides all of these benefits to the firm's owners. The owners of the firm employ the manager as an intermediary who transacts with the firm's customers, suppliers, creditors, and employees.

As with other types of specialized agents, the CEO brings the benefits of expertise to the firm's owners. A principal hires an agent to take advantage of specialized knowledge and abilities. An agent may offer technical knowledge of the industry or superior ability to conduct transactions. In the case of a company, the manager offers greater ability to conduct market transactions or to supervise the organization. The managers can offer owners greater information-gathering skills. The owners delegate to managers to achieve gains from trade in the market for human capital.

Closely connected to the use of expert agents are the benefits of specialization and division of labor. By being a full-time manager, the CEO develops specialized

---

7 See Casadesus-Masanell and Spulber (2005) on the role of trust and its relationship to incentives in agency.

skills that multiple owners cannot develop if they each devote only part of their time to management of the firm. In practice, the rise of the corporation accompanied the development of the professional manager.

Delegation to a manager also provides the unity of control necessary to supervision of a hierarchy. The manager delegates tasks to senior management specialists, who in turn supervise other managers and employees. The unity of central management avoids the confusion and conflicting signals that accompany an organization with multiple heads. Thus, a partnership is not an efficient structure for supervising a hierarchical organization. In practice, organizations invariably have a single CEO. Large professional services firms in law, accounting, consulting, or health care that are organized as partnerships approximate this structure with the title of managing partner and the designation of a hierarchy of authority relationships between partners. The result looks much more like the corporate form than a basic partnership.

Along with agency benefits come agency costs. The firm's owners are not able to observe the manager's effort perfectly, so that moral hazard problems emerge, as Jensen and Meckling (1976) pointed out. The firm's owners cannot observe the manager's private information about the manager's ability or the firm's productivity perfectly, so that adverse selection problems can occur. The corporate board may not exercise sufficient vigilance in monitoring the activities of the CEO. With asymmetric information within the organization, the CEO and other senior managers monitor the actions of middle managers and employees imperfectly. Considerable debate centers on whether executive pay is efficient or excessive. Bebchuk and Fried (2004) for example, argue that executive pay reflects influence on the corporate board rather than performance.

Agency costs affect managerial compensation. Managers receive compensation in the form of salary, benefits, and perks. To reduce shirking and address moral hazard, managerial compensation is based on the firm's performance adjusted for market data. In comparison with compensation under full information about effort, compensation with asymmetric information must provide additional rewards to reduce shirking. Because performance-based rewards shift some risk to the manager, the manager also must be compensated for the disutility of bearing risk. When there is asymmetric information about the manager's type or when managers have better information about the firm, managerial compensation includes information rents. Owners compensate managers for actions that indirectly reveal information. Owners can compensate managers for direct disclosure of information about the firm's performance beyond what is required by accounting rules and other disclosure regulations.[8]

---

8 Verrecchia (1990) examines the effect of the quality of internal information received by a manager on the manager's incentive to disclose that information to interested parties outside the firm. Wagenhofer (1990) allows for the possibility that information disclosed to investors may also be used strategically by a competitor and gives conditions for full and partial disclosure to occur.

Owners incur implicit agency costs in terms of managerial actions.[9] Jensen and Meckling (1976) point out that managers may take actions that increase their compensation at the expense of shareholders. Managers may reduce managerial effort that would have enhanced the firm's performance. Managers may avoid risky projects to reduce their personal risk even though the projects might have increased the firm's expected value.[10] Because of career concerns, managers may take decisions that improve the firm's short-run performance while reducing its expected value. Holmstrom and Ricart i Costa (1986) show that due to career concerns the manager can choose the wrong investment projects or avoid choosing investment projects. They also show that to prevent overinvestment, the firm's owners can ration capital investment. When corporate directors face liability based on the company's performance resulting from financial regulations, they may be reluctant to make decisions that create investment risks for the firm; see Pollock (2006).

The firm also incurs indirect agency costs when financial decisions are made to correct for agency problems. When the firm's managers have private information about the value of the firm that is not available to its investors, the capital structure of the firm may act as a signal that conveys information to investors. By observing the firm's capital structure, investors can draw inferences about the manager's private information. These inferences in turn affect the market value of the firm's equity, so that capital structure or dividends are no longer neutral. A variety of financial actions provide signals to financial markets.[11]

Capital structure and dividends are signals of private information about the firm's performance. In Grinblatt and Hwang (1989), the fraction of the new issue retained by the firm and its initial offer price convey information to investors. In Ambarish et al. (1987), firms signal with dividends and the level of investment (equivalently the net new issue of stock). Spiegel and Spulber (1997) show that regulated firms encounter countervailing incentives in signaling to two audiences, signaling higher costs to regulators and lower costs to capital markets. The capital structure of regulated firms thus can be uncorrelated with their expected values, reflecting the pooling of diverse firm types.

The market for corporate control affects the firm's managerial agency costs. The possibility of takeovers affects managerial incentives in decision making and revelation of information. They exercise a disciplinary effect on management according to Grossman and Hart (1982), Easterbrook and Fischel (1989), and Scharfstein (1988). Stein (1988) suggests that takeovers can result in managers choosing underinvestment. Laffont and Tirole (1988) find that the threat of takeovers can lead

---

9 On managerial compensation contracts, see for example Diamond and Verrecchia (1982), Holmstrom and Weiss (1985), and Holmstrom and Tirole (1993). For literature surveys, see Shleifer and Vishny (1997) and Vives (2000).

10 Lambert (1986) shows that a manager can either underinvest or overinvest in risky projects in comparison with the principal's desired outcome. See also Holmstrom and Weiss (1985).

11 See Ross (1977). See Harris and Raviv (1991) for a literature survey. See also Bhattacharya (1979), Miller and Rock (1985), John and Williams (1985), and Blazenko (1987).

managers to behave myopically. Schmidt (1997) identifies a "threat-of-liquidation effect" that stimulates managerial effort to avoid the disutility of liquidation. In addition, there is a "value-of-a-cost reduction effect" that creates a disincentive for managerial effort. The latter effect is analogous to the reduced incentives to innovate that are due to the lower returns under increased competition. If the market for managers clears, only the first effect is observed and competition increases managerial performance. With an excess supply of managers, and employed managers earning efficiency wages, both effects are observed, and the net effect of competition on managerial effort remains ambiguous.

Market competition provides incentives for managerial performance. Hart (1983), Scharfstein (1988), and Hermalin (1992) apply the theory of tournaments to examine market incentives for managerial performance.[12] They compare entrepreneurial sole proprietorships with firms in which owners delegate authority to managers. Their analysis shows that the proportion of entrepreneurial firms will affect managerial performance, although they disagree on the direction of the effect. Hart shows that with infinitely risk-averse managers, with no utility of income above a critical level, competition reduces managerial shirking. Scharfstein shows that competition can increase shirking when the manager's marginal utility of income is positive.

7.2.2 An Equilibrium Model of the Corporation

This section presents an equilibrium model of the corporation in which returns to investment are determined endogenously. A *corporation* is defined to be a financial structure in which one or more investors delegate management authority to a CEO. Investors provide finance capital to the firm. The firm contracts with the CEO. The manager's incentives take the form of a debt contract.[13]

Let the cost of setting up a firm exceed the endowment of an individual consumer, $K > h$, so that all entrepreneurs must obtain financing. The firm with outside finance is referred to as a corporation. After the firm is established, it consists of a CEO and a set of investors. It is equivalent whether the borrower is considered to be the entrepreneur, the CEO, or the firm itself. The corporation's investors share the firm's financing costs and earnings and delegate management authority to a CEO.

The CEO initially invests h in the company. This investment does not result in a linear return, but it is meant to represent the fact that the CEO owns assets in the firm. With standard CEO pay packages, CEOs may purchase stock and stock options,

---

12 See Lazear and Rosen (1981), Green and Stokey (1983), Nalebuff and Stiglitz (1983), and references therein. See also Bull and Ordover (1987).

13 The debt contract is not the optimal contract in the present framework; see Innes (1990) and Poblete and Spulber (2008a) for conditions under which debt contracts are optimal. The assumption of a debt contract does not affect the generality of the results because more complex efficient contracts would only strengthen the relative performance of the corporation in comparison to other forms.

but these assets are subject to contractual adjustments that decouple compensation from the initial investment. The CEO will associate with the smallest number of investors needed to finance the firm. Let $n^C - 1$ be the number of investors in the corporation, where $n^C - 1 = \lceil (K - h)/h \rceil$ is the largest integer greater than $(K - h)/h$. A corporation must have at least one investor, so that $n^C = \lceil K/h \rceil \geq 2$.

The face value of the debt is given by a return per unit of investment, R, multiplied by the total initial investment of the corporation's investors, $R(K - h)$. The return per unit of investment is determined endogenously at the market equilibrium. If the firm's realized income equals or exceeds the face value of the debt, the investors receive the full payment. If the firm's realized income is less than the face value of the debt, bankruptcy occurs, and because the firm's investors are the initial claimants, they receive all of the firm's realized income. Accordingly, the corporation's incentive contract for the manager equals

$$(9) \qquad \text{Manager's contract} = \max\{\tilde{x}F(z) - R(K - h), 0\}.$$

The return R must be sufficiently large to induce consumers to invest in the firm. The return must also be sufficiently small to induce the manager to provide managerial effort, so that the firm will be profitable. When the debt is small, there is no bankruptcy and the manager's effort is optimal.

The optimal debt contract will induce bankruptcy when the bad state is realized, if the debt is sufficiently large. As a consequence, the CEO's utility is given by

$$(10) \qquad u^M(R) = (1 - p)[F(z) - R(K - h)] - c(z).$$

The manager of the corporation chooses effort in order to solve the first-order condition

$$(11) \qquad (1 - p)F'(z^C) = c'(z^C).$$

Compare the CEO's effort with the first-best effort, z^S, which solves $E(\tilde{x})F'(z^S) = c'(z^S)$. Because investors are the residual claimants when the shock takes the low value, equation (11) shows that the CEO provides less effort than the first-best.

The net expected benefit of each investor is given by

$$(12) \quad u^C(R) = [pxF(z^C) + (1 - p)R(K - h) - (K - h)]/(n^C - 1) + h.$$

Investors set the rate of return to maximize their net benefits subject to the participation constraint of the CEO. The manager must obtain at least the same net benefits as investors; otherwise he would choose to be an investor. Formally the investors' problem is

$$\max_R u^C(R) \text{ subject to } \quad u^M(R) \geq u^C(R).$$

Because the net benefits of the CEO are decreasing in R and the benefits of investors are increasing in the relevant range, the constraint is always binding. The equilibrium return on investment, R, is such that the net benefits of investors and of the CEO are equal, $u^M(R) = u^C(R)$.

The investors' maximization problem uniquely determines the market equilibrium return,

$$(13) \quad R = \frac{(n^C - 1)(E(\tilde{x})F(z^C) - c(z^C)) - n^C pxF(z^C) + (K - n^C h)}{n^C(1 - p)(K - h)}.$$

The equilibrium return on investment R depends on individual endowments and the capital requirements of the firm, as well as the likelihood of the shock to production. As the likelihood of a shock increases, the agency problem worsens, and the expected benefit of an investor decreases. The equilibrium rate of return increases to compensate investors for the increased likelihood of bankruptcy.

The equilibrium net benefits of the corporation's CEO and its investors can be expressed as

$$(14) \quad u^C = [E(\tilde{x})F(z^C) - c(z^C) - K]/n^C + h.$$

Each participant in the corporation obtains the return of his initial investment plus a share of the expected output of the firm net of the costs of establishing the firm and the CEO's costs of effort. The returns to investors and the CEO reflect the costs of moral hazard, because the effort level is less than the efficient effort.

It is now shown that for a sufficiently large debt the optimal debt contract induces bankruptcy in the bad state. Let $x < \gamma(K - h)$. To induce participation by investors, it must be the case that when the shock takes the low value, bankruptcy occurs and investors receive all of the firm's income. To see why, suppose that the opposite is true and that bankruptcy never occurs, so that $xF(z) \geq R(K - h)$. Then, with $n^C - 1$ investors, each investor gets net benefits less than $[xF(z) - (K - h)]/(n^C - 1) + h$. Because there is at least one investor, $n^C \geq 2$, and effort is less than optimal, $z < 1$, each investor gets net benefits less than

$$[xF(z) - (K - h)]/(n^C - 1) + h \leq x/\gamma - (K - h) + h.$$

Because by assumption $x < \gamma(K - h)$, it follows that

$$x/\gamma - (K - h) + h < h.$$

Because investors receive less than their endowments, h, they are better off consuming their endowments. This is a contradiction, because investors would then choose not to invest in the corporation. Thus, the rate of return must be such that the low value of the shock induces bankruptcy, $xF(z) < R(K - h)$. Because there is only bankruptcy in the bad state, the effort of the manager is as described in equation (11).

The analysis can be extended by considering alternatives for investors that differ from the standard debt contract. It is well known that the optimal compensation scheme would be to "sell" the company to the manager; however, that is not feasible, because the CEO has limited endowment, h. The firm can compensate the CEO using an options contract. The corporation's owners offer the CEO a payment package that consists of an initial investment, a set of options of the firm that represent a fraction of equity, and a positive salary at the end of the period. The characterization of the market equilibrium obtained with debt financing carries over to the market equilibrium with equity financing. Corporations are established in a market equilibrium even with imperfectly designed incentives for the manager. The analysis is robust to changes in the incentive scheme that would improve or worsen corporate performance. The same forces that make the corporation perform better than the partnership still apply.

7.3 The Partnership in Equilibrium

Members of a partnership often manage the enterprise and contribute finance capital. When the partnership is self-financed by its members, ownership and control are combined. The objectives of the organization may not be separate from those of its members. The partnership's objective is to maximize the benefits of its members. When it obtains outside investment, the partnership introduces some separation between the objectives of the organization and those of its owners.

Partnerships must obtain outside investment when their members have limited liability and cannot fully self-finance the costs of establishing the partnership. Jensen and Meckling (1979) observe that labor-managed firms must obtain funds to train their members, to rent or purchase tangible assets such as manufacturing equipment, and to create or obtain intangible assets such as technology and product designs. They point out that labor-managed firms obtain such funds both from their workers and from issuing debt. Workers have (nontradeable) claims on future cash flows contingent on employment (1979, p. 482).

Outside investment changes the incentives of the partnership's members. Paying returns to outside investors breaks the budget-balancing constraint. Members of the partnership are no longer compensated with shares of the firm's total output, because outside investors also must be compensated. Under some conditions, different types of financing have the same effects on incentives. The partnership's members may retain ownership and finance their investment requirements with debt. Alternatively, the partnership's members may sell their ownership to outside investments. If outside investors compensate the partnership's managers with debt-style contracts, the incentives for performance will be similar to those observed when the partnership obtains financing with debt. Therefore, obtaining outside investment separates the objectives of the partnership from those of its owners.

7.3.1 The Self-Financing Partnership in Equilibrium

This section examines the self-financing partnership. Members provide both financing and managerial effort so that there is no separation between ownership and control. In the *basic partnership* without outside investment, n individuals equally share the costs of managing the firm and equally divide the residual returns. A partnership by definition must have at least two members. Self-financing requires that the endowments of the members cover the costs of establishing the partnership, $n \geq \lceil K/h \rceil$. The net benefits for each partner equal

$$(15) \qquad u^P(z_1, \ldots, z_n) = (1/n)E(\tilde{x})F\left(\sum_{i=1}^{n} z_i\right) - c(z_i) - K/n + h.$$

The partners play a Nash noncooperative game in effort levels. Denote the Nash equilibrium by z_i^P, $i = 1, \ldots n$.

Each partner determines his effort level by maximizing his net benefits given the Nash equilibrium strategies of the other partners. By symmetry, there is a unique Nash equilibrium in which all effort levels equal the same level, which solves

$$(16) \qquad E(\tilde{x})F'(nz^P)/n = c'(z^P).$$

The equilibrium effort levels of the partners depend on the number of members, $z^P = z^P(n)$. The first-order condition of partnerships (16) can be compared to the self-financing sole proprietorship. Partners choose efforts as a best response to the equilibrium efforts of the other partnerships and only receive a share of the returns to their efforts. Due to free riding, the partners provide less than optimal effort, $z^P(n) < z^S$.

Each partner's effort, $z^P(n)$, is decreasing in the number of partners, n. The costs of free riding are partly offset by the benefits from a diversity of managerial efforts, because the effort cost function is convex. The partnership's returns depend monotonically on aggregate managerial effort, $Z^P(n) = nz^P(n)$. With few partners, the marginal cost of managerial effort is high and adding more partners generates greater effort despite reductions in individual partners' efforts. As the number of members increases, the free rider problem eventually dominates the effect of more partners, and total productivity then decreases with the number of partners. The partnership's total effort, $Z^P(n)$, is single-peaked in the number of partners. Moreover, when the partnership becomes large, total effort approaches zero, $\lim_{n \to \infty} Z^P(n) = 0$.

The total surplus generated by the partnership equals

$$(17) \qquad U^P(n) = E(\tilde{x})F(nz^P(n)) - nc(z^P(n)) - K.$$

Each partner's benefits equal

$$(18) \qquad u^P(n) = U^P(n)/n + h.$$

Partners do not maximize the total surplus in equilibrium, because consumers can always form another partnership and obtain greater per-capita benefits. Partners choose the number of members to maximize per-capita benefits subject to endowment constraints. The optimal size of the self-financing partnership, n^P, solves

$$\max_n u^P(n) \quad \text{subject to} \quad n \geq K/h.$$

Let $n^P(K, h)$ denote the optimal size of the self-financing partnership.

Suppose that due to free riding, the partnership's total surplus with two members is less than or equal to the benefits of a self-financing sole proprietorship, $u^S = U^P(1) \geq U^P(2)$. This implies that $U^P(1) > U^P(2)/2$, so that as long as the self-financing sole proprietorship is feasible, $h \geq K$, no partnerships will form.

In what follows, assume that the total surplus created by a partnership of two people is greater than the surplus of the sole proprietorship, $U^P(2) > u^S = U^P(1)$. The condition holds for sufficiently small α and $\beta \geq 2$. The assumption does not guarantee the efficiency of partnerships, because the firm's financial structure is chosen to maximize utility per partner rather than total surplus. Define n^{PU} as the size that maximizes the self-financing partnership's *total* surplus. The maximum investment a partnership can sustain is equivalent to the partnership's maximum surplus,

$$K^P = E(\tilde{x})F(Z(n^{PU})) - n^{PU}c(Z(n^{PU})/n^{PU}) = U^P(n^{PU}, K = 0).$$

Consider first the optimal size of a partnership when individual consumers' endowment constraints are not binding.[14] There exists an optimal partnership size, $n^0(K)$. This equates the marginal total surplus to the average total surplus. The optimal partnership size is increasing in capital investment, K, because the partnership benefits from economies of scale and a diversity of efforts. If the optimal unconstrained size of the partnership is greater than or equal to the capital cost per partner, $n^0(K) \geq K/h$, then the optimal size of the self-financing partnership equals the unconstrained optimum, $n^P(K, h) = n^0(K)$.

Conversely, if the optimal unconstrained size of the partnership is less than the capital cost per partner, $n^0(K) < K/h$, the optimal size of the self-financing partnership is the highest integer given by the endowment requirement, $n^P = \lceil K/h \rceil$, which indicates the next integer higher than K/h. Because an agent's net benefit function is quasiconcave in n, once the endowment constraint becomes binding at $n^P = \lceil K/h \rceil$, it continues to be binding for larger n. As capital requirements increase, the equilibrium number of members of a self-financing partnership increases and the effects of free riding worsen. Thus, as capital requirements increase, the equilibrium number of partners begins to approach the minimum number of investors that can raise the necessary capital investment. The optimal size of a self-financing partnership, $n^P(K, h)$, is increasing in the capital requirement, K, and decreasing in partners' endowment, h.

As the number of partners increases, the partnership's surplus is reduced by the costs of free riding and is increased by the benefits of diverse efforts. These two effects can be summarized as follows:

(19)
$$U^{P\prime}(n) = E(\tilde{x})(F'(Z(n)) - c'(Z(n)/n))Z'(n)$$
$$-[c'(Z(n)/n)(Z(n)/n) - c(Z(n)/n)].$$

---

14 Maintaining the requirement that the size of a partnership have an integer value, note that the event that two different numbers of partners yield the same per capita surplus has measure zero. In the event of such a tie suppose that the smaller partnership size is chosen. This does not affect the net benefits that agents can get in partnerships.

The first term on the right-hand side of equation (19) is the total-production effect, whereas the second term is the diverse-efforts effect. As the partnership grows, free riding eventually causes overall production to decrease and the total-production effect overwhelms the diverse-efforts effect when the partnership is sufficiently large.

Recall that n^{PU} denotes the size of the partnership that maximizes total surplus, $U^P(n)$. Because the total surplus function is quasiconcave, it follows that the number of partners that maximizes the benefits per partner without the investment constraint is less than or equal to the size that maximizes total surplus, $n^0 \leq n^{PU}$. This implies that if $K/h > n^{PU}$, then the optimal size of a self-financing partnership is determined by the endowment constraints, $n^P(K, h) = \lceil K/h \rceil$. For $\beta \leq 2$, the maximum size is at $n^{PU} = 1$ and for $\beta > 2$ the maximum size is $n^{PU} \geq 1$.

7.3.2 The Partnership in Equilibrium with Outside Investors

The partnership may finance some portion of its capital costs by obtaining finance capital from outside investors. The partnership may obtain financing in the form of debt. Alternatively, the partnership may be owned by outside investors who provide an incentive contract to members of the partnership. The incentive contract is assumed to take the form of a debt contract. Let n represent the number of members of the partnership. If $n = 1$, the corporation is a special case of the partnership with outside investors.

Members of the partnership provide their initial endowment, h, to pay for the costs of establishing the partnership, K. Members of the partnership also provide management effort, z, to the partnership. Consider the situation in which the partnership cannot be self-financing, $nh < K$. If the total endowments of the partners are less than the costs of establishing the partnership, then the partnership must turn to outside investors. Let n^I be the sum of the number of members of the partnership and the number of outside investors, so that $n^I - n$ is the number of outside investors. The total of endowments of the partnership with outside investors must be sufficient to cover the costs of establishing the partnership, $n^I h \geq K$. The number of outside investors is the minimum number of investors whose endowments cover the additional capital costs, $n^I - n = \lceil (K - nh)/h \rceil$.

As with the corporation, the face value of the debt is given by a return per unit of investment, R, multiplied by the total initial investment of the partnership's outside investors, $R(K - nh)$. The return per unit of investment is determined endogenously at the market equilibrium. If the firm's realized income equals or exceeds the face value of the debt, the investors receive the full payment. If the firm's realized income is less than the face value of the debt, bankruptcy occurs, and because the firm's investors are the initial claimants, they receive all of the firm's realized income. Each member of the partnership receives an equal share of the

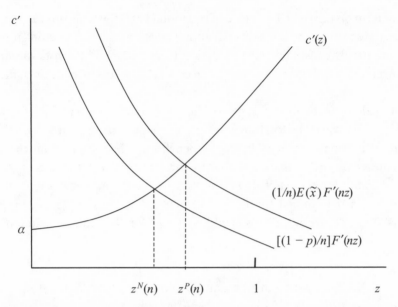

Figure 7.2. The managerial effort of members of the self-financing partnership and members of the partnership with outside investment.

returns of the firm net of the debt obligation. Accordingly, the incentive contract for each member of the partnership equals

(20)   Partner's contract $= \max\{[\tilde{x}F(Z) - R(K - nh)]/n, 0\}.$

When the debt is small there is no bankruptcy and the partners' efforts are not affected by debt.

The optimal debt contract will induce bankruptcy when the bad state is realized, if the debt is sufficiently large, as in the case of the corporation. As a consequence, each of the n partners' expected benefits are given by

$$(21) \quad u^N(z_1, \dots, z_n, R) = [(1 - p)/n]\left[F\left(\sum_{i=1}^{n} z_i\right) - R(K - nh)\right] - c(z_i).$$

The partners play a Nash noncooperative game in effort levels. Denote the Nash equilibrium for the partnership with outside investors by z_i^N, $i = 1, \dots, n$. By symmetry, the first-order condition for the effort levels of the members of the partnership with outside investors can be written as

$$(22) \qquad\qquad [(1 - p)/n]\,F'(nz^N) = c'(z^N).$$

The members of the partnership with outside investment provide less effort than the members of the self-financing partnership, $z^N(n) < z^P(n)$. This occurs because compensation of outside investors lowers the marginal return to members of the partnership; see Figure 7.2.

The net benefit of each outside investor is given by

(23) $u^I(R) = [pxF(nz^N(n)) + (1 - p)R(K - nh) - (K - nh)]/(n^I - n) + h.$

The members of the partnership must obtain at least the same net benefits as investors; otherwise they would choose to be investors. Formally the investors' problem is

$$\max_R u^I(R) \quad \text{subject to} \quad u^N(R) \geq u^I(R).$$

Because the net benefits of the members of the partnership are decreasing in the return R and the benefits of investors are increasing in the relevant range, the constraint is always binding. The equilibrium return on investment, R, is such that the benefits of investors and those of members of the partnership are equal, $u^N(R) = u^I(R)$.

Solving $u^N(R) = u^I(R)$ specifies the equilibrium rate of return as a function of the number of members of the partnership,

(24) $R(n) = \dfrac{(n^I - n)(E(\tilde{x})F(nz^N) - nc(z^N)) - n^I pxF(nz^N) + n(K - n^I h)}{n^I(1 - p)(K - nh)}.$

Substituting for the rate of return, the benefits of an outside investor equal

(25) $u^I(n, n^I) = (1/n^I)[E(\tilde{x})F(nz^N(n)) - nc(z^N(n)) - K] + h.$

The total surplus generated by the partnership depends on the number of members but not on the number of investors,

(26) $U^N(n) = E(\tilde{x})F(nz^N(n)) - nc(z^N(n)) - K.$

The individual benefits of outside investors or members of the partnership equal

(27) $u^I(n, n^I) = (1/n^I)U^N(n) + h.$

The form of the individual benefits function has an important implication.

Compare the corporation with the partnership that has outside investors. First, suppose that due to free riding, the partnership's total surplus with two members is less than or equal to the benefits of the corporation, $u^C = U^N(1) \geq U^N(2)$. This implies that $U^N(1) > U^N(2)/2$. Then, a partnership with outside investors will not be observed. If a sole proprietorship is feasible, $K \leq h$, there will only be self-financing sole proprietorships in equilibrium. If a self-financing sole proprietorship is not feasible, $K > h$, there will either be corporations or self-financing partnerships. Second, suppose that the total surplus created by a partnership of two people is greater than the surplus of the corporation, $u^C = U^N(1) < U^N(2)$. Then, partnerships may seek outside financing. This condition is assumed in this section.

Compare the self-financing partnership with the partnership that has outside investors. Let n^{NO} be the number of members of the partnership with outside investors that maximizes total surplus. The maximum surplus of the partnership

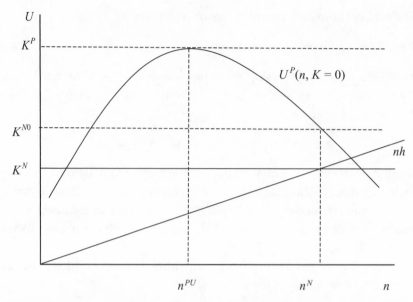

Figure 7.3. The critical values of capital investment determine when the partnership will self-finance. Here, K^{N0} equals the maximum capital investment of the partnership with outside finance and K^N is the critical capital investment above which it becomes desirable to seek outside finance, where $K^N < K^{N0}$.

with outside investors equals $U^N(n^{N0})$. Define the maximum investment that can be supported by the partnership with outside investors,

$$(28) \qquad K^{N0} = E(\tilde{x}) F(n^{N0} z^N(n^{N0})) - n^{N0} c(z^N(n^{N0})).$$

Because the effort of a member of the self-financing partnership is greater than the effort of a member of the partnership with outside investors, total surplus is greater in the self-financing partnership, $U^P(n) > U^N(n)$. The maximum investment that a self-financing partnership can sustain is greater than the partnership with outside investors, $K^P > K^{N0}$.

The size of the self-financing partnership is increasing in the cost of establishing the firm. As the size of the self-financing partnership increases, total surplus eventually declines due to free riding. Define n^N as the critical size of the self-financing partnership when surplus excluding establishment costs equals the maximum capital that can be supported by the partnership with outside finance,

$$(29) \qquad U^P(n^N, K = 0) = K^{N0}.$$

This is represented in Figure 7.3. This yields the fundamental relation that determines K^N,

$$(30) \qquad K^N = n^N h.$$

This is the level of capital investment at which it becomes desirable to separate ownership and control by switching from the self-financing partnership to the partnership with outside investors. Therefore, for $K < K^N$, the partnership will choose to self-finance. For $K^N \leq K \leq K^{N0}$, the partnership will obtain additional capital from outside investors. The partnership with outside finance chooses a return to maximize the benefits of outside investors subject to the participation constraint for members of the partnership. Obtaining outside finance changes the partnership's objectives. The partnership will choose to self-finance if $K^N \geq K^{N0}$, that is, endowments are sufficiently large, $h \geq K^{N0}/n^N$.

7.4 Market Equilibrium and Organizational Form

The results in this section formalize and prove an important conjecture due to Frank Knight, who identifies and ranks organizational forms from lowest to highest: the entrepreneurial sole proprietorship, the partnership, and the corporation. Knight's conjecture (1971, pp. 252–253) is as follows:

> Since it is capital which is especially at risk in operations based on opinions and estimates, the form of organization centers around the provisions relating to capital. It is undoubtedly true that the reduction of risk to borrowed capital is the principal desideratum leading to the displacement of individual enterprise by the partnership and the same fact with reference to both owned and borrowed capital explains the substitution of corporate organization for the partnership. The superiority of the higher form of organization over the lower from this point of view consists both in the extension of the scope of operations to include a larger number of individual decisions, ventures, or "instances," and in the more effective unification of interest which reduces the moral hazard connected with the assumption by one person of the consequences of another person's decisions.

Knight states that "It is the special 'risk' to which large amounts of capital loaned to a single enterpriser [entrepreneur] are subject which limits the scope of operations of this form of business unit by making it impossible to secure the necessary property resources." Knight adds that "it is the inefficiency of organization, the failure to secure effective unity of interest, and the subsequent large risks due to moral hazard when a partnership grows to considerable size, which in turn limit its extension to still larger magnitudes and bring about the substitution of the corporate form of organization."

7.4.1 Organizational Form in Equilibrium

Suppose that the partnership with outside investors will not form, so that the alternative organizational forms are the self-financing sole proprietorship, the self-financing partnership, and the corporation. The size of the corporation is given by n^C as defined previously. The size of the self-financing partnership that maximizes utility per partner is n^P. The self-financing sole proprietorship has a size $n^S = 1$. By symmetry all firms in an equilibrium will have the same financial structure and will be the same size. The market equilibrium financial structure is such that each consumer obtains net benefits $u = \max\{u^S, u^P, u^C\}$. In the event of ties, sole proprietorships cannot be blocked by partnerships or by corporations, and partnerships cannot be blocked by corporations. The market equilibrium consists of a financial structure in the set $\{S, P, C\}$ and a firm size n.

Each consumer must choose between four possible economic activities: (1) self-financing sole proprietor, (2) member of a self-financing partnership, (3) corporate CEO, or (4) corporate investor. Consider a market in which consumer-entrepreneurs can choose to form any type of organization: self-financing sole proprietorships, self-financing partnerships, and corporations. If an entrepreneur establishes a sole proprietorship, the entrepreneur chooses the optimal level of managerial effort. If a group of consumers establishes a partnership, they each choose the optimal level of effort to supply to the partnership. If a group of consumers establishes a corporation, they will choose the compensation scheme for the CEO who then chooses the level of managerial effort for the corporation.

Assume that $U^P(2) > U^P(1)$. In a corporation there must be more than one investor, since otherwise partnerships outperform the corporation. The need for at least a second investor implies that $K - h > h$. Also, recall that $x < \gamma h$, so that $x < \gamma(K - h)$. This again implies that the corporation's debt contract involves bankruptcy if the low-value of the shock occurs. The firm's ability to raise capital is limited by the return on investment, which can be represented for each financial structure by K^S, K^P, and K^C. The maximum capital that a corporation can raise equals

$$(31) \qquad\qquad K^C = E(\tilde{x})F(z^C) - c(z^C).$$

A comparison of partnerships and corporations shows that corporations earn more than self-financing partnerships when the partnership exceeds a critical size.

It can be shown that there exists a critical value n^*, such that total surplus before investment equals

$$(32) \qquad U^P(n, K = 0) = E(\tilde{x})F(nz^P(n)) - nc(z^P(n))$$
$$> E(\tilde{x})F(z^C) - c(z^C) = K^C,$$

if and only if $n \le n^*$. Intuitively when partnerships grow beyond a certain point, free riding outweighs the benefits of partnerships and the surplus created by partnerships is less than that created by corporations. The assumption that marginal cost of effort is positive plays a role here. From the Nash equilibrium condition for partnerships, $E(\tilde{x})F'(Z) = nc'(z)$, it follows that as the number of partners increases, and correspondingly the effort of individual partners decreases, total marginal costs eventually increase. This causes production in the partnership to decrease in the number of partners, and therefore makes partnerships undesirable for firms with many members.

Using the critical partnership size, n^*, we can determine a critical value of the consumer endowment level,

$$(33) \qquad h^* = K^C / n^*.$$

This relation is fundamental for our analysis. It is important because it specifies the relationship between the entrepreneurial sole proprietorship, the partnership, and the corporation. In particular, it tells us that there is a relationship between the endowment, the size of the organization, and the amount of capital that firms are able to support.

The critical value h^*, as given by the fundamental relation (33), relates the consumer's endowment to the decisions of an entrepreneur. By comparing the consumer's endowment to the critical value h^* it is possible to determine what organizational form the firm will have at the market equilibrium. At the market equilibrium, the only organization forms that exist are those that maximize the net benefits of their owners.

Effect of Capital Costs on Market Equilibrium When Endowments Are Large
Let $h \geq h^*$. Then there exists a unique market equilibrium. At the market equilibrium, there are no corporations and there exists a critical value of capital investment, $K_1 > 0$, such that if $K \leq K_1$, all firms are sole proprietorships and if $K > K_1$, all firms are self-financing partnerships.

This result is established as follows. Letting $h \geq h^*$, suppose to the contrary that a corporation exists at the market equilibrium. Then each of its investors and the CEO receive net benefits equal to $u^C = (E(\tilde{x})F(z^C) - c(z^C) - K)/n + h$. If these n consumers decide to form a partnership of size n, then because $h \geq h^*$ and $n < n^*$, it follows that $U^P(n, K = 0) > E(\tilde{x})F(z^C) - c(z^C) = K^C$. Each partner would obtain net benefits of

$$(34) \quad u^P(n) = U^P(n)/n + h > (E(\tilde{x})F(z^C) - c(z^C) - K)/n + h = u^C(n).$$

So the consumers would be better off by dissolving the corporation and forming a partnership, which contradicts the definition of the market equilibrium.

To prove a threshold K_1 exists, note that due to free riding in the partnership, when $K = 0$,

$$(35) \quad u^S = E(\tilde{x})F(z^S) - c(z^S) > E(\tilde{x})F(Z^P(n))/n - c(Z^P(n)/n) = u^P(n).$$

As K increases, the optimal size of the partnership increases, as shown previously. A sole proprietorship is formally equivalent to a partnership with only one member. Therefore, at some capital investment level $K \leq h$, the sole proprietorship is replaced either because the limited endowment condition becomes binding at $K = h$ or because partnerships are more productive due to diverse efforts and scale.

Consider now a general result that determines the organizational form in equilibrium. The result shows that the existence of corporations is due to a combination of limited endowment of individual consumers and limits on the growth of partnerships due to free riding.

Effect of Capital Costs on Market Equilibrium When Endowments Are Small

Let $h < h^*$. Then there exists a unique market equilibrium. At the market equilibrium there exist two critical levels of capital investment, K_1 and $K_2 = n^*h$. If $K < K_1$, all firms are sole proprietorships; if $K_1 < K \leq K_2$, all firms are self-financing partnerships; and if $K_2 < K \leq K^C$, all firms are corporations. If $K > K^C$ no firms exist.

This result proves that Knight's conjecture was correct. The proposition obtains the precise ordering of the three types of organizational forms that Knight identified. Also, the reasons for the transitions between the different organizational forms are exactly those that Knight predicted. The sole proprietorship is limited in size by the risks associated with capital investment requirements, which necessitate multiple decision makers, as in a partnership. In turn, the size of a partnership is limited by "the inefficiency of organization, the failure to secure effective unity of interest, and the subsequent large risks due to moral hazard." This leads to the substitution of the corporation for the partnership. The corporation provides sufficient investment to cover capital costs, secures a unity of interest through the separation of ownership and control, and mitigates the risks due to moral hazard in a partnership.

To understand this result, first notice that for $K \leq n^*h$, it is always possible for consumers to form partnerships of size $n = K/h \leq n^*$. By the definition of n^*, it must be the case that $U^P(n, K = 0) > E(\tilde{x})F(z^C) - c(z^C)$ and then

$$(36) \quad u^P(n) = (1/n)U^P(n) + h > [E(\tilde{x})F(z^C) - c(z^C) - K]/n + h = u^C.$$

Because partnerships give their members greater net benefits than corporations, corporations do not exist.

Since corporations do not exist whenever $K < n^*h$, organizations have to be either sole proprietorships or partnerships. The existence of the critical value K_1 is obtained in the same manner as in the previous result. If $K > n^*h$, the size of partnerships must be $n^P \geq \lceil K/h \rceil = n^C > n^*$. It follows that

$$(37) \quad u^P(n^P) = (1/n^P)U^P(n^P) + h \leq (1/n^C)U^P(n^P) + h$$
$$< (E(\tilde{x})F(z^C) - c(z^C) - K)/n^C + h = u^C.$$

This implies that in equilibrium, corporations cannot be blocked by a group of consumers forming a partnership, because the net benefits that consumers get in the best partnership are less than what they obtain in a corporation. Finally, when $K > K^C$, entrepreneurs prefer to keep their endowments rather than forming a corporation, but we have already proved that consumers are better off in corporations than in partnerships. Also, because sole proprietorships are not viable, no firm can exist.

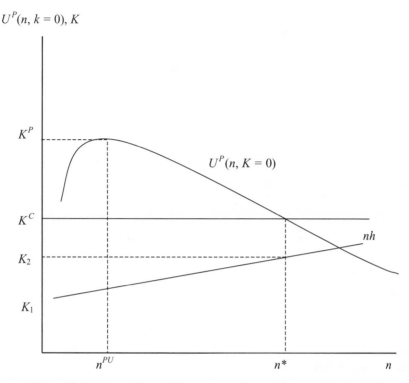

Figure 7.4. The critical values of capital investment determine organizational form at the market equilibrium. Notice that $K^C = E\,(\tilde{x})\,F(z^C) - c(z^C)$ equals the corporation's maximum capital investment.

The equilibrium is illustrated in Figure 7.4. There is a threshold level K_1, where $K_1 \leq h$, such that for lower levels of capital investment the entrepreneurial sole proprietorship is more efficient than the partnership. When the capital investment requirement exceeds K_1, the number of investors increases due to limited endowment constraints, the diverse-efforts benefits of the partnership and scale. For still larger values of capital investment K, the partnership is forced to add members and eventually the free rider problem becomes so severe that the total surplus of the partnership decreases. As shown in Figure 7.4, for n greater than n^*, the total surplus of the partnership is less than the profit of the corporation. The corporation forms to raise the necessary capital investment while providing unity of interest and reducing moral hazard relative to the partnership.

We now have the second fundamental equation for our analysis. As before, the size of partnerships is increasing in K. No firms operate if capital investment requirements exceed the level that can be supported by the corporation, K^C. As before, the size of partnerships is increasing in K. When consumer endowments are bounded, $h < h^*$, the result yields the fundamental relation

(38) $$K_2 = n^*h.$$

This is the level of capital investment at which it becomes desirable to separate ownership and control through the corporate form in contrast to the partnership.

Corporations are observed in equilibrium only when consumer endowments are below the critical value, h^*, that is determined by the maximum capital a corporation can support, divided by n^*. Recall that n^* is the biggest partnership such that a partnership earns more than a corporation. With small endowments and large capital requirements, corporations are observed in equilibrium. The market equilibrium yields an important insight regarding the effect of consumer endowments on organizational form at the market equilibrium. This allows us to contrast our analysis with standard results in corporate finance.

Effects of Endowments on the Market Equilibrium

For any given capital cost $K < K^C$, there exists a critical consumer endowment level, h_0, with the following properties. Corporations exist if and only if $h < h_0$. There exists a critical level of capital investment, K_0, such that when $K \leq K_0$, partnerships exist for $h_0 < h < K$ and sole proprietorships for $h \geq K$, and when $K > K_0$, only partnerships exist for $h > h_0$.

This result differs from the analysis in corporate finance of the effects of endowments on finance contracts. In the canonical model, the outside opportunity of investors is given exogenously. Financial contracts between investors and the borrower often are considered in isolation. In this setting, investors are more likely to lend money to borrowers who have large endowments than to borrowers who have small endowments. This is because the borrower's endowment plays a role in improving incentives to provide effort in improving the firm's expected output. Thus, when agents have smaller initial endowments, corporations are less likely to emerge.

In the present model, the sole proprietorship and the self-financing partnership provide endogenous outside opportunities for investors. At a market equilibrium, when consumers have smaller initial endowments, corporations are *more* likely to emerge. Small endowments limit the ability of consumers to finance capital investment, allowing corporations to emerge. Corporations are desirable because with smaller endowments partnerships must have more members, which leads to more severe free riding among partners. When endowments are large, and capital costs are low, the sole proprietorship becomes feasible due to the better incentives for managerial effort for the owner-manager. When endowments are large and capital costs are high, the partnership becomes desirable due to the advantages of combining diverse efforts. This establishes Knight's conclusion that greater individual wealth makes sole proprietorships and partnerships feasible.

7.4.2 Efficiency Comparisons

This section compares the financial structures of the firm in terms of the maximum capital costs that they can support, K^S, K^P, and K^P. The capital level that an entrepreneurial sole proprietorship can support equals the surplus that the organization is able to create,

$$(39) \qquad K^S = E(\tilde{x})F(z^S) - c(z^S).$$

Recall that the maximum capital that a corporation can raise is given by $K^C = E(\tilde{x})F(z^C) - c(z^C)$. In self-financing partnerships, the firm's production depends on the number of partners, which also depends on the capital requirements level. The maximum capital level it can sustain is defined as follows:

$$(40) \qquad \max_K \text{ such that } K \leq E(\tilde{x})F(Z(n^P)) - n^P c(Z(n^P)/n^P).$$

Note that in equation (37), n^P depends on the size of K^P.

Comparing the three types of organizations, we find that the corporation supports the *smallest* amount of capital investment. This is due in part to inefficient incentives for the CEO. The sole proprietorship induces the owner to devote greater managerial effort to the firm than does the corporate manager who only shares in the earnings of the firm. This is also due to the economies of scale in a partnership that result from diverse efforts. The partnership supports greater capital investment than the sole proprietorship since for a small size the diverse-efforts effect dominates the free rider effect, so that the size of the partnership that maximizes total surplus is greater than one member:

$$K^P > K^S > K^C.$$

Note that

$$K^S = \max_z E(\tilde{x})F(z) - c(z) > E(\tilde{x})F(z^C) - c(z^C) = K^C.$$

By the assumption that total surplus is greater with two partners than one,

$$K^P = U^P(n^{PU}, K = 0) \geq U^P(2, K = 0) > U^P(1, K = 0)$$
$$= E(\tilde{x})F(z^S) - c(z^S) = K^S.$$

This discussion establishes that the corporation in the present setting is a preferred organizational form but not because of its productivity, since the sole proprietorship and the partnership support greater capital investment. The result shows clearly that the order of organizations presented in our main proposition is not a result of the capital levels that the organizations support. Our main result depends instead on the connection between the size of the firm and the incentives that alternative forms of organizations can provide.

7.4.3 The Equilibrium Size of the Firm

This section examines the equilibrium size of the firm. The equilibrium ranges of sizes of the self-financing partnership and the corporation can be compared to show that firms are larger in market equilibria with corporations than in market equilibria with partnerships. To obtain this result requires additional characterization of the partnership.

In the present framework, corporations have the minimum number of investors to raise the necessary capital. Thus, at the capital switchpoint from partnerships to corporations, the size of the corporation will be greater than or equal to that of the partnerships. In practice, corporations have many investors because individuals may invest in many companies and can invest a small amount in any particular company, so that the number of investors will tend to be greater than the minimum number required. This result helps to explain the size difference of partnerships and corporations in a cross section of the economy. Partnerships tend to have few members. Corporations tend to involve large numbers of investors. The optimal size of the firm in partnerships is increasing in K not only because the endowment constraint becomes more binding, but also to take advantage of the diversification of efforts and to reduce the fixed costs per capita. The corporation is larger because of its ability to raise additional capital for investment without additional free rider effects of the self-financing partnership.

We can now characterize the equilibrium size of the firm. The size of the corporation is increasing in capital requirements, $n^C = \lceil K/h \rceil$. The size of the self-financing partnership also is increasing in capital requirements. This has the following important implication. *Firms are larger in market equilibria with corporations than in market equilibria with self-financing partnerships.*[15]

7.5 Conclusions

Firms offer benefits that derive from combining the productive efforts of many individuals and from sharing common costs of investment. Alternative organizational forms represent tradeoffs in terms of incentives for effort, risk allocation, cost efficiencies, and the ability to obtain capital investment. The equilibrium market model allows the three main types of organization to be determined endogenously. The analysis derives critical relationships between finance and the organization of the firm.

Depending on whether capital requirements are low, medium, or high, the market equilibrium organizational form consists of entrepreneurial sole proprietorships, partnerships, and corporations, respectively. Second, the market equilibrium organizational form will be either entrepreneurial sole proprietorships,

---

15   Consider the market equilibrium when individual endowments are bounded, $h < h^*$. Recall that if $K < K_1$, all firms are sole proprietorships; if $K_1 < K \leq K_2$, all firms are partnerships; and if $K_2 < K \leq K^C$, all firms are corporations. Thus, the range of sizes of partnerships is given by $n^P(K_1) \leq n \leq n^P(K_2)$. The range of sizes of corporations is given by $n^C(K_2) \leq n \leq n^C(K^C)$. From Figure 7.4, notice that $n^* > n^{PU}$. Because $n^* = K_2/h$, it follows that $K_2/h > n^{PU}$. Therefore, at $K = K_2$, $n^P(K) = \lceil K/h \rceil$ $n^C(K)$. This means that $n^P(K_2) > n^C(K_2)$, so that the range of sizes for corporations is above that for partnerships.

partnerships, or corporations depending on whether investor liability is high, medium, or low. This is important because it shows that greater corporate finance is associated with low endowments rather than with high endowments. The result differs from the standard analysis for two reasons. In the model, liability affects the incentive of investors rather than those of borrowers. Investors have endogenously determined opportunity costs that are given by the alternatives of forming sole proprietorships or partnerships. This analysis is robust to a range of management incentive contracts that reward the CEO on the basis of debt-style contracts or through options.

As Knight correctly predicted, increasing capital requirements and moral hazard create a ranking of organizational forms. When capital requirements are low, entrepreneurs form sole proprietorships. With medium capital requirements, consumer-entrepreneurs form partnerships, obtaining the benefits of joint investment and diverse efforts while bearing the inefficiencies of free riding. When capital requirements are high, consumer-entrepreneurs form corporations and face the tradeoffs between the benefits and costs of delegation to a CEO.

The analysis yields a very simple but fundamental formula for the critical consumer endowment level. This consumer endowment level determines the existence of corporations in equilibrium based on investor liability, the investment cost of establishing a firm. The critical consumer endowment level equals the ratio of the maximum capital that a corporation can support to the number of members of the largest partnership that still earns more than a corporation. This basic formula ties together the sole proprietorship, the partnership, and the corporation. Corporations only form when consumer endowments are below the critical cutoff.

This accords with Knight's (1971, p. 252) observation that "With the growth of large fortunes it becomes possible for a limited number of persons to carry on enterprises of greater and greater magnitude, and today we find many very large businesses organized as partnerships." With limited endowments, the corporation becomes the equilibrium mode of organization. Despite moral hazard in delegation to the CEO, so often emphasized in theory and in public policy debates, the corporation offers sharing of large-scale capital costs among many investors, unity of interest, and transferable ownership. The equilibrium analysis of the organization of the firm shows how corporations succeed in passing the market test.

PART IV

INTERMEDIATION BY THE FIRM

8

The Firm as Intermediary in the Pure-Exchange Economy

Achieving transaction benefits requires incurring transaction costs. Transaction costs arise in decentralized exchange because consumers must incur costs to gather information, find each other, negotiate the terms of trade, and carry out the trade. Transaction costs also arise when firms centralize exchange because establishing and operating markets requires costly communication and information processing. Firms are needed in the pure-exchange economy because they can improve the efficiency of transactions.[1] The purpose of this chapter is to show how firms contribute to the efficiency of the pure-exchange economy.

A fundamental impediment to trade in the pure-exchange economy is the absence of a double coincidence of wants. A consumer wishing to trade wheat for cloth must find another party willing to trade cloth for wheat. There may simply not be another consumer with the right preferences or endowments to be a trading partner. Even if such a consumer exists, consumers cannot obtain gains from trade unless they can meet at a convenient time. Potential trading partners may be separated by distance when travel and transportation are costly. Finally, preferences and endowments can be affected by random shocks so that consumers can only find trading partners in some states of the world. Consumers fail to capture gains from trade due to problems in finding the right trading partner. These lost gains from trade are implicit transaction costs.

The general theory of the firm provides insights into the role of money in the economy. Economic models of money introduce transaction costs into the pure-exchange economy as a means of understanding the role of money. Money performs three well-known functions. It serves as a unit of account, a store of value, and a medium of exchange. However, firms can perform many of the functions attributed to money, without the need to use money. Firms can provide units of

---

1 The general theory of the firm differs from the neoclassical view of the pure-exchange economy. The neoclassical pure-exchange economy does not have firms, because the only purpose of the firm would be to make production decisions. However, when transactions are costly, firms play an important role in a pure-exchange economy.

account by making exchanges in kind with economic agents. Firms can serve as a store of value through contracts with economic agents. Firms can provide a medium of exchange by serving as intermediaries in economic transactions between other economic agents. By replacing money, firms can solve the problem of the absence of a double coincidence of wants, an economic role traditionally attributed to money. Understanding how firms can perform some functions attributed to money yields insights into the economic role of the firm.

Firms reduce transaction costs associated with the problem of the absence of a double coincidence of wants. Acting as intermediaries, firms increase gains from trade and reduce the costs of trade when consumers are separated by time, distance, and uncertainty. Firms establish markets that provide centralized mechanisms for matching consumers more efficiently than decentralized exchange. Firms that are market makers stand ready to buy and sell, giving buyers and sellers immediacy that allows them to avoid trading delays and the risk of not finding a trading partner. In financial markets, market-making firms provide the corresponding assurance of liquidity by standing ready to buy and sell financial assets. Firms also provide transaction efficiencies by consolidating trades, allowing consumers to avoid the costs of finding multiple trading partners or mismatched transactions. Firms simplify the trading process by posting prices instead of more complex barter arrangements. Firms balance supply and demand by adjusting their purchases and sales, avoiding losses in gains from trade associated with market imbalances that can result in barter economies.

8.1 The Firm and Money

There are several important connections between firms and money. First, firms provide services that are complementary to money because they increase the efficiency of money. Second, firms create and manage money. Third, and perhaps most significantly, firms provide intermediation services that are substitutes for money, essentially performing the functions of money. The connections between the firm and money provide insights into the economic functions of both firms and money.

8.1.1 The Trading Post

Firms complement money by creating markets and organizations. Economic models used to study the role of money typically assume that consumers meet at a trading post. Consumers bring their monetary endowments and goods to the trading post, where they conduct exchange. These models further assume that trading posts are established exogenously and without cost. It is more reasonable to assume that there are costs to creating and managing a trading post. It is also more reasonable to assume that trading posts are created endogenously by economic actors. Governments, consumers, merchant associations, and firms create and manage trading posts.[2] Indeed, Starr (2003, p. 460) refers to a trading post as a "business firm" and a "market maker" that incurs transaction costs.

The presence of trading posts in monetary models raises the question of whether the efficiencies attributed to money are in part due to the trading post itself. Trading posts increase transaction efficiency by providing a place for traders to meet. It is reasonable to expect that firms will create and manage trading posts when it is profitable to do so. Firms can profitably establish trading posts when they can improve on the efficiency of alternative institutions. The firm can charge admission to the trading post or earn returns by intermediating transactions at the trading post. Trading posts are central marketplaces that provide value to traders by reducing search costs. The economic functions of money should be examined within the context of endogenous formation of trading posts.

By creating and managing markets, firms provide services that are complementary to money. Traders use money to facilitate exchange at the trading post. The trading post provides a central place of exchange where traders can use money. Firms provide many types of markets including stores, Web sites, banks, and organized financial exchanges. These marketplaces are complementary to the use of money. The existence of markets allows the use of money as a unit of account and a medium of exchange. The ability to use money to purchase goods and financial assets in market places makes it possible to use money as a store of value. Money cannot function without the existence of markets.

Firms also create money to obtain the returns from the resulting transaction efficiencies. By creating money, firms enhance their performance as intermediaries. Firms create money whether they operate in product markets or financial markets. In product markets, manufacturers, wholesalers, and retailers engage in some types of money creation. Firms that operate in financial markets, including banks, credit card companies, and clearinghouses, are the primary creators of money in the economy.

Firms perform many of the functions often attributed to money. This possibility has not been considered in the literature on money. For example, Wallace (1997) states that in models with the absence of a double coincidence of wants, "Nothing can happen unless some type of storable asset is put into the model." As the present discussion establishes, there are conditions under which money no longer is necessary because firms can solve the problem of the absence of a double coincidence of wants without the presence of money. Firms solve the problem of transferring assets when assets are not storable without the need for money in the overlapping-generations model. This solves the problem of having money as a store of value.

---

2 The Hudson's Bay Company, one of the earliest corporations, established trading posts across North America. These trading posts were known as "factories" after the intermediaries or "factors" who did business there; see Newman (2000). Historically, governments and merchants established trading posts associated with trading settlements, ports, warehouses, and open-air markets. Trading posts were found along the ancient trading routes and were associated with settlements, towns, and major cities.

In addition, firms solve the problem of the need for a unit of account because they can post prices in terms of tradable goods. This will be shown for an economy consisting of three consumers without the double coincidence of wants. Firms also solve the problem of the need for a medium of exchange by acting as counterparties for traders.

The firm's transactions with consumers effectively act as substitutes for money. Although the firm can perform many of the functions attributed to money, it bears emphasis that the presence of money does not replace the firm. The firm is needed even if there is fiat money. The firm performs additional related functions that money does not solve, including the creation of trading posts. The trading post in many monetary models is a market institution that is established exogenously without cost. The Theory of the Firm makes these trading posts endogenous because entrepreneurs establish firms, which in turn create trading posts. In addition, the firm posts relative prices, which addresses the problem of establishing prices and avoids the need for the Walrasian auctioneer. This contrasts with many monetary models that assume prices are established through the Walrasian mechanism.

8.1.2 Organizational Money

Although governments create fiat money, firms may be the main creators of money. Money that is created by fiat generally has no intrinsic value and is distinguished from commodity money, which has intrinsic value.[3] Governments create "public money" (also referred to as outside money) whose acceptance is based on trust in the government. Firms create "private money" (some of which is referred to as inside money) by fiat as well. Private money often is accepted based on trust in a particular firm's business reputation, which is sometimes backed by government guaranties and legal safeguards.

Firms create two types of private money: *organizational money* that is used within the firm and *market money* that is used in exchange between third parties outside the firm. Firms use both of these types of money to reduce transaction costs and improve the efficiency of exchange. The firm creates organizational money as a demand-side or supply-side complement to its own transaction mechanisms. Banks, which are a particular type of firm, create market money through deposit accounts and the fractional reserve system. Firms other than banks provide many other types of money.

Firms provide organizational money to enhance the value of their intermediation services and to improve the performance of their trading mechanisms. A firm can provide organizational money to allow consumers to transact more easily at its posted prices. Consider a firm that operates a trading post. Without the use of money, consumers can go to the trading post and barter goods with the firm that

---

3 Commodity money is bartered for other goods. Some types of commodity money, such as gold, also represent social conventions that designate them as a form of money.

operates the trading post. Also, without the use of money, consumers can enter the trading post and barter with each other. Alternatively, consumers can bring commodity money or fiat money to the trading post and use it to facilitate transactions there, either with each other or with the firm that operates the trading post.

Another possibility is for the firm that operates the trading post to offer consumers organizational money that they can use to transact within the trading post. This avoids some problems associated with the double coincidence of wants. Once in the trading post, consumers need not barter with each other because they can use the organizational money. The trading post firm serves as a market maker. Consumers can sell goods to the trading post firm in return for organizational money. They can purchase goods from the trading post firm in return for organizational money. Consumers can use the organizational money to transact directly with each other. In the next section of the chapter, it is shown that the firm can resolve the absence of a double coincidence of wants with and without creating organizational money.

In practice, firms often provide trade credit to customers and financing to suppliers. These forms of credit are used as a medium of exchange between the firm and its trading partners. Such credit facilitates exchange between the firm and its trading partners with accounting entries serving as a form of organizational money. The parties can transact frequently while settling the accounts occasionally.

There are various types of money that facilitate exchange within the firm. For example, casinos convert currency to poker chips that are used by customers to spend money placing bets, to receive payment for winning a gamble, and even to purchase goods offered by the firm. Amusement parks and fairs sell tickets that can be redeemed for rides, games, food, and merchandise. Club Med used plastic beads as internal money for vacationers. Many stores provide gift cards that are then used like money to make purchases. Firms also offer in-store credit for returned merchandise that is used to purchase other merchandise. Firms provide rewards to loyal customers in the form of organizational money. For example, airlines offer "miles" in return for customers' travel purchases that can be used to purchase additional travel. Credit card companies offer points that can be redeemed for goods and services within a network of stores.

Firms also create organizational money to keep track of transfers within the firm. For example, universities create budgets that can only be used for internal purchases such as computer time. These budgets, often referred to as "funny money," are denominated in terms of currency units of account, but no monetary transfers are involved. Generally speaking, accounting budgets for the divisions of a firm function as organizational money that is used for payments within the firm. The budgets are projections that are made for planning purposes within the firm, allowing managers to allocate capital and other resources within the firm. Actual expenditures and allocations typically depart from budget projections.

It is useful to observe that organizational money ceases to have value once the cycle of sales and purchases is complete. The process of money creation and destruction recalls early discussions of money as a circuit.[4] An important distinction between organizational money discussed here and the circuit theory is that no production is required for organizational money. The firm creates money to facilitate pure exchange. Also, in contrast to circuit theory, extending credit is not a necessary part of the life cycle of money. The monetary instrument can be created simply to enhance the firm's intermediation activities.

8.1.3 Market Money: Payment Systems

Financial firms provide many types of monetary instruments that are used for making payments. Some of these payment systems are not measured as part of the national money supply aggregates but they are nonetheless forms of money.

Whether or not banks hold fractional reserves, the checking accounts offered by banks provide convenience to depositors. This service is distinct from money creation associated with the bank's intermediation in the loan market. Checks reduce risks of loss and theft in comparison to handling cash and avoid the transaction costs of making trips to the bank to obtain cash for purchases. Checking accounts provide records of the depositor's financial transactions. Other firms that offer convenience and trust through retail payment systems include credit and debit card companies, electronic bill presentment and payment systems used to pay bills over the Internet, and electronic payment systems used to make purchases over the Internet.

Credit card companies address liquidity requirements by offering credit to buyers. They reduce transaction costs by consolidating payments both for buyers and for sellers. Buyers receive one monthly bill that combines their purchases from diverse sellers, and sellers receive payments that combine their sales to many customers. Credit card companies provide efficiencies through economies of scale in communication and accounting systems. In addition, it is more efficient for the credit card company to evaluate the creditworthiness of a buyer who makes many transactions than it would be for a seller who may only transact a few times with the buyer. Credit card firms also offer transaction efficiencies through relationships with sellers' banks, again allowing the consolidation of transactions across many buyers and many sellers.

Private payment networks offer transaction efficiencies at a wholesale level. Firms such as the Clearing House Interbank Payment System (CHIPS) make large-scale electronic payments.[5] Futures exchanges have associated clearinghouses that clear trades on a daily basis. Automated teller machine (ATM) networks are firms formed by bank joint ventures that allow individual customers of banks to transact through any ATMs in the network. Systems such as CHIPS or futures clearinghouses provide transaction efficiencies by periodic settlement of individuals' net positions rather than settlement of individual transactions.

---

4 See, for example, Wicksell (1936) and the overview in Graziani (2003).
5 CHIPS is a cooperative joint venture formed by a group of banks.

Firms that operate electronic payments systems create money that serves as a convenient medium of exchange. The electronic transfers are payment messages combined with credits or debits to the positions of participants. The bank participants in CHIPS, for example, provide approximately $2.8 billion in funding each day. CHIPS uses these funds to clear $1.4 trillion of transactions each day, over 500 times the initial outlay. In this manner, CHIPS handles over 285,000 transactions per day, with most of them clearing by the end of the day (www.chips.org). The transaction records of the electronic payments firm serve as money in the transactions of participants. An electronic payments system reduces the transaction costs of exchange for participants.

8.1.4 Market Money: Loans

Firms create most of the money that is used in markets. Banks are the main creators of money through their intermediation between borrowers and lenders. Banks, credit card companies, and clearinghouses also create money by providing payment systems that serve as media of exchange between buyers and sellers of goods, services, and financial assets.

Most of the money supply, as classified by the Federal Reserve System, is private money. Other than government currency, M1 consists of demand deposits, other checking accounts, and traveler's checks. M2 consists of M1 plus retail money market funds, small savings accounts, and small time deposits.[6]

Banks and other financial firms increase the aggregate money supply through intermediation between borrowers and lenders. A bank creates money by holding fractional reserves so that its loans exceed the bank's cash and other financial assets. These loans are given to the bank's customers in the form of demand deposits. The loans are added to the firm's assets, whereas the corresponding demand deposits are added to the firm's liabilities. Consider, for example, a bank that obtains $100 in cash from a depositor. The bank's initial position consists of an asset value of $100 in cash and liabilities of $100 in the form of a demand deposit. The bank creates $900 of additional money by making a loan of that amount to a borrower and creating a demand deposit in that amount for that borrower. The bank's balance sheet is then $1,000 in assets and $1,000 in liabilities. The bank's cash reserve of $100 is available for either customer, the initial depositor or the borrower, who needs cash.

The bank creates money as a byproduct of its intermediation in the market for debt. On the supply side, the bank obtains funds from depositors. The bank also obtains funds from investors through debt and equity to investors as with any other

---

6 The Board of Governors of the Federal Reserve Systems ceased publishing the M3 money aggregate, which adds in large-denomination time deposits, repurchase agreements, and Eurodollars; see Federal Reserve Statistical Release, revised March 9, 2006. The M3 aggregate is more than 50% greater than M2.

firm. On the demand side, the bank provides loans to consumers and firms. Banks are specialized firms that create and operate markets for loans.

The intermediation activities of banks have an important implication. Because money is already present in the economy, transaction costs in the market for loans are not entirely due to an absence of money. Even with money, the bank resolves other problems associated with the diverse wants of buyers and sellers.

The bank provides many distinct types of intermediation services in the market for loans. The bank mitigates the costs of search, communication, and negotiation between borrowers and lenders. The bank reduces adverse selection by screening borrowers and rationing credit.[7] The bank reduces moral hazard by devoting effort to monitoring borrowers and by efficiencies in monitoring many borrowers.[8] In the presence of moral hazard and adverse selection, the bank serves as a trust intermediary, substituting its reputation for that of borrowers.

Also, the bank addresses the problem of the absence of a double coincidence of wants in the loan market. Borrowers and lenders have wants that are incompatible in various ways. When they have different quantity requirements, the bank can consolidate or divide loan amounts to clear the market. When borrowers and lenders have different maturity requirements, the bank can consolidate or divide the duration of loans across time periods to clear the market. When borrowers and lenders have different risk tolerances, the bank can consolidate diverse loans or divide loans to adjust risks. These types of intermediation by banks are specialized forms of intermediation by firms.

8.2 The Firm and the Absence of a Double Coincidence of Wants

8.2.1 Immediacy

The absence of a double coincidence of wants increases transaction costs in a pure-exchange economy. The problem of the double coincidence of wants is a fundamental aspect of transaction costs that helps to explain the role of the firm in a pure-exchange economy. The firm reduces transaction costs by alleviating the cost of finding trading partners and by coordinating exchange between consumers. The associated transaction costs differ fundamentally from production costs because they affect what types of transactions consumers and firms choose. Transaction costs affect not only market outcomes but also the form of market mechanisms themselves. Thus, firms play an important role even in the pure-exchange economy.

---

7 See for example Stiglitz and Weiss (1981) on credit rationing. In Boyd and Prescott (1985), firms address adverse selection problems and produce information about the outcome of investment projects.

8 In Diamond's (1984) model of delegated monitoring, the intermediary benefits from risk pooling.

Consider a pure-exchange economy with three consumers.[9] There are three goods in the economy, designated as x, y, and z. Consumer 1 has utility

$$U^1(x, y, z) = x + vy$$

and an endowment of $(1, 0, 0)$. Consumer 2 has utility

$$U^2(x, y, z) = y + vz$$

and an endowment of $(0, 1, 0)$. Consumer 3 has utility of

$$U^3(x, y, z) = z + vx$$

and an endowment of $(0, 0, 1)$. Assume that $v > 1$. The three goods form a cycle, where each consumer has an endowment of a particular good in the cycle and wants to consume the next good in the cycle.

To illustrate the presence of transaction costs, suppose that trading takes time. Consumers can participate in only one pairwise meeting in a given time period. The endowments are perishable so that trade must take place in the current period. These assumptions guarantee that no trade will occur. It is evident that no pair of consumers has any basis for trade. Thus, the economy exhibits the problem of an absence of a double coincidence of wants. The consumers remain in a state of autarky. Each consumer receives utility equal to 1, which is the benefit they receive from consuming their initial endowments.

To solve the consumers' problem would require simultaneous exchange such that each consumer somehow received the good he wished to consume. Such an arrangement would give each consumer a utility of v and generate total gains from trade for the economy equal to $3(v - 1)$.

A firm can solve the problem of an absence of a double coincidence of wants. Assume that the firm is able to deal simultaneously with all three consumers. This gives the firm an advantage over pairwise meetings. The firm exercises monopoly power subject to the consumers' participation constraint given by the alternative of autarky. The firm sets up a trading post. At the trading post, the firm posts three prices: the price of good x in terms of good z, the price of good y in terms of good x, and the price of good z in terms of good y. These three prices are all equal:

$$p_{xz} = p_{yx} = p_{zy} = v.$$

The prices do not require money because they represent terms of trade between goods.

At these prices, consumers choose to spend their entire initial endowment, because doing so leaves them at least as well off as they were under autarky. Without redistribution of profit, each consumer purchases as much of his desired

---

9 The example is attributed to the discussion of Jevons (1871, 1875). Similar numerical examples appear in Wallace (1997) and Shubik (1999, p. 115).

good as his initial endowment will allow. The three consumer purchases are then equal to

$$q_y = q_z = q_x = 1/v.$$

This would result in the firm having a surplus amount of each good equal to $1 - 1/v$.

Suppose that the three consumers own the firm and that the firm redistributes its profit. Suppose that the firm redistributes its profit in the form of each consumer's most preferred good. Then, each consumer receives $1 - 1/v$ of his most preferred good. Their total consumption of their most preferred goods is then one unit and each consumer has utility equal to

$$U^1 = U^2 = U^3 = v.$$

Thus, the social optimum is attained through the operation of a firm. Each consumer obtains gains from trade relative to autarky equal to $v - 1$.

Instead of a monopoly firm, suppose that there are two or more firms that compete to serve the market. Then, if only one firm operates in equilibrium, it will offer better terms of trade, $p_{xz} = p_{yx} = p_{zy} = 1$. Each consumer will offer his entire initial endowment and purchase one unit of his most preferred good. The social optimum will be attained.

If the firm provides organizational money within the trading post, the traditional monetary solution is feasible. The cyclical consumer preferences and the allocation of endowments creates the problem of the absence of a double coincidence of wants since consumers cannot engage in bilateral trade. Organizational money reduces transaction costs for exchanges within a firm or exchanges between a firm and its trading partners.

The firm can set bid and ask prices for the three goods in terms of its organizational money. Suppose that the goods are x, y, and z. The bid prices are arbitrary and can be normalized to equal one, $w_x = w_y = w_z = 1$. Given that consumers value their most desired good with value $v > 1$, the ask prices are then

$$p_x = p_y = p_z = v.$$

Each consumer has one unit of a good that he values at 1 per unit. Consumers purchase q units of their preferred good,

$$q = 1/v.$$

The firm's organizational money can be distributed to its owners as a means of profit sharing. If each consumer owns an equal share of the firm each will receive $v - 1$ units of organizational money. The consumer will spend the remaining earnings on $(v - 1)/v$ units of their preferred good. The result is that each consumer obtains one unit of their preferred good and the socially optimal distribution of goods is achieved. The firm creates three units of organizational money. These units of money are used only to complete the various transactions between the firm and its customers, suppliers, and owners.

The basic model illustrates the role of the firm as an intermediary. By engaging in multiple transactions simultaneously, the firm saves time. The firm simplifies the process of exchange and provides consumers with immediacy. The simultaneous nature of exchange also avoids the problem of storing value and overcomes the perishable nature of the goods. Moreover, the presence of a firm solves the problem of a medium of exchange since the firm is a counterparty to multiple consumers and makes the necessary exchanges between goods without the need for money.

8.2.2 Intermediation with a Storable Good

Consider again the basic model, but suppose that the goods now are storable. Even though exchange takes time, consumers could achieve the efficient allocation through a series of exchanges. The efficient allocation could be attained in principle through only two trades.[10] The first consumer trades with the second consumer, giving a unit of good x, receiving a unit of good y, and attaining utility of v. The second consumer then trades the unit of good x with the third consumer, receiving a unit of good z and attaining utility of v. The third consumer also attains utility of v by receiving a unit of good x from the second consumer in return for a unit of good z. The sequence of trades requires one consumer to act as an intermediary and hold a good that he cannot consume.

The possibility of making two trades does not solve the problem of transaction costs, however. Repeated transactions are costly if consumers discount future benefits. Even if goods were storable, the sequence of two transactions takes time. To examine the time cost of transactions, suppose that all consumers discount the future with a positive discount rate ρ. Then, the two-period sequence of trades cannot occur if the discount rate is too high:

$$v < 1 + \rho.$$

If this condition holds, no consumer will wait to consume, so there will be no initial transaction, leading again to autarky. The firm could intermediate exchange between the three customers exactly as described previously.

Suppose instead that the discount rate is not too large:

$$v \geq 1 + \rho.$$

Then consumers potentially could engage in the series of two trades. Yet, the firm still can improve economic efficiency.

To examine the economic role of the firm when consumers can trade directly, it is necessary to specify how exchange between consumers takes place. Suppose that with three consumers, search is required. Search takes the form of random matching,

---

10 Shubik (1999) points this out.

so any two of the consumers can be matched in the first period. The consumer that acts as the intermediary automatically is matched with the remaining consumer in the second period.

Assume that consumers engage in Nash bargaining. The outcome is sensitive to how consumers negotiate with each other. The two negotiations occur sequentially. In the first period, a consumer negotiates with the intermediary consumer. In the second period, the intermediary consumer negotiates with the remaining consumer. The intermediary consumer must be compensated for delayed consumption. This affects the intermediary consumer's bargaining position in the first period. The intermediary consumer must hold some amount of the good that he cannot consume. This will affect his bargaining position in the second period. To be compensated for the cost of delay, the intermediary consumer must hold on to some of his initial endowment. This will create an inefficient distribution of the goods. This is an additional transaction cost of direct exchange.

Suppose that consumers 1 and 2 meet in the first period. Then consumer 2 must be the intermediary. Consumer 1 receives y units of good y and provides one unit of good x. Consumer 2 retains $1 - y$ units of good y and receives the unit of good x from consumer 1. Then, in the second period, the intermediary consumer 2 gives the unit of good x to consumer 3 and receives z units of the third good.

Apply backward induction to solve for the equilibrium. The outcome of bargaining in the second period is not affected by how much of the initial endowment of y that the intermediary consumer retains. The Nash bargaining solution for the amount of z received by the intermediary consumer solves

$$\max_z (vz)(1 - z + v - 1)$$

subject to $0 \leq z \leq 1$. If v is less than or equal to 2, then $z = v/2$. If v is greater than 2, then the intermediary consumer receives all of good z. Thus,

$$z = \min\{v/2, 1\}.$$

In the first period, the intermediary consumer bargains with the first consumer. The Nash bargaining solution for the amount of y received by the first consumer solves

$$\max_y (vy - 1)\left(\frac{1 - y + vz}{1 + \rho} - 1\right)$$

subject to $0 \leq y \leq 1$. Thus, consumer 1 receives

$$y = \min\{(1/2)(vz - \rho + 1/v), 1\},$$

where $z = \min\{v/2, 1\}$. It is readily verified that y is positive. The full transfer of the three goods need not take place. This is a departure from the efficient outcome which requires a full transfer of goods. Even if a full transfer of goods does take place, the outcome is inefficient simply because of the time cost of delay.

The firm again offers the advantage of simultaneous transactions. This addresses the time cost of delay. The firm also eliminates the distortion due to an incomplete transfer of goods. The firm competes with direct exchange and must offer benefits to consumers that exceed their expected payoff from direct exchange.

Due to random matching, all trading matches are equally likely. By symmetry, each consumer has the same expected benefit from direct exchange. It is sufficient to calculate the expected benefits from the matchings discussed previously. Then the total of expected benefits equals

$$EU = (1/3)(vy) + (1/3)(1 - y + vz)/(1 + \rho) + (1/3)(1 - z + v)/(1 + \rho),$$

where y and z are given by the equilibrium of direct exchange with sequential Nash bargaining. The firm posts prices

$$p_{xz} = p_{yx} = p_{zy} = v/EU.$$

The three consumers' purchases are equal to

$$q_y = q_z = q_x = EU/v.$$

The three consumers are indifferent between autarky and purchasing from the firm. In addition, if the firm is owned equally by the three consumers, and it redistributes $1 - EU/v$ of each consumer's most preferred good, the social optimum is attained.

To illustrate this outcome, suppose that direct exchange results in a complete transfer of goods, so that the only transaction cost is the delay. Then

$$EU = (1/3)v + (2/3)v/(1 + \rho).$$

So each consumer purchases $q = (1/3) + (2/3)/(1 + \rho)$ from the firm. Consumers know that they can buy and sell the goods when they are ready to transact, thus avoiding the time costs of waiting to trade and consume.

Maintaining the assumption that the good is storable, suppose now that consumers do not discount future utility, so that they can trade repeatedly without costs. Another problem with direct exchange persists, however. In the sequence of trades, the second consumer takes a risk by acting as an intermediary between the first and third consumer. The second consumer must hold an unwanted good x for a period and face the risk that the third consumer will not want the good or that the third consumer may not be available to trade in the next period. Shubik (1999, p. 117) points out that a consumer who acts as a broker or dealer in the sequence of trades faces unwanted exposure. This problem can be modeled by introducing uncertainty about whether the intermediary consumer will have a trading partner in the second period and the possibility that the intermediary consumer also may drop out of the market.[11]

The firm attracts all three consumers by eliminating any trading risk. The firm improves efficiency in comparison with direct exchange by acting as a market maker. The firm also posts prices and eliminates the need for negotiation between

---

11 This problem can be modeled in a straightforward way by assuming that there is some probability β that a consumer will not be in the market in the second period. This modifies the consumer's discount factor. The results are similar to the situation with delay that was discussed previously.

consumers. The role of the firm is to allow consumers to avoid transaction costs associated with intermediation.

A number of additional features of the equilibrium should be noted. The firm solves the problem of immediacy without the need for a medium of exchange. By trading in all three goods and posting the necessary terms of trade, the firm is able to trade with consumers without using a common unit of account and without money. This suggests that although money solves some problems associated with the absence of the double coincidence of wants, it is not a necessary solution. Firms can provide the required transactions without money. As will be seen later, there are situations in which money alone also is not sufficient to solve some types of problems of the double coincidence of wants. The role of the firm is distinct from that of a money instrument and much more complex. For example, firms serve as counterparties to trades, they calculate and post prices, and they communicate information to buyers and sellers.

The role of the firm is related to the notion of a trading post where consumers meet and engage in barter. Clower (1967), Shubik (1999), and others discuss the function of trading posts in barter economies. There are many types of market mechanisms that can operate at trading posts. For example, Shubik and Smith (2003) describe a game in which traders make bids in terms of the quantities of goods to be sold and the quantities of goods needed to buy them. The trading post serves as a mechanism for calculating prices based on these bids such that the market clears, much as the Walrasian mechanism depends on an exogenous auctioneer. If the trading post calculates prices or operates an auction, it should properly be viewed as a firm. The firm can be a dealer that buys and sells on its own account, a broker that arranges trades, or an organization that operates an exchange with specialists and pricing mechanisms. Given the complexity of these tasks, the firm should be treated as a player in the game, with pricing decisions chosen endogenously by the firm, as in the present discussion.

8.3 The Firm and Market Clearing

The firm clears markets by aggregating supply and demand, balancing purchases and sales, and posting market-clearing prices. This can be illustrated by a pure-exchange economy with four consumers and two goods, x and y, which are not storable. Two consumers have identical utilities, $U^i(x, y) = x + vy$, $i = 1, 2$, and endowments of $(1, 0)$ and $(3, 0)$, respectively. The third and fourth consumers have identical utilities $U^i(x, y) = x + y/v$, $i = 3, 4$, and identical endowments $(0, 2)$. Let $1 < v < 2$, so that the first two consumers wish to trade good x for good y with either of the second two consumers.

Again, suppose that trading takes time so that a consumer can participate in only one pairwise meeting per time period. Then two transactions will take place in the first period, between consumers 1 and 3 and consumers 2 and 4. Suppose that good x is divisible but good y is only tradable in discrete units.

Consumer 1 will exchange some amount of good x for one unit of good y with consumer 3. Consumer 3 has autarky utility of $2/v$. So for consumer 3 to receive gains from trade requires that

$$x^3 + y^3/v \geq 2/v.$$

If consumer 3 were to give up both units of good y to consumer 1, consumer 3 would need to receive $x^3 > 2/v > 1$, which is not possible, because consumer 1's endowment is equal to one unit of x. So consumers 1 and 3 will each consume one unit of good y, $y^1 = 1$ and $y^3 = 1$. Consumer 1's participation constraint is $x^1 + v \geq 1$. Because $x^3 = 1 - x^1$, x^1 is in the range

$$1 - v \leq x^1 \leq 1 - 1/v.$$

This defines the contract curve for consumers 1 and 3.

Consumer 2 will exchange some amount of good x for two units of good y with consumer 4. This is because consumer 2 has a higher marginal value for x than consumer 4 has for y and consumer 2 has an endowment of x that is greater than 2. So consumer 2 will consume both units of good y, $y^2 = 2$ and $y^4 = 0$. Consumer 4's participation constraint is $x^4 \geq 2v$. Given $y^2 = 2$, consumer 2's participation constraint is $x^2 + 2v \geq 3$, so that for $x^2 = 3 - x^4$, it follows that x^2 is in the range $3 - 2v \leq x^2 \leq 3 - 2/v$.

Taking utility as transferable in units of x, the total utility for the four consumers from the two trades equals

$$U^1 + U^2 + U^3 + U^4 = 3v + 4 + 1/v,$$

since $x^3 = 1 - x^1$ and $x^4 = 3 - x^2$. Gains from trade relative to autarky equal,

$$g = U^1 + U^2 + U^3 + U^4 - 4 - 4/v = 3(v - 1/v).$$

The maximum total utility for the four consumers would be $4 + 4v$, which is greater than the utility resulting from the two trades since $v > 1$. The total economic loss from the inability of individual consumers to engage in multiple trades per period equals

$$(4 + 4v) - (U^1 + U^2 + U^3 + U^4) = v - 1/v > 0.$$

This provides a measure of transaction costs due to the absence of the double coincidence of wants.

Suppose that a firm is not limited by the number of transactions per period. Then the firm can set bid and ask prices to clear the market. Suppose that the firm sets prices per unit of the discrete good y in terms of the divisible good x. The profit-maximizing ask and bid prices are

$$p^* = \frac{v}{2} + \frac{1}{2v}, \quad w^* = \frac{v}{4} + \frac{3}{4v}.$$

At the equilibrium prices, consumer 1 buys one unit of good y and consumer 2 buys three units of good y. To derive these prices, observe that both pairs of consumers must be at least as well off dealing with the firm as they were in direct exchange. Consumer 1 buys one unit of y from the firm and consumer 2 buys three units of y from the firm. Consumers 3 and 4 both sell two units of y to the firm. Because consumers 1 and 3 are able to engage in direct exchange, the joint participation constraint for the pair of consumers 1 and 3 is

$$U^1(1 - p, 1) + U^3(2w, 0) \geq 1 + v + 1/v.$$

Similarly, the joint participation constraint for the pair of consumers 2 and 4 is

$$U^2(3 - 3p, 3) + U^4(2w, 0) \geq 3 + 2v.$$

The profit-maximizing firm increases the bid-ask spread until these constraints are binding. Thus, we have

$$1 + v - p + 2w = 1 + v + 1/v,$$
$$3 - p + 3v + 2w = 3 + 2v.$$

Solving these constraints yields p^* and w^*.

The firm buys and resells four units of y, so the firm's profit in units of x is four times the bid-ask spread,

$$\Pi = 4(p^* - w^*) = v - 1/v.$$

The firm's profit exactly equals the transaction cost that is experienced by consumers due to the absence of a double coincidence of wants. The model can be closed by distributing shares of profits across consumers. This assumes that consumers do not take profits into account in their decision as to whether to deal with the firm or trade directly.

The presence of the profit-maximizing firm allows the economy to achieve the optimal outcome. The firm forms the market by aggregating demand and aggregating supply. Total demand and supply of good y at the equilibrium prices both equal four units of y. The profit-maximizing firm adjusts the ask and bid prices to clear the market. By engaging in multiple transactions, the firm clears the market and solves the problem of the absence of a double coincidence of wants.

8.4 The Firm and Time

The firm can provide a store of value that is a substitute for money. The overlapping-generations (OLG) model due to Allais (1947) and Samuelson (1958) offers a framework for studying the problem of the absence of a double coincidence of wants over time. Consider an infinite-horizon setting in which each generation of consumers lives for two time periods of equal duration, referred to as young and old. Generations are said to overlap because the young of any generation live during the same period of time as the old of the previous generation. All consumers have the same lifetime utility function,

$$u(c) + \frac{1}{1 + \rho} u(C),$$

where c is consumption while young and C is consumption while old. Consumers have a positive discount rate ρ. Let u be increasing, concave, and continuously differentiable, with $u(0) = 0$.

Consumers all have an endowment of the consumption good equal to 1 when they are young and equal to 0 when they are old. This represents the consumer's ability to work while young and inability to work during retirement. The key assumption of the OLG model is that the consumption good is not durable; that is, it cannot be stored. This means that with autarky, each generation can only consume when young. Thinking of the consumer as Robinson Crusoe, Samuelson (1958, p. 468) observes that because "no intertemporal trade with nature is possible . . . If Crusoe were alone, he would obviously die at the beginning of his retirement years." Thus, because $C = 0$, the consumer's utility under autarky is simply $u(1)$.

The question is whether Robinson Crusoe's lot is improved by being in the overlapping-generations society. Clearly, trade with one's own generation is not possible because preferences and endowments are identical. There is no possibility of trade with other generations either, because a young person with an endowment of 1 lives contemporaneously with old consumers of the previous generation who have nothing with which to trade. As Samuelson (1958) points out, it is impossible for any worker to find a younger worker who can be paid to support him in retirement. The young of any generation have nothing to offer the young of the next generation, even if they could somehow contract with them. The impossibility of trade between generations provides a clear illustration of the problem of the absence of a double coincidence of wants. The inability of generations to trade prevents the realization of potential gains from trade.

The combination of a good that cannot be stored and inability of generations to engage in trade illustrates an extreme type of transaction cost associated with time. Consumers of different generations are separated by time and so cannot realize gains from trade. The entry of a firm provides a solution to the transaction costs of the OLG model without the need for money. The firm is assumed to be infinitely lived. The firm has per-period operating costs per consumer equal to T. A young consumer pays the firm $C + p$ and in return receives a promise that the firm will deliver C in the consumer's old age. The firm does not store the good C because it promptly turns it over to the old consumers of the previous generation. The firm thus earns p from each young consumer. Thus, consumers pay the firm to provide a store of value.

The payment for storing value is like a negative interest rate. The consumer satisfies the budget constraint

$$c + C + p = 1,$$

where profits Π are not distributed to consumers. The firm's profit is $\Pi = p - T$ and the firm operates only if profit is nonnegative, so that resource constraints hold.

Taking profit as a given, the consumer maximizes utility subject to the budget constraint, so the consumer solves

$$\max_c u(c) + \frac{1}{1 + \rho} u(1 - c - p).$$

The consumer's demand for first-period consumption is $c^*(p)$, which solves

$$u'(c^*) = \frac{1}{1 + \rho} u'(1 - c^* - p).$$

If the firm is a monopolist, it raises the price until the consumer is indifferent between dealing with the firm and the autarky utility level,

$$u(c^*(p^*)) + \frac{1}{1 + \rho} u(1 - c^*(p^*) - p^*) = u(1).$$

If the firm faces Bertrand price competition from other firms, then $p = T$ and $\Pi = 0$.

The equilibrium price can be interpreted as a negative interest rate. From the consumers' budget constraint $1 - c^* = C^* + p^*$. Equivalently, the consumer obtains interest i on savings:

$$(1 - c^*)(1 + i) = C^*.$$

Combining these two equations, it follows that the interest rate is negative, and greater than -1:

$$i = \frac{-p^*}{C^* + p^*}.$$

The price paid to the firm has different incentives than an interest rate, because the price is a lump sum payment, whereas the interest rate is per unit of savings. The negative interest rate would discourage saving at the margin.

The equilibrium is characterized easily using the utility function $u(c) = c^{1/2}$. Thus, demand for consumption by young consumers equals

$$c^*(p) = \frac{(1 + \rho)^2 (1 - p)}{1 + (1 + \rho)^2}.$$

In the monopoly case, the consumer's participation constraint with $u(1) = 1$ yields the equilibrium price

$$p^* = \frac{1}{1 + (1 + \rho)^2}.$$

The equilibrium price is less than one and decreasing in the discount rate ρ. In the monopoly case, the young and old consumers' consumption levels equal

$$c^* = \frac{(1+\rho)^4}{[1+(1+\rho)^2]^2}, \quad C^* = \frac{(1+\rho)^2}{[1+(1+\rho)^2]^2}.$$

The monopoly firm is viable if and only if $p^* \geq T$, or

$$\frac{1}{1+(1+\rho)^2} \geq T.$$

The corresponding interest rate equals

$$i = -\frac{1+(1+\rho)^2}{1+2(1+\rho)^2}.$$

If the firm is a competitive firm, then the price falls to the firm's cost per period. A firm is viable at $p = T$ only if the consumer's participation constraint holds,

$$u(c^*(T)) + \frac{1}{1+\rho}u(1 - c^*(T) - T) \geq u(1),$$

which is equivalent to $1/[1 + (1 + \rho)^2] \geq T$, just as in the monopoly case. The consumption levels are then

$$c^* = \frac{(1+\rho)^2(1-T)}{1+(1+\rho)^2}, \quad C^* = \frac{1-T}{1+(1+\rho)^2}.$$

In the competitive case, consumption levels are decreasing in the firm's per-period cost T. As T goes to zero, consumption levels tend to the optimal consumption levels a consumer would choose with a fully storable good. The corresponding interest rate is

$$i = -\frac{T[1 + (1 + \rho)^2]}{1 + T(1 + \rho)^2}.$$

In either the monopoly or competitive cases, the greater is the consumer's discount rate, the lower must be the firm's operating cost for the firm to be viable. The firm alleviates the problem of the absence of a double coincidence of wants by providing a way to store value without money. The firm intermediates between generations, allowing consumers to transact over time. The firm's per-period costs T are explicit and reflect the transaction costs associated with storing value through contracts with a firm.

The classic OLG model assumes that goods cannot be stored, which exacerbates the absence of a double coincidence of wants. The role of the firm as a store of value holds even if the good can be stored at some cost. Suppose that the good is subject to some proportional reduction in value, γ, as a result of storage, $0 < \gamma < 1$. Then, under autarky, the consumer's savings are subject to some melting away:

$$(1 - c)(1 - \gamma) = C.$$

This corresponds to a negative interest rate, $i = -\gamma$. The consumer under autarky is able to consume while both young and old. Letting $u(c) = c^{1/2}$, the consumer under autarky chooses a consumption plan

$$c^0 = \frac{(1+\rho)^2}{1 - \gamma + (1+\rho)^2}, \quad C^0 = \frac{(1-\gamma)^2}{1 - \gamma + (1+\rho)^2}.$$

The utility of the consumer under autarky U^0 increases because of the possibility of storage,

$$U^0 = [1/(1+\rho)][1 - \gamma + (1+\rho)^2]^{1/2},$$

where $U^0 > 1$ for all $0 < \gamma < 1$.

The firm offers two advantages over autarky. First, transferring the good from the young to the contemporaneous old of the previous generation avoids any loss from storage. Second, the lump-sum price avoids the distortion of consumer decisions that a per-unit storage loss causes. The consumer demand $c^*(p)$ is the same as before. However, the monopolist must take account of the consumers' improved participation constraint, so that p^* solves

$$u(c(p^*)) + \frac{1}{1+\rho} u(C(p^*)) = U^0.$$

Thus, p^* equals

$$p^* = \frac{\gamma}{1 + (1+\rho)^2}.$$

This makes clear the tradeoff between the cost of storage in terms of the proportional loss γ versus the consumers' discount rate ρ. The effective interest rate when the firm acts as a store of value is

$$i = -\frac{p^*}{C^* + p^*} = -\frac{\gamma[1 + (1+\rho)^2]}{1 + \gamma(1+\rho)^2}.$$

The effective interest rate is less than $-\gamma$ because the firm can extract more rents through the lump-sum price, thus yielding benefits both as a store of value and by avoiding a proportional interest rate. Note that as γ approaches one, the effective interest rate also approaches one because the consumers' autarkic alternative improves with increases in γ.

Firms provide a market-based solution to the problem of costly transactions between consumers over time without the use of money. Some have proposed that governments could solve the problem of transacting in an overlapping-generations setting. One approach is for governments to tax the young and provide income transfers to retired workers. The costs of implementing such a solution are implicit or ignored in public policy discussions such as Samuelson (1958), but it is apparent that the direct and indirect cost of operating a taxation and retirement pension system would be significant.

Another solution proposed by Samuelson (1958) is the "social contrivance" of money. Either through government or by custom, society establishes fiat money.

The young consumers sell part of their endowment to the contemporaneous old consumers of the previous generation in return for money. The young then carry over the money into their old age, which they can use to buy the endowment from the young of the next generation. The use of money solves the problem of storing the good, or more to the point, the problem of storing value. This allows intergenerational gains from trade. Moreover, money provides a medium of exchange and a unit of account, which simplifies the transaction process. However, establishing a monetary system, while desirable and potentially efficient, is not costless. There are transaction costs associated with either government money or social customs. Thus, money only solves the OLG transaction cost problem if the benefits of using money exceed the costs of a monetary system. To evaluate these alternatives, the creation of a costly monetary system should be considered as endogenous to the economy.

Finally, an additional solution to the OLG problem would be possible if each generation were to live for multiple periods. In Samuelson's (1958) model, consumers live for three periods and have an endowment of 1 in each of the first two periods and an endowment of 0 in the final retirement period. The consumers in the middle period pay young consumers of the prior generation in return for payments in the following period. Then consumers of the prior generation reach their second period and can pay back consumers of the next generation who have reached their old age. The equilibrium interest rate is negative. The bilateral trades fail to achieve a socially optimal allocation. This solution, although imperfect, still requires the generations to line up just right with multiple productive periods.

Firms store value in many ways. They handle many types of storable commodities, including precious metals, energy resources, textiles, and grain and other agricultural goods. Modern forward contracts for grain are the descendants of the practice of issuing and lending warehouse receipts in wheat, corn, and oats in 1860s Chicago (Williams, 1986, p. 57). Futures markets reflect the standardization of forward contracts between individual buyers and sellers and the organization of formal exchanges; see Telser (1981) and Working (1953a, 1953b). By buying, selling, and storing commodities, firms help to transfer value over time. Firms create many types of contracts and financial assets. Firms issue securities and debt that allow the transfer of value over time. Insurance companies and banks provide mechanisms for consumers to transact across generations. These long-lived assets allow consumers to obtain the benefits of transactions between generations.

8.5 The Firm and Distance

8.5.1 Travel Costs and Centrally Located Firms

The most basic transaction costs are those associated with travel. Buyers and sellers who engage in direct exchange often expend time and resources in traveling to meet each other. Transportation of the goods that are exchanged also consumes

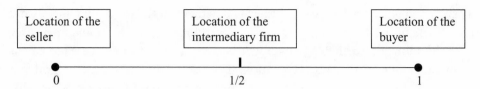

Figure 8.1. The basic model of a centrally located intermediary firm.

resources. International trade models incorporate transportation cost as *iceberg* costs by assuming that a proportion of the good is absorbed in the process of exchange (Samuelson, 1954b).

The firm reduces travel costs by intermediating between buyers and sellers. By providing a central place of exchange, a firm reduces travel costs and thus increases net gains from trade for buyers and sellers. In practice, buyers shop more conveniently at stores, shopping centers, and the central business districts of cities. In turn, sellers benefit from delivery to retail distributors, who in turn deliver to buyers. Buyers and sellers avoid travel costs because they rely on intermediation by firms.

Consider a basic model of intermediation with costly transportation. Suppose that the geographic space is the unit interval, with the seller located at the zero endpoint and the buyer located at one. The intermediary firm is located at $1/2$. This is represented in Figure 8.1.

The cost of a round trip is based on the one-way distance r. Suppose that travel costs are convex for either the buyer or the seller. Let travel costs have the quadratic form tr^2, where r is the distance between the origin and the destination. Convex travel costs reflect the costs of transporting perishable goods or information losses that increase with distance (Greenhut et al., 1987, p. 276). Convex travel costs also reflect the disutility of time spent on travel.

For a transaction to occur, it must take place at an established location. The seller can visit the buyer or the buyer can visit the seller, without the possibility of meeting in between the two locations. Because the distance that separates the buyer and seller equals one, total travel costs equal t. The buyer and seller will engage in direct exchange if and only if

$$v - c \geq t.$$

Thus, the net gains from direct exchange are

$$g = v - c - t.$$

If $t > v - c$, autarky results and the buyer and seller do not obtain any gains from trade. This situation can be interpreted as the absence of a double coincidence of wants. The two consumers are separated by distance, so neither consumer can find a suitable trading partner at their location.

Because marginal travel costs increase with distance, there are advantages to central location by a firm. By locating at $1/2$, an intermediary firm reduces the length of a trip for the buyer and the seller, although the total distance that needs to be traveled does not change. By substituting two short trips for one long trip, the firm reduces total travel cost to $2t(1/2)^2 = t/2$. The firm incurs fixed transaction costs, T. Thus, the total net gains from trade with intermediation by a firm equal

$$G = v - c - t/2 - T.$$

Entry of a firm increases gains from trade if the savings in travel costs exceed the firm's transaction costs,

$$T < t/2.$$

The centrally located firm can attract the buyer and the seller by offering the buyer an ask price p and offering the seller a bid price w such that the bid-ask spread is equal to the total travel cost the buyer and the seller would incur in direct exchange,

$$p - w = t.$$

The buyer and the seller choose to deal with the firm because they do not obtain any additional benefits from direct exchange. Note that for ease of presentation, it is assumed that the firm bears the travel cost of the buyer and the seller either by reimbursing them or by visiting them. Thus, the firm's profit equals the difference between savings in the travel costs and the firm's transaction costs, which is exactly the change in the total net gains from trade,

$$\pi = p - w - t/2 - T = t/2 - T.$$

The firm is profitable if and only if it increases net gains from trade. The convexity of travel costs helps to explain the establishment of retail firms as well as their central location in shopping malls and the central business districts of cities.

Suppose that two or more firms compete for the market. A firm's total costs include transportation costs, $t/2$, and fixed transaction costs, T. Bertrand price competition will drive profits to zero, so that the bid-ask spread will equal a firm's travel costs plus its transaction costs,

$$p - w = t/2 + T.$$

Competition will result in only one firm intermediating between the buyer and seller. The firm can only attract the buyer and the seller if the bid-ask spread is less than their travel costs in direct exchange, $p - w \leq t$, or equivalently, if the firm's transaction costs are less than the avoided travel costs, $T \leq t/2$.

8.5.2 Travel Costs and Market Making by Firms

The problem of the absence of a double coincidence of wants is a familiar explanation for the use of money as payment for goods. If consumers engage in barter, exchanging one good for another, it is unlikely that they will easily find a trading partner who has the right combination of endowments to carry out a particular

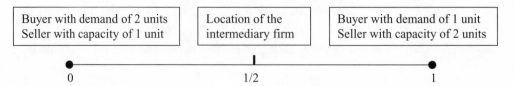

Figure 8.2. The absence of a double coincidence of wants with mismatches between demand and capacity.

trade. For example, a consumer wishing to trade apples for oranges is unlikely to find another consumer who wishes to trade oranges for apples. With many different goods and many potential trading partners, many bilateral trades would be needed to realize all potential gains from trade.

If there are travel costs, it is easy to imagine situations in which the problem of the absence of a double coincidence of wants cannot be solved without the use of exogenously provided currency. If (infinitely lived) trading partners meet only once in their lifetimes, and an agent with an endowment of one unit is always paired with an agent with an endowment of zero, there is no possibility of trade because there can be no extension of credit between trading partners. Each pair of trading partners is assumed to be located on a separate island, with no possibility of travel between islands within a time period. In each period, all agents are assigned to new islands, where they meet new trading partners. In such a setting, money is needed for the buyer, who is the agent with a commodity endowment of zero, to purchase a proportion of the good from the seller, who is the agent with a commodity endowment of one. Such island models with spatially separated agents are examined by Cass and Yaari (1966), Lucas (1972), and Townsend (1980). In particular, Townsend (1980) shows how money can solve the problem of the absence of a double coincidence of wants when agents are matched in various ways.

However, even with fiat money or commodity money, there remains the problem of the absence of a double coincidence of wants. In particular, buyers and sellers may not wish to trade at the same time or in the same amount. In this section, buyers and sellers are mismatched and it is too costly to find a better match due to travel costs. Firms act as market makers and solve the problem of the absence of a double coincidence of wants.

As before, let the geographic space be the unit interval. Let travel costs be quadratic and convex. Suppose that at the zero endpoint, there are a buyer with a two-unit demand and value v per unit and a seller with one-unit production capacity and unit cost c. At the other endpoint of the line, that is, at one, there are a buyer with a one-unit demand and value v per unit and a seller with two-unit capacity and unit cost c. The two endpoints can be thought of as islands separated by a distance of one. The locations of buyers and sellers are illustrated in Figure 8.2.

Assume that the good is perishable and cannot be stored. Assume further that it is not worth traveling between islands just to exchange one unit of the good:

$$v - c < t.$$

This implies that the buyer with the two-unit demand and the seller with the two-unit capacity will prefer to stay on their separate islands and trade with the one-unit seller and the one-unit buyer, respectively. This is because it is not worth traveling to trade the marginal unit. Thus, the two-unit buyer and the two-unit seller are always rationed by their local trading partners. This model generates an absence of a double coincidence of wants.

The result is autarky, with exchange being confined to the two islands. Total gains from trade equal the benefits of trading one unit of the good on each island, $g = 2(v - c)$. Because travel costs are convex, a firm that entered the market would locate centrally at $1/2$ to minimize travel costs. To further save on travel costs, the firm would travel to the two islands to trade, or equivalently, only the high-demand buyer and high-capacity seller would travel to visit the firm, trading one unit at home and one unit at the firm's location. Travel costs would be $2t(1/2)^2 = t/2$. Let the firm's fixed transaction costs equal T. Gains from trade with the entry of a firm equal

$$G = 3(v - c) - t/2 - T,$$

so that a firm increases gains from trade only if $v-c > t/2 + T$. If this condition holds and $v - c < t$, it follows that the travel cost saving is greater than the firm's transaction costs, $t/2 > T$. The entry of a firm means that the island with excess capacity exports one unit to the island with excess demand. The firm is a market maker, matching the high-demand buyer and high-capacity seller, who could not otherwise trade.

The bid-ask spread chosen by the firm extracts the full incremental gains from trade,

$$p - w = v - c,$$

if the firm bears the full cost of travel. This is because the high-demand buyer and high-capacity seller could not otherwise trade the incremental unit. Profits equal the increased gains from trade, $\pi = v - c - t/2 - T$. With multiple firms who engage in Bertrand price competition, only one firm serves the market. The firm's profit equals zero and the bid-ask spread equals transport costs plus transaction costs, $p - w = t/2 + T$.

8.5.3 Product Variety and One-Stop Shopping

With multiple buyers and sellers, a firm can provide efficiency gains even with linear travel costs. Suppose that there are four buyers who each demand at most one unit of the good that they each value at v per unit. Suppose also that there are two sellers, each of whom has the capacity to provide two units of the good at cost c per unit. The two sellers are located at the zero endpoint of the unit interval and the buyers are located at one. Suppose that travel costs are linear in distance tr. As before, r is the distance between origin and destination, not the full distance of the round trip. These travel costs exhibit economies of scale, because it is possible to engage in multiple transactions during a single trip to a particular location. Travel costs do not depend on quantity, because they reflect the costs associated with transactions rather than the costs of transporting goods. However, similar results hold if the analysis is extended to include transportation costs, which also tend to exhibit economies of scale in practice.

Because there are more buyers than sellers, and there are economies of scale in travel, it is more efficient for the sellers to visit the buyers. The cost of a round trip of one-way distance $r = 1$ is t. Thus, total gains from trade with direct exchange equal

$$g = 4(v - c) - 2t.$$

A firm can take advantage of the situation by consolidating travel. The firm can locate at any point along the unit interval because travel costs are linear. For example, the firm can locate at zero, purchase goods from sellers, and visit the buyers' locations to sell and deliver the goods. Alternatively, the firm can locate at one, open a store to serve the buyers, and travel to the sellers' location to purchase and receive the goods. The firm could locate a warehouse in between the two endpoints and engage in both pickup and delivery. The firm's fixed transaction costs equal T. If a firm intermediates trade between buyers and sellers, total gains from trade equal

$$G = 4(v - c) - t - T.$$

Thus, gains from trade increase when a firm intermediates exchange if the firm's transaction costs are less than the cost savings from consolidating travel,

$$T < t.$$

As before, the bid-ask spread equals the travel cost per transaction,

$$p - w = t/2.$$

So the firm is profitable if and only if it increases total net gains from trade,

$$\pi = 4(p - w) - t - T = t - T.$$

The preceding example is easily modified for transportation costs. Suppose that there are economies of scale in transportation, where K is the fixed cost of transportation and trQ is the variable cost of transporting Q units for distance r. As before, the two sellers would visit the four buyers, yielding total gains from trade with direct exchange of

$$g = 4(v - c) - 4t - 2K.$$

The firm would save on the fixed cost of transportation, so that

$$G - g = K - t.$$

Thus, gains from trade increase with intermediation by a firm if the fixed costs of transportation are greater than the firm's transaction costs, $K > T$. The bid-ask spread would reflect the per-unit transport cost of direct exchange:

$$p - w = t + K/2.$$

The firm's profit then would equal $\pi = K - T$.

The advantages of intermediation by a firm when there are travel costs also appear in a setting with differentiated products. The effects of consumer preference for product variety on the urban agglomeration of firms are examined by Stahl (1982), Fischer and Harrington (1996), and Fujita and Thisse (2002); see also the survey by Anas et al. (1998). Similar reasoning suggests that there are benefits from the central location of multiproduct firms.

Suppose that there are n buyers and m sellers. Each of the sellers produces a differentiated product with the same unit cost c. The goods are produced in discrete units. Each of the buyers has a maximum demand for exactly m units and has a preference for variety. A buyer prefers to consume one unit of every good rather than to concentrate demand on any subset of goods. An example of such preferences is the widely used constant elasticity of substitution (CES) utility function, for $s > 1$:

$$U(q_1, q_2, \ldots, q_m) = \left(\sum_{i=1}^{m} q_i^{\frac{s-1}{s}} \right)^{\frac{s}{s-1}}.$$

Thus, $v(m) = U(1, 1, \ldots, 1) = m^{s/(s-1)}$ is greater than the value the buyer would obtain by concentrating consumption on any subset of goods. Assume that there are gains from trade, $v(m) > mc$. To obtain a good a buyer must meet and transact with the seller who makes that good, so for all buyers to obtain the full variety of goods, each buyer must meet and transact with every seller. Suppose that each meeting requires fixed travel and transaction costs equal to t. Then total gains from trade with direct exchange equal

$$g = nv(m) - nmc - nmt.$$

Suppose that the incremental benefits of variety to consumers are greater than the incremental travel and transaction costs necessary to provide that variety, so that each buyer engages in direct exchange with every seller.

Suppose now that a firm establishes a store, such as a supermarket, department store, catalog, or Web site, that sells the full range of m goods. For ease of presentation, suppose that the firm bears the full travel and transaction costs of buyers and sellers, whether they visit the firm or the firm visits them. The firm offers the advantage of a reduced number of trips, because each buyer and each seller engage in transactions involving multiple units each time they interact with the store. Thus, by centralizing exchange, the store reduces the total number of transactions to $n + m$, so that travel and transaction costs are reduced to $(n + m)t$.

Suppose that the firm's fixed transaction costs equal T, so that net gains from trade increase by

$$G - g = [nm - (n + m)]t - T.$$

This implies that for any travel cost t and any fixed transaction costs T, there are *always* sufficiently large numbers of buyers and sellers such that establishing a firm increases net gains from trade; that is, for n and m sufficiently large, $G > g$. Firms offer product variety and the convenience of one-stop shopping.

Monopoly profit for a multiproduct firm equals the increase in gains from trade,

$$\pi = [nm - (n + m)]t - T.$$

The bid-ask spread equals the travel costs per transaction that the buyer and seller would incur in direct exchange,

$$p - w = t.$$

Bertrand competition between multiple firms drives profits to zero, so that the bid-ask spread equals the winning firm's travel costs plus fixed transaction costs divided by the number of units sold,

$$p - w = \frac{t(n + m) + T}{nm}.$$

The firm's unit costs are decreasing in the number of buyers and sellers. Firms have economies of scale in the number of transactions. Unit costs are decreasing in the number of products m, thus yielding economies of scope.

8.6 The Firm and Risk

8.6.1 Sharing Risk

The problem of the absence of the double coincidence of wants can occur as a consequence of economic shocks. Consider an economy with a single consumption good and three consumers, each with von Neumann-Morgenstern utility functions, where the utility of consumption is the concave function $u(q) = q^{1/2}$.

There are three states of the world, each occurring with equal likelihood of $1/3$. Each of the consumers has an endowment of one unit of an asset that offers an uncertain payoff of the consumption good that depends on the state of the world. The consumers have different assets, where the state-dependent payoff structures of the assets of consumers 1, 2, and 3 are respectively $(1, 0, 0)$, $(0, 1, 0)$, and $(0, 0, 1)$. The consumer endowments can be viewed, for example, as different types of human capital that have different productivity in different states of the world and thus delivers different payoffs of the consumption good.

The three consumers can only consume in all three states of the world if all three can trade. It is apparent that the problem of the absence of a double coincidence of wants exists. Any pair of consumers can engage in trade, each providing insurance to the other for the state of the world in which the other's endowment is zero. However, all three consumers are needed for each of the consumers to receive the good in all states of the world. This corresponds to the problem of incomplete markets in which there are only two assets with linearly independent returns and three states of the world. The endowments of the consumers are Arrow securities, because they pay a certain amount of the good in only a single state of the world (Arrow, 1953). The payoff structures of the assets are linearly independent. Only a combination of all three endowments would *span* the three states of the world. In this example, no two consumers can consume in all three states of the world.

To represent transaction costs, assume again that trade is time-consuming, so that a consumer can only engage in one trade per period of time. Assume further that consumers have only one time period to engage in trade before the state of the world is revealed. After the state of the world becomes known, there is no possibility of trade because only one consumer will have an endowment, so there is no double coincidence of wants *ex post*. Therefore, the only possibility of trade is *ex ante*, that is, before the state of the world is revealed.

Restricting attention to symmetric trades, two consumers will exchange 1/2 of a unit of each of their assets. If consumer 1 and consumer 2 were to trade their assets, they each would obtain payoffs of the consumption good equal to $(1/2, 1/2, 0)$. Their expected utility levels each equal

$$U = (1/3)u(1/2) + (1/3)u(1/2) = (2/3)(1/2)^{1/2}.$$

The third consumer, who does not engage in trade, has the payoff $(0, 0, 1)$ and expected utility of $(1/3)u(1) = 1/3$. Consumers are strictly better off with trade because they can reduce risk by spreading consumption across two states rather than having consumption concentrated in one state.

A firm can improve matters by trading simultaneously with all three consumers. This allows the firm to help consumers share risk more efficiently. The firm can offer consumers a riskless asset in the form of a commodity future contract that pays q units of the consumption good in each state of the world. The firm posts three prices for the riskless asset in terms of each of the three Arrow securities that consumers hold. The three prices of the riskless asset are all equal to one unit of the respective Arrow securities. Accordingly, each consumer obtains utility equal to $u(q) = q^{1/2}$. The firm sets the quantity of the consumption good q such that any two consumers are indifferent between dealing with the firm and trading with each other, so that q^* solves

$$u(q^*) = (2/3)(1/2)^{1/2}.$$

Thus, the amount of the consumption good provided by the commodity future is $q^* = 2/9$. Because consumers are indifferent between dealing with the firm and bilateral trade, and because consumers are strictly better off with bilateral trade than under autarky, it follows that the third consumer is strictly better off dealing with the firm.

The firm experiences no uncertainty because the firm obtains one unit of each asset and thus has one unit of the consumption good available in any state of the world. The firm pays out q^* units of the consumption good to each consumer in any state of the world. Therefore, the firm's profit equals

$$\Pi = 1 - 3q^* = 1/3.$$

The firm's profit can be distributed to consumers to close the model. Distributing equity shares of the firm does not add uncertainty because the firm's profit is the same in any state of the world.

8.6.2 Risk Pooling and Insurance

Firms reduce costs of transacting under uncertainty by facilitating multiple transactions. The greater the number of consumers that participate, the greater is the amount of risk pooling. Thus, lowering transaction costs under uncertainty allows firms to generate gains from trade by pooling risk. This explains the transaction efficiencies generated by insurance companies. Other financial firms such as banks pool risks of loan defaults by borrowers and of varying deposits of savers. Retailers and wholesalers pool risks that are due to demand fluctuations and supply variations by consolidating purchases and sales. Manufacturers pool demand risks by serving larger markets.

To illustrate transaction costs under uncertainty, consider an economy with $1 + 2m$ consumers. There is a single consumption good q that can also be interpreted as income. All consumers have an initial endowment ω of the consumption good, where $\omega > 1$. All consumers have the same von Neuman-Morgenstern utility function, $u(q) = q^{1/2}$.

There are $1 + m$ consumers who do not face a risk of loss and who can provide insurance. These consumers obtain $u(\omega)$ under autarky. The remaining m consumers face a risk of loss, where the losses are independently and identically distributed. Suppose that a loss of 1 unit of the consumption good occurs with probability β and no loss occurs with probability $1 - \beta$, where $0 < \beta < 1$. These consumers have expected utility $\beta u(\omega - 1) + (1 - \beta)u(\omega)$ under autarky.

Assume that transactions take time, so that a consumer can only engage in one bilateral transaction per period of time. Suppose that consumers have only one period of time to transact before the consumption loss is revealed. Then there will be exactly m transactions in which m consumers provide insurance to the m consumers who face a possibility of loss. Because there are more potential providers of insurance than consumers who face a loss, consumers providing insurance will obtain expected utility exactly equal to their autarky level $u(\omega)$. The results can easily be adapted if the relative numbers of insurers and insured are reversed. Let p

be the lump-sum premium paid by an insured consumer and let y be the level of coverage. Then an insurance contract between two consumers p, y solves

$$\max_{p,y} \beta u(\omega - 1 + y - p) + (1 - \beta)u(\omega - p)$$
$$\text{subject to } \beta u(\omega - y + p) + (1 - \beta)u(\omega + p) = u(\omega).$$

By standard arguments, an interior solution satisfies

$$\frac{u'(\omega - 1 + y - p)}{u'(\omega - y + p)} = \frac{u'(\omega - p)}{u'(\omega + p)}.$$

Applying the quadratic form of the utility function, and simplifying, the insurance premium is

$$p = \omega(2y - 1).$$

Substitute for p in the participation constraint for consumers providing insurance and apply the quadratic form of the utility function. This yields an expression for the coverage level,

$$y^* = \frac{\omega}{[\beta(2\omega - 1)^{1/2} + (1 - \beta)(2\omega)^{1/2}]^2}.$$

The insurance premium equals $p^* = \omega(2y^* - 1)$. The expected utility of the insured consumer simplifies to

$$U = \omega^{1/2}(1/y^* - 1)^{1/2}.$$

Assume that a firm can transact simultaneously with all consumers. The firm charges premium P to each insured consumer for coverage Y. The firm pays W to each consumer who provides insurance. All of the $1 + m$ consumers that do not face a loss provide coverage. The total coverage supplied to the m insured consumers is

$$Y \sum_{i=1}^{m} q_i,$$

where $q_i = 1$ if consumer i experiences a loss and $q_i = 0$ otherwise. The coverage provided by each of the $1 + m$ consumers that provide coverage is thus

$$\frac{Y}{m + 1} \sum_{i=1}^{m} q_i.$$

The *expected coverage* per consumer providing insurance is then

$$Y \frac{m}{m + 1} \beta,$$

because the expected value of q_i is β. The *variance* in coverage per consumer providing insurance equals

$$\frac{Y\beta(1 - \beta)}{m + 1}.$$

The firm's profit equals

$$\Pi = mP - (m+1)W.$$

It is easy to verify that the firm earns a positive profit. Suppose that the firm offered consumers who purchased insurance the same premium and the same coverage that they would obtain with bilateral exchange, $P = p^*$ and $Y = y^*$. Then insured consumers would be indifferent between bilateral exchange and dealing with the firm. Consumers providing insurance would be strictly better off than either under autarky or under bilateral trade with premium p^* and coverage y^* because the expected coverage per consumer providing insurance is strictly lower than with bilateral trade. This is the case for any $m \geq 1$, because adding one extra consumer to provide insurance improves matters. In addition, the variance in coverage per consumer is lower because risk is pooled across consumers that provide insurance, in contrast to bilateral exchange. Moreover, as m gets large, the variance in coverage tends to zero.[12]

Therefore, the firm can compensate consumers providing insurance with a payment W that is strictly less than p^*, so that the firm's profit is strictly positive. Accordingly, the firm can choose P^*, W^* to maximize profit, subject to the participation constraints for consumers who obtain insurance and consumers who provide insurance, such that the firm earns a strictly positive profit. The firm's profit is not subject to uncertainty because consumers who purchase insurance and consumers who provide insurance bear all the risks. The model can be closed by distributing profit shares to consumers, whether insurers or insured.

The analysis of insurance demonstrates that firms lower transaction costs under uncertainty by handling multiple transactions and increasing risk pooling. The firm plays an important economic role in enhancing the ability of consumers to share risk. Firms provide many types of mechanisms for allocating risk across consumers including standardized insurance policies and other types of state-contingent contracts. By transacting with many consumers, with uncertainty in preferences and endowments, firms create mechanisms for transferring value across states of the world.

8.6.3 Spanning States of the World

Consumers seeking to trade with each other in different states of the world need to have a means of transferring value. It is costly to write state-contingent contracts. The cost of writing such contracts is increased when there is not a sufficient number of assets with linearly independent returns. Markets are incomplete when the number of assets with linearly independent returns is less than the number of

---

12 These results are applications of the law of large numbers and generalize to other distributions
     of losses with finite variance.

states of the world. With incomplete markets, trading between consumers will be inefficient, so that not all potential gains from trade will be realized.

Consider the situation in which there are three states of the world and three consumers. All consumers are risk-averse, with concave utility of income w denoted by $u(w)$. Consumer 1 has two units of an asset x with the following returns in the three states: $(1, 2, 3)$. Such an asset cannot span the three states of the world by itself, there is a need for two other assets with linearly independent returns. The consumer would like to trade units of the asset x with other consumers, but faces the problem of separating out the state-dependent components of the asset. This could presumably be done by writing state-contingent contracts with other consumers, but this is likely to entail transaction costs of negotiation, contract specification, and state verification.

Suppose that the three states of the world have likelihood β_1, β_2, and β_3, where $\beta_1 + \beta_2 + \beta_3 = 1$. Under autarky, consumer 1's expected utility is $U = \beta_1 u(2) + \beta_2 u(4) + \beta_3 u(6) = u(w^0)$ where w^0 is a number less than the expected value of the two units of the asset by Jensen's inequality. The expected value of two units of the asset is $\beta_1 2 + \beta_2 4 + \beta_3 6$. The consumer would like to smooth out income fluctuations by increasing income in state 1 and reducing income in state 3.

Suppose that there are two other consumers. Consumer 2 has two units of a risky asset y with payoffs $(3, 2, 1)$ and consumer 3 has two units of a risky asset z with payoffs $(3, 3, 2)$. Consumer 1 would like to enter into contracts with the other two consumers to transfer income from state 3 to state 1. This presents some problems. To spread risk, consumer 1 would need to negotiate with both of the other consumers. Also, consumer 1 would need to write a contingent contract such that the consumer receives income in state 1 and makes payments to the other consumers in state 3, which requires writing a contingent contract based on the risky asset.

Consumers 1 and 2 could exchange one unit of each of their assets and fully eliminate their risk. However, this would leave consumer 3 with a risky asset and the allocation would be inefficient. Bilateral exchanges between consumers 2 and 3 or between consumers 1 and 3 would still leave all consumers with risk and would not represent efficient allocations.

Ross (1976) pointed out that an asset such as x with returns $(1, 2, 3)$ could be used as the basis for constructing two call options with exercise prices 1 and 2, respectively. A call option gives the buyer the right but not the obligation to purchase the asset. For the call option with an exercise price equal to 1, the buyer of the option will exercise the option only if the value of the underlying asset exceeds 1. Thus, the option with an exercise price of 1 will have a pattern of returns of $(0, 1, 2)$. For the call option with an exercise price equal to 2, the buyer of the option will exercise the option only if the value of the underlying asset exceeds 2. Thus, the option with an exercise price of 2 will have a pattern of returns of $(0, 0, 1)$. The three assets consisting of the original asset and the call options with exercise prices 1 and 2 have linearly independent returns and so span the three states of the world.

The creation of the options also entails transaction costs. Someone must design the options, establish prices for the options, sell the options, and then make sure that the contracts are properly executed when the strike price is attained. There is a role for a firm in a pure exchange economy to design and sell option contracts at prices p_1 and p_2, respectively. In the example, consumer 1 could sell both units of asset x to the firm for price p_x and then have no risk. The firm would then issue two units of an option with exercise price 1 and two units of an option with exercise price 2. Consumer 2 could purchase two units of the option with exercise price 1 and would then face no risk. Consumer 3 could purchase two units of the option with exercise price 2 and also face no risk.

The firm could set the purchase price for asset x and the prices for the options such that all three consumers are indifferent between holding their risky asset and dealing with the firm. Assuming that no exchange takes place under autarky, the firm would earn profits equal to the total insurance benefits that it provides to the three consumers.

In an economy with risky assets, the firm facilitates the transfer of risk by designing and issuing options. The firm allows the transfer of value across states of the world by taking apart the payoffs of risky assets. The firm offers simple option contracts. Consumers avoid the cost of writing more complex state-contingent contracts that would be based on their risky assets. Moreover, through pricing of the options, the firm facilitates exchange in comparison with bilateral trade. Through central clearing, the firm further simplifies the process of transferring risk. Creating complete markets requires transaction costs. The economic role of the firm includes creating and coordinating the transactions that are necessary to establish complete markets.

8.7 Conclusions

Firms play an important economic role in reducing transaction costs and increasing attainable transaction benefits. Firms address the problem of the absence of a double coincidence of wants. Firms perform functions traditionally attributed to money: providing a store of value, a medium of exchange, and a unit of account. Firms also create money and coordinate transactions that are substitutes for money. Firms help consumers achieve gains from trade by connecting them with the appropriate trading partners. Through their longevity, firms connect consumers over time, acting as a store of value and a counter party to trade between generations. Through their central location, firms connect consumers separated by geography and the costs of transportation. By creating contracts and pooling risk, firms help consumers to transfer value across states of the world and to obtain the benefits of sharing risk. The separation of objectives between the firm and its owners helps the firm to improve the efficiency of transactions in the pure-exchange economy.

9

The Firm versus Free Riding

The critical issue in the theory of the firm is determining what firms can do for consumers that consumers cannot do for themselves. Firms play an economic role when they increase efficiency in comparison to direct exchange between consumers. Consumers form organizations to take advantage of the benefits of joint production. The gains from joint production include economies of scale, public goods, common property resources, and externalities. However, consumer organizations can experience inefficiencies due to free riding. By separating the objectives of the organization from the consumption objectives of its owners, the firm addresses the free rider problem.

The chapter examines three types of gains from joint production: economies of scale, public goods, and extraction of common-property resources. Consumers can take advantage of the gains from joint production by forming a consumer organization. The consumer organization is a basic partnership, which can take the form of a buyers' cooperative, a workers' cooperative, a club, an association, or a syndicate. The consumer organization not only allocates goods, but also allocates total costs, so that its budget balances.[1] Due to the budget-balancing constraint, the consumer organization experiences inefficiencies due to free riding. The purpose of the chapter is to examine how firms can improve the efficiency of the organization engaged in joint production.

Assume that the consumer organization encounters transaction costs that limit contracting and monitoring. Also, members of the consumer organization have costs of communication and negotiation that limit their ability to form cooperative agreements. The members thus engage in strategic noncooperative behavior. The members of the consumer organization make consumption choices that are based

---

1 As is well known from the theory of mechanism design, budget balancing constrains the choice of allocation mechanisms. Dominant strategy mechanisms that satisfy a balanced budget will not be efficient. In many cases, a Bayes-Nash mechanism that satisfies a balanced budget and individual rationality also will not be efficient.

on their consumption benefits and the income effects of cost-sharing. Free riding creates a tradeoff between the benefits and the costs of joint production. A larger consumer organization obtains greater benefits from joint production. However, a larger consumer organization experiences greater transaction costs in the form of free riding.

The objectives of the consumer organization reflect the consumption objectives of its members. The firm separates the objectives of the organization from the consumption objectives of its owners. The firm's separation of objectives allows the firm to break the budget-balancing constraint for the organization. The firm can employ a wider range of incentive mechanisms, which alleviates the problem of free riding by members of the organization. The profit-maximizing firm need not attain full efficiency, due to distortions from monopoly pricing.

The comparison between the consumer organization and the firm depends on the tradeoff between free riding and profit maximization. This chapter shows that when there are few consumers, the consumer organization may be more efficient than the firm. When there are many consumers, the consumer organization may be less efficient than the firm. The comparison of the firm and the consumer organization determines when there are advantages to separating consumption decisions from production decisions.

The chapter compares the firm to a consumer organization that is owned by its members. To form a firm, the members of the consumer organization sell their ownership shares to outside investors. The firm's new owners do not have a consumption objective and receive income from the profits of the firm. The new owners unanimously prefer that the firm maximize profits. The discussion assumes that owners compete to acquire the organization, so that members of the cooperative receive bids equal to the profit of the cooperative after it is acquired. This results in separation of the consumption objectives of the members of the organization from the profit objectives of the firm.

The benefits of separation can be illustrated using a simple example. Suppose that there are two identical consumer cooperatives. Each cooperative obtains benefits from joint production. Each cooperative operates inefficiently because consumers engage in free riding. Suppose that each cooperative establishes a firm to manage joint production, with the members of the cooperative fully owning the shares of their cooperative's firm. Next, suppose that the members of two cooperatives trade all of their ownership shares for the ownership shares of the other cooperative. Because the cooperatives are identical, there will be an even trade. The swapping of shares represents diffuse ownership of shares in an economy with capital markets that serves to separate the objectives of consumers from those of firms. After the exchange, the two consumer cooperatives are entirely distinct from their owners. The owners of each of the cooperatives unanimously prefer profit maximization. Thus, the two cooperatives become firms that choose prices to maximize profits. The consumers served by the two cooperatives take prices as given in making consumption choices.

9.1 The Firm and Economies of Scale

Consumers have an incentive to produce jointly to take advantage of economies of scale. The consumer cooperative or buyers' cooperative is an organization that is owned and operated by its customers. The general absence of consumer cooperatives in the economy suggests that in practice firms provide significant advantages in coordinating transactions in comparison with associations of individual consumers. The discussion in this section examines conditions under which firms manage joint production and allocate resources better than do consumer cooperatives when there are economies of scale.

9.1.1 The Consumer Cooperative versus the Firm

The consumer cooperative encounters transaction costs that limit its choices of allocation mechanisms. Firms have the potential to improve the allocation of goods and services through the use of various pricing mechanisms. Price-setting firms exercise some measure of market power, depending on the extent of competition. Thus, there is a tradeoff between the allocative efficiencies offered by firms in coordinating production and potential allocative inefficiencies that result from market power.

The consumer cooperative is likely to experience several types of transaction costs that affect allocative efficiency. First, consumers encounter transaction costs in establishing the cooperative. These include the costs of negotiating the purpose, rules, procedures, governance structure, and membership of the cooperative. Second, consumers incur transaction costs in operating the cooperative, including record-keeping, price-setting, and the sharing of profits or losses. Third, consumers incur costs associated with managing the cooperative, including the time spent in meetings to decide policy, whether through negotiations or voting. In addition, the members of the cooperative bear the costs of monitoring each other to prevent free riding and fraud.

The transaction costs of the consumer cooperative are likely to increase with the number of members. There may be organizational diseconomies of scale for consumer cooperatives. Hansmann (1985) observes that consumer cooperatives require both repeated and large purchases because "otherwise the transaction costs of registering, keeping track of, and communicating with members will be disproportionate to the value of goods consumed." Hansmann adds that as a consequence "consumer cooperatives are typically small – to keep within bounds the consumer/members' incentive to free-ride on the monitoring efforts of other consumers – and serve primarily those consumers who reside near the cooperative" so that they can personally monitor its operations.

If the cooperative has few members, it appears more likely that it can maximize the well-being of its members through detailed bargaining. However, as the number of members increases, such detailed bargaining becomes more difficult. Achieving

Pareto-optimal allocations or allocations in the Core would place too great a burden on members in terms of communication, information gathering, calculation, voting, coalition formation, and negotiation. Accordingly, concepts from the theory of cooperative games are not a good fit for describing the consumer cooperative, despite the superficial appeal of applying complex solutions labeled as "cooperative." Ireland and Law (1983) observe that "In the case of the consumer cooperative, given weaker communication and cohesion, the myopic Cournot-Nash view of the consumer-member may be appropriate." They further suggest that a cooperative solution for consumption decisions is even less plausible in a consumer cooperative than it would be in a worker cooperative.[2]

The consumer cooperatives examined in this chapter operate through simple procedures. Given the basic rules, members of the cooperative play a Nash noncooperative game. The assumption of a noncooperative game is meant as a realistic portrayal of interaction within a group of consumers. The noncooperative game solution is not intended to prejudge the outcome in favor of allocation by firms. Many noncooperative games yield outcomes that do not maximize joint benefits. Each player's equilibrium action is a best response to the equilibrium actions of other players. Each player's action maximizes his own benefits given the equilibrium actions of other players. This generally differs from actions that maximize total benefits. Consumers in cooperatives share returns from the common enterprise and as a result are tempted to free ride on the other members.

Firms can perform better than cooperatives because they can employ different allocation mechanisms, such as prices and incentive mechanisms. There are costs to using these mechanisms, such as efficiency losses from the exercise of market power when firms set prices. There are also efficiency losses from distortions arising from the application of incentive-compatible revelation mechanisms under asymmetric information. The contribution of the firm depends on how centralized allocation of resources compares with noncooperative outcomes of a consumer cooperative. The comparison of the consumer cooperative and the firm shows how separating consumer and firm decisions can improve allocative efficiency.

Firms that maximize profits improve allocative efficiency through the use of price mechanisms. Thus, consumers are made better off when consumer decisions and firm decisions are separated. Not only is the allocation of resources more efficient, but also the firm's profit provides income for consumers. In contrast to the members of a cooperative, the firm's owners unanimously prefer profit maximization, because their consumption is not affected by the decision of the firm that they own. In turn, firms do not take into account the effect of profit on consumption decisions, because none of the consumers that they serve own their shares.

---

2 The application of cooperative solutions to the study of consumer cooperatives is common nevertheless; see Enke (1945), Sorenson et al. (1978), Anderson et al. (1979, 1980), Sandler and Tschirhart (1981), Sexton (1986), and Sexton and Sexton (1987); see also Pigou (1920a).

Even when the firm acts as a monopolist, it makes consumers better off in comparison to the consumer cooperative. This is due to the pricing instruments used by the firm. The allocation can be shown to satisfy a rationality constraint that consumers must prefer the allocation offered by the firm, plus profits earned from owning a firm, to the allocation offered by the consumer cooperative.

The divestiture of ownership shares by members of the consumer cooperative helps explain the role of firms in the separation of consumption and production decisions. The separation is motivated in part by allocative efficiencies offered by firms in contrast to consumer cooperatives. Second, the separation between consumers and firms through the swap of ownership mentioned earlier helps to explain profit-maximizing behavior by firms. This occurs without the need to assume that firms are price-takers, and without additional assumptions requiring firms to ignore the effects of profits on income or restricting consumer-owners to ignore the effects of firm decisions on their consumption. Third, the ownership swap helps explain the role of capital markets and the investor ownership of firms. Capital markets provide a way for consumers to trade ownership of firms without interference in the allocation decisions made by firms. Capital markets support profit maximization by firms.

To represent transaction costs, assume that consumers cannot attain a Core allocation. Consumers are restricted to average cost pricing. Consumers individually choose the amount that they wish to consume. Consumers are aware of the effects of their consumption on average costs. Consumers play a Nash noncooperative game in their choices of consumption levels. As a result, the allocation of consumption and the output that is produced need not be optimal. In contrast, firms can allocate the jointly produced output through price discrimination. The firm can shift shares of fixed costs toward those consumers with a greater willingness to pay. When there is asymmetric information about consumer preferences, firms can employ nonlinear pricing and general auction mechanisms to induce consumers to reveal their demand types and thus enhance allocative efficiency.

9.1.2 The Consumer Cooperative and Economies of Scale

One of the first and perhaps one of the most influential consumer cooperatives, the Rochdale Society of Equitable Pioneers, was established in 1844 by approximately 28 Lancashire weavers. The Rochdale Society set up a grocery store, among many other projects, including a factory and a textile mill. The cooperative sold to the public as well as to members at market prices. The profits of the cooperative were distributed to its members in proportion to their purchases.[3] Ireland and Law (1983) interpret the Rochdale distribution as average cost pricing. To see why proportional profit sharing corresponds to average cost pricing, consider the expenditure of a member of the consumer cooperative. Define the notation as follows: p is the output

---

3 See Reeves (1944) and the *Columbia Encyclopedia* (2001).

price, q_i is the purchase of member i, Q is total output, $C(Q)$ is total cost, and E_i is member i's net expenditure. Then

$$(1) \qquad E_i = pq_i - (q_i/Q)(pQ - C(Q)) = q_i C(Q)/Q,$$

so that each member pays average cost per unit of consumption. The profit share of a member i equals their share of total purchases, q_i/Q.

Suppose that there are n consumers indexed by i. A consumer of type i has a utility function $U(q, \mu_i)$, where q represents consumption and μ_i is a taste parameter that takes values in the unit interval. Let $u(q, \mu_i) = U_1(q, \mu_i)$ be the consumer's marginal utility. The consumer's utility function is twice differentiable and increasing in q and μ, and strictly concave in q, and marginal utility is increasing in μ, $u_2 > 0$. The utility function is positive for $q > 0$ for all μ and $U(0, \mu) = 0$ for all μ. Also, let $u_{22} < 0$ and $u_{21} > 0$. The consumer's utility function represents the benefits of consumption evaluated in units of a numeraire good. Define consumer i's demand function by $q_i(p) = q(p, \mu_i)$, which solves $u(q_i, \mu_i) = p$. Also, define aggregate demand as $Q(p) = \sum_{i=1}^{n} q_i(p)$.

The cost function $C(Q)$ is twice differentiable, increasing, and convex. Let $AC(Q) = C(Q)/Q$. The cost function is in units of the numeraire good. The optimal allocation of the consumption good across consumers solves

$$\max_{q_i} \sum_{i=1}^{n} U(q_i, \mu_i) - C\left(\sum_{i=1}^{n} q_i\right).$$

The maximization problem gives the standard solution that each consumer's marginal benefit should equal marginal cost,

$$(2) \qquad u(q_i^*, \mu_i) = C'\left(\sum_{i=1}^{n} q_i^*\right), \qquad \text{for } i = 1, \ldots, n.$$

Let q_i^* represent the efficient allocation, $i = 1, \ldots, n$. Define $Q^* = \sum_{i=1}^{n} q_i^*$ and note that $Q^* = Q(C'(Q^*))$.

Consider also an allocation in which prices are equal to average costs,

$$(3) \qquad u\left(q_i^{AC}, \mu_i\right) = AC\left(\sum_{i=1}^{n} q_i^{AC}\right),$$

for $i = 1, \ldots, n$ and $q_i^{AC} = q(AC, \mu_i)$. Define $Q^{AC} = \sum_{i=1}^{n} q_i^{AC}$ and note that $Q^{AC} = Q(AC(Q^{AC}))$. In regulatory economics, this is sometimes referred to as the "second-best" allocation.

The consumer cooperative allocates output based on average cost. However, this is not the same as average cost pricing. The members of the consumer cooperative are aware of the impact of their consumption on average cost. Consumers choose Nash-equilibrium consumption levels q_i^0. Let $Q_{(i)}^0$ be the total equilibrium consumption of all consumers other than i. Then consumer i's Nash equilibrium consumption level solves

$$\max_{q_i} U(q_i, \mu_i) - q_i \, AC\left(Q^0_{(i)} + q_i\right).$$

Suppose that the second-order sufficient condition for an interior maximum is satisfied, $u_1 - 2\,AC' - q\,AC'' < 0$. The first-order conditions for consumers' maximization problems are

$$(4) \qquad u\left(q_i^0, \mu_i\right) = \left(q_i^0 / Q^0\right) C'(Q^0) + \left(1 - q_i^0 / Q^0\right) AC(Q^0),$$

for $i = 1, \ldots, n$, where $Q^0 = \sum_{i=1}^{n} q_i^0$ is total equilibrium consumption for the consumer cooperative.

The marginal expenditure for a member of the consumer cooperative thus equals a weighted average of marginal cost and average cost. The consumer's marginal expenditure is greater than, equal to, or less than marginal cost if total equilibrium output Q^0 is less than, equal to, or greater than minimum efficient scale, Q_{MES}, defined by $C'(Q_{\text{MES}}) = AC(Q_{\text{MES}})$ for a U-shaped average cost curve. Varying the size of the membership of the cooperative will change its equilibrium output, as Ireland and Law (1983) observe in a setting with identical consumers.

With a large number of consumers, an individual consumer has a negligible effect on total output. With many consumers, therefore, an individual consumer does not recognize the marginal cost of his consumption. When there are many consumers, each consumer chooses consumption such that marginal utility equals average cost,

$$u\left(q_i^0, \mu_i\right) = AC(Q^0).$$

This outcome is equivalent to price-taking behavior with a price equal to average cost.

When the number of consumers is not large, and there is just the right number of consumers, total output at the equilibrium outcome equals the minimum efficient scale, $Q^0 = Q_{\text{MES}}$, and coincides with the first-best allocation and the allocation with average-cost pricing, $Q^0 = Q^* = Q^{AC}$. Suppose, however, that membership is low, so that $Q^0 < Q_{\text{MES}}$. Then the total output at the equilibrium outcome is between the first-best allocation and the allocation with average-cost pricing, $Q^{AC} < Q^0 < Q^*$. In this case, the consumer cooperative improves on average-cost pricing. If membership is high, then $Q^0 > Q_{\text{MES}}$ and $Q^* < Q^0 < Q^{AC}$. In this case, free-riding causes the total output to be greater than the efficient level but less than the output with average cost pricing.

The consumer cooperative performs better than average cost pricing. To see why, consider first the case where marginal cost is less than average cost at the equilibrium output, $C'(Q^0) < AC(Q^0)$. Then by the first-order conditions in (4), $C'(Q^0) < u(q_i^0, \mu_i) < AC(Q^0)$, for all i. This implies that

$$q(AC(Q^0), \mu_i) < q_i^0 < q(C'(Q^0), \mu_i)$$

for all i, so that, adding over i,

$$Q(AC(Q^0)) < Q^0 < Q(C'(Q^0)).$$

Because $Q(p)$ is decreasing and $AC(Q)$ is decreasing, $Q^{AC} < Q(AC(Q^0)) < Q^0$. Also, because $Q(p)$ is decreasing and $C'(Q)$ is increasing, $Q^0 < Q^* < Q(C'(Q^0))$, so that the cooperative's output is closer to the optimal output.

Next, consider the case where marginal cost is greater than average cost at the equilibrium output, $C'(Q^0) > AC(Q^0)$. As before, it follows that

$$Q(C'(Q^0)) < Q^0 < Q(AC(Q^0)).$$

Because $Q(p)$ is decreasing and $AC(Q)$ is increasing, $Q^0 < Q^{AC} < Q(AC(Q^0))$. Also, because $Q(p)$ is decreasing and $C'(Q)$ is increasing, $Q(C'(Q^0)) < Q^* < Q^0$, so that the cooperative's output again is closer to the optimal output.

As a result of their competitive consumption choices, total consumption moves closer to the first-best outcome. Consumers boost consumption above the average cost pricing level when average cost is decreasing because taking account of marginal costs reduces the price below average cost. Consumers reduce consumption below the average cost pricing level when average cost is increasing because taking account of marginal costs increases the price above average cost. The proportional sharing of average cost works like a nonlinear price schedule.

The consumer cooperative is better off sharing average costs and behaving noncooperatively than it would be taking as given an average cost price. To see why this is so, note that by Nash behavior,

$$\sum_{i=1}^{n} U(q_i^0, \mu_i) - C\left(\sum_{i=1}^{n} q_i^0\right) \geq \sum_{i=1}^{n} \left(U(q_i^{AC}, \mu_i) - q_i^0 AC(Q_{(i)}^0 + q_i^{AC})\right).$$

Add and subtract $C(Q^{AC})$:

$$\sum_{i=1}^{n} \left(U\left(q_i^{AC}, \mu_i\right) - q_i^{AC} AC\left(Q_{(i)}^0 + q_i^{AC}\right)\right)$$

$$= \sum_{i=1}^{n} U\left(q_i^{AC}, \mu_i\right) - C(Q^{AC}) + \sum_{i=1}^{n} q_i^{AC} \left(AC(Q^{AC}) - AC\left(Q_{(i)}^0 + q_i^{AC}\right)\right).$$

If average cost is decreasing, $Q^{AC} < Q^0$, it follows that $AC(Q^{AC}) > AC(Q^0)$, so that $q(AC(Q^{AC}), \mu_i) < q(AC(Q^0), \mu_i)$. Because $q_i^{AC} = q(AC(Q^{AC}), \mu_i)$ and $q(AC(Q^0), \mu_i) < q_i^0$, it follows that $q_i^{AC} < q_i^0$. Therefore, $Q^{AC} < Q_{(i)}^0 + q_i^{AC}$. This implies that the last term is positive. Conversely, if average cost is increasing, $q_i^{AC} > q_i^0$, so that the last term is also positive. This implies that

$$\sum_{i=1}^{n} U\left(q_i^0, \mu_i\right) - C\left(\sum_{i=1}^{n} q_i^0\right) > \sum_{i=1}^{n} U\left(q_i^{AC}, \mu_i\right) - C\left(\sum_{i=1}^{n} q_i^{AC}\right).$$

The consumer cooperative's pricing policies are constrained by the need to allocate costs. The budget-balancing restriction leads to free rider effects. The consumer cooperative effectively employs a quantity-based price schedule rather than a fixed price. When the number of members of the cooperative is not large, individual members recognize the effects of their consumption on average cost. Free rider effects perform a useful function in cost allocation. As a result, the average cost–sharing rule is sophisticated because it allows the consumer cooperative to price discriminate across its members.

Without any explicit transaction costs, the consumer cooperative performs better than a standard competitive firm that charges a constant per-unit price. Because the consumer cooperative does better than with average cost pricing, a competitive firm offering an average cost price would make consumers worse off unless the firm operated at minimum efficient scale. At the efficient scale, the consumer cooperative and the competitive firm would be equally efficient. Thus, a firm with market power that priced above average cost would not function as well as the consumer cooperative even if the firm operated at efficient scale. Therefore, for firms to perform better than a consumer cooperative, they must do more than operate production and offer consumers a linear price. This means that the theory of the firm must go beyond the perfectly competitive price-taking firm of neoclassical economics.

9.1.3 The Firm and Nonlinear Pricing

To compare the consumer cooperative with a price-setting firm, suppose that members of the consumer cooperative divest their ownership shares to outside investors. The members of the cooperative remain as customers and also receive payments from the outside investors. The separation of consumer objectives from owner objectives transforms the consumer cooperative into a firm. The firm can address scale economies by employing price discrimination. The firm offers various quantity-based pricing instruments including discrete multipart tariffs and non-linear price schedules. These pricing instruments help to explain why the economy is not organized by consumer cooperatives.

With a firm supplying the good, consumers take prices as given. By assumption, consumers have divested their ownership and receive bids equal to the firm's profit. The consumers' purchasing decisions are separate from the firm's pricing decisions. In contrast to the consumer cooperative, the firm can depart from budget-balancing pricing rules such as average cost pricing. The firm can discriminate across consumers to allocate payments for fixed costs. Through price discrimination, the firm can set marginal payments closer to marginal costs for some consumers, thus improving allocative efficiency. By generating greater consumer benefits through more efficient pricing at the margin, the firm can obtain additional revenues, recover fixed costs, and achieve greater economies of scale. Firms can employ more general price mechanisms than consumer cooperatives; it is also assumed that firms can commit credibly to price mechanisms.

The profit-maximizing firm addresses scale economies through nonlinear pricing. Let the cost function have fixed costs, K, and constant marginal costs, c:

$$C(Q) = cQ + K.$$

Because marginal costs are constant, there are no congestion effects.[4] The firm is able to meter the consumption levels of individual consumers, but the firm need not observe the demand types of individual consumers. Nonlinear pricing is useful for inducing individual consumers to reveal their private information.[5] Nonlinear pricing and other quantity-based pricing techniques are used widely in practice. Quantity discounts are standard for many types of consumer products. In addition, firms in a wide range of markets apply nonlinear pricing to allocate production capacity. These include electricity generation and transmission, natural gas transportation, access to airport facilities and landing rights, job-shop services, and computer scheduling.

To illustrate the basic issues, suppose for now that there are only two types of consumers, with demand parameters μ_1 and μ_2, with $\mu_1 < \mu_2$. Then the firm need offer at most two contracts, (q_1, P_1) and (q_2, P_2). The individual demand $q = D(p, \mu)$ is defined by equating marginal willingness to pay to a per-unit price $u(q, \mu) = p$. Assume that there exists $\overline{q} > 0$ such that $u(\overline{q}, 1) = c$, so that consumption is bounded above. Type-1 consumers are low-demand consumers with parameter μ_1 and type-2 consumers are high-demand consumers with parameter μ_2. Suppose that there are n_1 low-demand consumers and n_2 high-demand consumers, and let $n = n_1 + n_2$.

With average costs everywhere decreasing, the consumer cooperative chooses a price that is below the average-cost price and above the marginal-cost price. The consumer cooperative chooses outputs such that consumers pay a weighted average

---

4 When there are no congestion effects, nonlinear pricing is optimal even if the firm does not know the distribution of consumer types in the population. If marginal costs are increasing, there are congestion effects. Marginal cost is increasing in total output, so profit-maximizing consumption levels are interdependent. Nonlinear pricing is no longer optimal with congestion effects if the firm does not know the distribution of consumer types in the population. Thus, the firm's optimal pricing mechanism must take into account all of the consumer types. The optimal allocation mechanism is a generalized multiunit auction developed by Dasgupta and Spulber (1990). Spulber (1993a) shows, however, that even if the firm does not know the distribution of its customers' types and there are congestion effects, nonlinear pricing is approximately optimal. As the number of consumers served by the firm increases, the firm's knowledge of aggregate demand improves because the group of customers served is a larger sample from the population.

5 On nonlinear pricing, see particularly Spence (1977b), Mussa and Rosen (1978), Spulber (1979, 1981b, 1984a, 1984b, 1989a, 1989b, 1992), Maskin and Riley (1984), and Wilson (1993).

of marginal costs and average costs. With two types of consumers and constant marginal costs, the consumer cooperative outputs solve, from equation (4),

$$u\left(q_i^0, \mu_i\right) = \left(q_i^0/Q^0\right)c + \left(1 - q_i^0/Q^0\right)\left(c + K/Q^0\right)$$
$$= c + \left(1 - q_i^0/Q^0\right)K/Q^0, \quad i = 1, 2,$$

where $Q^0 = q_1^0 + q_2^0$. The benefits of the consumer cooperative are

$$g = n_1 \int_0^{q_1^0} u(q, \mu_1)dq + n_2 \int_0^{q_2^0} u(q, \mu_2)dq - cn_1 q_1^0 - cn_2 q_2^0 - K.$$

Consider a price-discriminating firm. The first-best contract provides a useful benchmark. Suppose that the firm charges all consumers a marginal cost price,

$$(5) \qquad\qquad q_i^* = D(c, \mu_i), \quad i = 1, 2.$$

Suppose further that all consumers bear an equal share of fixed cost. Then the first-best outcome is feasible if the consumer surplus of a low-demand consumer covers their share of fixed cost,

$$(6) \qquad\qquad \int_0^{q_1^*} u(q, \mu_1)dq - pq_1 \geq K/n.$$

For sufficiently large n, the first-best is attainable because fixed costs per person will be small.

Consider the more difficult case in which the first-best is not attainable. To induce consumers to self-select, the firm must find a way to lower the payment for lower demand consumers; see Maskin and Riley (1984). This requires a departure from marginal cost pricing. To illustrate why, consider for example a set of contracts that would correspond to first-degree price discrimination under full information:

$$(7) \qquad\qquad P_i^* = \int_0^{q_i^*} u(q, \mu_i)dq, \quad i = 1, 2.$$

Note that the low-demand consumer purchases less and pays less: $q_1^* < q_2^*$ and $P_1^* < P_2^*$.

The firm's profit-maximizing contracts are connected by the problem of adverse selection; that is, consumers may select contracts that were designed for others. The firm's contracts must be chosen to form a schedule that induces consumers to self-select the contracts intended for them. Under asymmetric information, the first-degree price-discrimination contracts would not separate consumers, because both types would prefer the low-priced contract. Adverse selection would occur. The high-demand consumer would obtain no gains from the high-payment high-output contract but would obtain positive gains from the low-payment low-output contract, because the high-demand consumer's surplus at any output is greater than that of the low-demand consumer; see Figure 9.1.

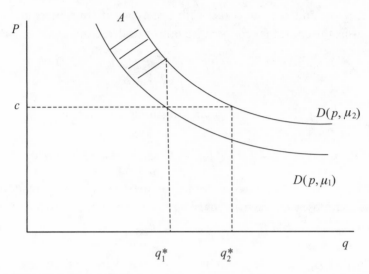

Figure 9.1. The high-demand consumer has greater surplus at any output level by an amount equal to the shaded area A.

To induce the high-demand consumer to choose the marginal cost price output, q_2^*, the firm would need to lower the fixed payment by the amount of consumer surplus gained from the low-output contract,

$$(8) \qquad\qquad\qquad \hat{P}_2 = P_2^* - A,$$

where A is the shaded area in Figure 9.1. This will result in consumers self-selecting, with low-demand consumers choosing (q_1^*, P_1^*) and high-demand consumers choosing $(q_2^*, \hat{P}_2)$.

The firm can easily obtain higher revenues, however. By slightly lowering the quantity offered to the low-demand consumers, the firm loses very little in terms of the fixed fee. This allows the firm to raise the fixed fee to higher-demand consumers substantially. This is illustrated in Figure 9.2.

By lowering the quantity below q_1^* to $\hat{q}_1$, the fixed fee charged to low-demand consumers must be reduced so that profit earned from low-demand consumers falls by E. At the same time, the fixed fee to high-demand consumers can be raised by an amount equal to B, which is always greater than E. The profit gained by the firm is the difference between the first-order effect on the fixed fee of the high-demand consumer B and the second-order effect on the profit earned from the low-demand consumer E. The area B represents the decrease in the shaded area A, which was the reduction in the fixed payment required for keeping the high-demand consumer indifferent between the two contracts. Moreover, the low-demand consumer continues to be charged a fixed fee equal to that consumer's benefit from output $\hat{q}_1$.

The largest fixed payment that leaves the low-demand consumer indifferent between purchasing from the firm and not purchasing the good is

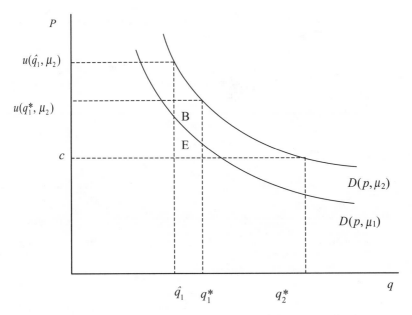

Figure 9.2. Adjusting the nonlinear price schedule to cover fixed costs.

$P_1 = \int_0^{q_1} u(q, \mu_1) dq$. The largest fixed payment that leaves the high-demand consumer indifferent between the two contracts is

$$(9) \qquad P_2 = \int_0^{q_2^*} u(q, \mu_2) dq - \left[\int_0^{q_1} u(q, \mu_2) dq - P_1 \right].$$

The firm's profit is

$$(10) \qquad \Pi = n_1(P_1 - cq_1) + n_2(P_2 - cq_2^*) - K.$$

After substituting for the payment schedules P_1 and P_2, the firm's profit-maximization problem can be written as a function of the consumption of the low-demand consumer:

$$(11) \quad \Pi(q_1) = n_1 \int_0^{q_1} u(q, \mu_1) dq - n_1 cq_1 + n_2 \int_0^{q_2^*} u(q, \mu_2) dq - n_2 cq_2^*.$$
$$- n_2 \int_{\mu_1}^{\mu_2} \int_0^{q_1} u_2(q, \mu) dq d\mu - K.$$

The profit-maximizing firm's first-order condition for the low-demand consumer's output is

$$(12) \qquad u\left(q_1^M, \mu_1\right) = c + (n_2/n_1) \int_{\mu_1}^{\mu_2} u_2\left(q_1^M, \mu\right) d\mu.$$

The output chosen by the profit-maximizing firm requires a greater distortion away from the output at which the marginal benefit of the low-demand consumer equals marginal cost; thus $q_1^M < \hat{q}_1 < q_1^*$. The profit-maximizing firm offers consumers the contracts (P_1^M, q_1^M) and (P_2^M, q_2^*), where

$$(13) \qquad\qquad P_1^M = \int_0^{q_1^M} u(q, \mu_1) dq,$$

$$(14) \qquad P_2^M = \int_0^{q_2^*} u(q, \mu_2) dq - \left[\int_0^{q_1^M} u(q, \mu_2) dq - P_1 \right].$$

The low-demand consumer chooses (P_1^M, q_1^M) and the high-demand consumer chooses (P_2^M, q_2^*).

The firm extracts all of the low-demand consumer's surplus and less than the high-demand consumer's surplus. The profit of the firm equals

$$(15) \qquad\qquad \Pi = n_1 P_1^M + n_2 P_2^M - \left(n_1 q_1^M + n_2 q_2^* \right) - K.$$

When consumers divest their ownership of the cooperative, they receive payments equal to the profits of the firm. Total consumer benefits equal

$$(16) \quad G = n_1 \int_0^{q_1^M} u(q, \mu_1) dq + n_2 \int_0^{q_2^*} u(q, \mu_2) dq - c n_1 q_1^M - c n_2 q_2^* - K.$$

Compare the benefits provided by the firm with those provided by the consumer cooperative. With the firm, the consumption of the high-demand consumer is optimal, so that the contribution of the high-demand consumer to total benefits is greater with a firm than with a consumer cooperative. In comparing the contribution of the low-demand consumer to total benefits, there are two possibilities. The low-demand consumer may consume more or less with the firm than with the consumer cooperative. Suppose first that the low-demand consumer consumes more with the firm than with the consumer cooperative, $q_1^M \geq q_1^0$. Then consumption with the firm is closer to the optimal output, and the contribution of the low-demand consumer to total benefits is greater with a firm than with a consumer cooperative. This implies that the total benefits are greater with a firm than with a consumer cooperative, $G > g$.

Suppose instead that the consumption of the low-demand consumer is lower with the firm than with the consumer cooperative, $q_1^M < q_1^0$. Then the consumption level is farther from the optimal output, and the contribution of the low-demand consumer to total benefits is lower with a firm than with a consumer cooperative. If the gain from the high-demand consumer is less than the loss from the low-demand consumer, the consumer cooperative yields greater total benefits. If the gain from the high-demand consumer is greater than the loss from the low-demand consumer, the firm yields greater total benefits.

The comparison depends on the relative numbers of the two types of consumers. From the firm's first-order condition (12), the quantity offered to the low-demand consumer may be increasing or decreasing in the ratio of the number of consumers of each type, n_2/n_1.[6] If the quantity offered to the low-demand consumer is increasing in the ratio of the number of consumers of each type or if it does not decrease too fast, and if the number of high-demand consumers, n_2, is sufficiently large relative to the number of low-demand consumers, n_1, then $G > g$. Under these conditions, total benefits are again greater with a firm than with a consumer cooperative, $G > g$.

9.1.4 The Firm and Nonlinear Pricing with Many Consumers

Consider the firm's nonlinear price schedule when there are many types of consumers. Suppose that consumer types are distributed on the unit interval μ_i, $i = 1, \ldots, n$, with $\mu_1 = 0$. The firm chooses contracts such that each consumer is exactly indifferent to the contract offered to a consumer of the next-lowest type:

$$(17) \quad P_i = \int_0^{q_i} u(q, \mu_i)dq - \left[\int_0^{q_{i-1}} u(q, \mu_i)dq - P_{i-1} \right], \quad i = 2, \ldots, n.$$

Substituting back into equation (17) recursively using the expressions for P_{i-1}, P_{i-2} and so on yields

$$(18) \quad P_i = \int_0^{q_i} u(q, \mu_i)dq - \sum_{j=0}^{i-1} \int_{\mu_j}^{\mu_{j+1}} \int_0^{q_j} u_2(q, \mu)dqd\mu, \quad i = 2, \ldots, n,$$

because $P_1 = \int_0^{q_1} u(q, \mu_1)dq$. The firm offers the n consumer types an equal number of contracts, (P_i, q_i), $i = 1, \ldots, n$. Consumers self-select by choosing the contracts designed for their demand types. Firms allocate scarce capacity without precise knowledge of aggregate demand in a wide variety of markets.

Consider the nonlinear pricing policy with many consumers. Suppose that consumer types are uniformly distributed on the unit interval. To find the nonlinear payment schedule, take the limit of the payments in the discrete-types case as μ_i approaches μ_{i-1}. The payment schedule is then

$$(19) \quad P(\mu_i) = \int_0^{q(\mu_i)} u(q, \mu_i)dq - \int_0^{\mu_i} \int_0^{q(\mu)} u_2(q, \mu)dqd\mu,$$

where the contract chosen by a type-μ consumer is $q_i = q(\mu_i)$.

---

6 Differentiating equation (12) implies that

$$dq_1^M/d(n_2/n_1) = \int_{\mu_1}^{\mu_2} u_2 \left(q_1^M, \mu \right) d\mu + (n_2/n_1) \int_{\mu_1}^{\mu_2} u_{21} \left(q_1^M, \mu \right) d\mu / u_1 \left(q_1^M, \mu_1 \right).$$

The denominator u_1 on the right-hand side is negative. The low-demand output is decreasing (increasing) if the numerator on the right-hand side u_{21} is positive (negative).

The firm's expected profits are the sum of consumer payments net of production costs. The payment of a consumer is derived by integrating equation (19) by parts. The firm's profit-maximization problem is as follows:

$$(20) \qquad \Pi = \max_{q(\mu)} \int_0^1 \left[\int_0^{q(\mu_i)} u(q, \mu) dq \right.$$

$$\left. - \int_0^{q(\mu)} u_2(q, \mu) dq (1 - \mu) - cq(\mu) \right] d\mu - K.$$

The firm maximizes profit subject to the constraints imposed by incentive compatibility and individual rationality. Under some conditions the solution to the unconstrained profit maximization problem satisfies the incentive compatibility and individual rationality conditions. The first-order condition for the firm's optimal output schedule therefore equates the consumer's virtual marginal willingness to pay to the firm's marginal cost:

$$(21) \qquad u(q^*, \mu) - (1 - \mu) u_2(q^*, \mu) = c.$$

The consumption $q^*(\mu)$ that solves the firm's first-order condition is nondecreasing in the taste parameter, so that the mechanism is incentive-compatible. The consumer's net benefit $U(\mu)$ is zero below some critical value of the taste parameter greater than or equal to zero, and positive and increasing for all higher values of the taste parameter.

By a change of variables, the nonlinear price schedule offered by the firm has the form

$$(22) \qquad P(q) = \int_0^q u(x, \mu^*(x)) dx,$$

where $\mu^*(x) = \min \{\mu : q^*(\mu) = x\}$. The consumer equates his marginal utility to the marginal nonlinear price schedule:

$$(23) \qquad P'(q) = u(q, \mu^*(q)).$$

The total gains from trade with nonlinear pricing by a firm equal

$$(24) \qquad G = \int_0^1 \left[\int_0^{q^*(\mu)} u(q, \mu) dq - cq^*(\mu) \right] d\mu - K.$$

The consumer's first-order condition can be written as

$$(25) \qquad u(q^*, \mu) = c + (1 - \mu) u_2(q^*, \mu).$$

With many consumers, recall that the consumer cooperative chooses an average cost price, so that the consumption of consumer μ equates marginal benefit to average cost:

$$(26) \qquad u(q^0, \mu) = c + K / \int_0^1 q^0(\mu) d\mu.$$

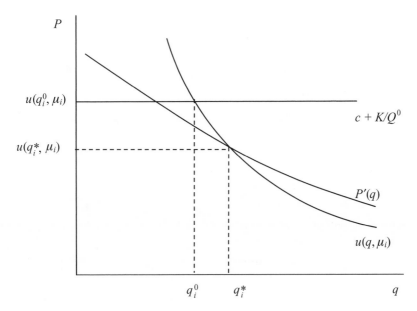

Figure 9.3. High-demand consumers consume more with a firm than with a consumer cooperative.

When fixed costs are zero, the consumer cooperative chooses a price equal to constant marginal cost, c. Increasing fixed costs, K, increases the average cost price and lowers consumption for each member of the cooperative, $q^0 = q^0(\mu K)$. Total gains from trade for the consumer cooperative can be expressed as a function of fixed costs:

$$(27) \qquad g(K) = \int_0^1 \left[\int_0^{q^0(\mu, K)} u(q, \mu) dq - c q^0(\mu, K) \right] d\mu - K.$$

A comparison of total benefits with a firm with total benefits with a consumer cooperative depends on consumption levels, because gains from trade are maximized when marginal benefits for each consumer equal marginal cost. The profit-maximizing firm offers greater total benefits than the consumer cooperative. For a consumer with sufficiently high taste parameter μ, the marginal price approaches marginal cost, so that consumption is greater with nonlinear pricing by a firm. Generally, let the critical value of the consumer taste parameter solve

$$(1 - \overline{\mu}) u_2(q, \overline{\mu}) = K / \int_0^1 q^0(\mu, K) d\mu.$$

Consumers with taste parameter greater than $\overline{\mu}$ face a marginal price that is less than average cost and consume more than they would if they were members of a cooperative. This possibility is shown in Figure 9.3. Because their consumption is greater, consumers with taste parameter greater than $\overline{\mu}$ make a greater contribution to total benefits with a firm than with a consumer cooperative. Consumers with taste parameter less than $\overline{\mu}$ consume more if they are members of a consumer cooperative. These consumers make a lower contribution to total benefits with a firm than with a consumer cooperative.

Compare the total benefits for a cooperative with the total benefits for the firm. The consumption levels of the members of the cooperative depend on fixed costs, in contrast to the consumption levels of the firm's customers. Therefore, total benefits for the consumer cooperative, $g(K)$, are decreasing in fixed costs due to the direct effect of fixed costs and the effect of fixed costs on the level of consumption. The total benefits with the firm are only subject to the direct effects of fixed costs, because consumption levels do not depend on fixed costs.

With fixed costs equal to zero, the consumer cooperative attains the social optimum, because it offers a marginal cost price. The firm does not attain the social optimum, because monopoly nonlinear pricing departs from marginal cost pricing. As fixed costs increase, the consumer cooperative experiences lower total benefits than the firm, because the average-cost price rises with fixed costs. There is a critical value of fixed costs, K^*, such that the consumer cooperative has higher total benefits for fixed costs less than K^*, and the firm has higher total benefits for fixed costs greater than K^*. Thus, the firm increases efficiency with sufficiently large fixed costs.

9.1.5 Competitive Pricing by Firms

When the total benefits generated by the firm are greater than with a consumer cooperative, consumers are made better off by selling their ownership of the consumer cooperative. The firm can generate greater benefits through price discrimination, although the benefits are offset by the firm's market power. The comparison between the consumer cooperative and the firm in the preceding discussion considered the firm in isolation and thus assumed that the firm had monopoly power. Suppose instead that the firm announces both prices and profit-share bids. The members of the cooperative will sell only if the firm will make them better off. This requires the firm to compete with the consumer cooperative and reduces its market power.[7]

The firm can improve on what the consumer cooperative offers by adjusting its prices. The firm will choose an output for the low-demand consumer that lies between q_1^M and q_1^0. This will raise the fixed payment of the low-demand consumer and lower the fixed payment of the high-demand consumer relative to that offered by the unconstrained monopolist. Therefore, there exists a set of contracts such that the firm is profitable, and the firm offers greater benefits than the consumer cooperative, $G > g$.

---

7 Demsetz (1968b) examines competition between firms for a franchise to operate a regulated firm. Demsetz's analysis is carried out for with linear pricing, with firms bidding the average-cost price to obtain the franchise. Spulber (1989b) extends this approach to free entry pricing with price discrimination and nonlinear pricing.

Next, consider free-entry competition between firms. Firms compete to serve customers, so that their profit is zero. A firm's break-even allocation determines the minimum distortion away from the efficient outcome for the low-demand consumer. Thus q_1^C solves

$$\Pi\left(q_1^C\right) = 0.$$

Because the consumer surplus of the low-demand consumers evaluated at the marginal cost price does not cover their share of fixed cost, it follows that the low-demand consumer's output when the firm breaks even must be less than the first-degree price-discrimination output level at which marginal willingness to pay equals marginal cost. The marginal price for the low-demand consumer is thus above marginal cost, $u(q_1, \mu_1) > c$, whereas that of the high-demand consumer equals marginal cost; see Figure 9.2. This is the minimum distortion needed to cover the firm's fixed costs. The departure from the first-best level of net benefits is

$$n_1 \int_{q_1^C}^{q_1^*} (u(q, \mu_1) - c)dq.$$

The price-discriminating firm generates greater total net benefits than the consumer cooperative operating with payments based on average cost, so that $G > g$.

9.2 The Firm and Public Goods

Public goods have the property of nonrivalrous consumption. Many consumers can obtain benefits from the same supply of the good without reducing the benefits each receive, that is, without congestion and without division of the good. Access to such goods often can be excluded, so that users must pay to have access to the goods. Excludable public goods include information, software, entertainment, education, television and radio programs transmitted by cable and satellite, Internet-based services, and global positioning satellite (GPS) location services. The discussion in this section applies to negative external effects, such as congestion, that can be addressed by consumer coordination. The discussion also applies to positive external effects, such as network effects, that provide consumers with incentives for joint production.

These types of public goods, also referred to as club goods, are provided by a variety of institutions. Consumers can form clubs and associations to establish recreational facilities or to sponsor an orchestra. Firms provide many types of non-rival but excludable public goods; for example, cable television companies charge for access to programming. Governments also provide public goods, including *pure* public goods that are both nonrivalrous and nonexcludable, such as national defense. Local governments provide local public goods that are confined to specific locations, so consumers can choose their locations taking into account the costs and benefits of the local public goods in different areas.[8]

Consider the role of the firm in the provision of public goods that are non-rivalrous but excludable. Suppose, as in the preceding section, that members of the consumer cooperative divest their ownership shares to outside investors. The members of the cooperative remain as customers and obtain the public good from the firm while also receiving payments from the outside investors. The separation of consumer objectives from owner objectives transforms the consumer cooperative into a firm. The firm overcomes the free rider problem that is faced by members of the consumer cooperative.

9.2.1 The Efficient Amount of the Public Good

Consider an economy with n consumers. Each consumer derives utility from consuming a public good Q and a private good x, which is the numeraire good. The consumer utility functions have the form

$$(28) \qquad U(Q, x, v_i) = v_i Q^{1/2} + x^{1/2}, \quad i = 1, \ldots, n,$$

where $v_i > 0$ is consumer i's taste parameter. Each consumer has an initial endowment of the private good ω. The mean of the consumer taste parameters equals

$$(29) \qquad v^* = (1/n) \sum_{i=1}^{n} v_i.$$

The technology for producing the public good is commonly available. The technology is represented by the cost function $C(Q) = cQ$.

The classic optimality condition for the provision of public goods is due to Samuelson (1954a). The sum of consumer marginal rates of substitution between the public and private good equals the marginal rate of transformation between the public and private good. The marginal rate of substitution for consumer i is

$$(30) \qquad \mathrm{MRS}_i = v_i Q^{-1/2} / x_i^{-1/2}.$$

The resource constraint is $\sum_{i=1}^{n} x_i = n\omega - cQ$. The marginal rate of transformation equals the marginal cost of producing the public good, $\mathrm{MRT} = c$. Thus, the optimality condition is $\sum_{i=1}^{n} \mathrm{MRS}_i = \mathrm{MRT}$, so that

$$(31) \qquad \sum_{i=1}^{n} v_i x_i^{1/2} / Q^{1/2} = c.$$

With equal welfare weights, the marginal utilities of consumption of the private good are equal across consumers, $\partial U_i / \partial x = \partial U_j / \partial x$. With the particular separable form of consumer utility functions assumed here, this implies that consumption

---

8 See the classic discussions in Tiebout (1956), Buchanan (1965), and McGuire (1974). See Cornes and Sandler (1986) for a survey and additional discussion.

levels of the private good are equal across consumers. Thus, each consumer pays an equal share of the public good,

(32) $$x_i = \omega - cQ/n, \quad i = 1, \ldots, n.$$

Substituting for x_i in equation (31), we can find the efficient level of the public good,

(33) $$Q^* = \frac{\omega n^2 v^{*2}}{c^2 + ncv^{*2}}.$$

Define the function $Q(v)$ as follows:

(34) $$Q(v) = \frac{\omega n^2 v^2}{c^2 + ncv^2}.$$

The efficient amount of the public good is $Q^* = Q(v^*)$. The function is increasing in v, so that the efficient level of the public good is increasing in the mean of the consumer taste parameters.

9.2.2 Production of the Public Good by a Consumer Cooperative

Because of the advantages of jointly producing the public good, consumers have an incentive to form a cooperative. Consumers benefit because consumption of the public good is nonrivalrous and production costs can be shared. Consumers jointly manage the public good cooperative. To represent transaction costs, assume that consumers employ a noncooperative allocating procedure. The preceding discussion showed the effects of noncooperative allocation with economies of scale. The effects of noncooperative allocation are substantially different with public goods.

Each consumer i proposes a number of units of the public good q_i and pays the costs of producing those units. The total of consumer proposals is the amount of the public good that is produced, $Q = \sum_{i=1}^{n} q_i$. All consumers derive utility from the public good. The Nash equilibrium proposals q_i^0 are the solutions to

$$\max_{q_i} \ v_i \left(q_i + Q_{(i)}^0\right)^{1/2} + (\omega - cq_i)^{1/2}, \quad i = 1, \ldots, n,$$

where $Q_{(i)}^0$ is the sum of the Nash equilibrium proposals of all consumers other than i.

The consumers' first-order conditions simplify to yield

(35) $$(c/v_i)^2 \left(q_i^0 + Q_{(i)}^0\right) = \omega - cq_i^0, \quad i = 1, \ldots, n.$$

Noting that $q_i^0 + Q_{(i)}^0 = Q^0$, sum both sides of equation (35) and solve for total production of the public good,

(36) $$Q^0 = \frac{n^2 \omega}{c^2 \left[n \sum_{i=1}^{n}(1/v_i)^2\right] + cn}.$$

To evaluate the efficiency of the consumers' cooperative, compare the amount of the public good produced by the consumer cooperative with the optimal amount of the public good. The cooperative's public good output can be written as $Q^0 = Q(v^0)$; the function $Q(v)$ is defined in equation (34), and

$$(37) \qquad v^0 = \left[n \sum_{i=1}^{n} (1/v_i)^2 \right]^{-1/2}.$$

It is sufficient to compare the term v^0 with the mean of the distribution of consumer taste parameters, v^*. By standard inequality arguments, it follows that

$$v^{*2} = \left[(1/n) \sum_{i=1}^{n} v_i \right]^2 > (1/n^2) \sum_{i=1}^{n} (v_i)^2 > \left[n \sum_{i=1}^{n} (1/v_i)^2 \right]^{-1} = (v^0)^2.$$

Because $v^* > v^0$ and the function $Q(v)$ is increasing in v, the cooperative produces a smaller than optimal amount of the public good, $Q^* > Q^0$. The net benefit generated by the consumer cooperative is given by

$$(38) \qquad g = \sum_{i=1}^{n} \left[v_i (Q^0)^{1/2} + (\omega - c q_i^0)^{1/2} \right].$$

Substituting from the consumers' first-order conditions (35), the net benefits generated by the consumer cooperative equal

$$(39) \qquad g = \sum_{i=1}^{n} (v_i + c/v_i)(Q^0)^{1/2}.$$

Consider the effect of the number of consumers on the consumer cooperative. Suppose, for example, that consumers are evenly divided between types v_1 and v_2, where $v_1 < v_2$. Then total output of the consumer cooperative equals

$$(40) \qquad Q^0(n) = \frac{\omega}{c^2 [(1/2)(1/v_1)^2 + (1/2)(1/v_2)^2] + c/n}.$$

As n gets large, the total output of the cooperative, $Q^0(n)$, increases to a finite limit.

Because the consumer cooperative is jointly managed by consumers and the level of public good production is chosen through a noncooperative equilibrium, production of the public good is suboptimal. Consumers engage in free riding, lowering their proposed bid amounts to shift costs to other consumers. In equilibrium, all consumers choose their proposals in anticipation of free riding by other consumers. Free riding, and the resulting reduction in output of the public good relative to a joint optimum, is a transaction cost of joint production in the consumer cooperative.

9.2.3 Production of the Public Good by a Firm

A firm can add value if it can alleviate the free rider problem. The firm can charge for access to the public good, because the good is excludable. Suppose that consumers in the cooperative sell their ownership shares to investors who bid the firm's anticipated profits in equilibrium. Each consumer in the cooperative receives an equal share of the firm's profits, Π/n, because the consumers are selling their ownership of the cooperative to investors. The firm charges all of its customers a lump-sum price P for access to the public good Q. So, $x = \omega + \Pi/n - P$.

The basic issues can be illustrated for the case of two types of consumers.[9] Suppose that the n consumers are evenly divided between types v_1 and v_2, where $v_1 < v_2$. Taking the firm's price and the share of profits as givens, a consumer of type i purchases the public good if

$$U(Q, x, v_i) = v_i Q^{1/2} + (\omega + \Pi/n - P)^{1/2} \geq (\omega + \Pi/n)^{1/2} \quad i = 1, 2.$$

The demand for the firm's output equals the number of consumers who benefit from purchasing the public good, $D(P; \Pi/n, Q) \leq n$.

The firm's profits are

$$(41) \qquad\qquad \Pi = PD(P; \Pi/n, Q) - cQ.$$

The firm chooses the price P and the quantity of the public good Q to maximize profits. This can be separated into two problems. First, the firm chooses the price to maximize revenue for a given amount of the public good. Second, the firm chooses the profit-maximizing output of the public good, trading off the revenue gained from increasing the amount of the public good against the additional production cost. The firm may choose a low price and sell to both types of consumers or the firm may choose a high price and sell only to the high-parameter consumers. It can be shown that with many consumers, the profit-maximizing firm will choose to sell to both types of consumers.

When selling to both types of consumers, the firm increases the price until the low-demand consumers are indifferent between purchasing and not purchasing the public good,

$$(42) \qquad U(Q, x, v_1) = v_1 Q^{1/2} + (\omega + \Pi/n - P)^{1/2} = (\omega + \Pi/n)^{1/2}.$$

This determines the price as a function of the quantity of the public good, $P = P(Q)$. Given the price function P, the firm's profit-maximization problem is

$$(43) \qquad\qquad \Pi = \max_Q P(Q)n - cQ.$$

The firm's first-order condition is then

$$(44) \qquad\qquad\qquad P'(Q)n = c.$$

---

9 The analysis can be extended to allow for many types of consumers. A similar comparison of pricing by a firm with cost-sharing by a consumer cooperative can be carried out when consumers have private information about their demand parameters.

Differentiating equation (42) gives the effect of the amount of the public good on the firm's price,

$$(45) \qquad P'(Q) = \frac{v_1 Q^{-1/2}}{(\omega + \Pi/n - P)^{-1/2}}.$$

To obtain the amount of the public good produced by the firm, substitute from equation (45) into the firm's first-order condition (44),

$$(46) \qquad (c/nv_1)^2 Q = \omega + \Pi/n - P.$$

Substituting for the equilibrium share of profits $\Pi/n = P - cQ/n$, the amount of the public good produced by the firm equals

$$(47) \qquad Q^F(n) = Q(v_1) = \frac{\omega n^2 (v_1)^2}{c^2 + nc(v_1)^2}.$$

The firm's output is less than the optimal amount, because the low-demand consumer's parameter is less than the mean. Substitute from equation (46) into equation (42) to obtain the firm's profit, $\Pi = nP - cQ$,

$$(48) \qquad \Pi = n[v_1 + c/(nv_1)]^2 Q^F - n\omega.$$

Profit is greater than if the firm were to sell only to high-demand consumers.[10]

The total benefits generated by the firm equal

$$(49) \qquad G = \sum_{i=1}^{n} [v_i(Q^F)^{1/2} + (\omega - \Pi/n - P)^{1/2}].$$

10 Consider the case in which the firm only sells to the high-demand consumers. The firm's profit equals $\Pi_H = nP/2 - cQ$, so that the firm's first-order condition is $P'(Q)n/2 = c$. The firm's profits are distributed to both types of consumers since they are selling the cooperative to outside investors. The firm exercises its market power by raising the price until the high-demand consumers are indifferent between purchasing and not purchasing the public good,

$$U(Q, x, v_2) = v_2 Q^{1/2} + (\omega + \Pi/n - P)^{1/2} = (\omega + \Pi/n)^{1/2}.$$

Differentiate the high-type consumer's indifference condition to obtain the effect of the amount of the public good on the firm's price. Substituting into the firm's profit-maximization condition gives

$$(2c/nv_2)^2 Q = \omega + \Pi/n - P.$$

Substitute into the high-type consumer's indifference condition to obtain

$$[v_2 + 2c/(nv_2)]^2 Q = \omega + \Pi/n.$$

Combine the prior two equations and apply the firm's profit function, $2\Pi/n = P - 2cQ/n$, to solve for the firm's output of the public good,

$$Q_H^F = \frac{\omega n^2 (v_2)^2}{2c^2 + nc(v_2)^2 + (1/2)[2c + n(v_2)^2]^2}.$$

The firm's profit equals $\Pi_H = n[v_2 + 2c/(nv_2)]^2 Q_H^F - n\omega$. Comparing with the firm's profit from serving both types of consumers, given in equation (48), implies that $\Pi > \Pi_H$ for all $n > c[1/(v_1)^2 - 4/(v_2)^2]$.

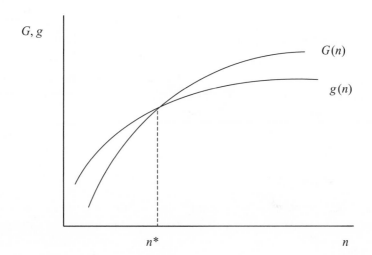

Figure 9.4. The firm generates greater gains from trade than the consumer organization when there are a large number of consumers.

Substituting from the firm's first-order condition, the total benefits of the firm equal

$$(50) \qquad G(n) = ((n/2)v_1 + (n/2)v_2 + c/v_1)(Q^F(n))^{1/2}.$$

The average benefits with the firm equal

$$(51) \quad G(n)/n = [(n^{1/2}/2)v_1 + (n^{1/2}/2)v_2 + cn^{-1/2}/v_1]\left[\frac{\omega(v_1)^2}{c^2/n + c(v_1)^2}\right]^{1/2}.$$

Average benefits are increasing in the number of consumers for large n. The first bracketed term is increasing in n for $n > c/(v_1)^2$. The second bracketed term is everywhere increasing in n. This implies that as n gets large, average benefits continue to increase.

Compare the equilibrium with a firm with the consumer cooperative. Total benefits for the consumer cooperative with two types of consumers equal

$$(52) \qquad g(n) = [(n/2)(v_1 + c/v_1) + (n/2)(v_2 + c/v_2)](Q^0(n))^{1/2}.$$

The average benefits with the consumer cooperative equal

$$(53) \qquad g(n)/n = [(1/2)(v_1 + c/v_1) + (1/2)(v_2 + c/v_2)](Q^0(n))^{1/2}.$$

Recall that total output for the consumer cooperative reaches a finite limit as n gets large. So, for large n, average benefits for members of the consumer cooperative are less than average benefits with a firm, $G(n)/n > g(n)/n$. This implies that for large enough n, total benefits are greater with a firm than with a consumer cooperative, $G(n) > g(n)$. This is illustrated in Figure 9.4.

The firm's output is greater than that of the consumer cooperative; that is, $Q^F > Q^0$ for all $n \geq 2$. The firm's output of the public good is increasing in the number of consumers, whereas the consumer cooperative's output approaches a finite limit due to free riding. The firm adds value by offering a fixed price for the public good. This coordinates consumption decisions and eliminates free riding. The use of prices for allocation lowers transaction costs and allows the firm to increase production of the public good. The firm's profits reflect the increased consumer benefits that result from greater output of the public good. By separating consumption decisions from production decisions, the firm increases economic efficiency in the provision of public goods.

9.2.4 The Firm and Public Goods: Mechanism Design

The firm can design a revelation mechanism to allocate the cost of the public goods under asymmetric information. The firm addresses asymmetric information about consumer types by designing a mechanism to induce consumers to reveal their private information. The firm uses the information to determine payments for the public good, to allocate access to the public good among consumers, and to decide how much of the public good to produce.

The firm can use revelation mechanisms in a manner consistent with profit maximization. The firm employs a profit-maximizing procedure that is based on the Vickrey (1961) auction for private goods; see also Clarke (1971) and Groves (1973).[11] An optimal mechanism auctions access to the public good. Vickrey-Clarke-Groves mechanisms, which use dominant strategies, not only are efficient mechanisms but also maximize revenues. The standard approach to public goods has focused on social welfare maximization. In that setting, mechanisms that allocate public goods with dominant strategies generally run a surplus; see Green and Laffont (1977). Most discussions characterize such mechanisms and the resulting allocations as inefficient. The allocation departs from Pareto efficiency because the mechanism designer's budget does not balance. The surplus cannot be returned to individual consumers because doing so would affect their incentives to report truthfully and thus alter the performance of the mechanism. Although Bayesian incentive-compatible mechanisms balance the social planner's budget, they may not satisfy individual rationality; see Arrow (1979) and d'Aspremont and Gérard-Varet (1979).[12]

For firms, however, the presence of a surplus is a positive feature of an allocation mechanism. Profit allows the firm to operate and obtain resources, while providing incentives for competition and entry. Thus, with profit-maximizing firms designing the mechanism, the surplus generated by the mechanism is a benefit rather than

11 There are many studies in the mechanism design literature that focus on the design of a mechanism by a social planner seeking Pareto-optimal outcomes; see for example Groves and Ledyard (1977), Green and Laffont (1977), Hurwicz (1979), Walker (1981), and Ledyard and Palfrey (1994).
12 Krishna and Perry (1998) show that there exists a socially efficient incentive-compatible and individually rational mechanism that balances the budget if and only if the Vickrey-Clarke-Groves mechanism results in an expected surplus.

a deadweight loss. Firms have a wider choice of mechanisms than the budget-balancing social planner.

Krishna and Perry (1998) point out that a generalized version of the Vickrey-Clarke-Groves mechanism maximizes expected revenues among all mechanisms that maximize social welfare. Although this property conflicts with social welfare maximization by a social planner, it does not conflict with profit maximization but rather enhances it. Profit-maximizing firms are not affected by the budget-balancing restriction, so that they can use mechanisms with dominant strategies. The profit-maximizing allocation need not be socially optimal, but it may be more efficient than allocations chosen by a budget-balancing consumer cooperative.

9.3 The Firm and Common-Property Resources

When there are common-property resources, a consumer cooperative will experience consumption externalities. With small numbers of consumers, cooperative solutions are possible and consumers can allocate the resource efficiently. With many consumers, there will be noncooperative usage of the resources. Free riding can be compared to a race in which consumers have an incentive to use more of the resource in anticipation of the usage of other consumers. Firms offer the advantage of allocating the resource among consumers using prices. When firms own and manage the resources, they can enhance allocative efficiency, because prices mitigate racing and conserve resources.

9.3.1 Allocation of Common-Property Resources by the Consumer Cooperative

Consumers may form a cooperative to allocate common-property resources. These might include exhaustible resources such as minerals, oil and natural gas, and renewable resources such as fish, game, lumber, and pastures. The ability of the consumer cooperative to allocate common-property resources depends on the transaction costs of coordination. When transaction costs are high, the result will be inefficient usage. When transaction costs are low, consumers may be able to coordinate their actions and allocate the resource efficiently.[13]

Inefficient competitive use of common-property resources often is referred to as the "tragedy of the commons." The expression is due to Garrett Hardin (1968), who cites a pamphlet written in 1833 by a mathematical amateur named William Forster Lloyd (1794–1852). Hardin discusses overpopulation, pollution, and resource depletion using a hypothetical story about overgrazing in the common area of medieval villages.

---

13 The discussion in this section draws from Spulber (2002a).

> Picture a pasture open to all. It is to be expected that each herdsman will try
> to keep as many cattle as possible on the commons. Such an arrangement
> may work reasonably satisfactorily for centuries because tribal wars, poaching,
> and disease keep the numbers of both man and beast well below the carrying
> capacity of the land. Finally, however, comes the day of reckoning, that is, the
> day when the long-desired goal of social stability becomes a reality. At this
> point, the inherent logic of the commons remorselessly generates tragedy.

If the common grazing area belongs to everyone it belongs to no one, the argument goes; villagers will have no incentive to preserve the resource and will put more farm animals to graze on it until the grass is depleted. The problem of overgrazing also appears in historical accounts such as Slater (1932), Gonner (1966), and Coleman (1977). For example, Gonner (1966, p. 25) states that "As many beasts are put on the common as possible . . . with the result that the common is overstocked."

Economists have written widely on the exhaustion of rents from common property resources; see for example Gordon (1954), Cheung (1970), and Spulber (1982). If property rights to a natural resource are not properly specified, individuals will compete to deplete the resource, whether it is a fishery, forest, or pool of crude oil underground. Even if the costs of extracting the resource prevent its depletion, competition without property rights will result in the dissipation of economic returns to the resource. If the resource were owned by one individual, then it would presumably be managed to maximize the economic returns from the resource. As with environmental pollution, which takes advantage of common ownership of air and water resources, the use of exhaustible resources is likely to depend on property rights.

How then to resolve the property rights problem? Rousseau's *Social Contract* and Hobbes' *Leviathan* address the origins of property rights and social agreements. One approach is to assign property rights to the government, which can exploit the resource itself, regulate access, or license private parties to use the resource in a controlled fashion. An important question is whether rent dissipation is inevitable in the absence of government assignments of property rights or the specification of property rights by a legal system with government enforcement.

The story of the feudal and medieval commons has been repeated often in public policy discussions of natural resources and environmental pollution and bears further examination. The notion that the enclosure acts were intended to replace an inefficient institution and that enclosure enhanced efficiency has been challenged. As Ostrom (1990, p. 224) notes, economic historians have provided a different picture of English land tenure before and after the enclosure acts that suggests a greater degree of cooperation in the management of agricultural land; see Thirsk (1967), McClosky (1976), Dahlman (1980), Yelling (1977), Allen (1982), and Fanoaltea (1988).

Ostrom (1990) identifies cooperative agreements as means of governing the commons, in contrast with the extremes of unified private ownership or government control. She distinguishes between open access resources and common property when managed by a clearly defined social group. Ostrom provides evidence that cooperative-choice arrangements for managing common property functioned well, in some cases for centuries, in Swiss alpine meadows, Japanese mountain commons, and irrigation institutions in the Spanish huertas or the Philippine zanjeras; see also Feeny et al. (1996). Ostrom also identifies problems that may arise by examining Turkish fisheries and groundwater allocation in California basins when access is not restricted and there are high transaction costs of cooperative agreements.

John Umbeck (1977) examines the private establishment of property rights in the context of the California gold rush of 1848 and 1849. There were no property rights, because California had just become a territory of the United States and the Governor, Colonel Mason, abolished Mexican laws pertaining to acquisition of mining rights on public lands without offering an alterative (Umbeck, 1977, p. 203). The gains from establishing property rights are likely to increase the more valuable is the resource. However, Umbeck suggests that the transaction costs of establishing property rights also will increase the more valuable is the resource. If the gains outweigh the costs for valuable resources, private parties may then establish property rights themselves without government intervention. In the case of the gold rush, the miners formed explicit contracts that allowed them to exploit their claims exclusively, to enforce their claims, and even to buy and sell those claims, thus creating a system of private property rights. Umbeck's analysis suggests that transaction costs can be more fundamental than property rights. Even if property rights are absent or not well defined, consumers or producers can create a system of property rights if transaction costs are sufficiently low relative to gains from trade to permit coordination.

This discussion is closely related to the insightful discussion of environmental pollution by Ronald Coase (1960) in "The Problem of Social Cost." Coase empha- sizes that if there were no transaction costs, private bargaining would alleviate the problem of external damages from pollution. Those generating pollution or neigh- borhood beautification, and the affected bystanders, could get together and reach an efficient bargain. The outcome of the bargain would be less pollution or more neighborhood beautification. Coase concludes that the problem of social cost stems from the presence of transaction costs.

Coase shows the importance of allocating property rights as a basis for private bargaining over external effects. Without an initial assignment of liability or estab- lishment of rights, "there can be no market transactions to transfer and recombine them." The main assertion, which has come to be known as the Coase theorem, is that "the ultimate result (which maximizes the value of production) is inde- pendent of the legal position if the pricing system is assumed to work without cost." With low transaction costs, the assignment of property rights affects the transfers between the parties in the negotiation but does not interfere with the efficiency of the outcome; see Spulber (1989b, Chapters 12 and 13) for further discussion.

Coase's insight into the way that bargaining adjusts to legal institutions to achieve an efficient outcome has proven to be fundamental to the economic analysis of law. Consumers and firms adjust the terms of their transactions and contracts in response to the particular form of legal rules. When transaction costs are low, alternative legal rules often have neutral effects on economic agreements as long as the law provides a clear assignment of rights. Moreover, when transaction costs are low, private bargaining can resolve problems of social costs without government intervention in the direct regulation of external effects.

Cheung's (1973) investigation of "The Fable of the Bees" provides a clear and compelling illustration of Coase's insight that private bargaining internalizes social benefits and costs. Beekeepers and farmers enter into voluntary agreements that capture the benefits of pollination provided by the bees and if applicable, the benefits to honey production from the orchard. Beekeepers and orchard owners can form pollination contracts when transaction benefits justify transaction costs. There is no market failure that calls out for correction by a government agency.[14] In practice, there are contracts for the rental of millions of bee colonies per year.[15]

In the allocation of common property resources or the management of environmental externalities, consumers can coordinate their activities when transaction costs are low. Thus, consumers may be able to create and enforce a system of property rights that improves the allocation of access to the commons. With environmental externalities, consumers may be able to create a system of property rights to allocate usage of the environment. If there are property rights for the environment, then with low transaction costs, consumers can potentially negotiate over environmental usage and payments to compensate each other for damages or benefits.

Coase (1960) emphasizes that a critical determinant of transaction costs is the number of parties to the negotiation. When there are many involved, bargaining costs are likely to increase. This suggests that with many consumers, access to common property resources and environmental resources is likely to be competitive rather than cooperative. When there are many consumers and the resulting costs of negotiation are significant, consumers will behave in a noncooperative fashion.

The problem of racing to deplete a renewable resource such as a fishery has been widely studied.[16] The comparison between the performance of the consumer cooperative and the monopoly firm in the case of renewable resources is closely related to the case of exhaustible resources. The fundamental difference is that

---

14 This is contrary to the discussions of Meade (1952) and Bator (1958) in the tradition of Pigou (1920b).

15 See Morse and Calderone (2000).

16 See for example Clark (1976, 1985) and Mirman and Spulber (1982). Levhari et al. (1982) examine a monopoly fishery of the type studied here. Levhari and Mirman (1980) present a noncooperative model of the open access fishery that is also related to the model considered in this section.

racing to deplete the stock of a renewable resource lowers the parent stock of the next generation and therefore impacts its prospects for growth.

Consider how noncooperative use of common property resources affects economic efficiency. Generally, the results of noncooperative behavior are a departure from Pareto optimality. In the case of common property resources, free riding behavior takes the form of racing. Consumers hurry to exploit the common resources before others do. Nash equilibrium consumption occurs more rapidly than is efficient.

To represent this situation, suppose that there are n consumers. All consumers have the same per-period utility function $U(q)$, where q is consumption of the common property resource. Consumers live for two periods and discount the utility at the common rate $\rho > 0$. Assume that extraction costs are zero.

Let K be the initial stock of the resource. Letting q_{it} be consumer i's consumption of the resource in period t, total initial period consumption cannot exceed the initial stock:

$$\sum_{i=1}^{n} q_{i1} \leq K.$$

Let K_2 be the amount of the resource at the beginning of the second period. If the resource is renewable, its biological growth function is $K_2 = K^\gamma$, where γ is a positive parameter less than one. If the resource is exhaustible, then $K_2 = K$, which corresponds to the case where $\gamma = 1$. Thus, in what follows, $\gamma < 1$ denotes the renewable resource case and $\gamma = 1$ denotes the exhaustible resource case. Thus, the amount of the resource in the second period is

(54)
$$K_2 = \left(K - \sum_{i=1}^{n} q_{i1} \right)^\gamma,$$

where $\gamma \leq 1$.

Consumption in the second period cannot exceed the amount of the resource that is available:

$$\sum_{i=1}^{n} q_{i2} \leq K_2.$$

Because utility is increasing and there are no extraction costs, consumers will prefer to use all of the resources remaining in the second period. Consumers are identical so the resources in the second period are divided equally,

(55)
$$q_{i2} = (1/n) \left(K - \sum_{j=1}^{n} q_{j1} \right)^\gamma,$$

for all $i = 1, \ldots, n$.

Let q_{i1}^0 be the Nash equilibrium consumption levels in the first period, and let $Q_{(i)}^0$ be the sum of the first-period consumption levels of all consumers other than i. Then the Nash equilibrium consumption of consumer i solves

$$\max_{q_{i1}} U(q_{i1}) + \frac{1}{1+\rho} U\left((1/n)\left(K - Q_{(i)}^0 - q_{i1}\right)^\gamma\right).$$

By symmetry, all consumers have the same consumption, $q_{i1}^0 = q^0$, $i = 1, \ldots, n$. Thus, the consumer's first-order condition implies that

(56) $$U'(q^0) = \frac{1}{1+\rho} U'((1/n)(K - nq^0)^\gamma)\frac{\gamma}{n}(K - nq^0)^{\gamma-1}.$$

The marginal rate of substitution between future and current consumption is less than the marginal rate of transformation:

(57) $$\frac{U'(q^0)}{[1/(1+\rho)]U'((1/n)(K - nq^0)^\gamma)} = \frac{\gamma}{n}(K - nq^0)^{\gamma-1}.$$

The reason is the presence of n on the right-hand side, which is due to free riding or racing behavior at the noncooperative equilibrium. In the case of an exhaustible resource, $\gamma = 1$, equation (57) implies that the marginal rate of substitution is equal to $1/n$. This is less than one, which is the marginal rate of transformation for an exhaustible resource.

Compare the rate of consumption chosen by the consumer cooperative with the efficient rate of consumption. The optimal rate of consumption maximizes the present value of benefits per consumer:

$$U(q) + \frac{1}{1+\rho} U((1/n)(K - nq)^\gamma).$$

The first-order condition is

(58) $$U'(q^*) = \frac{1}{1+\rho} U'((1/n)(K - nq^*)^\gamma)\gamma(K - nq^*)^{\gamma-1}.$$

Thus the marginal rate of substitution equals the marginal rate of transformation of the resource stock. It follows from equations (56) and (58), given the concavity of utility and $\gamma \leq 1$, that $q^0 > q^*$. Thus, a consumer cooperative with Nash strategies leads to racing behavior and faster consumption of common resources than is efficient.

9.3.2 Allocation of Common-Property Resources by the Firm

Firms provide an alternative to the consumer cooperative in the management of common-property resources. The firm separates consumption and allocation decisions. Consumers own the firm and receive its profits. The firm charges consumers prices for their consumption of the resource. A monopoly firm can improve the allocation of the common resource over time.

Suppose that consumer utility represents the consumer's money benefits. In period t, the firm offers consumers the price P_t, $t = 1, 2$. In each period, consumers maximize their consumption given the current price, $\max U(q_t) - P_t q_t$, so that

(59) $$U'(q_t) = P_t.$$

The firm thus faces a stationary inverse demand per consumer given by $P(q) = U'(q)$ and revenue $R(q) = U'(q)q$. As with the consumer cooperative, the firm does not have any costs of extracting the resource. The firm discounts future profits at rate ρ. The firm chooses first-period consumption q to maximize the present discounted value of profit per consumer,

$$\max_q R(q) + \frac{1}{1 + \rho} R((1/n)(K - nq)^\gamma).$$

The first-order condition for the monopoly consumption level is

(60) $$R'(q^M) = \frac{1}{1 + \rho} R'((1/n)(K - nq^M)^\gamma)\gamma(K - nq^M)^{\gamma - 1}.$$

With a general consumer utility function, the monopolist's rate of extraction of the resource may be less than, equal to, or greater than the efficient rate.[17] With extraction costs, the first-period marginal profit equals the discounted value of marginal profit times the marginal product of the remaining resource, so that again the monopolist's rate of extraction may be less than, equal to, or greater than the efficient rate. If the monopolist discounts future profits at a different rate than consumers, the monopolist's rate of extraction can again be less than, equal to, or greater than the efficient rate.

Consider the monopoly solution for the special case of constant-elasticity demand. Let consumer utility be $U(q) = q^\alpha$ for α less than one.[18] Then revenue equals $R(q) = \alpha q^\alpha$ and marginal revenue is proportional to the price $R'(q) = \alpha^2 q^{\alpha - 1} = \alpha P(q)$. In this case, the monopolist chooses consumption levels such that prices satisfy the efficiency condition

(61) $$P(q^M) = \frac{1}{1 + \rho} P((1/n)(K - nq^M)^\gamma)\gamma(K - nq^M)^{\gamma - 1}.$$

Because $P(q) = U'(q)$, it follows that the monopoly firm chooses a rate of consumption that is equal to the optimal rate of consumption, $q^M = q^* < q^0$. Thus, the monopoly allocates consumption of the resource efficiently over time and performs better than the consumer cooperative. The more consumers there are, the greater the impact of racing in the consumer cooperative. Thus, the more consumers there are, the greater the distortion in comparison with the efficient level. This means that with many consumers and constant-elasticity demand,

---

17 On efficient extraction of an exhaustible resource, see Hotelling (1931).
18 See Stiglitz (1976) for a related discussion of monopoly and exhaustible resources.

the greater is the advantage of the monopoly firm in comparison with the consumer cooperative. The monopolist conserves the resource relative to the consumer cooperative.

More consumers increases the transaction costs of the consumer cooperative leading to greater racing for general utility functions. Because the racing effect increases for the consumer cooperative, but not for the firm, the firm's allocation of resources is likely to be better than that of the consumer cooperative when there are many consumers.

Noncooperative behavior also can apply when the players are firms. For example, Libecap and Wiggins (1984, 1985) and Wiggins and Libecap (1985) examine problems that arise when firms encounter common-pool problems in oil fields. Firms can engage in noncooperative behavior in extracting the resource. Private negotiation to unitize oil fields can fail when firms experience high costs of bargaining and contracting and encounter asymmetric information. Libecap and Wiggins (1984) show that with many small firms, unitization is less likely than it is with greater industry concentration. This suggests that management of common resources by large firms is preferable to management by many small firms. The transaction-costs savings from consolidation of ownership would still apply if there were many small households that shared ownership of a resource. The households benefit by relying on one or more firms to manage the resource, with each household receiving a share of the firms' profits. Consolidation of ownership, as well as economies of scale, help to explain why large energy companies conduct much of oil and gas exploration and extraction.

9.4 Conclusions

The comparison between the firm and the consumer organization contrasts with the familiar dichotomy between private and public allocation of resources. In the presence of economies of scale, public goods, common-property resources, and externalities, market allocations may depart from the neoclassical ideal. This leads to various recommendations for public intervention in markets: price regulation and antitrust in the case of economies of scale, public provision in the case of public goods, and environmental regulation in the case of common-property resources and externalities. However, alleged market failures must be weighed against government failures, as Ronald Coase has cautioned.

The theory of the firm compares two private alternatives, the consumer organization and the firm. When transactions costs are low, consumers can find ways to allocate resources efficiently, handling potential problems associated with economies of scale, public goods, common-property resources, and externalities. When transaction costs are high, particularly when there are many consumers, firms provide alternative private solutions. Through prices, auctions, and other mechanisms, firms enhance the efficiency of resource allocation. Firms use quantity-dependent prices to allocate resources when there are economies of scale. If public goods are excludable, firms can use prices to allocate public goods and enhance efficiency in comparison to consumer cooperatives, thus reducing or avoiding free rider problems. With common-property resources and consumption externalities, firms combine ownership and control, avoiding excessive resource use that results from racing behavior.

In each case there are tradeoffs between the efficiencies of allocation through prices and inefficiencies due to distortions that result from market power. When there are many consumers, the consumer cooperative experiences greater free riding. As a consequence, the monopoly firm improves allocative efficiency in comparison to the consumer cooperative when there are many consumers. Competition between firms reduces market-power effects, making firms more efficient in comparison to consumer cooperatives. Competition between firms is likely to be greater in economies where entrepreneurs face low transaction costs of establishing firms and low regulatory barriers to entry.

The firm increases efficiency in the production economy by separating consumption and production decisions. When there are many consumers, free riding causes partnerships to perform less efficiently than firms. By separating the objectives of the organization from the consumption objectives of its owners, the firm alleviates the free rider problem. This allows the firm to increase the gains from joint production. Transaction efficiencies help to explain the observed rarity of consumer cooperatives and the prevalence of firms in economies with many consumers and low barriers to market entry.

PART V

MARKET MAKING BY THE FIRM

10

The Firm Creates Markets

Firms create and manage markets that enhance the efficiency of transactions. By creating markets, firms separate the economy's supply decisions from its demand decisions. Standing between sellers and buyers, firms coordinate their transactions. As matchmakers, firms bring buyers and sellers together. As market makers, firms operate central places of exchange, gather information about supply and demand, and adjust bid and ask prices. Firms make purchasing, sales, inventory, and production decisions that clear markets. This chapter examines the potential role of the firm as a market maker in comparison with direct exchange between consumers.

The essential contribution of firms to economic efficiency comes from the separation of decisions of sellers from the decisions of buyers. The firm offers market-making and matchmaking services that coordinate seller transactions and buyer transactions. Spulber (1999) emphasizes that by establishing transaction institutions, firms determine the market microstructure of the economy. Rather than engaging in direct exchange with each other, buyers and sellers can deal with market-making firms.

Firms enhance the efficiency of transactions by centralizing exchange. Centralization of exchange yields economies of scale in transaction technologies. Centralization of exchange allows the firm to aggregate individual supplies and to aggregate individual demands, avoiding mismatches of individual buyer demands with individual seller supplies. Market-making firms coordinate exchange between buyers and sellers by posting and adjusting prices. Market-making firms provide liquidity in financial markets and immediacy in product markets by standing ready to buy and sell, thus addressing the absence of a double coincidence of wants.

This chapter considers the market-making firm in comparison to search. The discussion considers both markets with homogeneous products and markets with differentiated products. With a homogeneous product, buyers with different valuations and sellers with different costs search for each other. Matches differ in terms of buyer valuations net of seller costs. The firm offers efficiencies in centralized matching by posting bid and ask prices or by establishing a double-auction process. The chapter considers Gehrig's (1993) model, in which a market-making firm competes with a decentralized search market when products are homogeneous.

With differentiated products, each seller offers a unique product. The preferences of each buyer are different from those of other buyers. A buyer receives different benefits from consuming each of the goods. For example, in a housing market, every house has unique features. Each potential home buyer views a house differently than other buyers. Any home buyer values each of the houses differently. With differentiated products, the firm also offers efficiencies in centralized assignment using brokers' fees and double-auction mechanisms. The chapter introduces a model with differentiated products in which a market-making firm competes with a decentralized search market.

The chapter examines competition between firms acting as dealers and a market-making firm. The model of competition between dealers is due to Spulber (1996a) and shows how equilibrium price distributions in a dealer market with search depend on the time costs of search. The chapter also considers extensions of Spulber (1996a) by Rust and Hall (2003) and Hendershott and Zhang (2006) that allow consumers to choose between dealers and a centralized market maker.

10.1 Market Making and Matchmaking by the Firm: Overview

The firm coordinates transactions between sellers and buyers. Through market-making and matchmaking activities, firms separate the economy's supply and demand decisions, thus creating and clearing markets. This section sets out the basic models of market making and matchmaking.

10.1.1 Market Making by the Firm

Market-making firms separate buyer decisions from seller decisions. To illustrate this, consider an economy in which individual consumers are either buyers or sellers. There is a continuum of buyers whose willingness to pay levels are uniformly distributed on the unit interval. Given an ask price $p \leq 1$, aggregate demand equals

$$(1) \qquad D(p) = \Pr\{x : x \geq p\} = 1 - p.$$

Seller opportunity costs are represented by c. There is a continuum of sellers whose costs are uniformly distributed on the unit interval. For a bid price $w \leq 1$, aggregate supply equals

$$(2) \qquad S(w) = \Pr\{y : y \leq w\} = w.$$

Suppose that there is a market-making firm that is a monopoly intermediary between buyers and sellers. The firm's profit function is

$$(3) \qquad \Pi(p, w) = pD(p) - wS(w).$$

The firm chooses the ask price p and the bid price w to maximize profit subject to the constraint that it sells no more than it buys, $D(p) \leq S(w)$. The profit-maximizing firm will always choose ask and bid prices such that the supply constraint is strictly binding.

Let $P(q)$ be the inverse demand function and let $W(Q)$ be the inverse supply function. Because the supply constraint is binding, the firm's profit function can be written as a function of the quantity of goods that are traded, Q:

(4)
$$\Pi(Q) = (P(Q) - W(Q))Q.$$

Define elasticities of demand and supply as $\eta(p) = -pD'(p)/D(p)$ and $\xi(w) = wS'(w)/S(w)$.

The firm's profit maximization problem yields the fundamental price-spread condition

(5)
$$p^* - w^* = p^*/\eta(p^*) + w^*/\xi(w^*)$$

and the market-clearing condition

(6)
$$Q^* = D(p^*) = S(w^*).$$

The firm equates the bid-ask spread to the sum of the reciprocal of the demand elasticity times the ask price and the reciprocal of the supply elasticity times the bid price. The profit-maximizing prices are set such that the bid-ask spread, $p^* - w^*$, is both positive and finite. The finiteness of the spread is significant since it shows that a monopolist earns arbitrage profits but does not increase the spread without bound. Solving the firm's maximization problem, the ask price is $p^* = 3/4$, the bid price is $w^* = 1/4$, and the quantity traded is $Q^* = 1/4$. The market equilibrium with a market-making firm is shown in Figure 10.1.

10.1.2 Matchmaking by the Firm with Homogeneous Products

Consider a firm that acts as a matchmaker. Let lump-sum subscription fees be P for buyers and W for sellers.[1] Let buyers and sellers engage in Nash bargaining after a match is made. If subscription fees are paid *after* a match is made, then only the total of subscription fees matters. Let b equal the total of subscription fees,

(7)
$$b = P + W.$$

If subscription fees are paid *before* a match is made, the greater of the buyer and seller fees determines their ex ante decisions to participate in the network. Because the higher of the two fees determines participation decisions by buyers and

---

1 Caillaud and Julien (2003) refer to ex ante fees as connection or registration fees and they refer to ex post fees as transaction fees. Their framework differs from the present one because in their model, all buyers are identical and all sellers are identical, and there is only one acceptable match for each individual.

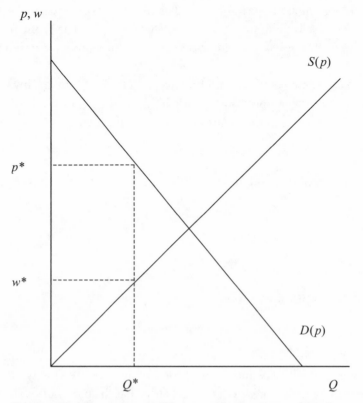

Figure 10.1. The market equilibrium with a market-making firm.

sellers, the firm will choose to set equal fees, $P = W = b/2$. Thus, the same level of participation will be observed under the two scenarios for the same total of the fees b.

Consider the firm's choice of the total of buyer and seller subscription fees, b. The monopoly matchmaker chooses b to maximize profit. Consider a continuum of buyers and a continuum of sellers, both of which are uniformly distributed on the unit interval with unit density. The total of the buyers' fee and the sellers' fee is b. For any b less than one, the marginal pair is such that the market clears and gains from trade equal the total fee:

$$(8) \qquad\qquad\qquad\qquad 1 - v = c,$$

$$(9) \qquad\qquad\qquad\qquad v - c = b.$$

Thus, the marginal pair is given by $v^{**} = (1 + b)/2$ and $c^{**} = (1 - b)/2$. Output is $Q(b) = (1 - b)/2$. Let $P^D(Q)$ and $P^S(Q)$ be inverse demand and supply.

A firm with transaction cost T per subscriber pair has profit equal to

$$(10) \qquad\qquad\qquad \Pi(b) = (b - T)(1 - b)/2.$$

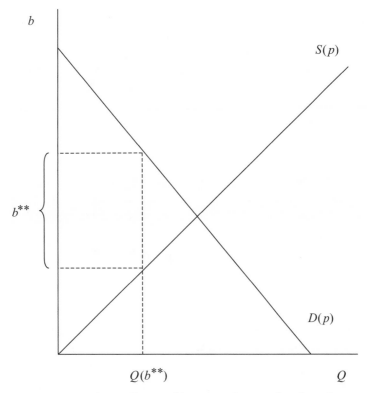

Figure 10.2. The market equilibrium with a matchmaking firm.

The firm's profit-maximizing fee is $b^{**} = (1 + T)/2$, the firm's profit is $\Pi = (1 - T)^2/8$, and the market-clearing output is $Q^{**} = (1 - T)/4$.

For any given commission rate b, consumers' surplus equals buyers' benefits minus sellers' costs and minus the firm's commissions:

$$(11) \qquad CS(b) = \int_0^{Q(b)} P^D(Q)dQ - \int_0^{Q(b)} P^S(Q)dQ - bQ(b)$$
$$= (1/4)(1 - b)^2.$$

The firm's fee b is a transaction cost that has two effects on gains from trade for buyers and sellers. There is a direct cost $bQ(b)$ and there is a deadweight loss due to those efficient transactions that cannot be completed. The deadweight loss to buyers and sellers is the transactions foregone in comparison with a situation in which the transaction cost b equals zero. The equilibrium with a matchmaking firm is shown in Figure 10.2.

Total surplus including the firm's profit equals

$$(12) \qquad V(b) = CS(b) + \Pi(b) = (1/4)(1 - b^2 - 2T + 2Tb).$$

Evaluated at the profit-maximizing rate $b^{**} = (1 + T)/2$, total surplus equals

$$(13) \qquad G = (3/16)(1 - T)^2.$$

10.1.3 Matchmaking by the Firm with Differentiated Products

Consider a market with differentiated products as represented by Becker's (1973) marriage market. Each buyer i has a productivity parameter z_i and each seller j has a productivity parameter y_j. Also, suppose that all sellers have zero costs. The value of a match is given by a multiplicative value function,

$$(14) \qquad\qquad a_{ij} = a(z_i, y_j) = z_i y_j.$$

Let subscription fees be paid *after* a match is made. The allocation of the subscription fees does affect the participation decision of buyers and of sellers since buyers and sellers make decisions about participation before paying the fees. This was already observed in the market for homogeneous products. Only the sum of subscription fees matters for participation decisions, not the amounts assigned to buyers or to sellers, $b = P + W$. The value of a match between buyer i and seller j with differentiated products is

$$(15) \qquad\qquad h_{ij} = \max\{0, a_{ij} - b\}.$$

Efficient matches in the marriage market consist of buyer-seller pairs with identical types. Matches form that yield benefits greater than or equal to the subscription fee,

$$(16) \qquad\qquad a(z_i, y_j) \geq b \quad \text{for } z_i = y_j.$$

Only those buyers and sellers that expect to be matched will subscribe to the network. Buyers and sellers will only choose to participate in the network if they can complete matches that generate sufficient gains from trade to cover the fee b.

When subscription fees are charged *before* a match is made in the marriage market, the greater of the buyer and seller fees determines participation in the network. The outcome of bilateral exchange affects the participation decision as well. Suppose that buyers and sellers engage in Nash bargaining and thus evenly divide the quasirents from exchange so that exchange between buyer i and seller j gives each party $a_{ij}/2$. Then, if buyer i anticipates trading with seller j, buyer i will become a member if and only if $a_{ij}/2 \geq P$. Also, if seller j anticipates trading with buyer i, seller j will become a member if and only if $a_{ij}/2 \geq W$. The effects of unequal fees are more complex with differentiated products than with homogenous products. Changes in the participation decisions of buyers or sellers can fundamentally change the configuration of efficient assignments and thus will affect buyer and seller expectations about participation on the other side of the market.

If the subscription fees are charged after a match is made, or if they are charged before a match is made but they are symmetric, $P = W = b/2$, the profit-maximizing firm is only concerned with the choice of the total fee b. To examine the firm's choice of a total fee, consider the marriage market with a continuum of buyers and a continuum of sellers, both of which are uniformly distributed on

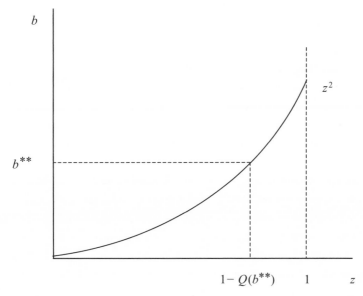

Figure 10.3. The market equilibrium with a matchmaking firm and differentiated products.

the unit interval. Since $z^2 \geq b$ for completed transactions, the firm's volume of transactions equals

(17) $$Q(b) = 1 - b^{1/2}.$$

Note that the marginal buyer and the marginal seller equal $z = y = 1 - Q(b)$. The firm chooses the subscription fee to maximize profits:

(18) $$\Pi(b) = (b - T)(1 - b^{1/2}).$$

Arranging terms in the first-order condition, the firm's profit-maximizing fee b^{**} solves

(19) $$3b^{**} - 2(b^{**})^{1/2} - T = 0.$$

The equilibrium is shown in Figure 10.3.

Given the firm's commission rate, b, consumers' surplus is the sum of the value of buyer-seller matches,

(20) $$CS(b) = \int_{b^{1/2}}^{1} (z^2 - b)dz = (2/3)b^{3/2} - b + 1/3.$$

Buyers and sellers pay a transaction cost in the form of a subscriber fee b. This fee has both a resource cost effect on total buyer and seller benefits $bQ(b)$ and a deadweight loss effect because it prevents efficient matches at the margin. Total surplus including the firm's profit equals

(21) $$G = V(b^{**}) = CS(b^{**}) + \Pi(b^{**}) = 1/3 - (1/3)(b^{**})^{3/2} + T(b^{**})^{1/2} - T.$$

10.1.4 The Literature on Market-Making Firms

This section reviews some of the relevant literature and terminology on market making and matching by firms. Economists have studied direct exchange between buyers and sellers for well over a century, at least since Böhm-Bawerk's (1923) famous market for horses. The analysis of transactions between individual buyers and individual sellers yields insights not only into direct exchange, but also helps define the economic contribution of the firm in coordinating exchange.

Direct Exchange, the Method of Marginal Pairs, and Stable Equilibrium

Rather than characterizing supply and demand as aggregates, Böhm-Bawerk's (1923) classic analysis examines transactions between individual buyers and individual sellers. He considers buyers' and sellers' subjective valuations and their formation of bilateral transactions. Böhm-Bawerk writes that "The case of two-sided competition is the most common in economic life, as it is the most important in the development of the Law of Price. It demands, therefore, our most careful attention." Böhm-Bawerk's "two-sided competition" framework provides an early model of direct exchange between buyers and sellers.

Böhm-Bawerk's (1923) *method of marginal pairs* is essentially a type of double auction that preceded Vickrey's (1961) landmark work. Böhm-Bawerk (1923, p. 213) observes that

> If all are to exchange at one market price, the price must be such as to suit all exchanging parties; and since, naturally, the price which suits the least capable contracting party suits, in a higher degree, all the more capable, it follows quite naturally, that the relations of the last pair whom the price must suit, or, as the case may be, the first pair whom it cannot suit, afford the standard for the height of the price.

The market-clearing price and quantity are determined by the marginal pair who trade, that is, the buyer-seller pair who have the smallest positive difference between the buyer's value and that of the seller, or by the marginal pair who are excluded from trade.

The two-sided market model is developed further by von Neumann and Morgenstern (1944). In their classic book *Games and Economic Behavior*, they apply Böhm-Bawerk's framework as their main, indeed their only, economic interpretation of general non-zero-sum games.[2] Lloyd Shapley (1961) introduces a related multiplayer market game. Shapley and Shubik (1972, p. 111) observe that

> Two-sided market models are important, as Cournot, Edgeworth, Böhm-Bawerk, and others have observed, not only for the insights they may give into

---

2 Von Neumann and Morgenstern (1944, p. 562) observe that "The size of the transaction, i.e. the number t_0 of units transferred, is determined in accord with Böhm-Bawerk's criterion of the 'marginal pairs.'"

more general economic situations with many types of traders, consumers, and producers, but also for the simple reason that in real life many markets and most actual transactions are in fact bilateral – i.e., bring together a buyer and a seller of a single commodity.

Gale and Shapley (1962) examine two-sided matching markets including students and universities, marriage partners, and renters and housing. Shapley and Shubik (1972) analyze two-sided markets for both homogenous and differentiated products. A substantial literature examines matching in two-sided markets. Much of this literature extends the work of Gale and Shapley (1962) and Shapley and Shubik (1972).[3]

Gale and Shapley (1962) introduce the concept of a "stable equilibrium" in a matching market. They develop an important algorithm for attaining a stable equilibrium that corresponds to Böhm-Bawerk's method of marginal pairs. Gale and Shapley consider a market in which equal numbers of buyers and of sellers have ordinal preferences over matches. An assignment of buyers to sellers is stable if it does not contain two buyers i_1 and i_2 who are assigned to sellers j_1 and j_2, respectively, such that buyer i_1 prefers seller j_2 to seller j_1 and buyer i_2 prefers seller j_1 to seller j_2. Gale and Shapley (1962) show that a stable assignment always exists.

Gale and Shapley's algorithm always finds a stable assignment. The Gale-Shapley algorithm does not involve central coordination because it involves only offers and acceptances or rejections between individual buyers and individual sellers. Individual buyers make offers to individual sellers and sellers can accept an offer to form a match. Sellers can break off a match if they get a better offer. Any buyer that does not have a match proposes a match to a seller that ranks highest among all sellers that have not yet rejected him. If the seller is not matched, the seller accepts the offer. If the seller is matched, the seller can either accept or reject the buyer's offer depending on whether or not it is preferred to the seller's existing match. The buyers can be chosen in any order. The algorithm continues until all buyers are matched with sellers.

The Gale-Shapley algorithm is useful for representing direct exchange because it characterizes interaction between individual buyers and individual sellers. Consider a modified Gale and Shapley (1962) market that allows money transfers within each buyer-seller pair.[4] Consider a market with homogeneous products. Let buyer

---

3 Hylland and Zeckhauser (1979) examine efficient assignments by a social choice mechanism in which individuals report their preference and the mechanisms assigns probabilities to position. Demange (1982), Leonard (1983), and Demange and Gale (1985) examine auction-based allocation mechanisms. For an overview of this literature see Roth and Sotomayor (1990). Two-sided matching markets include workers and employers, particularly at the entry level in such specialized professional markets as law, medicine, and business; see Roth and Xing (1994).

4 In their classic article, Gale and Shapley (1962) consider the assignment game in a two-sided market without money transfers. Shapley and Shubik (1972) consider the assignment game with money transfers. Gale and Shapley (1962) examine stable assignments whereas Shapley and Shubik (1972) focus on Core allocations. The stable outcome is not necessarily in the Core.

valuations be arranged in decreasing order, $v_1 > v_2 > \cdots > v_n$, and let seller costs be arranged in increasing order, $c_1 < c_2 < \cdots < c_m$. Buyers and sellers engage in Nash bargaining, evenly splitting the net benefits of exchange, so that each receives $(v - c)/2$. The following analysis holds for generalized Nash bargaining. Buyers and sellers have cardinal as well as ordinal preference rankings across matches.[5] The Gale-Shapley algorithm yields the following outcome. The highest-value buyer and the lowest-cost seller wish to trade with each other to obtain the greatest gains from trade. The highest-value buyer will match with the lowest-cost seller, the next-highest-value buyer will match with the next-lowest-cost seller, and so on, until there are no more subscriber pairs with nonnegative surplus. The Gale-Shapley algorithm yields an efficient assignment of buyers to sellers. The Gale-Shapley algorithm yields a stable matching that resembles Böhm-Bawerk's method of marginal pairs. The difference is that each pair trades at its own price, so that the outcome is not in the Core. Total net benefits of buyers and sellers are maximized by direct exchange between buyers and sellers when there is full information and costless matching.

Consider now the Gale-Shapley algorithm in a market with differentiated products. In Becker's (1973) marriage market, the production function is $a(z, y) = zy$. Let the buyer types z_i and the seller types y_j be arranged in decreasing order, $z_1 > z_2 > \cdots > z_n$ and $y_1 > y_2 > \cdots > y_n$, and let $z_i = y_j$ for $i = j$. Let seller costs equal zero. Buyer and seller types engage in Nash bargaining, evenly splitting the surplus, with each receiving $zy/2$. There is only one efficient assignment, which is to match each buyer with a seller of the same type. Applying the Gale-Shapley algorithm to describe the process of direct exchange, suppose that buyers make offers to sellers. Buyers and sellers will self-select, with the highest-value buyer matching with the highest-value seller and so on. Then, in Becker's marriage market, the Gale-Shapley algorithm yields the unique efficient assignment of buyers to sellers.

In the market with differentiated products represented by Becker's marriage market, direct exchange maximizes the total net benefits of buyers and sellers when there is full information and costless matching. The Gale-Shapley algorithm need not yield an efficient assignment with differentiated products. Consider a housing market example due to Shapley and Shubik (1972). The efficient assignment consists of the matches (1, 3), (2, 1), and (3, 2), which yields a total value of 16. This assignment is a stable equilibrium and is shown in bold in Table 10.1. The Gale-Shapley algorithm results in two matches, (2, 2) and (1, 1), with buyer 3 and seller 3 inactive. This outcome is indicated with asterisks in Table 10.1. This assignment yields only two transactions with a total value of 14 and so is not efficient. This implies that coordination by firms can improve allocative efficiency with differentiated products.

---

5 The values of matches in the assignment game with money transfers treat buyers and sellers symmetrically, as Shapley and Shubik (1972) observe.

Table 10.1. *The efficient assignment (in bold) and the outcome of the Gale-Shapley algorithm (with asterisks) in the housing market*

	Seller 1	Seller 2	Seller 3
Buyer 1	5*	7	**2**
Buyer 2	**8**	9*	3
Buyer 3	2	**6**	0*

Market Making by Firms

The firm enhances economic efficiency when it improves on direct exchange. With full information and costless search, direct exchange between consumers generally yields an efficient outcome with homogeneous products. Direct exchange between consumers may require central coordination in a market with differentiated products, even with full information and costless search. When buyers and sellers have incomplete information about the other side of the market and search is costly, firms can improve the efficiency of economic transactions. Firms offer potential efficiencies by offering communications services and centralizing matching of buyers with sellers. Market making by firms provides price signals, aggregates demands and supplies, and provides central places of exchange.

Spulber (1996a, 1996b, 1999, 2002b, 2002c, 2003) presents an analysis of models of market making by firms. Intermediation by firms can improve economic efficiency in a number of ways. By adding players to the economy, firms increase the number of potential matches. Rubinstein and Wolinsky (1987) consider a random matching model with buyers, sellers, and intermediaries that act as dealers. In a related setting, Yavas (1994b) examines the role of intermediaries that act as matchmakers in markets where both buyers and sellers search, considering such intermediaries as employment agencies and real estate brokers. In Yavas (1994b), the presence of the matchmaker affects the endogenously chosen search intensity of buyers and sellers.

As shown previously, the benefits of monopoly intermediary are partially offset by pricing inefficiencies. Competition between firms can improve the efficiency of intermediation. Stahl (1988) considers competition between firms engaged in Bertrand competition for inputs and subsequent Bertrand competition for outputs. Two firms bid for inputs in the first stage and then offer prices to buyers in the second stage. When the Nash equilibrium exists, the bid-ask spread is eliminated and bid and ask prices equal the Walrasian price.

Spulber (1999) examines competition between intermediaries in various settings including a two-sided circular market model with differentiated inputs and outputs, which is extended by Alexandrov et al. (2007). Buyers are located around a product circle and sellers are located around an input circle. In equilibrium, the bid-ask spread is positive and narrows depending on the number of firms that intermediate between buyers and sellers.

Gehrig (1993) allows Bertrand competition between intermediaries who also compete with the decentralized search market and shows that competition eliminates the bid-ask spread. Gehrig's model is presented in the next section. Loertscher (2004) introduces capacity constraints on intermediaries leading to rationing and positive bid-ask spreads. Spulber (1996a) obtains price dispersion in both bid and ask prices when intermediaries compete in a search setting. Shevchenko (2004) examines competition between intermediaries in a search setting when market makers can hold inventories of varying size. Weill (2005) examines how competing market makers provide liquidity in financial markets during financial disruptions.

Loertscher (2007) extends the two-sided spatial model in this section and in Spulber (1999). Loertscher looks at duopoly competition between market makers in a two-sided spatial model when buyers and sellers have the option of search. At the location of each of the market makers, buyers and sellers can engage in random matching, as in Gehrig's (1993) model. Because the market makers are differentiated in the sense of Hotelling, the equilibrium bid-ask spreads are positive, as in the model presented in this section. Positive bid-ask spreads allow search markets to operate at the two firms' locations. The two market makers compete with each other and with decentralized exchange between consumers in their respective local search markets. Loertscher's model shows that market-making firms make an economic contribution relative to direct exchange between consumers in a spatial setting. When search is costly, market-making firms with posted prices offer an alternative to search that is attractive for high-value buyers and low-cost sellers. Because the firms are differentiated by location, they earn profits from providing market-making services.

The firm as an intermediary can be observed in a wide variety of industry applications. Yavas (1996b) considers competition between a market maker and a search market when buyer and seller search intensities are endogenous. Yavas (1992) lets the intermediary choose between being a market maker and a matchmaker. Yavas (1996a) models the matching of buyers and sellers by real estate brokers and compare alternative commission structures; see also Yavas (1994a). Baye and Morgan (2001) study Internet intermediaries that act as information gatekeepers. Baye et al. (2004) consider Internet comparison sites that perform matchmaking functions in two-sided markets and their effects on price dispersion across online retailers. Lucking-Reiley and Spulber (2001) examine business-to-business intermediaries that act as dealers and operate online marketplaces. Ju et al. (2004) consider oligopolistic market makers in the natural gas industry. Bertrand competition between intermediaries is examined by Fingleton (1997), Spulber (1996a, 1999), Rust and Hall (2003), and Hendershott and Zhang (2006).

With many buyers and many sellers, direct exchange is likely to have high transaction costs. The costs to consumers of searching for the best trading partner are likely to be greater when there are many consumers than when there are few consumers. This means that the greater the number of consumers, the greater are the potential returns to centralized coordination of exchange. A greater number of consumers both increases the returns from centrally coordinating exchange and lowers the average costs implementing that central coordination. With a sufficiently large number of consumers it may thus be worthwhile for consumers to establish a market-making firm.

Firms add value if establishing a centralized exchange mechanism improves economic efficiency relative to an economy that relies exclusively on consumer search and direct bargaining. It should be emphasized that the benefits of market making by firms do not suggest a role for central planning by government. Hayek (1945, p. 519) emphasizes that

> The peculiar character of the problem of a rational economic order is determined precisely by the fact that the knowledge of the circumstances of which we must make use never exists in concentrated or integrated form but solely as the dispersed bits of incomplete and frequently contradictory knowledge which all the separate individuals possess.

Market making by firms is part of the private ordering of the economy. The market maker takes advantage of returns to centralization to improve on market allocation, without trying to identify all of the knowledge possessed by individual buyers and individual sellers.

Market making by firms is entirely distinct from central planning by government. The market-making firm addresses a very particular market, not the entire economy. The market-making firm may compete with other firms and well as direct exchange between buyers and sellers, rather than controlling the economy through government power. The market-making firm uses prices rather than command and control and central planning. A market-making firm has many ways of gathering and disseminating information, through commercial marketing, sales, and procurement activities that are entirely different from the activities of a government agency. The market-making firm can use such instruments as auctions for gathering buyer and seller bids. Finally, the market-making firm maximizes profit, in contrast to government agencies that pursue all kinds of other objectives. Finally, the market-making firm can go out of business if it makes unprofitable decisions.

Two-Sided Markets, Networks, and Network Effects

The term "two-sided competition" dates back to Böhm-Bawerk's 1891 book, whereas the term "two-sided market" dates back at least to Shapley and Shubik (1972). A *two-sided market* generally designates a situation in which individual buyers seek matches with individual sellers or individual sellers seek matches with individual buyers. A two-sided matching market can be decentralized, as represented by Böhm-Bawerk's method or marginal pairs, or by the Gale-Shapley algorithm.

A two-sided matching market also can be centralized, with matchmaking firms coordinating exchange and providing networks for communication.

Network theory provides a useful framework for examining the effects of limited communication on decentralized matching markets. Kranton and Minehart (2000, 2001) examine the effects of incomplete communication networks. In their framework, buyers have different valuations of a homogenous good. Sellers are identical because they have the same cost of supplying the good to a buyer. Kranton and Minehart (2001) show that with costless auctions, the equilibrium allocation of goods is efficient since the highest-value buyers receive the goods, subject to constraints imposed by incomplete communications networks.

Spulber (2006) examines the effects of incomplete communications networks on allocative efficiency when buyers have different valuations and sellers have different costs. Spulber considers markets both with homogeneous products and with differentiated products. Buyers and sellers face costly communication due to incomplete communications networks. Buyers and sellers also face costly computation because they must search for partners to engage in bilateral exchange. Firms improve allocative efficiency by providing centralized networks that improve communication. Firms also can improve allocative efficiency by offering matchmaking services.

Some economists use the term "two-sided market" to designate a market with "network effects"; see for example Rochet and Tirole (2003).[6] A "network effect" is said to occur when individuals obtain benefits from the consumption of others.[7] In a two-sided market, a "network effect" is said to occur when buyers obtain benefits from the participation of sellers and sellers obtain benefits from the participation of buyers. Firms acting as intermediaries in such a two-sided market take network effects into account when choosing prices. Competition between networks is discussed in Caillaud and Jullien (2001, 2003). Rysman (2004) presents an empirical study of competition between providers of Yellow Pages that examines network effects. For a critical analysis of "network effects" see Liebowitz (2002), Liebowitz and Margolis (1994, 1999), and Spulber (2008a). Spulber (2008b) considers the interplay between social networks and the private networks that are provided by firms.

10.2 Market Making by the Firm versus Consumer Search

Market making by the firm centralizes exchange and thus contrasts with decentralized exchange between consumers. Whether acting as buyers or as sellers, consumers engage in costly search to find trading partners. Consumers devote time and effort to negotiating the terms of trade. This section compares market making by the firm

---

6 The "network effects" literature on two-sided markets tends not to reference the earlier literature on "two-sided markets."

7 See Farrell and Saloner (1985, 1986) and Katz and Shapiro (1985, 1986, 1994).

with direct exchange between consumers. The market-making firm competes with a search market. The firm is viable if and only if it can attract consumers away from a market with decentralized exchange.

The view of the firm as a market maker contrasts with the neoclassical notion of the firm as a price-taker. In the neoclassical model, the exogenous Walrasian auctioneer takes on market-making functions. Industrial organization analysis, in the tradition of Bertrand, recognizes price setting by firms. However, IO economists traditionally have taken such market-making activities as evidence of imperfect competition that would require government intervention in the form of regulation and antitrust. Instead, the theory of the firm views market making as an alternative to consumer search.

Firms set most prices in the economy. To select prices, firms must calculate demand schedules for their outputs, and supply schedules for their inputs. Firms must perform the calculations needed to select profit-maximizing prices. In addition, firms must communicate the appropriate prices to buyers and sellers and provide many other types of information including product features, guarantees, the firm's location, complementary services, and methods of delivery. Moreover, firms need to continually adjust prices to respond to changes in market conditions.

Suppose that the firm has the ability to post prices. Individual buyers and sellers often take prices as given in their dealings with the firm when there are many competing buyers and many competing sellers. In contrast, if buyers and sellers meet to carry out bilateral exchange, there is only one buyer and seller in an individual match. Accordingly, after being matched in the search market, a buyer and a seller necessarily bargain over the terms of exchange. This section examines whether a firm that posts prices offers advantages over bilateral exchange in a search market. The model in this section is based on Gehrig (1993).

The sequence of events is as follows. The firm selects prices and communicates those prices to buyers and sellers. After observing those prices, buyers and sellers decide whether to visit a firm or to go to the matching market. If buyers and sellers choose to visit the firm, they trade with the firm at the posted prices. If there is a difference between the number of buyers and the number of sellers that trade with the firm, some of the traders on the long side of the market will be quantity-rationed by the firm and then become inactive. If buyers and sellers choose to enter the matching market, buyers and sellers meet randomly and bargain over the terms of trade. For ease of discussion, assume that after being matched, buyers and sellers observe each others' characteristics and engage in full-information Nash bargaining, so buyers and sellers evenly divide the gains from trade.[8]

---

8 This contrasts with Gehrig's (1993) more general model in which asymmetric information persists after a match is made. The buyer still does not know the seller's opportunity cost and the seller does not know the buyer's willingness to pay. The uncertainty in the bargaining process affects the search process by making the returns to search uncertain. The model with full information and the model with asymmetric information at the bargaining stage have similar properties.

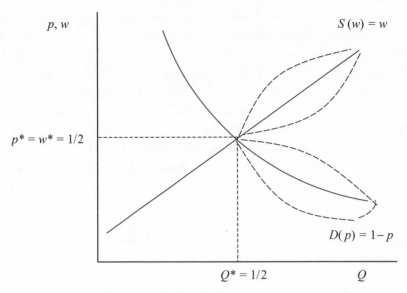

Figure 10.4. Supply and demand and efficiency in a search market.

Consumers are either buyers or sellers. Buyer willingness-to-pay levels are represented by v. Thus at price p, the buyer with willingness-to-pay level v has utility $U(v) = v - p$. There is a continuum of buyers whose willingness-to-pay levels are uniformly distributed on the unit interval. For $p \leq 1$, aggregate demand equals $D(p) = 1 - p$. Seller opportunity costs are represented by c. The seller with cost c has net benefit at price w equal to $R(c) = w - c$. There is a continuum of sellers whose costs are uniformly distributed on the unit interval. For $w \leq 1$, aggregate supply equals $S(w) = w$.

Buyer willingness-to-pay levels and seller costs are their private information, although aggregate demand and supply are common knowledge. This helps to explain the fundamental distinction between the firm and a search market. In the search market, buyers and sellers do not know the characteristics of their potential trading partners. The firm offers the certainty of posted prices.

Consider the search market without any firm. The search market is inefficient due to the vagaries of random matching. To examine the search market, consider the supply-and-demand diagram in Figure 10.4. Efficient matching requires that the marginal buyer's willingness to pay and the marginal seller's costs are equal. This means that it is efficient to match high-value buyers $v \geq v^*$ with low-cost sellers $c \leq c^*$. Buyers with low value, $0 < v < v^*$, should be inactive and sellers with high cost, $c^* < c < 1$, also should be inactive. Efficient matching thus requires the marginal buyer's value to equal the marginal seller's cost,

$$v^* = c^*.$$

In addition, the total amount demanded and the total amount supplied should be equal,

$$D(p^*) = S(w^*).$$

Given the distribution of buyer types and seller types, it follows that the marginal buyer's valuation and the marginal seller's cost should equate supply and demand as in the standard Walrasian model,

$$v^* = c^* = p^* = w^* = 1/2.$$

Moreover, demand and supply are equal to output Q^* given by

$$Q^* = D(p^*) = S(w^*) = 1/2.$$

With efficient matching, the active buyers are those on the left-hand side of the supply-and-demand picture. Any random matching of buyers and sellers on the left-hand side of the supply-and-demand diagram yields the same net benefits. Total net benefits with efficient matching equals

(22) $$g^* = \int_{v^*}^{1} v\,dv - \int_{0}^{c^*} c\,dc = 1/4.$$

Buyers and sellers on the right-hand-side of the supply-and-demand diagram are inactive with efficient matching; see Figure 10.4.

With random matching, a buyer and a seller trade if $v \geq c$. Total expected benefits with random matching equal

(23) $$g = \int_{0}^{1} \int_{0}^{v} (v - c)\,dc\,dv = 1/6.$$

The total expected volume of trade with random matching is $Q = \int_{0}^{1} \int_{0}^{v} dc\,dv = 1/2$. The matching market yields lower net benefits than efficient matching because with random matching low-value buyers and high-cost sellers can find trading partners. Let buyers and sellers who trade in the matching market evenly split the gains from trade. The expected utilities of buyers and sellers in the matching market equal

(24) $$U(v) = (1/2) \int_{0}^{v} (v - c)\,dc = v^2/4,$$

$$R(c) = (1/2) \int_{c}^{1} (v - c)\,dv = (1 - c)^2/4.$$

With random matching all buyers and sellers are active.

Consider now the role of a firm that offers buyers an ask price p and sellers a bid price w. There are three stages in the market-making process. First, the firm selects prices to maximize profit. Then, buyers and sellers choose between dealing with the firm and entering the matching market. Those rationed by the firm also enter the matching market. Finally, the matching market clears and those buyers and sellers with positive gains from trade conclude their exchange.

Let $\varphi(v)$ and $\psi(c)$ represent the conditional distribution of buyer types and seller types respectively who are active in the matching market. Suppose for the moment that neither buyers nor sellers are rationed on the matching market. Then the buyer and seller expected benefits in the matching market are

$$(25) \qquad\qquad U(v) = (1/2)\int_0^v (v - c)d\psi(c),$$

$$(26) \qquad\qquad R(c) = (1/2)\int_c^1 (v - c)d\varphi(v).$$

The market equilibrium with a market-making firm consists of the firm's bid and ask prices (p, w), buyer and seller expectations $(\varphi(v), \psi(c))$, and buyer and seller choices of whether to trade with the firm or to enter the matching market.

   The firm sets an ask price p and a bid price w, in competition with the matching market. The firm randomly rations the long side of the market if the number of buyers and sellers that go to the firm are not equal. Let q equal the number of buyers and x the number of sellers. Then the firm's profit is

$$(27) \qquad\qquad \Pi = (p - w)\min\{q, x\}.$$

The value to buyers of trading with the firm, $v - p$, and the value to sellers, $w - c$, are contingent on not being quantity-rationed by the firm.

   For any positive bid-and-ask spread, there will be an active matching market. This is because buyers with willingness to pay v such that $w < v < p$, and sellers with opportunity cost c such that $w < c < p$, will expect positive gains from trade from entering the matching market. Consumers in the matching market have positive expected gains from trade since they anticipate benefits from making a match and bargaining. Suppose that a buyer expects to find a partner in the matching market with likelihood γ. Then the buyer of type v will choose to trade with the firm rather than enter into the matching market if

$$v - p \geq \gamma U(v).$$

If a seller expects to find a partner in the matching market with likelihood γ, the seller of type c will choose to trade with the firm rather than enter into the matching market if

$$w - c \geq \gamma R(c).$$

These inequalities assume that the firm does not choose prices that would ration buyers or sellers.

   In equilibrium, buyers with high willingness to pay and sellers with low cost choose to trade with the firm. Buyers with moderate willingness to pay and sellers with moderate cost enter the matching market. Buyers with low willingness to pay and sellers with high cost are inactive.

   The market equilibrium is defined fully by the four critical values $v_0, \overline{v}, \overline{c},$ and c_0. The sets of *inactive* buyers and sellers are intervals representing the lowest-value buyers $[0, v_0)$ and the highest-cost sellers $(c_0, 1]$. To see why, observe that if buyer v_0 is inactive, then any buyer with a lower willingness to pay must also be inactive, because otherwise buyer v_0 could imitate buyer v and secure at least the same payoff. This is a contradiction, because then buyer v_0 would no longer be inactive. The same reasoning applies to the high-cost sellers.

The set of *active* buyers and sellers are as follows. Buyers with moderate willingness-to-pay levels $[v_0, \overline{v}]$ and sellers with moderate costs $[\overline{c}, c_0]$ enter the decentralized matching market. Buyers with a high willingness to pay $(\overline{v}, 1]$ buy from the firm and sellers with low costs $[0, \overline{c})$ sell to the firm.

The proof that these intervals define participation in the two markets follows from the monotonicity of the payoff functions $U(v)$ and $R(c)$. A sketch of the argument is sufficient to understand the approach. First note that in equilibrium, only one side of the market can be rationed by the firm. Consider the decision of buyers, as the case for sellers is the same. Suppose that a buyer with a willingness to pay v chooses to enter the matching market. Then any buyer with a higher willingness to pay would either enter the matching market or trade with the firm rather than remain inactive, because otherwise he could imitate buyer v and still obtain positive gains from trade.

Suppose that a buyer v' chooses to enter the matching market. It can be shown that any buyer with a *lower* willingness to pay also would enter the matching market (or be inactive). This will establish that the set of buyers visiting the firm are all those buyers with willingness to pay greater than v'. There are two possibilities: either the number of buyers visiting the firm is less than or equal to the number of sellers, or the number of buyers visiting the firm exceeds the number of sellers. Consider the case where the number of buyers visiting the firm is less than or equal than the number of sellers. It is not necessary to review the other case, which is similar. Since the number of buyers visiting the firm is less than or equal to the number of sellers, the firm does not ration buyers, so that the expected value to a buyer v of visiting the firm is simply $v - p$. On the other hand, there may be more buyers than sellers on the matching market, so that the buyer expects to be rationed on the matching market with some likelihood $1 - \gamma$. The expected returns from entering the matching market are thus $\gamma U(v')$.

Since it is assumed that the type v' buyer chooses the matching market rather than the firm, it must be the case that expected returns from the matching market exceed the surplus obtained by trading with the firm,

$$\gamma U(v') > v' - p.$$

Now, consider a buyer with a lower willingness to pay, $v < v'$. By the definition of $U(v)$, note that $\gamma U'(v) = (\gamma/2)\psi(c) < 1$, so that

$$\gamma U(v) - (v - p) > \gamma U(v') - (v' - p) > 0.$$

Therefore, the type-v buyer will also prefer the matching market to trading with the firm. This shows that all buyers with willingness to pay in $(\overline{v}, 1]$ will choose to buy from the firm. A similar argument establishes that all sellers with costs in $[0, \overline{c})$ will choose to sell to the firm.

The set of consumers that are active in equilibrium includes an equal number of buyers and sellers so that $v_0 = \overline{c}$ and $c_0 = \overline{v}$, because a buyer with $v < \overline{c}$ or a seller with $c > \overline{v}$ will find no counterpart in the matching market. Thus, the interval $[\overline{c}, \overline{v}]$ defines the set of buyers and the set of sellers in the matching market.[9]

So, in equilibrium, no rationing occurs in the matching market. The distributions of agents in the matching market are equal to the uniform distribution on $[\overline{c}, \overline{v}]$,

$$\varphi(v) = (v - \overline{c})/(\overline{v} - \overline{c}) \quad \psi(c) = (c - \overline{c})/(\overline{v} - \overline{c}).$$

Therefore, the expected benefits of buyers and sellers in the matching market are

$$(28) \qquad U(v) = \frac{1}{4}\frac{(v - \overline{c})^2}{\overline{v} - \overline{c}}, \quad R(c) = \frac{1}{4}\frac{(\overline{v} - c)^2}{\overline{v} - \overline{c}}.$$

Note that the critical payoffs are equal, $U(\overline{v}) = R(\overline{c}) = (1/4)(\overline{v} - \overline{c})$. For the marginal buyer and the marginal seller, benefits are equal:

$$(29) \qquad U(\overline{v}) = \frac{1}{4}\frac{(\overline{v} - \overline{c})^2}{\overline{v} - \overline{c}} = \overline{v} - p,$$

$$(30) \qquad R(\overline{c}) = \frac{1}{4}\frac{(\overline{v} - \overline{c})^2}{\overline{v} - \overline{c}} = w - \overline{c}.$$

Because $U(\overline{v}) = R(\overline{c})$, it follows that $\overline{v} - p = w - \overline{c}$.

The profit-maximizing monopolist will choose prices to balance purchases and sales:

$$(31) \qquad q = 1 - \overline{v} = \overline{c} = x.$$

From $\overline{v} - p = w - \overline{c}$, it follows that the ask and bid prices are symmetric around the Walrasian price of $1/2$, and the firm does not ration either side of the market:

$$(32) \qquad 1 - p = w.$$

---

9 Gehrig (1993) observes that there are a multiplicity of equilibria arising from the coordination problem between buyers and sellers and from their beliefs about the likelihood of rationing. The particular market equilibrium that is shown is appealing because it weakly dominates the no-trade equilibrium (and any other equilibrium). This occurs because visiting the firm is costless. Traders do not incur direct costs of visiting the firm, nor does observation of the firm's posted price require foregoing the matching market. If it were costly to visit the firm and observe the posted prices, there might be a weakly dominating equilibrium with less trade or no trade with the firm, or possible indeterminacy in the model. The use of coordination mechanisms other than the firm's posted prices also could affect the equilibrium outcome. In addition, inventory holding by firms could reduce buyer and seller concerns about being rationed, which could also alter the equilibrium outcome.

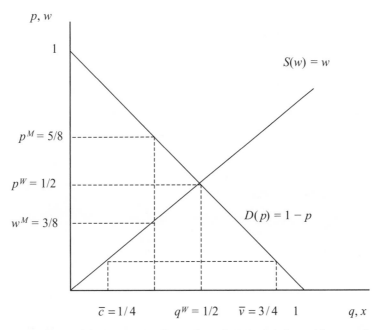

p, w

1

$S(w) = w$

$p^M = 5/8$

$p^W = 1/2$

$w^M = 3/8$

$D(p) = 1 - p$

$\bar{c} = 1/4$ $q^W = 1/2$ $\bar{v} = 3/4$ 1 q, x

Figure 10.5. The equilibrium prices chosen by a firm competing with a search market.

The monopolist's profit can be rewritten as

(33) $$\Pi = (p - w)q = (2p - 1)q.$$

From equations (28), (29), and (31), output can be written as a function of the ask price,

(34) $$q = 3/2 - 2p.$$

So the monopolist's profit-maximizing ask price solves

$$\max{}_p(2p - 1)(3/2 - 2p).$$

The equilibrium prices chosen by the firm are thus $p^M = 5/8$ and $w^M = 3/8$. The market-clearing quantity is $q = 1/4$. The solution is illustrated in Figure 10.5.

    The firm trades with buyers in the interval $[3/4, 1]$ and sellers in the interval $[0, 1/4]$. Buyers and sellers in the interval $[1/4, 3/4]$ enter the matching market. The beliefs of buyers and sellers that they will not be quantity-rationed by the firm are confirmed in equilibrium. The firm's price spread $p - w = 1/4$ reflects the inefficiency of the consumers' decentralized bargaining and matching market. The monopoly firm's price spread is less than what it would choose in the absence of competition from the matching market. The unconstrained monopoly prices are $p = 3/4$ and $w = 1/4$.

    The profitability of the firm shows that it plays a role in improving market efficiency. The firm improves allocative efficiency in comparison to the matching market without the presence of a firm. Total benefits of buyers and sellers with market making by a firm are equal to the sum of gains from trading with the firm and gains from trade in the matching market,

$$(35) \qquad G = \int_{\underline{v}}^{1} v \, dv - \int_{0}^{\overline{c}} c \, dc + \int_{\overline{c}}^{\overline{v}} U(v) \, dv + \int_{\overline{c}}^{\overline{v}} R(c) \, dc = 11/48.$$

The firm's profit equals

$$(36) \qquad\qquad \Pi = (2p - 1)(3/2 - 2p) = 1/16.$$

Recall from equation (23) that the benefits to consumers in a random matching market when there is no market-making firm equal $g = 1/6$. The firm provides total benefits equal to

$$(37) \qquad\qquad G - g = 11/48 - 1/6 = 1/16.$$

Therefore, the firm captures all of the increased benefits to consumers that result from market making,

$$(38) \qquad\qquad \Pi = G - g.$$

The firm improves economic efficiency relative to a search market by efficiently matching high-value buyers and low-cost sellers. In addition, the firm improves economic efficiency by rendering low-value buyers and high-cost sellers inactive. By competing with a search market, the firm also improves the efficiency of the search market, because fewer buyers and sellers choose to search and those buyers and sellers have more similar values and costs than the general population of buyers and sellers. The profit-maximizing firm's bid-ask spread is sufficient to capture all of these increases in gains from trade relative to a stand-alone search market.

10.3 Matchmaking by the Firm versus Consumer Search

Firms provide various centralized mechanisms for matching buyers and sellers when products are differentiated. Such mechanisms can reduce search costs significantly in comparison to decentralized exchange. Centralized matching mechanisms have several common features. First, firms exclude buyers and sellers through access prices. Second, firms offer buyers and sellers a means of searching for trading partners among subscribers, often through a computerized search engine. Third, buyers or sellers provide information to the firm that is shared with other subscribers.

This section presents a model of market making with differentiated products. Buyer types z and seller types y are uniformly distributed on the unit interval. As in Becker's (1973) marriage market, suppose that the value of a match is multiplicative,

$$(39) \qquad\qquad a(z, y) = zy.$$

The firm's subscribers are assumed to have perfect information about the other side of the market. This means that if a set of buyers and a set of sellers are among the firm's subscribers, then they can find prospective matches costlessly. If the set of buyers corresponds exactly to the set of sellers, recall that the efficient assignment is to match buyers and sellers with the same parameter values, $z = y$. If the two sets are not identical, the highest-value buyer should be matched with the highest-value seller and so on until the smaller set has been fully assigned. The firm can ration the long side of the market that it serves by sending the excess buyers or sellers to the search market. It can be shown that the firm will choose prices so that it serves the same number of buyers and of sellers.

The firm charges an access price p to buyers and an access price r to sellers. After paying the access prices, buyers and sellers observe the types of other subscribers. Because there is full information among subscribers, there is an efficient assignment. Each buyer-seller pair bargains over the division of the surplus. Suppose that each buyer-seller pair divides their surplus evenly so that each receives $zy/2$. Notice that the access prices do not enter into the division of the surplus since these prices are sunk costs for buyers and sellers. The value of the match is the quasirent that must be divided between the buyer and the seller.

Buyers and sellers must choose between dealing with the firm and entering a decentralized search market with random matching. Let $\varphi(z)$ and $\psi(y)$ represent equilibrium beliefs about the conditional distribution of buyer and seller types in the decentralized market. Then, the expected benefits of buyers and sellers in the decentralized search market, contingent on finding a match, equal

$$(40) \qquad U(z) = (1/2) \int_0^1 zy\,d\psi(y),$$

$$(41) \qquad R(y) = (1/2) \int_0^1 zy\,d\varphi(z).$$

The equilibrium with a market-making firm thus consists of three things: the firm's access fees p and r, the buyer and seller expectations $(\varphi(z), \psi(y))$, and buyer and seller choices about whether to subscribe to the firm's service or to enter the search market.

The firm sets its access prices p and r to maximize profit. Let q and x equal the number of buyers and sellers respectively who subscribe to the firm's service. The firm's profit is thus

$$(42) \qquad \Pi = pq + rx.$$

The value to a buyer z of dealing with the firm and finding a match y is

$$zy/2 - p.$$

The value to a seller y of dealing with the firm and finding a match z is

$$zy/2 - r.$$

Because any match in the search market has positive benefits, there are no inactive buyers or sellers (setting aside the buyer and the seller with parameter value of zero, who have zero measure). Because the firm serves the same number of buyers as the number of sellers, it follows that the number of buyers in the search market will equal the number of sellers in the search market. There is no rationing in equilibrium. Also, buyers and sellers served by the firm are assigned efficiently.

The equilibrium can be described by the number of buyers and sellers in the search market z_0, with $1 - z_0$ buyers and $1 - z_0$ sellers served by the firm. To verify that this is an equilibrium, consider the decision of a buyer of type z. The buyer's conditional beliefs about the equilibrium distribution of sellers in the search market, $\psi(y)$, are the uniform distribution on the interval $[0, z_0]$. Thus,

$$(43) \qquad U(z) = (1/2) \int_0^{z_0} zy \, dy / z_0 = (1/4) z z_0.$$

The buyer z_0 obtains benefits $z_0^2/2 - p$ from dealing with the firm. Then, if z_0 is the marginal buyer, he is indifferent between dealing with the firm and entering the search market if

$$(44) \qquad z_0^2/2 - p = U(z_0) = z_0^2/4.$$

This implies that z_0 solves

$$(45) \qquad z_0^2/4 = p.$$

Therefore, the net benefit to buyer z from dealing with the firm equals

$$(46) \quad z^2/2 - p - U(z) = z^2/2 - z_0^2/4 - z z_0/4 = (1/4)(2z^2 - z_0^2 - z z_0).$$

This expression is less than, equal to, or greater than zero as z is less than, equal to, or greater than z_0. So the buyer of type $z \geq z_0$ prefers to deal with the firm and the buyer of type $z < z_0$ prefers to enter the search market.

By symmetry, prices are the same for buyers and for sellers $p = r$, and $q = x = 1 - z_0$, so that the firm's profit is

$$(47) \qquad \Pi = 2p(1 - z_0) = (1/2) z_0^2 (1 - z_0),$$

where $p = z_0^2/4$. The firm chooses the marginal buyer or seller to maximize profit, so that $z_0 = 2/3$. The subscription rate for buyers or sellers is $p = 1/9$. Thus, the firm's profit is $\Pi = 2/27$. Total benefits to consumers without distributing profits equal

$$(48) \quad G = \int_{z_0}^1 z^2 \, dz + \int_0^{z_0} \int_0^{z_0} zy \, dz \, dy = 1/3 - z_0^3/3 + z_0^4/4 = 23/81.$$

Compare the firm's centralized matching market with a random matching market. In the random matching market, because all buyers and sellers can trade with each other, total gains from trade equal

$$(49) \qquad g = \int_0^1 \int_0^1 zy \, dx \, dy = 1/4.$$

The matchmaking firm's contribution to consumer benefits equals

$$(50) \qquad G - g = 23/81 - 1/4 = 11/324.$$

The firm's profit is greater than the total increase in consumer benefits, $\Pi > G - g$. This is because efficient matching creates winners and losers. The winners are the high-value types, that is, those with parameter values above z_0. Their gains from trade are

$$\begin{aligned} G_H - g_H &= \int_{z_0}^1 z^2 dz - \int_{z_0}^1 \int_0^1 zy \, dz \, dy \\ &= \left(1/3 - z_0^3/3\right) - \left(1/4 - z_0^2/4\right) = 31/324. \end{aligned}$$

The firm captures only some of the economic gains it creates for the high-type buyers and high-type sellers:

$$\Pi < G_H - g_H.$$

The low-value types, that is, those with parameter values below z_0, have expected losses because the high-value traders exit the search market:

$$G_L - g_L = \int_0^{z_0} \int_0^{z_0} zy \, dz \, dy - \int_0^{z_0} \int_0^1 zy \, dz \, dy = z_0^4/4 - z_0^2/4 = -5/81.$$

The firm creates aggregate benefits by efficiently matching its subscribers.

10.4 Competition between Market-Making Firms

Firms create and manage markets by adjusting prices and balancing demand and supply. By setting ask and bid prices, wholesale and retail firms act as intermediaries, coordinate transactions, clear markets, and establish relative prices in the economy; see Spulber (1996a). Firms choose ask and bid prices for capital, labor, manufactured inputs, resources, and technology. Manufacturing firms often combine production with related market-making activities. This section examines how the market equilibrium with endogenous entrepreneurs and endogenous price setting by firms differs from the frictionless Walrasian framework.

The market equilibrium with endogenous price setting by competing firms contrasts with the traditional supply-and-demand model. This section presents a model of market making by price-setting firms with consumers searching for the lowest ask price and suppliers searching for the highest bid price. Contrary to the "law of one price," and consistent with some search models, the equilibrium with market-making firms features nondegenerate distributions of ask prices and bid prices.

Transaction cost frictions give firms market power, so that the buy and sell prices offered by a firm are not equal in equilibrium. Instead, market-making firms set buy and sell prices with ranges that are respectively above and below the Walrasian market-clearing price. Furthermore, as a consequence of market frictions, total output lies below the Walrasian output. The market equilibrium is also compared to monopoly intermediation. The equilibrium buy and sell pricing policies are respectively below and above those of a monopoly intermediary, and total output lies above the expected monopoly level. The model in this section is due to Spulber (1996b).

The model highlights the role of *time* as a transaction cost. There are no explicit costs of search. Rather, because search is time-consuming, and buyers, sellers, and firms discount future returns with a common discount rate, a buyer may settle for a higher price, or a seller may accept a lower offer, instead of continuing to search. Firms examine the tradeoff between current and future sales in committing to a price. The equilibrium depends on the discount rate in a crucial way. As the discount rate goes to zero, thus eliminating the time cost of search, output at the market equilibrium with price-setting firms approaches the Walrasian outcome. Conversely, as the discount rate becomes high, thus increasing the time cost of search, output at the equilibrium with price-setting firms approaches the monopoly intermediation outcome. Increases in the discount rate lead to an increase in the equilibrium number of active firms, profit per firm, the mean spread between ask and bid prices, and the variance of ask and bid prices, while lowering the number of active consumers and suppliers.

Entrepreneurs have different transaction technologies, which affects their decision about whether or not to establish a firm. Consumers and suppliers enter the market in the initial period and exit when they have purchased or sold the good. Assume that firms commit to stationary pricing policies and choose prices before search begins, as in most search models. The discount rate directly affects the firm's decision problem because demand is nonstationary. Firms are concerned about the tradeoff between pricing for high demand in the early periods, when there are many searchers, and pricing in the later periods, when there is low demand because many searchers have left the market. There exists a unique symmetric equilibrium at which firms' bid and ask pricing policies depend on their transaction costs.

Consumers and suppliers do not engage in direct exchange. This occurs when market-making firms have sufficient transaction cost advantages so that search markets are inactive. For retailers and wholesalers, these advantages could consist of specialized technologies for effecting transactions that yield absolute cost advantages, such as computer processing of transactions, bar code scanners, automated warehousing, and transportation. George Stigler, in his classic 1961 article "The Economics of Information," recognized that because the efficiency of personal search is low for both buyers and sellers, there arises a need for specialized traders. For manufacturers, the advantage could include not only lower transaction costs but also knowledge of manufacturing technology that is not readily available to consumers and suppliers. The purpose of the discussion is to explore competition between intermediaries rather than comparing intermediation with direct transactions between consumers and suppliers.

Consumers differ from each other in terms of their willingness to pay for the final good, so that reservation values differ. Suppliers differ from each other in terms of the opportunity costs of supplying their good or service so that their reservation values differ as well. This heterogeneity of consumers and suppliers has the advantage of making it possible to derive the traditional supply and demand curves and to compare the results with the Walrasian framework. The search framework is particularly useful in that it makes clear the connection between transaction costs and market equilibrium. Finally, firms differ from each other in terms of transaction or production costs. The analysis shows how heterogeneity leads to market equilibrium distributions of bid and ask prices.

The model contrasts with standard search models that differentiate between agents on the search side of the market strictly in terms of the costs of search, so that consumers have the same demands or workers have the same outside opportunities. The exception to this approach is Diamond (1987), who examines a search model in which consumers can differ in their willingness to pay for the good. In Diamond's model, search is costly because it takes time and consumers discount future returns. Search models with bilateral heterogeneity have been given limited attention. The search analysis here is closely related to that of MacMinn (1980) and the extension by Benabou (1993), who study a search model in which consumers have different search costs whereas price-setting firms have different production costs, although they do not consider intermediation. In a search model, Hogan (1991) introduces a monopoly arbitrageur that competes with producers and shows that arbitrage may reduce efficiency. His model does not address competition between intermediaries or search across intermediaries as in the present model.

Gehrig (1990) presents an intermediation model in which there are heterogeneous consumers and suppliers who have the opportunity to be randomly matched with each other or to visit intermediaries whose posted prices are commonly observable. In contrast to the present model of time-consuming search, Gehrig allows consumers and suppliers to meet costlessly and trade based on first-and-final offers. His finding that the intermediary trades with consumers with high willingness to pay and suppliers with low cost is similar to the set of active consumers and suppliers in the present model. Gehrig's model is similar to the present one in that consumers and suppliers are heterogeneous, and the monopoly intermediary posts both ask and bid prices. Gehrig's model differs from the present one in that his matching process is *static*, and because posted prices are commonly observable, there is no search across intermediaries. Unlike the present model, Gehrig is concerned with price setting by a monopolist competing with direct matches between consumers and suppliers. Gehrig further shows that Bertrand competition between identical intermediaries results in Walrasian prices. This contrasts with the market equilibrium here, where search across heterogeneous intermediaries results in a departure from the ideal Walrasian outcome, but corresponds with an important limiting case.

Rubinstein and Wolinsky (1987) observe that "Despite the important role played by intermediation in most markets, it is largely ignored by the standard theoretical literature." They present an intermediation model based on a stochastic, time-consuming matching process. In their model the terms of trade are the result of a split-the-difference bargaining process between buyers, sellers, and intermediaries, rather than the search and price-setting considered here. The advantage of the present model is that relative prices are set by intermediaries. In both models, the matching process is exogenously determined and buyers and sellers form reservation values. In my model, consumers and suppliers make optimal search decisions based on the market equilibrium distribution of ask or bid prices. Finally, in their model, consumers, suppliers, and middlemen are each identical. This has the advantage of permitting simple stochastic matches of consumers and suppliers with each other or with the middlemen. The assumption of identical agents does not permit the general demand and supply framework developed here that allows a comparison with the Walrasian framework. Moreover, the present framework emphasizes that firms perform a dual role of making markets and transforming inputs into outputs. Thus, their role is not simply reduction of market frictions.

Models of financial market microstructure generally obtain a bid-ask spread by assuming commonly observable prices, that is, without search, either in a perfect competition setting (e.g., Copeland and Galai, 1983, and Glosten and Milgrom, 1985) or in a monopoly setting (e.g., Garman, 1976). Similarly, Dennert (1993) presents a static equilibrium model of oligopoly competition between dealers in financial markets when there are informed insiders and uninformed liquidity traders, and shows that only randomized pricing strategies exist in equilibrium. Although the present search model is substantially different, the heterogeneity of intermediaries plays a related role in generating equilibrium price distributions. Also, Yanelle (1989a, 1989b) presents a static, financial intermediation model without search in which the intermediary has an advantage over direct transactions due to economies of scale. Bhattacharya and Hagerty (1987) extend Diamond (1982) to examine bid-ask price setting by identical dealers who set prices and choose the number of permanent clients that they will visit. Their setting, and the other financial intermediation models, are substantially different from the present one.

10.4.1 Entrepreneurs, Buyers, Suppliers, and Firms

Firms post constant ask prices, p, for sales to consumers and constant bid prices, w, for purchases from suppliers. The ask and bid prices can be observed only after time-consuming search. Consumers search across firms for the best ask price, whereas suppliers search across firms for the best bid price. We begin by characterizing the three kinds of economic agents and deriving the supply and demand functions faced by individual firms. Then we set out the firms' optimization problem and define the market equilibrium.

All economic agents discount future net benefits at a positive rate δ. There are no explicit costs of search. Because search is a time-consuming process for both consumers and suppliers, the only cost of search is due to the time spent searching and the discounting of delayed benefits. In each period, consumers and suppliers visit one firm and observe the firm's posted ask or bid price, respectively. Thus, the cost of search for consumers and suppliers is due to discounting future gains from trade. Firms discount future earnings as well, which affects their pricing policies in the case of price commitment.

Firms, such as large retailers, typically deal with millions of consumers and thousands of suppliers. The purchases of consumers from such firms and the sales of suppliers to such firms typically are very small relative to the firm's overall sales and purchases. To represent this, and to facilitate aggregation, the model assumes that consumers have unit demands and suppliers have unit supplies, whereas firms purchase multiple units from suppliers and sell multiple units to consumers.

By setting ask and bid prices and by purchasing inputs from suppliers and selling outputs to consumers, firms make the market. They stand ready to sell products and to buy inputs at their posted prices. Firms establish and operate the market mechanism by sending price signals to suppliers and consumers that determine their search decisions and their production or consumption choices. The firm is restricted to posting prices and cannot ration consumers or suppliers by quantity. Free disposal is allowed so that the firm can overstock. Firms cannot hold inventories across periods (inventory costs are too high or the goods are perishable). Thus, prices must be set such that the quantity purchased is greater than or equal to the quantity sold in each round. The market equilibrium consists of distributions of ask and bid prices across firms. The equilibrium distributions of ask and bid prices are represented by cumulative probability distributions $F(p)$ and $G(w)$ defined on the nonnegative real line.

Assume that firms choose stationary bid and ask prices. The assumption of stationary price paths is made to simplify the analysis and implies that the market equilibrium price distributions are also stationary. The equilibrium of the model without the assumption of constant price paths would lead to complex nonstationary price distributions and nonstationary decision problems for consumers and suppliers as well. In the model with one-time entry of consumers and suppliers, this assumption corresponds to most search models in which prices remain constant until the search process is completed.

Consumers and suppliers are assumed to be price-takers, whereas the firms acting as intermediaries are price-makers. In particular, assume that consumer and supplier decisions are not based on the solvency of the intermediary or the possibility of being rationed. This rules out situations in which sellers might refuse to supply a low-cost intermediary resulting in an intermediary rationing buyers more than anticipated. This further eliminates the possibility of bankruptcy for the intermediary, resulting from buyers not making purchases. Given the continuum of buyers and sellers, we do not consider "off equilibrium" behavior that might arise in other settings. Thus, intermediaries set prices based on their supply and demand functions, which depend on equilibrium market price distributions.

To highlight the competition between firms acting as market makers, consumers and suppliers do not trade directly with each other due to the intermediary's cost advantages in managing transactions. If the firms are manufacturers, then they may employ production technology that is not readily available to customers and suppliers. The analysis shows the effects of costly search on the market equilibrium with competing intermediaries.

Entrepreneurs

There is a continuum of potential entrepreneurs that is represented by a uniform distribution of types k on the unit interval. The entrepreneur's type k represents the per-unit transaction costs of the firm that the entrepreneur can establish. Differences in transaction costs represent differences in the entrepreneur's knowledge of transaction technology and the entrepreneur's ability. Different values of start-up costs k represent inventions of new transaction technologies and new business methods. By establishing a firm, an entrepreneur creates an innovation, because the firm implements the new transaction technology. Entrepreneurs do not incur any explicit costs to establish a firm.

The potential firms can be thought of as either merchants or manufacturers. As merchants, the firms sell the same number of units that they purchase. As manufacturers, it is assumed that the firm's technology exhibits constant returns to scale. Then, without loss of generality, it can be assumed that the technology converts inputs to outputs on a one-to-one basis. Firms have a constant marginal cost k of carrying out a transaction and stocking or manufacturing a unit of output.

Buyers

Consumers who are buyers have a willingness to pay v for the good purchased from a firm. The population of consumers is represented by a uniform distribution of willingness-to-pay levels on the unit interval. Differences in willingness-to-pay levels represent differences in consumer tastes. This representation of consumer preferences differs from most search models, in which consumers have an identical willingness to pay for the good but differ in terms of the cost of search. In these search models, price distributions are obtained on the basis of varying search costs. The present model, by assuming heterogeneous tastes, addresses the basic issue of how to allocate goods across consumers with differing valuations and allows a comparison with traditional market models. Because consumers have differing valuations of the good and because the costs of search are deferred gains from trade, it follows that consumers will also have differing costs of search.

Consumers know the equilibrium distribution of ask prices $F(p)$ but not the particular firms associated with each price. Depending on the consumer's willingness to pay and on the distribution of ask prices, some consumers will choose to refrain from search. Active consumers search across firms and observe a single asking price in each period. After observing a price, an active consumer decides whether to purchase the good or to continue searching.

The buyer's optimal search rule is to compare the net value of current consumption with the returns to search. The buyer purchases the good if and only if the ask price p is less than or equal to the reservation value. The reservation value is defined by a standard recursive equation,

$$(51) \qquad v - r = \frac{1}{1 + \delta} \left[\int_0^r (v - p) dF(p) + \int_r^\infty (v - r) dF(p) \right],$$

where a solution exists. Simplifying the recursive equation with integration by parts yields

$$(52) \qquad v = L(r) \equiv r + \frac{1}{\delta} \int_0^r F(p) dp.$$

Buyers with a higher willingness to pay engage in less search.[10] A buyer with willingness to pay equal to 1 has the maximum reservation value $\bar{r}$.[11] For any given F, a less patient buyer engages in less shopping.

Suppliers

Consumers who are suppliers have an initial endowment of one unit that can represent labor, capital, land, resources, or a manufactured input. Suppliers have an opportunity cost c for the good or service supplied to a firm. The population of suppliers is represented by a uniform distribution of opportunity costs on the unit interval. Different opportunity costs can represent differences in suppliers' outside opportunities, disutilities of effort, or abilities. The model addresses the question of how the market allocates production across suppliers with differences in opportunity costs. Because suppliers have different opportunity costs and because the costs of search are deferred gains from trade, it follows that, like buyers, suppliers will have differing costs of search.

Suppliers know the equilibrium distribution of bid prices $G(w)$ but not the particular firm associated with each price. The suppliers' decision problem parallels that of consumers. The supplier sells a good or service to a firm if and only if the

---

10 This follows because the function $L(r)$ is continuous and strictly increasing on $[0, \infty)$.

11 Because the function $L(r)$ is continuous and strictly increasing on $[0, \infty)$, it has an (increasing) inverse R. For any v in $[0, 1]$, equation (52) has a unique solution $r \equiv R(v; \delta, F)$ for every δ and F. The maximum reservation value is $\bar{r} = R(1; \delta, F)$.

firm's bid price w is greater than or equal to the supplier's reservation value. Suppliers have a reservation value t defined by

$$(53) \qquad t - c = \frac{1}{1+\delta}\left[\int_0^t (t-c)dG(w) + \int_t^\infty (w-c)dG(w)\right],$$

where a solution exists. The recursive equation simplifies to

$$(54) \qquad\qquad c = Y(t) \equiv t - \frac{1}{\delta}\int_t^\infty [1 - G(w)]dw.$$

A higher-opportunity-cost supplier engages in more search. The lowest-cost firm has a minimum reservation value of $\hat{t}$.[12] For any given G, a less-patient supplier engages in less search.

Firms

Firms are market makers that clear markets by posting ask and bid prices before the search process begins. The rigidity of prices during search is a standard assumption in search models. Firms set prices to maximize the present discounted value of profits, trading off net revenues from current and future transactions. Thus the firm's pricing policy depends directly on the discount rate, as well as indirectly though the demand and supply decision of buyers and suppliers.

The density of buyers with reservation value r can be represented by $h(r)$, which is given by

$$(55) \qquad\qquad h(r) = dL(r)/dr = 1 + F(r)/\delta.$$

Let m represent the endogenous density of active firms, so that the per-firm density of buyers equals $h(r)/m$. Each active firm receives an equal share of searchers.

By the law of large numbers, the number of active buyers with reservation value r who visit the firm can be calculated. The number of buyers with reservation value r who visit the firm equals the density of buyers per firm times 1 for the first round of searches, $1 - F(r)$ for the second round of searches, $[1 - F(r)]^2$ for the third round of searches, and so on. The firm's demand in the ith round of searches is obtained by integration over the set of buyers with reservation values higher than the firm's ask price for all $p \leq \bar{r}$,

$$(56) \qquad\qquad D^i(p) = \int_p^{\bar{r}} [1 - F(r)]^i \frac{h(r)}{m}dr.$$

The situation is similar on the supply side. The density of suppliers with reservation value t is represented by $l(t)$, which is given by

$$(57) \qquad\qquad l(t) = dY(t)/dt = 1 + [1 - G(t)]/\delta.$$

---

12 The function $Y(t)$ is continuous and strictly increasing in t on $[0, \infty)$ so that it has an (increasing) inverse T. For any c in $[0, 1]$, equation (54) has a unique solution $t = T(c; \delta, G)$ for every δ and G. The minimum reservation value is $\hat{t} \equiv T(0; \delta, G)$.

The per-firm density of suppliers thus equals $l(t)/m$. The supply in the ith round of searches for all $w \geq \hat{t}$ is

(58) $$S^i(w) = \int_{\hat{t}}^{w} (G(t))^i \frac{l(t)}{m} dt.$$

Define weighted demand and supply functions $D(p)$ and $S(w)$, respectively, as

(59) $$D(p) \equiv \sum_{i=0}^{\infty} \frac{D^i(p)}{(1+\delta)^i},$$

(60) $$S(w) \equiv \sum_{i=0}^{\infty} \frac{S^i(w)}{(1+\delta)^i}.$$

These functions will be useful in characterizing the market equilibrium. Given constant posted prices, the price-distribution functions $F(p)$ and $G(w)$ are the same in each period. Substitute for $h(r)$ from equation (55) into equation (56) and apply the convergence of the sum of a geometric series to equation (59). For any market price-distribution functions, the weighted demand has a linear form,

(61) $$D(p) = \sum_{i=0}^{\infty} \int_{p}^{\bar{r}} \frac{[1 - F(r)]^i}{(1+\delta)^i} \frac{[\delta + F(r)]}{\delta m} dr = (\bar{r} - p)\frac{(1+\delta)}{\delta m}.$$

Substitute for $l(t)$ from equation (57) into equation (58) and apply the convergence of the sum of a geometric series to equation (60). For any market price-distribution function, the weighted supply also has a linear form,

(62) $$S(w) = \sum_{i=0}^{\infty} \int_{\hat{t}}^{w} \frac{(G(t))^i}{(1+\delta)^i} \frac{[\delta + 1 - G(t)]}{\delta m} dt = (w - \hat{t})\frac{(1+\delta)}{\delta m}.$$

The firm's present discounted value of profits Π is defined as

(63) $$\Pi(p, w, k) \equiv p \sum_{i=0}^{\infty} \frac{D^i(p)}{(1+\delta)^i} - (w + k) \sum_{i=0}^{\infty} \frac{S^i(w)}{(1+\delta)^i}.$$

Because firms cannot ration customers or hold inventories, prices must be set such that $D^i(p) \leq S^i(w)$. The firm chooses prices p, w to solve the following program:

(64) $$\max_{p,w} \Pi(p, w, k) \text{ subject to } D^i(p) \leq S^i(w), i = 1, 2 \ldots.$$

10.4.2 Market Equilibrium

The market reaches equilibrium as a result of the pricing policies of firms acting as intermediaries between consumers and suppliers. This section solves the firm's optimization problem and characterizes the equilibrium price distributions. The constraints in expression (64) are difficult to handle. The problem can be analyzed by solving a relaxed program in which the constraints are replaced by a single less restrictive constraint. After characterizing the equilibrium, given the firm's optimal actions in the relaxed program, we show that the constraints in original program (64) are satisfied at equilibrium. This establishes that equilibrium applies to firm behavior in the original problem.

When the weighted demand and supply functions in equations (59) and (60) are used, the firm's relaxed program is

(65) $\max_{p,w} \Pi(p, w, k)$ subject to $D(p) \le S(w)$.

The profit-maximizing firm that solves the relaxed program chooses prices such that the weighted demand and supply are equal. Otherwise, the firm could increase its profit by lowering the bid price w. Therefore, the constraint in expression (65) is strictly binding. Because $D(p)$ is continuous and downward-sloping, it has a unique inverse $p = P(q)$. Also, the weighted supply $S(w)$ has a unique inverse $w = W(q)$. Then the firm chooses q to maximize profit:

(66) $\Pi(q) = [P(q) - W(q) - k]q.$

Each firm equates the price-spread net of transaction costs with the sum of the reciprocals of the elasticities of demand and supply times the ask and bid prices, respectively.[13] Define $\eta(p) = -pD'(p)/D(p)$ and $\xi(w) = wS'(w)/S(w)$ as the elasticities of the weighted demand and supply functions. The firm's profit-maximizing ask and bid prices $p(k)$ and $w(k)$, respectively, satisfy the following fundamental equation:

(67) $p(k) - w(k) - k = \dfrac{p(k)}{\eta(p(k))} + \dfrac{w(k)}{\xi(w(k))}.$

The solution is represented in Figure 10.6. At the profit-maximizing ask and bid prices, weighted demand and supply are equal:

(68) $D(p(k)) = S(w(k)).$

To obtain the equilibrium pricing policies, we derive the pricing policies that solve the firm's relaxed program (65) and then show that the constraints in the general program (64) are satisfied in equilibrium. Given equations (61) and (62), the profit function in equation (66) has the form

$$\Pi(q) = \{\bar{r} - \hat{t} - k - q[2\delta m/(1 + \delta)]\}q,$$

13 The problem of prices bunching at some price, as in Diamond-type equilibria, does not occur here in equilibrium. Because there are no explicit costs of search, consumers have different willingness-to-pay levels, so a lower ask price increases demand. A higher bid price raises the amount offered by suppliers who have different opportunity costs. In this setting, differences in transaction costs of firms lead to different prices. Bunching of equilibrium prices in search models is discussed by Reinganum (1979), Stiglitz (1987a), and Benabou (1993).

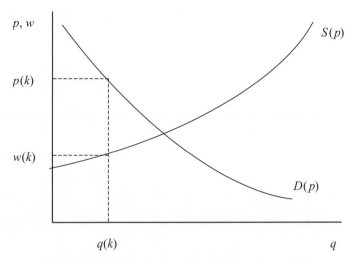

Figure 10.6. Profit-maximizing price setting by firms.

which is strictly concave, with a unique maximum at

$$q(k) = (\bar{r} - \hat{t} - k)(1 + \delta)/(4\delta m)$$

for all $k \leq \bar{r} - \hat{t}$. This is strictly decreasing in k for $k \leq \bar{r} - \hat{t}$. Prices are given by

$$p^*(k) = P(q(k)) = (3\bar{r} + \hat{t} + k)/4,$$

$$w^*(k) = W(q(k)) = (\bar{r} + 3\hat{t} - k)4.$$

The firm's pricing policy is unique.

The profit of the firm is strictly decreasing in the transaction cost k because

$$\Pi(q^*(k)) = (\bar{r} - \hat{t} - k)^2(1 + \delta)/(8\delta m).$$

Therefore the set of active firms is convex. No consumer is willing to pay more than $\bar{r}$ and no supplier will sell for less than $\hat{t}$, so that the marginal entrepreneur is m:

$$m = \bar{k} = \bar{r} - \hat{t}.$$

Given the pricing policies, a unique closed-form solution is obtained for the equilibrium distribution.[14] Substitute for $k = \bar{k}$ and $k = 0$ so that

$$\hat{p} = (3\bar{r} + \hat{t})/4, \quad \bar{p} = \bar{r},$$

$$\hat{w} = \hat{t}, \quad \bar{w} = (\bar{r} + 3\hat{t})/4.$$

14 The market equilibrium consists of ask and bid price distributions (F, G) defined by the functional mappings $H(p; F, G) = Pr\{p^*(k) \leq p\}$ for $p < \bar{r}$, $H(p; F, G) = 1$ for $p \geq \bar{r}$, $J(w; F, G) = Pr\{w^*(k) \leq w\}$ for $w > \hat{t}$, and $J(w; F, G) = 0$ for $w \leq \hat{t}$. The firm pricing policies $p(k)$ and $w(k)$ depend on the equilibrium price distribution through the values of $\bar{r}$ and $\hat{t}$. The pair of price distributions is a market equilibrium if and only if it is a fixed point of the functional mapping $(H, J) : (F, G) \rightarrow (H(.; F, G), J(.; F, G))$.

For $p \in [\hat{p}, \overline{p}]$ and $w \in [\hat{w}, \overline{w}]$, the equilibrium ask and bid price distributions are obtained as follows:

(69) $$F(p) = \Pr\{p^*(k) \le p\} = \frac{4p - 3\overline{r} - \hat{t}}{\overline{r} - \hat{t}},$$

(70) $$G(w) = \Pr\{w^*(k) \le w\} = 1 - \frac{\overline{r} + 3\hat{t} - 4w}{\overline{r} - \hat{t}}.$$

Now substitute the equilibrium ask and bid price distributions into equations (52) and (54) to calculate the highest reservation value for consumers and the lowest reservation value for suppliers. From equation (52), for $v = 1$ and $\overline{r} = R(1)$,

(71) $$1 = \overline{r} + \frac{1}{\delta} \int_{\hat{p}}^{\overline{r}} F(p) dp$$

$$= \overline{r} + \frac{1}{\delta} \int_{(3\overline{r}+\hat{t})/4}^{\overline{r}} \frac{4p - 3\overline{r} - \hat{t}}{\overline{r} - \hat{t}} dp$$

$$= \frac{(1 + 8\delta)\overline{r} - \hat{t}}{8\delta}.$$

From equation (54), for $c = 0$ and $\hat{t} = T(0)$,

$$0 = \hat{t} - \frac{1}{\delta} \int_{\hat{t}}^{\overline{w}} \frac{\overline{r} + 3\hat{t} - 4w}{\overline{r} - \hat{t}} dw$$

$$= \frac{(1 + 8\delta)\hat{t} - \overline{r}}{8\delta}.$$

Solving for $\overline{r}$ and $\hat{t}$ yields

$$\overline{r} = (1 + 8\delta)/(2 + 8\delta), \quad \hat{t} = 1/(2 + 8\delta).$$

Therefore the price ranges are

$$\hat{p} = (1 + 6\delta)/(2 + 8\delta), \quad \overline{p} = (1 + 8\delta)/(2 + 8\delta),$$

$$\hat{w} = 1/0(2 + 8\delta), \quad \overline{w} = (1 + 2\delta)/(2 + 8\delta).$$

Because the weighted demand and supply are equal, $D(p(k)) = S(w(k))$, it follows that

$$p(k) + w(k) = \overline{r} + \hat{t}.$$

Substituting for w in equation (70), note that

$$1 - G(w(k)) = [4p(k) - 3\overline{r} - \hat{t}]/(\overline{r} - \hat{t}) = F(p(k)).$$

Therefore, $D^i(p(k)) = S^i(w(k))$ for all i, so that the firm's equilibrium strategies satisfy the general optimization problem (64).

The unique symmetric equilibrium-pricing policy functions for $k \leq \bar{r} - \hat{t}$ are

$$p(k) = (1 + 6\delta)/(2 + 8\delta) + k/4,$$

$$w(k) = (1 + 2\delta)/(2 + 8\delta) - k/4.$$

The equilibrium set of active entrepreneurs is the convex set of $[0, \bar{k}]$, with the transaction cost of the marginal firm equal to the difference between the highest consumer reservation value and the lowest supplier reservation value,

$$m = \bar{k} = \bar{r} - \hat{t}.$$

The unique market-equilibrium ask and bid price distributions are as follows. The distribution of ask prices is

(72) $$F(p) = \frac{p(2 + 8\delta) - (1 + 6\delta)}{2\delta} \quad \text{for } p \in [\hat{p}, \overline{p}],$$

with $F(p) = 0$ for $p \leq \hat{p}$ and $F(p) = 1$ for $p \geq \overline{p}$, where

$$\hat{p} = (1 + 6\delta)/(2 + 8\delta), \quad \overline{p} = (1 + 8\delta)/(2 + 8\delta).$$

The distribution of bid prices is

(73) $$G(w) = \frac{w(2 + 8\delta) - 1}{2\delta} \quad \text{for } w \in [\hat{w}, \overline{w}],$$

with $G(w) = 0$ for $w \leq \hat{w}$ and $G(w) = 1$ for $w \geq \overline{w}$, where

$$\hat{w} = 1/(2 + 8\delta), \quad \overline{w} = (1 + 2\delta)/(2 + 8\delta).$$

At the market equilibrium, both the bid and the ask prices have nondegenerate distributions. The price distributions are functions of the rate of discount. This serves to emphasize the role played by time-consuming search in price setting.

A buyer is active if and only if the buyer's willingness to pay is greater than or equal to the minimum support price of the price distribution. Therefore, if a buyer is active, so are buyers with a greater willingness to pay. Active buyers thus have high reservation prices in the convex set $[\hat{v}, 1]$, where $\hat{v} \geq 0$ is the marginal buyer. From equation (52), $\hat{v} = \hat{p} = R(\hat{v}) \equiv \hat{r}$. For suppliers, from equation (54), $\bar{c} = \overline{w} = T(\bar{c}) \equiv \hat{t}$, and active suppliers have low opportunity costs $[0, \bar{c}]$. In equilibrium, the number of active buyers and suppliers and total output Q is

(74) $$1 - \hat{v} = \bar{c} = Q = (1 + \delta)/(2 + 8\delta).$$

The number of entrepreneurs in equilibrium equals

(75) $$m = 4\delta/(1 + 4\delta).$$

The greater transaction costs are, the greater is the number of entrepreneurs in equilibrium. A higher cost of time δ raises the value of the firm and induces entrepreneurs to establish more firms. The equilibrium is illustrated in Figure 10.7.

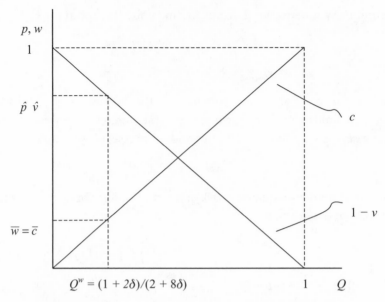

Figure 10.7. The market equilibrium with stationary pricing.

10.5 Competition between Market-Making Firms: Characterization of Equilibrium

Market making by price-setting firms results in a spread that straddles the single-price Walrasian equilibrium and is less than the monopoly bid-ask spread. These benchmarks are represented in Figure 10.8. The price spread separates the economy's demand decisions from its supply decisions. This section examines the effects of transaction costs on the characteristics of the market equilibrium.

10.5.1 Comparison with the Walrasian Equilibrium

The Walrasian framework assumes a frictionless economy with exogenous price setting. In the Walrasian equilibrium, supply and demand are equalized at a single price and transaction costs are zero. A consumer is able to observe the market-equilibrium price without engaging in search. A consumer thus purchases the good at the market-equilibrium price if and only if the price is less than the consumer's willingness to pay for the good. It is interesting to determine whether this is a limiting case of market equilibrium with price-setting firms.

Given a uniform distribution of consumer willingness-to-pay levels on the unit interval, the number of consumers willing to purchase the good is given by those consumers with willingness to pay between p and 1. Thus aggregate demand is simply $D^W(p) = 1 - p$. Similarly, given a uniform distribution of supplier opportunity costs on the unit interval, the aggregate supply is $S^W(p) = p$. Equating demand and supply, we find that the Walrasian price and quantity are $p^W = 1/2$ and $Q^W = 1/2$.

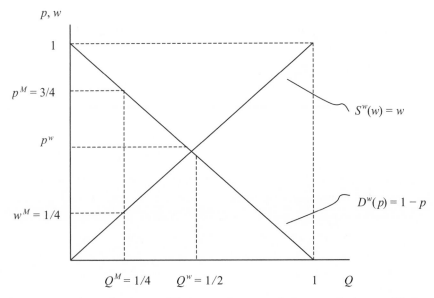

Figure 10.8. The Walrasian equilibrium and monopoly intermediation equilibrium.

The equilibrium price ranges for bid and ask prices straddle the Walrasian price for all positive δ,

$$\hat{w} < \overline{w} < p^W < \hat{p} < \overline{p}.$$

The properties of the bid-ask spread that are observed in financial market-monopoly models (Garman, 1976) carry over to search markets with competing intermediaries. Competition between intermediaries does not lead to the Walrasian outcome, because search is costly. Moreover, the spread of prices around the Walrasian price is not due here to inventory costs, but rather is due to the local market power of firms as a consequence of consumer search costs.

Bid and ask prices that straddle the Walrasian price imply that the total output with price-setting firms is strictly less than the Walrasian output levels for all positive $\delta : Q(\delta) < Q^W$. This shows that transaction costs cause aggregate output to fall below the perfectly competitive output.

As the discount rate goes to zero, the range of bid prices and the range of ask prices converge to the Walrasian price:

$$\lim_{\delta \to 0} \hat{w} = \lim_{\delta \to 0} \overline{w} = \lim_{\delta \to 0} \hat{p} = \lim_{\delta \to 0} \overline{p} = p^W.$$

Also, the aggregate output with price-setting firms converges to the Walrasian equilibrium output: $\lim_{\delta \to 0} Q(\delta) = Q^W$. This result illustrates the effects of the time costs of search on the market equilibrium.

When the cost of time becomes very low, that is, the discount rate falls, total output rises toward the Walrasian equilibrium. However, with a low cost of time, search costs are lowered, so that only firms with very low transaction costs remain active. This means that there are relatively fewer firms in an equilibrium with a lower discount rate. Because consumers search more, price competition between firms becomes much more vigorous and the spread between the ask and bid prices approaches zero. Thus, the market equilibrium with price-setting firms approaches the textbook market equilibrium. In the limit, the only active firms are low-transaction-cost firms posting prices in a manner that resembles that of the Walrasian auctioneer.

10.5.2 Comparison with Monopoly

In the monopoly equilibrium there is a single price setter and the market clears in the first period without search taking place. The costs of market clearing are just monopoly profits and do not include search costs. A monopoly firm with transaction cost k sets prices so that demand and supply are equal, $D^W(p^M) = S^W(w^M)$, and the markup satisfies the fundamental equation (67). The firm equates the markup over cost to the sum of the reciprocal of the demand elasticity times the ask price and the reciprocal of the supply elasticity times the bid price:

$$p^M - w^M - k = p^M/\eta^M(p^M) + w^M/\xi^M(w^M).$$

Note that, in contrast to the firm's optimization condition, which was already derived, the monopolist's prices are based on the Walrasian supply and demand functions. The monopolist's optimal ask and bid prices are therefore equal to $p^M(k) = (3 + k)/4$ and $w^M(k) = (1 - k)/4$. The monopoly output is $Q^M(k) = (1 - k)/4$, so that expected output is $Q^M = 1/8$.

For any finite discount rate δ, the price spread for each firm is within the monopoly price spread for the same transaction cost k:

$$w^M(k) < w(k) < p(k) < p^M(k).$$

For any finite discount rate δ, the total output with price-setting firms is strictly greater than the expected output under monopoly: $Q^M < Q(\delta)$. Thus, for any finite positive δ, each competitive firm offers a lower ask price and a higher bid price than the monopoly and the total output with price-setting firms lies between the monopoly and the Walrasian output levels:

$$Q^M < Q(\delta) < Q^W.$$

As the discount rate goes to infinity, all firms are active, with each firm's pricing strategy tending toward the monopoly pricing policy:

$$\lim_{\delta \to \infty} p(k) = p^M(k) \quad \text{and} \quad \lim_{\delta \to \infty} w(k) = w^M(k).$$

Also, as the discount rate goes to infinity, the aggregate output with price-setting firms converges to the expected monopoly ouput: $\lim_{\delta \to \infty} Q(\delta) = Q^M$.

As the discount rate rises, the cost of search to buyers and suppliers rises as well. This causes the equilibrium output to fall toward the monopoly output. With high costs of time, search costs increase for buyers and suppliers, so that firms with higher transaction costs can operate profitably. This implies that when search costs are high, many firms will operate in equilibrium, but price competition will be less vigorous. The spread between ask and bid prices increases as a consequence of reduced price competition.

10.5.3 Properties of the Market Equilibrium

The equilibrium spread between a firm's ask price and bid price exceeds the firm's per-unit transaction cost for all but the marginal firm:

$$p(k) - w(k) - k = (\overline{k} - k)/2 > 0,$$

for all $k < \overline{k}$. This is important because it demonstrates the existence of positive arbitrage profit in equilibrium. This occurs because firms set prices and face downward-sloping demand functions and upward-sloping supply functions as a consequence of the time costs of search. This result demonstrates that arbitrage profit is observed in equilibrium with a continuum of competitive price-setting firms.

The form of the firm's pricing-policy functions is particularly interesting because it shows that the less efficient firms offer a higher ask price and a lower bid price. Thus the firm's ask and bid prices are inversely correlated, and a firm with a higher transaction cost k has a higher price spread. This testable proposition shows that high prices and low factor payments are due to inefficiency rather than to market power. Moreover, the markup $p(k) - w(k) - k$ is decreasing in k, so that less efficient firms have smaller markups.

Consider now the effect of the discount rate on the market equilibrium. The discount rate affects buyers' and suppliers' search decisions and determines the firm's pricing policy. A higher rate of discount lowers the number of active buyers and suppliers and raises the number of active firms. The intuition is that a higher rate of discount raises the costs of additional search to consumers. This increases the returns to intermediation by firms, thus increasing the marginal transaction cost at which firms can operate profitably, which increases the number of firms that are active in equilibrium.

The means of the ask and bid price distributions are $Ep = (1 + 7\delta)/(2 + 8\delta)$ and $Ew = (1 + \delta)/(2 + 8\delta)$. The variances of prices are equal on the input and the output sides of the market:

$$\sigma_p^2 = \sigma_w^2 = (1/3)[\delta/(2 + 8\delta)]^2.$$

The price means and variances have the following properties. An increase in the discount rate raises the mean ask price, lowers the mean bid price, and raises the variances of the ask and bid prices.

The expected spread between ask and bid prices thus is increased by a higher discount rate. A higher discount rate, by raising the cost of search, also increases price dispersion. Because a higher rate of discount also raises the number of active firms, it follows that the number of entrepreneurs that choose to establish firms is positively correlated with the expected bid-ask spread. This means that increased competition is associated with greater expected spreads and higher variance. The reason for this correlation is that a higher cost of search raises the returns to intermediation.

The equilibrium price spread and profit per firm are now characterized. The net equilibrium price spread is

$$p(k) - w(k) - k = [4\delta - k(1 + 4\delta)](1 + \delta)/(16\delta^2).$$

A higher discount rate increases the markup for all active firms, $k < \bar{k}$. This result reflects the value of information. A higher discount rate increases the cost of time-consuming search for buyers and suppliers. Firms raise ask prices and lower bid prices because consumers and suppliers are willing to pay a premium to avoid further search.

The effect of the discount rate on profit per firm depends on the firm's level of cost. Profits for a firm with transaction cost k are

$$\Pi(k) = [(1 + \delta)/(2 + 8\delta)16\delta^2][4\delta - k(1 + 4\delta)]^2.$$

The reason is that although a higher discount rate increases the markup for all firms, the effect on quantity sold per firm differs. A higher discount rate raises quantity sold for higher-cost firms and lowers quantity sold for lower-cost firms.

Entrepreneurs establish firms that intermediate between buyers and sellers and adjust prices. The model of firms presented here combines intermediation between input and output markets with price setting. Intermediation between buyers and suppliers often is the primary economic activity of firms, whether they are merchants or manufacturers. Even in the neoclassical setting, firms coordinate input purchases, production, distribution, and output sales, thus implicitly helping to clear markets. However, because the neoclassical firm takes prices as given, the firm only intermediates on the quantity side by transforming inputs into outputs. In the neoclassical framework, market making takes place outside the firm through exogenous price adjustment represented by the Walrasian auctioneer.

Models of imperfect competition in the field of industrial organization have brought the price-setting role of firms to center stage, but ignore the intermediation role of firms by emphasizing competition in product markets. The analysis presented here shows how price-setting firms make the market by acting as intermediaries between consumers and suppliers. It shows that market clearing can involve distributions of both ask and bid prices when price-setting firms act as intermediaries, and establishes conditions under which the standard model of supply and demand is a limiting case of a market with costly search.

Buyers and suppliers have incomplete information about ask and bid prices. Search is costly because search across firms is a time-consuming process and economic agents discount future returns. Equilibrium bid and ask prices set by firms depend on the discount rate. The level of the discount rate can be viewed as a determinant of the value of information. A higher rate of discount raises the cost of search and increases the spread between bid and ask prices as well as the dispersion of ask and bid prices. This in turn raises the profits of firms. In the equilibrium of the single-entry model with stationary pricing policies, the number of active firms is increasing in the discount rate. This result demonstrates that there are greater returns to intermediation when search is more costly. The time cost of obtaining price information thus creates economic rents for firms acting as market makers.

Microeconomic and finance models often assume that a price spread cannot be sustained due to the incentives for unlimited purchase and resale. The no-arbitrage condition is predicated in part on the assumption that firms are price takers with prices set by a Walrasian auctioneer. In the present model, with market making by competing price-setting firms, the price spreads set by firms are positive at the market equilibrium.

The equilibrium with competing intermediaries contrasts with the standard Walrasian supply and demand framework. For any rate of discount, the market clears in the sense that supply equals demand. The range of ask prices is above the Walrasian price and the range of bid prices is below it, and total output is less than the Walrasian output. As the discount rate goes to zero, thus lowering the time cost of search, the market equilibrium with price-setting firms approaches the Walrasian equilibrium. This result confirms the familiar textbook characterization of supply and demand as an ideal or limiting case of a market with price-setting firms.

As the discount rate goes to zero, transaction costs fall, reducing the number of entrepreneurs. There are fewer entrepreneurs because only the most efficient firms operate. These firms serve the market with very narrow bid-ask spreads and high trade volumes and approximate the efficiency of ideal markets.

10.5.4 The Equilibrium with a Centralized Exchange

This section examines what effect establishing a centralized exchange will have on the search-market equilibrium. A market-making firm creates and operates the centralized exchange. The centralized exchange firm posts prices that are observed by all buyers and sellers. The firm that operates the centralized exchange competes with a decentralized dealer market composed of many market-making firms. Search in the dealer market creates inefficiencies that create returns for the centralized exchange. The model in this section is due to Rust and Hall (2003), who extend Spulber (1996a). The model of the market-making firm that operates the centralized exchange market is similar to that of Gehrig (1993) that was discussed earlier.

Buyers and sellers can trade on the centralized exchange without incurring search costs. This adds a fourth option for each buyer and each seller. A buyer or seller chooses between the following options: (i) he can be inactive, in which case his utility is zero, (ii) he can buy or sell immediately from the centralized exchange at posted ask or bid prices, (iii) he can enter the dealer market, engage in search, and accept an offer, or (iv) he can reject the offer obtained in the dealer market and continue to search in the dealer market while retaining the option of accepting the central exchange price.

Assume that the most efficient dealer has cost $\underline{k} = 0$. This ensures that for any positive bid-ask spread set by the market maker, the dealer market will be active. This rules out complications arising from the possibility that the centralized exchange firm might engage in limit pricing in order to drive dealers out of the market.

Consider the buyer's decision. The decision of a seller is similar. Let p^E represent the posted ask price in the exchange market and let w^E represent the posted bid price in the exchange market. The buyer who trades in the exchange market obtains benefits $v - p^E$. The buyer who trades in the dealer market at price p obtains benefits $v - p$. Optimality requires that $p \le r(v) < v$, where $r(v)$ is the reservation price in the search market that solves the recursive equation (52). Because, with positive probability, trade does not take place in the first period, this consumer's expected utility from being active in the dealer market is strictly less than $v - p$. Therefore, there exists an ask price $p^E > p$ such that the consumer would be indifferent ex ante between searching in the dealer market and receiving and accepting at some uncertain future date the offer p or immediately buying the good from the market maker at ask price p^E. Therefore, the market maker can attract buyers and sellers by offering immediate trade at publicized ask and bid prices.

The value function for a buyer with valuation v who has received an offer p in the dealer market and who observes the posted price p^E in the exchange market equals

(76) $\quad V^B(p, p^E, v)$

$$= \max \left\{ 0, v - p, v - p^E, [1/(1+\delta)] \int_{\underline{p}}^{\overline{p}} V^B(x, p^E, v) dF(x) \right\}.$$

It follows immediately that for an offer p in the dealer market ever to be acceptable, $p \le p^E$ must hold, for otherwise $v - p$ can never be greater than $v - p^E$. Thus, the ask price p^E set by the centralized exchange is the upper bound of the support of equilibrium prices in the dealer market; i.e., $\overline{p} = p^E$. An analogous result holds for sellers, establishing that $\underline{w} = w^E$.[15] Therefore, in the dealer market, buyers pay ask prices that are uniformly lower than p^E and sellers receive bid prices that are uniformly higher than w^E. Though this is common knowledge, these better offers will only materialize after one period. As we will demonstrate, due to this delay the most efficient sellers and the buyers with the highest valuations prefer to trade immediately rather than to wait for more favorable terms.

Substitute $\overline{p} = p^E$ and $\underline{w} = w^E$ in the profit equation (66) for $\overline{r}$ and $\hat{t}$ respectively, as defined in footnotes 11 and 12. Recall the assumption that $\underline{k} = 0$. Then,

---

15 This is Theorem 3 in Rust and Hall (2003).

applying previous arguments, the ask and bid prices in the dealer markets will be uniformly distributed. The ask and bid price distributions are given by

$$F(p) = \frac{4p - 4p^E - w^E}{p^E - w^E}, \quad G(w) = \frac{4w - 4w^E}{p^E - w^E},$$

for $p \in [\underline{p}, \overline{p}] = [(3/4)p^E + (1/4)w^E, p^E]$ and $w \in [\underline{w}, \overline{w}] = [w^E, (3/4)w^E + (1/4)p^E]$.

Let $v^E(p^E)$ be the marginal buyer who is indifferent between trading in the dealer market and buying from a market maker at the ask price p^E. For this buyer, the exchange price is a reservation value for searching in the dealer market,

$$(77) \qquad v^E(p^E) - p^E = \frac{1}{\delta} \int_{\underline{p}}^{p^E} F(p)dp.$$

If the marginal buyer is less than one, $v^E(p^E) < 1$, then the set of buyers can be divided into three groups. Buyers with a low willingness to pay, $v \in [0, \underline{p})$ are inactive, buyers with an intermediate willingness to pay, $v \in [\underline{p}, v^E(p^E))$, search in the dealer market, and buyers with a high willingness to pay, $v \in [v^E(p^E), 1]$, buy from the exchange.

The intuition for the buyer strategies is as follows. A buyer with valuation v_0 has a net value of searching across dealers in the dealer market equal to $v_0 - r(v_0)$, whereas his net utility of buying from the exchange equals $v_0 - p^E$. Thus, consumer v_0 is indifferent between going to the dealer market or trading with the exchange if and only if $r(v_0) = p^E$. Next, consider a buyer with a slightly higher valuation. Since $d(v - p^E)/dv = 1$ and $d(v - r(v))/dv < 1$, it follows that any buyer with a higher valuation strictly prefers to buy from the exchange. A buyer with a lower valuation strictly prefers to search in the dealer market or strictly prefers to be inactive.

The result that all buyers with $v \geq v^E(p^E)$ will buy from the exchange at ask price p^E implies that the demand function facing the exchange is

$$(78) \qquad Q^D(p^E, w^E) \equiv 1 - v^E(p^E) = 1 - p^E - \frac{1}{\delta} \int_{\underline{p}}^{p^E} F(p)dp.$$

Note that the buyer's demand Q^D also depends on the bid price because the bid price affects the range of ask prices, $[(3/4)p^E + (1/4)w^E, p^E]$.

By symmetry, the seller of type $c^E(w^E)$ is indifferent between entering the dealer market and selling to the exchange at price w^E if and only if

$$(79) \qquad v^E(w^E) = w^E - \frac{1}{\delta} \int_{w^E}^{\overline{w}} (1 - G(w))dw.$$

Hence, seller c prefers to sell to the exchange if and only if $w^E - c > t(c) - c$. Let c_0 be the seller who is just indifferent between joining the dealer market or selling to the exchange. Because $d(w^E - c)/dc = -1 < d(t(c) - c)/dc < 0$, it follows that all sellers with cost $c < c_0$ will prefer to sell to the exchange and all sellers with $c > c_0$ will prefer to enter the dealer market or to be inactive.

As with buyers, there are three sets of sellers if $c^E(w^E) > 0$. Sellers with a high cost, $c \in (\overline{w}, 1]$, are inactive, sellers with an intermediate cost, $c \in (c^E(w^E), \overline{w}]$, search in the dealer market, and sellers with a low cost, $c \in [0, c^E(w^E)]$, sell to the exchange. As all sellers with $c \leq c^E(w^E)$ trade with the exchange, the supply function faced by the exchange is

$$(80) \qquad Q^S(w^E, p^E) \equiv c^E(w^E) = w^E - \frac{1}{\delta} \int_{w^E}^{\overline{w}} (1 - G(w)) dw.$$

The exchange's supply function depends on the ask price because the range of bid prices depends on the ask price, $[w^E, (3/4)w^E + (1/4)p^E]$. Substituting for $\underline{p} = (3/4)p^E + (1/4)w^E$ and $\overline{w} = (3/4)w^E + (1/4)p^E$ in equations (78) and (80) and using the equilibrium price distributions F and G gives

$$(81) \qquad Q^D(p^E, w^E) \equiv 1 + w^E/(8\delta) - [1 + 1/(8\delta)] p^E,$$

$$(82) \qquad Q^S(w^E, p^E) = -p^E/(8\delta) + [1 + 1/(8\delta)] w^E.$$

Consider the optimization problem of the firm that manages the exchange. Replacing $p^E = 1 - w^E$ in either (81) or (82) and solving yields the bid price as a function of the output at which the exchange market clears, Q:

$$(83) \qquad W(Q) = \frac{1}{2} \frac{1}{1 + 4\delta} + \frac{4\delta}{1 + 4\delta} Q.$$

Using $p^E = 1 - w^E$, the exchange's ask price function is

$$(84) \qquad P(Q) = 1 - \frac{1}{2} \frac{1}{1 + 4\delta} - \frac{4\delta}{1 + 4\delta} Q.$$

The bid-ask spread is $p^E - w^E = 1 - 2w^E$ and the spread as a function of output Q equals

$$(85) \qquad P(Q) - W(Q) = \frac{4\delta}{1 + 4\delta} (1 - 2Q).$$

The exchange firm's profits as a function of output equal

$$(86) \qquad \Pi(Q) = (P(Q) - W(Q)) Q = \frac{4\delta}{1 + 4\delta} (1 - 2Q) Q.$$

The profit-maximizing sales of the exchange equal $Q^E = 1/4$. The equilibrium prices are

$$p^E = 1 - w^E = 1 - \frac{3}{4} \frac{1}{1 + 4\delta}.$$

The establishment of a centralized exchange creates competition for the dealer market. The maximum ask price in the dealer market when there is not an exchange market equals $\overline{p} = (1 + 8\delta)/(2 + 8\delta)$. Competition from the centralized exchange market reduces the maximum ask price to p^E, which is strictly less than $\overline{p}$ for all values of the discount rate. Similarly, competition from the centralized exchange raises the minimum bid price in the dealer market.

The centralized exchange that competes with a dealer market has half the output of the Walrasian market, $Q^W = 1/2$. The ask price of the centralized exchange firm, p^E, is greater than, equal to, or less than the Walrasian price, $p^W = 1/2$, depending on whether the discount rate, δ, is greater than, equal to, or less than $1/8$. In the model with competition between an exchange market and a dealer market, the discount rate represents transaction costs because it is the time cost of search. Thus, the time costs of search in the dealer market determine whether the exchange price is greater than or less than the Walrasian price.

Compare the market outcome when the centralized exchange market maker competes with the decentralized dealer market with the market outcome when a centralized exchange market maker competes with decentralized search market without dealers. Competition between centralized exchange and a decentralized search market is Gehrig's (1993) model described earlier. From equation (34) earlier in the chapter, the inverse demand function is $P(q) = 3/4 - q/2$ and the inverse supply function is $W(q) = 1 - P(q) = 1/4 + q/2$. The profit function of the centralized exchange market maker that competes with decentralized search equals

$$(87) \qquad \Pi(Q) = (P(Q) - W(Q))Q = (1 - 2Q)Q.$$

It follows that the market-clearing output is the same in both cases, $q = Q = 1/4$. The equilibrium prices chosen by the monopoly market maker are $p^M = 5/8$ and $w^M = 3/8$. The ask price set by the monopoly market maker, p^M, is greater than, equal to, or less than the ask price set by the exchange firm, p^E, depending on whether the value of the discount rate, δ, is less than, equal to, or greater than $1/4$.

The discount rate affects the equilibrium of the model of competition between an exchange market and a dealer market. Note that there are no search costs in the model with a monopoly market maker and decentralized consumer search. When transaction costs are low (δ less than $1/4$), an exchange firm competing with dealers chooses a bid-ask spread that is smaller than that of a monopoly market maker competing with decentralized search. When transaction costs are high (δ greater than $1/4$), an exchange firm competing with dealers chooses a bid-ask spread that is smaller than that of a monopoly market maker competing with decentralized search.

10.5.5 The Choice between Direct Sales and Intermediated Sales

This section summarizes Hendershott and Zhang (2006), which develops a model related to Spulber (1996a) that examines a firm's choice of marketing channels. An upstream firm can engage in retail sales to consumers, possibly through online sales. The upstream firm also can sell to consumers through heterogenous intermediaries. Consumers choose between purchasing from the upstream firm and searching across intermediaries. Purchasing from the upstream firm may be more or less convenient than purchasing from retail intermediaries in the search market. The upstream firm offers the convenience of a more rapid purchase but the inconvenience associated with not observing products before purchase.

The upstream firm offers consumers the retail price, p^U, and offers intermediaries the wholesale price, w. The intermediary firms have different unit costs, k, that take values in the interval $[\underline{k}, 1]$. The intermediary firms serving the search market choose different retail prices, $p(k)$. Let p represent the entire vector of retail prices in the search market. Consumers have different levels of willingness to pay, v, which are uniformly distributed on the unit interval. The description of the retail search market follows the model in Spulber (1996a) as outlined earlier in this section.

A consumer that purchases directly from the upstream firm encounters greater difficulty in choosing a product with the right specifications. Accordingly, the consumer faces the likelihood α that the product does not fit properly. The consumer returns items that do not fit properly and does not obtain a replacement. In contrast, the consumer is able to obtain items that fit properly when shopping in the search market. This represents a contrast between ordering over the Internet, where the consumer does not experience the item before purchase, and buying from a retailer after experiencing the item.

The consumer is able to purchase with greater speed when buying from the upstream firm than when shopping on the retail search market. Let δ^U represent the appropriate discount rate for the time it takes to purchase from the upstream firm. Let δ represent the appropriate discount rate for the time period needed to observe one price in the search market. To represent the greater speed of purchase from the upstream firm in comparison to the search market, suppose that $\delta^U > \delta$.

The upstream firm has unit production costs k^U. The upstream firm also has a cost c for each good that is returned. The upstream firm's retail demand is $D^U(p^U, w)$, and the upstream firm's wholesale demand from the intermediary firms is $D^W(p^U, w)$. Therefore, the upstream firm's profit function can be written as

$$\Pi^U(p^U, w) = [(1-\alpha)p^U - k^U - \alpha c]D^U(p^U, w) + w D^W(p^U, w).$$

The upstream firm chooses the prices p^U and w to maximize profits. It can be shown that if the upstream firm's unit costs, k^U, are in an intermediate range, both sales channels will be active in equilibrium. The upstream firm charges a wholesale price equal to the monopoly price minus one-half of the costs of the lowest-cost intermediary, $w = (1 - \underline{k})/2$. The upstream firm chooses to sell to consumers at a retail price equal to

$$p^U = 1/2 + (k^U + \alpha c)/[2(1-\alpha)].$$

The equilibrium has the following properties. Consumers with a low willingness to pay are inactive, with $[0, v_0)$ being the set of inactive consumers. Consumers with an intermediate willingness to pay, in the interval $[v_0, v_1)$, purchase from intermediaries in the search market. Finally, consumers with a high willingness to pay, in the interval $[v_1, 1]$, purchase from the upstream firm. The high-value consumers are willing to incur the inconvenience of possibly returning purchases in return for the convenience of making purchases more rapidly.

The upstream firm competes with downstream intermediaries by making retail sales to consumers. Online sales by the upstream firm reduce the number of active intermediaries, and lower the prices and mark-ups of each intermediary. When the upstream firm engages in online sales, each consumer obtains a greater surplus and more consumers make purchases. Online sales by the upstream firm increase total consumer surplus.

These results help to explain the proliferation of sales channels offered by firms. The development of the Internet significantly lowers the costs of selling to consumers without intermediaries. Consumers can benefit from rapid purchase online with lower costs of search. This need not displace retail intermediaries, because they offer the convenience of experiencing products before purchase. The addition of online sales by the upstream firm improves transaction efficiency by allowing consumers to choose their most preferred marketing channel. By competing with retail intermediaries, the upstream firm's online sales increase overall consumer benefits.

10.6 Conclusions

Firms offer transaction methods that may improve on those that are feasible for consumers. By being third parties in transactions, often as intermediaries between buyers and sellers, firms add degrees of freedom to the transactions. Through specialization and economies of scale, firms can provide transaction technologies at a lower unit cost than bilateral exchange. Firms improve exchange relative to direct exchange between consumers by providing central places of exchange. Firms offer longevity that resolves some problems of exchange over time. Firms offer assets and monetary instruments that improve the efficiency of exchange. Firms create networks with communications and computation technologies that lower the costs of matchmaking between consumers.

Firms establish markets and operate them by adjusting prices and balancing supply and demand. Markets offer benefits in comparison with decentralized exchange between consumers in various ways. Centralized market makers avoid costly search and the associated inefficiencies of imperfect matches. Posted prices allow buyers and sellers to avoid the uncertainties in the terms of trade that would occur in a market with search and bilateral negotiation. The market maker stands ready to buy or sell, providing the market with liquidity or immediacy, and assures buyers and sellers that they will find a trading partner.

The discussion demonstrated the relationship between transaction costs and the number of entrepreneurs. The greater are transaction costs, the greater is the number of entrepreneurs in equilibrium. A higher cost of time raises the value of the firm and induces more entrepreneurs to establish firms.

The role of the firm as market maker makes the important connection between the entrepreneur and economic equilibrium. Entrepreneurship is consistent with economic equilibrium. Entrepreneurs establish firms, and in turn, firms make markets. Entrepreneurs play a fundamental role in economic equilibrium because they create the institutions that are responsible for market equilibrium.

11

The Firm in the Market for Contracts

Firms are intermediaries in the market for contracts. By coordinating contracts, firms create a "nexus of contracts."[1] The firm provides an alternative to direct exchange between consumers. There are many types of bilateral contracts including buyer-seller, principal-agent, borrower-lender, and investor-entrepreneur. Firms offer advantages over bilateral contracts through market making and coordination across multiple contracts. This chapter compares bilateral contracts between consumers with multilateral transactions managed by the firm. The discussion examines transaction costs associated with adverse selection, moral hazard, and contract hold-up.

Competition provides a major source of benefits from multilateral contracts. Buyers compete with each other to obtain the firm's goods. Sellers compete with each other to provide goods to the firm. The firm is able to manage competition between its customers and between its suppliers. This allows the firm to do much more than extract rents from its trading partners. By orchestrating competition, the firm can promote efficient behavior.

Competition between the firm's trading partners provides a number of useful incentives that are absent from bilateral contracts. Competition induces buyers and sellers to invest in increasing benefits or reducing costs, thereby mitigating the effects of hold-up observed in bilateral contracts. Competition allows the firm to use group incentives that aggregate information, thus alleviating moral hazard problems that are present in bilateral contracts. Competition also allows the firm to obtain economies of scale in monitoring performance, evaluating quality, or observing agent characteristics, thus reducing adverse selection problems that arise from asymmetric information in bilateral contracts. Multilateral transactions,

---

1 Jensen and Meckling (1976) argue that the firm is a "nexus of contracts" and find that "[t]he 'behavior' of the firm is like the behavior of the market, i.e., the outcome of a complex equilibrium." In contrast to their analysis, the theory of the firm suggests that the firm is not a passive result of the equilibrium, but instead actively coordinates contracts.

intermediated by the firm, therefore provide many opportunities to improve upon bilateral relationships between consumers.

The firm also improves efficiency relative to bilateral exchange by being the *residual claimant* in its transactions. The firm breaks the budget-balancing problem that is inevitable in bilateral transactions. By maximizing profit, the firm seeks to extract as much rent as possible from its set of transactions. This enhances efficiency in various ways. In the hold-up problem, parties to a contract renegotiate its terms to obtain a new division of quasirents after investments have been sunk. The firm extracts rents ex ante through prices offered to buyers and to sellers. Buyers and sellers, although experiencing disincentives due to the firm's market power, are able to capture the marginal returns to their investment, taking the firm's prices as given. This contrasts with bilateral exchange when there is renegotiation, because the two parties to a contract fully share the quasirents. Thus, buyers or sellers are only able to capture a share of the marginal returns to their investment, leading to the classic underinvestment problem.

The firm's role as residual claimant also improves efficiency relative to bilateral agency contracts. The terms of a principal-agent contract necessarily involve a division of surplus. Any incentives for performance must satisfy a balanced budget condition. Put differently, there are no residual claimants in bilateral exchange. This limits the types of incentive contracts available to contracting parties. In the principal-agent relationship, increases in performance incentives require compensating a risk-averse agent for bearing risk. The agent's tradeoff between incentives and risk is reflected directly in the benefits received by the principal as a direct consequence of budget balancing. Thus, the moral hazard problem in bilateral contracting is closely related to the budget-balancing problem.

A third-party residual claimant who intermediates between the principal and the agent can decouple the principal's benefits from those of the agent. The firm decouples the benefits of principals and agents through multilateral contracts. By managing competition between agents, the firm aggregates information and improves incentives for performance. The firm can use the improved information to induce greater agent performance with less risky payments, thus reducing the amount of compensation that must be paid to risk-averse agents.

Finally, the firm can take advantage of economies of scale in contracting to improve efficiency relative to bilateral contracts. At the contract formation stage, standard contract terms reduce the costs of writing contracts. This allows the firm to include more contract contingencies that improve the efficiency of contracts.[2] At the contract performance stage, economies of scale in monitoring performance let the firm include performance incentives that might not be feasible with bilateral contracting. The firm can also obtain economies of scale in information gathering, allowing the firm to monitor the performance of agents in principal-agent relationships, so that the firm intermediates between principals and agents. In the market

---

2 On costly contract contingencies, see Townsend (1979), Dye (1985), and Luca and Felli (1994).

for lemons, the firm mitigates adverse selection problems. Through economies of scale in monitoring, the firm can determine the quality of goods offered to sellers and certify product quality to its customers.

11.1 Contracts and Incentives to Invest: Firms Create Markets

Consider an economy in which consumers form bilateral contracts, acting either as buyers or as sellers. Buyers and sellers encounter many types of transaction costs associated with bilateral exchange. This section examines those costs and discusses how firms can use multilateral contracts to improve economic efficiency.

11.1.1 Contracting Costs

We examine how the firm can alleviate transaction costs in comparison to bilateral exchange. Consider the initial stage of contracting in which buyers and sellers must find a trading partner. Costly search introduces inefficiencies in the matching process itself, as discussed in earlier chapters. Mismatches between buyers and sellers reduce the potential surplus from the exchange. This in turn reduces incentives to form a contract. If a contract is formed, lower surplus can reduce incentives for the buyer and the seller to invest in improving the contractual relationship. Thus, lower contract surplus can mean departures from optimal investment levels, further reducing the value of the relationship.

Costly search before contracts form also can affect the contract terms once a buyer and seller have met. If finding a new partner is costly, the buyer and the seller encounter inertia. Search costs reduce the value of outside options. This affects the bargaining positions of the buyer and the seller, potentially altering relative bargaining power and the division of the surplus.

Search costs and the resulting inertia also affect the efficiency of the contract in the final performance phase. By reducing the contract surplus due to mismatches between buyers and sellers, inefficient assignments weaken incentives to perform. This can lead to inefficient effort levels and inefficient performance decisions. By reducing the value of contracts due to mismatches, costly search can affect the degree to which contracts are honored. Costly search also affects contract performance by changing the value of outside options. If contracting parties must search for new trading partners, they may be stuck in an inefficient contractual relationship. Costly search may serve to enforce performance when there might be mutual benefits to dissolving the relationship. For example, suppose that after the contract has formed, a buyer and a seller discover that the seller has high costs of performance relative to other sellers. The buyer might not find it worthwhile to breach the contract because the buyer would take into account both the possible offer of another seller and the transaction costs of finding the other seller. A similar problem would arise if a buyer and a seller discovered that other buyers had a higher willingness to pay. The seller would not find it worthwhile to breach because the seller would take into account the possible offer of an outside buyer net of the transaction costs of finding the other seller. If trading partners have asymmetric search costs, one party with lower search costs may take advantage of the reliance of the other contracting party, who finds outside options less attractive.

The costs of search can complicate investment in contractual relationships. The contracts literature has emphasized the problem of relationship-specific investment. Such investment makes a party to a contract potentially subject to renegotiation after the investment has been committed. In legal terms, one party takes advantage of the reliance of the other party. In practice, many factors mitigate the risks of one party taking advantage of the other party's reliance. Contract law of course provides penalties and remedies for breach. Expectations damages make the breaching party restore the other party to the same position as if the contract had been honored. In addition, the loss of business reputation and social pressures reduce incentives for breach.

It is useful to emphasize that transaction-specific investment need not be the problem. The investment may be general; that is, the investment may be equally well suited to many alternative contractual relationships. What makes the investment appear to be transaction-specific is that search and negotiation costs make it difficult for the buyer and the seller to change trading partners. Thus, hold-up can be a result of bilateral contracts themselves. Trading partners are stuck with each other due to high transaction costs in search and negotiation. Thus, hold-up need not be the result of the properties of capital equipment or human capital. The capital investment may be general, but the transaction costs of forming the relationship are sunk costs. High switching costs make the investment relationship-specific. Multilateral contracts help to correct this problem.

The firm can address many of the transaction costs associated with bilateral contracts. The firm improves buyer-seller assignments through many types of matching and market-making activities. The firm improves allocative efficiency both in markets with homogeneous products and in markets with differentiated products. The efficient assignment of buyers to sellers or of sellers to buyers increases the returns from exchange and thereby improves incentives for investment. Buyers invest more in increasing benefits and sellers invest more in reducing costs. With general investments, this chapter shows that investment is more efficient when the market-making firm improves market allocations. Thus, when firms improve allocative efficiency, they also improve dynamic efficiency relative to bilateral contracts.

Market organization significantly affects incentives for investment. In a market with decentralized exchange, contracts are formed through bilateral negotiation. Buyers and sellers do not have incentives to invest efficiently prior to forming contracts because they must share any quasirents generated by the investment with prospective trading partners. Because buyers and sellers do not obtain the full marginal return to their investment, they will invest less than the efficient amount, which will in turn further reduce market efficiency. In contrast, in a market with a price-setting firm, buyers and sellers face fixed terms of exchange. If the firm's market power is constrained, buyers and sellers retain more of the marginal return to investment. As a result, the firm improves the efficiency of investment.

Compare two alternative forms of market organization. In a market with decentralized exchange, buyers and sellers search for each other, negotiate the terms of exchange, and enter into contracts. In a market with transactions organized and intermediated by firms, buyers and sellers face posted prices for goods that are bought and sold. As shown in the previous chapter, the presence of a market-making firm can improve the allocation of goods when the firm competes with the search market. In a market with search and random matching, total output is excessive and there are incentives for inefficient under investment. In a market with a monopoly dealer, total output is insufficient and underinvestment also occurs. Competition between a firm and the search market improves incentives to invest both for buyers and for sellers. Competition between firms narrows the price spread and eliminates search, thus resulting in efficient total output and investment. Firms play an important role in the economy by providing an alternative to bilateral contracts.

The hold-up problem is said to occur when buyers and sellers make relationship-specific investments without binding contractual agreements. When buyers and sellers cannot make binding agreements, but must make irreversible investments, they will negotiate the terms of exchange after making their investments. Because negotiation takes place after investments are made, the buyer and the seller share the surplus from exchange and thus do not obtain the full returns to their investment. Anticipating this outcome, buyers and sellers will reduce their investments and will thus be worse off relative to a situation with efficient investment levels.

Contrary to the situation depicted in the story of the hold-up problem, there are many reasons to expect that buyers and sellers can enter into binding contracts. If the value of the transaction is greater than the transaction cost of forming a contract, there are many circumstances under which buyers and sellers can make credible commitments. The institution of contract law provides for enforcement of efficient contracts and remedies for breach of contract. For those contracts that are efficient, contract law preserves investment incentives even when contracts are renegotiated (Rogerson, 1984). In addition, buyers and sellers can enter into binding contracts through repeated interaction and long-term contractual relationships. Social and business reputation also serve to enforce contracts. Buyers and sellers honor their contractual obligations to avoid hurting their reputations in order to preserve future business opportunities. Finally, social institutions that enforce contractual commitments and build trust create incentives to honor contracts.

The market for contract formation may not be efficient if the institutions of contractual enforcement somehow do not operate effectively. Alternatively, certain types of transactions may not lend themselves to contract formation. In particular, the transaction costs of forming binding contracts can exceed the value of the transactions. When there is uncertainty, it may be relatively costly to negotiate and monitor performance for complete contingent contracts, thus leading buyers and sellers to enter into incomplete contracts. The economics literature on contracts has tended to focus on situations in which buyers and sellers cannot make binding contractual commitments because contractual performance cannot be observed or verified by a third party such as a court; see for example Williamson (1975), Klein et al. (1978), Grout (1984), Williamson (1985), Hart and Moore (1988), Rogerson (1992), Nöldeke and Schmidt (1995), and Che and Hausch (1999).

The economics literature generally considers transaction-specific investment within bilateral relationships. In the contracts framework, investment incentives are ex post; that is, they depend on expectations about how the contract will allocate the gains from trade between the contracting parties. When contracts are incomplete or nonbinding, renegotiation leads to contract hold-up, which creates incentives for underinvestment relative to the outcome that maximizes joint gains from trade for the buyer and seller. Williamson (1985) speaks of the "fundamental transformation" that takes place when buyers and sellers form binding commitments to each other. Although the buyer and the seller are committed to the relationship, this paradoxically exposes each one to hold-up by the other because the terms of exchange are assumed to be nonbinding.

The firm provides an important way to eliminate the fundamental transformation from competitive markets to bilateral exchange. The firm does this not by internalizing transactions, but rather by market making. By dealing with many individual buyers and sellers, the market-making firm provides an alternative to bilateral exchange. This has a number of important advantages. Buyers and sellers make general investments, that is, investments that are not specific to a particular bilateral exchange but rather apply to exchange with one or more firms. Buyers and sellers do not engage in bilateral negotiation, but rather take bid and ask prices offered by the firm as given. The firm, for its part, also does not engage in negotiations with individual investors because it uses price mechanisms to deal with many buyers and many sellers. The firm does not revise its prices to take advantage of investment commitments of buyers and sellers because the firm is able to commit itself to posted prices. The firm improves incentives for investment by buyers and sellers by making markets for goods more efficient.

The standard model of bilateral exchange between a buyer and a seller subject to uncertainty is closely related to a market with many different types of buyers and sellers who search for each other. By law-of-large-numbers arguments, random matching of buyers and sellers in a search market is formally equivalent to a single buyer and a single seller who have independent random draws of types. Bilateral contract models, such as Hart and Moore (1988), generally feature bilateral trade between a single buyer and a single seller who enter into a contract and then make investments before learning their own types. After learning their own types, the buyer and the seller then decide whether or not to renegotiate the contract and whether or not to trade. In that literature, the standard ex post efficiency criterion is used: trade occurs if and only if $v \geq c$. However, with many diverse buyers and sellers, such an efficiency notion is second best. Efficiency would require that buyers and sellers be matched so that total gains from trade were maximized, as in the standard supply and demand framework, in which gains from trade are exhausted at the margin and high-cost suppliers and low-value buyers are excluded from the matching process.

Thus, the investment efficiency benchmark in the contracts literature corresponds to second-best efficiency. As will be shown, the second-best efficient investment levels are higher than the first-best efficiency levels. Therefore, the investment efficiency criterion in the contracts literature that is used to show underinvestment due to hold-up requires investment above first-best levels. Note further that the investment levels obtained in the contracts literature, in which buyers and sellers with transaction-specific investments cannot make binding contractual commitments, correspond formally to investment levels obtained here in the case where buyers and sellers are matched randomly in the search market. Accordingly, underinvestment in the bilateral contracts framework corresponds to underinvestment relative to the second-best criterion when buyers and sellers are matched in the search market.

The hold-up problem in the contracts literature is due to splitting the surplus in ex post bargaining; see Klein et al. (1978), Williamson (1985), and Grossman and Hart (1986). The contracts literature suggests that firms should vertically integrate when investment is transaction-specific, to avoid contractual hold-up between primary input suppliers and companies buying those primary inputs. In the bilateral contracts setting, the boundaries of the firm would then be determined by contractual inefficiencies and the specificity of investment. In contrast, by posting prices, the firm alleviates problems due to splitting the surplus. More generally, firms reduce the problems associated with ex post bargaining by offering binding commitments to bid and ask prices.

Firms have incentives to honor contracts because they deal with many buyers and sellers. Because firms enter into many transactions, they can make commitments that cannot be made by individual buyers and sellers. Thus, the solution to underinvestment is not necessarily vertical integration but rather the entry of firms that enhance market efficiency and reduce or eliminate contract hold-up.

Markets with competing firms provide incentives for efficient investment that can be greater than those with decentralized direct exchange between individual buyers and sellers. The entry of competing firms in business-to-business markets is likely to enhance complementary investments by buyers and sellers in a wide range of industries. The benefits from increased investment and the improved efficiency of trade create market returns to the entry of intermediaries. Rather than engage in costly search and bilateral bargaining, buyers and sellers turn to firms to handle exchange at posted prices.

With decentralized exchange in a search market, underinvestment has several sources. The inefficiency of search creates uncertainty about the likelihood of finding a suitable trading partner. Moreover, random matching lowers the expected gains from trade in successful matches. Finally, bargaining with the trading partner means that buyers and sellers divide the gains from trade so that companies do not obtain the full marginal return to their irreversible investment, which is similar to the contract hold-up problem. By posting prices, firms alleviate these three effects: reducing uncertainty about finding a trading partner, reducing uncertainty about the gains from trade, and reducing the hold-up problem, because buyers and sellers that trade with the dealer keep the returns to their investment. Market microstructure matters for the investment efficiency.

Buyers and sellers often make these investments before knowing the identity of future trading partners and without being tied contractually to specific trading partners, so that these investments are general rather than transaction-specific. Buyers make investments that enhance the value of purchased inputs and sellers make investments that reduce the cost of providing inputs. The expectations of buyers and sellers regarding prices, transaction costs, the likelihood of completing a transaction, and the characteristics of potential trading partners will have important effects on the marginal value of complementary investment. The expected returns to investment thus depend on the institutions of exchange that buyers and sellers encounter, that is, on the microstructure of business-to-business markets. Knowing the effects of market microstructure on investment makes possible the design of more efficient markets. The purpose of this section is to examine the impact of different market microstructures on buyer and seller incentives to invest. The results suggest that the entry of dealers should stimulate investment by businesses and enhance the efficiency of trade.

Markets with general investments provide ex ante incentives to invest; that is, anticipated terms of trade with potential trading partners affect returns to investment. Buyers and sellers often do not know the identities of potential trading partners when making investments, which suggests that many types of capital investment by buyers and sellers are not transaction-specific in practice.[3] The

3 A number of related papers examine investment incentives in a competitive framework with general investments, although they do not consider the effect of intermediaries on the market equilibrium; see Acemoglu (1996, 1997), Acemoglu and Shimer (1999), and Felli and Roberts (2000). The large search literature recognizes inefficiencies from random matching but does not consider investment or intermediation; see the discussion in Osborne and Rubinstein (1990) and Pissarides (2000, pp. 183–203). There is a growing literature on ex ante investment in a competitive framework. MacLeod and Malcomson (1993) allow contracting parties to switch trading partners after they have made investments, although the outside option is specified exogenously. Acemoglu and Shimer (1999) and Holmstrom (1999) also consider general investments and examine conditions for efficiency. In Felli and Roberts (2000), workers make complementary investments before being matched. In their model, workers make competitive wage bids, so that matches are efficient; that is, the worker of the kth highest quality is matched with the firm of the kth highest quality. When both workers and firms invest, there are coordination failure inefficiencies in the form of multiple equilibria, some of which are inefficient. Acemoglu (1996) examines the interaction between ex ante investments and costly search in a labor market. Workers make human capital investments before finding out what firms will employ them and

analysis shows that firms, in tandem with informal search markets, improve economic efficiency in comparison to decentralized search markets alone. Competition between firms narrows the price spread and crowds out the search market, leading to first-best investment and to an efficient volume of trade.

11.1.2 Market-Making by the Firm Affects Incentives to Invest

We compare three alternative market microstructures: a search market, a market-making firm, and competition between a market-making firm and direct exchange in a search market. These market organizations affect investment efficiency because they impact the marginal return to investment. Market inefficiency reduces incentives to invest. The market-making firm in competition with search improves efficiency and increases incentives to invest.

The Basic Model of Investment in a Search Market
Consider a search market with many heterogeneous buyers and sellers. Buyers and sellers meet and bargain over the terms of trade. Random matching is inefficient because low-value buyers can complete trades successfully, as can high-cost sellers, possibly excluding high-value buyers or low-cost sellers. This lowers the total gains from trade and results in a volume of trade that is greater than the efficient level. The inefficiency of random matching reduces the returns to investment, contributing to underinvestment at the market equilibrium. Buyers and sellers in the search market engage in bilateral exchange. Dividing the surplus through bilateral exchange also reduces incentives to invest.

Buyers and sellers make irreversible investments before entering the search market. Investments are general; that is, they do not depend on the identity or characteristics of prospective trading partners. Buyer investments enhance their expected willingness to pay and seller investments lower their expected production costs. As a result, buyers and sellers make investments based on the effects of those investments on expected returns in the search market. The search market thus affects the incentives to invest for buyers and for sellers.

The sequence of events is as follows. Buyers and sellers invest before entering the market, so all buyers have the same investment level and all sellers have the same investment level. Then, buyers and sellers learn their own willingness to pay and costs, respectively. Finally, buyers and sellers make trading decisions and complete transactions.

firms invest before hiring, with workers being identical ex post. Acemoglu (1996) interprets the underinvestment that results from random matching as "social increasing returns in human capital accumulation." Acemoglu (1997) also looks at labor market imperfections that lead to underinvestment in training. Based on the present analysis, the entry of labor market intermediaries should improve human capital accumulation. Internet-based job search sites, for example, alleviate some search inefficiencies and improve the job matching process, possibly enhancing the incentives of both workers and firms to make complementary investments.

There is a continuum of buyers with uncertain willingness to pay v for a unit of a good determined by $v = x + V(b)$. The parameter x represents the buyer's type and is uniformly distributed with unit density on the unit interval. The buyer's value is increasing in the investment b. The function $V(b)$ is positive, strictly concave, and twice continuously differentiable. At price p, the aggregate demand function is $D(p, b) = \Pr\{x : x + V(b) \geq p\}$. The aggregate demand function is thus

$$D(p, b) = \begin{cases} 1 & \text{for } p < V(b), \\ 1 + V(b) - p & \text{for } V(b) \leq p \leq 1 + V(b), \\ 0 & \text{for } 1 + V(b) < p. \end{cases}$$

There is a continuum of sellers with uncertain cost c of supplying a unit of the good, determined by $c = y + C(k)$. The parameter y represents the seller's type and is uniformly distributed with unit density on the unit interval. The seller's cost is decreasing in the investment k. The function $C(k)$ is positive, strictly convex, and twice continuously differentiable. At price w, the aggregate amount supplied by sellers is $S(w, k) = \Pr\{y : y + C(k) \leq w\}$. The aggregate supply function equals

$$S(w, k) = \begin{cases} 1 & \text{for } w > 1 + C(k), \\ w - C(k) & \text{for } C(k) \leq w \leq 1 + C(k), \\ 0 & \text{for } w < C(k). \end{cases}$$

To guarantee that the market demand function $D(p, b)$ and the market supply function $S(w, k)$ cross, assume that $0 < \delta < 1$ for all b, k, where $\delta(b, k) \equiv V(b) - C(k)$. The requirement that $0 < \delta$ implies that market demand cannot be everywhere below market supply, so there exist some feasible matches. The assumption holds, for example, if $V(b) = 1 - 1/(b + 2)$ and $C(k) = 1/(k + 3)$. The requirement that $\delta < 1$ implies that market demand cannot be everywhere above market supply, thus ruling out the case in which all random matches would result in trade. This rules out the complete viability condition discussed in Chapter 9.

Buyers invest before observing their value parameter and sellers invest before observing their cost parameter. Before they observe their own types, all buyers are identical to each other and all sellers are identical to each other. Thus, we can restrict attention to symmetric investment equilibria. Individual investment levels b and k equal total investment levels because the measure of buyers and that of sellers equals one.

Each buyer's value parameter and each seller's cost parameter remains private information prior to trade. After a match is made, the buyer and the seller learn each other's private information. Investment levels impact expected gains from trade by affecting the likelihood of trade and the available net benefits to be allocated through negotiation.

First-best efficiency maximizes social welfare. First-best efficiency has two components: Investments must be efficient and the market mechanism must be efficient as well. For the market mechanism to be efficient, the marginal buyer's willingness to pay must equal the marginal seller's cost, as in the basic supply and demand framework. For investment levels to be efficient, they must maximize total expected gains from trade. Moreover, the market mechanism must be efficient given investment efficiency and investment must maximize total gains from trade given efficient matching.

Efficient matching requires that there exist parameter values x^F and y^F such that low-willingness-to-pay buyers of type $x < x^F$ and high-cost sellers of type $y > y^F$ are inactive. It is then efficient to match randomly any buyer in $[x^F, 1]$ with any seller in $[0, y^F]$. With efficient matching, the marginal buyer's willingness to pay and the marginal seller's cost are equal:

$$(1) \qquad x^F + V(b) = y^F + C(k).$$

Also, the total amount demanded should equal the total amount supplied: $1 - x^F = y^F$. Thus, using equation (1), the first-best volume of trade equals

$$(2) \qquad Q^F(b, k) = 1 - x^F = y^F = (1 + \delta(b, k))/2.$$

Total expected gains from trade with efficient matching equal $G^F(b, k)$, where

$$(3) \qquad G^F(b, k) = \int_{x^F}^{1} (x + V(b))dx - \int_{0}^{y^F} (y + C(k))dy = (1 + \delta)^2/4.$$

First-best investment levels (b^F, k^F) maximize expected gains from trade net of investment costs, $G^F(b, k) - b - k$. Assume that there exist interior maximizers.

After a match is made, the buyer and the seller learn each other's type. If there are potential gains from trade, the buyer and the seller bargain over the division of the surplus. Bargaining is represented by the Nash bargaining solution, so that buyers and sellers evenly divide the gains from trade. The analysis carries through with uneven divisions of the surplus. Similar results can be obtained when the buyer and the seller divide the surplus under asymmetric information; see for example Gehrig (1993) and Spulber (1999) for alternative versions of matching.

If a buyer of type x and a seller of type y are matched, trade occurs if and only if gains from trade are positive:

$$(4) \qquad x + V(b) \geq y + C(k).$$

The *second-best outcome* is defined as the investment levels that maximize the expected gains from trade in a search market net of investment costs. With random matching, a high-value buyer of type x in $[\tilde{x}, 1]$, where $0 < \tilde{x} = 1 - V(b) + C(k) < 1$, is able to trade with any seller. A low-value buyer of type x in $[0, \tilde{x}]$ is only able to trade with low-cost sellers of type $y \leq x + V(b) - C(k)$. The total expected gains from trade in a search market $G^S(b, k)$ are defined by

$$(5) \quad G^S(b, k) = \int_{1-\delta}^{1} \int_{0}^{1} (x - y + \delta)dydx + \int_{0}^{1-\delta} \int_{0}^{x+\delta} (x - y + \delta)dydx$$
$$= (1 + 3\delta + 3\delta^2 - \delta^3)/6.$$

Second-best investment levels (b^S, k^S) maximize $G^S(b, k) - b - k$. Assume that there exist interior maximizers.[4]

Random matching in a search market satisfies the ex post efficiency criterion that buyer value exceeds seller cost, as in equation (4). Random matching is not ex ante efficient because trade should be restricted to higher-value buyers and lower-cost sellers, with marginal buyers and sellers as specified in equation (1). For any given investment levels b and k, the efficiency loss from random matching relative to efficient matching equals

$$(6) \qquad G^F(b, k) - G^S(b, k) = (1 - 3\delta^2 + 2\delta^3)/12 > 0.$$

Random matching is inefficient because demand and supply cross, so that the complete viability condition does not hold. The difference is positive because the right-hand side is decreasing in δ for $\delta > 0$ and zero at $\delta = 1$. Random matching would be efficient if and only if the market demand curve were everywhere above the market supply curve. The inefficiency of random matching results from the presence in the market of high-cost sellers and low-value buyers who are to the right of the crossing point of the supply and demand curves. For example, a buyer with a low willingness to pay, $x = (1 - \delta)/3 < x^F$, who would not buy under efficient matching might be matched with a low-cost seller of type $y = (1 + \delta)/4 < y^F$, so that a high-value buyer could fail to find a match.

It may be surprising to observe that too many matches occur with random matching. With random matching, the expected volume of trade equals $Q^S(b, k) = (1 + 2\delta - \delta^2)/2$. Thus, the second-best volume of trade is greater than the first-best volume of trade evaluated at the same investment levels, $Q^S(b, k) > Q^F(b, k)$. The possibility of successful matches for buyers or sellers who are to the *right* of the crossing point of supply and demand raises the expected number of matches. This shows that the inefficiency of random matching is due to the presence of low-value buyers and high-cost sellers, leading to excessive trade.

Now compare first-best and second-best outcomes. First-best investment levels with efficient matching are less than second-best investment levels with random matching, $(b^F, k^F) < (b^S, k^S)$. The first-best trading volume is less than the second-best trading volume, $Q^F < Q^S$.[5] Because of the inefficiency of random

---

4 By the assumption that $0 < \delta < 1$ for all b, k, where $\delta(b, k) \equiv V(b) - C(k)$, it follows that $G^F(b, k)$ and $G^S(b, k)$ are positive for all b and k. By the assumption of interior maximizers, it follows that $G^F(b^F, k^F) - b^F - k^F > 0$ and $G^S(b^S, k^S) - b^S - k^S > 0$.

5 The analysis applies standard monotone comparative statics techniques; see Athey et al. (1996). Let $J(\delta) = \min_{b,k} b + k$ subject to $\delta = V(b) - C(k)$. Note that the minimizers b and k are increasing in δ. The first-best and second-best problems reduce to one-dimensional problems, $\max_\delta G^F(\delta) - J(\delta)$ and $\max_\delta G^S(\delta) - J(\delta)$. Because $G^S(\delta) - G^F(\delta)$ is strictly increasing in δ, from equation (6), standard monotone comparative statics analysis implies that every maximizer of the first-best problem is smaller than every maximizer of the second-best problem, $\delta^F < \delta^S$. The indicators for the first- and second-best problems serve as parameters. By monotone comparative statics, $\delta^F < \delta^S$ implies that $(b^F, k^F) < (b^S, k^S)$. Because $\delta < 1$, $Q^F(\delta) = (1 + \delta)/$

matching, the second-best criterion requires greater investment than does the first-best criterion. The result that first-best investment is less than second-best investment is unexpected because the returns to investment would appear to be greater with efficient matching. The reason that second-best investment levels are higher is that greater investment increases the likelihood of trade. In a search market, the second-best investment levels are higher than with the first-best investment with efficient matching, because the additional investment is needed to overcome the inefficiency of random matching. Random search with bilateral trade satisfies only the ex post efficiency standard that buyer value exceeds seller cost. The resulting trading inefficiency leads to an investment efficiency criterion that is *too strict*. Efficient markets require *less* investment because there is no need for higher investment to overcome transaction inefficiencies.

The Search Market

Before observing their types, and before entering the search market, the buyer and the seller choose investment levels to maximize their expected gains from trade. The sequence of events is as follows.

Period 1a: At the beginning of the period, each buyer chooses investment b and each seller chooses investment k.

Period 1b: At the end of the period, each buyer i observes their type x_i and each seller j observes their type y_j, which remain private information before a match is made.

Period 2: Buyers and sellers are matched randomly. After a match is made, the trading partners observe each other's type and decide whether or not to trade. If gains from trade are positive, they bargain over the terms of trade. Otherwise, the trading partners exit the market.

Buyers and sellers play a Nash noncooperative game in investment levels. Let (b^R, k^R) represent the Nash equilibrium investment levels with random matching in a search market.

After a successful match, the buyer and the seller engage in Nash bargaining and divide the gains from trade equally, so that the expected gains from trade for a buyer or for a seller equal $(1/2)G^S(b, k)$. Accordingly, buyers choose b to maximize $(1/2)G^S(b, k^R) - b$ and sellers choose k to maximize $(1/2)G^S(b^R, k) - k$. Assume that there exist interior maximizers.[6]

$2 < [1 + 2\delta - \delta^2]/2 = Q^S(\delta)$. Because $Q^F(\delta)$ is increasing in δ and $\delta^F < \delta^S$, it follows that $Q^F = Q^F(\delta^F) < Q^F(\delta^S) < Q^S(\delta^S) = Q^S$.

6 By the assumption that $0 < \delta < 1$ for all b, k, $G^S(b, k)$ is positive for all b and k. Given the assumption of interior maximizers, it follows that individual rationality is satisfied in equilibrium so that $(1/2)G^S(b^R, k^R) - b^R > 0$ and $(1/2)G^S(b^R, k^R) - k^R > 0$. Otherwise, a buyer or seller could choose zero investment and obtain positive benefits.

Consideration of the Nash equilibrium shows that underinvestment occurs in a search market relative to the first-best and second-best levels:

$$(b^R, k^R) < (b^F, k^F) < (b^S, k^S).$$

Buyers and sellers have an incentive to invest not only to improve their net benefits but to increase the likelihood of a successful match in the search market. Greater investment increases the chances that the net benefits from a random match will be positive. However, in the search market equilibrium with random matching, buyers and sellers invest before bargaining over the division of surplus. They correctly anticipate that they will not capture the full marginal returns to their investments. Accordingly, they have an incentive to scale back their investment levels, thus reducing the value of a match relative to the second-best optimum. The buyer and the seller underinvest relative to the first-best and the second-best investment levels because they must divide the quasirents in direct exchange. This effect overcomes any incentive to invest to improve the likelihood of a successful match.

The Nash equilibrium trading volume in the search market with random matching is less than the second-best trading volume, $Q^R < Q^S$.[7] The Nash equilibrium trading volume in a search market may be greater than or less than the first-best trading volume. Although the trading volume in the search market is greater than the trading volume with efficient matching for the same investment levels, the underinvestment at the Nash equilibrium with search may reduce the trading volume below the first best level.

Investment Incentives with a Market-Making Firm

Consider a market for contracts in which a firm acts as a monopoly dealer. The dealer transacts with many buyers and sellers. The dealer posts an ask price p for buyers and a bid price w for sellers. Buyers and sellers choose their investment levels before observing prices and the dealer chooses prices without observing investment levels.

Unlike random matching, the dealer's price spread excludes low-value buyers and high-cost sellers. Buyers and sellers invest before observing the intermediary's prices, whereas the intermediary sets prices without observing investments. Prices and investments are determined at a Nash equilibrium; that is, equilibrium investments and equilibrium prices represent strategic best responses. This contrasts with bilateral exchange, in which a buyer and a seller renegotiate the terms of exchange after investments have been made. The firm's prices are a best response to the equilibrium investment levels of all buyers and sellers. The firm's prices cannot be affected by changes in the investment of any single buyer or seller, because each individual has measure zero.

7 Nash equilibrium investment levels in a search market must maximize $(1/2)G^S(\delta) - J(\delta)$. Since $G^F(\delta) - (1/2)G^S(\delta)$ is strictly increasing in δ, every maximizer of $(1/2)G^S(\delta) - J(\delta)$ is smaller than every maximizer of the first-best problem, so that $\delta^R < \delta^F$. By the definition of δ, it follows that $(b^R, k^R) < (b^F, k^F)$. The trading volume is less than the second-best trading volume because $Q^S(\delta) = [1 + 2\delta - \delta^2]/2$ is increasing in δ and $\delta^R < \delta^S$, so that $Q^R = Q^S(\delta^R) < Q^S(\delta^S) = Q^S$.

The dealer, the buyers, and the sellers play a Nash noncooperative game in prices and investment levels. The sequence of events is as follows.

Period 1a: At the beginning of the period, each buyer chooses investment b and each seller chooses investment k. The dealer posts prices p, w.

Period 1b: At the end of the period, each buyer i observes their type x_i and each seller j observes their type y_j.

Period 2: Buyers and sellers decide whether or not to transact with the dealer. Transactions are completed.

Nash equilibrium investment levels are (b^D, k^D) and the dealer's Nash equilibrium ask and bid prices are (p^D, w^D).

The aggregate demand function is $D(p, b) = \Pr\{x : x + V(b) \geq p\}$, so that the dealer's inverse demand is $P^D(Q, b) = 1 + V(b) - Q$. For the aggregate supply function $S(w, k) = \Pr\{y : y + C(k) \leq w\}$, the dealer's inverse supply is $W^D(Q, k) = C(k) + Q$. The dealer's profit-maximizing prices balance the amounts demanded and supplied. The dealer's profit can be stated as a function of output:

$$(7) \qquad \Pi(Q; b^D, k^D) = (P^D(Q, b^D) - W^D(Q, k^D))Q$$
$$= (1 + V(b^D) - C(k^D) - 2Q)Q.$$

The dealer's profit-maximizing output is a unique best response to the Nash equilibrium investment levels (b^D, k^D):

$$(8) \qquad Q^D = (1/4)(1 + V(b^D) - C(k^D)).$$

From equation (8) and the inverse demand and supply functions, the Nash equilibrium ask and bid prices are

$$(9) \qquad p^D = (1/4)(3 + 3V(b^D) + C(k^D)),$$

$$(10) \qquad w^D = (1/4)(1 + V(b^D) + 3C(k^D)).$$

The dealer's equilibrium ask and bid prices straddle the Walrasian equilibrium price P^W evaluated at the equilibrium investment levels,

$$w^D < P^W = (1 + V(b^D) + C(k^D))/2 < p^D.$$

The buyer and the seller choose investment levels as best replies to the dealer's Nash equilibrium prices. The buyer and seller have expected benefits defined by

$$(11) \qquad h^B(b, k) = \int_{p^D - V(b)}^{1} (x + V(b) - p^D)\,dx,$$

$$(12) \qquad h^S(b, k) = \int_{0}^{w^D - C(k)} (w^D - y - C(k))\,dy.$$

The buyer maximizes $h^B(b, k^D) - b$ and the seller maximizes $h^S(b^D, k) - k$.[8]

---

8 Assume that there are interior solutions and that individual rationality holds in equilibrium, $h^D(b^D, k^D) - b^D \geq 0$, and $(1/2)h^S(b^D, k^D) - k^D \geq 0$.

Intermediation reduces investment relative to direct exchange. Because the buyers and the sellers play a Nash noncooperative game with the dealer, the buyers' and the sellers' investments are best responses to the dealer's equilibrium prices. The dealer's prices are in turn a best response to the buyers' and sellers' equilibrium investments. Accordingly, the buyers, the sellers, and the dealer have no incentive to revise their equilibrium choices. Because the buyers and the sellers take the dealer's equilibrium prices as given, they capture the full marginal returns to their investments unlike in the search market. However, the underinvestment problem is exacerbated when the search market is replaced by a monopoly dealer because of the possibility that the buyer or the seller will not be able to trade at the dealer's posted prices. The dealer's market power reduces the returns to investment.

There may be multiple Nash equilibria of the investment game. Because the buyers' and the sellers' benefit functions are increasing in each other's investment, equilibria with higher investments are Pareto preferred to equilibria with lower investments.[9] Nash equilibrium investment levels in the dealer market are less than Nash equilibrium investment levels in the search market with random matching, and therefore less than the first-best levels and less than the second-best levels:

$$(b^D, k^D) < (b^R, k^R) < (b^F, k^F) < (b^S, k^S).$$

The volume of trade in the dealer market is less than the first-best volume of trade, $Q^D < Q^F$, less than the volume of trade in the search market, and therefore less than the second-best volume of trade, $Q^D < Q^R < Q^S$.[10]

---

9 To simplify matters, we restrict attention to the Pareto-preferred equilibrium of the investment game; see Milgrom and Roberts (1994).

10 From the investment problems of the buyers and the sellers, equations (11) and (12), the Nash equilibrium investment levels must maximize $G^D(b, k) - b - k$, where $G^D(b, k) = h^B(b, k) + h^S(b, k)$. The buyer and the seller investments in the search market (b^R, k^R) must maximize $(1/2)G^S(b, k) - b - k$. The function $(1/2) G^S(b, k)$ is monotonically increasing in b and k, and it is supermodular because $\partial^2(1/2)G^S/\partial b \partial k = (1/2)[1 - (V - C)]$ $(-C')V' > 0$. Note that $\partial(1/2)G^S(b, k)/\partial b = (1/4)[1 + 2(V(b) - C(k)) - (V(b) - C(k))^2]$ $V'(b)$ and $\partial G^D(b, k)/\partial b = [1 + V(b) - p^D]V'(b)$. Substituting for p^D from equation (9) into the first derivative of G^D yields $\partial G^D(b, k)/\partial b = (1/4)[1 + V(b) - C(k)]V'(b)$, so that $\partial(1/2)G^S(b, k)/\partial b > \partial G^D(b, k)/\partial b$. The same analysis applies for k. Also, after substituting for p^D from equation (9) into the first derivative and differentiating with respect to k, it follows that $\partial^2 G^D(b, k)/\partial k \partial b = -C'(k)V'(b)/4 > 0$. By Topkis (1978), the maximum best-reply function for the investment game in the search market is above the maximum best-reply function for the investment game in the dealer market. By Theorem 4 of Milgrom and Roberts (1994), the buyer and seller investment levels in the high-investment Nash equilibrium of the search market are greater than their investment levels in the high-investment Nash equilibrium of the dealer market, so that $(b^D, k^D) < (b^R, k^R)$. Recall that the volume of trade for the first-best problem is $Q^F(\delta) = (1 + \delta)/2$ where $\delta = V(b) - C(k)$. The volume of trade in the dealer market is $Q^D(\delta) = (1 + \delta)/4$ from equation (8). Note that $Q^D(\delta) < Q^F(\delta)$. Since δ is increasing in b and k and $Q^F(\delta)$ and $Q^D(\delta)$ are increasing in δ, then $(b^D, k^D) < (b^F, k^F)$ implies that $Q^D < Q^F$. The volume of trade for the second-best problem is $Q^S = [1 + 2\delta - \delta^2]/2$, so $Q^D(\delta) < Q^S(\delta)$. Because $Q^D(\delta)$ and $Q^S(\delta)$ are increasing in δ, then $(b^D, k^D) < (b^R, k^R)$ implies that $Q^D < Q^R$.

The reason investment is lower in the dealer market than in the search market is that the dealer's price spread lowers the likelihood of trade, reducing the marginal return to investment, because only the highest-willingness-to-pay buyers and lowest-cost sellers will transact with the dealer. This monopoly effect dominates the benefits of the dealer market for buyers and sellers who receive the full returns to their investment when trade occurs. The intermediated equilibrium resembles efficient matching except that it also excludes buyers and sellers whose willingness to pay and cost levels fall within the dealer's price spread. A combination of direct exchange and intermediation would address this inefficiency by allowing direct exchange between buyers and sellers whose valuations are within the price spread.

Competition between the Search Market and the Market-Making Firm

This section considers competition between a dealer and the search market. Competition between the decentralized search market and dealer market improves incentives to invest for buyers and sellers. Competition between direct and intermediated exchange reduces the intermediary's market power and narrows the bid-ask spread. Moreover, competition allows buyers and sellers to self-select, with high-willingness-to-pay buyers and low-cost sellers trading with the intermediary, and buyers and sellers with valuations within the spread entering the search market. The self-selection of buyers and sellers reduces the economic impact of costly searching and matching. Very-high-cost sellers and very-low-value buyers are inactive in equilibrium. This means that they do not enter the matching market, which alleviates the inefficiency of random matching within that market. Moreover, because they are dealing with the intermediary, high-value buyers and low-cost sellers do not face any risk of exclusion from the market. The combination of the reduced market power of the intermediary and the self-selection of buyers and sellers choosing between the two markets increases the marginal return to investment relative to either the search market or the dealer market alone, thus increasing equilibrium investment.[11]

As before, buyers and sellers invest before observing their types. After observing their types, buyers and sellers decide whether to enter the search market or to purchase from, respectively sell to, the dealer at the posted prices. Buyers and sellers

---

11 The model of a dealer posting bid and ask prices follows standard models of financial intermediaries beginning with Garman (1976); see Spulber (1996b, 1999) for a more comprehensive survey of market microstructure models. We extend Gehrig's (1993) basic model of competition between a dealer and a search market by considering a two-stage setting with investment by buyers and sellers in the first stage and Nash bargaining in the second-stage search market. Gehrig (1993) does not consider investment and assumes first-and-final-offer bargaining under asymmetric information. Rubinstein and Wolinsky (1987) allow intermediaries to compete with direct exchange in a random matching model with bilateral bargaining but also without investment. Spulber (1996a) examines competition between dealers when buyers and sellers search across dealers.

entering the search market are matched randomly. The sequence of events is as follows.

Period 1a: At the beginning of the period, each buyer chooses investment b, each seller chooses investment k, and the dealer posts prices p, w.
Period 1b: At the end of the period, each buyer i observes their type x_i and each seller j observes their type y_j.
Period 2: Buyers and sellers decide whether to transact with the dealer, to enter the search market, or to be inactive. Transactions are completed.

The Nash equilibrium with competition between a dealer and a direct-exchange market is denoted by (p^*, w^*, b^*, k^*). We begin by considering the second-stage market subgame, taking the investment levels (b^*, k^*) as given.

The analysis of the market game is based on Gehrig (1993), who examines competition between a dealer and a search market, but does not consider investment. The dealer rations the long side of the market so that the dealer's purchases and sales balance and buyers and sellers who cannot trade with the dealer exit the market. Once a buyer and a seller are matched in the search market, they learn each others' types and the gains from trade are allocated by Nash bargaining.

The market equilibrium is defined by four critical values: X_0, X_1, Y_0, and Y_1. In equilibrium, low-value buyers with types in the interval $[0, X_0)$ are inactive and high-cost sellers with types in $(Y_1, 1]$ are inactive. To see why, observe that if a buyer X_0 is inactive, all buyers with a lower value x must be inactive as well. Otherwise the buyer of type X_0 could follow the strategy of the buyer of type x and secure at least the same payoff.

Active buyers and sellers are defined as follows. Buyers with type in $[X_0, X_1)$ enter into the search market and high-value buyers with type in $[X_1, 1]$ buy from the dealer. Sellers with type in $(Y_0, Y_1]$ enter into the search market and low-cost sellers with type $[0, Y_0]$ sell to the dealer. Let $\psi(y)$ be the equilibrium distribution of sellers in the search market, so that $\psi(Y_0) = 0$ and $\psi(Y_1) = 1$. Let $\varphi(x)$ be the equilibrium distribution of buyers in the search market, so that $\varphi(X_0) = 0$ and $\varphi(X_1) = 1$. The equilibrium distributions can be shown to be uniform.

To see why the equilibrium is defined by these intervals, consider the buyers' decision problem, because that of the sellers is similar. A buyer's expected value from entering the search market is

(13) $\quad U(x, b^*, k^*, \psi) = \int_{y \leq x + V(b^*) - C(k^*)} (1/2)(x + V(b^*) - y - C(k^*)) d\psi(y).$

Suppose that the buyer of type X_1 prefers to enter the search market rather than to trade with the dealer: $U(X_1) > X_1 + V(b^*) - p$. Then any buyer with a lower type x also prefers to enter the search market, because $U(x) - x - V(b^*) - p^*$ is strictly decreasing in x. The properties of the equilibrium hold even if the buyer (or seller) expects to be rationed in the search markets. Such rationing does not occur in equilibrium; see Gehrig (1993) and Spulber (1999) for further discussion.

In equilibrium, both the dealer market and the search market balance. Thus, the critical values of buyer value and seller cost are such that the marginal buyer's value and the marginal seller's cost are equal:

$$(14) \qquad\qquad X_0 + V(b) = Y_0 + C(k),$$

$$(15) \qquad\qquad X_1 + V(b) = Y_1 + C(k).$$

These relationships hold because a seller with cost $c = y + C(k)$ greater than $X_1 + V(b)$ will find no trading partners in the matching market, so the highest-cost seller that is active has cost $Y_1 + C(k) = X_1 + V(b)$. Similarly, a buyer with value $v = x + V(b)$ less than $Y_0 + C(k)$ will find no trading partners in the search market, so that the lowest-value buyer that is active has value $X_0 + V(b) = Y_0 + C(k)$.

To examine the dealer's problem, it is useful to derive aggregate demand and supply. The buyer of type x who enters the direct-exchange market has expected benefits equal to

$$(16) \qquad U(x, b, k, Y_0, Y_1) = \int_{Y_0}^{x+\delta} (1/2)(x + V(b) - y - C(k))d\psi(y)$$

$$= \frac{(x - Y_0 + \delta)^2}{4(Y_1 - Y_0)}.$$

The buyer of type x purchases from the dealer if and only if the net benefits equal or exceed those expected from search. The dealer faces the market demand $D(p; b^*, k^*) = \Pr\{x : x + V(b^*) - p \geq U(x, b^*, k^*, Y_0, Y_1)\}$, so that

$$(17) \qquad D(p; b^*, k^*) = 1 + V(b^*) - p - U(X_1, b^*, k^*, Y_0, Y_1).$$

The seller of type y sells to the dealer if and only if the net benefits from doing so equal or exceed those expected from direct exchange:

$$(18) \qquad R(y, b, k, X_0, X_1) = \int_{y+\delta}^{X_1} (1/2)(x + V(b) - y - C(k))d\phi(x)$$

$$= \frac{(X_1 - y + \delta)^2}{4(X_1 - X_0)}.$$

The seller of type y sells to the dealer if and only if the net benefits equal or exceed those expected from search. The dealer faces the market supply $S(w; b^*, k^*) = \Pr\{y : w - y - C(k^*) \geq R(y, b^*, k^*, X_0, X_1)\}$, so that

$$(19) \qquad S(w; b^*, k^*) = w - C(k^*) - R(Y_0, b^*, k^*, X_0, X_1).$$

The dealer's profit function is $\Pi(q) = [P(q) - W(q)]q$, where $P(q)$ is inverse demand and $W(q)$ is inverse supply from equations (17) and (19), suppressing b and k. The dealer's prices are the unique best response to equilibrium investments (b^*, k^*). The dealer's bid-ask spread is positive and there is an active search market in equilibrium.

With competition between a dealer and the search market, the equilibrium bid-ask spread straddles the Walrasian price evaluated at the equilibrium investment levels; that is,

$$w^* < P^W = (1 + V(b^*) + C(k^*))/2 < p^*.$$

This is obtained in the following way. The quantity demanded by buyers is $1 - X_1$, and the quantity offered by sellers is Y_0. The dealer chooses prices that equate the amount demanded and supplied, so that $q = 1 - X_1 = Y_0$. From equations (14) and (15), note that $X_0 = q - V(b) + C(k)$ and $Y_1 = 1 - q + V(b) - C(k)$. Then, from equations (16)–(19), the inverse demand and supply functions are

$$P(q) = (1/4)(3 + 3V(b^*) + C(k^*) - 2q),$$
$$W(q) = (1/4)(1 + V(b^*) + 3C(k^*) + 2q).$$

The dealer's profit can then be written as follows:

$$\Pi(q) = (1/2)(1 + V(b^*) - C(k^*) - 2q)q.$$

Setting marginal profit equal to zero, the dealer's first-order condition can be solved for the dealer's equilibrium output:

$$q^* = (1/4)(1 + V(b^*) - C(k^*)).$$

The second-order sufficient condition for a unique interior maximum is satisfied, so the dealer's output q^* is the unique solution to the dealer's profit-maximization problem for any investments (b^*, k^*). The dealer's Nash equilibrium prices (p^*, w^*) are obtained by substituting the dealer's profit-maximizing output into the inverse demand and supply functions:

$$p^* = (1/8)(5 + 5V(b^*) + 3C(k^*)),$$
$$w^* = (1/8)(3 + 3V(b^*) + 5C(k^*)).$$

So, $p^* - P^W = w^* - P^W = (1/8)(1 + V(b^*) - C(k^*)) > 0$.

Having characterized the market game in the second period, we now derive the first-period Nash equilibrium investment strategies of the buyers and sellers. A buyer chooses investment b as a best response to the Nash equilibrium prices p^* and w^* and the equilibrium investment of the sellers, k^*. A seller chooses investment k as a best response to the Nash equilibrium prices p^* and w^* and the equilibrium investment of the buyers, b^*. The buyer's and the seller's expected benefits combine the expected returns from direct and intermediated exchange:

$$(20) \quad g^B(b, k^*) = \int_{X_1}^{1} (x + V(b) - p^*)dx + \int_{X_0}^{X_1} U(x, b, k^*, Y_0, Y_1)dx,$$

$$(21) \quad g^S(b^*, k) = \int_{0}^{Y_0} (w^* - y - C(k))dy + \int_{Y_0}^{Y_1} R(y, b^*, k, X_0, X_1)dy.$$

The buyers choose investment b to maximize the expected net benefit, $g^B(b, k^*) - b$, and the sellers choose investment k to maximize the expected net benefit, $g^S(b^*, k) - k$.[12]

Competition between the dealer and the search market increases the returns to investment. The high-value buyer and the low-cost seller avoid the risk that they will not find a good match in the search market. The firm's posted prices offer better terms than they expect to obtain in the search market. The high-value buyer and the low-cost seller pay a premium to the firm to avoid the search market. Intermediate-value buyers and sellers who do not transact with the dealer still realize a return on their investment by entering the search market. The search market adds contingencies that allow the intermediate-value buyer and intermediate-cost seller the option of search.

Nash equilibrium investment levels with competition between a dealer and a search market are higher than Nash equilibrium investment levels with search alone and higher than the Nash equilibrium investment levels in a market with a dealer alone, $(b^D, k^D) < (b^R, k^R) < (b^*, k^*)$. The equilibrium volume of trade with competition between a dealer and a search market is greater than the equilibrium volume of trade in a market with search alone or in a market with a dealer alone, $Q^D < Q^R < Q^*$.

The search market is active and the volume of trade on the search market is positive and equals

$$X_1^* - X_0^* = Y_1^* - Y_0^* = (1/2)(1 + V(b^*) - C(k^*)).$$

The total volume of trade equals the sum of the dealer's volume and the search market volume:

$$Q^* = q^* + X_1^* - X_0^* = (3/4)(1 + V(b^*) - C(k^*)).$$

The volume of trade with competition between a dealer and a search market exceeds the second-best and first-best volumes of trade when evaluated at the same investment levels: $Q^*(\delta) > Q^S(\delta) = Q^F(\delta)$.[13]

---

12 Assume that there are interior solutions and that individual rationality holds in equilibrium, $g^B(b^*, k^*) - b^* \geq 0$ and $g^S(b^*, k^*) - k^* \geq 0$.

13 In the individual buyer's problem, X_1 solves $X_1 + V(b) - p^* = U(X_1, b, k^*, Y_1, Y_0)$ and X_0 solves $U(X_0, b, k^*, Y_1, Y_0) = 0$. From the definition of U, $\partial U(x, b, k^*, Y_1, Y_0)/\partial b = V'(b)(x + V(b) - Y_0 - C(k^*) - Y_0)/2(Y_1 - Y_0)$. Applying the envelope theorem, and using equation (16) and the values of X_1, X_0, the buyer's value is monotonically increasing in b:

$$\partial g^B(b, k^*)/\partial b = (1 + V(b) - p^*)V'(b) > 0.$$

In the individual seller's problem, Y_0 solves $w^* - Y_0 - C(k) = R(Y_0, b^*, k, X_0, X_1)$ and Y_1 solves $R(Y_1, b^*, k, X_0, X_1) = 0$. As before, the seller's value is monotonically increasing in k:

$$\partial g^S(b^*, k)/\partial b = -(w^* - C(k))C'(k) > 0.$$

The comparison of output levels is made given the equilibrium investment levels. Accordingly, it is necessary to substitute for p^* and w^* to obtain $\partial g^B(b, k^*)/\partial b = (3/8)(1 + V(b) - C(k^*))V'(b)$

Competition between the dealer and the search market enhances incentives for investment. The introduction of search enhances incentives to invest because buyers and sellers with valuations within the spread trade with each other, thus raising the expected returns to investment relative to an equilibrium in which those buyers and sellers would not trade. The presence of the search market allows buyers and sellers within the spread to have some chance of completing an exchange. Thus, in comparison with the market with only a dealer, the mixed market allows buyers and sellers to realize the returns to their investment by trading with the dealer and by entering the search market.

The combination of a dealer market and a search market has another advantage in that it enhances the efficiency of the matching process in the search market. The dealer's price spread diverts high-value buyers and low-cost sellers from the search market and guarantees that they will be able to complete a transaction without being displaced by matches with lower gains from trade. The combination of intermediated and direct exchange has an additional and more subtle effect on matching. The low-value buyers and high-cost sellers, whose values are outside the spread, are inactive since they would not find a suitable match in the search market. Because these traders do not enter the search market, the inefficiency of that market is mitigated, even if it is not fully eliminated. The enhanced performance of the search market further increases the returns to investment.

Competition between a dealer and a search market reduces the dealer's market power and thus narrows the bid-ask spread. This raises the gains from trading with the dealer for buyers and sellers. The narrower spread also increases incentives to invest. Moreover, the narrower spread reduces the number of buyers and sellers entering the search market thus reducing search inefficiencies. The Nash equilibrium with competition between the dealer and the search market results in a lower ask price and a higher bid price than the Nash equilibrium prices in a dealer market without a search market, $w^D < w^* < p^* < p^D$.[14]

---

and $\partial g^S(b^*, k)/\partial b = (3/8)(1 + V(b^*) - C(k))(-C'(k))$. The value functions are supermodular in b and k, $\partial^2 g^B(b, k)/\partial k \partial b = \partial^2 g^S(b, k)/\partial k \partial b = -(3/8)V'(b)C'(k)$. Compare the equilibrium with the search market with random matching. Recall that the buyer and the seller investments in the search market (b^R, k^R) must maximize $(1/2)G^S(b, k) - b - k$. As already noted, the function $(1/2)G^S(b, k)$ is monotonic increasing in b and k, and it is supermodular because $\partial^2(1/2)G^S(b, k)/\partial b \partial k = (1/2)(1 - \delta)(-C'(k))V'(b) > 0$. Because $\partial(1/2)G^S(b, k)/\partial b = (1/4)(1 + 2\delta - \delta^2)V'(b)$ and $\partial g^B(b, k)/\partial b = (3/8)(1 + \delta)V'(b)$, it follows that $\partial g^B(b, k)/\partial b > \partial(1/2)G^S(b, k)/\partial b$. The same analysis applies for k. So, by Topkis (1978) and Theorem 4 of Milgrom and Roberts (1994), $(b^*, k^*) > (b^R, k^R)$. Recall that the volume of trade with a dealer and a search market is $Q^*(\delta) = (3/4)(1 + \delta)$ and the volume of trade in the search market with no dealer is $Q^S(\delta) = [1 + 2\delta - \delta^2]/2$, so $Q^S(\delta) < Q^*(\delta)$. Because $Q^S(\delta)$ and $Q^*(\delta)$ are increasing in δ, $(b^R, k^R) < (b^*, k^*)$ implies that $Q^R = Q^S(\delta^R) < Q^*(\delta^R) < Q^*(\delta^*) = Q^*$.

14 Recall that $\partial g^B(b, k)/\partial b = [1 + V(b) - p]V'(b) > 0$, so that $g^B(b, k) - b$ is supermodular in b and $-p$. The seller's value is monotonically increasing in k, $\partial g^S(b, k)/\partial b = -[w - C(k)]C'(k) > 0$, so that $g^S(b, k) - k$ is supermodular in k and w. In the market with a dealer

The presence of a dealer alleviates the problems with investment incentives that arise under direct exchange. However, underinvestment is still present. Nash equilibrium investment levels with competition between a dealer and a search market are less than the first-best efficient investment levels and the second-best efficient levels:[15]

$$(b^*, k^*) < (b^F, k^F) < (b^S, k^S).$$

Underinvestment persists with competition between intermediated and direct exchange. When making investment choices, buyers and sellers take into account the possibility that they will wind up in the matching market and strategically underinvest. Moreover, the bid-ask price spread set by the dealer also reduces the marginal returns to investment.

For any given investment levels the volume of trade with competition between a dealer and a search market is greater than the second-best and the first-best efficient volume of trade: $Q^*(\delta) > Q^S(\delta) > Q^F(\delta)$. This occurs because of the excessive amount of trade in the search market. Even though the size of the search market is smaller due to the presence of a dealer, the total of trade with the dealer and trade in the search market is larger than the efficient levels. It is not possible to evaluate the efficiency of the equilibrium volume of trade with competition between a dealer and a search market. Because underinvestment is observed, and because the volume of trade is increasing in equilibrium investment levels, the equilibrium volume of trade may be greater or less than the efficient levels.

Competition between dealers eliminates the price spread thus rendering the search market inactive. Competition results in the Walrasian equilibrium price, so that matching of buyers and sellers is efficient. By Bertrand competition arguments, Gehrig (1993) shows that with competing dealers, there is an equilibrium that corresponds to the Walrasian outcome, although it is not necessarily unique. Then, the market price equals the Walrasian price evaluated at the equilibrium investment levels, $p^{**} = w^{**} = P^{**} = (1/2)(1 + V(b^{**}) + C(k^{**}))$, and the volume of trade equals the Walrasian equilibrium output.

Buyers and sellers choose investments at a Nash equilibrium, taking market equilibrium prices as given. Let $(p^{**}, w^{**}, b^{**}, k^{**})$ represent the Nash equilibrium prices and investments. With competition between dealers, there is a Nash

---

but no search, note that $h^B(b, k) - b$ is supermodular in b and $-p$ and $h^S(b, k) - k$ is supermodular in k and w. Note further that for any given p and w, $\partial g^B(b, k)/\partial b = \partial h^B(b, k)/\partial b$ and $\partial g^S(b, k)/\partial k = \partial h^S(b, k)/\partial k$. Because $(b^*, k^*) > (b^D, k^D)$ in equilibrium, it must be the case that $p^* < p^D$ and $w^* > w^D$.

15 The function G^F is monotonically increasing in b and k, and it is supermodular because $\partial^2 G^F/\partial b \partial k = -C'V'/2 > 0$. The buyer's value $g^B(b, k)$ is monotonically increasing in b and supermodular in b, k. The seller's value $g^S(b, k)$ is monotonically increasing in k and supermodular in b, k. Further, $\partial g^B(b, k)/\partial b = (3/8)(1 + \delta)V'(b) < (1/2)(1 + \delta)V'(b) = \partial G^F(b, k)/\partial b$ and similarly $\partial g^S(b, k)/\partial k < \partial G^F(b, k)/\partial k$. So by Topkis (1978) and Theorem 4 of Milgrom and Roberts (1994), $(b^*, k^*) < (b^F, k^F)$.

equilibrium at which dealers choose bid and ask prices equal to the Walrasian price and buyer and seller investment levels are efficient, $(b^{**}, k^{**}) = (b^F, k^F)$. Competition between firms provides incentives for efficient investment by buyers and sellers. Suppose that dealers have constant marginal cost t per transaction, so that the equilibrium price spread with competing dealers equals $p - w = t$. Then a search market would still exist because of the price spread, assuming that direct exchange was costless. As the unit cost t approaches zero, the search market is displaced and the volume of trade and investment levels approach the efficient outcome. Lower transaction costs in the market for contracts improve incentives to invest. Intermediation by firms addresses the problem of contracting faced by buyers and sellers in direct exchange.

11.2 Moral Hazard: Firm Management of Tournaments versus Bilateral Agency Contracts

Consider a market in which consumers are either principals or agents. To obtain a good, a principal must enter into a contract with an agent. A principal can only contract with one agent and an agent can only contract with one principal. The agent devotes costly effort to producing the good. The agent's effort level is unobservable to the principal. The production process is subject to uncertainty. The output produced by an agent is only observable to the principal with whom the agent has entered into a contract. The principal and the agent choose the terms of the contract before production takes place. The contract rewards the agent based on the realized output. Rewards cannot be based on the agent's effort because effort is not observable. The contract does not depend on the output of other agents since those outputs are not observable to the parties to a contract.

All principals are identical to each other initially, as are all agents. Thus, any principal can be matched with any agent. After matches are made, the principal and the agent encounter the traditional moral hazard problem. The principal can induce the agent to increase productive effort, but that requires increasing rewards for production. Rewards based on production increase the agent's exposure to risk because output is subject to random shocks. The greater the risk faced by a risk-averse agent, the more the principal must compensate the agent. Accordingly, the principal and the agent face a tradeoff between the benefits of productive efficiency and the costs of risk.

Firms can structure their rewards to managers and employees by taking relative performance into account. By serving as a contracting hub, the firm can contract simultaneously with many principals and many agents. To compare the performance of coordinated contracting with that of individual contracts, suppose that the firm rewards relative performance using a rank-order tournament. This limits the firm because the rank-order tournament does not perform as well as the optimal incentive scheme, which effectively uses piece rates adjusted for aggregate performance. However, by establishing a rank-order tournament, the firm can enjoy the benefits of information aggregation while inducing competition between agents. Even though the tournament need not be the optimal multiagent compensation scheme, the discussion derives a condition under which the tournament performs better than optimal bilateral contracts. With sufficient correlation between output shocks, the firm improves productive efficiency.[16] This illustrates how the firm can use competitive transactions to improve efficiency relative to bilateral agency contracts.

11.2.1 Principal-Agent Contracts

To illustrate the contrast between bilateral contracts and the firm, we examine a market with two principals and two agents. Principals are risk-neutral and have a willingness to pay equal to v per unit of output. To obtain q units of output, a principal must enter into an exclusive bilateral contract with an agent. The principal offers a payment schedule to the agent before production takes place. The agent devotes effort to a production process that is subject to random shocks. The principal receives the output of the product process and makes the payment to the agent.

The agents are identical ex ante. They have utility of income I given by a von Neumann-Morgenstern utility function with constant absolute risk aversion,

$$u(I) = -e^{-rI}.$$

The parameter r is the agent's coefficient of absolute risk aversion. For ease of presentation, consider the agent's *certainty equivalent reward*, which is the certain reward that would leave the agent indifferent in comparison with an uncertain alternative. The certain reward is represented as a transferable utility consisting of an expected payment and an adjustment for the cost of risk,

$$(22) \qquad U = EI - (1/2)r \operatorname{var}(I).$$

If the certainty equivalent of random income I is I^{CE}, then $u(I^{CE}) = Eu(I)$. The certainty equivalence approximation holds exactly when income is normally distributed and the von Neumann-Morgenstern utility function u is exponential.

We restrict attention to linear contracts that reward the agent using a commission α per unit of output q and a fixed payment β. Thus, the agent receives a payment based on a linear schedule,

$$(23) \qquad p(q) = \alpha q + \beta,$$

for q units of output. The payment $p(q)$ is the agent's incentive schedule.

---

16 On tournaments, see Lazear and Rosen (1981), Holmstrom (1982), Nalebuff and Stiglitz (1983), Green and Stokey (1983), Malcolmson (1986), Dixit (1987), Battacharya and Guasch (1988), Drago and Heywood (1989), Kräkel (2002), and Tsoulouhas and Vukina (2004). The tournament literature has not compared tournaments with bilateral contracts, although there have been comparisons between tournaments and piece rates that are optimal in a multiagent setting.

The agents produce output by devoting effort a_i, $i = 1, 2$, with cost of effort equal to $C(a) = a^2$. The production process is subject to an idiosyncratic shock x_i, $i = 1, 2$, and a common shock y,

$$(24) \qquad\qquad q_i = a_i + x_i + y, \quad i = 1, 2.$$

The idiosyncratic shocks x_i are normally distributed with mean zero and variance σ_x^2. The common shock is normally distributed with mean zero and variance σ_y^2. Principals and agents cannot observe either type of shock. Agents must choose their effort before the realization of the shocks. An agent can infer the sum of the shocks after output is observed. The agent's income is given (dropping seller subscripts) by

$$(25) \qquad\qquad I = \alpha(a + x + y) + \beta - a^2.$$

The agent's certainty-equivalent utility of income thus equals

$$(26) \qquad\qquad U = \alpha a + \beta - a^2 - (1/2)r\alpha^2\left(\sigma_x^2 + \sigma_y^2\right).$$

Each principal receives an expected net benefit of $vEq - Ep$, so the expected net benefit equals

$$(27) \qquad\qquad V = va - \alpha a - \beta.$$

Consider a decentralized market for contracts. Principals and agents engage in bilateral exchange. Each principal contracts with a different seller. Bilateral exchange causes contracts to be independent because principals cannot observe the output of any agent other than the one with whom they have contracted. Each contract only depends on the information revealed by the output of an individual agent.

The terms of a bilateral contract consist of the per-unit payment α and the fixed payment β. The choice of the per-unit payment α will not depend on the allocation of total surplus between the principal and the agent. The fixed payment β is used to allocate the total surplus between the principal and the agent. Because effort is unobservable, the agent chooses effort to maximize expected benefits:

$$\max_a \alpha a + \beta - a^2 - (1/2)r\alpha^2\left(\sigma_x^2 + \sigma_y^2\right).$$

Thus, the agent's optimal effort is a function of the per-unit payment,

$$a^0 = \alpha/2.$$

The total benefits for the principal and the agent-and-seller equal

$$(28) \qquad\qquad U + V = va^0 - (a^0)^2 - (1/2)r\alpha^2\left(\sigma_x^2 + \sigma_y^2\right).$$

The principal and the agent choose the per-unit payment to maximize total surplus, given that the agent chooses effort to maximize expected utility, so that

$$v/2 - \alpha/2 - r\alpha\left(\sigma_x^2 + \sigma_y^2\right) = 0.$$

Thus, the optimal per-unit payment is positive and solves

(29) $$\alpha^0 = v/\left[1 + 2r\left(\sigma_x^2 + \sigma_y^2\right)\right].$$

This is perhaps the most significant aspect of the market for contracts. Optimal bilateral contracts necessarily involve a piece-rate payment.

In the equilibrium of the market for contracts, an agent's effort equals

(30) $$a^0 = (v/2)/\left[1 + 2r\left(\sigma_x^2 + \sigma_y^2\right)\right].$$

Total surplus for a principal and an agent equals

(31) $$U^0 + V^0 = (v^2/4)/\left[1 + 2r\left(\sigma_x^2 + \sigma_y^2\right)\right].$$

Individual rationality requires that both the principal and the agent be better off or at least as well off as their best alternative. Suppose that the returns from their best alternative are normalized to zero for both the principal and the agent. So the individual rationality conditions are $U \geq 0$, $V \geq 0$. Suppose further that the principal and the agent evenly split the expected gains from trade, so that

(32) $$U^0 = V^0 = (U^0 + V^0)/2 = (v^2/8)/\left[1 + 2r\left(\sigma_x^2 + \sigma_y^2\right)\right].$$

From equation (27), the equilibrium fixed payment can be obtained as

$$\beta^0 = (v - \alpha)a^0 - V^0.$$

Substitute for the equilibrium effort level a^0 from equation (30) and for the agent's share of expected gains from trade V^0 the equilibrium value of the fixed payment β:

$$\beta = \frac{v^2}{8\left[1 + 2r\left(\sigma_x^2 + \sigma_y^2\right)\right]^2}\left[6r\left(\sigma_x^2 + \sigma_y^2\right) - 1\right].$$

11.2.2 The Firm and the Tournament

The firm designs a rank-order tournament between agents offering a set of prizes W_1 and W_2, where the larger prize goes to the winning agent, $W_1 > W_2$. The agent with the greater output q wins the tournament. The discussion of tournaments is similar to that of Lazear and Rosen (1981), although they assume that the firm is competitive and earns zero profit. Here, we allow the firm to maximize profit subject to the individual rationality constraints of the principals and the agents.

Let q_1 be the output of agent 1 and let q_2 be the output of agent 2. Then the probability that worker 1 wins the tournament is

(33) $$\begin{aligned} \Pr\{q_1 > q_2\} &= \Pr\{a_1 + x_1 + y > a_2 + x_2 + y\} \\ &= \Pr\{a_1 - a_2 > x_2 - x_1\}. \end{aligned}$$

Notice that the additive common shock plays no role in determining the winner of the tournament. If x_1 and x_2 are independently and identically distributed with density $f(x)$, the density of the difference $X = x_2 - x_1$ equals

$$h(X) = \int_{-\infty}^{\infty} f(X + y) f(y) dy,$$

with cumulative distribution function $H(X)$. Thus,

(34) $\Pr\{q_1 > q_2\} = H(a_1 - a_2).$

This specifies the probability that agent 1 wins the tournament as a function of the difference between the effort levels of the two agents.

Recall that $f(x)$ is a normal distribution with mean zero and variance σ_x^2. Thus, the distribution of the difference has mean zero and variance $2\sigma_x^2$, because by standard arguments $E(x_2 - x_1) = 0$ and var $(x_2 - x_1) = 2\sigma_x^2$. By a change of variables, note that

(35) $h(0) = \int_{-\infty}^{\infty} (f(y))^2 dy = 1/(2\sigma_x\sqrt{\pi}),$

where π is the numerical constant. Two agents with equal efforts have the same likelihood of winning the tournament, $H(0) = 1/2$.

Let payment W be a random variable that takes the value W_1 with probability $H(a_1 - a_2)$ and takes the value W_2 with probability $1 - H(a_1 - a_2)$. The expected income of agent 1 from the tournament is

(36) $E I = E\left(W - a_1^2\right) = E W - a_1^2.$

The variance of agent 1's income is

(37)   var $(I) =$ var $\left(W - a_1^2\right) =$ var (W)
$$= H(a_1 - a_2) W_1^2 + (1 - H(a_1 - a_2)) W_2^2 - (E W)^2.$$

If effort levels are equal, then $E W = (W_1 + W_2)/2$ and var $(W) = (W_1 - W_2)^2/4$. The effects of agent 1's effort on the mean and on the variance of payment are as follows:

(38) $\dfrac{\partial E W}{\partial a_1} = h(a_1 - a_2)(W_1 - W_2),$

(39) $\dfrac{\partial \text{ var } (W)}{\partial a_1} = h(a_1 - a_2)[(W_1)^2 - (W_2)^2 - 2 E W(W_1 - W_2)].$

The effects of effort on mean and variance evaluated at $a_1 = a_2$ are

$$\left. \frac{\partial E W}{\partial a_1} \right|_{a_1 = a_2} = (W_1 - W_2)/(2\sigma_x\sqrt{\pi}),$$

$$\left. \frac{\partial \text{ var } (W)}{\partial a_1} \right|_{a_1 = a_2} = 0.$$

For ease of presentation, consider the agents' problems using certainty equivalence. The mean-variance certainty equivalence is only an approximation because income is a two-state random variable. The two agents play a Nash noncooperative game in effort levels. Let a_1^* and a_2^* be the Nash equilibrium effort levels. Then agent 1 chooses effort a_1 given a_2^* to maximize the certainty-equivalent utility,

$$(40) \qquad U = E\,W - a_1^2 - (1/2)r\,\text{var}\,(W).$$

The agent's first-order condition gives

$$\frac{\partial E\,W}{\partial a_1} - \frac{r}{2}\frac{\partial \text{var}\,(W)}{\partial a_1} = 2a_1.$$

At the symmetric Nash equilibrium, effort levels are equal, $a_1^* = a_2^*$. This implies that in equilibrium, risk aversion does not affect effort levels because $\partial \text{var}\,W/\partial a_1 = 0$ when efforts are equal. The efforts of the agents are thus equal to

$$(41) \qquad a_1^* = a_2^* = (W_1 - W_2)/(4\sigma_x\sqrt{\pi}).$$

The risk-averse agents' certainty equivalent evaluated at the equilibrium effort levels must satisfy the agents' individual rationality condition,

$$(42) \quad U = (W_1 + W_2)/2 - (W_1 - W_2)^2/(4\sigma_x\sqrt{\pi})^2 - (1/2)r(W_1 - W_2)^2/4 \geq U^0.$$

This constrains the firm's choice of prizes W_1 and W_2. If the individual rationality condition holds with equality, then $U = U^0$ implicitly defines W_2 as a function of W_1. Differentiating $U = U_0$ with respect to W_1 gives

$$(43) \qquad W_1 - W_2 = \frac{1 + \partial W_2/\partial W_1}{1 - \partial W_2/\partial W_1}\frac{1}{1/(2\sigma_x\sqrt{\pi})^2 + r/2}.$$

The firm offers principals a contingent contract to deliver output at a per-unit price P. The firm offers to give each principal half of the total output that is produced by the two agents. Given the equilibrium agent effort levels, total expected output equals

$$(44) \qquad E(q_1 + q_2) = 2a^* = (W_1 - W_2)/(2\sigma_x\sqrt{\pi}).$$

The risk-neutral principal's individual rationality condition specifies that the principal must receive at least the same expected utility as in the decentralized market,

$$(45) \qquad (v - P)E(q_1 + q_2)/2 \geq V^0.$$

If the principal's individual rationality condition is binding, the contract price is a function of the payments in the tournament,

$$(46) \qquad \begin{aligned} P &= v - 2V^0/E(q_1 + q_2) \\ &= v - 2V^0(2\sigma_x\sqrt{\pi})/(W_1 - W_2). \end{aligned}$$

The firm designs a tournament by choosing prizes W_1 and W_2. The firm maximizes profit subject to the principals' and the agents' individual rationality conditions. The firm's profit is

(47) $$\Pi = PE(q_1 + q_2) - W_1 - W_2.$$

The profit-maximizing firm will adjust the contract price and the prizes such that the principals' and the agents' individual rationality conditions are binding. Substituting from the principals' individual rationality condition, the firm's profit can be written as a function of the prizes,

(48) $$\Pi = v(W_1 - W_2)/(2\sigma_x\sqrt{\pi}) - 2V^0 - W_1 - W_2.$$

The agents' individual rationality condition specifies W_2 as a function of W_1. Thus, profit can be written as a function of W_1. Maximizing profit over W_1 gives

(49) $$[v/(2\sigma_x\sqrt{\pi})](1 - \partial W_2/\partial W_1) - (1 + \partial W_2/\partial W_1) = 0.$$

Using equation (43) to substitute for $\partial W_2/\partial W_1$ yields the difference in prizes,

(50) $$W_1 - W_2 = \frac{v/(2\sigma_x\sqrt{\pi})}{1/(2\sigma_x\sqrt{\pi})^2 + r/2}.$$

We now determine whether or not the firm plays an economic role in the presence of moral hazard. Substitute for $W_1 + W_2$ in the firm's profit equation (50) using the principals' individual rationality condition (48). Then substitute for $W_1 - W_2$ in the firm's profit equation using equation (50). The firm's profit is then

(51) $$\Pi = \frac{v^2/2}{1 + 2r\sigma_x^2\pi} - 2(U^0 + V^0).$$

The total gains from trade without the firm equal

(52) $$g = 2(U^0 + V^0) = \frac{v^2/2}{1 + 2r\left(\sigma_x^2 + \sigma_y^2\right)}.$$

Value created by the firm is $G = (v^2/2)(1 + 2r\sigma_x^2\pi)$. The firm is profitable and thus adds value if and only if $G \geq g$ or equivalently if and only if

$$\sigma_y^2 \geq (\pi - 1)\sigma_x^2.$$

This condition is necessary and sufficient for the rank-order tournament offered by the firm to improve efficiency relative to agency contracts. Competition between agents improves efficiency if and only if the variance of the common shock is sufficiently large relative to the variance of the idiosyncratic shock. This means that there must be sufficient returns to aggregation of information by the firm to overcome the inefficiency of the tournament.

The tournament has the advantage of eliminating risks from the common shock for risk-averse agents; see equation (33). There is no need to compensate agents for that risk in contrast to bilateral agency contracts. The risks of the common shock are shifted onto risk-neutral principals. The prize structure reflects these considerations. The difference in prizes is decreasing in the agents' risk aversion parameter r. A higher principal willingness to pay increases the difference between the prizes. The agents' optimal effort with a tournament is obtained by combining equations (44) and (50):

$$(53) \qquad a^* = \frac{v/2}{1 + 2r\sigma_x^2\pi}.$$

Optimal effort is increasing in principal willingness to pay, decreasing in agent risk aversion, and decreasing in the variance of the idiosyncratic shocks. The prize structure and optimal effort are independent of the variance of the common shock.

11.3 Adverse Selection: The Firm Monitors Performance

Consider an economy with entrepreneurs who need capital to invest in projects and lenders with capital available for making investments. The entrepreneurs and the lenders can engage in direct exchange, with lenders negotiating contracts with entrepreneurs. A firm competes with direct exchange by acting as an intermediary between the lenders and the entrepreneurs. The model is based on Diamond (1984).

Consider first direct exchange between lenders and entrepreneurs. Suppose that there are N entrepreneurs in the economy and mN lenders. An entrepreneur requires one unit of investment and each lender has available $1/m$ units of investment capital.[17] For the direct-exchange case, it is sufficient to examine the decision of a single entrepreneur. Each entrepreneur undertakes an investment with an uncertain payoff y, which is uniformly distributed on the unit interval, so that $Ey = 1/2$. After making the investment, the entrepreneur observes the realized value of y. The value of y is the entrepreneur's private information so that it is not observable by lenders. After observing y, the entrepreneur makes a payment z to his lenders, where $z \le y$.

Because each entrepreneur has an incentive to understate the outcome of the investment project so as to reduce the payment to lenders, the debt contract includes a nonpecuniary penalty function $H(z)$. The penalty function can represent a loss of reputation for the entrepreneur. The entrepreneur chooses an optimal penalty function that maximizes the entrepreneur's net benefits, subject to two constraints. First, the entrepreneur's payment strategy must be incentive-compatible.

---

17 The investment is normalized to one and the competitive return is less than one without loss of generality. The assumption could be interpreted as an assumption that investment is the only store of value, with money depreciating at a faster rate. Alternatively, the required investment level could be normalized to equal some number less than the competitive return.

The entrepreneur's strategy maximizes the entrepreneur's expected net benefit subject to the performance of the investment project,

$$\max_{z(y)} E[y - z - H(z)] \quad \text{subject to } z \leq y.$$

Second, the expected payment by the entrepreneur must be greater than or equal to the competitive interest rate available to lenders r:

$$E z(y) \geq r.$$

The entrepreneur's incentive-compatible strategy, $z(y)$, depends on the penalty function, H. The optimal penalty function maximizes the entrepreneur's expected profit, $E[y - z(y) - H(z(y))]$, subject to the lender's individual-rationality constraint.

The optimal contract between the entrepreneur and the lenders has the form of a debt contract with face value h and a penalty function $H^*(z)$ equal to the shortfall from h,

$$H^*(z) = \max\{h - z, 0\},$$

where $h = 1 - (1 - 2r)^{1/2}$.

To see why the penalty function is optimal, observe first that, given H^*, the entrepreneur's optimal strategy is

$$z(y) = \begin{cases} y & \text{if } y < h \\ h & \text{otherwise.} \end{cases}$$

Given this strategy, the lender's individual rationality constraint is satisfied exactly; that is,

$$E z(y) = r.$$

The penalty function maximizes the entrepreneur's net benefits. This is because H^* gives the smallest penalties such that the entrepreneur's incentive-compatible strategy satisfies the lender's individual-rationality constraint.

Observe that, by construction, h is the smallest number such that if the constraint $z \leq y$ and $z \leq h$ are satisfied, then $E z(y) \geq y$. So there must exist some payment $h^+ \geq h$ that is incentive-compatible. If $z = h^+$ is incentive-compatible given contract $H(z)$, then

$$y - h^+ - H(h^+) \geq \max_{z' \in [0, h^+]}[y - z' - H(z')].$$

Thus, for all $z' \in [0, h^+]$, it follows that

$$H(z') \geq h^+ + H(h^+) - z'.$$

Since $h^+ \geq h$ and $H(z) \geq 0$ for all z, it follows that

$$H(z') \geq h - z' = H^*(z').$$

Note that $H^*(z) = 0$ for $z \geq h$. Thus H^* gives the smallest penalties such that the entrepreneur's incentive-compatible strategy satisfies the lender's individual-rationality constraint. So H^* is the optimal penalty function.

Under direct exchange, entrepreneurs earn the expected profit

$$\pi = E[y - z(y) - H^*(z(y))] = E[y - h] = \tfrac{1}{2} - h.$$

Entrepreneurs are profitable if $h \leq 1/2$. Since $h = 1 - (1 - 2r)^{1/2}$, this requires that the interest rate not be too high, $r \leq 3/8$.

Now consider a firm that acts as a monopoly intermediary between lenders and entrepreneurs. The firm has a fixed cost of monitoring, k. Assume that monitoring allows the firm to observe the outcome of each entrepreneur's project, y. Thus the firm does not need to impose (nonpecuniary) penalties on the entrepreneurs, avoiding the deadweight loss from such penalties. The firm can write a simple debt contract with face value g with the entrepreneur:

$$g(y) = \begin{cases} y & \text{if } y < g \\ g & \text{otherwise.} \end{cases}$$

The firm lends to all N entrepreneurs and earns a total return equal to $G = \sum_{i=1}^{n} g(y_i)$. Assume that the returns to projects are independently distributed.

Although the firm can observe the outcome of the project, lenders cannot observe the firm's income. It follows that the optimal contract with lenders must include a deadweight nonpecuniary penalty function, which is the same as the optimal penalty function derived in the case of direct exchange. Suppose that the firm pays Z to lenders. The firm's objective is expected returns net of the investment costs of monitoring:

$$\Pi = E[G - Z - H(Z)] - Nk.$$

By the same reasoning as in the case of direct monitoring, the optimal penalty function for the firm is of the form

$$H(Z) = \max\{f^N - Z, 0\},$$

where f^N depends on the number of loan contracts N. The firm's payment strategy $Z(G)$ is a function of total receipts and depends on the penalty function,

$$Z(G) = \begin{cases} G & \text{if } G < f^N \\ f^N & \text{otherwise.} \end{cases}$$

The expected payment made by the firm to lenders must at least equal their opportunity cost of capital. Thus, the optimal contract for the firm exactly satisfies the lender's individual-rationality constraint,

$$E\,Z(G) = Nr.$$

This equation determines the value of the critical parameter f^N.

The entrepreneurs must earn at least what they could earn with direct exchange. With intermediation, an entrepreneur earns

$$E[y - g(y)] = \tfrac{1}{2} - g + g^2/2.$$

The firm increases the face value g until the entrepreneur is exactly indifferent between direct exchange and intermediated exchange:

$$\tfrac{1}{2} - h = \tfrac{1}{2} - g + g^2/2,$$

so that $g = 1 - (1 - 2h)^{1/2}$. The face value exceeds the penalty in the direct-exchange case, which in turn exceeds the competitive rate of return:

$$g > h > r.$$

Substitute for the repayment policy $Z(G)$ and the optimal nonpecuniary penalty function $H(Z)$ in the firm's expected net return of the investment costs of monitoring. The firm's profit equals

$$\Pi = E[G - f^N] - Nk.$$

Because the outcomes of the entrepreneur's investment products are independently distributed, $EG = N(g - g^2/2) = Nh$. So the firm's expected net return equals the number of loan contracts times the difference between the penalty parameter in the direct-exchange case and the cost of monitoring by the firm, minus the penalty parameter in the delegated-monitoring case. The firm's profit is then

$$\Pi = N[h - k - f^N/N].$$

Therefore, the firm is profitable if and only if

$$h - k - f^N/N \geq 0.$$

If the firm makes only one loan to a single entrepreneur, then $f^1 = h$ and the firm is not profitable because $\Pi = -k$. By the (weak) law of large numbers, it can be shown for large N that the penalty parameter divided by N falls below h and tends toward the interest rate r. Using the form of $Z(G)$, rewrite the individual-rationality constraint $E Z(G) = Nr$ in terms of the distribution of the sample mean G/N on $[0, g]$,

$$P^N E[G/N | G/N < f^N/N] + (1 - P^N) f^N/N = r,$$

where $P^N = \Pr\{G/N < f^N/N\}$. By the weak law of large numbers there exists $N^* < \infty$ such that $P^N < \delta$ for all $\delta > 0$, because $E G/N = h > f^N/N$ for $N > 1$; see Diamond (1984, p. 401). Thus, for large N, f^N/N approaches r. Thus, given $h > r + k$, the firm is profitable for sufficiently large N. Since $h = 1 - (1 - 2r)^{1/2}$, this means that $1 - r - (1 - 2r)^{1/2} > k$.

The firm is able to compete against direct exchange due to the ability to monitor project outcomes and economies of scale in monitoring multiple loans. The firm observes a sample of realizations of loan projects rather than a single project.

By the central limit theorem, the variance of the average payment received from entrepreneurs falls as the number of loans increases. As a result, the cost to lenders of monitoring the firm is lower the more loans the firm makes. The firm with more loans then earns a spread that is sufficient to cover the costs of observing entrepreneur performance.

11.4 Adverse Selection: The Firm Certifies Quality

Asymmetric information about product quality creates transaction costs, as in Akerlof's (1970) well-known model of a market for lemons. Akerlof showed that a market with bilateral trade can fail to exist if customers are less well informed than suppliers about product quality. In equilibrium, low-quality used cars drive out high-quality used cars, because consumers are only willing to pay an "average" price for cars of unknown quality, and only sellers of low-quality cars can trade at that price. As a result of unobservable product quality, there can be returns to centralized quality certification by firms. Because there are foregone gains from trade, there are economic returns to investment in capital equipment or expertise needed to certify the quality of the product. By investing in the technology needed to verify product quality, and certifying product quality, firms can supply useful information to the market.

Biglaiser (1993) shows that introducing a firm into a market with adverse selection enhances efficiency.[18] His analysis suggests that the firm has a greater incentive to invest in monitoring quality than does an individual buyer, since the firm buys more goods. In addition, the firm's incentive to report accurately the quality of goods stems from the returns to building a good reputation. Biglaiser's model has three types of agents: buyers, suppliers, and a firm. When two agents meet, they bargain over the terms of trade. A buyer entering the market decides whether to go to a seller or to a firm. In equilibrium, the firm has no incentive to sell a low-quality good as a consequence of the returns to reputation. All high-quality suppliers sell through the firm, whereas all low-quality suppliers sell directly to consumers, so that a separating equilibrium exists.

The classic adverse selection problem is Akerlof's market for lemons, in which suppliers know product quality but buyers do not. Sellers of low-quality goods have an incentive to overstate quality. Biglaiser (1993) introduces a firm that plays the role of an expert in determining product quality. The firm has an incentive to invest in skills to detect the quality of the product because it buys many more goods than an individual buyer. In addition, the firm has a greater incentive to report the quality of the good accurately than does a supplier who sells only a few goods. Therefore, the firm becomes an expert because of the returns to investment in detecting quality and the returns to investment in reputation. This section reviews

18 See also Garella (1989).

some of the main conclusions of Biglaiser's analysis, without reproducing the full details of his model.

There are three types of agents in the market: buyers, sellers, and a monopoly firm. All agents are infinitely lived and discount returns with a factor $\rho = e^{-\gamma}$, where γ is the rate of discount. Each seller is endowed with one unit of the good, which can be of two quality levels, high or low. The seller knows the quality of his good, but the quality is unobservable to buyers. The firm is able to monitor the quality of any seller's good by becoming an expert at a one time entry cost of T. For ease of discussion, normalize to zero the cost of meeting a buyer or seller and the cost to the firm of testing individual goods. The firm does incur a cost of verifying product quality in that testing delays the sale of the good by one period.

A buyer or seller that has the good receives a return equal to its value in each future period. A buyer values a low-quality good at v_L per period and a high-quality good at v_H per period, where $0 < v_L < v_H$. A seller values the low-quality good at zero and the high-quality good at u_H per period, where $u_H < v_H$. This implies that under full information there are always gains from trade between a buyer and a seller regardless of the quality of the good.

In each period a measure i of sellers and buyers enter the market. A proportion λ of sellers have a high-quality good, whereas a proportion $1 - \lambda$ have a low-quality good. The analysis is restricted to a steady-state equilibrium where the measure of agents entering and leaving the market are equal. Furthermore, each player's strategy maximizes that player's utility given the strategies of other players and all players of the same type use the same strategies.

Following Akerlof (1970), assume that a buyer values the average quality of goods less than a high-quality seller's valuation,

$$(54) \qquad\qquad (1 - \lambda)v_L + \lambda v_H < u_H.$$

This "market-for-lemons" condition (54) makes it impossible for high-quality goods to be in the market when the price for all goods is the same. Note that the condition implies $v_L < u_H$. The condition is more likely to hold if the proportion of low-quality goods is high.

Consider first the market without a firm. Suppose that buyers and sellers are matched randomly and bargain over the price of the good. The bargaining game is not specified. However, assume that if the buyer thinks that the seller has a low-quality good and if that belief is accurate, then the buyer and seller immediately come to an agreement. The buyer and the low-quality seller trade at some price p. Otherwise, bargaining is subject to asymmetric information. A seller can signal that he holds a high-quality good only by waiting to trade. Given these assumptions, two outcomes are possible: there are only low-quality goods in the market or there are both low- and high-quality goods.

Suppose that both goods are traded in the market. What is the highest possible price of the low-quality good? The price must be such that the low-quality seller does not have an incentive to delay and thereby represent the good as a high-quality good. To determine the value of representing the good as being of high quality, let t be the delay in trading with a high-quality seller. Suppose that high-quality sellers receive the lowest possible price that keeps them in the market, namely u_H. The low-quality seller will reveal truthfully the quality of his good if and only if the price p is less than or equal to the present discounted value of what the high-quality seller receives, $\rho^t uH$. The low-quality seller's incentive compatibility condition is strictly binding if

$$(55) \qquad p = \rho^t u_H.$$

Again, assuming that the high-quality seller receives exactly u_H with delay t, the highest price that can be paid for the low-quality good and still keep the buyer in the market equates the buyer's expected net benefit to zero:

$$(56) \qquad (1 - \lambda)(v_L - p)\lambda\rho^t(v_H - u_H) = 0.$$

Solving equations (55) and (56) yields an upper bound on the price for the low-quality good and a delay in trading the high-quality good such that there are both low- and high-quality goods in the market. The equilibrium delay t solves

$$(57) \qquad \rho^t = (1 - \lambda)v_L/(u_H - \lambda v_H).$$

From the market-for-lemons condition (54) it follows that ρ^t is between zero and one. Also, $p = \rho^t u_H < u_H$.

If low-quality goods drive out high-quality ones, that is, if only low-quality sellers enter the market, gains from trade equal

$$(58) \qquad g_L = (1/(1 - \rho))[(1 - \lambda)v_L + \lambda u_H].$$

If both types of sellers enter the market, then gains from trade equal

$$(59) \qquad g_H = (1/(1 - \rho))[(1 - \lambda)v_L + \lambda\rho^t(v_H - u_H) + \lambda u_H],$$

where $g_L < g_H$ because $v_H > u_H$. There may not be an equilibrium with high-quality goods in the market.

Now, compare the market outcome with an infinitely lived firm. Assume that the firm has no more bargaining power than does a buyer. The firm can offer a warranty. Suppose that it is common knowledge whether or not the firm has honored warranties in the past. Also, suppose that another firm always can enter the market and supplant the incumbent. Although the warranty is not enforceable, the offer is credible because the firm is concerned about the consequences of a reputation for not honoring warranties.

Assume that the expected time when a buyer and a low-quality seller will trade is the same whether or not the firm is in the market if the buyer's belief about the seller's type is the same. The price at which they trade may vary depending on the presence or absence of the firm within the market.[19]

Biglaiser (1993) constructs a market equilibrium with the following properties. The market is segmented. All high-quality sellers sell their goods through the firm and *most* low-quality sellers sell their goods directly to buyers. Sellers of low-quality goods need not go through the firm because their claim to have a low-quality good is credible. The firm receives a high enough payment for the good so that the firm accurately represents the quality of the goods that it sells. There are sufficiently high profits so that the firm has an incentive to represent correctly the quality of goods over time.

Biglaiser (1993) obtains an equilibrium with a firm such that the firm chooses to inspect a portion of the goods offered by sellers. High-quality sellers always choose to sell to the firm. Low-quality sellers are indifferent between entering the search market or selling to the firm, where they can earn a premium if they are not inspected or experience a delay in returning to the search market if they are inspected. As the cost of inspection approaches zero, the equilibrium approaches a limit in which the number of low-quality sellers that choose to visit the firm approaches zero. For ease of presentation, consider only the limit of the equilibrium in which all low-quality sellers are in the search market and all high-quality sellers sell to the firm.

The firm pays high-quality sellers a price w_H and sells to buyers at price p_H with a delay of one period that is necessary for the firm to complete inspections. Thus, the firm's profit is

$$(60) \qquad \Pi = [1/(1 - \rho)]\lambda(\rho p_H - w_H) - T.$$

With only low-quality sellers in the search market, the equilibrium price in the search market is z_L, where $v_L \geq z_L \geq 0$. The firm chooses a price for the high-quality good such that the buyer is indifferent between buying the low-quality good in the search market and buying the high-quality good from the firm,

$$(61) \qquad v_H - p_H = v_L - z_L,$$

so that $p_H = v_H - v_L + z_L$. The firm pays the high-quality seller a price equal to the value of holding the good to the high-quality seller, $w_H = u_H$. Thus, the firm's profit equals

$$(62) \qquad \Pi = [1/(1 - \rho)]\lambda[\rho(v_H - v_L + z_L) - u_H] - T.$$

The firm's profit is positive for all ρ sufficiently close to one. For a sufficiently high discount factor, it is worthwhile for the firm to incur the entry cost needed to observe quality.

---

19 Biglaiser (1993) also assumes that when bargaining with a low-quality seller, the price that the buyer and the low-quality seller will agree to makes the buyer indifferent between purchasing from the low-quality seller or from the firm.

Total gains from trade with the firm, when evaluated at the limit of the equilibrium with all low-quality sellers in the search market, equals

$$(63) \qquad G = [1/(1-\rho)][(1-\lambda)v_L + \lambda v_H + \lambda u_H] - T$$

since all goods are traded. The difference between gains from trade with and without a firm equals

$$(64) \qquad G - g_H = [1/(1-\rho)]\lambda[v_H - \rho^t(v_H - u_H)] - T.$$

As ρ approaches one, $G - g_H$ is positive for any value of entry cost T. Since $g_L < g_H$, it follows that $G - g_L$ is also positive. This implies that a firm improves allocative efficiency for a sufficiently high discount factor. The reason is that the discounted value of the increased gains from trade of the high-quality good exceeds the set-up cost that the firm incurs to enter the market. The increased gains from trade from sales of the high-quality good are due to the firm certifying quality and equal $v_H - \rho^t(v_H - u_H)$.

Compare the firm's profit with the increase in gains from trade,

$$(65) \qquad G - g_H - \Pi = [1/(1-\rho)]\lambda[v_H - \rho^t(v_H - u_H)$$
$$- \rho(v_H - v_L + z_L) + u_H].$$

Because the price in the search market z_L is less than or equal to v_L, note that

$$(66) \qquad G - g_H - \Pi \geq [1/(1-\rho)]\lambda[v_H(1-\rho) + u_H - \rho^t(v_H - u_H)].$$

For ρ approaching one and $v_H < 2u_H$, the increase in gains from trade is strictly greater than the firm's profit. The firm may not fully capture the efficiency gains due to quality certification.

The greater the gains from trade of the high-quality good, the higher the value of the firm's intervention. Moreover, the greater the proportion of low-quality goods, the more likely the "market-for-lemons" condition is to be satisfied and thus the more likely an expert will enter the market. With a relatively low discount rate or a relatively low set-up cost for experts, the firm will be profitable and the welfare gain from quality certification by the firm will be increased.

Biglaiser's analysis shows that in markets where goods are sold directly both by producers and by intermediaries that certify their quality, the firm's goods will have a higher average price and a higher average quality. Thus, quality certification by experts in markets with adverse selection helps to explain part of the commonly observed bid-ask spread between wholesale and retail prices. It also explains the presence of retail guarantees for some manufacturers' products, because consumers in the model have the choice of whether to purchase the good directly from the manufacturer or through a firm.

In a dynamic setting, Biglaiser and Friedman (1994) consider middlemen as guarantors of the product quality of their suppliers. Because firms handle the products of two or more suppliers, their incentives to sell a lower-quality good differ from those of individual suppliers. The firm that sells a low-quality product suffers a loss of reputation and thus loses customers for all other products. They characterize the long-run equilibrium of a competitive market in which the presence of firms acting as intermediaries lowers the threshold prices that are required to sustain high quality production.

Biglaiser and Friedman (1997) extend the analysis of adverse selection to allow for free-entry competition between experts. Firms have an infinite time horizon, unlike individual buyers and sellers, who are only active for at most one period. This gives firms incentives to learn from experience, to invest in expertise, and to earn returns to building a reputation for truthfulness. Through these activities, firms alleviate adverse selection relative to decentralized trade between short-lived buyers and sellers. Firms address adverse selection by offering nonlinear price schedules to buyers and sellers. Nonlinear pricing induces buyers to reveal their valuation through purchases of higher-quality goods and induces sellers to reveal product quality though premiums for higher quality. They show that decentralized trade cannot yield an optimum allocation and they provide conditions under which intermediated trade achieves the optimum.

Adverse selection is a common feature of transactions and contracts in any market. Buyers have unobservable characteristics such as income, location, risk aversion, impatience, and valuation of quality that affect willingness to pay. Sellers have unobservable characteristics such as opportunity costs, production costs, and product quality that affect their supply decisions. Dealing with the effects of incomplete information creates costs for both buyers and sellers. The firm improves the allocation of goods under asymmetric information. Generally, asymmetric information creates distortions such that the output is below the Walrasian quantity. Product market intermediaries address adverse selection by evaluating product characteristics and by certifying product quality. By dealing with greater number of buyers and sellers, as compared with decentralized trade, firms have incentives to invest in product testing and in reputation. Longer-lived firms have incentives to test products and to build a reputation for accurate representation of product quality.

11.5 Conclusions

Contracts between individual consumers, acting as buyers and as sellers, can be inefficient for various reasons. There are costs to search and negotiation that make assignments of buyers to sellers or sellers to buyers inefficient. Search and bargaining costs make it difficult for buyers and sellers who are already in a contractual relationship to seek new trading partners. Institutions such as contract law, social pressures, and business reputation help to enforce efficient contracts. Transactions costs of recontracting increase incentives for contractual performance. The inefficiencies of bilateral exchange are not necessarily the result of contractual commitments, but rather the underlying inefficiencies of the decentralized exchange mechanism that precedes contracting.

The chapter shows that the firm can serve as an alternative to bilateral contracts. The firm need not substitute vertical integration with buyers or sellers for bilateral contracts. The firm can improve economic efficiency by intermediating between buyers and sellers. The firm substitutes multilateral transactions with many buyers and with many sellers for bilateral contracts. This preserves competition between buyers and between sellers and maintains incentives for efficient performance. Thus, the firm substitutes competitive transactions for bilateral contracting between consumers.

When buyers and sellers invest in contractual relationships, the firm improves the efficiency of assignments and thus improves incentives to invest relative to bilateral contracting. Thus, the firm reduces the hold-up problem due to bilateral contracts. When buyers and sellers form bilateral principal-agent contracts, the firm improves incentives to invest by aggregating information. The firm mitigates moral hazard problems by basing rewards on aggregate information and designing tournaments.

When there is asymmetric information, buyers and sellers encounter adverse selection problems. In markets with bilateral principal-agent contracts, the firm improves efficiency by intermediating between lenders and entrepreneurs. Lenders invest in the firm through debt contracts and the firm in turn lends to the entrepreneurs. By pooling risk and by obtaining economies of scale in monitoring, the firm improves efficiency in the market for loans. In markets with bilateral exchange of goods of unobservable quality, the firm improves efficiency by monitoring and certifying product quality. By taking advantage of economies of scale in monitoring technology and by fostering competition among suppliers of products with different quality levels, the firm reduces the problem of adverse selection.

12

Conclusion

The *Theory of the Firm* provides a general framework for introducing institutions into microeconomics. Firms, markets, and organizations arise endogenously through the optimization decisions of economic actors. Individuals choose to become entrepreneurs and establish firms. In turn, firms create and manage markets and organizations. These institutions are part of the economic equilibrium and their features depend on the preferences, endowments, knowledge, and transaction costs of individuals. Microeconomics with transaction costs and endogenous institutions offers a more complete picture of the economy.

12.1 The Firm

The general theory of the firm presented here offers a formal method of identifying what is a firm. The separation criterion asks whether the objectives of an institution can be separated from those of its owners. The firm is a transaction institution whose objectives are separate from those of its owners. The separation of objectives provides the basis for profit maximization by firms. The separation of objectives supports the development of financial markets that allocate ownership of firms and corporate control.

The separation criterion offers a bright line distinction between the firm and the many types of consumer organizations that also engage in economic transactions. Consumer organizations include clubs, merchants' associations, exchanges, buyers' cooperatives, workers' cooperatives, nonprofits, basic partnerships, and public enterprises. These organizations are not firms because their objectives are closely tied to the consumption or production interests of their members. For example, a club's objectives are to provide for the recreation, social interaction, cultural development, or other interests of its members. As another example, a basic partnership's objectives are to apply the human capital and financial capital contributions of its members. Other consumer organizations that are not specifically formed to engage

458

in economic transactions, such as political parties, also have objectives that depend on those of their owners.

The separation criterion allows the application and generalization of the Fisher Separation Theorem. The Fisher Separation Theorem offers several crucial insights. First, the theorem shows why firms maximize profits. Consumers who own a firm obtain income from the firm's profits and unanimously prefer that the firm maximize profits. Consumers choose consumption to maximize their benefits given prices and their budget constraints.

Second, the Separation Theorem shows that the separation provides gains from trade. The firm's owners are made better off by trading with other economic actors rather than relying on the firm for their consumption interests. The consumers who own the firm turn to markets for their consumption, saving, and labor supply activities. In turn, the firm earns a greater profit by trading with other economic actors rather than adjusting its production to serve its owners' consumption interests. The firm maximizes profits through transactions with its customers, employees, investors, and suppliers.

Finally, the Separation Theorem provides the basis for markets to separate consumption decisions from production decisions. Markets are institutions that stand between buyers and sellers. Markets coordinate consumption decisions and production decisions though centralization and price adjustment. Rather than relying on the ownership of firms to achieve consumption interests, consumers obtain gains from trade in the marketplace. Firms in turn maximize profits by obtaining gains from trade through markets.

The separation criterion presented here extends the Fisher Separation Theorem beyond its neoclassical setting. The Fisher Separation Theorem depends on price-taking behavior by both consumers and firms, with markets clearing through the Walrasian auctioneer. Our discussion relaxes this requirement, allowing firms to choose prices. By addressing price setting by firms, the general separation theorems are consistent with firms acting as market makers, adjusting prices to clear markets.

The Theory of the Firm extends the separation to the formation of organizations. By separating their objectives from those of their owners, consumer organizations can be transformed into firms. A worker cooperative maximizes the average benefits of its members, but changes its objective to profit maximization when there is a market for memberships. The profit-maximizing firm chooses a different-sized workforce than the worker cooperative.

The objectives of the partnership change when it must obtain outside financing. When investment costs are relatively low in comparison to the endowments of the partnership's members, the partnership can self-finance. When the capital investment exceeds a critical size, it becomes desirable to separate ownership and control by switching from a self-financing partnership to a partnership with outside investors. The partnership must provide a sufficient return to attract investors so that obtaining outside finance changes the partnership's objectives.

Firms are assets whose owners receive both residual returns and residual rights of control. Delegation of authority to managers allows for the development of professional managers. The separation between ownership and control allows the formation of a market for corporate control which improves incentives to managerial performance. Firms have an economic identity that is distinct from their customers, suppliers, owners, managers, and employees. The firm's economic identity is distinct because it takes part in transactions independently, which allows limited liability of its owners and protection of the firm's assets. The firm's distinct identity fosters the development of a business reputation in financial markets, labor markets, and product markets.

The ability of firms to provide transaction efficiencies stems from the separation of objectives from its owners. The firm becomes an independent economic actor, which adds degrees of freedom to the economy. Profit maximization motivates the firm to seek efficiencies in production, investment, and innovation. The firm breaks the budget-balancing constraint of consumer organizations. Much additional work remains to understand when the separation theorem might apply in more complex economic environments.

The firm differs from consumer organizations in many ways. The entrepreneur chooses the firm's initial objectives, business plan, production technology, and transaction methods. The entrepreneur, the firm's owners, and its managers can endow the firm with features and capabilities that differ from those of individual consumers or consumer organizations. The firm offers longevity exceeding human lifetimes. The firm benefits from specialization of function that cannot be achieved by individual consumers or groups of consumers. The firm provides transaction mechanisms that improve communication and information processing. The firm performs many of the economic functions traditionally identified with money. Through market making and organization design, firms improve the efficiency of transactions. These capabilities make firms essential to the allocation of resources in the modern economy.

12.2 The Entrepreneur

The general theory of the firm explains how firms are established. The entrepreneur plays a central role in the general theory of the firm. The formal definition of a firm provides a basis for defining the entrepreneur. Entrepreneurs are individuals who establish firms. This defines the objectives, activities, capabilities, costs, and rewards of the entrepreneur.

The concept of the foundational shift helps to clarify entrepreneurship. The entrepreneur becomes an owner of the firm once it is established. The activities of the entrepreneur are those required to establish a firm, including the choice of the firm's products, technology, and transaction methods. The entrepreneur must assemble the financing, personnel, and technology necessary to launch the firm.

The entrepreneur's capabilities are those required to design the firm and to engage in the transactions to establish the firm. The costs of the entrepreneur are the transaction costs of establishing the firm. The entrepreneur's reward is his share of the value of the firm once it is established. The entrepreneur has an incentive to establish a firm only if his share of the value of the firm exceeds the costs of establishing the firm.

The foundational shift is based on the separation of the firm's objectives from those of its owners. The entrepreneur and the firm generally are not separate during the process of conception, development, and establishment of the firm. The firm is a work in progress and depends on the entrepreneur's skills and effort. When the firm is established, the entrepreneur may continue to contribute to the firm as an owner, manager, employee, or consultant. However, these functions can be performed by contracting with individuals who were not involved in founding the firm. The firm's objectives are separate from those of its owners, including its founders. After it is established, the firm takes on a life of its own.

The discussion identifies three types of entrepreneurial competition. Entrepreneurs compete with each other to establish firms. As a result, the success of entrepreneurs will depend on how individual entrepreneurs differ in terms of preferences, endowments, knowledge, and abilities. Entrepreneurs compete with consumer organizations and direct exchange. The success of entrepreneurs will then depend on whether the firms they establish improve the efficiency of transactions relative to direct exchange between consumers. Entrepreneurs compete with existing firms. As a result, the success of entrepreneurs will be affected by the competitive advantage the new firm gains over incumbent firms. It is interesting to examine the relative effects of these types of entrepreneurial competition on the formation and growth of firms.

Much more work remains to be done to understand entrepreneurship. A consistent definition of entrepreneurship may be useful as a guide to empirical studies. The entrepreneur's task is distinct from the commercialization of invention. An invention can be commercialized by other means, including the establishment of a consumer organization or licensing the invention to an existing firm. What distinguishes the entrepreneur's task from these alternatives is that he establishes a firm to commercialize an invention. The entrepreneur forms the firm to commercialize the new product, manufacturing process, or business method. It is the means of commercialization that distinguishes the entrepreneur.

Similarly, the entrepreneur's task is distinct from generic risk bearing. Many other types of economic actors bear risk: inventors bear risk by investing in R&D, investors bear risk by providing financial capital, individuals bear risk by investing in their education, and firms bear risk by developing projects. Entrepreneurs bear a particular kind of risk – that associated with establishing a firm.

The entrepreneur's task also is distinct from self-employment. The entrepreneur has alternative ways to be self-employed, including acting as an independent contractor. Also, an individual has alternative forms of employment in the labor market.

Although the opportunity costs of the entrepreneur can affect his decisions, the task of establishing a firm is a very specific activity. The potential entrepreneur's decision must evaluate the value of the new firm and the transaction costs of establishing the firm.

12.3 The Intermediation Hypothesis

The "intermediation hypothesis" summarizes some of the main empirical implications of the Theory of the Firm. When consumers who engage in direct exchange encounter greater transaction costs, in comparison to firms' transaction costs, firms are more likely to intermediate exchange between consumers.

Empirical analyses of the firm have tended to emphasize the effect of transaction costs on the internalization of transactions. Increased outsourcing by firms suggests that other forces are at work. The entry of many new types of intermediaries, particularly Internet firms, suggests the need for greater understanding of the effects of transaction costs on the organization of firms. By intermediating market transactions, firms offer an alternative to internalization of transactions.

A wide variety of transaction costs can create opportunities for intermediation by firms. These include the costs of communication, information processing, search, matching, bargaining, moral hazard, adverse selection, free riding, and contracting. When consumers experience relatively greater increases, or relatively smaller reductions, in these costs, firms can enhance economic efficiency. This suggests the need to examine how variations in these costs affect both the growth of existing firms and the establishment of new firms.

The size of the market affects transaction costs. This is particularly significant if the size of the market has an impact on the transaction costs of direct exchange that differs from its impact on the firm's transaction costs. As the size of the market expands, the transaction costs of search and matching may increase the transaction costs of direct exchange substantially. In a larger market, the costs of coordination required to establish consumer organizations may also increase. In contrast, larger markets allow firms to achieve economies of scale in intermediation activities. The "intermediation hypothesis" suggests that increases in the extent of the market explain greater intermediation by firms.

Economic growth appears to be positively associated with the establishment of firms. As economies develop, many different types of firms arise, including large-scale manufacturing enterprises. Increased economic development seems to generate many types of highly specialized intermediaries, including retailers and wholesalers. In addition, economic development generates financial intermediaries such as insurance companies, investment banks, brokerages, dealers, and organized financial exchanges. It is worthwhile to examine how the extent of the market affects the size and function of these transaction institutions.

12.4 Markets and Organizations

The scope of a firm includes both its market-making activities and its organizational activities. The firm creates markets and designs its organization to intermediate transactions. The profit-maximizing firm selects an efficient mix of market transactions and organizational transactions. Through markets and organizations, firms centralize exchange and offer an alternative to direct exchange between consumers.

Because they are intermediaries, firms separate the decisions of buyers from those of sellers in the economy. Firms stand between supply and demand, matching sellers with buyers, aggregating demands and supplies, adjusting prices, and clearing markets. The firm coordinates the transactions of buyers and sellers and improves the efficiency of exchange. Neoclassical economics identifies markets as separating the decisions of buyers from those of sellers. Because firms create and operate markets and organizations, they separate buyer decisions from seller decisions in a similar manner.

Firms generally have a spread between ask prices and bid prices. The price spread separates the marginal benefits of buyers from the marginal costs of sellers. The spread is due to many factors including transaction costs, asymmetric information, and market power. Technological change that reduces transaction costs improves economic efficiency by reducing the bid-ask spread. Increased competition between market-making firms also can reduce the bid-ask spread and improve economic efficiency.

By separating the decisions of buyers and sellers, firms coordinate buyers and sellers. Traders can choose between trading with the intermediary at posted prices or entering decentralized markets. The option of centralized exchange provides efficiencies for traders that deal with the firm. Under some conditions, the option of centralized exchange also improves the efficiency of the decentralized search market by narrowing the range of buyer types and seller types that enter into direct exchange.

Firms also improve the efficiency of the market for contracts through intermediated exchange. Buyers and sellers engaged in bilateral exchange may face contracting costs that include the costs of writing contingent contracts, the costs associated with incomplete contracts, the costs of underinvestment and contract renegotiation, and the costs of moral hazard and adverse selection. As market makers, firms engage in multilateral contracting, which can improve efficiency in comparison to bilateral contracts.

The firm also separates buyer decisions from seller decisions through its organization. The vertically integrated firm carries out a variety of internal transactions for labor services, finance capital, and other resources. Through its management activities, firms coordinate these internal transactions. The firm's management transactions complement its set of transactions with investors, suppliers, and customers.

The firm's extent of vertical integration is based on a comparison of the net benefits of market transactions and organizational transactions. The firm increases its extent of vertical integration for a given scope of activities by substituting organizational transactions for market transactions. This is the "make-or-buy" choice between market transactions and organizational transactions.

The separation criterion extends the traditional separation theorem to the formation of organizations. Basic partnerships do not maximize profits because they maximize the benefits of their members. However, when owners of basic partnerships can sell their memberships, the owners will then unanimously prefer profit maximization. For example, when owners of worker cooperatives can sell their memberships, the size of the worker cooperative is that of a profit-maximizing firm.

The organizations established by firms improve incentives in comparison to consumer organizations under some conditions. Consumers benefit from joint production when there are economies of scale, public goods, and common property resources. However, joint production is subject to free rider problems because consumer organizations have balanced budgets. Separation allows the firm to obtain the benefits of joint production while alleviating free rider problems. The firm has a wider range of allocation mechanisms that allow it to improve incentives for customers and employees.

The discussion of the theory of the firm presented here shows that firms exist to improve the efficiency of economic transactions. Firms are established through the efforts of entrepreneurs. Firms perform an essential economic role by creating markets and organizations. Much work remains to be done to understand the impact of initial economic conditions on the establishment of firms. The analysis of the firm raises fundamental questions about the effects of social relationships, public policy, and the legal context on the formation of economic institutions. The theory of the firm poses a challenge to researchers seeking to understand the structure and function of economic institutions.

References

Abernathy, W. J., and J. M. Utterback, 1978, "Patterns of Industrial Innovation," *Technology Review*, 80, June/July, pp. 41–47.

Acemoglu, D., 1996, "A Microfoundation for Social Increasing Returns in Human Capital Accumulation," *Quarterly Journal of Economics*, 111, August, pp. 779–804.

Acemoglu, D., 1997, "Training and Innovation in an Imperfect Labor Market," *Review of Economic Studies*, 64, July, pp. 445–464.

Acemoglu, D., and R. Shimer, 1999, "Holdups and Efficiency with Search Frictions," *International Economic Review*, 40, November, pp. 827–849.

Aghion, P., and P. Bolton, 1992, "An Incomplete Contracts Approach to Financial Contracting," *Review of Economic Studies*, 59, 3, July, pp. 473–494.

Aghion, P., and P. Howitt, 1992, "A Model of Growth through Creative Destruction," *Econometrica*, 60, March, pp. 323–351.

Agrawal, A., and G. N. Mandelker, 1987, "Managerial Incentives and Corporate Investment and Financing Decisions," *Journal of Finance*, 42, 4, pp. 823–837.

Akerlof, G. A., 1970, "The Market for 'Lemons': Quality Uncertainty and the Market Mechanism," *Quarterly Journal of Economics*, 84, pp. 488–500.

Alchian, A. A., 1950, "Uncertainty, Evolution, and Economic Theory," *Journal of Political Economy*, 58, pp. 211–221.

Alchian, A. A., and H. Demsetz, 1972, "Production, Information Costs, and Economic Organization," *American Economic Review*, 62, 5, December, pp. 777–795.

Alderson, W., 1954, "Factors Governing the Development of Marketing Channels," in R. M. Clewett, ed., *Marketing Channels for Manufactured Products*, Homewood, IL: Irwin.

Aldous, J. M., and R. J. Wilson, 2000, *Graphs and Applications: An Introductory Approach*, New York: Springer.

Alexandrov, A., G. Deltas, and D. F. Spulber, 2007, "Competition between Differentiated Intermediaries," Northwestern University Working Paper.

Allais, M., 1947, *Economie et Intérêt*, Paris: Imprimerie Nationale.

Allen, R. C., 1982, "The Efficiency and Distributional Implications of 18th Century Enclosures," *Economic Journal*, 92, pp. 937–953.

Ambarish, R., K. John, and J. Williams, 1987, "Efficient Signaling with Dividends and Investments," *Journal of Finance*, 42, pp. 321–343.

American Law Institute, 1958, *Restatement Second of Agency*, Vol. 1 and Vol. 2, St. Paul, MN: American Law Institute Publishers.

Anas, A., R. Arnott, and K. A. Small, 1998, "Urban Spatial Structure," *Journal of Economic Literature*, 36, September, pp. 1426–1464.

Anderson, E., 1985, "The Salesperson as Outside Agent or Employee: A Transaction Cost Analysis," *Marketing Science*, 4, Summer, pp. 234–254.

Anderson, E., and D. Schmittlein, 1984, "Integration of the Sales Force: An Empirical Examination," *Rand Journal of Economics*, 15, Autumn, pp. 385–395.

Anderson, J. E., and E. van Wincoop, 2003, "Gravity with Gravitas: A Solution to the Border Puzzle," *American Economic Review*, 93, 1, March, pp. 170–192.

Anderson, J. E., and E. van Wincoop, 2004, "Trade Costs," *Journal of Economic Literature*, 42, 3, September, pp. 691–751.

Anderson, R. K., P. K. Porter, and S. C. Maurice, 1979, "The Economics of Consumer-Managed Firms," *Southern Economic Journal*, July, pp. 119–130.

Anderson, R. K., P. K. Porter, and S. C. Maurice, 1980, "Factor Usage by Consumer-Managed Firms," *Southern Economic Journal*, October, pp. 522–530.

Andrews, K. R., 1971, *The Concept of Corporate Strategy*, Homewood, IL: Irwin.

Ang, J. S., R. A. Cole, and J. W. Lin, 2000, "Agency Costs and Ownership Structure," *Journal of Finance*, 55, 1, February, pp. 81–106.

Anton, J. J., and D. A. Yao, 1995, "Starts-Ups, Spin-Offs, and Internal Projects," *Journal of Law, Economics, and Organization*, 11, October, pp. 362–378.

Aoki, M., 1986, *The Co-operative Game Theory of the Firm*, New York: Clarendon Press.

Arora, A., 1997, "Appropriating Rents from Innovation: Patents, Licensing and Market Structure in the Chemical Industry," *Research Policy*, 27, pp. 391–403.

Arrow, K. J., 1951, "An Extension of the Basic Theorems of Classical Welfare Economics," in J. Neyman, ed., *Proceedings of the Second Berkeley Symposium on Mathematical Statistics and Probability*, Los Angeles: University of California Press, pp. 507–532.

Arrow, K. J., 1953, "Le Rôle des valeurs boursières pour la répartition la meilleure des risques," *Econometrie*, Colloques Internationaux du Centre National de la Recherche Scientifique, Vol. XI, Paris, pp. 41–47, reprinted as 1963–1964, "The Role of Securities in the Optimal Allocation of Risk-Bearing," *Review of Economic Studies*, 31(2), pp. 91–96.

Arrow, K. J., 1962, "Economic Welfare and the Allocation of Resources for Invention," in R. R. Nelson, ed., *The Rate and Direction of Inventive Activity*, Princeton, NJ: Princeton University Press, pp. 609–625.

Arrow, K. J., 1964, "Control in Large Organizations," *Management Science*, 10, pp. 397–408.

Arrow, K. J., 1968, "The Economics of Moral Hazard: Further Comment," *American Economic Review*, 58, June, pp. 531–537.

Arrow, K. J., 1974, *The Limits of Organization*, New York: Norton.

Arrow, K. J., 1975, "Vertical Integration and Communication," *Bell Journal of Economics*, 6, pp. 173–183.

Arrow, K. J., 1979, "The Property Rights Doctrine and Demand Revelation under Incomplete Information," in M. Boskin, ed., *Economics and Human Welfare*, New York: Academic Press, pp. 23–39.

Arrow, K. J., and G. Debreu, 1954, "Existence of an Equilibrium for a Competitive Economy," *Econometrica*, 22, pp. 265–290.

Arrow, K. J., and F. H. Hahn, 1971, *General Competitive Analysis*, San Francisco: Holden-Day.

Arrow, K. J., T. Harris, and J. Marschak, 1951, "Optimal Inventory Policy," *Econometrica*, 19, pp. 230–272.

Arrow, K. J., and L. Hurwicz, 1960, "Decentralization and Computation in Resource Allocation," in R.W. Pfouts, ed., *Essays in Economics and Econometrics*, Chapel Hill: University of North Carolina Press, pp. 34–104.

Arvan, L. D., and L. N. Moses, 1982, "Inventory Investment and the Theory of the Firm," *American Economic Review*, 72, March, pp. 186–193.

Astrachan, J. H., and Shanker, M. C. (2003). "Family Businesses' Contribution to the U.S. Economy: A Closer Look," *Family Business Review*, 16, 3, pp. 211–219.

Athey, S., P. Milgrom, and J. Roberts, 1996, "Robust Comparative Statics," manuscript, Cambridge, MA: Massachusetts Institute of Technology.

Athey, S., and A. Schmutzler, 2001, "Innovation and Market Dominance," *Rand Journal of Economics*, 32, Spring, pp. 1–26.

Audretsch, D. B., M. C. Keilbach, and E.E. Lehmann, 2006, *Entrepreneurship and Economic Growth*, Oxford: Oxford University Press.

Bagwell, K., G. Ramey, and D. F. Spulber, 1997, "Dynamic Retail Price and Investment Competition," *Rand Journal of Economics*, 28, Summer, pp. 207–227.

Baiman, S., 1982, "Agency Research in Managerial Accounting: A Survey," *Journal of Accounting Literature*, 1, pp. 154–213.

Baiman, S., 1989, "Agency Research in Managerial Accounting: A Second Look," Carnegie Mellon University working paper.

Baiman, S., and J. S. Demski, 1980, "Economically Optimal Performance Evaluation and Control Systems," *Journal of Accounting Research*, Supplement, 18, pp. 184–220.

Bain, J. S., 1956, *Barriers to New Competition*, Cambridge, MA: Harvard University Press.

Bain, J. S., 1959, *Industrial Organization*, New York: Wiley.

Bain, J. S., 1972, *Essays on Price Theory and Industrial Organization*, Boston: Little, Brown and Company.

Bakos, Y., 2001 "The Emerging Landscape for Retail E-Commerce," *Journal of Economic Perspectives*, 15, Winter, pp. 69–80.

Ball, J. N., 1977, *Merchants and Merchandise: The Expansion of Trade in Europe 1500–1630*, New York: St. Martin's Press.

Barabási, A.-L., 2002, *Linked: The New Science of Networks*, Cambridge, MA: Perseus Publishing.

Barnard, C., 1938, *The Functions of the Executive*, Cambridge, MA: Harvard University Press.

Baron, D. P., and D. Besanko, 1984, "Regulation, Asymmetric Information, and Auditing," *Rand Journal of Economics*, 15, pp. 447–470.

Baron, D. P., and R. B. Myerson, 1982, "Regulating a Monopolist with Unknown Cost," *Econometrica*, 50, pp. 911–930.

Bartelsman, E. J., and M. Doms, 2000, "Understanding Productivity: Lessons from Longitudinal Microdata," *Journal of Economic Literature*, 38, September, pp. 569–594.

Bartlett, R. P., III, 2006, "Venture Capital, Agency Costs, and the False Dichotomy of the Corporation," *UCLA Law Review*, 54, October, pp. 37–115.

Barzel, Y., 1987, "The Entrepreneur's Reward for Self-Policing," *Economic Inquiry*, 25, January, pp. 103–116.

Barzel, Y. and T. R. Sass, 1990, "The Allocation of Resources by Voting," *Quarterly Journal of Economics*, 105, pp. 741–771.

Baskin, J. B., and P. J. Miranti, Jr., 1997, *A History of Corporate Finance*, Cambridge: Cambridge University Press.

Basu, A., R. Lal, V. Srinavasan, and R. Staelin, 1985, "Salesforce Compensation Plans: An Agency Theoretic Perspective," *Marketing Science*, 4, pp. 267–291.

Bator, F. M., 1958, "The Anatomy of Market Failure," *Quarterly Journal of Economics*, 72, August, pp. 351–379.

Baumol, W. J., 1968, "Entrepreneurship in Economic Theory," *American Economic Review, Papers and Proceedings*, 58, May, pp. 64–71.

Baumol, W. J., 1993, *Entrepreneurship, Management, and the Structure of Payoffs*, Cambridge, MA: MIT Press.

Baumol, W. J., 2002, *The Free-Market Innovation Machine: Analyzing the Growth Miracle of Capitalism*, Princeton, NJ: Princeton University Press.

Baumol, W. J., 2006, "Entrepreneurship and Invention: Toward Their Microeconomic Value Theory," Special Session on Entrepreneurship, Innovation and Growth I: Theoretical Approach, American Economic Association Meetings.

Baumol, W. J., R. E. Litan, and C. J. Schramm, 2007, *Good Capitalism, Bad Capitalism, and the Economics of Growth and Prosperity*, New Haven, CT: Yale University Press.

Baye, M. R., and J. Morgan, 2001, "Information Gatekeepers on the Internet and the Competitiveness of Homogeneous Product Markets," *American Economic Review* 91, June, pp. 454–474.

Baye, M. R., J. Morgan, and P. Scholten, 2001, "Price Dispersion in the Small and in the Large: Evidence from an Internet Price Comparison Site," Indiana University working paper, July.

Baye, M. R., J. Morgan, and P. Scholten, 2004, "Price Dispersion in the Large and in the Small: Evidence from an Internet Price Comparison Site," *Journal of Industrial Economics*, December, 52, pp. 463–496.

Baysinger, B. D., and H. N. Butler, 1985, "Antitakeover Amendments, Managerial Entrenchment, and the Contractual Theory of the Corporation," *Virginia Law Review*, 71, November, pp. 1257–1303.

Bayus, B. L., and R. Agarwal, 2007, "The Role of Pre-Entry Experience, Entry Timing, and Product Technology Strategies in Explaining Firm Survival," *Management Science*, 53, December, pp. 1887–1902.

Bebchuk, L., and J. M. Fried, 2004, *Pay without Performance: The Unfulfilled Promise of Executive Compensation*, Cambridge, MA: Harvard University Press.

Becker, G., 1973, "A Theory of Marriage, Part I," *Journal of Political Economy*, 81, pp. 813–846.

Bellas, C. J., 1972, *Industrial Democracy and the Worker-Owned Firm: A Study of Twenty-One Plywood Companies in the Pacific Northwest*, New York: Praeger Publishers.

Benabou, R., 1993, "Search Market Equilibrium, Bilateral Heterogeneity, and Repeat Purchases," *Journal of Economic Theory*, 60, pp. 140–158.

Ben-Ner, A., 2006, "For-Profit, State and Nonprofit: How to Cut the Pie among the Three Sectors," in J.-P. Touffut, ed., *Advancing Public Goods*, Cheltenham, UK: Edward Elgar, pp. 40–67.

Ben-Ner, A., and B. Gui, 2003, "The Theory of Nonprofit Organizations Revisited," in H. Anheier and A. Ben-Ner, eds., *The Study of the Nonprofit Enterprise: Theories and Approaches*, New York: Kluwer Academic/Plenum Publishers, pp. 3–26.

Ben-Ner, A., and D. Jones, 1995, "Employee Participation, Ownership, and Productivity: A Theoretical Framework," *Industrial Relations*, 34, 4, October, pp. 532–554.

Benninga, S., M. Helmantel, and O. Sarig, 2005, "The Timing of Initial Public Offerings," *Journal of Financial Economics*, 75, pp. 115–132.

Ben-Porath, Y., 1982, "Individuals, Families, and Income Distribution," *Population and Development Review*, 8, Supplement: Income Distribution and the Family, pp. 1–13.

Ben-Porath, Y., 1980, "The F-Connection: Families, Friends, and Firms in the Organization of Exchange," *Population and Development Review*, 6, March, pp. 1–30.

Bergemann, D., and U. Hege, 1998, "Venture Capital Financing, Moral Hazard, and Learning," *Journal of Banking and Finance*, 22, pp. 703–735.

Berglöf, E., 1994, "A Control Theory of Venture Capital Finance," *Journal of Law, Economics, and Organization*, 10, October, pp. 247–267.

Berhold, M., 1971, "A Theory of Linear Profit-Sharing Incentives," *Quarterly Journal of Economics*, 85, 3, pp. 460–482.

Berle, A. A., Jr., 1928, *Studies in the Law of Corporation Finance*, Chicago: Callaghan and Company.

Berle, A. A., Jr., 1954, *The 20th Century Capitalist Revolution*, New York: Harcourt, Brace and Company.

Berle, A. A., Jr., and G. C. Means, 1932, *The Modern Corporation and Private Property*, New York: Commerce Clearing House.

Berle, A. A., Jr., and G. C. Means, 1967, *The Modern Corporation and Private Property*, revised edition, New York: Harcourt, Brace & World.

Berman, K. V., 1967, *Worker-Owner Plywood Companies: An Economic Analysis*, Pullman, WA: Bureau of Economic and Business Research, Washington State University Press.

Bewley, T., 1999, *Why Wages Don't Fall during a Recession*, Cambridge, MA: Harvard University Press.

Bhattacharya, S., 1979, "Imperfect Information, Dividend Policy and the Bird in the Hand Fallacy," *Bell Journal of Economics*, 10, pp. 259–270.

Bhattacharya, S., and J. L. Guasch, 1988, "Heterogeneity, Tournaments, and Hierarchies," *Journal of Political Economy*, 96, pp. 867–881.

Bhattacharya, S., and K. Hagerty, 1987, "Dealerships, Trading Externalities, and General Equilibrium," in Edward C. Prescott and Neil Wallace, eds., *Contractual Arrangements for Intertemporal Trade*, Minneapolis: University of Minnesota Press, pp. 81–104.

Biais, B., and C. Casamatta, 1999, "Optimal Leverage and Aggregate Investment," *Journal of Finance*, 54, pp. 1291–1323.

Biglaiser, G., 1993, "Middlemen as Experts," *Rand Journal of Economics*, 24, 2, Summer, pp. 212–223.

Biglaiser, G., and J. W. Friedman, 1994, "Middlemen as Guarantors of Quality," *International Journal of Industrial Organization*, 12, pp. 509–531.

Biglaiser, G., and J. W. Friedman, 1999, "Adverse Selection with Competitive Inspection," *Journal of Economics & Management Strategy*, 8, pp. 1–32.

Bilodeau, M., and R. Steinberg, 2006, in S.-C. Kolm and J. M. Ythier, eds., *Handbook on the Economics of Giving, Reciprocity, and Altruism*, vol. 2, Amsterdam: North Holland, pp. 1271–1334.

Black's Law Dictionary, seventh edition, 1999, St. Paul, MN: West Group.

Blair, M. M., 1995, *Ownership and Control: Rethinking Corporate Governance for the Twenty-First Century*, Washington, DC: Brookings Institution.

Blair, M. M., 2003a, "Locking in Capital: What Corporate Law Achieved for Business Organizers in the Nineteenth Century," *UCLA Law Review*, 51, pp. 387–455.

Blair, M. M., 2003b, "Why Markets Chose the Corporate Form: Entity Status and the Separation of Asset Ownership from Control," Georgetown University Law Center, Business, Economics and Regulatory Policy Working Paper No. 429300.

Blair, M. M., 2004, "The Neglected Benefits of the Corporate Form: Entity Status and the Separation of Asset Ownership From Control," in *Corporate Governance and Firm Organization: Microfoundations and Structural Forms*, Oxford: Oxford University Press, pp. 45–66.

Blair, M. M., and L. A. Stout, 1999, "A Team Production Theory of Corporate Law," *Virginia Law Review*, 85, 2, March, pp. 247–328.

Blanchard, O. J., and S. Fischer, 1989, *Lectures on Macroeconomics*, Cambridge, MA: MIT Press.

Blanchflower, D. G. and A. J. Oswald, 1998, "What Makes an Entrepreneur?" *Journal of Labor Economics*, 16, January, pp. 26–60.

Blau, D. M., 1987. "A Time-Series Analysis of Self-Employment in the United States," *Journal of Political Economy*, 95, June, pp. 445–467.

Blazenko, G. W., 1987, "Managerial Preference, Asymmetric Information and Financial Structure," *Journal of Finance*, 42, pp. 839–862.

Bodnaruk, A., E. Kandel, M. Massa, and A. Simonov, 2007, "Shareholder Diversification and the Decision to Go Public," *Review of Financial Studies*, forthcoming.

Boemer, C. S., and J. T. Macher, 2001, "Transaction Cost Economics: An Assessment of Empirical Research in the Social Sciences," Georgetown University Working Paper.

Böhm-Bawerk, E., 1923 [1891 in German New York: G. E. Stechert], *Positive Theory of Capital*, translated from the German, London: Macmillan.

Bollobás, B., 1998, *Modern Graph Theory*, New York: Springer-Verlag.

Bollobás, B., 2001, *Random Graphs*, 2nd edition, Cambridge: Cambridge University Press.

Bolton, P., and D. S. Scharfstein, 1990, "A Theory of Predation Based on Agency Problems in Financial Contracting," *American Economic Review*, 80, pp. 93–106.

Bolton, P., and D. S. Scharfstein, 1996, "Optimal Debt Structure with Multiple Creditors," *Journal of Political Economy*, 104, pp. 1–25.

Bonaccorsi, A., and P. Giuri, 2000, "When Shakeout Doesn't Occur: The Evolution of the Turboprop Engine Industry," *Research Policy*, 29, pp. 847–870.

Bourgeois, L. J., III, 1985, "Strategic Goals, Perceived Uncertainty, and Economic Performance in Volatile Environments," *Academy of Management Journal*, 28, 3, September, pp. 548–573.

Boyd, J., and E. Prescott, 1985, "Financial Intermediary Coalitions," *Journal of Economic Theory*, 38, pp. 211–232.

Boyer-Xambeu, M.-T., G. Deleplace, and L. Gillard, 1994, *Private Money and Public Currencies: The 16th Century Challenge*, Armonk, NY: M. E. Sharpe.

Bresnahan, T. F., and S. M. Greenstein, 1997, "Technical Progress and Co-invention on Computing and in the Uses of Computers," *Brookings Papers on Economic Activity: Microeconomics*, pp. 1–78.

Bresnahan, T. F., and S. M. Greenstein, 1999, "Technological Competition and the Structure of the Computer Industry," *Journal of Industrial Economics*, 47, March, pp. 1–40.

Bresnahan, T. F., 1989, "Empirical Studies of Industries with Market Power," in R. Schmalensee and R. Willig, eds., *Handbook of Industrial Organization*, Amsterdam: North Holland, pp. 1011–1058.

Bresnahan, T. F., and D. M. G. Raff, 1991, "Intra-industry Heterogeneity and the Great Depression: The American Motor Vehicles Industry, 1929–1935," *Journal of Economic History*, 51, June, pp. 317–331.

Britnell, R. H., 1993, *The Commercialisation of English Society, 1000–1500*, Cambridge: Cambridge University Press.

Brito Ramos, S., 2006, "Why Do Stock Exchanges Demutualize and Go Public," Swiss Finance Institute, Research Paper Series No. 06-10.

Bromberg, A. R., and L. E. Ribstein, 1988, *Partnership*, 1st ed., Boston: Little, Brown.

Brown, S. A., 1997, *Revolution at the Checkout Counter: The Explosion of the Bar Code*, Cambridge, MA: Harvard University Press.

Brune, N., G. Garrett, and B. Kogut, 2004, "The International Monetary Fund and the Global Spread of Privatization," Yale University working paper.

Buchanan, J. M., 1965, "An Economic Theory of Clubs," *Economica*, 32, pp. 1–14.

Bull, C., and J. A. Ordover, 1987, "Market Structure and Optimal Management Organizations," *Rand Journal of Economics*, 18, 4, winter, pp. 480–491.

Bulow, J., J. Geanakoplos, and P. Klemperer, 1985, "Multimarket Oligopoly: Strategic Substitutes and Complements," *Journal of Political Economy*, 93, pp. 488–511.

Butler, H. N., 1989, "Contractual Theory of the Corporation," *George Mason University Law Review*, 11, pp. 99–123.

Cabral, L., and M. H. Riordan, 1994, "The Learning Curve, Market Dominance, and Predatory Pricing," *Econometrica*, 62, pp. 1115–1140.

Caillaud, B., and B. Jullien, 2001, "Competing Cybermediaries," *European Economic Review*, 45, 4–6, May, pp. 797–808.

Caillaud, B., and B. Jullien, 2003, "Chicken and Egg: Competition Among Intermediation Service Providers," *Rand Journal of Economics*, 34, pp. 309–328.

Camp, L. J., 2000, *Trust and Risk in Internet Commerce*, Cambridge, MA: MIT Press.

Cantillon, R., 1755, *Essai sur la nature du commerce en général*, http://cepa.newschool.edu/het/profiles/cantillon.htm.

Carcopino, J., 1968 [1940], *Daily Life in Ancient Rome: The People and the City at the Height of the Empire*, H. T. Rowell, ed., New Haven, CT: Yale University Press.

Casadesus-Masanell, R., and D. F. Spulber, 2000, "The Fable of Fisher Body," *Journal of Law and Economics*, 43, April, pp. 67–104.

Casadesus-Masanell, R., and D. F. Spulber, 2005, "Trust and Incentives in Agency," *Southern California Interdisciplinary Law Journal*, 15, 1, pp. 45–104.

Cass, D., and M. Yaari, 1966, "A Re-examination of the Pure Consumption Loans Model," *Journal of Political Economy*, 74, pp. 353–367.

Casson, M., 1982, *The Entrepreneur: An Economic Theory*, Totowa, NJ: Barnes & Noble Books.

Casson, M., 1987, *The Firm and the Market*, Cambridge, MA: MIT Press.

Casson, M., 1997, *Information and Organization: A New Perspective on the Theory of the Firm*, New York: Clarendon Press.

Casson, M., 2003, *The Entrepreneur: An Economic Theory*, 2nd ed., Cheltenham, UK: Edward Elgar.

Caves, R. E., 1996, *Multinational Enterprise and Economic Analysis*, 2nd ed., New York: Cambridge University Press.

Chandler, A. D., 1962, *Strategy and Structure*, Cambridge, MA: MIT Press.

Chandler, A. D., 1977, *The Visible Hand: The Managerial Revolution in American Business*, Cambridge, MA: Harvard University Press.

Chandler, A. D., 1990a, "Fin de Siècle: Industrial Transformation," Mikulas Teich and Roy Porter, eds., *Fin de Siècle and Its Legacy*, New York: Cambridge University Press.

Chandler, A. D., 1990b, *Scale and Scope: The Dynamics of Industrial Capitalism*, Cambridge, MA: Harvard University Press.

Che, Y.-K., and I. Gale, 2003, "Optimal Design of Research Contests," *American Economic Review*, 93, pp. 646–671.

Che, Y.-K., and D. Hausch, 1999, "Cooperative Investments and the Value of Contracting: Coase vs. Williamson," *American Economic Review* 89, March, pp. 125–147.

Chenery, H. B., 1953, "Process and Production Functions From Engineering Data," Chapter 8 in W. Leontief, ed., *Studies in the Structure of the American Economy*, New York: Oxford University Press, pp. 297–325.

Cheney, G., 1999, *Values at Work: Employee Participation Meets Market Pressure at Mondragon*, Ithaca, NY: ILR Press, Cornell University Press.

Cheung, S. N. S., 1970, "The Structure of a Contract and the Theory of a Non-exclusive Resource," *Journal of Law and Economics*, 13, April, pp. 49–70.

Cheung, S. N. S., 1973, "The Fable of the Bees: An Economic Investigation," *Journal of Law and Economics*, 16, pp. 11–33.

Chuang, J. C.-I., and M. A. Sirbu, 2000, "Network Delivery of Information Goods: Optimal Pricing of Articles and Subscriptions," in Kahin, B., and H. Varian, eds., *Internet Publishing and Beyond: The Economics of Digital Information and Intellectual Property*, Cambridge, MA: MIT Press, pp. 138–166.

Chuang, J. C.-I., and M. A. Sirbu, 2001, "Pricing Multicast Communications: A Cost-Based Approach," *Telecommunication Systems*, 17, July, pp. 281–297.

Clark, C. W., 1976, *Mathematical Bioeconomics: The Optimal Management of Renewable Resources*, New York: Wiley.

Clark, C. W., 1985, *Bioeconomic Modelling and Fisheries Management*, New York: Wiley.

Clark, J. B., 1894, "Insurance and Profits," *Quarterly Journal of Economics*, 7, pp. 40–54.

Clarke, E., 1971, "Multipart Pricing of Public Goods," *Public Choice*, 2, pp. 19–33.

Clemons, E., and L. Hitt, 2001, "The Internet and the Future of Financial Services: Transparency, Differential Pricing, and Disintermediation," in Brookings Task Force on the Internet, *The Economic Payoff from the Internet Revolution*, Brookings Institute Press, Washington, DC, pp. 87–128.

Clotfelter, C. T, ed., 1992, *Who Benefits from the Nonprofit Sector?* Chicago: University of Chicago Press.

Clower, R., 1967, "A Reconsideration of the Microfoundations of Monetary Theory," *Western Economic Journal*, 6, pp. 1–8.

Clower, R., and A. Leijonhufvud, 1975, "The Coordination of Economic Activities: A Keynesian Perspective," *American Economic Review*, 65, pp. 182–188.

Coase, R. H., 1937, "The Nature of the Firm," *Economica*, 4, pp. 386–405.

Coase, R. H., 1960, "The Problem of Social Cost," *Journal of Law and Economics*, 3, pp. 1–44.

Coase, R. H., 1988, "The Nature of the Firm: Origin, Meaning, Influence," *Journal of Law, Economics and Organization*, 4, reprinted in Oliver E. Williamson and Sidney G. Winter, eds., 1991, *The Nature of the Firm: Origin, Meaning, Influence*, Oxford: Oxford University Press, pp. 34–74.

Coase, R. H., 1994, "The Institutional Structure of Production," The 1991 Alfred Nobel Memorial Prize Lecture in Economic Sciences, in Ronald H. Coase, *Essays on Economics and Economists*, Chicago: University of Chicago Press, pp. 3–14.

Coase, R. H., 2000, "The Acquisition of Fisher Body by General Motors," *Journal of Law and Economics*, 43, 1, April, pp. 15–32.

Coase, R. H., 2006, "The Conduct of Economics: The Example of Fisher Body and General Motors," *Journal of Economics and Management Strategy*, 15, 2, Summer, pp. 255–278.

Coleman, D. C., 1977, *The Economy of England, 1450–1750*, Oxford: Oxford University Press.

Committee T1A1 [renamed Network Performance, Reliability and Quality of Service Committee (PRQC)], 2000, *ATIS Telecom Glossary 2000*, Washington, DC: Alliance for Telecommunications Industry Solutions.

Commons, J. R., 1931, "Institutional Economics," *American Economic Review*, 21, pp. 648–657.

Cooter, R., and B. J. Freedman, 1991, "The Fiduciary Relationship: Its Economic Character and Legal Consequences," *New York University Law Review*, 66, pp. 1045–1075.

Copeland, T. E., and D. Galai, 1983, "Information Effects on the Bid Ask Spread," *Journal of Finance*, 38 (5), December, pp. 1457–1469.

Cornelli, F., and O. Yosha, 2003, "Stage Financing and the Role of Convertible Securities," *Review of Economic Studies*, 70, pp. 1–32.

Cornes, R., and T. Sandler, 1986, *The Theory of Externalities, Public Goods, and Club Goods*, Cambridge: Cambridge University Press.

Coughlan, A. T., and S. K. Sen, 1989, "Salesforce Compensation: Theory and Managerial Implications," *Marketing Science*, 8, pp. 324–342.

Courant, R., and F. John, 1989, *Introduction to Calculus and Analysis*, vol. 1, New York: Springer.

Cox, W. M., and R. Alm, 1999, "The Churn among Firms: Recycling America's Corporate Elite," *Southwest Economy Federal Reserve Bank of Dallas*, Issue 1, January/February, pp. 6–9.

Craswell, R., and M. R. Fratrik, 1985–1986, "Predatory Pricing Theory Applied: The Case of Supermarkets vs. Warehouse Stores," *Case Western Reserve Law Review*, 36, pp. 49–87.

Crocker, K. J., 1983, "Vertical Integration and the Strategic Use of Private Information," *Bell Journal of Economics*, 14, pp. 236–248.

Cyert, R. M., and J. G. March, 1963, *A Behavioral Theory of the Firm*, Englewood Cliffs, NJ: Prentice Hall.

Dahl, G., 1998, *Trade, Trust, and Networks: Commercial Culture in Late Medieval Italy*, Lund, Sweden: Nordic Academic Press.

Dahlman, C., 1980, *The Open Field System and Beyond: A Property Rights Analysis of an Economic Institution*, Cambridge: Cambridge University Press.

Danø, S., 1966, *Industrial Production Models: A Theoretical Study*, New York: Springer.

Dantzig, G. B., 1963, *Linear Programming and Extensions*, Princeton, NJ: Princeton University Press.

Dantzig, G. B., and P. Wolfe, 1960, "A Decomposition Principle for Linear Programs," *Operations Research*, 8, pp. 101–111.

Danzon, P., and M. Furekawa, 2001, "E-Health: Effects of the Internet on Competition and Productivity in Health Care," in Brookings Task Force on the Internet, *The Economic Payoff from the Internet Revolution*, Washington, DC: Brookings Institute Press, pp. 189–234.

Dasgupta, P., P. Hammond and E. Maskin, 1979, "The Implementation of Social Choice Rules: Some General Results on Incentive Compatibility," *Review of Economic Studies*, 46, pp. 185–216.

Dasgupta, S., and D. F. Spulber, 1990, "Managing Procurement Auctions," *Journal of Information Economics and Policy*, 4, pp. 5–29.

Dasgupta, P., and J. E. Stiglitz, 1980, "Industrial Structure and the Nature of Innovative Activity," *Economic Journal*, 90, pp. 266–293.

d'Aspremont, C., and L. A. Gérard-Varet, 1979, "Incentives and Incomplete Information," *Journal of Public Economics*, 11, pp. 25–45.

Davis, J. S., 1965 [1917], *Essays in the Earlier History of American Corporations*, New York: Russell & Russell.

Davis, L. E., and D. C. North, 1971, *Institutional Change and American Economic Growth*, Cambridge: Cambridge University Press.

Day, J., 1987, *The Medieval Market Economy*, Oxford: Basil Blackwell.

DeAngelo, H., 1981, "Competition and Unanimity," *American Economic Review*, 71, March, pp. 18–27.

Debreu, G., 1959, *The Theory of Value*, New Haven, CT: Yale University Press.

Deily, M. E., 1991, "Exit Strategies and Plant-Closing Decisions: The Case of Steel," *Rand Journal of Economics*, 22, summer, pp. 250–263.

De Ligt, L., 1993, *Fairs and Markets in the Roman Empire: Economic and Social Aspects of Periodic Trade in a Pre-industrial Society*, Amsterdam: J. C. Gieben.

Demange, G., 1982, "Strategy Proofness in the Assignment Market Game," working paper, Laboratoire d'Econometrie de l'Ecole Polytechnique, Paris.

Demange, G., and D. Gale, 1985, "The Strategy Structure of Two-Sided Matching Markets," *Econometrica*, 53, pp. 873–888.

Demange, G., D. Gale, and M. Sotomayor, 1986, "Multi-item Auctions," *Journal of Political Economy*, 94, pp. 863–872.

DeMott, D. A., 1998, "A Revised Prospectus for a Third Restatement of Agency," *U.C. Davis Law Review*, 31, summer, pp. 1035–1062.

DeMott, D. A., 1991, *Fiduciary Obligation, Agency and Partnership: Duties in Ongoing Business Relationships*, St. Paul, MN: West Publishing Co.

Demsetz, H., 1968a, "The Cost of Contracting," *Quarterly Journal of Economics*, 87, February, pp. 33–53.

Demsetz, H., 1968b, "Why Regulate Utilities?," *Journal of Law and Economics*, 11, April, pp. 55–65.

Demsetz, H., 1983, "The Structure of Ownership and the Theory of the Firm," *Journal of Law and Economics*, 26, June, pp. 375–390.

Demsetz, H., 1991, "The Theory of the Firm Revisited," in Oliver E. Williamson and Sidney G. Winter, eds., *The Nature of the Firm*, Oxford: Oxford University Press, pp. 159–178.

Demsetz, H., and K. Lehn, 1985, "The Structure of Corporate Ownership: Causes and Consequences," *Journal of Political Economy*, 93, 6, December, pp. 1155–1177.

Demski, J. S., and D. E. M. Sappington, 1986, "Line-Item Reporting, Factor Acquisition, and Subcontracting," *Journal of Accounting Research*, 24, pp. 250–269.

Demski, J. S., and D. E. M. Sappington, 1987, "Delegated Expertise," *Journal of Accounting Research*, 25, pp. 68–89.

Dennert, J., 1993, "Price Competition between Market Makers," *Review of Economic Studies*, 60, pp. 735–751.

De Roover, R., 1965, "Italian Hegemony in the Fourteenth and Fifteenth Centuries," Chapter III in M. M. Postan, E. E. Rich, and E. Miller, eds., *The Cambridge Economic History of Europe, v. III, Economic Organization and Policies in the Middle Ages*, Cambridge: Cambridge University Press, pp. 70–105.

De Roover, R., 1974, *Business, Banking, and Economic Thought in Late Medieval and Early Modern Europe*, J. Kirshner, ed., Chicago: The University of Chicago Press.

Deutsch, C. H., 1995, "For Law Firms, the Shakeout in the Business World Has Finally Hit," *New York Times*, February 17, p. B13.

Diamond, D. W., 1984, "Financial Intermediation and Delegated Monitoring," *Review of Economic Studies*, 51, pp. 393–414.

Diamond, D. W., and P. H. Dybvig, 1983, "Bank Runs, Deposit Insurance, and Liquidity," *The Journal of Political Economy*, 91, 3, June, pp. 401–419.

Diamond, D. W., and R. E. Verrecchia, 1982, "Optimal Managerial Contracts and Equilibrium Security Prices," *Journal of Finance*, 37, pp. 275–287.

Diamond, P. A., 1965, "National Debt in a Neoclassical Growth Model," *American Economic Review*, 55, pp. 1126–1150.

Diamond, P. A., 1967, "The Role of a Stock Market in a General Equilibrium Model with Technological Uncertainty," *American Economic Review*, 57, pp. 759–773.

Diamond, P. A., 1982, "Aggregate Demand Management in Search Equilibrium," *Journal of Political Economy*, 90, pp. 881–894.

Diamond, P. A., 1987, Consumer Differences and Prices in a Search Model, *Quarterly Journal of Economics*, 102, pp. 429–436.

Dicey, A. V., 1905, *Lectures on the Relation between Law and Public Opinion in England during the Nineteenth Century*, London: Macmillan.

Diestel, R., 2000, *Graph Theory*, 2nd edition, New York: Springer.

Dixit, A. K., 1980, "The Role of Investment in Entry-Deterrence," *Economic Journal*, 90, pp. 95–106.

Dixit, A. K., 1983, "Vertical Integration in a Monopolistically Competitive Industry," *International Journal of Industrial Organization*, 1, pp. 63–78.

Dixit, A. K., 1987, "Strategic Behavior in Contests," *American Economic Review*, 77, December, pp. 891–898.

Dixit, A. K., and R. S. Pindyck, 1994, *Investment under Uncertainty*, Princeton, NJ: Princeton University Press.

Dixit, A. K., and J. E. Stiglitz, 1977, "Monopolistic Competition and Optimum Product Diversity," *American Economic Review*, 67, June, pp. 297–308.

Doeringer, P., and M. Piore, 1971, *Internal Labor Markets and Manpower Analysis*, Lexington, MA: Heath.

Domar, E., 1966, "The Soviet Collective Farm as a Producer Cooperative," *American Economic Review*, 56, 4, part 1, September, pp. 743–757.

Donne, J., 1975 [1572–1631], *Devotions upon Emergent Occasions,* edited, with commentary, by Anthony Raspa, Montreal: McGill-Queen's University Press.

Dorfman, R., P. A. Samuelson, and R. M. Solow, 1958, *Linear Programming and Economic Analysis*, New York: McGraw-Hill.

Dow, G. K., 1993, "Why Capital Hires Labor: A Bargaining Perspective," *American Economic Review*, 83, 1, March, pp. 118–134.

Dow, G. K., 2003, *Governing the Firm: Workers' Control in Theory and Practice*, Cambridge: Cambridge University Press.

Drago, R., and J. S. Heywood, 1989, "Tournaments, Piece Rates, and the Shape of the Payoff Function," *Journal of Political Economy*, 97, August, pp. 992–998.

Drake, J. H., 1917, "Partnership Entity and Tenancy in Partnership: The Struggle for Definition," *Michigan Law Review*, 15, June, pp. 609–630.

Drèze, J. H., 1976, "Some Theory of Labor Management and Participation," *Econometrica*, 44, 6, November, pp. 1125–1139.

Drèze, J. H., 1989, *Labour Management, Contracts and Capital Markets: A General Equilibrium Approach*, Oxford: Blackwell.

Drèze, J. H., and F. Modigliani, 1972, "Consumption Decisions under Uncertainty," *Journal of Economic Theory*, 5, pp. 308–335.

Drucker, P. F., 1946, *Concept of the Corporation*, New York: John Day.

Dutta, B., and M. O. Jackson, eds., 2003, *Networks and Groups: Models of Strategic Formation*, Berlin: Springer.

Dutta, B., and S. Mutuswami, 1997, "Stable Networks," *Journal of Economic Theory*, 76, pp. 322–344.

Dyck, A., and L. Zingales, 2004, "Private Benefits of Control: An International Comparison," *Journal of Finance*, 59, pp. 537–600.

Dye, R. A., 1985, "Costly Contract Contingencies," *International Economic Review*, 26, pp. 233–250.

Dye, R. A., 1986, "Optimal Monitoring Policies in Agencies," *Rand Journal of Economics*, 17, pp. 339–350.

Easterbrook, F. H., and D. R. Fischel, 1989, "The Corporate Contract," *Columbia Law Review*, 89, pp. 1416–1448.

Easterbrook, F. H., and D. R. Fischel, 1991, *The Economic Structure of Corporate Law*, Cambridge, MA: Harvard University Press.

eBay, 2001, *Annual Report 2000*, http://www.shareholder.com/ebay/annual/2000_annual_10K.pdf, accessed November 6, 2008.

Economides, N., 1996, "The Economics of Networks," *International Journal of Industrial Organization*, 14, 2, March, pp. 673–699.

Edgeworth, F. Y., 1967, *Mathematical Psychics: An Essay on the Application of Mathematics to the Moral Sciences*, New York: Augustus M. Kelley. [Originally published 1881, London: C. Kegan Paul & Co.].

Edmonds, C. C., 1923, "Tendencies in the Automobile Industry," *American Economic Review*, 13, pp. 422–441.

Eisenberg, M. A., 2000, *An Introduction to Agency, Partnerships and LLCs*, 3rd ed., New York: Foundation Press.

Ekelund, R. B., Jr., and R. Burton, 1996, *Sacred Trust: The Medieval Church as an Economic Firm*, New York: Oxford University Press.

Engels, F., 1989, *Socialism: Utopian and Scientific*, New York: Pathfinder Press.

Enke, S., 1945, "Consumer Cooperatives and Economic Efficiency," *American Economic Review*, 35, March, pp. 148–55.

Erdös, P., and A. Rényi, 1960, "On the Evolution of Random Graphs," *Publications of the Mathematical Institute of the Hungarian Academy of Sciences*, 5, pp. 17–61.

Erdös, P., and A. Rényi, 1961, "On the Strength of Connectedness of Random Graphs," *Acta Mathematica Hungarian Academy of Sciences*, 12, pp. 261–267.

Eriksen, L., 2000, "Online Vertical Markets: Not a One-Size-Fits-All World," in *The Report on Manufacturing* (March), Boston: AMR Research.

Euler, L., 1736, "Solutio Problematis ad Geometriam Situs Pertinentis" [The Solution of a Problem Relating to the Geometry of Position], 8 *Commentarii Academiae Scientiarum Imperialis Petropolitanae* 128 (1736, pp. 128–140), reprinted in N. L. Biggs, E. K. Lloyd, and R. J. Wilson, 1976, *Graph Theory 1736–1936*, London: Oxford University Press, pp. 3–11.

Evans, D. S., and B. Jovanovic, 1989, "An Estimated Model of Entrepreneurial Choice under Liquidity Constraints," *Journal of Political Economy*, 97, August, pp. 808–827.

Evans, D. S., and L. S. Leighton, 1989, "Some Empirical Aspects of Entrepreneurship," *American Economic Review*, 79, June, pp. 519–535.

Fama, E. F., 1980, "Agency Problems and the Theory of the Firm," *Journal of Political Economy*, 88, 2, pp. 288–307.

Fama, E. F., and M. C. Jensen, 1983a, "Agency Problems and Residual Claims," *Journal of Law and Economics*, 26, June, pp. 327–349.

Fama, E. F., and M. C. Jensen, 1983b, "Separation of Ownership and Controls," *Journal of Law and Economics*, 26, June, pp. 301–325.

Fanoaltea, S., 1988, "Transaction Costs, Whig History, and the Common Fields," *Politics and Society*, 16, pp. 171–240.

Farrell, J., and G. Saloner, 1985, "Standardization, Compatibility, and Innovation," *Rand Journal of Economics*, 16, pp. 70–83.

Farrell, J., and G. Saloner, 1986, "Installed Base and Compatibility: Innovation, Product Preannouncements, and Predation," *American Economic Review*, 76, pp. 940–955.

Farrell, J., and S. Scotchmer, 1988, "Partnerships," *Quarterly Journal of Economics*, 103, 2, pp. 279–297.

Favier, J., 1998, *Gold and Spices: The Rise of Commerce in the Middle Ages*, New York: Holmes & Meier.

Feeny, D., S. Hanna, and A. F. McEvoy, 1996, "Questioning the Assumptions of the 'Tragedy of the Commons' Model of Fisheries," *Land Economics*, 72, May, pp. 187–205.

Fein, A. J., 1998, "Understanding Evolutionary Processes in Non-manufacturing Industries: Empirical Insights from the Shakeout in Pharmaceutical Wholesaling," *Journal of Evolutionary Economics*, 8, pp. 231–270.

Felli, L., and K. Roberts, 2000, "Does Competition Solve the Hold-Up Problem?" manuscript, London: London School of Economics, February.

Ferrier, G. D., and C. A. K. Lovell, 1990, "Measuring Cost Efficiency in Banking: Econometric and Linear Programming Evidence," *Journal of Econometrics*, 46, pp. 229–245.

Fershtman, C., 1985, "Managerial Incentives as a Strategic Variable in a Duopolistic Environment," *International Journal of Industrial Organization*, 3, pp. 245–253.

Fershtman, C., and K. L. Judd, 1987, "Equilibrium Incentives in Oligopoly," *American Economic Review*, 77, pp. 927–940.

Fershtman, C., K. L. Judd, and E. Kalai, 1991, "Observable Contracts: Strategic Delegation and Cooperation," *International Economic Review*, 32, pp. 551–559.

Fershtman, C., V. Mahajan, and E. Muller, 1990, "Marketshare Pioneering Advantage: A Theoretical Approach," *Management Science*, 36, pp. 900–918.

Fine, C., and D. Raff, 2001, "Internet-Driven Innovation and Economic Performance in the American Automobile Industry," in Brookings Task Force on the Internet, *The Economic Payoff from the Internet Revolution*, Washington, DC: Brookings Institute Press, pp. 62–87.

Fingleton, J., 1997, "Competition among Middlemen When Buyers and Sellers Can Trade Directly," *Journal of Industrial Economics*, 45, 4, pp. 405–427.

Fischel, D. R., 1982, "The Corporate Governance Movement," *Vanderbilt Law Review*, 38, pp. 1259–1292.

Fischer, J. H., and J. E. Harrington, Jr., 1996, "Product Variety and Firm Agglomeration," *Rand Journal of Economics*, 27, Summer, pp. 281–309.

Fishburn, P., 1974, "Convex Stochastic Dominance with Continuous Distribution Functions," *Journal of Economic Theory*, 7, pp. 143–158.

Fisher, I., 1906, *The Nature of Capital and Income*, New York: Macmillan.

Fisher, I., 1907, *Rate of Interest: Its Nature, Determination and Relation to Economic Phenomena*, New York: Macmillan.

Fisher, I., 1930, *The Theory of Interest: As Determined by Impatience to Spend Income and Opportunity to Invest It*, New York: Macmillan.

Fisher, I., 1933, "The Debt-Deflation Theory of Great Depressions," *Econometrica*, 1, October, pp. 337–357.

Flaherty, T. M., 1980, "Industry Structure and Cost-Reducing Investment," *Econometrica*, 48, pp. 1187–1209.

Frank, L. K., 1925, "The Significance of Industrial Integration," *Journal of Political Economy*, 33, April, pp. 179–195.

Frisch, R., 1965, *Theory of Production*, Dordrecht: Reidel.

Fudenberg, D., and J. Tirole, 1986, "A Theory of Exit in Oligopoly," *Econometrica*, 54, 943–960.

Fujita, M., and J.-F. Thisse, 2002, *Economies of Agglomeration: Cities, Industrial Location and Regional Growth*, Cambridge: Cambridge University Press.

Furubotn, E. G., and R. Richter, 2000, *Institutions and Economic Theory: The Contribution of the New Institutional Economics*, Ann Arbor: University of Michigan Press.

Gabel, M., and H. Bruner, 2003, *Global Inc.: An Atlas of the Multinational Corporation*, New York: The New Press.

Gale, D., and L. Shapley, 1962, "College Admissions and the Stability of Marriage," *American Mathematical Monthly*, 69, 1, pp. 9–15.

Gal-Or, E., 1992, "Vertical Integration in Oligopoly," *Journal of Law, Economics, and Organization*, 8, pp. 377–393.

Gal-Or, E., 1993, "Internal Organization and Managerial Compensation in Oligopoly," *International Journal of Industrial Organization*, 11, pp. 157–183.

Gal-Or, E., 1997, "Multiprincipal Agency Relationships as Implied by Product Market Competition," *Journal of Economics and Management Strategy*, 6, 2, Summer, pp. 235–256.

Gans, J. S., and S. Stern, 2000, "Incumbency and R&D Incentives: Licensing the Gale of Creative Destruction," *Journal of Economics & Management Strategy*, 9, Winter, pp. 485–511.

Garcia, B. E., 2004, "Family-Owned Businesses Make Up Important Base for U.S., World Economy," *The Miami Herald*, June 12, Knight Ridder/Tribune Business News.

Garella, P., 1989, "Adverse Selection and the Middleman," *Economica*, 56 (223), August, 395–400.

Garicano, L., and S. N. Kaplan, 2001, "The Effects of Business-to-Business E-Commerce on Transaction Costs," working paper, July, Graduate School of Business, University of Chicago.

Garman, M. B., 1976, "Market Microstructure," *Journal of Financial Economics*, 3, June, pp. 257–275.

Geanakoplos, J., and P. Milgrom, 1991, "A Theory of Hierarchies Based on Limited Managerial Attention," *Journal of the Japanese and International Economies*, 5, pp. 205–225.

Gehrig, T., 1993, "Intermediation in Search Markets," *Journal of Economics and Management Strategy*, 2, Spring, pp. 97–120.

Gehrig, T. P., 1996, "Natural Oligopoly and Customer Networks in Intermediated Markets," *International Journal of Industrial Organization*, 14(1), pp. 101–118.

Geroski, P. A., 1995, "What Do We Know about Entry?" *International Journal of Industrial Organization*, 13, pp. 421–440.

Gertner, R. H., D. S. Scharfstein, and J. C. Stein, 1994, "Internal Versus External Capital Markets," *Quarterly Journal of Economics*, 109, 4, November, pp. 1211–1230.

Ghemawat, P., and B. Nalebuff, 1985, "Exit," *Rand Journal of Economics*, 16, pp. 184–194.

Gies, J., and F. Gies, 1972, *Merchants and Moneymen: The Commercial Revolution, 1000–1500*, New York: Crowell.

Gilligan, T., M. Smirlock, and W. Marshall, 1984, "Scale and Scope Economies in the Multi-product Banking Firm," *Journal of Monetary Economics*, 13, May, pp. 393–405.

Glosten, L. R., and P. R. Milgrom, 1985, "Bid, Ask and Transaction Prices in a Specialist Market with Heterogeneously Informed Traders," *Journal of Financial Economics*, 14, pp. 71–100.

Goldberg, P. K., and M. M. Knetter, 1997, "Goods Prices and Exchange Rates: What Have We Learned?" *Journal of Economic Literature*, 35, September, pp. 1243–1272.

Goldstein, P., 1992, "Copyright," *Law and Contemporary Problems*, 55, Spring, pp. 79–91.

Gompers, P. A., 1995, "Optimal Investment, Monitoring, and the Staging of Venture Capital," *Journal of Finance*, 50, 5, December, pp. 1461–1489.

Gompers, P. A., and J. Lerner, 1999, *The Venture Capital Cycle*, Cambridge, MA: MIT Press.

Gonner, E. C. K., 1966, *Common Land and Inclosure* [1912], reprinted, New York: Kelly.

Gordon, H. S., 1954, "The Economic Theory of the Common Property Resource: The Fishery," *Journal of Political Economy*, 62, April, pp. 124–142.

Gort, M., and S. Klepper, 1982, "Time Paths in the Diffusion of Product Innovations," *Economic Journal*, 92, September, pp. 630–653.

Graham, R. L., and J. Nesetril, eds., 1997, *The Mathematics of Paul Erdös*, Berlin: Springer.

Granovettor, M., 1985, "Economic Action and Social Structure: The Problem of Embeddedness," *American Journal of Sociology*, 91, pp. 451–510.

Graziani, A., 2003, *The Monetary Theory of Production*, Cambridge: Cambridge University Press.

Green, J., and J.-J. Laffont, 1977, "Characterization of Satisfactory Mechanisms for the Revelation of Preferences for Public Goods," *Econometrica*, 45, pp. 427–438.

Green, J. R., and J.-J. Laffont, 1979, *Incentives in Public Decision Making*, Amsterdam: North Holland.

Green, J. R., and N. L. Stokey, 1983, "A Comparison of Tournaments and Contracts," *Journal of Political Economy*, 91, pp. 349–364.

Greenhut, M. L., G. Norman, and C.-S. Hung, 1987, *The Economics of Imperfect Competition: A Spatial Approach*, Cambridge: Cambridge University Press.

Greenstein, S. M., 1998, "Industrial Economics and Strategy: Computing Platforms," *IEEE Micro*, 18, May–June, pp. 43–53.

Greif, A., 1989, "Reputation and Coalitions in Medieval Trade: Evidence on the Maghribi Traders," *Journal of Economic History*, 49, December, pp. 857–882.

Greif, A., 1993, "Contract Enforceability and Economic Institutions in Early Trade: The Maghribi Traders' Coalition," *American Economic Review*, 83, pp. 525–548.

Greif, A., 2001, "Impersonal Exchange and the Origins of Markets: From the Community Responsibility System to Individual Legal Responsibility in Pre-modern Europe," in

M. Aoki and Y. Hayami, eds., *Communities and Markets in Economic Development*, Oxford: Oxford University Press, pp. 3–41.

Greif, A., P. Milgrom, and B. R. Weingast, 1994, "Coordination, Commitment, and Enforcement: The Case of the Merchant Guild," *Journal of Political Economy*, 102, August, pp. 745–776.

Grinblatt, M., and C. Y. Hwang, 1989, "Signalling and the Pricing of New Issues," *Journal of Finance*, 44, pp. 393–420.

Gromb, D., and D. Scharfstein, 2005, "Entrepreneurship in Equilibrium," working paper 9001, June, National Bureau of Economic Research.

Gross, J., and J. Yellen, 1998, *Graph Theory and Its Applications*, Boca Raton, FL: CRC Press.

Gross, J., and J. Yellen, eds., 2004, *Handbook of Graph Theory*, Boca Raton, FL: CRC Press.

Grossman, S. J., and O. D. Hart, 1982, "Corporate Financial Structure and Managerial Incentives," in J. McCall, ed., *The Economics of Information and Uncertainty*, Chicago: University of Chicago Press.

Grossman, S. J., and O. D. Hart, 1986, "The Costs and Benefits of Ownership: A Theory of Vertical and Lateral Integration," *Journal of Political Economy*, 94, August, pp. 691–719.

Grout, P. A., 1984, "Investment and Wages in the Absence of Binding Contracts: A Nash Bargaining Approach," *Econometrica*, 52, March, pp. 449–460.

Groves, T., 1973, "Incentives in Teams," *Econometrica*, 41, 4, pp. 617–631.

Groves, T., and J. Ledyard, 1977, "Optimal Allocation of Public Goods: A Solution to the 'Free Rider' Problem," *Econometrica*, 45, May, pp. 783–810.

Groves, T., and M. Loeb, 1975, "Incentives and Public Inputs," *Journal of Public Economics*, 4, pp. 211–226.

Guttman, J. M., 1978, "Understanding Collective Action: Matching Behavior," *American Economic Review*, 68, pp. 251–255.

Guttman, J. M., 1987, "A Non-Cournot Model of Voluntary Collective Action," *Economica*, 54, pp. 1–19.

Haavelmo, T., 1960, *A Study in the Theory of Investment*, Chicago: The University of Chicago Press.

Hall, P., 1935, "On Representatives of Subsets," *Journal of the London Mathematical Society*, 10, pp. 26–30.

Hansmann, H., 1980, "The Role of the Nonprofit Enterprise," *Yale Law Journal*, 89, 3, pp. 835–901.

Hansmann, H., 1985, "The Organization of Insurance Companies: Mutual versus Stock," *Journal of Law, Economics, and Organization*, 1, 1, spring, pp. 125–153.

Hansmann, H., 1988, "Ownership of the Firm," *Journal of Law, Economics, and Organization*, 4, autumn, pp. 267–304.

Hansmann, H., 1996, *The Ownership of Enterprise*, Cambridge, MA: Harvard University Press.

Hansmann, H., and R. Kraakman, 2000a, "The Essential Role of Organizational Law," *The Yale Law Journal*, 110, 3, December, pp. 387–440.

Hansmann, H., and R. Kraakman, 2000b, "Organization Law as Asset Partitioning," *European Economic Review*, 44, pp. 807–817.

Hansmann, H., R. Kraakman, and R. Squire, 2006, "Law and the Rise of the Firm," European Corporate Governance Institute Working Paper Series in Law, No. 57/2006, pp. 1–63.

Hardin, G., 1968, "The Tragedy of the Commons," *Science*, 162, December 13, pp. 1243–1248.

Harrigan, K. R., 1980, *Strategies for Declining Businesses*, Lexington, MA: Heath.

Harris, L., 2003, *Trading and Exchanges: Market Microstructure for Practitioners*, New York: Oxford University Press.

Harris, M., and A. Raviv, 1991, "The Theory of Capital Structure," *Journal of Finance* 46, pp. 297–355.

Hart, O. D., 1983, "The Market Mechanism as an Incentive Scheme," *Bell Journal of Economics*, 14, pp. 366–382.

Hart, O. D., 1995, *Firms, Contracts and Financial Structure*, Oxford: Oxford University Press.

Hart, O. D., and B. Holmström, 1986, "The Theory of Contracts," in T. F. Bewley, ed., *Advances in Economic Theory Fifth World Congress*, Cambridge: Cambridge University Press, pp. 71–155.

Hart, O. D., and J. Moore, 1988, "Incomplete Contracts and Renegotiation," *Econometrica*, 56, July, pp. 755–785.

Hart, O. D., and J. Moore, 1996, "The Governance of Exchanges: Members' Cooperative versus Outside Ownership," *Oxford Review of Economic Policy*, 12, 4, pp. 53–69.

Hart, O. D., and J. Moore, 1998, "Default and Renegotiation: A Dynamic Model of Debt," *Quarterly Journal of Economics*, 113, pp. 1–41.

Hart, O. D., and J. Moore, 1990, "Property Rights and the Nature of the Firm," *Journal of Political Economy*, 98, December, pp. 1119–1158.

Hart, O. D., and J. Tirole, 1990, "Vertical Integration and Market Foreclosure," *Brookings Papers on Economics Activity, Microeconomics*, pp. 205–286.

Hawley, F. B., 1893, "The Risk Theory of Profit," *Quarterly Journal of Economics*, 7, July, pp. 459–479.

Hawley, F. B., 1901, "Final Objections to the Risk Theory of Profit: A Reply," *Quarterly Journal of Economics*, 15, August, pp. 603–620.

Hawley, F. B., 1907, *Enterprise and the Productive Process*, New York: G. P. Putnam's Sons.

Hayek, F. A., 1941, *The Pure Theory of Capital*, Chicago: The University of Chicago Press.

Hayek, F. A., 1945, "The Use of Knowledge in Society," *American Economic Review*, 35, September, pp. 519–530.

Hayek, F. A., 1976, *Law, Legislation and Liberty*, v. 2: *The Mirage of Social Justice*, Chicago: The University of Chicago Press.

Hayek, F. A., 1977, "The Creative Powers of a Free Civilization," in F. Morley, ed., *Essays on Individuality*, Indianapolis: The Liberty Fund.

Hayek, F. A., 1985, "Richard Cantillon," Translated from the 1931 article in German by M. Ó Súilleabháin, *Journal of Libertarian Studies*, 7, 2, Fall, pp. 217–247.

Hayek, F. A., 1988, *The Fatal Conceit: The Errors of Socialism, The Collected Works of F. A. Hayek*, v. 1, edited by W. W. Bartley, London: Routledge.

Hayek, F. A., 1991, "Spontaneous ('Grown') Order and Organized ('Made') Order," in G. Thompson, J. Francis, R. Levacic, and J. Mitchell, eds., *Market, Hierarchies and Networks: The Coordination of Social Life*, London: Sage Publications, pp. 293–301.

Heflebower, R., 1908, *Cooperatives and Mutuals in the Market System*, Madison: University of Wisconsin Press.

Hellman, T., 1998, "The Allocation of Control Rights in Venture Capital," *Rand Journal of Economics*, 29, pp. 57–76.

Hellmann, T., 2005, "When Do Employees Become Entrepreneurs?" working paper, April , University of British Columbia.

Hellmann, T., 2007, "Entrepreneurs and the Process of Obtaining Resources," *Journal of Economics and Management Strategy*, 16, Spring, pp. 81–110.

Hellmann, T., and M. Puri, 2000, "The Interaction between Product Market and Financing Strategy: The Role of Venture Capital," *Review of Financial Studies*, 13, Winter, pp. 959–984.

Hendershott, T., and J. Zhang, 2006, "A Model of Direct and Intermediated Sales," *Journal of Economics and Management Strategy*, 15, pp. 279–316.

Hermalin, B. E., 1992, "The Effects of Competition on Executive Behavior," *The Rand Journal of Economics*, 23, 3, autumn, pp. 350–365.

Hillman, R. W., 2005, "The Bargain in the Firm: Partnership Law, Corporate Law, and Private Ordering within Closely-Held Business Associations," research paper No. 37, April, School of Law, University of California, Davis.

Hirshleifer, J., 1965, "Investment Decisions under Uncertainty: Choice-Theoretic Approaches," *Quarterly Journal of Economics*, 79, pp. 509–536.

Hobbes, T., 1991, *Leviathan*, edited by Richard Tuck, New York: Cambridge University Press.

Hogan, S., 1991, "The Inefficiency of Arbitrage in an Equilibrium-Search Model," *Review of Economic Studies*, 58, pp. 755–775.

Holmes, O. W., 1952, "Agency II," (1891) *Harvard Law Review*, 5, reprinted in Oliver Wendell Holmes, *Collected Legal Papers*, New York: Peter Smith.

Holmes, T. J., and J. A. Schmitz, 1990, "A Theory of Entrepreneurship and Its Application to the Study of Business Transfers," *Journal of Political Economy*, 98, April, pp. 265–294.

Holmes, T. J., and J. A. Schmitz, 1995, "On the Turnover of Business Firms and Business Managers," *Journal of Political Economy*, 103, October, pp. 1005–1038.

Holmes, T. J., and J. A. Schmitz, 1996, "Managerial Tenure, Business Age, and Small Business Turnover," *Journal of Labor Economics*, 14, January, pp. 79–99.

Holmstrom, B., 1979, "Moral Hazard and Observability," *Bell Journal of Economics*, 10, pp. 74–91.

Holmstrom, B., 1982, "Moral Hazard in Teams," *Bell Journal of Economics*, 13, pp. 324–340.

Holmstrom, B., 1985, "Managerial Incentives, Investment and Aggregate Implications: Scale Effects," *Review of Economic Studies*, pp. 403–425.

Holmstrom, B., 1999, "The Firm as a Subeconomy," *Journal of Law, Economics and Organization*, 15, April, pp. 74–102.

Holmstrom, B., and P. Milgrom, 1991, "Multitask Principal Agent Analyses: Incentive Contracts, Asset Ownership and Job Design," *Journal of Law, Economics and Organization*, 7, special issue, pp. 24–52.

Holmstrom, B., and J. Ricart i Costa, 1986, "Managerial Incentives and Capital Management," *Quarterly Journal of Economics*, 101, November, pp. 835–859.

Holmstrom, B., and J. Roberts, 1998, "The Boundaries of the Firm Revisited," *Journal of Economic Perspectives*, 12, 4, Fall, pp. 73–94.

Holmstrom, B., and J. Tirole, 1993, "Market Liquidity and Performance Monitoring," *Journal of Political Economy*, 101, pp. 678–709.

Holmstrom, B., and L. Weiss, 1985, "Managerial Incentives, Investment, and Aggregate Implications: Scale Effects," *Review of Economic Studies*, 52, pp. 403–426.

Holmstrom, M., 1989, *Industrial Democracy in Italy: Workers' Co-ops and the Self-Management Debate*, Aldershot, UK: Avebury.

Holtz-Eakin, D., D. Joulfaian, and H. S. Rosen, 1994a, "Entrepreneurial Decisions and Liquidity Constraints," *Rand Journal of Economics*, 25, summer, pp. 334–347.

Holtz-Eakin, D., D. Joulfaian, and H. S. Rosen, 1994b, "Sticking it Out: Entrepreneurial Survival and Liquidity Constraints," *Journal of Political Economy*, 102, February, pp. 53–75.

Hopenhayn, H., 1992, "Entry, Exit, and Firm Dynamics in Long Run Equilibrium," *Econometrica*, 60, pp. 1127–1150.

Horvath, M., F. Schivardi, M. Woywode, 2001, "On Industry Life-Cycles: Delay, Entry, and Shakeout in Beer Brewing," *International Journal of Industrial Organization*, 19, July, pp. 1023–1052.

Hotelling, H., 1931, "The Economics of Exhaustible Resources," *Journal of Political Economy*, 39, 2, pp. 137–175.

Huddart, S., and P. J. Liang, 2005, "Profit Sharing and Monitoring in Partnerships," *Journal of Accounting and Economics*, 40, December, pp. 153–187.

Hunt, E. S., 1994, *The Medieval Super-companies: A Study of the Peruzzi Company of Florence*, Cambridge: Cambridge University Press.

Hunt, E. S., and J. M. Murray, 1999, *A History of Business in Medieval Europe, 1200–1550*, New York: Cambridge University Press.

Hurwicz, L., 1979, "Outcome Functions Yielding Walrasian and Lindahl Allocations at Nash Equilibrium Points," *Review of Economic Studies*, 46, pp. 217–225.

Hylland, A., and R. Zeckhauser, 1979, "The Efficient Allocation of Individuals to Positions," *Journal of Political Economy*, 87, 2, pp. 293–314.

Innes, R. D., 1990, "Limited Liability and Incentive Contracting with Ex-ante Action Choices," *Journal of Economic Theory*, 52, pp. 45–67.

Ireland, N. J., and P. J. Law, 1983, "A Cournot-Nash Model of Consumer Cooperative," *Southern Economic Journal*, 49, 3, January, pp. 706–716.

Jackson, M. O., and S. Wilkie, 2005, "Endogenous Games and Mechanisms: Side Payments among Players," *Review of Economic Studies*, 72, pp. 543–566.

Jackson, M. O., and A. Wolinsky, 1996, "A Strategic Model of Social and Economic Networks," *Journal of Economic Theory*, 71, pp. 44–74.

Janson, S., T. Luczak, and A. Ruciński, 2000, *Random Graphs*, New York: Wiley.

Jensen, M. C., 1986, "Agency Costs of Free Cash Flow, Corporate Finance and Takeovers," *American Economic Review*, 76, pp. 323–339.

Jensen, M. C., 2000, *A Theory of the Firm: Governance, Residual Claims, and Organizational Forms*, Cambridge, MA: Harvard University Press.

Jensen, M. C., and W. Meckling, 1976, "Theory of the Firm: Managerial Behavior, Agency Costs and Ownership Structure," *Journal of Financial Economics*, 3, pp. 305–360.

Jensen, M. C., and W. H. Meckling, 1979, "Rights and Production Functions: An Application to Labor-Managed Firms and Codetermination," *Journal of Business*, 52, 4, October, pp. 469–506.

Jevons, W. S., 1871, *The Theory of Political Economy* [reprinted 1970], London: Penguin.

Jevons, W. S., 1875, *Money and the Mechanism of Exchange*, London: Macmillan.

Johansson, D., 2004. "Economics without Entrepreneurship or Institutions: A Vocabulary Analysis of Graduate Textbooks," *Econ Journal Watch*, Atlas Economic Research Foundation, 1, 3, December, pp. 515–538.

John, K., and J. Williams, 1985, "Dividends, Dilution, and Taxes: A Signaling Equilibrium," *Journal of Finance*, 40, pp. 1053–1070.

Johnson, H. T., and R. S. Kaplan, 1986, *Relevance Lost: The Rise and Fall of Managerial Accounting*, Cambridge: Harvard Business School Press.

Jones, G., 2000, *From Merchants to Multinationals: British Trading Companies in the Nineteenth and Twentieth Centuries*, Oxford: Oxford University Press.

Joskow, P., 2005, "Regulation and Deregulation after 25 Years: Lessons Learned for Research in Industrial Organization," *Review of Industrial Organization*, 26, December, pp. 169–193.

Jovanovic, B., 1982, "Selection and the Evolution of Industry," *Econometrica*, 50, May, pp. 649–670.

Jovanovic, B., 1994, "Firm Formation with Heterogeneous Management and Labor Skills," *Small Business Economics*, 6, June, pp. 185–191.

Jovanovic, B., and G. M. MacDonald, 1994, "The Life Cycle of a Competitive Industry," *Journal of Political Economy*, 102, April, pp. 322–347.

Ju, J., S. C. Linn, and Z. Zhu, 2004, "Price Dispersion in a Model with Middlemen and Oligopolistic Market Makers: A Theory and an Application to the North American Natural Gas Market," working paper, University of Oklahomat.

Kamara, A., 1993, "Production Flexibility, Stochastic Separation, Hedging, and Futures Prices," *Review of Financial Studies*, 6, pp. 935–957.

Kandel, E., and Lazear, E, 1992, "Peer Pressure and Partnerships," *Journal of Political Economy*, 100, pp. 801–817.

Kaplan, S. N., B. A. Sensoy, and P. Strömberg, 2005, "What Are Firms? Evolution from Birth to Public Companies," discussion paper No. 5224, September, Center for Economic Policy Research.

Kaplan, S. N., and P. Strömberg, 2003, "Financial Contracting Theory Meets the Real World: An Empirical Analysis of Venture Capital Contracts," *Review of Economic Studies*, 70, 2, pp. 281–315.

Kaplan, S. N., and P. Strömberg, 2004, "Characteristics, Contracts, and Actions: Evidence from Venture Capital Analyses," *Journal of Finance*, 59, 5, pp. 2177–2210.

Katz, M. L., 1989, "Vertical Contractual Relations," in R. Schmalensee and R. Willig, eds., *Handbook of Industrial Organization*, Amsterdam: North Holland, pp. 655–721.

Katz, M. L., 1991, "Game-Playing Agents: Unobservable Contracts as Precommitments," *Rand Journal of Economics*, 22, pp. 307–328.

Katz, M. L., and C. Shapiro, 1985, "Network Externalities, Competition, and Compatibility," *American Economic Review*, 75, June, pp. 424–440.

Katz, M. L., and C. Shapiro, 1987, "R&D Rivalry with Licensing or Imitation," *American Economic Review*, 77, pp. 402–420.

Katz, M. L., and C. Shapiro, 1986, "Technology Adoption in the Presence of Network Externalities," *Journal of Political Economy*, 94, pp. 822–841.

Katz, M. L., and C. Shapiro, 1994, "Systems Competition and Network Effects," *Journal of Economic Perspectives*, 8, 2, Spring, pp. 93–115.

Khanna, T., 2008, *Billions of Entrepreneurs: How China and India Are Reshaping Their Futures–And Yours*, Cambridge, MA: Harvard Business School Press.

Kihlstrom, R. E., and J.-J. Laffont, 1979, "A General Equilibrium Entrepreneurial Theory of Firm Formation Based on Risk Aversion," *Journal of Political Economy*, 87, August, pp. 719–748.

Kihlstrom, R. E., and J.-J. Laffont, 1982, "A Competitive Entrepreneurial Model of a Stock Market," in J. J. McCall, *The Economics of Information and Uncertainty*, NBER Conference Report No. 32, Chicago: University of Chicago Press.

Kindleberger, C. P., 1996, *Manias, Panics, and Crashes: A History of Financial Crises*, New York: Wiley.

King, S. R., 1998, "Staying in Vogue," *New York Times*, November 4, p. C1.

Kirzner, I. M., 1973, *Competition and Entrepreneurship*, Chicago: University of Chicago Press.

Kirzner, I. M., 1979, *Perception, Opportunity, and Profit: Studies in the Theory of Entrepreneurship*, Chicago: The University of Chicago Press.

Kitch, E. W., 2000, "Elementary and Persistent Errors in the Economic Analysis of Intellectual Property," *Vanderbilt Law Review*, 53, pp. 1727–1741.

Klein, B., R. G. Crawford, and A. A. Alchian, 1978, "Vertical Integration, Appropriable Rents, and the Competitive Contracting Process," *Journal of Law and Economics*, 21, October, pp. 297–326.

Klein, P. G., 2005, "The Make-or-Buy Decision: Lessons from Empirical Studies," in Claude Menard and Mary Shirley, eds., *Handbook of New Institutional Economics*, New York: Springer, pp. 435–464.

Klepper, S., and E. Graddy, 1990, "The Evolution of New Industries and the Determinants of Market Structure," *Rand Journal of Economics*, 21, spring, pp. 27–44.

Knight, F. H., 1965, "Understanding Society through Economics," *American Behavioral Scientist*, 9, September, pp. 37–39.

Knight, F. H., 1971 [Houghton, Mifflin, 1921], *Risk, Uncertainty and Profit*, Chicago: University of Chicago Press.

Koolman, G., 1971, "Say's Conception of the Role of the Entrepreneur," *Economica*, New Series, 38, 151, August, pp. 269–286.

Koopmans, T. C., 1957, *Three Essays on the State of Economic Science*, New York: McGraw-Hill.

Kornhauser, L. A., 1989, "The Nexus of Contracts Approach to Corporations: A Comment on Easterbrook and Fischel," *Columbia Law Review*, 89, pp. 1449–1460.

Kranton, R. E., and D. F. Minehart, 2000, "Competition for Goods in Buyer-Seller Networks," *Review of Economic Design*, 5, pp. 301–331.

Kranton, R. E., and D. F. Minehart, 2001, "A Theory of Buyer-Seller Networks," *American Economic Review*, 61, pp. 485–508.

Kräkel, M., 2002, "Tournaments versus Piece Rates under Limited Liability," University of Bonn working paper.

Krasa, S., and A. P. Villamil, 1992, "Monitoring the Monitor: An Incentive Structure for a Financial Intermediary," *Journal of Economic Theory*, 57, pp. 197–221.

Krishna, V., 2002, *Auction Theory*, San Diego: Academic Press.

Krishna, V., and M. Perry, 1998, "Efficient Mechanism Design," working paper, Pennsylvania State University, April.

Krouse, C. G., 1985, "Competition and Unanimity Revisited, Again," *American Economic Review*, 75, December, pp. 1109–1114.

Krugman, P. R., 1979, "Increasing Returns, Monopolistic Competition, and International Trade," *Journal of International Economics*, 9, November, pp. 469–479.

Krugman, P. R., 1996, *Rethinking International Trade*, Cambridge, MA: MIT Press.

Kuan, J. W., 2001, "The Phantom Profits of the Opera: Nonprofit Ownership in the Arts as a Make-Buy Decision," *Journal of Law, Economics, and Organization*, 17, pp. 507–520.

Laffont, J.-J., and D. Martimort, 1997, "The Firm as a Multicontract Organization," *Journal of Economics and Management Strategy*, 6, 2, summer, pp. 201–234.

Laffont, J.-J., and J. Tirole, 1988, "The Dynamics of Incentive Contracts," *Econometrica*, 56, 5, September, pp. 1153–1175.

Lafontaine, F., 1992, "Agency Theory and Franchising: Some Empirical Results," *Rand Journal of Economics*, 23, pp. 263–283.

Lafontaine, F., and S. Bhattacharrya, 1995, "The Role of Risk in Franchising," *Journal of Corporate Finance*, 21, pp. 39–74.

Lafontaine, F., and M. Slade, 2007, "Vertical Integration and Firm Boundaries: The Evidence," *Journal of Economic Literature*, 45, September, pp. 629–685.

Lal, R., 1986, "Delegating Pricing Responsibility to the Salesforce," *Marketing Science*, 5, pp. 159–168.

Lambert, R. A., 1986, "Executive Effort and Selection of Risky Projects," *Rand Journal of Economics*, 17, spring, pp. 77–88.

Lancaster, K., 1980, "Intra-industry Trade under Perfect Monopolistic Competition," *Journal of International Economics*, 10, pp. 151–175.

Landes, D., 2006, *Dynasties: Fortunes and Misfortunes of the World's Great Family Businesses*, New York: Viking.

Lange, O., and F. M. Taylor, 1964, *On the Economic Theory of Socialism*, B. E. Lippincott, ed., New York: McGraw-Hill.

Latham, S., 2000, "Evaluating the Independent Trading Exchanges," in *The Report on E-Commerce Applications*, March, Boston: AMR Research.

Lazear, E., and S. Rosen, 1981, "Rank Order Tournaments as Optimum Labor Contracts," *Journal of Political Economy*, 89, pp. 841–864.

Lazear, E. P., 2004, "Balanced Skills and Entrepreneurship," *American Economic Review*, 94, 2, May, pp. 208–211.

Lazear, E. P., 2005, "Entrepreneurship," *Journal of Labor Economics*, 23(4), pp. 649–680.

Ledyard, J., and T. Palfrey, 1994, "Voting and Lottery Drafts as Efficient Public Goods Mechanisms," *Review of Economic Studies*, 61, pp. 327–355.

Legros, P., and S. A. Matthews, 1993, "Efficient and Nearly-Efficient Partnerships," *Review of Economic Studies*, 60, 3, July, pp. 599–611.

Leonard, H. B., 1983, "Elicitation of Honest Preferences for the Assignment of Individuals to Positions," *Journal of Political Economy*, 91, 3, pp. 461–479.

Lerner, A. P., 1944, *The Economics of Control: Principles of Welfare Economics*, New York: Macmillan.

Lerner, J., and P. A. Gompers, 2001, *The Money of Invention: How Venture Capital Creates New Wealth*, Cambridge, MA: Harvard Business School Press.

Levhari, D., R. Michener, and L. Mirman, 1982, "Dynamic Programming Models of Fishing: Monopoly," in L. J. Mirman and D. F. Spulber, eds., *Essays in the Economics of Renewable Resources*, Amsterdam: North-Holland, pp. 175–186.

Levhari, D., and L. J. Mirman, 1980, "The Great Fish War," *Bell Journal of Economics*, 11, Spring, pp. 322–334.

Levi, S. C., 2002, *The Indian Diaspora in Central Asia and Its Trade 1550–1900*, Leiden: Brill.

Levin, J., 2002, "Multilateral Contracting and the Employment Relationship," *Quarterly Journal of Economics*, 117, August, pp. 1075–1103.

Levin, J., 2003, "Relational Incentive Contracts," *American Economic Review*, 93, 3, June, pp. 835–857.

Levin, J., and S. Tadelis, 2005, "Profit Sharing and the Role of Professional Partnerships," *Quarterly Journal of Economics*, 120, February, pp. 131–171.

Levitt, T., 1960, "Marketing Myopia," *Harvard Business Review*, 38, July–August, pp. 24–47.

Lewis, W. D., 1915, "The Uniform Partnership Act," *Yale Law Journal*, 24, May, pp. 617–641.

Lewis, W. W., 2004, *The Power of Productivity*, Chicago: University of Chicago Press.

Libecap, G. D., and S. N. Wiggins, 1984, "Contractual Responses to the Common Pool: Prorationing of Crude Oil Production," *American Economic Review*, 74, 1, March, pp. 87–98.

Libecap, G. D., and S. N. Wiggins, 1985, "The Influence of Private Contractual Failure on Regulation: The Case of Oil Field Unitization," *Journal of Political Economy*, 93, 4, August, pp. 690–714.

Lieberman, M. B., 1990, "Exit from Declining Industries: 'Shakeout' or 'Stakeout'?" *Rand Journal of Economics*, 21, winter, pp. 538–554.

Liebowitz, S. J., 2002, *Rethinking the Network Economy*, New York: American Management Association.

Liebowitz, S. J., and S. E. Margolis, 1994, "Network Externality: An Uncommon Tragedy," *Journal of Economic Perspectives*, 8, pp. 133–150.

Liebowitz, S. J., and S. E. Margolis, 1999, *Winners Losers and Microsoft: Competition and Antitrust in High Technology*, Oakland, CA: The Independent Institute.

Lilien, G. L., P. Kotler, and K. S. Moorthy, 1992, *Marketing Models*, Englewood Cliffs, NJ: Prentice-Hall.

Lilien, G. L., and E. Yoon, 1990, "The Timing of Competitive Market Entry: An Exploratory Study of New Industrial Products," *Management Science*, 36, pp. 68–585.

Lim, C., 1981, "Risk Pooling and Intermediate Trading Agents," *Canadian Journal of Economics*, 14, 2, May, pp. 261–267.

Lindahl, E., 1958, "Just Taxation – A Positive Solution," in Richard Musgrave and Alan Peacock, eds., *Classics in the Theory of Public Finance*, London: Macmillan, pp. 98–123.

Lindley, N. L., 1888, *A Treatise on the Law of Partnership*, 5th edition, Boston: C. H. Edison.

Lloyd, W. F., 1883, *Two Lectures on the Checks to Population*, Oxford: Oxford University Press.

Loertscher, S., 2004, "Market Making Oligopoly," University of Bern, working paper.

Lu, X., and R. P. McAfee, 1996, "Matching and Expectations in a Market with Heterogeneous Agents," in M. Baye, ed., *Advances in Applied Microeconomics*, v. 6, Greenwich, CT: JAI Press, pp. 121–156.

Luca, A., and L. Felli, 1994. "Incomplete Written Contracts: Undescribable States of Nature," *Quarterly Journal of Economics*, 109, November, pp. 1085–1124.

Lucas, R. E., Jr., 1972, "Expectations and the Neutrality of Money," *Journal of Economic Theory*, 4, pp. 103–124.

Lucas, R. E., Jr., 1978, "On the Size Distribution of Business Firms," *Bell Journal of Economics*, 9, Autumn, pp. 508–523.

Lucking-Reiley, D., 2000, "Auctions on the Internet: What's Being Auctioned, and How?" *Journal of Industrial Economics*, 48, September, pp. 227–252.

Lucking-Reiley, D., and D. F. Spulber, 2001, "Business-to-Business Electronic Commerce," *Journal of Economic Perspectives*, 15, winter, pp. 55–68.

Lutz, F., and V. Lutz, 1951, *The Theory of Investment of the Firm*, Princeton, NJ: Princeton University Press.

Lyon, J. M., 2004, "Payments Evolution or Revolution? Views from the Federal Reserve," *The Region*, June, pp. 6–9 and 38–41.

MacAvoy, P. W., and I. M. Millstein, 2003, *The Recurrent Crisis in Corporate Governance*, New York: Palgrave Macmillan.

MacLeod, W. B., and J. M. Malcomson, 1993, "Investment, Holdup, and the Form of Market Contracts," *American Economic Review*, 83, September, pp. 811–837.

MacMinn, R. D., 1980, "Search and Market Equilibrium," *Journal of Political Economy*, 88, pp. 308–327.

MacMinn, R. D., 1987, "Forward Markets, Stock Markets, and the Theory of the Firm," *Journal of Finance*, 42, December, pp. 1167–1185.

Macneil, I. R., 1974, "The Many Futures of Contracts," *Southern California Law Review*, 47, pp. 691–816.

Macneil, I. R., 1978, *Contracts: Exchange Transactions and Relations; Cases and Materials*, Mineola, NY: Foundation Press.

Macneil, I. R., 1980, *The New Social Contract: An Inquiry into Modern Contractual Relations*, New Haven, CT: Yale University Press.

Makowski, L., and L. Pepall, 1985, "Easy Proofs of Unanimity and Optimality without Spanning: A Pedagogical Note," *Journal of Finance*, 40, September, pp. 1245–1250.

Malcomson, J. M., 1986, "Rank-Order Contracts for a Principal with Many Agents," *Review of Economic Studies*, 53, October, pp. 807–817.

Malinowski, B. K., 1966 [1922], *Argonauts of the Western Pacific: An Account of Native Enterprise and Adventure in the Archipelagoes of Melanesian New Guinea*, New York: Dutton.

Malinvaud, E., 1967, "Decentralization Procedures for Planning," in *Activity Analysis in the Theory of Growth and Planning*, E. Malinvaud and M. O. L. Bacharach, eds., London: Macmillan, pp. 107–208.

Maney, K., 1995, *Megamedia Shakeout: The Inside Story of the Leaders and the Losers in the Exploding Communications Industry*, New York: Wiley.

Manne, H. G., 1965, "Mergers and the Market for Corporate Control," *Journal of Political Economy*, 73, 2, April, pp. 110–120.

Manne, H. G., 1966, "Insider Trading and the Stock Market," New York: Free Press.

Mansfield, E., 1962, "Entry, Gibrat's Law, Innovation, and the Growth of Firms," *American Economic Review*, 52, pp. 1025–1051.

March, J. G., and H. A. Simon, 1958, *Organizations*, New York: John Wiley.

Marino, A. M., and J. Zábojník, 2004, "Internal Competition for Corporate Resources and Incentives in Teams," *Rand Journal of Economics*, 35, 4, winter, pp. 710–727.

Markovits, C., 2000, *The Global World of Indian Merchants 1750–1947: Traders of Sind from Bukhara to Panama*, Cambridge: Cambridge University Press.

Marschak, J., and R. Radner, 1972, *Economic Theory of Teams*, New Haven: Yale University Press.

Marshall, A., 1922, *Principles of Economics*, 8th ed., New York: Macmillan.

Marx, K., 1992, *Capital: A Critique of Political Economy*, New York: Penguin Classics.

Mas-Colell, A., M. D. Whinston, and J. R. Green, 1995, *Microeconomic Theory*, New York: Oxford University Press.

Maskin, E., and J. Riley, 1984, "Monopoly with Incomplete Information," *Rand Journal of Economics*, 15, pp. 171–196.

Mason, E. S., 1939, "Prices and Production Policies of Large-Scale Enterprise," *American Economic Review*, Supplement, 29, March, pp. 61–74.

Mason, E. S., 1949, "The Current State of the Monopoly Problem in the United States," *Harvard Law Review*, 62, June, pp. 1265–1285.

Masten, S. E., 1988, "A Legal Basis for the Firm," *Journal of Law, Economics, and Organization*, 4, 1, Spring, pp. 181–198.

Masten, S., J. W. Meehan, Jr., and E. A. Snyder, 1991, "The Costs of Organization," *Journal of Law, Economics and Organization*, 7(1), Spring, pp. 1–25.

Mathewson, G. F., and R. A. Winter, 1983, "Vertical Integration by Contractual Restraints in Spatial Markets," *Journal of Business*, 56, pp. 497–517.

Mauss, M., 1954, *The Gift. Forms and Functions of Exchange in Archaic Societies*, Glencoe, IL: Free Press.

McAfee, R. P., and J. McMillan, 1995, "Organizational Diseconomies of Scale," *Journal of Economics & Management Strategy*, 4, Fall, pp. 399–426.

McClellan, S. T., 1984, *The Coming Computer Industry Shakeout: Winners, Losers, and Survivors*, New York: Wiley.

McClosky, D. N., 1976, "English Open Fields as Behavior toward Risk," in P. Uselding, ed., *Research in Economic History: An Annual Compilation*, v. 1, Greenwich, CT: JAI Press, pp. 124–170.

McGuire, M.C., 1974, "Group Segregation and Optimal Jurisdictions," *Journal of Political Economy*, 82, pp. 112–132.

McKenzie, L. M., 1959, "On the Existence of General Equilibrium for a Competitive Market," *Econometrica*, 27, January, pp. 54–71.

McKenzie, L. M., 1981, "The Classical Theorem on Existence of Competitive Equilibrium," *Econometrica*, 49, June, pp. 819–841.

Meade, J. E., 1952, "External Economies and Diseconomies in a Competitive Situation," *Economic Journal*, 62, pp. 54–67.

Meade, J. E., 1970, *The Theory of Indicative Planning*, Manchester: Manchester University Press.

Meade, J. E., 1972, "The Theory of Labour-Managed Firms and of Profit Sharing," *Economic Journal*, 82, 325, pp. 402–428.

Means, G. C., 1934, "The Consumer and the New Deal," *The Annals of the American Academy of Political and Social Science*, 173, May, pp. 7–17.

Means, G. C., 1935, "The Major Causes of the Depression," in F. S. Lee and W. J. Samuels, eds., reprint 1992, *Heterodox Economics of Gardiner C. Means: A Collection*, Armonk, NY: M. E. Sharpe, Inc., pp. 73–92.

Means, G. C., 1939, *The Structure of American Economy*, Washington, DC: National Resources Committee, reprint 1966, New York: Augustus M. Kelley Publisher.

Means, G. C., 1940, "Big Business Administered Prices, and the Problem of Full Employment," *Journal of Marketing*, 4, pp. 370–381.

Mechem, F. R., 1896, *Elements of the Law of Partnership*, Chicago: Callaghan and Company.

Mechem, F. R., 1914, *A Treatise on the Law of Agency*, v. 1, 2nd ed., Chicago: Callaghan.

Melumad, N., and D. Mookherjee, 1989, "Delegation as Commitment: The Case of Income Tax Audits," *Rand Journal of Economics*, 20, pp. 139–163.

Melumad, N., and S. Reichelstein, 1987, "Centralization versus Delegation and the Value of Communication," *Journal of Accounting Research*, supplement, 25, pp. 1–21.

Melumad, N., D. Mookherjee, and S. Reichelstein, 1995, "Hierarchical Decentralization of Incentive Contracts," *Rand Journal of Economics*, 26, pp. 654–672.

Melumad, N., D. Mookherjee, and S. Reichelstein, 1997, "Contract Complexity, Incentives, and Value of Delegation," *Journal of Economics and Management Strategy*, 6, 2, Summer, pp. 257–290.

Mesenbourg, T. L., 2001, "Measuring Electronic Business," working paper, U.S. Bureau of the Census, August, Washington, DC.

Milgrom, P., and J. Roberts, 1988, "An Economic Approach to Influence Activities in Organizations," *American Journal of Sociology*, 94, supplement, pp. S154–S179.

Milgrom, P., and J. Roberts, 1990, "Bargaining Costs, Influence Costs, and the Organization of Economic Activity," in J. Alt and K. Shepsle, eds., *Perspectives on Positive Political Economy*, Cambridge: Cambridge University Press, pp. 57–89.

Milgrom, P., and J. Roberts, 1992, *Economics, Organization, and Management*, Englewood Cliffs, NJ: Prentice Hall.

Milgrom, P., and J. Roberts, 1994, "Comparing Equilibria," *American Economic Review*, 84, June, pp. 441–459.

Milgrom, P. R., and R. J. Weber, 1982, "A Theory of Auctions and Competitive Bidding," *Econometrica*, 50, September, pp. 1089–1122.

Mill, J. S., 1848, *Principles of Political Economy*, Boston: Little Brown.

Miller, M. H., and F. Modigliani, 1961, "Dividend Policy, Growth, and the Valuation of Shares," *Journal of Business*, 34, 4, October, pp. 411–433.

Miller, M. H., and K. Rock, 1985, "Dividend Policy under Asymmetric Information," *Journal of Finance*, 40, pp. 1031–1051.

Miller, N. H., 1997, "Efficiency in Partnerships with Joint Monitoring," *Journal of Economic Theory*, 77, pp. 285–299.

Mirman, L. J., and D. F. Spulber, eds., 1982, *Essays in the Economics of Renewable Resources*, Amsterdam: North-Holland Publishing Company.

Mirrlees, J., 1974, "Notes on Welfare Economics, Information, and Uncertainty," in M. Balch, D. McFadden, and S. Wu, eds., *Essays in Economic Behavior under Uncertainty*, Amsterdam: North Holland, pp. 243–258.

Mirrlees, J., 1976, "The Optimal Structure of Authority and Incentives within an Organization," *Bell Journal of Economics*, 7, pp. 105–131.

Mirrlees, J. A., 1999, "The Theory of Moral Hazard and Unobservable Behaviour: Part I," *Review of Economic Studies*, pp. 3–21.

Miwa, Y., and J. M. Ramseyer, 2000, "Rethinking Relationship-Specific Investments: Subcontracting in the Japanese Automobile Industry," *Michigan Law Review*, Vol. 98 , April, pp. 2636–2667.

Modigliani, F., and M. H. Miller, 1958, "The Cost of Capital, Corporation Finance and the Theory of Investment," *The American Economic Review*, 48, 3, June, pp. 261–297.

Monteverde, K., and D. J. Teece, 1982, "Appropriable Rents and Quasi-Vertical Integration," *Journal of Law and Economics*, 25, 2, October, pp. 321–328.

Moore, K., and D. Lewis, 1999, *Birth of the Multinational*, Copenhagen: Copenhagen Business School Press.

Moriwaki, L., 1996, "Shakeout Brewing," *Seattle Times*, November 3.

Morrison, A., and W. Wilhelm, Jr., 2005, "Partnership Firms, Reputation, and Human Capital," *American Economic Review*, 94, pp. 1682–1692.

Morrison, S. A., and C. Winston, 1995, *The Evolution of the Airline Industry*, Washington, DC: Brookings Institution.

Morse, R. A., and N. W. Calderone, 2000, "The Value of Honey Bees as Pollinators of U. S. Crops in 2000," Cornell University working paper, March.

Muris, T. J., D. T. Scheffman, and P. T. Spiller, 1992, "Strategy and Transaction Costs: The Organization of Distribution in the Carbonated Soft-Drink Industry," *Journal of Economics and Management Strategy*, 1, pp. 83–128.

Mussa, M., and S. Rosen, 1978, "Monopoly and Product Quality," *Journal of Economic Theory*, 18, pp. 310–317.

Myers, S., and N. Majluf, 1984, "Corporate Financing and Investment Decisions When Firms Have Information That Investors Do Not Have," *Journal of Financial Economics*, 13, pp. 187–221.

Myerson, R. B., 1977, "Graphs and Cooperation in Games," *Mathematics of Operations Research*, 2, pp. 225–229.

Myerson, R. B., 1979, "Incentive Compatibility and the Bargaining Problem," *Econometrica*, 47, pp. 61–73.

Myerson, R. B., 1981, "Optimal Auction Design," *Mathematics of Operations Research*, 6, pp. 58–73.

Myerson, R. B., 1983, "Mechanism Design by an Informed Principle," *Econometrica*, 51, pp. 1767–1797.

Myerson, R. B., and M. Satterthwaite, 1983, "Efficient Mechanisms for Bilateral Trading," *Journal of Economic Theory*, 29, pp. 265–281.

Nalebuff, B. J., and J. E. Stiglitz, 1983, "Prizes and Incentives: Towards a General Theory of Compensation and Competition," *Bell Journal of Economics*, 14, pp. 21–43.

Nelson, R. R., and S. G. Winter, 1982, *An Evolutionary Theory of Economic Change*, Cambridge, MA: Harvard University Press.

Newman, P. C., 2000, *Empire of the Bay: The Company of Adventurers That Seized a Continent*, New York: Penguin.

Nickerson, J., and B. Silverman, 2003, "Why Aren't Truck Drivers Owner-Operators? Asset Ownership and the Employment Relation in Interstate For-Hire Trucking," *Journal of Economics and Management Strategy*, 12, Spring, pp. 91–118.

Nöldeke, G., and K. M. Schmidt, 1995, "Option Contracts and Renegotiation: A Solution to the Hold-Up Problem," *Rand Journal of Economics*, 26, Summer, pp. 163–179.

Obstfeld, M., and K. Rogoff, 2000, "The Six Major Puzzles in International Macroeconomics," in B. S. Bernanke and K. Rogoff, eds., *NBER Macroeconomics Annual 2000*, 15, Cambridge, MA: MIT Press, pp. 339–390.

O'Hara, W. T., and P. Mandel, 2002, "The World's Oldest Family Companies," *Family Business Magazine*, http://www.familybusinessmagazine.com/oldworld.html. accessed September, 2006.

Osborne, M. J., and A. Rubinstein, 1990, *Bargaining and Markets*, San Diego: Academic Press.

Ostrom, E., 1990, *Governing the Commons: The Evolution of Institutions for Collective Action*, Cambridge: Cambridge University Press.

Pareto, V., 1896–1897, *Cours d'économie politique*, 2 volumes, Lausanne.

Parks, T., 2006, *Medici Money: Banking, Metaphysics, and Art in Fifteenth-Century Florence*, New York: W. W. Norton.

Pastor, L., L. Taylor, and P. Veronesi, 2006, "Entrepreneurial Learning in the IPO Decision, and the Post-IPO Drop in Firm Profitability," working paper 12792, Cambridge, MA: National Bureau of Economic Research, December, pp. 1–45.

Pauly, M. V., 1968, "The Economics of Moral Hazard: Comment," *American Economic Review*, 58, June, pp. 531–537.

Penrose, E. T., 1959, *The Theory of the Growth of the Firm*, Oxford: Basil Blackwell.

Perotti, E. C., and E.-L. von Thadden, 2006, "The Political Economy of Corporate Control and Labor Rents," *Journal of Political Economy*, 114, 1, pp. 145–174.

Perry, M. K., 1989, "Vertical Integration: Determinants and Effects," in R. Schmalensee and R. Willig, eds., *Handbook of Industrial Organization*, Amsterdam: North Holland, pp. 181–255.

Perry, M. K., and R. H. Groff, 1985, "Resale Price Maintenance and Forward Integration into a Monopolistically Competitive Industry," *Quarterly Journal of Economics*, 100, pp. 1293–1311.

Peterson, B. S., and J. Glab, 1994, *Rapid Descent: Deregulation and the Shakeout in the Airlines*, New York: Simon and Schuster.

Phlips, L., 1983, *The Economics of Price Discrimination*, Cambridge: Cambridge University Press.

Pigou, A. C., 1920a, "Cooperative Societies and Income Tax," *Economic Journal*, June, pp. 156–162.

Pigou, A. C., 1920b, *The Economics of Welfare*, London: Macmillan.

Pigou, A. C., 1922, "Empty Economic Boxes: A Reply," *Economic Journal*, 32, pp. 458–465.

Pirrong, S. C., 1999, "The Organization of Financial Exchange Markets: Theory and Evidence," *Journal of Financial Markets*, 2, pp. 329–357.

Pissarides, C. A., 2000, *Equilibrium Unemployment Theory*, 2nd ed., Cambridge, MA: MIT Press.

Poblete, J., and D. F. Spulber, 2008a, "Investors, Entrepreneurs, and Tycoons: The Effect of the Distribution of Wealth on the Establishment of Firms," Northwestern University working paper.

Poblete, J., and D. F. Spulber, 2008b, "Entrepreneurs, Partnerships, and Corporations: Incentives, Investment and the Financial Structure of the Firm," Northwestern University working paper.

Poitevin, M., 1989, "Financial Signalling and the Deep Pocket Argument," *Rand Journal of Economics*, 20, pp. 26–40.

Polanyi, K., 2001 [1944], *The Great Transformation: The Political and Economic Origins of Our Time*, Boston: Beacon Press.

Pollock, A. J., 2006, "What Should Society Want from Corporate Governance?" American Enterprise Institute for Public Policy Research, *Financial Services Outlook*, February, pp. 1–6.

Pozen, D. E., 2008, "We Are All Entrepreneurs Now," *Wake Forest Law Review*, 43, pp. 283–340.

Posner, R. A., 1986, *Economic Analysis of Law*, 3rd edition, Boston: Little Brown.

Postan, M. M., 1973, *Medieval Trade and Finance*, Cambridge: Cambridge University Press.

Pounds, N. J. G., 1994, *An Economic History of Medieval Europe*, 2nd edition, London: Longman.

Povel, P., and M. Raith, 2004, "Optimal Debt with Unobservable Investments," *Rand Journal of Economics*, 35, 3, Autumn, pp. 599–616.

Prendergast, C., 1999, "The Provision of Incentives in Firms," *Journal of Economic Literature*, 37, 1, March, pp. 7–63.

Prescott, E. S., and R. M. Townsend, 2006, "Firms as Clubs in Walrasian Markets with Private Information," *Journal of Political Economy*, 114, pp. 644–671.

Price, J. M., 1991, "Transaction Costs: A Note on Merchant Credit and the Organization of Private Trades," in J. D. Tracy, ed., *The Political Economy of Merchant Empires*, Cambridge: Cambridge University Press, pp. 276–297.

Qian, Y., 1994, "Incentives and Loss of Control in an Optimal Hierarchy," *Review of Economic Studies*, July, 61, pp. 527–544.

Radner, R., 1986, "The Internal Economy of Large Firms," *Economic Journal*, 96, supplement: Conference Papers, pp. 1–22.

Ramakrishnan, R. T. S., and A. V. Thakor, 1984, "Information Reliability and a Theory of Financial Intermediation," *Review of Economic Studies*, 51, pp. 415–432.

Rao, R. C., 1990, "Compensating Heterogeneous Salesforces: Some Explicit Solutions," *Marketing Science*, 19, pp. 319–341.

Rapoport, A., and R. Solomonoff, 1950, "Structure of Random Nets," *Proceedings*, International Congress of Mathematicians, p. 674.

Rapoport, A., and R. Solomonoff, 1951, "Connectivity of Random Net," *Bulletin of Mathematical Biophysics*, 13, pp. 107.

Rasmusen, E., 1987, "Moral Hazard in Risk-Averse Teams," *Rand Journal of Economics*, 18, 3, Autumn, pp. 428–435.

Rasmusen, E., 1989, *Games and Information*, Oxford: Basil Blackwell.

Reeves, J., 1944, *A Century of Rochdale Co-operation, 1844–1944*, London: Lawrence and Wishart.

Reinganum, J. F., 1979, "A Simple Model of Equilibrium Price Dispersion," *Journal of Political Economy*, 87, pp. 851–858.

Reinganum, J. F., 1981, "Dynamic Games of Innovation," *Journal of Economic Theory*, 25, pp. 1–41.

Reinganum, J. F., 1982, "A Dynamic Game of R and D: Patent Protection and Competitive Behavior," *Econometrica*, 50, pp. 671–688.

Reinganum, J. F., 1989, "The Timing of Innovation: Research, Development, and Diffusion," ch. 14 in R. Schmalensee and R. D. Willig, eds., *Handbook of Industrial Organization*, v. 1, New York: Elsevier Science Publishers, pp. 849–908.

Repullo, R., and J. Suarez, 2004, "Venture Capital Finance: A Security Design Approach," *Review of Finance*, 8, pp. 75–108.

Reyerson, K., 2002, *The Art of the Deal: Intermediaries of Trade in Medieval Montpellier*, Leiden, Netherlands: Boston Brill.

Reynolds, P. D., 1997, "Who Starts New Firms? Preliminary Explorations of Firms-in-Gestation," *Small Business Economics*, 9, no. 5, October, pp. 449–462.

Reynolds, P. D., 2000, "National Panel Study of U. S. Business Startups: Background and Methodology," *Databases for the Study of Entrepreneurship*, 4, pp. 153–227.

Reynolds, P. D., N. M. Carter, W. B. Gartner, and P. G. Greene, 2004, "The Prevalence of Nascent Entrepreneurs in the United States: Evidence from the Panel Study of Entrepreneurial Dynamics," *Small Business Economics*, 23, 4, November, pp. 263–284.

Reynolds, R. L., 1952, "Origins of Modern Business Enterprise: Medieval Italy," *Journal of Economic History*, 12, pp. 350–365.

Reynolds, S. S., 1988, "Plant Closings and Exit Behavior in Declining Industries," *Economica*, 55, pp. 493–503.

Ribstein, L. E., 2004, "Why Corporations?" *Berkeley Business Law Journal*, 2, pp. 183–232.

Ribstein, L. E., 2006, "Should History Lock In Lock-In?" Illinois Law and Economics Working Papers Series, Working Paper No. LE06-005, February, pp. 1–19.

Ribstein, L. E., 2007, "Rise of the Uncorporation," July, University of Illinois Law & Economics Research Paper No. LE07-026.

Ricart i Costa, J. E., 1988, "Managerial Task Assignment and Promotions," *Econometrica*, 56, 2, pp. 449–466.

Riordan, M. H., 1990a, "Asset Specificity and Backward Integration," *Journal of Institutional and Theoretical Economics*, 46, pp. 133–146.

Riordan, M. H., 1990b, "What Is Vertical Integration?" in M. Aoki, B. Gustafsson, and O. E. Williamson, eds., *The Firm as a Nexus of Treaties*, London: Sage Publications, pp. 94–111.

Riordan, M. H., 1991, "Ownership without Control: Toward a Theory of Backward Integration," *Journal of Japanese and International Economies*, 5, pp. 101–119.

Riordan, M. H., and D. E. M. Sappington, 1987, "Information, Incentives, and Organizational Mode," *Quarterly Journal of Economics*, 102, pp. 43–263.

Rob, R., 1991, "Learning and Capacity Expansion under Demand Uncertainty," *Review of Economic Studies*, 58, pp. 655–676.

Rochet, J.-C., and J. Tirole, 2003, "Platform Competition in Two-Sided Markets," *Journal of the European Economic Association*, 1, 4, pp. 990–1029.

Rogerson, W. P., 1984, "Efficient Reliance and Damage Measures for Breach of Contract," *Rand Journal of Economics*, 15, pp. 39–53.

Rogerson, W. P., 1992, "Contractual Solutions to the Hold-Up Problem," *Review of Economic Studies*, 59, October, pp. 777–794.

Rogoff, K., 1996, "The Purchasing Power Parity Puzzle," *Journal of Economic Literature*, 34, June, pp. 647–668.

Rosenberg, N., 1992, "Economic Experiments," *Industrial and Corporate Change*, 1, pp. 181–203.

Rosin, G. S., 1989, "The Entity-Aggregate Dispute: Conceptualism and Functionalism in Partnership Law," *Arkansas Law Review*, 42, pp. 395–466.

Ross, S. A., 1973, "The Economic Theory of Agency: The Principal's Problem," *American Economic Review*, 63, May, pp. 134–139.

Ross, S. A., 1974, "On the Economic Theory of Agency and the Principle of Similarity," in M. Balch, D. McFadden, and S. Wu, *Essays on Economic Behavior under Uncertainty*, Amsterdam: North-Holland, pp. 215–233.

Ross, S. A., 1976, "Options and Efficiency," *Quarterly Journal of Economics*, 90, February, pp. 75–89.

Ross, S. A., 1977, "The Determination of Financial Structure: The Incentive-Signalling Approach," *Bell Journal of Economics*, 8, pp. 23–40.

Roth, A. E., and M. A. O. Sotomayor, 1990, *Two-Sided Matching: A Study in Game Theoretic Modeling and Analysis*, Cambridge: Cambridge University Press.

Roth, A. E., and X. Xing, 1994, "Jumping the Gun: Imperfections and Institutions Related to the Timing of Market Transactions," *American Economic Review*, 84(4), September, pp. 992–1044.

Rousseau, J.-J., 1948, *The Social Contract, or Principles of Political Right*, translated with introduction and notes by Henry J. Tozer, 3rd ed., London: Allen & Unwin.

Ruback, R. S., and M. C. Jensen, 1983, "The Market for Corporate Control: The Scientific Evidence," *Journal of Financial Economics*, 11, pp. 5–50.

Rubinstein, A., 1998, *Modeling Bounded Rationality*, Cambridge, MA: MIT Press.

Rubinstein, A., and A. Wolinsky, 1987, "Middlemen," *Quarterly Journal of Economics*, 102, August, pp. 581–593.

Rural Business-Cooperative Service, 2002, "Agricultural Cooperatives in the 21st Century," Cooperative Information Report 60, Washington, DC: United States Department of Agriculture.

Rust, J., and G. Hall, 2003, "Middlemen versus Market Makers: A Theory of Competitive Exchange," *Journal of Political Economy*, 111(2), pp. 353–403.

Rysman, M., 2004, "Competition between Networks: A Study of the Market for Yellow Pages," *Review of Economic Studies*, 71, April, pp. 483–512.

Sahlins, M., 1974, *Stone Age Economics*, London: Tavistock.

Sahlman, W. A., 1990, "The Structure and Governance of Venture-Capital Organizations," *Journal of Financial Economics*, 27, 2, pp. 473–521.

Saint-Simon, H., 1975, *Selected Writings on Science, Industry and Social Organization*, trans. and ed. by K. Taylor, London: Croom Helm.

Salant, S.W., 1984, "Preemptive Patenting and the Persistence of Monopoly: Comment," *American Economic Review*, 74, pp. 247–250.

Samuelson, P. A., 1954a, "The Pure Theory of Public Expenditure," *Review of Economics and Statistics*, 36, pp. 387–389.

Samuelson, P. A., 1954b, "The Transfer Problem and Transport Costs II: Analysis of Effects of Trade Impediments," *Economic Journal*, June, 64, pp. 264–289.

Samuelson, P. A., 1958, "An Exact Consumption-Loan Model of Interest with or without the Social Contrivance of Money," *Journal of Political Economy*, 66, 6, December, pp. 219–234.

Samuelson, P. A., 1980, *Principles of Economics*, 11th ed., New York: McGraw Hill.

Sandler, T., and J. Tschirhart, 1981, "On the Number and Membership Size of Consumer Managed Firms," *Southern Economic Journal*, 47, 4, April, pp. 1086–1091.

Say, J.-B., 1841, *Traité d'Économie Politique*, 6th edition, Paris: Guillaumin.

Say, J.-B., 1852, *Cours Complet d'Économie Politique: Pratique*, volumes I and II, 3rd edition, Paris: Guillaumin.

Scarpetta, S., P. Hemmings, T. Tressel, and J. Woo, 2002, "The Role of Policy and Institutions for Productivity and Firm Dynamics, Evidence from Micro and Industry Data," working paper No. 329, April, Organization for Economic Co-operation and Development.

Scharfstein, D., 1988a, "The Disciplinary Role of Takeovers," *Review of Economic Studies*, April, pp. 185–199.

Scharfstein, D., 1988b, "Product-Market Competition and Managerial Slack," *Rand Journal of Economics*, 19, pp. 147–155.

Scharfstein, D., and J. C. Stein, 2000, "The Dark Side of Internal Capital Markets: Divisional Rent-Seeking and Inefficient Investment," *Journal of Finance*, 55, 6, pp. 2537–2564.

Scherer, F. M., 1970, *Industrial Organization and Economic Performance*, Chicago: Rand McNally.

Schiesel, S., 1997, "Web Publishers Start to Feel Lack of Advertising, An On-line Shakeout Has Affected Mainstream Media and Start-Ups," *New York Times*, March 25, p. C1.

Schmalensee, R., 1989, "Inter-industry Studies of Structure and Performance," in R. Schmalensee and R. Willig, eds., *Handbook of Industrial Organization*, Amsterdam: North-Holland, pp. 951–1010.

Schmidt, K. M., 1997, "Managerial Incentives and Product Market Competition," *Review of Economic Studies*, 64, pp. 191–213.

Schmidt, K. M., 2003, "Convertible Securities and Venture Capital Finance," *Journal of Finance*, 58, June, pp. 1139–1166.

Schramm, C. J., 2006a, "Entrepreneurial Capitalism and the End of Bureaucracy: Reforming the Mutual Dialog of Risk Aversion," presented at the American Economic Association meetings, Boston, MA.

Schramm, C. J., 2006b, *The Entrepreneurial Imperative: How American's Economic Miracle Will Reshape the World (and Change Your Life)*, New York: HarperCollins.

Schramm, C. J., 2006c, "Law outside the Market: The Social Utility of the Private Foundation," *Harvard Journal of Law and Public Policy*, 30, Fall, pp. 355–415.

Schumpeter, J. A., 1942, *Capitalism, Socialism, and Democracy*, New York: Harper & Row.

Schumpeter, J. A., 1947, *Capitalism, Socialism and Democracy*, 2nd ed., London: Allen and Unwin.

Schumpeter, J. A., 1964, *Business Cycles: A Theoretical, Historical, and Statistical Analysis of the Capitalist Process*, reprinted in 1989, abridged version of first edition published in 1939, Philadelphia: Porcupine Press.

Schumpeter, J. A., 1966, *History of Economic Analysis*, New York: Oxford University Press.

Schumpeter, J. A., 1997 [1934], *The Theory of Economic Development*, New Brunswick, NJ: Transaction Publishers.

Sealey, C., Jr., and J. T. Lindley, 1977, "Inputs, Outputs, and a Theory of Production and Cost at Depository Financial Institutions," *Journal of Finance*, 32, pp. 1251–1266.

Segal, I., 1999, "Contracting with Externalities," *Quarterly Journal of Economics*, 114, 2, May, pp. 337–388.

Sexton, R. J., 1986, "The Formation of Cooperatives: A Game-Theoretic Approach with Implications for Cooperative Finance, Decision Making, and Stability," *American Journal of Agricultural Economics*, 68, 2, May, pp. 214–225.

Sexton, R. J., and T. A. Sexton, 1987, "Cooperatives as Entrants," *The Rand Journal of Economics*, 18, 4, winter, pp. 581–595.

Shaffer, S., 1997, "Network Diseconomies and Optimal Structure," July, working paper No. 97–19, Federal Reserve Bank of Philadelphia.

Shane, S., 2001, "Technological Opportunities and New Firm Creation," *Management Science*, 47, February, pp. 205–220.

Shane, S., 2003, *A General Theory of Entrepreneurship: The Individual-Opportunity Nexus*, Cheltenham, UK: Edward Elgar.

Shapiro, C., and J. E. Stiglitz, 1983, "Equilibrium Unemployment as a Worker Discipline Device," *American Economic Review*, 74, June, pp. 433–444.

Shapley, L. S., 1961, "Values of Large Games V: An 18-Person Market Game," research project, Santa Monica, CA: The Rand Corporation, RM-2860, November.

Shapley, L. S., 1962, "Complements and Substitutes in the Optimal Assignment Problem," *Naval Research Logistics Quarterly*, 9, pp. 45–48.

Shapley, L. S., and M. Shubik, 1972, "The Assignment Game I: The Core," *International Journal of Game Theory*, 1, 2, pp. 111–130.

Shapley, L. S., and M. Shubik, 1976, "Trade Using One Commodity as a Means of Payment," research report, Santa Monica, CA: Rand.

Sheshinski, E., and Y. Weiss, 1977, "Inflation and Costs of Price Adjustment," *Review of Economic Studies*, 44, June, pp. 287–303.

Shevchenko, A., 2004, "Middlemen," *International Economic Review*, 45, 1, pp. 1–24.

Shimer, R., and L. Smith, 2000, "Assortive Matching and Search," *Econometrica*, 68, March, pp. 343–369.

Shleifer, A., and R. Vishny, 1997, "A Survey of Corporate Control," *Journal of Finance*, 52, pp. 737–783.

Shubik, M., 1982, *Game Theory in the Social Sciences: Concepts and Solutions*, Cambridge, MA: MIT Press.

Shubik, M., 1984, *A Game-Theoretic Approach to Political Economy*, Cambridge, MA: MIT Press.

Shubik, M., 1999, *The Theory of Money and Financial Institutions*, v. 1, Cambridge, MA: MIT Press.

Shubik, M., and E. Smith, 2003, "Structure, Clearinghouses and Symmetry," Cowles Foundation Discussion Paper No. 1419, May, Yale University, New Haven, CT.

Silk, A. J., and E. R. Berndt, 1994, "Costs, Institutional Mobility Barriers, and Market Structure: Advertising Agencies as Multiproduct Firms," *Journal of Economics and Management Strategy*, 3, Fall, pp. 437–480.

Simon, H. A., 1955, "A Behavioral Model of Rational Choice," *Quarterly Journal of Economics*, 69, pp. 99–118.

Simon, H. A., 1972, "Theories of Bounded Rationality," in C. B. McGuire and R. Radner, eds., *Decisions and Organizations*, Amsterdam: North Holland, pp. 161–176.

Simon, H. A., 1976, *Administrative Behavior*, 3rd ed., New York: Free Press.

Simon, H. A., 1989, *Price Management*, Amsterdam: North Holland.

Sklivas, S. D., 1987, "The Strategic Choice of Managerial Incentives," *Rand Journal of Economics*, 18, pp. 452–458.

Slater, G., 1932, *The Growth of Modern England*, London: Constable.

Sloan, A. P., Jr., 1963, *My Years with General Motors*, New York: Doubleday.

Smith, A., 1998 [1776], *An Inquiry into the Nature and Causes of the Wealth of Nations*, Washington, DC: Regnery Publishing.

Smith, D. G., 1999, "Team Production in Venture Capital Investing," *Journal of Corporation Law*, 24, Summer, pp. 949–974.

Smith, J. E., 1996, "Fisher Separation and Project Valuation, in Partially Complete Markets," working paper, Duke University.

Smith, M., J. Bailey, and E. Brynjolfsson, 1999, "Understanding Digital Markets: Review and Assessment," in E. Brynjolfsson and B. Kahin, eds., *Understanding the Digital Economy*, Cambridge, MA: MIT Press, pp. 99–136.

Solomonoff, R., 1952, "An Exact Method for the Computation of the Connectivity of Random Nets," *Bulletin of Mathematical Biophysics*, 14, p. 153.

Solomonoff, R., and A. Rapoport, 1951, "Connectivity of Random Nets," *Bulletin of Mathematical Biophysics*, 13, pp. 107–117.

Sorenson, J. R., J. T. Tschirhart, and A. B. Whinston, 1978, "Private Good Clubs and the Core," *Journal of Public Economics*, 10, 1, August, pp. 77–95.

Sowell, T., 2006, *On Classical Economics*, New Haven, CT: Yale University Press.

Spence, A. M., 1977a, "Entry, Investment and Oligopolistic Pricing," *Bell Journal of Economics*, 8, Autumn, pp. 534–544.

Spence, A. M., 1977b, "Nonlinear Prices and Welfare," *Journal of Public Economics*, 8, pp. 1–18.

Spiegel, Y., and D. F. Spulber, 1997, "Capital Structure with Countervailing Incentives," *Rand Journal of Economics*, 28, pp. 1–24.

Spulber, D. F., 1979, "Noncooperative Equilibrium with Price Discriminating Firms," *Economics Letters*, 4, pp. 221–227.

Spulber, D. F., 1980, "Research, Development and Technological Change in a Growing Economy," *Energy Economics*, 2, 4, October, pp. 199–207.

Spulber, D. F., 1981a, "Capacity, Output, and Sequential Entry," *American Economic Review*, 71, pp. 503–514.

Spulber, D. F., 1981b, "Spatial Nonlinear Pricing," *American Economic Review*, 71, December, pp. 923–933.

Spulber, D. F., 1982, "A Selective Survey," in L. J. Mirman and D. F. Spulber, eds., *Essays in the Economics of Renewable Resources*, Amsterdam: Elsevier-North Holland Publishing, pp. 3–26.

Spulber, D. F., 1984a, "Competition and Multiplant Monopoly with Spatial Nonlinear Pricing," *International Economic Review*, 25, pp. 425–439.

Spulber, D. F., 1984b, "Nonlinear Pricing, Advertising and Welfare," *Southern Economic Journal*, April, pp. 1025–1035.

Spulber, D. F., 1985, "Risk Sharing and Inventories," *Journal of Economic Behavior and Organization*, 6, pp. 55–68.

Spulber, D. F., 1988a, "Bargaining and Regulation with Asymmetric Information about Demand and Supply," *Journal of Economic Theory*, 44, April, pp. 251–268.

Spulber, D. F., 1988b, "Optimal Environmental Regulation under Asymmetric Information," *Journal of Public Economics*, 35, pp. 163–181.

Spulber, D. F., 1989a, "Product Variety and Competitive Discounts," *Journal of Economic Theory*, 48, pp. 510–525.

Spulber, D. F., 1989b, *Regulation and Markets*, Cambridge, MA: MIT Press.

Spulber, D. F., 1992a, "Economic Analysis and Management Strategy: A Survey," *Journal of Economics and Management Strategy*, 1, Fall, pp. 535–574.

Spulber, D. F., 1992b, "Optimal Nonlinear Pricing and Contingent Contracts," *International Economic Review*, 33, 4, November, pp. 747–772.

Spulber, D. F., 1993a, "Monopoly Pricing," *Journal of Economic Theory*, 59, 1, pp. 222–234.

Spulber, D. F., 1993b, "Monopoly Pricing of Capacity Usage under Asymmetric Information," *Journal of Industrial Economics*, 41, I, 3, September, pp. 241–257.

Spulber, D. F., 1994, "Economic Analysis and Management Strategy: A Survey Continued," *Journal of Economics and Management Strategy*, 3, Summer, pp. 355–406.

Spulber, D. F., 1995, "Bertrand Competition When Rivals' Costs Are Unknown," *Journal of Industrial Economics*, 43, pp. 1–12.

Spulber, D. F., 1996a, "Market Making by Price Setting Firms," *Review of Economic Studies* 63, pp. 559–580.

Spulber, D. F., 1996b, "Market Microstructure and Intermediation," *Journal of Economic Perspectives*, 10, Summer, pp. 135–152.

Spulber, D. F., 1998, *The Market Makers: How Leading Companies Create and Win Markets*, New York: McGraw Hill/ Business Week Books.

Spulber, D. F., 1999, *Market Microstructure: Intermediaries and the Theory of the Firm*, New York: Cambridge University Press.

Spulber, D. F., 2002a, "Introduction: Economics Fables and Public Policy," in D. F. Spulber, ed., *Famous Fables of Economics: Myths of Market Failure*, Malden, MA: Blackwell Publishers, pp. 1–31.

Spulber, D. F., 2002b, "Market Microstructure and Incentives to Invest," *Journal of Political Economy*, 110, April, pp. 352–381.

Spulber, D. F., 2002c, "Transaction Innovation and the Role of the Firm," in M. R. Baye, ed., *The Economics of the Internet and E-commerce*, Advances in Applied Micro-economics, v. 11, Oxford, UK: JAI Press/Elsevier Science, pp. 159–190.

Spulber, D. F., 2003a, "The Intermediation Theory of the Firm: Integrating Economic and Management Approaches to Strategy," *Managerial and Decision Economics*, 24, pp. 253–266.

Spulber, D. F., 2003b, *Management Strategy*, New York: McGraw Hill.

Spulber, D. F., 2006, "Firms and Networks in Two-Sided Markets," in T. Hendershott, ed., *The Handbook of Economics and Information Systems*, 1, Amsterdam: Elsevier, pp. 137–200.

Spulber, D. F., 2007, *Global Competitive Strategy*, Cambridge: Cambridge University Press.

Spulber, D. F., 2008a, "Consumer Coordination in the Small and in the Large: Implications for Antitrust in Markets with Network Effects," *Journal of Competition Law and Economics*, 4, June, pp. 1–56.

Spulber, D., 2008b, "The Interplay between Private Networks and Social Networks," Northwestern University Discussion Paper.

Spulber, D. F., and C. S. Yoo, 2005, "Network Regulation: The Many Faces of Access," *Journal of Competition Law and Economics*, 1, 4, December, pp. 635–678.

Spulber, N., 2003, *Russia's Economic Transitions: From Late Tsarism to the New Millennium*, Cambridge: Cambridge University Press.

Stahl, D. O., 1988, "Bertrand Competition for Inputs and Walrasian Outcomes," *American Economic Review*, 78, pp. 189–201.

Stahl, K., 1982, "Location and Spatial Pricing Theory with Nonconvex Transportation Cost," *Bell Journal of Economics*, 13, autumn, pp. 575–582.

Starr, R. M., 2003, "Why Is There Money? Endogenous Derivation of 'Money' as the Most Liquid Asset: A Class of Examples," *Economic Theory*, 21, pp. 455–474.

Steffen, R., 1977, *Agency – Partnership*, St. Paul, MN: West Publishing.

Steil, B., 2002, "Changes in the Ownership and Governance of Securities Exchanges: Causes and Consequences," *Brookings-Wharton Papers on Financial Services 2002*, pp. 61–91.

Stein, J. C., 1988, "Takeover Threats and Managerial Myopia," *Journal of Political Economy*, 96, 1, February, pp. 61–80.

Stern, L. W., and A. I. El-Ansary, 1988, *Marketing Channels*, 3rd. edition, Englewood Cliffs, NJ: Prentice-Hall.

Stigler, G. J., 1949, *The Theory of Price*, New York: Macmillan.

Stigler, G. J., 1961, "The Economics of Information," *Journal of Political Economy*, 69, pp. 213–225.

Stiglitz, J. E., 1974, "Incentives and Risk Sharing in Sharecropping," *Review of Economic Studies*, 41, p. 219.

Stiglitz, J. E., 1976, "Monopoly and the Rate of Extraction of Exhaustible Resources," *American Economic Review*, 66, 4, September, pp. 655–661.

Stiglitz, J. E., 1987, "The Causes and Consequences of the Dependence of Quality on Price," *Journal of Economic Literature*, 25, March, pp. 1–48.

Stiglitz, J. E., and A. Weiss, 1981, "Credit Rationing in Markets with Imperfect Information," *American Economic Review*, 71, June, pp. 393–410.

Stinchcombe, A. L., 1990, *Information and Organization*, Berkeley: University of California Press.

Stoljar, S. J., 1961, *The Law of Agency: Its History and Present Principles*, London: Sweet & Maxwell Limited.

Stoll, H., 2002, "Comment on Steil," *Brookings-Wharton Papers on Financial Services 2002*, pp. 83–91.

Stoll, H. R., 1985, "Alternative Views of Market Making," in Yakov Amihud, Thomas S. Y. Ho, and Robert Schwartz, eds., *Market Making and the Changing Structure of the Securities Industry*, Lexington, MA: Heath, pp. 67–92.

Sutton, J., 1991, *Sunk Costs and Market Structure*, Cambridge, MA: MIT Press.

Taylor, C. R., 1995, "Digging for Golden Carrots: An Analysis of Research Tournaments," *American Economic Review*, 85, September, pp. 872–890.

Tedeshi, B., 2000, "E-commerce Report," *New York Times*, May 1, p. C10.

Teilhac, E., 1927, *L'Oeuvre Économique de Jean-Baptiste Say*, Paris: Librairie Félix Alcan.

Telser, L.G., 1981, "Why There Are Organized Futures Markets," *Journal of Law and Economics*, 24, pp. 1–22.

Temin, P., 2001, "A Market Economy in the Early Roman Empire," MIT Department of Economics working paper 01-08, February, Cambridge, MA.

Temin, P., 2002, "Financial Intermediation in the Early Roman Empire," MIT Department of Economics working paper 02-39, November, Cambridge, MA.

The Columbia Encyclopedia, 6th edition, 2001, New York: Columbia University Press.

Thirsk, J., 1967, *The Agrarian History of England and Wales*, Cambridge: Cambridge University Press.

Tiebout, C. M., 1956, "A Pure Theory of Local Expenditures," *Journal of Political Economy*, 64, pp. 416–424.

Tinbergen, J., 1967, *Development Planning*, New York: McGraw Hill.

Tirole, J., 1986, "Procurement and Renegotiation," *Journal of Political Economy*, 94, pp. 235–259.

Tirole, J., 1988, *The Theory of Industrial Organization*, Cambridge, MA: MIT Press.

Topkis, D. M., 1978, "Minimizing a Submodular Function on a Lattice," *Operations Research*, 26, March–April, pp. 305–321.

Topkis, D. M., 1998, *Supermodularity and Complementarity*, Princeton, NJ: Princeton University Press.

Townsend, R. M., 1978, "Intermediation with Costly Bilateral Exchange," *Review of Economic Studies*, 55, 3, pp. 417–425.

Townsend, R. M., 1979, "Optimal Contracts and Competitive Markets with Costly State Verification," *Journal of Economic Theory*, 21, 2, pp. 265–293.

Townsend, R. M., 1980, "Models of Money with Spatially Separated Agents," in J. Karelsen and N. Wallace, eds., *Models of Monetary Economics*, Minneapolis, MN: Federal Reserve Bank of Minneapolis, reprinted in Robert M. Townsend, *Financial Structure and Economic Organization*, 1990, Cambridge, MA: Basil Blackwell, ch. 2, pp. 53–100.

Tracy, J. D., ed., 1990, *The Rise of Merchant Empires: Long-Distance Trade in the Early Modern World, 1350–1750*, Cambridge: Cambridge University Press.

Tsoulouhas, T., and T. Vukina, 2004, "Regulating Broiler Contracts: Tournaments Versus Fixed Performance Standards," North Carolina State University working paper.

Tullock, G., 1966, "Information without Profit," *Public Choice*, 1, December, pp. 141–159.

Tutte, W. T., 2001, *Graph Theory*, Cambridge: Cambridge University Press.

Tybout, J. R., 2000, "Manufacturing Firms in Developing Countries: How Well Do They Do, and Why?" *Journal of Economic Literature*, 38, March, pp. 11–44.

Umbeck, J., 1977, "The California Gold Rush: A Study of Emerging Property Rights," *Explorations in Economic History*, 14, pp. 197–226.

United Nations Conference on Trade and Development, 2003, *World Investment Report, 2003 FDI Policies for Development: National and International Perspectives*, New York: United Nations.

United States Census Bureau, 2000, *1997 Economic Census, Wholesale Trade, Geographic Area Series*, March, Washington, DC: U.S. Department of Commerce.

United States Small Business Administration, Office of Advocacy, 2001, *Small Business Economic Indicators: 2000*, Washington, DC: SBA.

Vanek, J., 1970, *The General Theory of Labor-Managed Market Economies*, Ithaca, NY: Cornell University Press.

Verlinden, C., 1965, "Markets and Fairs," in M. M. Postan, E. E. Rich, and E. Miller, eds., *The Cambridge Economic History of Europe, v. III, Economic Organization and Policies in the Middle Ages*, Cambridge: Cambridge University Press.

Verrecchia, R., 1990, "Information Quality and Discretionary Disclosure," *Journal of Accounting and Economics*, 12, pp. 365–380.

Vickers, J., 1984, "Delegation and the Theory of the Firm," *Economic Journal*, 95, supplement, pp. 38–147.

Vickrey, W., 1961, "Counterspeculation, Auctions and Competitive Sealed Tenders," *Journal of Finance*, 16, pp. 8–37.

Vickrey, W., 1962, "Auctions and Bidding Games," in *Recent Advances in Game Theory*, Conference Proceedings, Princeton, NJ: Princeton University Press, pp. 15–27.

Vives, X., 2000, "Corporate Governance: Does It Matter?" in X. Vives, ed., *Corporate Governance: Theoretical and Empirical Perspectives*, Cambridge: Cambridge University Press.

Von Mises, L., 1998 [1949], *Human Action: A Treatise on Economics*, Auburn, AL: Ludwig von Mises Institute.

Von Neumann, J., and O. Morgenstern, 1944, *Theory of Games and Economic Behavior*, Princeton, NJ: Princeton University Press.

Von Thunen, J. H., 1966, *The Isolated State*, translated by C. M. Wartenberg and P. Hall, Oxford: Pergamon Press.

Votaw, D., 1965, *Modern Corporations*, Englewood Cliffs, NJ: Prentice-Hall.

Vulkan, N., 1999, "Economic Implications of Agent Technology and E-commerce," *Economic Journal*, 109, February, pp. F67–F90.

Wagenhofer, A., 1990, "Voluntary Disclosure with a Strategic Opponent," *Journal of Accounting and Economics*, 12, pp. 341–363.

Walker, M., 1981, "A Simple Incentive-Compatible Scheme for Attaining Lindahl Allocations," *Econometrica*, 49, pp. 65–71.

Wallace, N., 1997, "Absence-of-Double-Coincidence Models of Money: A Progress Report," *Federal Reserve Bank of Minneapolis Quarterly Review*, 21, winter, pp. 2–20.

Walras, L., 1938, "Recherches sur les principes mathematiques de la theorie des richesse," Paris: Librarie des Sciences Politiques et Sociales.

Walras, L., 1954, *Elements of Pure Economics*, translated by William Jaffe, Homewood, IL: Irwin.

Waltzing, J. P., 1979 [1895–1900], *Étude historique sur les corporations professionnelles chez les romains*, v. I–IV, New York: Arno Press.

Ward, B., 1958, "The Firm in Illyria: Market Syndicalism," *American Economic Review*, 48, 4, September, pp. 566–589.

Watts, D. J., 2003, *Six Degrees: The Science of a Connected Age*, New York: Norton.

Weber, Max, 1968, *Economy and Society: An Outline of Interpretive Sociology*, v. 3, G. Roth and C. Wittch, eds., New York, NY: Badminster Press.

Weill, P.-O., 2005, "Leaning against the Wind," Department of Finance, New York University Stern School of Business, working paper.

Weisbrod, B. A., 1988, *The Nonprofit Economy*, Cambridge, MA: Harvard University Press.

Weisbrod, B. A., 1998, *To Profit or Not to Profit: The Commercial Transformation of the Nonprofit Sector*, New York, NY: Cambridge University Press.

Weiss, L. W., 1974, "The Concentration-Profits Relationship and Antitrust," in H. J. Goldschmid, H. M. Mann, and J. F. Weston, eds., *Industrial Concentration: The New Learning*, Boston: Little, Brown.

Whinston, M. D., 1988, "Exit with Multiplant Firms," *Rand Journal of Economics*, 19, pp. 568–588.

Wicksell, K., 1936, *Interest and Prices*, London: Macmillan.

Wiggins, S. N., and G. D. Libecap, 1985, "Oil Field Unitization: Contractual Failure in the Presence of Imperfect Information," *American Economic Review*, 75, 3, June, pp. 368–385.

Williams, J., 1986, *The Economic Function of Futures Markets*, Cambridge: Cambridge University Press.

Williamson, O. E., 1970, *Corporate Control and Business Behavior*, Englewood Cliffs, NJ: Prentice-Hall.

Williamson, O. E., 1975, *Markets and Hierarchies*, New York: Free Press.

Williamson, O. E., 1985, *The Economic Institutions of Capitalism*, New York: Free Press.

Williamson, S. D., 1986, "Costly Monitoring, Financial Intermediation, and Equilibrium Credit Rationing," *Journal of Monetary Economics*, 18, pp. 159–179.

Williamson, S. D., 1987, "Costly Monitoring, Loan Contracts, and Equilibrium Credit Rationing," *Quarterly Journal of Economics*, 102, pp. 135–145.

Wilson, R. B., 1993, *Nonlinear Pricing*, New York, Oxford University Press.

Woodruff, C., 2002, "Non-contractible Investment and Vertical Integration in the Mexican Footwear Industry," *International Journal of Industrial Organization*, 20, pp. 1197–1224.

Working, H., 1953a, "Futures Trading and Hedging," *American Economic Review*, 43, pp. 314–343.

Working, H., 1953b, "Hedging Reconsidered," *Journal of Farm Economics*, 35, pp. 544–561.

Wright, R., 2002, *The Wealth of Nations Rediscovered: Integration and Expansion in American Financial Markets, 1780–1850*, Cambridge: Cambridge University Press.

Yanelle, M.-O., 1989a, "Increasing Returns to Scale and Endogenous Intermediation," University of Basel, WWZ Discussion Paper 8908.

Yanelle, M.-O., 1989b, "The Strategic Analysis of Intermediation: Asymmetric Information and the Theory of Financial Markets," *European Economic Review*, 33 (2/3), March, pp. 294–301.

Yavas, A., 1992, "Marketmakers versus Matchmakers," *Journal of Financial Intermediation*, 2, March, pp. 33–58.

Yavas, A., 1994a, "Economics of Brokerage: An Overview," *Journal of Real Estate Literature*, 2, July, pp. 169–195.

Yavas, A., 1994b, "Middlemen in Bilateral Search Markets," *Journal of Labor Economics*, 12, July, pp. 406–429.

Yavas, A., 1996a, "Matching of Buyers and Sellers by Brokers: A Comparison of Alternative Commission Structures," *Real Estate Economics*, 24, pp. 97–112.

Yavas, A., 1996b, "Search and Trading in Intermediated Markets," *Journal of Economics and Management Strategy*, 5, pp. 195–216.

Yelling, J. A., 1977, *Common Field and Enclosure in England 1450–1850*, Hamden, CT: Archon.

Yoo, C. S., 2004, "Copyright and Product Differentiation," *New York University Law Review*, 79, April, pp. 212–280.

Zbaracki, M. J., M. Bergen, S. Dutta, D. Levy, and M. Ritson, 2002, "Beyond the Costs of Price Adjustment: Investments in Pricing Capital," working paper, University of Pennsylvania.

Zbaracki, M. J., M. Ritson, D. Levy, S. Dutta, and M. Bergen, 2004, "Managerial and Customer Costs of Price Adjustment: Direct Evidence from Industrial Markets," *Review of Economics and Statistics*, 86, May, pp. 514–533.

Zender, J. F., 1991, "Optimal Financial Instruments," *Journal of Finance*, 46, pp. 1645–1663.

Zingales, L., 1995, "Insider Ownership and the Decision to Go Public," *Review of Economic Studies*, 62, July, pp. 425–448.

Zingales, L., 2000, "In Search of New Foundations," *Journal of Finance*, 55, 4, pp. 1623–1653.

Author Index

Subject Index

511